KING
EDWARD
VIII

PHILIP ZIEGLER

SUTTON PUBLISHING

First published in 1990 by William Collins Sons & Co. Ltd

This new revised edition first published in 2001 by
Sutton Publishing Limited · Phoenix Mill
Thrupp · Stroud · Gloucestershire · GL5 2BU

British Library Cataloguing in Publication Data
A catalogue record for this book is available from the British
Library

ISBN 0 7509 2747 X

Printed and bound in Great Britain by
J.H. Haynes & Co. Ltd, Sparkford.

Contents

KING
EDWARD
VIII

List of Illustrations

Preface

In the ten years since my biography of King Edward VIII first appeared the fascination evoked by this ill-fated monarch and his much publicized romance seems in no way to have diminished. There have been more than a dozen new books dealing with his life or aspects of it, newspaper articles, plays, television documentaries, even a musical comedy. The last of these was reasonably generous in its interpretation of his behaviour and his motives; in almost every other case the approach has been critical if not flagrantly hostile.

The main line of attack has related to his attitude towards Germany between 1935 and 1945. As Prince of Wales, it is argued, he was pro-German, condoning if not actively encouraging the rise of National Socialism. As King, he was an arch-appeaser, energetically intervening to make sure that his ministers did not react robustly to the German occupation of the Rhineland. As Duke of Windsor he wittingly betrayed secrets of military importance to the Germans in 1939 and 1940, while in Spain and Portugal he flirted with German emissaries who suggested that he remain in Europe and hold himself in readiness for a return to an occupied Britain. At any time he would have been ready to supplant his brother and take back the throne if the opportunity had arisen. Until well on into the war he maintained that Britain must inevitably be defeated and that a negotiated peace was the only sane way forward. Such attacks culminated in a television programme entitled 'Edward, the Traitor King', without even the courtesy of a question mark.

The curious feature of all these publications is that no fact of any significance was adduced which was not to be found in my biography. From the book which follows this preface it is clear, sometimes painfully clear, that Edward VIII could be silly and indiscreet, that he did see considerable merits in the practice of

Preface

National Socialism in Germany, that in 1940 and 1941 he not merely favoured a negotiated peace but spoke his mind in public at a time when solidarity with the British government or at least silence was incumbent on him. His behaviour was such as to give German agents – anxious to feed their superiors in Berlin the news that they wanted to hear – some cause for hoping that he might rally to the Axis cause if the circumstances were right. But German official documents published since the war show that this was no more than supposition and that there is no hard evidence to support the thesis of his treachery, be it actual or potential.

Ah, yes, say the Duke's detractors, but the published documents do not tell the whole story. King George VI sent the royal librarian, Owen Morshead, and the art historian (and, as it later transpired, Communist spy) Anthony Blunt on a secret mission to Germany to secure the papers that would have proved the Duke's guilt and bring them back for destruction or incarceration in some inaccessible vault at Windsor. The fact that the mission was far from secret; that its task was to bring back certain nineteenth century family papers – mainly letters from Queen Victoria to her eldest daughter, the Empress Frederick; that all these papers were eventually returned to Germany; and that a complete inventory exists of everything that was brought back has not been allowed to spoil a good story.

To reach the conclusion that the Duke of Windsor was a traitor it is necessary to credit every surmise of those who wanted him to be so and to ignore the testimony of all those who worked with him and knew him best. Even then there would be no proof. It is a cardinal principle of British law – indeed, of the law of any civilized society – that an accused is assumed innocent until proved guilty. In the case of the Duke of Windsor the reverse has been true, he has been assumed guilty because he cannot positively be proved innocent. And yet to prove that somebody did *not* do something is notoriously difficult: for a single crime an alibi can with luck be established but if a pattern of behaviour or of thought is in question it is generally impossible to do more than establish a balance of probabilities, based on one's knowledge of the person concerned. I make no claim to omniscience, but I probably know more about the Duke of

Windsor than anyone else alive. I am absolutely certain that, with his all faults, he was a patriot who would never have wished his country to be defeated or would have contemplated returning to an occupied Britain as a puppet king. I accept that I cannot prove my contention, but I have much better grounds for maintaining it than any of the writers who have asserted the contrary over the last decade. Nothing that they have written has caused me to change my mind.

The other thing that has surprised me over the last ten years has been the number of people who have written to state – with varying degrees of confidence – that their mother, their uncle, the woman who keeps a boarding house down the road, was an illegitimate child of the Prince of Wales. Here too there can be no proof – or no proof, at least, that the Prince *was* the father; sometimes the facts of chronology or geography make it certain that he was innocent. In no case is the physical resemblance between putative father and son so striking as to provide conclusive evidence. This biographer, at least, views each claim in the same spirit as he would the alleged apparition of a ghost: each individual sighting should be treated with extreme scepticism but at the end of the day it is easier to believe in the existence of ghosts than to seek to explain them all on rational or scientific grounds. There is no reason to believe that the Prince of Wales was incapable of siring children; he was notoriously promiscuous, and if people choose to believe that they are his descendants then good luck to them. It seems supremely unlikely that any evidence could now turn up which would prove their contention justified and, except to them, it would matter very little if it did.

Acknowledgements

By generous permission of Her Majesty The Queen I was accorded unrestricted access to the Royal Archives at Windsor, as well as allowed to reproduce those photographs mentioned in the list of illustrations. For this I am profoundly grateful, as also for the privileged access which I have enjoyed to certain restricted papers in the Public Record Office, the Bodleian Library, Lambeth Palace Library, Cambridge University Library, the Library of the University of Birmingham, and Churchill College Library. References to these papers are supplied even in those cases where they will not be opened in the Public Record Office or elsewhere for a considerable time to come.

I am most grateful to Her Majesty Queen Elizabeth and those other members of the royal family who were kind enough to talk to me and allow me to use unpublished copyright material.

Sir William Heseltine, former Private Secretary and Keeper of the Archives to Queen Elizabeth II, was an unfailing source of encouragement and wise advice over the years in which I was at work on this book. Of him, and of Mr Oliver Everett, the Queen's Librarian at Windsor, I can say literally that without their help this biography would never have been written. Miss Elizabeth Cuthbert, Lady de Bellaigue, Miss Pamela Clark, Miss Frances Dimond and all the staff of the Royal Archives confirmed my belief that nowhere in the world can greater expertise be found married to equal patience and benevolence.

Before I embarked on this book it was my conviction that every biographer must owe *something* to those who had worked in the field before him. My study of certain recent books dealing with the Duke and Duchess of Windsor disabused me of this impression. My reference notes, however, make clear how much I have derived from other earlier works on the subject. Two writers must be specially mentioned:

King Edward VIII

Frances Donaldson's *Edward VIII*, published in 1974, appears as perceptive and brilliantly written today as when it first appeared. The immense volume of additional manuscript material which I have been enabled to read has inevitably led to some differences of emphasis or interpretation but I would not dispute her central thesis. It is characteristic of Lady Donaldson's generosity that access to some of that manuscript material was obtained thanks to her advice and help. Her kindness to one whom she might reasonably have considered an unwelcome interloper was repeated and exemplary.

Michael Bloch has equally gone out of his way to help me. I have not invariably agreed with his interpretation of events but his writing is always intelligent and stimulating and his scholarship impressive. Much of his research, particularly into the Duke of Windsor's period as Governor of the Bahamas and his adventures in Spain and Portugal in 1940, could not have been duplicated. My debt to him will be self-evident.

It would be invidious to pick out books which I have found of especial value but I must express my gratitude to those other official biographers who have written of recent monarchs or members of the royal family: Sir Harold Nicolson and Mr Kenneth Rose on King George V (the latter not strictly speaking 'official' but none the less refulgent for that); Sir John Wheeler-Bennett on King George VI, Mr James Pope-Hennessy on Queen Mary. They have demonstrated that it is possible to be 'official' without being ponderously decorous or slavishly discreet.

I hesitate, too, to single out any individuals amongst those who have allowed me to read manuscript material, but because of the immense importance of the letters as well as her personal kindness I must express especial gratitude to the late Lady Laycock for letting me read and quote freely from the two thousand-odd letters written to her mother, Freda Dudley Ward, by the Prince of Wales in the decade beginning in 1921. I recollect the moment at which Lady Laycock told me that these letters still existed as being one of the most exciting in my life as a biographer. Lady Alexandra Metcalfe not only let me use manuscript material of crucial importance, but as one of the very few survivors of those who knew King Edward VIII well when he was Prince of Wales was an invaluable guide to me along my way.

Acknowledgements

Almost half the illustrations in this book come from the collection of photographs then preserved at the Duke of Windsor's former house in Paris, then sumptuously restored by Mr Mohamed Al Fayed to the glories which it knew in the Windsors' heyday. Mrs Christiane Sherwen put this remarkable collection in order and researched its components with meticulous scholarship.

My gratitude to the above in no way diminishes my thanks to those others who allowed me to use manuscript material in their possession or whose copyright they controlled, or to reproduce photographs from their private collections: Sir John Aird, the Earl of Airlie, Mr Julian Amery, Sir John Baring, Maître Suzanne Blum and the Trustees of the Pasteur Institute, the Marquis de Breteuil, Lord Brownlow, Sir Edward Cazalet, Mr Peregrine Churchill, Mr Winston Churchill, Mrs Norman Colville, Lord Crathorne, the Earl of Cromer, the Earl of Dudley, Lady De L'Isle and Dudley, Lady Donaldson, Mrs Grace du Reitz, Mrs David Erskine, Sir Robert Fellowes, Hon. Lady Goulding, Mr John Grigg, the Earl of Halifax, Mrs David Hankinson, Lord Hardinge of Penshurst, Sir Rupert Hart-Davis, Lady Mary Harvey, Commander Michael Hutchinson, Lady Johnston, Mrs Pamela Karslake. Lord Lambton, the Earl of Leicester, H.E. Mr Leif Leifland, Viscount Monckton, Lady Murray, Viscount Norwich, Sir Patrick Reilly, Mr Kenneth Rose, Sir Michael Thomas, Mr Hugo Vickers, Lord Wigram.

Many others were prodigal of their time and hospitality and in one way or another aided me immeasurably along my way. The list is far from comprehensive but I must mention Mr Alfred Amos, Mr Thomas Beddard, Mr Peter Begent, Mr A.D. Bowyer, Mr W.E.A. Callender, Lord Charteris of Amisfield, Mrs Sibilla Clarke, Mr Michael Cole, Sir John Colville, Miss Irma Cosworth, the Earl of Derby, Vice Admiral Sir Kaye Edden, Miss Marlene Eilers, Mr Alan Fisher, the Rev. D.C. Flatt, Mr Alastair Forbes, Sir Dudley Forwood, Mr Joe Friedman, Lord and Lady Glendevon, General Sir Michael Gow, the Dowager Lady Hambleden, Mr Duff Hart-Davis, Captain David Horn, Lady Laura Howard, Rear Admiral C.D. Howard-Johnston, Baroness Nancy von Hoyningen-Huene, Mr Miles Huntingdon-Whiteley, Mr David Irving, Mr Len Jakeman, Mr Walter Lees, Mr Jonathan Leiserach, Mr and Mrs Julian Loyd, Mr Andrew Lyell, Mr T.S. Matthews, Lady Audrey Morris, Hon. Lady Mosley, Count Raymond de Nicolay, Mr and

Mrs Willoughby Norman, Group-Captain H.W. Pearson-Rogers, Mr Jeremy Pilcher, Mr John Pringle, Mr Robert Rhodes James, Mr Oris Russell, Mr Alfred Shaughnessy, Lord Tennyson, Mr Richard Wells, Colonel Jeffery Williams, Lord and Lady Zuckerman.

Librarians are traditionally the most helpful and patient of mortals; I owe a particular debt to Mr Correlli Barnett and Miss Elizabeth Bennett of Churchill College, Dr B.S. Benedikz of the University of Birmingham, Dr Geoffrey Bill of the Lambeth Palace Library, Mr Douglas Matthews of the London Library, Dr J. Orbell, archivist of Baring Brothers, Mr A.E.B. Owen of the Cambridge University Library, Dr David Vaizey of the Bodleian.

I am most grateful to my editors, Mr Richard Ollard, Miss Carol O'Brien and Miss Lucinda McNeile of Collins and Mrs Carol Janeway of Knopf. My agent Mrs Diana Baring performed her customary miracles. Mrs Wilber typed my manuscript with skill and striking patience.

My family showed their habitual tolerance of an author on the premises. My wife Clare, by her wisdom and generosity of mind, brought to my understanding of King Edward VIII a depth that would otherwise have been lacking.

Picture Credits

King Edward VIII

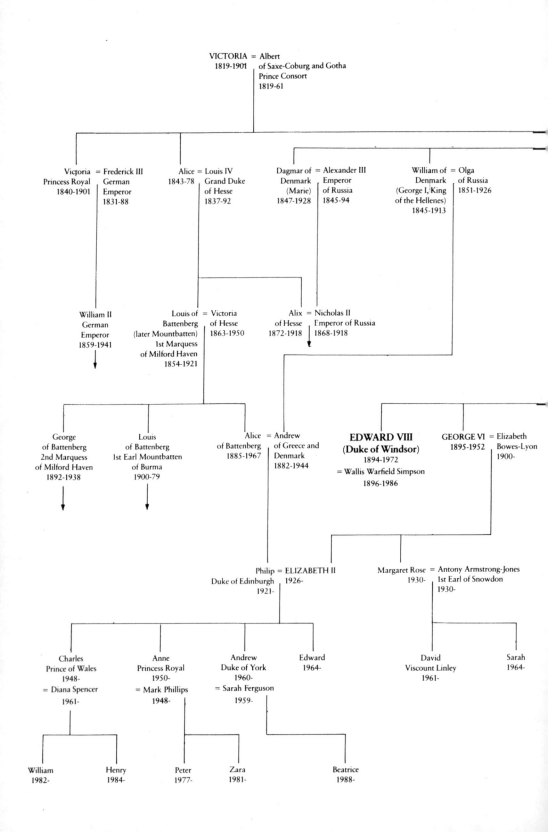

VICTORIA = Albert
1819-1901   of Saxe-Coburg and Gotha
            Prince Consort
            1819-61

Victoria = Frederick III   Alice = Louis IV   Dagmar of = Alexander III   William of = Olga
Princess Royal   German   1843-78   Grand Duke   Denmark   Emperor   Denmark   of Russia
1840-1901   Emperor   of Hesse   (Marie)   of Russia   (George I, King 1851-1926
                 1831-88   1837-92   1847-1928   1845-94   of the Hellenes)
                                                                                       1845-1913

William II   Louis of = Victoria   Alix = Nicholas II
German   Battenberg   of Hesse   of Hesse   Emperor of Russia
Emperor   (later Mountbatten) 1863-1950   1872-1918   1868-1918
1859-1941   1st Marquess
                    of Milford Haven
                    1854-1921

George   Louis   Alice = Andrew   EDWARD VIII   GEORGE VI = Elizabeth
of Battenberg   of Battenberg   of Battenberg   of Greece and   (Duke of Windsor)   1895-1952   Bowes-Lyon
2nd Marquess   1st Earl Mountbatten 1885-1967   Denmark   1894-1972   1900-
of Milford Haven   of Burma   1882-1944   = Wallis Warfield Simpson
1892-1938   1900-79   1896-1986

                                        Philip = ELIZABETH II   Margaret Rose = Antony Armstrong-Jones
                                        Duke of Edinburgh   1926-   1930-   1st Earl of Snowdon
                                        1921-   1930-

Charles   Anne   Andrew   Edward   David   Sarah
Prince of Wales   Princess Royal   Duke of York 1964-   Viscount Linley   1964-
1948-   1950-   1960-   1961-
= Diana Spencer   = Mark Phillips   = Sarah Ferguson
1961-   1948-   1959-

William   Henry   Peter   Zara   Beatrice
1982-   1984-   1977-   1981-   1988-

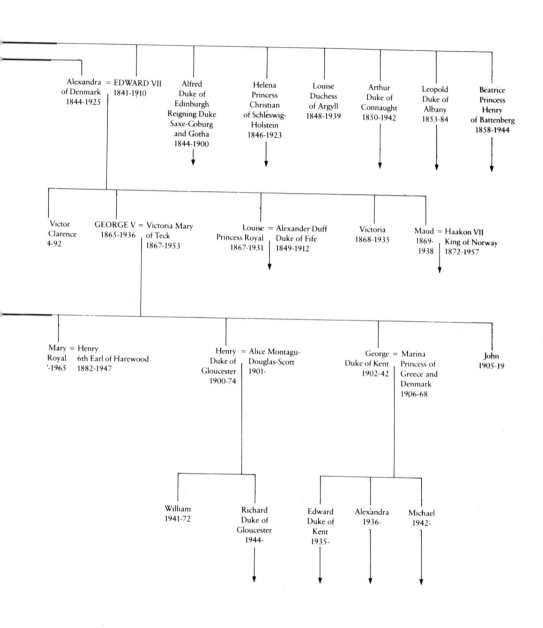

Alexandra = EDWARD VII
of Denmark   1841-1910
1844-1925

Alfred
Duke of
Edinburgh
Reigning Duke
Saxe-Coburg
and Gotha
1844-1900

Helena
Princess
Christian
of Schleswig-
Holstein
1846-1923

Louise
Duchess
of Argyll
1848-1939

Arthur
Duke of
Connaught
1850-1942

Leopold
Duke of
Albany
1853-84

Beatrice
Princess
Henry
of Battenberg
1858-1944

Victor
Clarence
4-92

GEORGE V = Victoria Mary
1865-1936   of Teck
1867-1953

Louise = Alexander Duff
Princess Royal   Duke of Fife
1867-1931   1849-1912

Victoria
1868-1935

Maud = Haakon VII
1869-   King of Norway
1938   1872-1957

Mary = Henry
Royal   6th Earl of Harewood
'-1965   1882-1947

Henry = Alice Montagu-
Duke of   Douglas-Scott
Gloucester   1901-
1900-74

George = Marina
Duke of Kent   Princess of
1902-42   Greece and
Denmark
1906-68

John
1905-19

William
1941-72

Richard
Duke of
Gloucester
1944-

Edward
Duke of
Kent
1935-

Alexandra
1936-

Michael
1942-

1

The Child

E VEN IN THE TWILIGHT OF THE TWENTIETH CENTURY to be one of the 540 or so* living and legitimate descendants of Queen Victoria is a matter of some moment. To have been born in 1894, eldest son of the eldest surviving son of the eldest son of the Queen Empress, was to be heir to an almost intolerable burden of rights and responsibilities.

Queen Victoria had then been on the throne for fifty-seven years. The great majority of her subjects had no recollection of another monarch. She had weathered the unpopularity which had grown up when she retreated into protracted seclusion after the death of the Prince Consort and now enjoyed unique renown. The Widow of Windsor, ruler of a vast empire and grandmother to half the crowned heads of Europe, was a bewitching figure; her obstinate refusal to play to the gallery had eventually won her the reverent respect of all but a tiny republican minority among her people. She had become a myth in her own lifetime.

To have a myth as a mother is not necessarily a prescription for a happy family life. In 1894 the future King Edward VII had already been Prince of Wales for more than fifty years. The role is never an easy one to fill, and in Edward's case was made almost impossible by the carping censoriousness of his parents. The Prince of Wales gave them something to censure – he was self-indulgent, indolent and licentious – but he was also uncommonly shrewd and well able to do a useful job of work if given the chance. The Queen gave him as few chances as possible. She treated him as an irresponsible delinquent, and in doing so ensured that his irresponsibility and delinquency became more marked. It was not

---

* The latest figure prepared in January 1990 by Marlene Eilers, author of *Queen Victoria's Descendants* (New York, 1987), was 536 but they are a philoprogenitive lot and the number has by now probably increased.

until he at last succeeded to the throne that his qualities as a statesman were given a proper chance to flourish.

In 1863 he married Princess Alexandra of Denmark – 'Sea-King's daughter from over the sea' – radiantly beautiful and with a sweetness of nature which enabled her to endure her husband's infidelity with generosity and dignity. She was capable of great obstinacy and occasional selfishness but she was still one of the most endearing figures to have sat upon the British throne. She rarely read, her handwriting would have disgraced an intoxicated spider, increasing deafness cut her off from society, but she enjoyed a vast and justified popularity until the day she died.

The first duty of an heir to the throne is to ensure the succession. The Prince and Princess of Wales did their best, producing two sons, three daughters, and then another short-lived son. Unhappily, however, their eldest son, Prince Albert Victor, always known as Eddy, proved an unhopeful heir for the throne of England. Languid and lymphatic – '*si peu de chose*, though as you say a "Dear Boy"', the Grand Duchess of Mecklenburg-Strelitz brutally dismissed him[1] – he deplored the strident jollity of his family and preferred to trail wistfully in the wake of whatever unsuitable woman had attracted his attention. A determined and reliable wife seemed the only hope for his redemption, and a paragon was found in Princess Victoria Mary – May to the family – only daughter of the Duke and Duchess of Teck.

The Tecks were professional poor relations. The Duke was haunted by the fact that his father's morganatic marriage had deprived him of his claim to the throne of Württemberg, and all his life attached to the rituals of rank and precedence an importance which seemed extravagant even to the courtiers who surrounded him. His mountainous wife Mary Adelaide, 'Fat Mary', was by no means unaware that she was a granddaughter of King George III, but she bore her royal blood more lightly. She devoted her energies to entertaining lavishly beyond her means and then recouping the family finances by ferocious economies and periods of exile in the relative cheapness of Florence. There Princess May spent some of her most formative years, learning the value of money the hard way, but also learning to appreciate beauty and acquiring a range of aesthetic interests which to her English cousins seemed odd if not actively undesirable. From her parents she inherited a respect

2

for the blood royal which led her to regard the occupant of the British throne with something close to reverence.

The Tecks were protégés of the British royal family, who let them occupy rooms in Kensington Palace and make their home in the pleasant, rambling grace-and-favour White Lodge, in the heart of Richmond Park. The Princess of Wales was particularly fond of the Duchess, and it was hardly surprising that May's name should have come to the fore when the quest began for a wife for Prince Eddy. It was not a spectacular match but it was respectable, and Queen Victoria considered that a future King of England needed no extra *réclame* in his bride to secure his immortality. To the Tecks the marriage was all that they had dreamed of; May's morganatic blood would have proved an impediment to an alliance with any of the grander continental royal families, while the upper reaches of the British aristocracy had shown little eagerness to embrace this peripherally royal and penniless princess. Only May hesitated. 'Do you think I can really take this on?' she asked her mother. 'Of course you can,' was the robust reply, and of course she did.[1] Her future husband was given equally little opportunity to object. 'I do not anticipate any real opposition on Prince Eddy's part if he is properly managed and told he *must* do it,' wrote the Prince of Wales's private secretary, Francis Knollys, '– that it is for the good of the country etc. etc.'[2]

May was spared what must have seemed an unappealing match. The engagement was announced at the end of 1891; the wedding fixed for February; early in January 1892 Prince Eddy contracted influenza, pneumonia developed, within a few days he was dead. His place in the line of succession was taken by his brother George. The change was in every way to the benefit of the country. In 1873 Queen Victoria had sent Prince George a watch, 'hoping that it will serve to remind you to be very punctual in everything and very exact in all your duties . . . I hope you will be a good, obedient, truthful boy, kind to all, humble-minded, dutiful and always trying to be of use to others!'[3] Few precepts can have been taken more earnestly to heart. Prince George had been conscientious, hard-working and responsible as a boy; he was no different as a man. The Royal Navy, for which he had been trained, can claim many men of cultivation and even a few eccentrics and intellectuals among the officers, but it takes considerable independence of mind to maintain such characteristics in a mainly unsympathetic environment. Prince George had neither the wish nor the ability to stand apart. He was an arch-conformist; bored by books, pictures, music; wholly without intellectual curiosity or imagination; suspicious of new ideas; entertained only by his stamp collection and the slaughter of ever greater quantities of pheasants, partridges and the like.

Yet his bluff and phlegmatic exterior was to some extent illusory. He was a worrier, an insomniac, a man whose sense of duty often stood between him and the enjoyment of his role in life. In 1892 his duty was to marry quickly and to provide heirs to a crown which would otherwise eventually fall into the unpromising hands of his sister Louise, Duchess of Fife. With a suitable bride for a future British monarch already selected, the solution seemed obvious to the Tecks and to his parents. The wedding planned for Prince Eddy should take place, only the date and the bridegroom would be changed. Prince George took little convincing that this was his destiny; May felt slightly greater qualms, but she too was soon persuaded. In May 1893 the Duke of York, as Prince George had been created the previous year, dutifully proposed to his late brother's fiancée. He was as dutifully accepted. On 6 July the couple, by now very much, if undemonstratively, in love, were married in the Chapel Royal. A year later, on 23 June 1894, their first child, a boy, was born at the Tecks' home in Richmond Park. He was not Victoria's first great-grandchild but in her eyes he was beyond measure the most important.

The original plan had been for the baby to be born in Buckingham Palace but an early heatwave drove the couple to the comparative cool of White Lodge. The Duke of York was in the library, pretending to read *Pilgrim's Progress*, when the birth took place at 10 p.m.; his father, the Prince of Wales, was holding an Ascot Week ball in the Fishing Temple at Virginia Water. The telephone that had recently been installed to link White Lodge to East Sheen was used to give him the news and enable him to propose a toast to the new prince.[1] 'My darling May was not conscious of pain during those last 2½ terrible hours,' the Duke of York wrote to Victoria; in terms that sound as if the end of the operation had

4

been not so much the cradle as the grave. 'The baby weighed 8 lbs when he was born, and *both grandmothers* . . . pronounce him to be a most beautiful, strong and healthy child.'[1] Fifteen hundred people signed their names on the following day in the book which had been placed in a marquee for the occasion, and the Duchess of Teck's sister, the Grand Duchess of Mecklenburg-Strelitz, announced that she 'went – mentally – on my knees, tears of gratitude and happiness flowing, streaming, and the *hugging* followed'.[2]

The bickering that normally accompanied the naming of a royal child now ensued. The Queen took it for granted that a daughter would be called Victoria and a son Albert. The Duke of York said it had long been decided 'that if it was a boy, we should call him Edward after *darling Eddy*. This is the dearest wish of our hearts, dearest Grandmama, for Edward is indeed a *sacred* name to us, and one which I know would have pleased *him* beyond anything.'[3] 'You write as if *Edward* was the *real* name of dear Eddy,' retorted the Queen severely; everyone knew that he had in fact been christened Albert Victor.[4] The Duke proved unusually obstinate and the baby was called Edward Albert Christian George Andrew Patrick David. Christian was the name of the baby's godfather, the King of Denmark; the other four names represented England, Scotland, Ireland and Wales. Some reports state that David was an afterthought, introduced to gratify the aged and moribund Marchioness of Waterford. There are differing views about her motives: that assiduous and well-informed courtier Lord Esher said it was because 'she had some fad about restoring the Jews to the Holy City';[5] the Prince of Wales's friend the Marquis de Breteuil recorded that the old lady had dreamed of an ancient Irish legend according to which there would be a great king over the water and his name would be David.[6]

The christening took place with all the pomp befitting a baby who stood third in line to the British throne. Twelve godparents, mainly German, attended; as well as the Prime Minister, Lord Rosebery. The gold bowl used as a font was brought from Windsor Castle. The cake, thirty inches high and five feet in circumference, was made by McVitie and Price in Edinburgh. 'I have two bottles of Jordan water,' the Duke proudly told his old tutor, Canon Dalton, and both were lavished on the occasion.[7] The only discordant note was struck by the first socialist member of parliament,

Keir Hardie. When it was proposed that the House of Commons should congratulate the Queen on the happy event, Hardie opposed the motion. 'From his childhood onward,' he said, with what to some will seem dreadful prescience, 'this boy will be surrounded by sycophants and flatterers by the score . . . A line will be drawn between him and the people he is to be called upon some day to reign over. In due course . . . he will be sent on a tour round the world, and probably rumours of a morganatic alliance will follow, and the end of it will be the country will be called upon to pay the bill.'[1]

Prince Edward, who from birth was always known to his family as David, was followed eighteen months later by a brother, Albert George, who was in due course to become Duke of York and, less predictably, King George VI. Edward attended his sibling's christening and behaved impeccably until Prince Albert, in the arms of the Bishop of Norwich, began to yell. Edward, evidently seeing this as a challenge to his primacy, yelled louder and was removed. 'Of course he is very young to come to church,' the Duke of York told the Queen, 'but we thought that in years to come it would give him pleasure to know that he had been present at his brother's christening.'[2] A daughter, Mary, was born in 1897; then came a gap of three years, after which Henry – future Duke of Gloucester – was born in 1900 and George – future Duke of Kent – in 1902. The youngest child, John, born in 1905, was an epileptic who lived in seclusion and was to die at the age of fourteen.

The three elder children were close enough in age to be much together; Princes Edward and Albert – David and Bertie – being in particular inseparable. Lord Esher, visiting Sandringham, played with the children in the garden and noted that: 'The second boy is the sharpest – but there is something rather taking about Prince Edward.'[3] Most other observers agree it was Edward who was the sharper and who habitually took the lead – 'because as the eldest son he had the highest status in the family,' explained the Duchess of York's close friend, Lady Airlie.[4] He found that he could easily manage his tractable and worshipping younger brother, but that Princess Mary was an independent-minded tomboy who was disinclined to do the bidding of any mere boy.

It has often been alleged – not least by the subject of this biography – that the Duke and Duchess of York were cold and

6

distant parents. It would be foolish to pretend that the relationship between the future King George V and his sons, in particular his eldest son, was a happy one. When they were babies, however, all the evidence is that he was a doting father; far more ready to take an interest in his children than was true of most English parents of the upper and upper middle classes. 'I have got those two photographs of you and darling Baby on my table before me now,' he wrote to his wife from Cowes in August 1894. '. . . I like looking at my Tootsums little wife and my sweet child, it makes me happy when they are far away.'[1]* 'Baby is very flourishing. He walks about all over the house, he has 14 teeth,' he boasted to Canon Dalton. A month later Prince Edward still walked about all over the house but had sixteen teeth.[2] The Duchess was more critical in her attitude. Her baby, she told her brother, was 'exactly what I looked like as a baby, consequently *plain*. This is a pity and rather disturbs me.'[3] She does not seem to have had much idea of what was to be expected from a small child: 'David was "jumpy" yesterday morning,' she wrote when he was a little over two years old, 'however he got quieter after being out, what a curious child he is.'[4] When Edward began to get letters from his parents, the Duke of York was always the more demonstratively affectionate. He was coming to Sandringham on Saturday, he told his three-year-old son, and would be 'so pleased to see our darling little chicks again'. When the chicks had chickenpox; 'I hope none of you have grown wings and become little chickens and tried to fly away, that would be dreadful and we should have to go up in a balloon to catch you.'[5]

The trouble began when his children reached an age at which mature conduct might reasonably – or unreasonably – be expected of them. Admiral Fisher, at Balmoral in 1903, noted: 'The two little Princes are splendid little boys and chattered away the whole of their lunch-time, not the faintest shyness.'[6] The comment is notable as marking one of the last occasions on which father and sons were observed together without something being said about the constraint and fear which dominated the atmosphere. Kenneth Rose has convincingly challenged the story by which King George V is supposed to have told Lord Derby: 'My father was

---

* An ambiguous remark; presumably the Duke derived comfort from the photograph rather than the distance.

frightened of his mother, I was frightened of my father, and I'm damned well going to see that my children are frightened of me!'[1] But though the tale may well be apocryphal, like most apocryphal tales it contains an essential truth. The Duke of York loved and wanted the best for his children but he was a bad-tempered and often frightening man; he was never cruel, but he was a harsh disciplinarian who believed that a bit of bullying never did a child any harm; he shouted, ranted, struck out both verbally and physically to express his displeasure. A summons to the library almost always heralded a rebuke, and a rebuke induced terror in the recipient. His banter was well-intentioned but it could also be brutal. On the birth of Prince Henry: 'David of course asked some very funny questions. I told him the baby had flown in at the window during the night, and he at once asked where his wings were and I said they had been cut off.'[2] Prince Edward was six at the time, and he claimed the vision of his brother's bleeding wings disturbed his sleep for weeks afterwards.

The Duke of York had rigid ideas, invested with almost totemic significance, about punctuality, deportment, above all dress. The children were treated as midshipmen, perpetually on parade. Any deviation from the approved ritual was a fall from grace to be punished for the sake of the offender. 'I hope your kilts fit well, take care and don't spoil them at once as they are new,' wrote the Duke to his eldest son. 'Wear the Balmoral kilt and grey jacket on week days and green kilt and black jacket on Sundays. Do not wear the red kilt till I come.'[3] Inevitably they got things wrong, wore a grey jacket with a green kilt or a Balmoral kilt on Sundays. Retribution was swift and fearful. 'The House of Hanover, like ducks, produce bad parents,' the royal librarian, Owen Morshead, told Harold Nicolson. 'They trample on their young.' 'It was a mystery,' said a royal private secretary, Alec Hardinge, 'why George V, who was such a kind man, was such a brute to his children.'[4]

Prince Albert, more nervous and slow-witted than his elder brother, suffered as much, but Edward, both because of his status and his tendency to carelessness, came in for the most censorious attention. His father took due pride in his achievements. David recited a poem 'quite extraordinarily well', he noted in his diary. 'He said Wolseley's farewell (Shakespeare) without a mistake.'[5]

The Child

But he felt correspondingly sharp dismay at his son's backslidings. 'The real difficulty had been with the Duke of Windsor, never with the present King,' Queen Mary told Nicolson many years later.[1] She deluded herself if she thought that Prince Bertie had escaped unscathed, but she was right in her belief that her elder son, from whom so much was expected and who found acquiescence in his father's shibboleths so much more uncongenial, was the principal victim in the generation war. Prince Edward certainly saw himself as such, a conviction that was fortified as his childhood slipped farther into the past. He told Freda Dudley Ward's daughter Angela how lucky she was to have a loving mother. His own childhood had been dreadful, he said; he had received no love and no appreciation for his achievements.[2] 'I had a *wretched* childhood!' he told his authorial assistant, Charles Murphy. 'Of course there were short periods of happiness but I remember it chiefly for the miserableness I had to keep to myself.'[3] That this misery was exaggerated in retrospect seems evident, that it was real and painful at the time is hardly less so.

His mother did her best to provide a refuge from the Duke's harshness. 'We used to have a most lovely time with her alone — always laughing and joking,' Edward remembered, '. . . she was a different human being away from him.'[4] But though she made manifest her sympathy for her children, she did little to protect them from their father's wrath, or to try to change his attitude. Though to later generations she appeared the quintessence of intractable strong-mindedness, she held her husband in awe, as an individual and still more as a future monarch. 'I always have to remember that their father is also their King,'[5] she was later to pronounce, and the King-to-be deserved almost the same reverence. She saw her role as that of loyal support; to argue with, or still more, criticize her husband was something to be done rarely, and then only with extreme caution.

The Duke and Duchess were not the only people of significance in the children's lives. It is curious that almost all the nannies who feature in the pages of childhood memoirs are either saints or sadists. Edward had one of each. The sadist delighted in pinching him or twisting his arm just before his evening visit to his parents' drawing room; as a result he would cry and find himself peremptorily banished.[6] The saint, Charlotte 'Lalla' (or, to Edward, 'Lala')

Bill, came later as nurse to Princess Mary and extended her attention to the boys. Neither had any great importance in Edward's upbringing. More influential was the stalwart Finch, a nursery footman whose father had been in the service of the great Duke of Wellington and who shared some of that dignitary's resolution and resourcefulness. From male nanny he stayed on to serve his master as valet and then butler, dependable, devoted, totally loyal, always respectful yet blunt sometimes to the point of rudeness. He allowed his youthful charge to take no liberties and on one occasion spanked him for teasing Lalla Bill. Edward threatened to denounce him to his father, but Lalla Bill got her story in first and insult was added to injury when the Prince was made to apologize to Finch for being such a nuisance.[1]

But it was his grandparents who provided the most striking contrast to his father's stern regime. The Prince of Wales could be quite as bad-tempered and as much a stickler for protocol as his son, and possessed a streak of meanness which was missing in the Duke of York, but to his grandchildren he was almost as indulgent as he was to himself. Edward basked in his obvious affection and endured with equanimity outbursts that would have terrified him in his father. Once he infuriated his grandfather by fidgeting at luncheon and finally knocking something off the table. 'Damn you, boy!' roared the Prince, smashing a melon to the floor. 'David surveyed the debris in silence and then turned to his grandfather with an irresistibly funny expression of polite enquiry. Then the two burst out laughing.'[2] His grandmother was still less alarming. 'We saw dear Grannie yesterday,' Edward wrote in 1897, in a letter presumably dictated to a nursemaid, 'and she had a funny cock and an owl which she blowed out of a pipe.'[3] With Queen Alexandra, as she was shortly to become, it was always cocks and owls and laughs and demonstrative affection.

It amused the Waleses to subvert their son's austerity. In August 1900 the Yorks set off on an extensive imperial tour. The grandparents were left in charge, and reports were soon reaching the royal tourists of the way the children were being pampered and their education neglected. The last straw came when the woman supposed to be teaching Edward French was left behind when the family moved to Sandringham. The Duchess protested, but got little satisfaction. 'The reason we did not take her,' wrote Queen

The Child

Alexandra, 'was that [Doctor] Laking particularly asked that he might be left more with his brothers and sister – for a *little while* – as we all noticed how *precautious* [sic – "precocious" is presumably what she had in mind] and *old-fashioned* he was getting – and quite the *ways* of a "*single child*"! which will make him ultimately a "tiresome child" – laying down the law and thinking himself far superior to the younger ones. It did him a great deal of good – to be treated the *same* as Bertie . . .'[1]

The charge that Edward was being brought up as an only child does not seem well founded. The three elder children were much together, and, in spite of their father's insistence on correct clothing on every occasion, enjoyed a freedom to roam the countryside on foot or bicycle which would seem enviable to contemporary princes. Edward felt protective towards his siblings; it is said that once, when he heard that his father was on the way to inspect the flower beds that they were encouraged to look after at Windsor, he covered up for his sister's inadequacy as a gardener by running ahead and transplanting some flowers from his plot to hers.[2] Lord Esher spent some time with them in 1904 and noted: 'The youngest is the most riotous. The eldest a sort of head nurse.' Looking through a magazine together the children chanced on a picture of Prince Edward labelled 'Our Future King'. 'Prince Albert at once drew attention to it – but the elder hastily brushed his brother's finger away and turned the page. Evidently he thought it bad taste.'[3]

But outside the family his social horizons were severely limited. Occasional visits to cousins of his age was the utmost permitted him. The children of the Duke and Duchess of Fife were favoured companions. 'He was so pleased to be with them,' reported a governess. 'They wanted to take his hand and he wanted to take their ball' – an exchange which he must have felt greatly to his advantage.[4] But he seems to have had no aversion to girls. 'So dear David is precocious,' wrote his great-aunt Augusta. 'He was so from the first. I have a vivid and pleasing recollection of the only time I saw him this year at White Lodge, when he *flirted* with the nice Lady Cousins.'[5]

The Duke of York was a man of habit and, imperial tours apart, he liked the year to unroll to an unchanging pattern. In January the whole family was at York Cottage, Sandringham, the children staying on there in February and March while their parents were in London. At Easter they were reunited at York Cottage or Frogmore House, Windsor. They stayed together in London for May and June, and then in July and August the children with their mother would retreat to Frogmore while the Duke shot or yachted. September and the first half of October were spent near Balmoral; then it was back to York Cottage for the rest of the year.

York Cottage was thus as near to a permanent home as the children knew. It had been built by the Prince of Wales to hold the overflow from his vaster shooting parties and given to the Duke of York as a wedding present. The word 'Cottage' hardly conveys a true picture. Harold Nicolson, who must have visited it on a cold, wet day, described it as 'a glum little villa . . . separated by an abrupt rim of lawn from a pond at the edge of which a leaden pelican gazes in dejection upon the water lilies and bamboos'.[1] In sunnier circumstances the pond is a more than respectable lake and the life-size pelican looks contented if not exuberant. As for the glum little villa – villa perhaps, but large enough to provide today spacious estate offices, storage rooms for the Sandringham shop and five decent-sized flats. The rooms were small – the nursery being barely large enough to accommodate a medium-sized rocking horse – but the Duke liked small rooms, which reminded him of naval cabins. 'Very nice to be in this dear wee house again,' he wrote in his diary, and when his father offered to rent for him Lord Cholmondeley's palace at nearby Houghton, he rejected the proposal with alacrity. As a child Edward was fond enough of its cosy and suburban comfort, as he grew older it came more and more to symbolize all that he disliked about family life.

His education was at first desultory. Reading, writing and a little history were given priority; Latin, mathematics and the sciences were eschewed; French and German were deemed essential, with enforced recitations of poems in both languages on his parents' birthdays, turning these festivals into nightmares. 'I am a good boy. I know a lot of German,' Edward proudly told his father in 1901.[2] He was less good when it came to French, mainly from dislike of his teacher, a podgy Alsatian lady called Hélène Bricka whom he described as 'a dreadful old person'.[3] Religious instruction, such as it was, came from Canon Dalton; it failed to enthral the young prince. Cecil Sharp, expert in folklore, song and dancing, was supposed to have taken charge of Edward's 'social education' and first inspired in him a passion for 'physical jerks' and other forms of violent and uncomfortable exercise.[1] Geography was picked up largely as a by-product of the Yorks' travels. 'I am very pleased to get a present from Christchurch and a whip from Tasmania,' he wrote when his parents were in the Antipodes. 'I know where these places are . . . Fancy Papa shooting peacocks.'[2] He learned the art of crochet from his mother and picked up some general knowledge from forays into the royal palaces. 'There are such a lot of books,' he remarked in awe after a visit to the library at Windsor. 'I saw the first book Caxton printed. I read all about him in *Arthur's History*.'[3] It was not a bad beginning, but it did not add up to the formal education required by a future king. His father knew that something more was called for, but could not convince himself that the matter was of any urgency, until January 1901 when Queen Victoria died. The Prince of Wales succeeded as King Edward VII; the Duke of York became Duke of Cornwall and ten months later added the title of Prince of Wales.

Prince Edward, aged six, was now second in line to the throne. The event meant little to him; he was dimly aware that something of vast significance had occurred, an era had ended, hushed and reverent mourning was in order, but he had hardly known his great-grandmother and felt no personal grief at her disappearance. Of the funeral he remembered only 'the piercing cold, the interminable waits, and of feeling very lost'.[4] He made a clearer impression on others than the ceremony did on him. His aunt Maud, Princess Charles of Denmark and later Queen of Norway, remembered that 'Sweet little David behaved so well during the service and was supported by the little Hesse girl who took him under her protection and held him most of the time round his neck. They looked such a delightful little couple!'[5] King Edward's Coronation the following year meant little more to him. Edward remembered only the longueurs of the service in the Abbey, mitigated by the clatter when one of the great-aunts dropped her book programme over the edge of her box into a gold cup below. Once only did the ceremony come alive, when his mother whispered to him, 'Now Papa will do homage to Grandpapa.'[6] For a moment the relevance of what was going on to himself and to his country became dramatically apparent.

13

Grumbling, the Duke of Cornwall – or Prince of Wales, as it is easier to style him without more ado – moved from his modest apartments in St James's Palace to the massive grandeur of Marlborough House. He took over Frogmore House at Windsor and Abergeldie near Balmoral. These changes made little difference to his son's way of life. But a far more significant event had already occurred. In the spring of 1902 the Prince of Wales engaged as tutor to his elder sons Henry Hansell, a thirty-nine-year-old schoolmaster and son of a Norfolk country gentleman, who had taken his degree at Magdalen College, Oxford, and had recently been tutor to the Duke of Connaught's son, Prince Arthur.

There were a lot of good things about Hansell. Six foot three inches tall and strikingly handsome, he had played football for Oxford and was an excellent shot. Shane Leslie, who was taught by him, describes him as uproariously funny, to small boys at least, convulsing all around him by the comical goose step with which he would advance from his goal in a football match.[1] He liked his charges and served them with loyalty and devotion. The Princess of Wales thought he taught history well and managed to engage the boys' interest: 'This pleases me immensely as you know how devoted I am to history.'[2] He made an excellent impression on many people who should have been competent judges. Lord Derby said of him: 'Never have I found a man who understands boys better. Admirably straight, but very broadminded. I can imagine no man better able to guide rather than drive a boy.'[3] '*Mon impression sur M. Hansell fut excellente du premier coup,*' wrote the Marquis de Breteuil. '*Je le jugeai de suite un homme intelligent, plein de tact, bon et complètement dévoué à son élève.*'[4]

And yet it is impossible to doubt that this good, honest, conscientious man had a disastrous effect on the intellectual development of his pupils. Without imagination, with only the most rudimentary sense of humour, pedestrian in mind, aesthetically unaware, Hansell represented everything that was most philistine and blinkered about the English upper middle classes. Whatever adventurous instincts Edward might have had were blanketed by his tutor's smug and unquestioning self-assurance. Harry Verney worked with Hansell during the First World War and told Edward that what had struck him was 'his commanding presence . . . his savoir faire coupled with the most incredible stupidity in dealing with the business of the office . . . I am amazed to read that he got a Second in history at Oxford, but I expect you are right. With it all what a very charming man he was, and devoted to you.'[1] Edward's final view was not dissimilar. He told Harold Nicolson in 1953 that Hansell had been 'melancholy and inefficient'. 'He never taught us anything at all,' he went on. 'I am completely self-educated.'[2]

Prince Edward had a naturally enquiring mind. He was ready to question any dogma and investigate any phenomenon which he did not immediately comprehend. He was hungry for exact information, and wanted to know not only how things worked, but why, and whether they could work better. He did not lose this freshness of approach but, thanks in part at least to Hansell, it was never harnessed to an intellectual apparatus which would have made it an effective instrument. It was the mark of Hansell's tuition that the Duke of Windsor could admit fifty years later that he had 'always preferred learning history from pictures than from script, and it's amazing how much one can learn from pictures'.[3] That his father should think his progress under Hansell all that could be desired was perhaps to be expected; that his mother was equally approving is more surprising. Yet she appears to have had no qualms. 'I do so hope our children will turn out common-sense people, which is so important in this world,' she told her aunt Augusta early in 1907. 'We have taken no end of trouble with their education and they have very nice people round them so one feels all is being done to help them.'[4]

To be fair to Hansell, he saw the claustrophobic limitations in the system of education imposed upon his charges. He wanted them sent to a preparatory school, preferably Ludgrove where he himself had taught. When this proposal was brusquely vetoed by the Prince of Wales, he at least tried to open their social horizons a little way by organizing football matches in which the princes and boys from the local village played against teams from nearby schools. Edward enjoyed both the games and the conviviality which accompanied them. His father was dubious, not so much over the principle as over the choice of sport. He complained to Hansell that the Prince much preferred 'football to golf, which is a pity, and dislikes playing golf now, probably because his brother beats him, but I want you to encourage him all you can. I have already told him he will have more opportunities of playing golf when he grows up than football or cricket.'[1] But Edward was always hesitant about fresh experiences: 'How funny he is about trying anything new like hockey,' remarked his father. 'We must try to get him over it.'[2]

> You'll be glad to hear
> That the Cuckoo is hear!
>   That is poetry.[3]

wrote Edward proudly from Frogmore in April 1904. It was a solitary foray into an art form that was to hold little appeal for him in later life. But in some ways his education was less inadequate. He took a keen interest in the 1906 general election, which Hansell turned into a game. Edward backed Campbell-Bannerman, the Liberal leader; Prince Albert favoured the Conservative Balfour. When Campbell-Bannerman, duly elected Prime Minister, visited Windsor, the eleven-year-old Prince asked whether being at the top of the ladder would not make him feel giddy. 'Is this not delightful and promising for his future!' exclaimed his doting great-aunt Augusta.[4] His memory for names and faces was trained from a very early age – after going into a room with some fifty people in it he was rigorously grilled on the identity of every one he had met. He was encouraged to take an interest in any part of the world visited by his parents. When the Prince of Wales was in India: 'Mr Holland Hibbert came to lecture to us. The part that interested me most was when he told us about the holy men of Benares. He said that some of them hold their arms up all their lives. I think it must be rather tiresome.' Some of them also lie on a bed of nails, replied his father. 'I thought them rather nasty kind of people.'[5]

But the Prince never learned to read for pleasure or acquired even a superficial knowledge of the English classics. Tommy Lascelles, then his private secretary, speculated many years later about what Hansell could have taught his charge. 'I recollect the Prince of Wales years ago, coming back from a weekend at Panshanger and saying to me, "Look at this extraordinary little book wh. Lady Desborough says I ought to read. Have you ever heard of it?"' The extraordinary little book was *Jane Eyre*. Another time he asked Hardy to settle an argument he had had with his mother about whether the novelist had written a book called *Tess of the D'Urbervilles*; 'I said I was sure it was by somebody else.' Hardy answered politely that it had indeed been one of his earlier books.[1] A working knowledge of English literature is perhaps unnecessary to a monarch, but to be totally ignorant of its greatest monuments is surely undesirable.

In the many accounts that survive of Edward at this period, it is his quickness, brightness and anxiety to please which are most often remarked on. 'A delightful child, so intelligent, nice and friendly,' said Queen Victoria;[2] 'a sweet little person' was Esher's judgment;[3] 'he had a look of both intelligence and kindness, and a limpid clarity of expression,' observed the Aga Khan.[4] His formal courtesy and consideration for others were unusual in one so young, as also 'the look of Weltschmerz in his eyes' which Lord Esher detected when he was only eleven years old. He was soft-hearted, telling Lord Roberts that when he was King he would pass a law against cutting puppy dogs' tails and forbid the use of bearing reins on horses. 'Those two things are very cruel.'[5] When he caught his first fish he danced for joy, then handed it to the boatman and said: 'You must *not* kill him, throw him back into the water again!'[6] (Such sensibilities did not endure. Only a year later he was recording in triumph, 'We caught such a lot of fishes! and had them for breakfast this morning.'[7]) But his benevolence, though sincere, was sometimes remote from the realities of human existence. The first recorded story that he told his brothers was about an extremely poor couple living on a deserted moor. They were starving. One day the man heard his wife moan, 'I'm so hungry.' '"Very well," said her husband. "I'll see to it." So he rang the bell and, when the footman came, ordered a plate of bread and butter.'[8]

In June 1904 Prince Edward's skull was inspected by Bernard Holländer, an eminent phrenologist. Most of the comments could have been made by anyone of a sycophantic nature without reference to the cranium, but there are some interesting points. The Prince, said Holländer, was eager to acquire knowledge and a keen observer, but 'he would show his talents to greater advantage were he possessed of power of concentration and greater self-confidence'. He had a good eye for painting and would like music, though mainly of the lighter kind, 'for example songs and dancing tunes'. He would have little use for organized religion himself but would respect the views of others. 'Persons with the Prince's type of head are never guilty of either a mean or dishonest action; they are just-minded, kindly disposed and faithful to their word.' He had strong 'feelings of humanity and sympathy for the welfare of others . . . He will seek to alleviate the sufferings of the poor.' He would be uneasy in company, dislike public appearances, accept responsibilities with reluctance. He would not, it was clear, find it easy to be King.[1] Even at the age of ten he seemed to cherish doubts about his fitness for the role that his birth had thrust on him. More than thirty-two years later, after the abdication, Lalla Bill wrote in high emotion to Queen Mary. 'Do you remember, Your Majesty, when he was quite young, how he didn't wish to live, and he never wanted to become King?'[2]

2

The Youth

THERE WERE GOOD REASONS FOR CHOOSING THE Royal Navy as a training ground for future monarchs. Careers open to princes at the beginning of the twentieth century were rare indeed, and the armed services provided one of the few in which they could find employment. The Navy, as the senior, was the obvious choice. It was a cherished national institution, its officers were recruited largely from the gentry or aristocracy, it offered less opportunities for debauchery or any kind of escapade than its land-based counterpart, it inculcated those virtues which it was felt were above all needed in a future king: sobriety, self-reliance, punctuality, a respect for authority and instinct to conform. A few years at sea would do harm to few and most people a lot of good. But to thrust a boy into the Navy at the age of twelve and leave him there until he was nineteen or twenty, if not longer, was unlikely to produce the rounded personality and breadth of mind needed to cope with the plethora of problems which afflict the constitutional monarch. When Edward's father and uncle went to sea, Queen Victoria complained that the 'very rough sort of life to which boys are exposed on board ship is the very thing not calculated to make a refined and amiable Prince'.[1]

The risk seemed more that the Navy would blinker rather than brutalize a prince. The curious thing was that the Prince of Wales himself was aware of the limitations of a naval education. He knew that he had grown up without any understanding of international affairs, any knowledge of society or politics, any facility for languages. He deplored these handicaps. And yet when it came to his own sons, he condemned them to the same sterile routine. At least when he had joined the Navy it had not seemed likely that he would become King. Prince Edward was destined for the throne, yet still the same formula was applied. It was almost as if the Prince of Wales was determined that, as he had himself been deprived of proper training for his life work, his son should suffer equally; and yet in fact no thought could have been further from his mind.

The best hope for Edward seemed to be that he would fail to pass the entrance examination. Everyone agreed that he should be subjected to the same ordeal as any other candidate, though he was to be medically inspected by the royal doctors – 'I may perhaps add that he is a particularly strong, healthy boy,' wrote Hansell.[1] He had no Latin, but at a pinch could have offered German as an alternative. No one doubted that he was intelligent enough, but his spelling was appalling and his knowledge of mathematics exiguous. The Prince of Wales was apprehensive, then delighted and relieved to be told his son had passed the *viva voce* examination with flying colours. 'Palpably above the average,' said Sir Arthur Fanshawe,[2] while another examiner, Lord Hampton, said that of the three hundred boys he had seen, Edward had been equal to the best.[3] 'This has pleased us immensely,' wrote the Princess of Wales proudly.[4] But the overall results of the written examination were not so flattering. In fact he 'failed by a few marks to pass the qualifying examination, an Admiralty official reported in 1936. 'Prince Edward obtained 291 marks out of 600 . . . but I notice that 5 candidates with lower marks were entered.'[5]

At all events, he did well enough to be admitted without imposing too great a strain on the examiners' consciences. In May 1907 his father took him to the Naval College at Osborne in the Isle of Wight. 'I felt the parting from you very much,' the Prince of Wales wrote two days later, 'and we all at home miss you greatly. But I saw enough . . . to assure me that you would get on capitally and be very happy with all the other boys. Of course at first it will all seem a bit strange to you but you will soon settle down . . . and have a very jolly time of it.'[6] It seems unlikely that Prince Edward saw jolly times ahead when he received this letter. For any small boy the first exile to boarding school must be a scarifying experience; for Edward the ordeal was worse since he had been evicted abruptly from a cloistered family circle in which the existence of other children was hardly known. He shared a dormitory with thirty others, adjusting himself painfully to the fact that the day began at six, discipline was rigid, all work and play were conducted in a hectic bustle. He slept between the sons of Lord Spencer and

Admiral Curzon-Howe. They had been chosen because their parents were well known to the Prince of Wales, but to Edward they seemed at first as alien as if they had been visitors from Mars. He had no idea how to relate to his contemporaries and had to learn not only new manners but almost a new language. It was much to his credit that he managed to look cheerful when his father left and to write proudly a few days later: 'I am getting on very well here now . . . I think nothing of going up the mast as I am quite used to it.'[1] His mother gratefully took his protestations at face value. 'He has fallen into his new life very quickly,' she told her aunt Augusta, 'which is such a blessing.'[2]

The Prince of Wales's instructions were that his son was to be treated exactly like any other naval cadet. Edward asked for nothing better, his ruling desire was to conform and to be accepted by his peers. But there was no chance that he would be able to escape altogether from his identity. He was subjected to mild bullying by small boys determined to show that he was not anything very special; red ink was poured down his neck, his hands were tied behind his back and he was guillotined in the sash window of his classroom. But his inoffensiveness and obvious determination not to trade on his rank soon led to his acceptance. Within a few weeks he had won through, was given a nickname – 'Sardines', presumably because he was the son of the Prince of W[h]ales – and became a tolerated if not leading member of society.

'Perhaps the actual hours of work at Osborne are not excessive,' the Prince of Wales wrote to Hansell, with greater perception than might have been expected, 'but the whole life is a very strenuous one and they are never alone and therefore never quiet from the time they get up till the time they go to bed.'[3] Sociable by nature, Edward survived the hurly-burly well, but the gaps left by Hansell's teaching quickly became apparent. He did well in French but even special coaching in mathematics failed to raise him from the bottom ten places in the Exmouth term of sixty or so cadets. On the whole he settled respectably, if without great distinction, a little above the halfway mark; more important, he worked steadily throughout his two years at Osborne, reaching his peak after eighteen months and then only slipping back because of ill health. His father applauded his achievements and was decently consolatory about his setbacks. 'I am delighted with the good reports that were sent me about you and that you are now 24th in your term,' he wrote at the end of 1907, '. . . that is splendid, and I am sure you must be very pleased about it too and it will make you more keen about your mark.'[1]

Edward's letters to his parents were short and uncommunicative even by the standards of schoolboys, consisting mainly of excuses for not having written before or at greater length: 'I am in a bean-bag team and I had to practise every morning,' was one explanation; 'I have had to practise Swedish drill every morning,' occurred a few weeks later; then, in desperation, 'I have been doing such a lot of things lately that I have not had much time.'[2] His father tolerated brevity but not a failure to write at all. 'You must be able to find time to write to me once a week,' he protested, '. . . I am anxious to hear how you are getting on.'[3] Edward endured stoically the separation from his family, but felt it a bit hard when his mother announced that she intended to visit Germany during the first two weeks of his first holidays. The Princess of Wales was apologetic but unrelenting; Aunt Augusta was eighty-five and unable to travel. 'I hope we shall have great fun when we *do* meet,' she wrote.[4] In spite of the demands on their time the Waleses generally did manage to make the holidays fun. 'We miss you most dreadfully,' the Prince of Wales wrote when his son returned to Osborne. 'I fear you felt very sad at leaving home. I know I did when I was a boy, it is only natural that you should, and it shows that you are fond of your home.'[5]

By the time Prince Albert followed his brother to Osborne, Edward was in his last term and a figure of some consequence. 'I hope you have "put him up to the ropes" as we say,' wrote their father. 'You must look after him all you can.'[6] Opportunities for such tutelage were limited, boys from different terms were not supposed to mix at Osborne and when the brothers wanted to talk together surreptitious assignations had to be made in the further reaches of the playing fields. Prince Edward was expected to do more than just give comfort to his sibling; the Prince of Wales frequently instructed him to make sure Bertie worked harder or to pass on complaints about his failure to concentrate. Edward seems to have relished the quasi-parental role, especially since his brother did conspicuously worse than him. 'Bertie was 61st in the order which was not so bad,' he wrote later from Dartmouth. 'I really think he is trying to work a bit. This is an excellent thing . . .'[1]

Though Edward had hardly been an outstanding success at Osborne, let alone a hero, he had profited by his time there. He had gained immeasurably in confidence and found that it was possible to get on well with his contemporaries. 'He is wonderfully improved,' noted Esher, 'Osborne has made him unshy, and given him good manners.'[2] His father, after only one term, found him 'more manly' and much more able to look after himself.[3] It had been sink or swim; anyone who could not look after himself in the maelstrom of Osborne life would not have survived for long. But he had swum, and even got some pleasure out of doing so. When he got home to Frogmore at the beginning of his first holidays he had found the entrance beflagged and a large banner reading '*Vive l'amiral!*' No banners flew on his final departure from Osborne but a sense of achievement possessed him just the same.

Dartmouth follows Osborne as the day the night, and giving something of the same impression of light following dark. Though the discipline seemed almost as harsh, the bullying as mindless, the tempo of life as relentless as at Osborne, the cadets were that much nearer to maturity and their troubles easier to endure. 'This is a very nice place, much nicer than Osborne . . .' wrote Edward in relief in May 1909. 'There is a very nice Chapel here and I think I am going to join the Choir.' But the pressure was still on. 'There is an awful rush here and everything has to be done so quickly. We are allowed 3 minutes to undress in the evening.'[4] His mother was alarmed by this last piece of information. How could he do a proper job of cleaning his teeth in so short a time? 'This is so important and I want to know. Don't forget to answer this question.'[5] Edward's reply was tinged with the exasperation that a boy of fifteen properly feels towards a fussing mother. The three minutes did not include time for brushing teeth. 'We are allowed *plenty* of time for that. There is also *plenty* of time in the morning, and I am taking great care of my teeth.'[6]

He had moved on to Dartmouth with his contemporaries from Osborne, so the process of adjustment was less painful than at the junior college. Stephen King-Hall, who was a cadet in the same year, recorded that he was 'rather shy but generally liked'. In his first terms he was sometimes seen staggering back from the football fields with a load of boots, victim of the wish of some senior cadet to be able to say in later life: 'The King once carried my boots.'[1] His academic strengths and weaknesses did not greatly change. In May 1909 he reported proudly that he was top in German, second in history, top in English, third in French, but only thirty-seventh in the overall order, still dragged down by his inability to manage any branch of mathematics.[2] In the exams in March 1910 he was forty-eighth in geometry and forty-fifth in trigonometry out of a term of fifty-nine: 'That is quite good for me,' he wrote defensively.[3] He found exams difficult and regularly produced worse results than he had in class. Lord Knutsford stayed at York Cottage early in 1911 and spoke to Edward about the examination system. The Prince praised it, in spite of his own inadequacy. As to the final exams, he said, 'I dare say I shall take some time, as I am not at all clever, but I might pass.' Knutsford found him 'a really charming boy, very simple and keen'. He taught him card tricks and found that 'he could do the "French drop" fairly well'.[4]

The previous year his Easter holidays had been unexpectedly extended by the sudden illness of the King. During the night of 6 May 1910 Edward VII died. The first Edward knew of it was when Bertie saw from their window in Marlborough House that the Royal Standard over Buckingham Palace was at half mast. He mentioned this to his father who muttered, 'That's all wrong,' and ordered the Standard to be transferred to Marlborough House and flown 'close up'.[5] King Edward VII might be dead but the King lived.

With his father now King George V, Edward automatically inherited the Dukedom of Cornwall. Life at Dartmouth in theory was unchanged but the cadets would have been less than human if they had not recognized that only one life stood between their fifteen-year-old contemporary and the throne.

Perhaps in deference to his presence, the authorities at Dartmouth had introduced a course of Civics. He told his father that he was much enjoying it and discovering a great deal about the constitution: 'It is such a useful subject for me to learn.'[6] He began to follow the daily papers, taking the *Morning Post* and the *Westminster Gazette*. It was 'a very good thing, I think', he told his mother. 'It is about time I read the papers, as in years to come, when I am obliged to follow politics, I shall know something about it.'[1] The King saw this letter and at once wrote to insist that *The Times* be substituted for the *Morning Post* – 'the views and opinions expressed are much sounder in every way'. The *Westminster Gazette* was excellent and moderate – 'You should always try and form moderate opinions about things, and never extreme ones, especially in politics.'[2] He must have written with special feeling since Britain was involved in a constitutional crisis over the powers of the House of Lords in which moderate opinions were hard to find. 'It must have been so very hard for Papa to say the right thing, and yet show at the same time that he was not partial to one party or the other,' wrote Edward sympathetically.[3]

The succession of his father to the throne with all the attendant ceremonies reduced the usefulness of Edward's last term at Dartmouth. His parents were sorry that he should find himself thrust into the position of heir to the throne 'without being older and having more preparation'. Still, the Queen told her aunt Augusta, 'we have done our best for him and we can only hope and pray we may have succeeded and that he will ever uphold the honour and traditions of our house'.[4] The Rev. H. Dixon Wright, who prepared Edward for confirmation, had the same cause at heart. The Prince's mind, he told Archbishop Davidson, was 'absolutely innocent and uncontaminated'. With the consent of the King Wright had 'warned him on the subject of "the sinful lusts of the flesh", that he may be forearmed'.[5] The Archbishop was somewhat dismayed to find that the King expected him to 'examine' the Prince in the presence of his parents and suggested some relaxation of the procedure. 'I have no wish whatever for the examination which my dear brother and I had to undergo in the presence of the Queen and my parents,' wrote George V cheerfully. 'I thought it a terrible ordeal, but was under the impression it was always done with the members of my family. Delighted to hear that it is not necessary.'[6] The confirmation passed off none the worse for this breach with precedent. 'The impression made upon me by the quiet boyish simplicity, the clear and really thoughtful attitude, and the wistful keenness of the young Prince is one which can never be effaced,' wrote the Archbishop, a tribute that would have been still more impressive if it had been written to anyone but the Queen.[7]

The Coronation was fixed for 22 June 1911. Being still only

sixteen Edward could not wear a peer's robes, so his father created him a Knight of the Garter. For one who was soon to show an almost pathological dislike of dressing up, Edward donned the somewhat fanciful costume with striking calm, in his diary noting merely that it would 'look very well when ready' and that it was lucky that his father no longer needed his, since the expense would otherwise have been considerable.[1] The Queen told her aunt that he had carried off the ceremony with great sang-froid and dignity: 'David wore the Garter dress white and silver with the cloak and big hat and feathers. He really looked too sweet.'[2]

The Coronation followed a few days later. The children paid their usual morning visit to their parents and found the King brusque and conspicuously nervous. He showed Edward the Admiralty Order in *The Times* gazetting him a midshipman and handed him the dirk that went with the rank.[3] The children then processed together to the Abbey in one of the state coaches. Queen Alexandra had thought this a poor idea and was proved right when the younger princes began to giggle and play the fool. George tried to tickle Mary and fell on the floor. On the return journey things got so bad that only Edward's threats to hit his brothers maintained any sort of order.[4] In the Abbey, however, all was decorous. Edward was conducted to his stall, his brothers bowed as they filed in front of him, Princess Mary curtsied deeply 'and the Prince rose and gravely bowed to her'.[5] When the moment came for him to do homage he was consumed by nerves; if he blundered or behaved clumsily, he believed his father would feel that he had failed him.[6] He did not blunder. That night George V wrote in his diary: 'I nearly broke down when dear David came to do homage to me, as it reminded me so much [of] when I did the same thing to beloved Papa. He did it so well.'[7]

By then Edward was already Prince of Wales, given the title on his sixteenth birthday. There had been no formal investiture of a Prince of Wales for more than three hundred years, but the Empress Frederick had suggested the ceremony should be revived; the Bishop of St Asaph espoused the idea; and Lloyd George, Chancellor of the Exchequer and Constable of Caernarvon Castle, saw a chance to gratify Welsh national pride and win political support.[8] Some time-honoured traditions were hurriedly invented, Caernarvon Castle refurbished, gold quarried from the Merionethshire hills to make the Prince's regalia, and a quaint costume of white satin breeches and purple velvet surcoat devised for the occasion. At this point Edward struck. What, he asked, 'would my Navy friends say if they saw me in this preposterous rig?'[1] The Queen talked him into grudging acquiescence and Lloyd George taught him some Welsh phrases for the occasion. He practised in the garden at Frogmore, bellowing '*Mor o gan yw Cymru i gyd*' – all Wales is a sea of song – to Hansell fifty yards away. He could hear every word, reported Hansell.[2]

The ceremony was a great success; the only people who recorded their displeasure were the Mayor and Aldermen of Chester, who felt that since Prince Edward was among other things Earl of Chester, the investiture should have happened there. The leading man earned himself a crop of compliments. Winston Churchill, the Home Secretary, congratulated him on possessing a voice 'which carries well and is capable of being raised without losing expressiveness'.[3] Lloyd George assured him that he had forged a lasting bond of affection with the Welsh 'and won the admiration of all those who witnessed the spectacle'.[4] Queen Mary told Aunt Augusta that he had played his part to perfection, 'It was very émouvant for George and me.'[5] To the youthful Harry Luke he seemed 'the incarnation of all the Fairy Princes who have ever been imagined'.[6] The last description encapsulated everything that disquieted Edward about the ceremony. He was not sure he wanted to be a prince at all, certainly he did not wish to be a fairy prince. He hated anything which made him a man apart, which set him on a pedestal for his fellows to goggle at and worship. If to be Prince of Wales meant to put on fancy dress and strike attitudes in remote Welsh castles, then it was not a job for him.

There were good points about the position too. As Duke of Cornwall, he now enjoyed the revenues of the Duchy of Cornwall, derived from much valuable property in London and huge estates in the West Country. These amounted to some £90,000 a year, far more than he could possibly require before he came of age and set up his own establishment. The Treasurer of the Duchy of Cornwall, Walter Peacock, estimated that by the end of his minority savings would probably amount to £400,000; say, very roughly, £10 million at current values.[7] With new wealth and consequence came new responsibilities. J. C. Davidson, some time in 1912, was

summoned from his work in the Colonial Office to St James's
Palace to be looked over as a prospective private secretary. He
quickly decided it was no job for him: 'I would have made a very
poor courtier, nor did I quite like the character of the Prince of
Wales, charming in some ways as he was.'[1] The Prince possibly
reciprocated the mild dislike; certainly no job was offered to
Davidson, nor any private secretary appointed.

Meanwhile his naval career was running to its close. His last
term at Dartmouth had been truncated by a fierce attack of measles.
He retreated to Newquay to convalesce and to pay a few perfunctory visits to his recently acquired estates in the vicinity. On 29
March 1911 he returned briefly to Dartmouth to give presents and
signed photographs to the officers, masters and a few particularly
close friends. On the same day he presented to the town of Dartmouth the silver oar which symbolized the ancient rights of the
Duke of Cornwall over the adjoining waters: 'This was my first
function, and I think it went off very well,' he noted in his diary.[2]
Neither he nor his father appeared to have any doubts about the
value of the education he had received. 'I certainly think the College
is the best school in England,' wrote the King.[3] The Prince echoed
the sentiment when he visited Winchester in 1913. 'I believe it is
a very good school,' he told his father. '... It is amusing to see
the difference between an ordinary school and Dartmouth. The
boys talk of discomfort, but in the dormitories they have cubicles
and they sit about in studies all day. Their life is not half as
strenuous as it is at Dartmouth and we were more contented. There
can be no better education than a naval one.'[4]

The Dartmouth course ended with a training cruise. The Coronation made it impossible for the Prince to take part, but as a
consolation in the autumn of 1911 he was sent on a three-month
tour in the battleship *Hindustan*. The Prince served as a midshipman as the ship sailed along the south coast to Portland, Plymouth
and Torbay, then for a month to Queensferry and back to Portland
for the final weeks. The Captain, Henry Campbell, was a shining
example of those bluff sailor men who maintain a conspicuous
independence of attitude while keeping a weather eye always open
to the wishes of those likely to further their careers. 'Not the
smallest exception or discrimination has been made in his favour,'
he wrote in his final report on the Prince.[5] Up to a point it was

true. The Prince did work hard, get up at 6 a.m. to do rifle drill or P.T., receive the same pay – 1/9d (9p) a day – as the other midshipmen, keep his watches, do a stint in the coal bunkers – 'the atmosphere is thick with coal dust and how the wretched stokers who have to remain down there can stand it, I do not know'.[1] But not many midshipmen ate regularly with their captain, went for walks ashore with him when the ship was near land, lunched in their stately homes with Lord Mar, Lord Rosebery and Lord Mount Edgcumbe. He was always the Prince of Wales and though he seems to have been genuinely welcome in the gunroom by the other midshipmen, he was there as a guest, not as a member.

'I like the Captain very much indeed, he is always so interesting,' wrote the Prince in his diary. 'The Chaplain had a talk with me . . . and gave me some tracts to read.'[2] The Chaplain, one suspects, was found less interesting than the Captain. Campbell reciprocated the boy's affection, and, though he was not above flattery, his letter to Queen Mary has the ring of sincerity:

> We in the Navy rate a man for what he does, not for what he is; from the highest to the lowest he was looked upon with affection and respect. His character has formed; it is strong but very gentle and is best described in the old Scotch words 'Ye can break but ye canna bend me.' In spite of his very happy nature he thinks a great deal and he one day made it quite clear to me that he was fully alive to the fact that false speech and fond hopes do not alter facts . . . The Prince said to me one day; 'If I have learnt nothing else since I have been with you, I have learnt what inconvenience is and what it means to be really tired.' I thought of my promise to you and felt that it had been fulfilled.[3]

When he went ashore for the last time the ship's company sang 'God Bless the Prince of Wales' and 'Auld lang syne'. The Prince knew it was the end of his naval life. 'I only wish it was possible for you to continue serving in what I consider the finest service in the world,' his father had written to him.[4] But it was not possible. The first year of his reign had finally convinced George V that life aboard a ship could not equip a prince to be King. Edward must travel, he must learn languages, he must study history and the constitution, he must serve in the Army, he must become the very model of a modern monarch. The Prince of Wales was disconsolate, but he knew his father was right.

'You know, I think father now is quite a nice man,' Edward had said in apparent surprise to his mother in the summer of 1910.[1] That George V was in fact quite a nice man is hardly in question; that his son continued to think him quite a nice father is more doubtful. The trouble was partly that the King tried too hard. 'Now that you are leaving home, David, and going out into the world,' he said when he deposited his son for the first time at Osborne, 'always remember that I am your best friend.'[2] The same refrain reverberated down the years: in 1908, 'I wish you always to look upon me as your *best friend*, when in doubt and want advice, come to me'; in 1913, 'I want you always to look upon me as your *best friend*'; in 1914, 'I want you to treat me as your best friend.'[3] It is possible that some boys may indeed regard their fathers as their best friends, but even if they did it is unlikely that they would relish being constantly reminded of the fact.

There was a sententiousness about the King's approach which must have grated on its victim. 'I trust that you will always remember . . .' wrote George V just after his accession, 'that now you must always set a good example to the others by being very obedient, respectful to your seniors and kind to everyone.'[4] 'May God spare you for many, many years and may you grow up to be a happiness and a credit to your parents and your Country,' was the message for the Prince's thirteenth birthday.[5] The sentiments were unexceptionable, but no teenage boy could be expected to pay much attention to such exhortations. In later life Edward was apt to say that his father never said anything nice about him, always it was carping criticism and rebuke. This is not altogether fair. The King did sometimes congratulate his son on his manners, his letter-writing or some new achievement. But such occasions were the exception. 'Papa has been so nice to me since my return . . .' wrote the Prince in his diary in 1913. 'No faults have been found . . . Such a change!!' It was too good to last. Within a few days there was 'an awful row' when the King took exception to his sons going out for a walk with small rifles and shooting rabbits. 'Those things are always a great bore,' noted the Prince wearily.[1] His recreations were a frequent source of recrimination: 'You seem to be having too much shooting and not enough riding or hunting. I can't understand why you didn't hunt when Sir G. Fitzwilliam came expressly for that . . . What on earth were you doing? . . . I must say I am disappointed.'[2]

A less sensitive or more self-confident boy might have recognized the genuine solicitude which lay behind the King's captiousness and have responded to the spirit rather than the manner. The Prince did not. His health provided grounds for constant skirmishes. 'Do smoke less, take less exercise, *eat more* and rest more,' wrote the King, in despair at his eighteen-year-old son's increasingly eccentric train of life. 'You are just at the critical age from now till you are 21 and it is most necessary that you should develop properly, both in mind and body. It all depends . . . whether you develop into a strong, healthy man or remain a sort of puny, half grown boy.'[3] The Prince paid little attention. He had, for reasons difficult to follow, concluded that he was teetering always on the verge of fatness, and to avoid such a fate submitted his body to much violent physical exercise and ate with ill-judged frugality. He considered his parents' efforts to modify this regime to be fussy and interfering, and dismissed the injunctions of the royal doctors as the vapourings of the King's hired lackeys. He found it hard to credit what to the outsider seems the patent sincerity of his father's heartcry: 'I am only telling you these things for your own good and because I am so devoted to you and take such an interest in everything.'[4] There were interludes of harmony: 'We now understand each other so well,' wrote the Prince of Wales in July 1913;[5] a conversation with the King at York Cottage a few months later 'made a difference to my life and made me look on everything in a totally different light';[6] but soon there would be more grumbles and recriminations and all the good would be undone.

Queen Mary's role in the relationship was curiously remote. In the future mother and son were to develop a close rapport, but though there are occasional references in these years to 'charming talks' or 'wise advice', she played very much a secondary role. When the Prince's equerry, William Cadogan, urged her to use her influence with the King to ensure that he sometimes addressed a word of encouragement to his son, she accepted that such advice was badly needed but could not bring herself to proffer it.[7] One of the few fields where she seemed ready to take an initiative was in the selection of Christmas or birthday presents. Here she avoided any possible disappointment by acting both as donor and recipient. 'I must just tell you,' she wrote in May 1912, 'that I have got for you to give me as a birthday present 2 charming old Chinese cloisonné cups (price £12) for my Chinese Chippendale room.' The King adopted the same somewhat curious practice. For Christmas the same year he wanted a gold soup bowl. It was 'awfully expensive, £150', the Queen told her son, 'but Papa is very anxious to have it and has ordered it, and I only hope you won't mind'.[1]

Prince Albert remained Edward's closest ally. At Osborne and Dartmouth Edward's role had been that of protector or occasional critic, but with the Navy behind him the Prince of Wales was able to develop a close companionship with his younger brother. 'Bertie is a delightful creature and we have so many interests in common,' wrote the Prince in his diary in 1913, and then a fortnight later, 'I am so miserable it is dear old Bertie's last night; we have been so much together of late and I shall miss him terribly.'[2] Prince George too, though eight years younger, was now becoming a friend. At first the relationship was very much *de haut en bas*; the Prince of Wales rather patronizingly explained to his brother about the Royal Navy or made him exercise – 'George got stitches all the time . . . he is too fat for running.'[3] By 1914 he had become 'a capital boy',[4] they spent much time together and chatted freely. Bertie was still the real support, however, with whom the Prince of Wales formed a common front against the assaults of unreasonable parents. At dinner with Queen Alexandra, 'Bertie and I did our best to be funny and we succeeded';[5] at Christmas in York Cottage, 'it is hard work keeping 3 wild brothers in order; well I should say two, as my 2nd brother helps me. He is nearly as tall as I am and weighs more.'[6]

Oxford in the autumn of 1912 was to be the next phase of the Prince's education, but before he went up it was decided he should spend a few months in France. He was reasonably fluent in French but had picked up 'a very John Bull intonation' while at Dartmouth, and this called for improvement.[7] The Marquis de Breteuil, an anglophile French aristocrat with an American wife and two sons of the Prince's age, somewhat reluctantly allowed himself to be selected as host. He was summoned to Buckingham Palace to inspect his future charge and found him 'very thin, younger in appearance than his years, puny [*chétif*], timid but most attractive'. He insisted that Hansell, by whom he was much impressed, should accompany the Prince. George V emphasized that the visit must be entirely informal; the Marquis pointed out that his guest could hardly fail to call on the President. 'You're right,' said the King. 'I can't get used to the idea that in a few months he will be eighteen, and that he's already the Prince of Wales.'[1]

He had some excuse for his failure. Everyone agrees that both physically and mentally the Prince was slow to develop. The image of the slight, shy, wistful figure which was to become imprinted in the public consciousness over the next twenty years was already well established. In 1912 he still seemed conspicuously ill-equipped to grapple with the demands imposed on him by his position. Any boy of his age would have been discomfited by the 'huge and most alarming' luncheon given by the prefect of police, Louis-Jean Lépine – 'it was rather trying and the food was nasty,' but most would have coped better with the informal dance which the Breteuils held in his honour: 'They were mostly young folk who went on to a ball. I danced once or twice but it bores me to a degree. I went to bed at 10.15.'[2] There is no evidence from his diary that he met any girl in France who engaged his attention for more than a few minutes.

How much French he learnt is another matter. An amiable French scholar, Maurice Escoffier, had been engaged to conduct the Prince around France and supervise his studies; not surprisingly he reported on his protégé's amazing progress. To judge, however, from the Prince's dislike of the language and reluctance to speak it, an aversion which persisted even after he had lived in France for many years, the progress must have been limited, or at least not maintained. The most that can be said of his three months in France was that he mildly enjoyed them and learnt quite a lot about the country's history and political structure. More important still, he made himself well liked. 'He charmed everyone during his stay,' read a letter which was the more convincing for not being intended for the eyes of his parents. 'Old and young, rich and poor, were equally impressed by his frankness. The Breteuils could not say enough about his generous and open [*belle et franche*] nature.'[1]

'French customs are very curious, but I suppose I shall get used to them in time,' wrote the Prince resignedly.[2] He was happiest at the Breteuil château in the valley of the Chevreuse, shooting, bathing in the lake, and generally behaving as if he was at home. 'We hope you will treat him exactly like your own son,' the King had written. 'He is a good boy and I know he will always do at once what you tell him.'[3] The Marquis's real sons may not have been best pleased by the imposition on them of this unexpected extra brother but they played their part gallantly. The Prince liked both of them: 'Even the eldest who likes music is very nice.'[4] Fortunately François made up for this aberrant taste by liking tennis too. In Paris the Prince saw the sights; watched Sarah Bernhardt play *L'Aiglon* – 'she is about 70 and takes the part of a boy of 18. I think she ought to stop acting now';[5] visited the Jardin d'Acclimatation – 'a rotten kind of zoo';[6] was received by President Fallières and presented with the grand cordon of the Légion d'honneur – 'Nothing could have been better or more self-possessed and tactful than the Prince's manner,' wrote the British Ambassador. 'He did not hesitate at all in his French'; and visited the studio of the painter Monsieur Gillot – 'The Yacht's foremast is about half the height it ought to be,' he told the King. 'I think M. Gillot is one of these impressionist artists, but I know that you hate that sort of painting.'[7]

He was not greatly impressed by the capital, telling the Aga Khan that he could not imagine what his grandfather had seen in it.[8] The press did not make it more agreeable for him. For the first time he found himself assailed by importunate photographers, and he did not relish the experience. His father sympathized. Unless the reporters behaved better, he decreed, 'drastic steps must be taken to get rid of them'.[9] It would be interesting to know what he had in mind. The Premier and future President, Raymond Poincaré, met him several times during his stay in Paris and was struck by his 'thoughtful character, eagerness to learn, interest in practical problems, and a real knowledge of industrial possibilities'. He was a poor trencherman, however, 'the choicest menus being treated by him with complete indifference'.[10] What the Prince enjoyed most of all was the week he spent with the French Mediterranean fleet: he had a passion for the sea, wrote the Marquis de

Breteuil, and would happily have made this part of his visit twice as long.[1]

And so it was back to England and the final preparations for his life at Oxford. It seems to have been Hansell and Lord Derby who urged the merits of a university education on the King, probably with some encouragement from Lord Esher. Not everyone approved. 'Surely this cannot be true,' expostulated his great-aunt Augusta. 'It is too democratic.'[2] That was one of the reasons that the King favoured it: 'I have always been told that one can have the best time of one's life at College if one makes up one's mind,'[3] he told his son. The Prince was sceptical. He accepted that the time would probably pass well enough, at least provided Hansell came along, but he remained unenthusiastic.[4] When his mother tried to get him to make some choices about the furnishing of his rooms, he noted gloomily in his diary, 'I am afraid it does not interest me much. I am just about fed up with the whole affair.'[5] The root of his woe became apparent when his brother Bertie remarked how much he envied him and the Prince retorted that the feeling was mutual. Oxford might be tolerable in its own way but it was not where he wished to be: 'It is an awful situation and I only wish I was back quietly in the only service – the navy.'[6]

As a Magdalen man himself, Hansell naturally urged its merits as a haven for the Prince. George V appealed to Lord Derby for advice. Starting from the very reasonable hypothesis that only three colleges were worth consideration, Derby dismissed New College as being at that moment beset by troubles and Christ Church as the haunt of *nouveaux riches*. That left Magdalen.[7] The King concurred. An additional argument was that Derby was ready to send his own son, Edward Stanley, to the same college. 'David is certainly a most loyal boy and I am sure would always do his best to be keen and get on wherever he was,' the King told Hansell.[8] In fact Magdalen does not seem to have been a bad choice. It had a reputation for independence of mind, the eschewing of anything that seemed smart or extravagant and a robust indifference to rank.[9] It was well suited for the somewhat special needs of an undergraduate who was also heir to the throne.

With Oxford as with Dartmouth, George V decreed that his son should be treated exactly like his contemporaries and then took steps to ensure that this would be impossible. The Prince was to be attended at Oxford not merely by Hansell and his valet Finch but also by an equerry. This last appointment caused some cogitation. Esher commented how difficult it would be to find somebody who would be 'watchful but not seem to be so; instructive and not a bore; moral and not a prig; high spirited and not reckless. It would be an interesting task for a young man with imagination.'[1] The King preferred horses to imagination. He chose William Cadogan, a gallant and honourable soldier who was almost wholly without intellectual interests and whose chief function was to persuade his charge to hunt. 'Not a very exciting sort of chap,' commented the Prince when they first met.[2] As if this entourage did not sufficiently separate him from the common herd, the Prince was settled in his own suite of rooms, furnished by the Queen with Sheraton pieces of furniture and good watercolours. Odder still for Oxford, he had his own bathroom. It may not have been very luxurious – 'a cold, converted torture chamber' one of his contemporaries described it[3] – but it still set its owner apart from his fellows.

The real problem, however, was summed up by Cosmo Lang, then Archbishop of York. The object of the Prince going to Oxford, he assumed, was that he should enter 'naturally and simply' into college life. His life might be simple but would never be natural if his friends were selected for him. Yet if something of the sort was not done, the best men in college would hang back in the fear that they might seem royal toadies, while less desirable companions, 'often agreeable and plausible enough', would thrust themselves forward. The solution must be to persuade a few of the 'leading and best men' to ease the Prince's passage into college society.[4] Derby's son Stanley should obviously be a member of any such group.

On the whole the system worked. The Prince was still shy. Lord Grantley remembered his 'characteristic way of coming into a room, jerking forward from the hips and fingering his tie the whole time . . . It looked as if it was torture to him to meet strangers.'[5] He was further handicapped by the fact that most of his contemporaries had moved on in a group from their respective public schools, while there were few if any naval cadets at Oxford. 'The junior common room is something like a gunroom,' he noted nostalgically in his diary. 'At 7.00 I dined in hall . . . I got on fairly well, only my drawback is not knowing anyone. It lasted ½ hour and then Stanley and a chap called Higham sat in my room till 9.45. They are very nice and we talked about many things.'[1] It was not easy at first, but he was friendly and ready to become sociable. He forced himself out of his shell, attending the celebrated entertainments in the common room and marvelling at the amount people drank. 'We were all pretty dead at the end and I had almost a drop too much. However, I managed all right . . . It is a good thing to do as one gets to know people.'[2] After the first few nights he spent almost every evening in the rooms of one of his friends, smoking, singing, talking or playing cards. Barrington-Ward, a future editor of *The Times*, remembered him calling in on his rooms when an impromptu concert was in progress. A number of cardboard trumpets were lying around. 'The Prince promptly took one and made as much noise as anyone. He said he liked a "good row". So we had a ragtime, comic songs and choruses, and he joined in merrily like a man . . . It was impossible not to like him. He is clean-looking and jolly, with no side at all.'[3]

The friends he made, however, were not necessarily those whom his father or Hansell would have chosen. His opinion of Stanley varied from day to day, but his considered judgment in 1916, by which time they had become close friends, was that Stanley had greatly improved but that he had never really liked him as an undergraduate. 'I wish you had rooms opposite mine, it would be great,' he wrote to an old naval friend. 'As it is, I have that chap Stanley, who I don't know very well, and who is coshy!! That is the worst of all crimes!!'[4] Coshy meant stuck-up, putting on airs. Lord Cranborne was 'very nice' but Lord Ednam – who, as the Earl of Dudley, was in time to become one of his closest friends – was undoubtedly coshy; a period in a gunroom would have done him good.[5] The Prince's friends tended to be more home-spun, people who would have fitted naturally into the Royal Navy. One or two were intellectuals; in February 1913 he dined for the first time with a man who was to play a critical role in his life, 'the President of the Union debating society, W. Monckton, a very nice man'.[6] A few were deemed unsuitable. Hansell and Cadogan warned him against one in particular: 'They say that Ronnie is a bad lot, he is a gt friend of mine and of course this is a gt blow to me. However I shall in no way chuck him but merely not be seen about with him.'[1] Unfortunately he made the mistake of inviting the delinquent Ronnie to meet his brother Prince Harry when the latter visited Oxford. Hansell 'was very sick with me . . . I am an awful failure in this life and always do the most idiotic things.'[2]

Such moods of contrition became more frequent after his first few months at Oxford. The Prince did nothing very wicked but for the first time in his life he found it possible to slip his leash, and it would have been surprising if he had not celebrated the fact with mild excess. Many years later he told the American journalist Cy Sulzberger that he had found Oxford quite agreeable 'because we were drunk all the time'.[3] He exaggerated, but though not drunk all the time, he managed it not infrequently. On 10 November 1912 he drank too much port, fell, made his nose bleed, and had to be put to bed by two friends who distracted Hansell while he got undressed. But he had the resilience of youth. He was walking round the garden by 7.30 the following morning and apologizing to his friends not long afterwards – 'They were awfully nice about it.'[4] Usually there was more noise than alcohol: 'There were 25 of us and we went up to Somerville's rooms where we danced and made a row . . . It was a great evening.'[5] He eschewed the chic world of Evelyn Waugh's Bollinger Club baying for broken glass. He was elected to the Bullingdon – in its own eyes at least the most elite of Oxford dining clubs – went to a dinner, was made to drink too much, and retired furious and the worse for wear: 'I will have nothing more to do with the filthy riding men, they are a beastly set.'[6]

He never joined the set, but within a few months of making this entry in his diary he had become a riding man himself. His father considered that this was a part of his education quite as important as learning French or studying the constitution. 'If you can't ride, you know, I'm afraid people will call you a duffer,' he told his son. Hunting was the only way to learn properly. 'The English people like riding and it would make you very unpopular if you couldn't do so.'[7] Cadogan was in charge of the training and found his pupil at first recalcitrant. A year before, the Prince had hunted near Sandringham and had stood about all day 'soaked through and petrified with cold. And then they wonder why one does not like hunting!'[8] Now he grumblingly let himself be dragged off to ride in the neighbourhood but showed plainly that he thought it a bore – 'deadly as usual'.[1] To his surprise he found that he was beginning to enjoy the riding more and more. He went out with the South Oxfordshire hunt, was in the saddle for seven hours without falling off, was awarded the brush and enjoyed his day.[2] 'Until a few months ago I was terrified of riding and loathed the sight of a horse,' he told a friend, 'but it suddenly came to me, and under Cadogan's instruction and tuition, I have now plenty of confidence and jump everything!!'[3] Some time that spring he graduated to that horseman's nirvana, the Pytchley hunt. The King's private secretary, Lord Stamfordham, congratulated him with all the gravity befitting so august an occasion. 'I solemnly believe that few things will tend more to endear you to the people who some day by God's will will be your subjects.'[4]

Riding was only one of the Prince's sporting pursuits. He golfed, played squash and went for gruelling runs. He played cricket at Radley, made a duck, and commented sourly: 'It's a poor game.'[5] He was a regular member of the Magdalen football second XI, and appeared occasionally in the first. He shot from time to time on estates near Oxford. Lord Crawford met him in October 1913 with the Wantages at Lockinge. 'The Prince of Wales seems over-burdened with his duties which he performs with meticulous precision,' he noted. 'Poor boy, somehow he made me feel very sorry for him ... If only he would bolt with a ballet girl, say for twenty-four hours!'[6] The poor boy still found time to gamble several evenings a week, though he rarely lost or won more than £10 or so; to acquire and drive a 39-horse-power touring model blue Daimler; to learn the bagpipes with Pipe-Major Ross of the Scots Guards. He joined the Officers' Training Corps, whose adjutant was the future Field Marshal Jumbo Wilson, and scored 96 out of 100 shooting at a static target and 86 at a moving. Fifty would have earned a pass, and 75 been enough for qualification as a marksman. He took part in night manoeuvres in Blenheim Park and spent a hectic few days in the annual camp, rising at 5 a.m. to act as breakfast orderly and having a ride in an airship. 'It was the first time I had ever flown and the sensation is wonderful.'[7]

Into the interstices of these activities he fitted his academic life. Some further education was badly needed; his mind in 1912 was a ragbag of miscellaneous information and his power of expressing what he knew was limited. He spelt deplorably; in one letter alone writing 'chaplin' for chaplain, 'chapple' for chapel, 'colision', 'dammaged' and 'explaned'. He was supposed to go regularly to lectures and follow a programme of special studies with tutors. The lectures he frequently eschewed. He went once to hear Walter Raleigh on English literature and complained, 'It was very hard to understand and I do not think I shall go to any more.'[1] The Rev. Lancelot Phelps on political economy proved more attractive: 'Political Economy interests me more the more that I do it and I think I have quite got hold of the line of thought.'[2] But the individual tuition was more important. The Prince studied history with Charles Grant Robertson, French with Monsieur Berthon, German with Professor Fiedler and constitutional law with Sir William Anson, the Warden of All Souls. Anson probably taught the Prince almost everything of importance which he retained from his time at Oxford; a brilliant expositor, a man of charm, humour and generosity, he was liked as well as admired by the Prince – 'a remarkable and distinguished little man,' he called him affectionately.[3]

Unfortunately, the central figure, to whom the Prince had to read an essay every week, was the President of Magdalen, Sir Herbert Warren. Warren had a good mind and no doubt many other redeeming features, but what most struck the undergraduates was that he was a bore and a snob. The Prince loathed him – 'an awful old man' he described him.[4] Reading an essay to a critical and often supercilious pedagogue is always an ordeal; it is made worse if one dislikes one's auditor. The Prince dreaded his weekly session. He knew, with reason, that essay-writing was not his forte and rarely got any pleasure from their composition. Most of his efforts survive;[5] on St Anselm, Beaconsfield, Chatham, Nelson, 'The Relation of Democracy to War', Tennyson. They were conscientious, superficial and unimaginative. Cromwell was 'one of England's greatest statesmen and generals'; on 'Ambition' he commented: 'The most ideal form of ambition is when it is used for the sake of one's country. That patriotism should be the genuine motive is the most perfect thing conceivable.'

His best essay, and the subject which he most cared about, dealt with the explorer Scott. He had read *Scott's Last Expedition* while on holiday at York Cottage, a laborious process, since he read slowly and it kept him up until 1 a.m. for almost a month, but a rewarding one: 'It is a most fascinating book and a wonderful story of pluck in the face of ghastly hardship and suffering.'[1] His essay reflected this enthusiasm; Warren thought well enough of it to send it to the King, who passed it on to the historian and former prime minister, Lord Rosebery. Rosebery was predictably enthusiastic: 'It was really admirable . . . a clear, sympathetic and vigorous narrative through which one can see the author's heart. I am quite astonished at it . . .' He wrote more as courtier than critic, but the essay did deserve praise. The Prince's final comment was characteristic: 'It bears out the fact that Englishmen can endure hardships and face death as it should be faced.'[2]

It cannot be said that Oxford widened his cultural horizons. 'We listened to classical music till 10.00. It was very dull,' he wrote gloomily in his diary; and again after the Russian ballet, 'That form of entertainment, like most stage things, leaves me stone cold.'[3] Nor did he become a reading man. His tutors constantly praised his efforts but pointed out that his knowledge was too superficial; 'he must read more and think more for himself which is most necessary in his position,' was his mother's verdict.[4] 'Bookish he will never be,' wrote Warren in an otherwise unctuous article in *The Times*. Unsurprisingly, he went on: 'The Prince of Wales will not want for power of ready and forcible presentation, either in speech or writing.'[5] Lord Esher had long talks with the Prince at Balmoral and found: 'His memory is excellent and his vocabulary unusual, and above all things, he thinks his own thoughts.'[6] (The compliments were not returned. The Prince wrote of Esher: 'That man has a finger in every pie and one cannot trust him.'[7]) A quick mind, a retentive memory, considerable curiosity, facility for self-expression: they were not everything but they were a lot.

The Prince admitted he owed something to Oxford but he was never fond of it nor ceased to think he would be better off in the Navy. His diary is pitted with groans about the awfulness of his life, increasing in violence as his second year wore on: 'I'm absolutely fed up with the place and it has got on my nerves'; 'It is pretty rotten to be back here'; 'Back again in this hole!'[8] Warren pressed him to stay on for another term and get a degree. 'The

answer to the 1st is NO and the second doesn't interest me at all!!'[1]
At least in the spring and summer vacations of 1913 he escaped,
both from Oxford and from his parents, to visit Germany. In later
life he said that he had felt more at home in Germany than in
France, 'because there I stayed mostly among relations'.[2] His diary
suggests that he enjoyed himself more because he was that much
older and had correspondingly greater liberty. Cadogan replaced
Hansell and saw himself more as companion than as tutor, while
Professor Fiedler, who was also in the entourage, was a 'jolly old
chap' who was easily disposed of. Once in Berlin the Prince locked
the professor in the bathroom and escaped with a friend to sample
the night life, giving the porter the key and saying that something
seemed to be wrong with the lock.[3]

His two longest stays were in Württemberg and Strelitz. He
arrived at Württemberg in travelling clothes to find the King and
his staff in full dress uniform, but soon settled in comfortably to
this slow, sleepy court. Every day after a heavy lunch he and the
King would drive around the city and adjoining countryside. At
first the King would acknowledge the salutes of his subjects but
'gradually movements of hand became shorter – eyes closed – all
stopped – King sound asleep until horses pulled up at home and
groom said "Majestät, ist zu Hause."'[4] There was no golf, no tennis,
no fishing, one day shooting capercaillie – 'It is a curious sport . . .
but I am glad to have seen it' – too much sightseeing and too many
visits to the opera. 'I am getting fed up with life here to say the
least of it.' He was taken to Das Rheingold – 'such a waste of
time'; Siegfried – 'appallingly dull'; Der Freischutz – 'not exciting'.[5]
The King perhaps took in more than his young guest realized. The
Prince had enjoyed his visits to an officers' mess and to the Daimler
factory, he told Queen Mary, 'but visiting Museums he did not
seem to like quite so much'.[6]

Possibly word of this visit got through to Neustrelitz, for the
Grand Duchess Augusta wrote in some alarm to say that she feared
the Prince would be bored, 'there being no sports nor Games of
any kind'.[7] There was no reason to fear anything of the sort, replied
Queen Mary firmly: 'He is quite a contented person and never
rushes about after amusement.'[8] Her brother Alge, future Earl of
Athlone, who was there for the visit, was less confident: 'Strelitz,
as you can imagine, after a short time is more than a young person

42

can stand. A week is enough for Alice and me.' He found his nephew 'a mixture of extreme youth and boyishness with the ways of a man over forty . . . We both, as everyone, liked him extremely. He is so *liebenswürdig* [lovable] and simple, too much so, he should now realize he is "The Prince" and not require so much pushing forward.'[1]

Berlin proved the most enjoyable of his visits, mainly because he was entrusted for his entertainment to a young attaché at the British Embassy, Godfrey Thomas, who took him to funfairs, night clubs and the Palais de Danse, 'where we remained till 2.00. It is a large public place frequented by very doubtful women with whom you go and dance, but it is devoid of all coarseness and vulgarity. I danced a good deal . . .'[2] He spent one night with Kaiser Wilhelm II and was startled to find him seated behind his desk on a military saddle mounted on a wooden block. The Emperor 'explained condescendingly that he was so accustomed to sitting on a horse he found a saddle more conducive to clear, concise thinking'.[3] The Prince found his host unexpectedly easy to talk to and quite enjoyed his visit;[4] the Emperor, according to the Prince's future biographer, Hector Bolitho, considered his guest charming and unassuming but 'a young eagle, likely to play a big part in European affairs because he is far from being a pacifist'.[5]

The Prince must have been uneasily aware that wherever he went in Germany he would be sized up as a potential husband for unmarried daughters. The courts of Germany had provided so many spouses for the British royal family that it was reasonable to assume the precedent would again be followed. He had experienced his first taste of what he could expect when the Emperor's daughter, Victoria Louise, visited London in 1911. The press reported rumours that an engagement was imminent.[6] Dynastically it would have been most suitable and Princess Victoria Louise had many good points. A young maid of honour, Katherine Villiers, pronounced her wholly without good looks but with much sweetness and *joie de vivre*.[7] The Prince himself found her 'most easy to get on with'.[8] But there is no reason to think that he or his parents gave any serious thought to marriage. Nor did Victoria Louise; she found the Prince 'very nice' but 'terribly young, younger than he actually was'.[9]

More real was the putative romance with Princess May, or more formally Caroline Matilda, of Schleswig-Holstein. The couple got on particularly well when they were staying together at Gotha. May was 'such a nice girl', Alge's wife Alice reported, 'much like the others only taller and very slim'.[1] Her brother-in-law August Wilhelm, son of Kaiser Wilhelm II, was sufficiently encouraged to write directly to the Prince in June 1914 to suggest that a match should be made. The nineteen-year-old Prince consulted his mother and with some difficulty constructed a reply – 'an awkward job'.[2] His letter does not survive, probably he pleaded that he was too young to contemplate matrimony at the moment. The war put an end to the possibility but in 1915 he remarked rather wistfully to Godfrey Thomas, 'Well, I could very easily have done worse.' Thomas commented that, though Princess May's teeth needed attention and her nose was too red, a dentist and a little powder would soon have put things to rights. 'HRH was really very much attracted to her, and I am perfectly certain that if the War hadn't come, it would have been brought off. It is difficult to see now who he will marry or when, but whoever it is, I know that he will often think with affectionate regret of Princess May as the might have been.'[3]

It has been said that the sympathy for Germany which the Prince of Wales showed in the 1930s stemmed from the success of his pre-war visits. All the evidence is that, though he enjoyed his stay there and liked some of his relations, he was not particularly struck by the country or its people. 'The Germans as a race,' he told a friend, 'are fat, stolid, unsympathetic, intensely military, and all the men have huge cigars sticking out of their faces at all times.'[4] 'The trip was very interesting,' he reflected when he got back to London, 'but I don't care much about the Germans.'[5] Of the countries which he visited before the First World War, the one that pleased him most was Norway, where he loved the skiing, the open-air existence and the informality of court life – 'a lovely country with a charming people,' he found it. 'It was just like home.'[6] This last comment betrayed his real priorities. Far though he might wander, and much pleasure though he might derive from his wanderings, whether as Prince, as King, or as Duke of Windsor, there was always for him to be no place like home.

*

The Youth

By the summer of 1914 the King had agreed that his son should spend the last few months of the year travelling and should join the Grenadier Guards the following year. The prospect was pleasing enough, but already shades of the prison house were beginning to close upon the growing Prince. The first dread intimation of what was to come had struck him in June 1912, when he got back at lunch time from his stay in France to find that the same afternoon he had to go with the King and Queen to a St John's Ambulance Parade – 'rather, if not very dull'; at 6.30 p.m. he was receiving the Khedive of Egypt and at 8.30 he was taking the wife of the Bishop of Winchester in to dinner.[1] From then on public functions multiplied. He quickly decided that the more formal and decorous they were, the more he would dislike them. He attended his first court in March 1914 and found it 'mighty poor fun . . . I went in with the parents to the ballroom and stood till 11.00 while hundreds of women went by, each one plainer than the last . . . I don't mind if I never go to one again.' He did go, of course, and resented it even more: 'a bum show. This court etiquette is intolerable.' As for the state visit of the King and Queen of Denmark: 'What rot and a waste of time, money and energy all these state visits are.'[2]

When he had a proper job to do, however, he did it conscientiously and well. He was sent by the King to greet Poincaré, now President of the Republic, on his arrival at Portsmouth. The French statesman was impressed by his 'charm of manner and vivacity'. The Prince had 'lost none of his former delightful simplicity' but had '"come on" a good deal'.[3] The King was delighted by the reports he was given of his son's performance: 'It gave both Mama and me great pleasure . . . I may sometimes find fault with you but I assure you it is only for your own good and because I am so devoted to you.'[4] The Prince's first important solo performance came in June 1914 when he opened the new church of St Anselm on the Duchy of Cornwall estates in south London. He took endless trouble with his speech and carried it off well: 'I had a wonderful sense of confidence in the audience, who I felt would make allowances for it being my 1st public function.'[5] At present, he told his audience, he knew little of the difficulties which beset those who were concerned with housing for the working classes, 'but by studying the comfort and happiness of my tenants I hope to gain experience'. Congratulations flowed in, on his diction, his pace, his obvious sincerity; the one that would have pleased him most because it was not intended for his eyes was sent to one of the ladies-in-waiting, Lady Fortescue. 'It was a wonderful success. He did it quite beautifully. At first he seemed a little nervous but it wore off and his speech was quite charming. He said it as if he really meant it . . . and in such a firm, charming voice. Everyone was tremendously enthusiastic . . . He looked *so* young among all those elderly prelates, but so dignified.'[1]

For the first time he began to talk seriously to politicians and form opinions of them. Churchill was his hero, mainly because he was now First Lord of the Admiralty and arch advocate of a larger Navy: 'He is a wonderful man and has a great power of work.' Asquith, the Prime Minister, he liked, though he found Mrs Asquith 'rather tiring and never stops talking'; Esher and Lulu Harcourt (the Colonial Secretary) were particularly tiresome.[2] If he had any preference between the parties he did not confide it to his diary, though on certain issues he feared the Liberal government would be insufficiently firm. He had strong views about the suffragettes and told his father that he hoped 'the woman suffrage bill will never be passed. It is curious how divided the present cabinet is on the subject.'[3] To his relief Asquith held firm. 'I really think that at last some drastic measures are to be taken as regards those bl--d-suffragettes, whose conduct is becoming more and more infamous every day,' he told Godfrey Thomas in the summer of 1914.[4] He was as strongly opposed to Home Rule for Ireland. 'I hope it will not pass,' he wrote in his diary when the Home Rule Bill was introduced in 1912.[5] His parents shared his views on the future of Ulster. Queen Mary wrote him outspoken letters in March and April 1914 about the weakness of the government and the deplorable way they had treated the Army.[6] 'Although we aren't supposed to have any politics,' the Prince responded, 'there does come a time when all that outward nonsense must be put aside, and that time has come.'[7]

Socially his life was transformed in that last summer before the war. His parents had had a party for him at Buckingham Palace in March 1913. 'I had to dance, a thing I hate,' he wrote forlornly in his diary: 'The whole thing was a great strain.' He did not change his views for a year at least; then in July 1914 as a twenty-year-old he went to the Londesboroughs' ball. 'I stuck out to the bitter end and got back at 2 a.m. It was really great fun,' he recorded in mild astonishment. Next night it was the turn of the Portlands: 'The floor was perfect and my dancing is improving.' He stayed till 3.45, and did the same the following night at the Salisburys'.[1] A looker-on at the Salisburys' dance who did not know about his change of heart commiserated on his sad plight: 'The Prince is no dancer . . . It was something of an ordeal for so young a boy and of so retiring a disposition.'[2] The sympathy was uncalled for: 'I have now become fond of dancing and love going out!'[3] But he was still discriminating. Baroness Orczy saw him at a court ball in mid-July, dancing the *quadrille d'honneur* with one of his aunts and looking 'moody and somewhat bored'.[4] Nor did he allow his new-found enthusiasm in any other way to change his train of life. He was up at 6 a.m. after the Londesborough ball, rose at 7 a.m. for a swim after the Portlands' and was playing squash by 7 a.m. after the Salisburys': 'I've had only 8 hours sleep in the last 72 hours.'[5]

The ferocious social round was combined with a course with the Life Guards – riding school, sword drill, care of horses and equipment, marching. 'Not very exciting but anyhow a definite job which is the gt thing!!' he wrote in his diary. 'Military life and ways are curious.'[6] He still pined for the Navy. Halfway through his cavalry course he went with the King to Portsmouth for the naval review and visited old friends aboard HMS *Collingwood*. It was 'glorious. God what a life this is compared to my attachment.'[7] But he knew that it was a paradise not to be regained. The plan was that he should spend 1915 with the Grenadier Guards, 1916 with the Royal Horse Artillery, and then join the 10th Hussars on their return from South Africa. Meanwhile he danced the summer away and made plans for another grand tour of Europe in the autumn. A break in the routine came at the end of June when he spent a week with the Officers' Training Corps and manoeuvred vigorously about the plains near Aldershot. 'When in camp I make it a rule *never* to open a newspaper,' he wrote to a friend, 'so am completely ignorant of all happenings in the outer World, except that the Austrian Archduke and his wife have been assassinated. I expect it has caused a stir in Germany.'[8]

3

'Oh!! That I Had a Job'

T HAT IN 1914 THE YOUTH OF BRITAIN WENT EXULT-
antly to war is one of the stranger features of that agonizing conflict. The Prince of Wales had even less reason than
most to share in this exultation. For one thing, many of his close
relations, whom he had grown to know and like over the past few
years, were now numbered among the enemy. For another, his
position as heir to the throne set him apart from his contemporaries: they set off with armour shining to defeat the Huns and be
home by Christmas, he knew that his armour was likely to be more
ornamental than useful and that he had only a slim chance of
wearing it in battle. Yet when he heard that he was to join the
Army in France, he wrote to Sir George Arthur of this 'wonderful
and joyous surprise'. Twenty-five years later he was shown this
letter and commented how terrifying he found it, coming as it did
from an average boy of twenty. He had conceived war almost as
a holiday, 'a glorious adventure'. 'How disillusioned we all were
at the end of it,' he commented ruefully. 'One wonders if the
generation of that age today feel as we did, or are they conscious
of the appalling consequences of another World war and its futility?
No! far worse than that how it would utterly destroy civilization.'[1]
    The run-up to war found the Prince incredulous and baffled.
The murder of the Archduke Franz Ferdinand at Sarajevo em-
broiled first Austria and Serbia, then Germany and Russia, finally
France and Britain. The Prince was inclined to believe that Russia
and Germany were behaving reasonably and that Austria was the
prime offender, but admitted, 'I must stop talking all this rot, for
I know nothing about it.'[2] As war between France and Germany
became inevitable, his chief fear was lest the government should
stay neutral. 'That will be the end of us; we shall never be trusted
by any power again.'[3] The decision to stand by our allies came as
a great relief but 'Oh!! God; the whole thing is too big to compre-

hend!! Oh!! That I had a job.'[1] That last expostulation was to be his constant refrain for the next four years. He went on to the balcony with his parents at Buckingham Palace to acknowledge the cheers of the crowd. The King wrote in his diary that night that he prayed to God he would protect dear Bertie's life.[2] It never occurred to him that his eldest son might be exposed to danger. How could he be? He was the Prince of Wales.

The Prince poured out his woes to his closest confidant, his brother Bertie:

> Well, this is just about the mightiest calamity that has ever or will ever befall mankind ... To think that but 17 days ago we were together with everything working peacefully in Europe, and now we are at the commencement of a most hideous and appalling war, the duration or issue of which are impossible to predict ... 'England at war with Germany!!' that seems a sentence which would appear nowhere but in a mad novel.
>
> The Germans could never have chosen a worse moment, and serve them right too if they are absolutely crushed, as I can but think they will be. The way they have behaved will go down to history as about the worst and most infamous action of any govt!! Don't you agree? I bet you do.
>
> I am as good as heartbroken to think I am totally devoid of any job whatsoever and have not the faintest chance of being able to serve my country. I have to stay at home with the women and children, a passenger of the worst description!! Here I am in this bloody gt palace, doing absolutely nothing but attend meals ... Surely a man of 20 has higher things to hope for? But I haven't apparently! Oh God it is becoming unbearable to live this usual life of ease and comfort at home, when you my dear old boy, and all naval and army officers, are toiling under unpleasant conditions, suffering hardships and running gt risks with your lives, for the defence and honour of England ... At such a time you will picture me here, depressed and miserable and taking no more part in this huge undertaking than Harry and George, 2 irresponsible kids who run about playing inane games in the passage. However, enough about my rotten self, for I am a most bum specimen of humanity, and so must not be considered.[3]

The self-disparagement in the last sentence is a constant feature of his letters and his diary; consciously overstated, yet nonetheless sincere. He knew that it was not his fault that he was not among the first of the volunteers to fight for King and country, but he still condemned himself for being left behind. In fact his period of misery hanging around 'this awful palace where I have had the worst weeks of my life'[1] was quickly over. On 6 August 1914, only the day after he had written in such anguish to his brother, he asked for and was given a commission in the Grenadier Guards. He was only 5 feet 7 inches tall instead of the regulation 6 feet, but recorded in triumph: 'I am to go to the King's Company but shall be treated just like an ordinary officer, thank goodness, and am to share a room in barracks.'[2] In fact his treatment for the first fortnight was far worse than the ordinary officer, let alone the ordinary Guards officer, would have expected while serving at home. The 1st Battalion was training at Warley Barracks in Brentwood. The officers' mess was a 'filthy hole', the rooms were garrets, there was no furniture and no carpet. 'But what does one care when living under war conditions? I am so glad to have joined up and to have escaped from the palace!!'[3]

When the battalion moved back to London his euphoric mood persisted. He established that he was the first Prince of Wales ever to carry the colours on the King's Guard at Buckingham Palace, and accepted with relish what in peacetime he would have dismissed as a piece of pompous ritual, as well as positively welcoming the long, boring route marches from Wellington Barracks through Kensington and Fulham returning down the King's Road. 'It is pretty rotten in London,' he told Godfrey Thomas, 'and we can't do any training. But anyhow we are on the spot and feel that this is a stepping stone to getting out!! How we long for it.'[4] He deluded himself that he would continue to be treated 'just like an ordinary officer' and would soon go to France and the front with his fellow officers. His delusion was quickly dispelled. On 8 September, a week before the 1st Battalion sailed, his father told him that he would not accompany it. Instead he would join the 3rd Battalion and remain in London. 'This is a bitter disappointment,' he wrote in his diary.[5] When the time came for him to watch the battalion march off from the barracks, his bitterness was still greater. 'I am a broken man,' he told his friend Jack Lawrence. 'It is terrible being left behind!!'[1]

His closest friend in the Grenadiers, Lord Desmond Fitzgerald – one of the very few contemporaries who was invited to call him 'Eddie' – wrote to console him and tell him how much he had admired 'the way you have borne your disappointment . . . However, it is not the fact of going to war, when thousands are doing so, that needs bravery; but to cheerfully accept the unpleasant things of life needs the greatest strength of character. And thus you have been able to set a wonderful example of how to do one's duty.'[2] The Prince was unconvinced. In public he put a good face on it, but his misery was too acute to conceal from his friends. Indeed, he was anxious to advertise it; he would have been less than human if he had not wanted everyone to know that he was eager to share the dangers of war and stayed behind against his will. How real those dangers were became rapidly apparent; by 2 November only six officers of his beloved 1st Battalion remained unwounded.

He appealed to the Secretary of State for War, Lord Kitchener, and called on him with his father's assistant private secretary, Clive Wigram. 'He is now a gt fat bloated man,' he wrote vengefully in his diary, who put forward what seemed to the Prince most unconvincing reasons for refusing him leave to return to the 1st Battalion, but held out vague hopes of his joining the staff of the Commander-in-Chief of the British Expeditionary Force, Sir John French, in a few months when the line had been stabilized. 'A pretty rotten contrast to my gt wish,' commented the Prince, adding grudgingly: 'He is a rough customer but mighty strong, and is just the man to boss these politicians at such a time!!'[3] The King told Esher that his son had argued that he was expendable; if he were killed there were four brothers to take his place. 'What if you were not killed, but taken prisoner?' Kitchener asked drily.[4]

While eating his heart out in London with the 3rd Battalion of the Grenadiers – 'strictly *entre nous*,' he told Lady Glenusk, 'there are not many *really* nice people in the 3rd Batt . . . The junior ensigns are a poor lot!!'[5] – he made himself useful in other ways. Shortly before the outbreak of war he had become President of a National Fund for providing food for the poor, and had published an appeal in the daily papers. A quarter of a million pounds came in on the first day and within a week the total was more than £1 million. Most of the work was done by a Liberal member of parliament, Ernest Benn – future Lord Stansgate – whom the Prince judged 'a nice, capable little man'.[1] Public relations were entrusted to a Mr Pearson, who wanted the Prince to be painted by the military artist Caton Woodville at the head of his regiment, and the resultant poster to be exhibited on every available hoarding. This idea was quashed (as also was a still more eccentric suggestion that a certain celebrated music hall artist should be drawn in a cart to Trafalgar Square where he would delight the populace by playing patriotic airs on a piano with his nose).[2] The King approved the principle of the Fund, but insisted that whatever publicity there was should stress that his son had nothing to do with its administration. Otherwise he foresaw the disgruntled poor blaming the Prince if their applications for relief were rejected.[3] The Prince took the point and fully shared his father's apprehension. All his life he disliked the role of patron, lending his name to some enterprise over which he had no real control. At the end of 1915 he became Chairman of the Statutory Committee of the Patriotic Fund, a body set up to concern itself with the care of sailors and soldiers who had suffered during the war. 'Its work will, alas!, be carried into long years to come . . .' explained Lord Stamfordham. 'It will indeed be a vast machine of National Relief.'[4] Few projects could have appealed more strongly to the Prince, but after the inaugural meeting he still wrote gloomily: 'It's such a rotten show for me; just a mere figurehead with the name of P of Wales as usual!!'[5]

Major Cadogan had rejoined his regiment when war broke out, and to help him with the Fund and his other duties the Prince persuaded Godfrey Thomas to take time off from the Foreign Office and join him as part-time equerry. His chief function, in Stamfordham's eyes at any rate, was to persuade his master to eat more and take less exercise. Thomas tried dutifully but soon admitted defeat. He won the King's confidence, however, and was held to be a healthy influence on his employer. Towards the end of 1914 he spent a weekend with the royal family at York Cottage. After dinner everyone sat around while the King, in big tortoise-shell spectacles, read extracts from the newspapers, 'generally adding explosive comments about the Germans'. When the Queen and Princess Mary had gone to bed, the party adjourned to the billiard room, where the Prince of Wales and Prince Albert played while the King read his telegrams. Next day they went for a long walk. On the way back they met the epileptic Prince John and his nurse. 'The Prince of Wales took him for a run in a kind of push-cart he had, and they both disappeared from view.'[1]

The Prince's initial distaste for the idea of a job on French's staff lessened as other possibilities faded, and when the King finally told him the time had come he was ecstatic: 'This seems almost too good to be true, for once across the Channel lots of things are possible.'[2] Stamfordham told French that the King wanted his son 'to gain practical experience of the vast machinery employed in the conduct of a Campaign'. He was to be attached to the various sections of the headquarters and to attend talks with the Chief of Staff – 'You will find him an attentive, silent listener, absolutely reticent and discreet.'[3] This was not at all how the Prince saw his future, and Thomas observed that he was in a notably bad temper when he had to put aside his normal regimental kit and don the staff uniform with red tabs and cap to match;[4] but he comforted himself with the thought that once in France it would surely be possible to get to the front. The most serious danger seemed to be that the fighting would be over before he could be in the thick of it. His comments on the progress of the war were resolutely optimistic. 'Those bloody Germans are fairly getting it in the neck and no mistake,' he told Jack Lawrence on 20 August,[5] and a month later assured his aunt Alice: 'It really looks as if the allies were getting a proper grip of the situation and that the German downfall has commenced.'[6]

With the declaration of war the Germans had become unequivocally 'bloody', guilty of 'savage barbarism'[7] and 'infamous conduct'; 'As for the Emperor's conduct, words fail me!!'[8] When words did fail him, he filled the gap with obscenities. Writing after gas had just been used he told his friend Houston-Boswell: 'One can't be surprised at anything those German buggers do. One really can't believe we are fighting European christians ... I am a great advocate of the principle of taking no prisoners or as few as possible!!'[9] Godfrey Thomas commented on the Prince's propensity at this time to use bad language and tell filthy stories: 'It is a phase that most people go through at their public school and I hope that it has merely come a bit late in his case and that he'll soon get out of it.'[1] He did, but in the years that followed his escape from the Palace he felt bound to emphasize his independence by larding his diary and letters to his contemporaries with the more conventional expletives.*

The Prince's arrival in France, General Lambton told the King, had given universal pleasure: 'I will try to keep him well occupied and as far from shells as possible.'[2] In this sentence were encapsulated the Prince's two principal causes for woe over the next eighteen months – indeed, for the duration of the war; he *was* kept far from shells, he was *not* well occupied. The latter was not the fault of French or Lambton. A stray and untrained second lieutenant in supreme headquarters will inevitably be at a loose end and overworked senior officers cannot always be inventing tasks for him. If he had not been the Prince of Wales he might have been of modest use at the most menial level; if he had possessed a forceful personality and administrative skills he might have worked himself into a position unjustified by his rank; but he *was* the Prince, he was far from forceful, his skills were limited. 'It's a pretty rotten life for me,' he complained to Thomas. 'I feel I'm the only man out here without a job, and it's true; thus I am but an onlooker in uniform, and become less like an officer every day.'[3] To have been an orthodox ADC to French would at least have involved regular duties, but the King felt it was improper for the Prince of Wales to act in such a role.[4] Instead he was in attendance but with no real function: 'I merely sloped along astern, looking a bloody fool and very much in the way.'[5]

Occasionally he was given some proper work to do. Once he was allowed to use his German in the interrogation of prisoners. The peasants were the most ready to talk, and, even if taciturn originally, could usually be persuaded to tell all they knew by a show of amazement at their ignorance. The more educated prisoners he found 'all lie, and one can't blame them'. In such a case the approved technique was to give the prisoner a good meal with plenty of wine. This loosened his tongue. 'Rather a beastly idea, perhaps, but still it is necessary.'[6] He hoped that similar work

---

* To retain these in quotation, except in the few cases where they add something to the sense, would lengthen the book to little purpose and impose an unnecessary burden on the reader.

would follow, but it never did. When, very occasionally, he found himself doing something useful, his gratification was obvious. In March 1915 he reconnoitred the defences around Le Quesnoy. 'The work is really rather responsible,' he told his father proudly, 'as it is v. necessary that the staff should have detailed information . . .'[1]

Stamfordham urged him not to admit to the King that he was bored and under-employed lest he found himself called back to England. 'You are so terribly keen and full of "go" that you wish always to be doing something . . .'[2] More cheeringly, Desmond Fitzgerald insisted that he *was* always doing something: 'You have little idea what an enormous amount of good you do and how much everyone admires and loves you.'[3] But it was not the sort of love and admiration the Prince wanted. Shortly after his arrival he was made to inspect some Indian troops. He accepted that his visit had done wonders for their morale but, 'I hated this, as I haven't come out for that sort of thing.'[4] French was restrained in his use of the Prince as popular figurehead, but he knew well that 'that sort of thing' was what the Army wanted.

Hospital visiting was another valuable service. 'It pleases the men and shows you take a sympathetic interest in their welfare,' George V told his son.[5] The sympathy was real, and though the Prince felt he should be playing a more valiant role, the warmth and generosity of his nature ensured that the memory of his visits was cherished by all those who experienced them. There is a story, often recounted, of the occasion when the Prince noticed that one patient had been segregated behind curtains. He asked why, and was told that the man had been so fearfully mutilated that it was thought better to keep him out of the way. The Prince insisted on seeing him, stood by his bed, then leant over and kissed him. Lady Donaldson in her admirable biography, properly sceptical of such picturesque but unsubstantiated anecdotes, dismissed it as apocryphal.[6] It does sound too good to be true. But many years later Gordon Selwyn, the chaplain of the hospital and later Dean of Winchester, told Shane Leslie how well he recalled the scene. 'Remember,' the Dean said, 'men have gone to heaven for less. Never can we forget that action.'[7]

Keeping on good terms with the French was another way the Prince could help significantly. He was frequently despatched on liaison visits to French headquarters. The reports which he drafted on his return were of slight value. The cavalry were 'not bad riders . . . but they are about the worst horse masters in the world!!'; the officers were markedly inferior to their British counterparts: 'They are brave enough and some of them very capable, but they don't possess that personality or refineness [sic] which the British officer does, giving the latter complete control over his men, who will generally respect him and follow him anywhere!! How can this ideal state of affairs be reached when frequently the officer is of much lower birth than some of his men?' In spite of this, he concluded in some surprise, 'discipline in the French army is good one would say'.[1] But what mattered was not his somewhat jejune judgment of the French Army but the impression he left behind him. 'I only hope I did some good,' the Prince wrote to his father . . . 'I went out of my way to be civil and always called on any general or senior officer at any place I passed.'[2] Staunch republicans usually make the most fervent royalists and the French military warmed to their shy, friendly and unassuming visitor. '*Il a su ravir tout le monde par sa simplicité, sa bonne grace et sa belle jeunesse,*' wrote General Huguet. '*Il sait par ses charmantes qualités gagner les coeurs autour de lui.*'[3] Huguet was an anglophile; more remarkable was the notoriously rebarbative and anti-British general who, after a visit by the Prince, admitted reluctantly: '*Il parait que parmi vous autres, il y a quand même des gens civilisés.*'[4]

But this was not why he had come to France. Endlessly he reproached himself for the comfort and ease of his existence, compared with the rigours of 'the poor people in the trenches. I fear this is going to be a very soft life.'[5] His initial impression of Sir John French was good – 'he seems a charming man, so human' – but he could not say as much for the rest of the staff; 'a d—d uninteresting crowd and no mistake'.[6] In a less atrabilious mood he would admit that it was not so much that the staff were boring as that they were twenty years older than him. At GHQ a colonel was small fry; young men of twenty were unheard of. Osbert Sitwell, who sometimes found himself similarly out of place at large gatherings of dignitaries, remembered 'the very young, slight figure of the Prince of Wales . . . with his extreme charm, his melancholy smile and angry eyes, trying like myself, I expect, to pretend he was enjoying himself'.[1] The Prince was lonely, and the loneliness was only exacerbated by the constant presence of the officer charged with his day-to-day wellbeing, the middle-aged and portly Colonel Barry. Only when Barry was joined in January 1915 by a young Grenadier captain, Lord Claud Hamilton, was the Prince's desolation mitigated: 'He is such a good chap and has done very well in the 1st batt and got a DSO. It is very nice for me having him here.'[2]

The sharpest pain lay in the knowledge that his contemporaries, in particular in the Grenadiers, were dying in their tens of thousands while he sat safely behind the line. Thirty-five Grenadier officers were killed in the fighting at Neuve Chapelle in March 1915: 'Isn't it too ghastly to think of . . .' he wrote to his closest confidante, Lady Coke. 'But of course I never went near the fighting; kept right away as usual!!'[3] Godfrey Thomas got the same complaint: 'I do hate being a prince and not allowed to fight!!'[4] On his birthday Desmond Fitzgerald said that he could not think of any suitable present: 'The only thing I know of that you would really like, I cannot give you, and that is that you would become an ordinary person.'[5]

He strove endlessly to get permission to join his regiment, or to serve even for a few days in the front line. Briefly he was posted to General Charles Monro's divisional headquarters near Bethune, only to be moved back promptly when an attack was imminent. But he did win at least half his point. In February 1915 the King agreed that he might visit the trenches 'provided that you are with responsible people . . . I want you to do exactly what other young officers on the Staff do, but not to run unnecessary risks, no "joy-rides" or looking for adventure . . . I want you to gain an insight into the life they lead in the trenches. I hope now your mind will be at rest and that you will not be depressed any more. You can do anything within reason except actually fighting in the trenches.'[6] It was something, a great deal indeed, but opportunities for a young officer at GHQ to approach the front line were still few and far between. There are plenty of accounts which describe his hair-breadth 'scapes i' the imminent deadly breach. The future Lord Lee wrote that 'his main desire appeared to be to get either killed or wounded. At intervals he had to be retrieved from advanced trenches and dugouts, whither he had escaped by one

57

subterfuge or another.'[1] A fellow officer described him complaining he had never seen a shell burst within a hundred yards of him. Claud Hamilton remarked that one had burst nearer than that. 'Yes, but dash it, I never saw it!' exclaimed the Prince.[2] 'He loved danger,' said the Rev. Tubby Clayton.[3]

Clayton's comment, at least, is nonsense. The Prince never courted danger, still less loved it. He found shelling terrifying and freely admitted as much. General Sir Ian Hamilton denied that he ever flouted his instructions or took unnecessary risks. 'He *did* take risks, but they were always in the line of duty. We *did* worry about him ... but not because of any insubordination on his part.'[4] Whenever he left the trenches to return to headquarters, he did so with relief. But he did so with shame as well. The ferocious battering to which he subjected his body, with a regime of endless walks and runs, a minimum of food and sleep, must have been in part a mortification of the flesh to assuage this conviction of his inadequacy. If he had been able to change places with a subaltern in the most exposed part of the line he would have done so with alacrity, though also with dismay and trepidation. The moans that fill his diary and letters to his friends about his unlucky lot are wearisome to read and seem sometimes overdone. Their constant refrain, however, was that he was being denied the chance to do as his friends and contemporaries were doing and risk his life for his country. He never stopped trying and it is impossible not to feel respect for his efforts.

His brief sojourn with Monro and the 2nd Division at Bethune included a visit to the Guards Brigade – 'The best day I have had since I've been out, for it was a real treat to be with my brother officers and away from the staff.' The treat was cut short when Monro decided he was too close to the line and sent him back: 'It did bring it home to me how wretched it is to be the Prince of Wales!! I almost broke down.'[5] Shortly after his father's new dispensation, he got within a hundred yards of the German lines, but heard only a few snipers' shots. Then, at Givenchy in March 1915, he came under shellfire for the first time and saw the aftermath of a fierce battle: 'It was a marvellous 2 hrs for me; in my wildest dreams I never thought I sh'd see so much. There are masses of corpses in the open swampy space; a terrible sight.'[6] His excitement was tempered by the horror of the battle. Six officers of the 1st Battalion of the Grenadier Guards were killed in a single day and he felt only relief when a halt was called: 'The operations of the last two days have seemed madness to me. Just sheer murder to attack now.'[1] For him it was back to GHQ. 'I am in the depths of depression, realizing at last that there is no job I can take on out here, so am really the only man who has nothing to do, or anything to work for.'[2]

He was inevitably a prime exhibit for visitors to GHQ. Churchill was one of the more regular. Like most immature young men of twenty, the Prince tended to take his opinions from those around him. Regular Army officers viewed Churchill with mingled distrust and distaste. The Prince followed suit. His initially mild complaints at the frequency of Churchill's visits when he had 'other and more important work to perform'[3] became more splenetic and the Minister was categorized as an 'interfering politician', bothering the overworked naval and military authorities.[4] By the time the First Lord resigned in 1915 he had become an 'intriguing swine';[5] 'Thank God both Winston and Fisher have gone;' he exclaimed to Godfrey Thomas, 'the former is nothing short of a national danger.'[6] On the whole he thought it a good thing that politicians should come out to France 'to see a few realities',[7] but the visits renewed his sense of grievance: 'Mr Bonar Law arrived last night ... and of course went out today with the express purpose of visiting a trench; he will have seen more of the actual fighting than I have in three months!!'[8]

In May 1915 his ceaseless efforts to get closer to the front met with some success when he was transferred to the HQ of 1st Army Corps, to whose command Sir Charles Monro had been promoted. It was still staff work but, at least, he told Thomas, 'now I am out a gt deal and never get into a car if I can possibly help it, doing all my work riding, biking or on foot. That keeps me fairly fit ...'[9] The luxury was less oppressive than at GHQ: 'No tap, no pump, the only source of [water] is from a v. deep open well and it takes 3 mins to draw a small tub!!'[10] Best of all, the work was more satisfying. He was now on the administrative side, concerned mainly with the supply of ammunition. 'I like this so much better than on the Intelligence branch where I was before as one is dealing with facts and *not* theories; I'm not a theorist and what I am doing now interests me.'[11] His new job made him particularly resentful of the shortage of ammunition and other resources caused by the Dardanelles campaign. 'It makes me sick to think of 10 ruddy DIVS killing old Turks instead of Boches!!' he told Thomas. 'That won't help us.' The campaign had been a mistake, he told the Marquis de Breteuil, though he reluctantly accepted that *'une fois commencée, il faut la finir, et vaincre les Turcs.'*[1]

Oliver Lyttelton met the Prince at 1st Army Corps HQ. 'He was,' wrote Lyttelton, 'the most charming and delightful being that I had ever known.' The two men were invited by Desmond Fitzgerald to dine with the Irish Guards about four miles away. Lyttelton was relieved at the thought that the Prince's car would be available but instead found he was expected to bicycle. Worse still: '"I never get off," said HRH, as we faced a mile or two of hilly road. "It is one of the ways that I keep fit." I was in good training, but after a mile I had sweated through my Sam Browne belt and had begun to entertain some republican inclinations. However, we had a gay and delightful evening: the Prince was happy and in the highest spirits; we replaced our lost tissue with some old brandy, and free-wheeled home to our cage like school-boys.'[2] 'The prince eats little and walks much,' Lyttelton told his mother. 'We eat much and walk little.'[3]

On 23 June 1915 the Prince of Wales came of age. The two trustees of his minority, Lord Balfour of Burleigh and Lord Revelstoke, retired; so also did the Treasurer of the Duchy of Cornwall, Walter Peacock. Sydney Greville was appointed Treasurer and the Prince's Comptroller. But no festivities marked what would normally have been an occasion for fastuous celebration. 'It was a sad and depressing occasion,' the Prince told Lady Coke, 'with this ghastly war on and so many of one's best friends killed. In fact I did my utmost to forget it altogether.'[4] His gloom was alleviated but far from dispelled by his new posting. He had barely arrived at Monro's HQ before the 1st Army attacked and was repelled. 'It is bloody when there is any fighting,' he wrote in his diary, 'as everyone is too busy to bother about a . . . useless ullage like myself and the result is that I'm the only man in N France who is unemployed and has no job!!'[5]

In July 1915 he spent his first night in the trenches. 'My impressions that night were of constant close proximity to death, repugnance from the stink of the unburied corpses . . . and general

gloom and apprehension,' he told his father. 'It was all a real eye
opener to me, now I have some slight conception of all that our
officers and men have to go thro!! The whole life is horrible and
ghastly beyond conception.' And this was an uneventful summer
night. 'Think what it must have been like during a night of fighting
in the winter? It does make one think.'[1] The King first heard of
his son's adventures at second hand and was indignant, then
received a letter from the Prince himself and decided all was in
order; 'which shows,' concluded Stamfordham, 'that so long as
the King hears of your doings direct from yourself it is all right'.[2]
He rarely had cause to complain; the Prince wrote to his father
regularly and at inordinate length, sometimes spending two or
three hours a night over these compositions before moving on to
the rest of his extensive correspondence. 'Your letters are capital
and everything very well described,' the King complimented him,
going on to complain about the number of words omitted or
misspelt.[3] Stamfordham took up the point: 'I know you will curse
me as an interfering old ass,' he told the Prince; 'but realizing how
devoted you are to the King, and how strongly these feelings are
reciprocated . . . I want to put to rights a small matter which causes
a slight, tho' of course only temporary annoyance.'[4] The Prince
did take more care after this rebuke but his spelling remained
disastrous; it improved gradually over the years but was shaky till
the day he died.

Kitchener came out in the same month. 'He is fatter than ever
and as red as usual, but seemed pleased with everything,' the Prince
noted in his diary – adding rather cryptically, 'Wow!! Wow!!'[5]
Troops lined the road for the visit, a mark of grandeur which the
Prince felt should have been reserved for his father – 'Unless you
looked inside the car it might have been you driving round, which
I thought absolutely wrong.' Still, the troops did not cheer as
vigorously as they had for the King, 'and I happen to know that
they were all v. bored at being turned out to line the roads'.[6] He
thought both Kitchener and French were to be criticized for the
embittered bickering between them which made so difficult the
conduct of the war – 'It does seem a disgrace that people in high
positions can't put away all thoughts for themselves at such a
time!!' – but put most of the blame on French: 'an odd little man
and far from clever'.[7]

When the King visited France, the Prince of Wales was in attendance. He would have preferred to be with his battalion, but it was a welcome break from GHQ. George V was delighted with his son's performance. 'I am glad to say he is very popular with everyone and is tremendously keen to do anything he can,' he told the Queen.[1] The Prince had told his father that one of the worst features of life in France was the ignorance of and hostility to the Navy shown by most senior officers. He was often asked whether the Navy was doing anything at all. 'Although I am now serving in the army, I never forget that I was brought up in the Navy . . . So it grieves . . . me much to hear these things said of my beloved service.'[2] Every time he saw the King he pleaded that he should be allowed to visit the fleet at Scapa Flow. The King, for some reason that neither Stamfordham nor the Queen could understand, at first took strong exception to the idea. Queen Mary was stirred to unwonted activity on the subject: 'There can be no possible objection to your going now . . . You may certainly count on my support.'[3] They won the day. In August 1915 the visit took place. Godfrey Thomas accompanied the Prince and recorded his delight and child-like enthusiasm for all he saw.

On the return journey they were cajoled into breaking their journey at Dunrobin, home of the Duke of Sutherland. They had insisted the visit should be informal, but when the train arrived, wrote Thomas, there were 'rows and rows of people in kilts. I don't wonder the Prince was rather annoyed. He couldn't find his cap or his cigarettes or anything and eventually rushed down the corridor to the carriage door using such fearful language that I'm almost certain the Duke and Duchess . . . must have had the benefit of the end of it.' The drive to the castle was lined with troops; the Prince travelled with the Duke 'looking perfectly furious and hardly uttering'. This visit over, the Prince and Thomas spent a few days stalking at Abergeldie where Princes Harry and George were also staying. On the last day they all packed into a car to go to the railway station. 'I can't say we behaved very well en route, as any female passing us was waved and yelled at, and they sang loudly most of the way . . . By the time we reached Ballater, one of the strings of HRH's deerstalker had broken, and the flap was hanging down in a drunken way. We were all dirty, sweaty and dishevelled, and must have looked like a lot of tramps.'[4] It had been a marvellous break from France, but it left the Prince dejected: 'How I long to be back at sea again and infinitely prefer being a sailor to a soldier!!'[1]

George V used his son as a source of information on the senior generals. 'I want to know privately if the C in C has had a row with Genl Smith-Dorrien,' he asked in March 1915. 'You might find out and let me know.'[2] The Prince had little useful information on this point but he did not spare Sir John French in his correspondence and his testimony must have contributed to the strong support George V gave Kitchener against the Commander-in-Chief. When Monro was succeeded by Sir Hubert Gough, the Prince was cautiously enthusiastic. At first he was dismayed by the new Corps Commander's reluctance to let him visit the front line, then he became more approving as the rules were relaxed. 'There is no doubt he is an able tactician and a good "pushing" general,' he wrote in July. 'He talks too much; that is his gt fault to my mind.'[3]

His views on most matters were orthodox and strident. He was strongly in favour of conscription, feeling that the whole nation must be mobilized if the war was ever to be won.[4] He welcomed as irresistible the call to arms which his father delivered in October 1915. Who would have the heart to ignore such an appeal? 'But no doubt there are thousands of these foul unpatriotic brutes about!! One almost begins not to think so highly of one's country as one did!!'[5] Conscientious objectors were 'loathsome'; he had twelve hundred of them working in the Duchy, 'Disgusting looking men with long hair and they never wear hats; they loaf about the place and look at one with a very contemptible air!!'[6] Miners who struck for higher pay were still more loathsome, they should be put 'straight into the trenches and send the whole crowd out patrolling, the first night they go in!!'[7] As for Roger Casement, the Irishman who sought to lead a German-inspired rising, he deserved least sympathy of all: 'He should be publicly hung in Hyde Park or some open space where there is room for a large crowd.'[8]

His father and brothers would have echoed these views, as indeed would 90 per cent of the officers of the British Army. On most issues, though his parents might from time to time irritate him, he differed from his family very little. Increasingly it seemed to him that he had most in common with Prince Albert. The two had grown particularly close; 'more so perhaps than most brothers, as our interests are the same,' wrote the Prince of Wales early in 1915. 'I am sure he will always do very well in the future; in fact I often feel that if I do as well as he does I shall be all right!!'[1] Prince Albert's naval career was suffering from his ill health and he had been forced to work in the Admiralty, a dreary job which he performed uncomplainingly. 'I must say I admire him tremendously for this and don't hesitate to tell you he's one of the best,' the Prince wrote to Godfrey Thomas, knowing well that uncomplaining acceptance of ill fortune was not his own forte.[2] Prince Albert, however, was not so uncomplaining when it came to the conduct of his parents. The two Princes united in a chorus of criticism. Prince Albert wailed about the 'awful prison' of Buckingham Palace: 'The parents have got funny ideas about us, thinking we are still boys at school or something of that sort, instead of what we are.'[3] The Prince of Wales was no more enthusiastic about life in the Palace, especially after the King imposed a teetotal regime for the duration of the war: 'Awful balls the whole thing. I don't think it will have much effect on the drinking community. Lloyd George forced it on Papa.'[4]

As he grew older he became more adept at avoiding the sombre dignity of the family circle. By 1917 he was able to come and go more or less at pleasure. He was summoned for two weeks to Sandringham. 'This little boy somehow says NO,' he told Lady Coke. 'He might possibly spend two or three days there, but not more, not for nobody, and he knows a bit too much for that!!!!'[5] – a point so close to his heart as to demand even more than his usual allotment of two exclamation marks. In London he still stayed always at Buckingham Palace, but tried to time his periods of leave so that he had at least a few days there without his parents. This did not always work out. 'I am sorry your style was rather cramped during your leave in London,' Lord Burghersh wrote sympathetically. 'It's exactly the same with me. Family *so* inquisitive.'[6] But it would be wrong to attach too much significance to such flights from the family nest. The Prince was far from rejecting his parents or demanding total independence. On his twenty-first birthday his father wrote to tell him: 'You will have about

£246,000 which . . . is a splendid sum of money which will go on increasing until you marry and set up house. Until then, I hope you will consider my home as your home.' The Queen echoed her husband's words: 'I hope that for some years to come you, my darling Son, will continue to live under our roof, where you are and ever will be "*le bienvenu*".'[1] The Prince in his reply told his mother how pleased he would be to remain with his parents 'until the fateful day arrives when I shall have to think about finding me a wife, and I trust that day is as yet afar off!!'[2] Privately he had probably made up his mind that he must set up on his own once the war was over, but he had no wish to confront his parents on such an issue while the war was still raging and long-term plans seemed impossible to make.

In June 1915 the Prince had first speculated about the possibility that a Guards division might be formed under the command of Lord Cavan, 'an ideal state of things'.[3] A month later the ideal became reality; 'It ought to be the finest division in the world,' the King wrote proudly.[4] The Prince had no doubt that this was where he belonged. In his eyes the Guards were as far above the other line regiments as the Navy was above the Army. He admitted to the King that he and the other Guards officers were apt to think that their men were the only ones of any use, 'which is v. wrong and which one must avoid above all things, but it's not an unnatural point of view to take really!!'[5] But though his transfer to this martial empyrean brought some relief and moved him a little closer to the fighting, it did not prove entirely satisfactory. Life at Cavan's headquarters was no less sybaritic than in his previous postings; Raymond Asquith visited the headquarters in November 1915 and was given 'a good dinner and an excellent bottle of champagne . . . the Prince of Wales was there and gave me a long and fragrant cigar'.[6] Nor was the work more enlivening; a typical day in December had him devoting the morning to pursuing a missing consignment of gum boots and the afternoon to bargaining for the use of a piece of land on which to build bathing huts: 'Heavens, the unparalleled monotony of this life!! . . . I shall go mad soon!!'[7] Worst of all, though he liked and admired 'Fatty' Cavan, he deplored the General's reluctance to let him get near the trenches:

'I think Fatty is going to shut me up in my glasshouse more than ever.'[1] Only a week after this entry he escaped from his glasshouse and visited the front line during a lull in the battle of Loos. The 1st Guards Brigade had charged three hundred yards across open ground towards the enemy line and had been massacred by machine-gun fire as they reached the final wire, 'too cruel to be killed within a few yards of yr. objective . . . This was my first real sight of war and it moved and impressed me most enormously.' On the way back the party had to jump into a trench to avoid a storm of shrapnel, fifty yards away the Prince's car was damaged and his driver killed: 'He was an exceptionally nice man, a beautiful driver and a 1st rate mechanic; it's an absolute tragedy and I can't yet realize that it has happened.'[2]

The Commander-in-Chief, told that the Prince had been in the car beside his driver, promptly ordered that he should return to Corps headquarters. The Prince wrote in dismay to his father. 'What did you have me appointed to Guards DIV for? That I should be removed as soon as there is any fighting? . . . I can assure you it is one of the biggest blows I have ever had . . . My dearest Papa, I implore of you to have this most unfortunate and deplorable order from GHQ cancelled *as soon as* possible.'[3] French reconsidered his decision and the Prince stayed with the Guards. The King ruled, however, that his son should only go up to the front if it was 'absolutely necessary', otherwise Cavan would be placed in an impossible position.[4] It all depended on what was meant by 'necessary', and the Prince eventually saw his interpretation of the word accepted: if it was necessary for the General to go to the front line it must be necessary for his staff officers to accompany him. But he was not content with what he had gained. 'If *only* I could spend 48 hours in the line;' he told his father, '. . . I should get an idea of what trench life is like, which it is absolutely impossible to do otherwise . . . I suppose you wouldn't like to make permission for me to do this a form of Xmas present to me?'[5]

It had not needed the sight of the mounds of dead in front of the German lines at Loos to make the Prince doubtful of the allied strategy. The endless, hideously costly attacks, achieving nothing except at the best the occupation of a few trenches, seemed to him futile. The commanders had promised great advances, the breaking of the German line: 'When is all this? Ask of the winds, and I call it sheer murder!!' He had lost all confidence in French. 'The sooner we get a new C in C the better.'[1] But when a new Commander-in-Chief was appointed it was Douglas Haig, a man as wedded to the policy of bloody attrition as ever French had been. 'He is *very* unpopular,' the Prince told Stamfordham. 'I can't stand the man myself, so hard and unsympathetic.'[2] Towards the end of the war he was to revise his views, and even find Haig 'human and sympathetic',[3] but at the end of 1915 it seemed to him that the new C.-in-C. treated men 'as mere fighting tools',[4] and that, in the Prince's eyes, was almost the ultimate accusation.

Shortly before French departed George V came to France for one of his periodic visits to his troops. Startled by the cheering of the men the King's horse reared, threw its rider and fell heavily on top of him. The Prince rushed to his father's side, to find him winded and unable to breathe. Doctors arrived and pronounced that there were no internal injuries, only shock and severe bruising. It had been a lucky escape; the ground where the King fell was soft, otherwise he would have been crushed beyond recognition.[5] The Prince hurried back to London with Claud Hamilton to reassure the Queen. 'Thank God Papa is all right,' he wrote in his diary, 'it's an ill wind that blows nobody any good, and little did Claudie and I think in the morning that we shd be on our way home in less than 12 hrs.'[6]

Before this episode the Prince had been in slightly bad odour at court because of his reluctance to wear some foreign medals which he had been awarded. He apologized to the King, 'but you know how distasteful it is to me to wear these war decorations having never done any fighting and having always been kept well out of danger'.[7] The sense of inferiority which he felt in the presence of fighting men was redoubled when he was flaunting honours which they had been denied. His discomfort was redoubled in mid-1916 when he was awarded the Military Cross. Lady Coke wrote to congratulate him. 'I don't feel I deserve it *in the least*,' the Prince replied crossly. 'There are *so* many gallant yet undecorated officers who should have MCs long before me.'[8] He was promoted Captain at about the same time but got no pleasure from it 'as I have no command'. 'You'll be saying to yourself "What a gloomy view of

67

life he does take",' he admitted to Stamfordham. 'Well, I fear that is the case . . .'[1]

He was craving for change, and when it became clear that he could not expect to stay with the Guards division when it went into the line at Ypres, he concluded that he had much better leave France altogether. He conceived the idea of visiting the allied forces in the Middle East and Kitchener agreed that a report on the defences in the Canal Zone would be of use. The King initially opposed the idea on the grounds that the danger from submarines in the Mediterranean was too great. His reluctance made the Prince's wish to go become almost overpowering. 'D—n the risk of . . . torpedoes,' he wrote to Stamfordham, 'it is such rot, isn't it? But all these family fears have to be considered!'[2] The King relented, and at once the Prince began to wonder whether he was doing the right thing. 'I do feel such a miserable worm,' he told his uncle. 'Of course it will be very interesting and pleasant in Egypt, but I shan't be able to enjoy it in the least, when I know where I ought to be and where my friends are.'[3]

He suggested that Desmond Fitzgerald should accompany him as equerry. The proposal was rejected, Fitzgerald was too junior for such a role. A week before the Prince sailed, Fitzgerald was training with his regiment near Calais. The padre took a turn at throwing a hand grenade and somehow bungled it. Fitzgerald was fatally injured. It was the worst experience the Prince had suffered during the war. 'It is a fearful blow to lose one's greatest friend, and he was that to me.'[4] In wartime those whose friends are in daily danger must either learn to accept their loss with relative equanimity or themselves break under the strain. The Prince had built a carapace of resignation with which to confront the awful massacre of his contemporaries. Fitzgerald's death, though, broke down his guard. He left for Egypt in a mood as depressed as he had ever known, and the tragedy was to cast a blight over what would otherwise have been a pleasant escapade.

4

The Captain

THE PRINCE OF WALES'S EXPEDITION TO THE MIDDLE
East proved a welcome break in the four black years that
he spent on the Western Front. He would not have been the
man he was if he had not striven to diminish his pleasure by endless
doubts and self-accusations. 'I feel such a swine having a soft
comfortable time out here while the Guards Division is up at
Ypres,' he told Lady Coke;[1] and he found little comfort in the
knowledge that he would never have been allowed near the battle
himself and that his presence with the allied forces in the Canal
Zone was a badly needed boost to the morale of those who felt
themselves to be members of a forgotten army.

His last days in London had been hectic. He called on Kitchener
to get his instructions – 'He talked a lot, quite interesting in a
way, but I'm frightened of the man'[2] – acquired the mountain of
impedimenta thought necessary for such a journey, and spent the
last night in mingled work and revelry. He, Prince Albert and
Godfrey Thomas, recorded the latter, 'played the gramophone till
the small hours and when we thought it was time for some song
that we hadn't got among the records, we were obliged to sing it.
After a lot of exercise dancing round and round the room, Prince
Bertie proceeded to go to bed, but his brother got into his bed with
all his clothes on, so by the time he'd been pulled out by us, there
wasn't much left of the bed . . . So we turned the gramophone on
again. I got away just before two. HRH was starting at 9 the next
morning, and had done practically no packing as usual, and also
had about 20 letters to write. The result, as I heard afterwards,
was that he had exactly 1¼ hours sleep that night and went off
without any breakfast, which is entirely typical.' Thomas got this
last information in a letter from Prince Albert, who added: 'A
wonderful chap. I don't know how he does it, do you?'[3]

The King had been convinced that even in comparatively temperate March the Prince would find the heat in the Canal Zone intolerable, but his son relished hot weather and was inspired by it to undertake still more strenuous physical exercise. He enjoyed the life in Ismalia, 'strafing up and down the Canal', visiting the troops and preparing a report on the supply system. On his first day at GHQ he went to hear General Birdwood address the Australian and New Zealand Brigades. His presence was announced to the men, 'at which they gave 3 cheers, bloody fools!!'[1] At first he had been slightly deterred by their reputation for drunkenness and indiscipline but he was quickly overwhelmed by their exuberance; they had committed undreamt-of atrocities in the red-light districts of Cairo and Alexandria, but 'they have fought so d—d hard and are *so* keen, that it is hard to deal severely with them'. What moved him most was the 'marvellous imperial spirit' that had called them up, 'for they aren't fighting for themselves or their own country either; only for the Empire'. 'As you know,' he told his friend Captain Bailey, 'I'm not often given to these highflown ideas, but really these Anzacs have impressed me so much!!'[2] On the banks of the Suez Canal the Prince conceived a reverence for the idea of Empire that was to sustain him during the rigorous tours that lay ahead.

Not everyone reciprocated his enthusiasm. Among the many men he spoke to when he visited the Anzac troops at Tel-el-Kebir, was John Monash, a Brigadier General who had been one of the heroes of Gallipoli and was to become the most prominent Australian soldier of the First World War. 'What he said to me was "M-m-m-m",' wrote Monash. 'The fact was the youngster was completely bewildered, and most evidently ill at ease.'[3] His was a minority voice, however; every other account of the visit was lyrical in tone. Birdwood maintained that the men took him to their hearts; the Prince's equerry, Malcolm Murray, spoke of the warmth of their reception – 'They would rush across to wherever the Prince was coming up, make a line for him and cheer time after time.'[4] One eye-witness account was passed on at third hand to Queen Mary: '. . . the enthusiasm knew no bounds, and the cheering was perfectly overwhelming. Our friend said that men looked at him so intently that they forgot to salute! and added "I'm not exaggerating when I say that some of them gazed at him with tears rolling down their cheeks."'[5]

The Captain

The Prince of Wales had been in crowds many times before, but this was the first time that he had experienced the adulation that was so often to be his lot over the next twenty years. It could be argued that any young, personable and smiling prince would have had the same effect. The contrary can hardly be proved, but so many reports by men and women who prided themselves on being not easily impressed testify to the extraordinary potency of his personality that it is impossible to dismiss them all. To the seasoned veterans of Gallipoli his youth, charm, simplicity and friendliness, his patent sincerity and concern for their wellbeing, proved irresistible. Many millions were to find the same combination as effective in the future.

For the Prince it was exhilarating, disconcerting and slightly alarming. He for his part had no doubt that it was his royal blood and not his personal qualities which won him such applause. The idea displeased him. 'Oh!! to be out here privately and not as the P of W,' he moaned to Godfrey Thomas. 'That's what ruins my life and ever will!!!!' This particular complaint was provoked by a projected visit to Khartoum. He had pleaded to be allowed to go there but typically at once began to have doubts once permission had been conceded. If he could have gone as a common tourist he would have been delighted, but he was travelling officially as heir to the throne: 'You know how I hate all those bulls at any time, so think how odious it is to me in wartime!!'[1] In the Governor – the Sirdar – Reginald Wingate, he found a man determined to milk the situation to the last drop: 'A little snob,' he called him in his diary; 'He is HRHing the whole time and never relaxes a moment.'[2] Yet he had to admit that Wingate knew his job superlatively well and that the pomp was well deployed to make the greatest possible impression on the Sudanese. 'I am throwing my heart and soul into it all to make it a success, though it goes against the grain,' he told his father.[3] To Malcolm Murray it sometimes seemed that heart and soul were not as energetically deployed as might have been hoped for. The Prince, he complained to Stamfordham, 'always wanted to efface himself, and hates any kind of formal thing. This is exactly what he wants practice in – he is rather naughty about going up to speak to people etc.'[4]

The Prince's always weak stomach for sightseeing was quickly over-taxed. Even before he reached Luxor on his return journey

71

down the Nile he was confessing in his diary: 'I'm utterly fed up with visiting temples and never want to see another one again.' He found an itinerant snake-charmer decidedly more interesting than Karnak by moonlight. The ancient and eminent Egyptologist Professor Le Grain lavished his learning on the young visitor but gained little gratitude for his pains. 'I wasn't sorry to see him go, for he . . . nearly killed me with his detailed descriptions.'[1] It is unlikely, however, that the professor guessed how little pleasure he had given; the Prince's manners rarely fell below excellence and he would have gone to great pains to put a good face on his sufferings. When Ronald Storrs conducted the Prince round Cairo a few days later, he wrote that he had never met a visitor 'who entered more swiftly into the spirit of the place . . . I have met none with equal vitality or with more appreciation of Eastern life'.[2] Perhaps Storrs was a more congenial cicerone than the professor, certainly the Prince found Cairo much jollier than the Upper Nile and agitated to be allowed to pay it a second visit. The King for some reason objected and the Prince wrote in injured innocence: 'I don't want to go galivanting about in Cairo, far from it. I'm not even going to ask you for a night there . . . just a few hours so that I may go to the bazaars and do some shopping for you and Mama.'[3]

In Cairo he met Lord Edward Cecil, a fellow Grenadier, shrewd judge of character and author of the exquisitely witty *The Leisure of an Egyptian Official*. 'He is a nice boy of fifteen, rather immature for that age,' Lord Edward wrote to his wife. 'He cannot get in or out of a room except sideways and he has the nervous smile of one accustomed to float. I hope he will grow up, but he is leaving it till late. He is curiously decided, even obstinate, and happily there is no sign of weakness of character. His main terror is getting fat. He adores the Regiment and would talk all day about it, but beyond love of all military matters, an outspoken hatred of politicians and a very fine English accent when he speaks French, he has no apparent special characteristics. I think one day he will fall in love and then he will suddenly grow up.'[4]

He never got back to Cairo nor was he allowed to stay on in the Middle East after the onset of the hot season. Malcolm Murray direly prophesied sunstroke and probably enteric fever if he lingered on, and the King ordered his return: 'You have had a nice change and have enjoyed some nice warm weather; think of the many thousands of poor fellows who are obliged to remain in France without a break...'[1] The Prince might justifiably have retorted that he thought constantly about them, that he had done all he could to be treated like them, and that his return to a job on the staff would not improve their lot by an iota. Instead, he accepted his recall with moderately good grace. On the way back, in May 1916, he called on King Victor Emmanuel at his head-quarters near the Italian front at Udine. He found the King a 'dear and charming little man' but it was the same story as in France; as soon as the royal party got anywhere near any scene of possible action, the cars would turn round and speed back to a safer section of the line.[2]

On his return he submitted a report on the supply and transport arrangements in the Canal Zone which Kitchener forwarded to the King; it did the Prince great credit, commented Kitchener, 'and shows his grasp of details, and military knowledge'.[3] 'A really excellent report,' George Arthur, then an official in the War Office, described it.[4] The praise seems high for a somewhat cursory state-ment of the existing position, in twelve hundred words, with little detail and no recommendations, but it showed at least that he had kept his eyes open and not treated the expedition as a joy ride. The King had good reason to be pleased with his son's performance. Wingate had written that the Prince's visit had done enormous good in the Sudan; the GOC reported that the morale of the troops in the Canal Zone had been notably improved; it was not the sort of war the Prince wanted to wage, but this time even he had to admit that he had been of use.

Back in France the Prince rejoined Lord Cavan's staff with the 14th Army Corps. He was no nearer having a proper job. 'He holds a very junior appointment of course,' commented the future Field Marshal Montgomery loftily, 'and I can't imagine that he does much real work.'[5] Lord Newton, then a junior minister at the Foreign Office, found him 'an undeveloped youth with pleasant and unassuming manners' and ascribed his lack of any important staff job to the fact that he could not be induced to read.[6] The charge of immaturity was certainly justified, but when the Prince

73

was given something to do, he did it conscientiously. His complaint was that he was left in idleness or burdened with unnecessary and clearly improvised duties. After less than a week back in headquarters he was exclaiming bitterly that he was 'thoroughly fed up'. 'God knows how long the Lord Claud and I will be stuck here,' he wrote to Captain Bailey; 'it couldn't be very long as I sh'd go mad after a few months . . . How I do grouse . . . !!'[1]

Claud Hamilton was at first his only real friend at Corps HQ. The Prince recognized that Hamilton's military career was jeopardized by his absence from his regiment and readily agreed to make up his pay to the level it might have reached in other circumstances. 'Of course I should *hate* not to help him as I ought to,' he wrote to Stamfordham, 'and am only wondering whether £150 is sufficient.'[2] Hamilton repaid this generosity with loyalty and an unflinching readiness to tell his master the truth, however unpalatable it might be. One of the Prince's more attractive characteristics was his readiness to accept any amount of criticism from those whom he liked and who, he believed, had his interests at heart. In May 1918 he ran foul of Hamilton over some unspecified matter, probably relating to an escapade with some women from the Voluntary Aid Detachment. 'I have had a straight talk and said it must stop or I shall go,' Claud Hamilton told Lady Coke. 'He thoroughly realized he was in the wrong and promised to turn over a new leaf. Now it is much better.'[3] Some months later he was still gossiping to his friends about 'the Prince and the VADs, which, if known, would cause some trouble', but the offence seems to have been in the past.[4] Hamilton remained with the Prince for several more years, though in the end the two men decided they could not work together.

Early in 1917 Hamilton was reinforced by the arrival of Piers 'Joey' Legh, another Grenadier and a son of Lord Newton. Legh was to remain with the Prince for twenty years and accompany him into exile after the abdication. More than ten years again after that he was still talking of the man 'whom he had loved and whose charm was so great that he would thrill with emotion if the Duke entered the room just now'.[5] As with Claud Hamilton, the Prince accepted from him rebukes which a vainer or more touchy man would have resented. In June 1917 General Cavan told him off for devoting too much time to his interminable runs, neglecting the newspapers and paying no attention to world affairs. 'Of course he is right really and I don't attempt to be a P of W or prepare for being so,' the culprit admitted ruefully, 'but how I hate all that sort of thing and how unsuited I am for the job!!' Yet he persisted with his runs. Legh spoke to him 'like a father', and threatened to report him to Cavan. The Prince continued to offend, whereupon Legh did report him and Cavan categorically forbade further runs. 'That old shit Joey,' the Prince wrote in his diary, 'but I'm none the less fond of him and forgive him *all* as he's only done it for my good . . .'[1]

Hamilton and Legh, the Prince told his mother, were 'my 2 *great* friends who are and have been *real* friends to me; I'm devoted to them!!'[2] Without their companionship he would have found intolerable the gloom and, as he saw it, uselessness of his life in Cavan's headquarters; even with them his depression sometimes almost overcame him. One day when he had been refused a visit to the front line, he remained in his room, writing letters till 1 a.m. 'I could not face . . . any company. I wanted to be alone in my misery!! I feel quite ready to commit suicide and would if I didn't think it unfair on Papa.'[3] He no doubt over-dramatized his misery, but he was an unhappy and frustrated man. More and more he dreaded the next 'push', when he knew there would be yet further massacres, more friends killed, more shame for him. He went to a staff meeting at which an attack was ordered on a certain hill. The General involved protested, but Cavan insisted the hill must be taken. 'He must have hated doing this as I could see he was worried. Several people have told me that the whole plan of attack seems to them impossible and mad. Of course Haig doesn't think of the poor buggers who will have to pay the price for this . . .'[4] He tried to convince himself that a war of bloody attrition held the only hope of victory, but signally failed. 'These continuous heavy casualty lists make me sick,' he wrote during the battle of the Somme, 'it all seems such a waste for of course it doesn't matter if we don't push on another few miles as regards the end of the war, we only push to kill Huns and help our allies. I'm afraid I can't bring myself to look on the situation in such a big way; I can't keep the wretched infantry being slaughtered out of my thoughts.'[5]

It was just before this battle that the Prince went with Cavan's deputy, General Morland, to see the first 'tanks', a code word for 'these new land submarines'. He was impressed by their ingenuity, admired the bravery of their crews, but was sceptical of their value: 'They are good toys but I don't have much faith in their success.'[1] He told his father of his doubts and was duly crushed: 'With regard to the "Tanks" which you scoffed at when you first saw them . . .' retorted the King, reports were so good that several hundred had been ordered.[2] The King was proved right in the end, but the performance of the tank in the First World War, at least before the battle of Cambrai more than a year later, did something to support the Prince's scepticism.

The progress of the war over its last two years is marked by his ever growing respect for the fighting men; not just for the officers or the Guardsmen but 'for the British conscript . . . for he hates the whole thing and isn't fired with the same spirit as were the first hundred thousand'. And yet they managed to keep 'so marvellously cheery' and to prepare for each new scene of carnage with renewed determination. They were marvels, 'it does make one feel so proud of being an Englishman'. More was being asked of them than had ever been asked of British troops before. And he felt humble as well as proud: 'No one can realize what these . . . battles are like till they've been in one, and I don't, as I never have.'[3]

He never stopped trying to get forward to the front line, never stopped hating it when he was there. In June 1917 he rose at 4 a.m. to go to the trenches: 'and how I loathed it!! But frightened tho' I am, I should honestly loathe it still more if I never went forward!!'[4] Shortly before that he told Lady Coke that in recent months he had only once been within range of enemy shellfire since his return, 'so you need have no thoughts for my safety'.[5] The worst danger he had confronted was in October 1916, when he was at the front with General Gathorne Hardy. A shell fell forty yards in front, then one thirty yards behind. Fortunately the German gunners did not complete the bracket: 'I've never been so near becoming a casualty before, though it did me worlds of good, frightening me properly.'[6] Four days later they were still more comprehensively shelled. 'That strafing we got has taught me more than anything ever has during my 2 years out here; it gives me a slight impression of what our men have to go through these days.'[7]

Gathorne Hardy was the last person with whom the Prince would have chosen to die; 'he is so unfair to all his subordinates that I feel ashamed to be out with him!!'[1] The Prince's dislike for Gathorne Hardy had started one particularly cold and wet night when the Grenadiers were moving up to the front. A staff officer remarked, 'Lord, I'm sorry for those poor devils going up.' 'Oh well, they've got their ground sheets,' retorted Gathorne Hardy. 'Pass the port.'[2] The remark probably signified little, but to the Prince it showed unforgivable callousness. His respect for the fighting men would never have allowed him to speak of them so indifferently. Indeed he would never have made a First World War general; he was too soft-hearted, too squeamish, too concerned about the safety and comfort of the men. 'I'm v keen on the fighting troops being made as *comfortable* as possible always . . .' he told Wigram. 'Poor devils, they have a bloody enough time in the trenches . . . they are absolutely marvellous and I'd do anything for them.'[3]

As a weapon of war, he rated the aeroplane far ahead of the tank. Early in September 1917 he visited the *Cigognes*, the crack French squadron which included Guinemeyer, the ace who had shot down over fifty German planes. 'They are fine fellows,' he told Lady Coke, 'and all gentlemen, to put it snobbishly, which makes such a difference really.' The visit was of particular interest to him because a few weeks before he had been given permission by the King to go up in an aeroplane himself, provided it was nowhere near the line. He had had his first flight on 17 July: 'It's a wonderful feeling up there,' he wrote, 'but I don't feel I ever want to learn to fly.'[4] In fact he was soon eager to do so, and though he took no steps to learn until long after the war, he went up quite frequently over the next two years. One account says that his permission to fly was withdrawn because he flew with a Canadian war ace who was photographed piloting the aircraft with one arm in a sling.[5] There is nothing in the Prince's diary about this, though in September 1918 he did fly up to 10,000 feet with a Canadian called Barker. 'It is really the safest thing in the world, far safer than motoring!!' he told his mother.[6]

After the exhilaration of flying, he found little to thrill him in the course he did with the Royal Artillery. It seems to have been a pointless exercise; the course was designed for officers who had done a year or more with an artillery battery, and, since he hardly knew one end of a gun from another, he understood nothing of what was going on. The drills were incessant and tedious, the other students uninspiring, the food disastrous. This last at least he could put right, with a weekly hamper from Fortnum and Mason containing a ham, two tongues and a Stilton. 'You know I attach very little importance to my food,' he told his mother, 'and I have always taken the view that most people eat too much . . . But I must confess that I like the small amount of food that I eat to be good.'[1] The contents of the hamper were shared out around the mess and the Prince's departure was a cause for sincere regret.

At the end of 1916 Asquith fell and Lloyd George succeeded him as Prime Minister. Only six months before, the Prince had told his father that he did not care for Lloyd George 'as a man, a statesman or anything' but by December 1916 he had concluded that 'everyone has gt confidence in him and feels that he is really out to win the war and that he has no thought for himself'.[2] He welcomed the change, believing that a strong government was essential and that 'old Squiff' could never have provided the necessary leadership.[3] He was particularly gratified that Churchill was not in the reformed government and disgusted when he reappeared as Minister of Munitions six months later – 'I suppose he has silently wormed his way in again.'[4] Grudgingly he admitted to the King that Churchill would probably do the job well and 'perhaps it is safer to give him a job than to have him hanging around unemployed'.[5]

By this time hopes of a rapid victory had been dashed by the collapse of the Russian empire. 'Let us hope that the new Govt will get the upper hand and smash the socialists,' the King wrote to his son in April 1917. 'I should imagine that a republic in Russia is an impossibility.'[6] To the Prince the blow struck at the allied war effort by the defection of the Russians seemed more catastrophic than the murder of his relatives whom he had hardly met. 'Oh! this ———— war . . . I feel as if we are in for at least another 10 years of it!!' The Russian revolution, followed by the crumbling of the monarchies at the end of the war, caused him to think about the future of the British royal family. 'Ours is by far the most solid,' he told his father, 'tho of course it must be kept so and I more than realize that this can only be done by keeping in the closest possible touch with the people and I can promise you that this point is always at the back of [my] mind and that I am and always will make every effort to carry it out . . . I also feel that we have good reason to be confident of the good sense and calmness of our race, anyhow just now, tho of course one knows there are many and great dangers, and one mustn't shut one's eyes to them even if they don't really become formidable till 2 or 3 years after the declaration of peace when the race will have got over the joy and novelty of "no war on".'[1]

His relationship with his father had been better since his visit to the Middle East, and he wrote in his diary in March 1917 that 'the parents are more charming to me than ever, and seem glad to see me again'.[2] But though he was getting on well with his father, it was his mother with whom he felt closest. His letters and diary abound in references to cosy and confidential talks about every aspect of his life: 'It's so wonderful to feel that we can really talk things over now, and vital and *intime* things, and I can assure you, darling Mama, that this makes all the difference to me.'[3] The Queen responded warmly: 'I think I *do* understand and can enter into other people's feelings,' she wrote in mingled gratification and surprise.[4]

She seemed to relish the fact that she was closer than the King to her sons, and was not beyond making a little mischief to emphasize the difference. She complained to the Prince that she had not been present when important decisions were made about his future, 'such a pity, as first of all I ought to know and secondly it makes it more difficult for me just to hear in a cursory way from Papa'. She urged her son to write his 'secret and intimate views' on a separate sheet of paper, so that the King should not realize he was being kept in the dark. She evolved an elaborate plot to get the Prince back on leave for Christmas: 'I cannot help laughing to myself at the *mystery* which surrounds any new plan which . . . we have to put before Papa, it all requires such a lot of thought, writing, choosing the right moment etc, really comical in a way but so tiresome.'[5] Yet though she would enter into conspiracy with her sons, an open confrontation with the King was still out of the question. Never did she doubt that his will must prevail.

One issue on which she consulted her son without reference to the King was the future of Princess Mary. The Prince constantly pressed the Queen to allow his sister friends of her own age and greater liberty to move around outside the palaces. Princess Mary bravely insisted that life at Buckingham Palace was not too bad:

'You need not feel so sorry for me . . . The only things I object to are those rather silent dinners you know so well, when Papa will read the paper.'[1] Her brother knew that she was lonely and, in everything except material terms, underprivileged. He joined eagerly in what his mother called the 'all important matter' of finding the Princess a husband who would be both socially acceptable and tolerable to live with.[2] Hopefully he put forward the names of friend after friend, only to find that his mother always shrank from proposing them to the King. Princess Mary did not find a husband until 1922 and then it was by no doing of the Prince of Wales.

Early in 1919 his epileptic brother, Prince John, finally died. The young invalid's always frail grasp on reason had been failing rapidly and it had been obvious for some months that he could not survive for long. The Prince of Wales hardly knew him; saw him as little more than a regrettable nuisance. He wrote to his mother a letter of chilling insensitivity. She did not reply but he heard from others how much he had hurt her. He was conscience-stricken. 'I feel such a cold hearted and unsympathetic swine for writing all that I did . . .' he told the Queen. 'No one can realize more than you how little poor Johnnie meant to me who hardly knew him . . . I can feel so much for you, darling Mama, who was his mother.'[3] His overture was gratefully received. At first she had thought his attitude a little hard-hearted, she confessed, but now felt that he was only taking the common-sense view.[4] The King fully shared his attitude: 'the greatest mercy possible,' he called John's death, his youngest son had been spared endless suffering.[5]

Stamfordham had urged the King to bring the Prince back to London in the winter of 1917. 'Time is slipping away and these years are valuable and important ones in His Royal Highness's life. He should be mixing with leading men other than soldiers, doing some useful reading and *gradually* getting accustomed to speaking in public.'[6] Cavan concurred. Then suddenly the Italian line collapsed. German troops, set free by the collapse of Russian resistance, had come to the aid of their Austrian allies and quickly turned the tide of the campaign. It seemed that Italy might be knocked out of the war if British and French reinforcements were

80

not rushed south. The 14th Army Corps was chosen for the task. Cavan pleaded that if the Prince of Wales accompanied the Corps the moral effect in Italy would be great. Against this, he had to admit that the Corps might arrive too late to save the Italians, in which case anything might happen and the risk to the Prince be considerable.[1] The King decided the risk must be run and by 8 November the Prince had joined the Corps HQ at Mantua. '. . . and here we stay indefinitely,' he told Lady Coke. 'The whole show is the vaguest thing on record and we know nothing of our future . . . as it all depends on where the Italians stop the Huns.'[2]

At first it was uncertain whether the Italians would stop the Huns at all. The Prince arrived in time to see the wreckage of the Italian 2nd Army retreating by way of Treviso and Padua. It was a kind of mobile warfare which he had never witnessed, and even though the allied forces were patently coming off worst, he found it irresistibly exciting: 'This is real campaigning, not the stale old warfare in Flanders, and it's all a great experience for me.'[3] His initial opinion of the Italian armies could hardly have been less favourable: 'contemptible soldiers,' he described them, who didn't understand the elements of modern warfare and retreated so fast that the enemy was unable to keep contact with them.[4] Inevitably his opinion changed when the Italians made a stand: 'fine stout-hearted fellows' they then became, though of course 'one mustn't forget that they are a Latin race!!'[5] He complained about those French and British officers who criticized the Italians too overtly, and though he referred to them privately as 'Ice-creamers', was at pains to speak of them politely in public. But a constant refrain of his diary and letters was the superiority of the French, Britain's leading and natural ally. 'They are a grand people, the French, and I'm more fond of them than ever now,' he told the King; 'what a far finer and nicer nation than the Italians. If *only* they had a monarchy!!!!'[6]

His views of Italian cuisine and culture were as jaundiced as of their military prowess. He could not stand macaroni, spaghetti or Chianti and hadn't seen a single pretty woman, he told Lady Coke, so 'I'm rather off Italy just now'.[7] The monuments were little better: Mantua was 'a deadly dull and antiquated little town', Bologna had lots of picturesque buildings 'tho I can't say that I spent much time looking at them'; the Veronese paintings in the

Villa Giacometti were 'interesting as being over 300 years old . . . but I can't say that actually they appeal to me enormously, and are, of course, typically Italian'.[1]

He was more impressed by Rome, which he visited in May 1918 to attend the celebrations of the third anniversary of the Italian declaration of war (a cause for jollification which the Prince was not alone in thinking somewhat far-fetched). The main function took place in the Augusteum, and in the course of his speech the Italian President, Orlando, spoke of the Prince as having come to Italy to share their dangers and defend their country. 'The whole audience rose, faced the Prince and cheered madly,' Henry Lygon told the Queen.[2] The Prince's speech from the royal box was delivered, wrote the Ambassador, Sir James Rodd, 'in a clear voice which carried well, with just a little touch of boyish shyness that went straight to the hearts of his audience'.[3] Claud Hamilton told Lady Coke that he had done it very well, 'everybody could easily hear him, he received a great ovation'.[4] It was a period at which Hamilton was inclined to be critical of his employer so his judgment that the Prince 'played his part better than I have ever seen him do before' can be taken seriously. The Prince was no less ready to judge his own performances harshly but he told the King that he felt his visit had done some good and had helped cement the alliance with Italy; 'it has been rather a trying week but very interesting and it has taught me a lot'.[5] His parents were delighted by his achievements: the King told him how much he appreciated the excellent way he had carried out the visit, while the Queen wrote of his 'wonderful success . . . I feel prouder of my dearest son than ever.'[6]

The King had objected to the proposal that the visit to Rome should include a call on the Pope but Balfour, the Foreign Secretary, insisted that this was essential.[7] Dutifully, the Prince paraded at the Vatican. He was not greatly struck by what he saw: he found Pope Benedict XV unprepossessing in his appearance, 'tho intelligent and well informed and he talks fairly decent French'. The Prince kept the conversation to generalities; 'and I most certainly did *not* kiss his ring,' he told the Queen proudly. 'Nothing would have induced me to!!'[8] This sturdy independence availed nothing with the *Daily Express*, who reported that the Prince 'appeared to be greatly gratified by his visit'. Under the headline 'Visit which should not have been made', the *Express* condemned the King for not having stepped in to veto it.[1] George V considered the report a direct attack on the Crown, all the worse because the proprietor, Lord Beaverbrook, was a member of the government.[2]

'Much tho one loathes the ——— Huns, one can't help admiring the way they are sticking out the war,' the Prince wrote to King George V in October 1917.[3] Their first offensive subsided, but there were signs that it was about to be renewed when the time came to celebrate the royal Silver Wedding in London. The last thing the Prince wanted was to become involved in what promised to be wearisome festivities. He persuaded Cavan to cable the King arguing that it would make a bad impression in Italy if the Prince left at so critical a moment.[4] The King agreed, but little in the way of a German attack ensued, indeed, within a few weeks the enemy lines were crumbling all across Europe.

The war was clearly ending. The plan had been for the Prince to spend three months at the end of 1918 taking a staff course at Cambridge, but with time running out Haig pleaded that he should instead visit the Dominion and American troops in France. The King left the final decision to his son, who had been looking forward to three relatively easy months at home. 'Of course I never hesitated as to what was the right thing,' the Prince wrote. '. . . one has to sink one's personal feelings and wishes on these occasions.'[5] He was being disingenuous as well as priggish; Cambridge might have been enjoyable but nothing would have induced him to leave the continent with final victory so close.

He hoped that he would be able to visit the Dominion forces with a minimum of fuss. He was quickly disabused by Lord Stamfordham. The Prince of Wales could not visit Canadian or Anzac troops unofficially: 'On the contrary these visits . . . have an undoubted political significance and may have far-reaching effects upon the Empire and Crown. You will be there as . . . Heir to the Throne and every word and deed will have its own particular influence.' Pressmen would follow him everywhere and the coverage they gave him would affect the reception he received when he visited the Dominions after the war. He would be constantly in the public eye.[6] It was a melancholy reminder to the Prince that with the armistice a new form of penal servitude would begin and that this time the sentence would be for life.

The Canadians were the first on whom he called. He was euphoric about his reception. 'They are great lads these old "Knucks",' he told Joey Legh, 'real, husky stout-hearted fellows for whom I've a great admiration.'[1] He was overwhelmed by their cheerfulness and friendly informality: 'How I wish I had been across to Canada, and living amongst them makes me just long to go there.'[2] His only complaint was that they tended to assume that they had done all the serious fighting and to speak with some disdain of the 'Imperial' or British troops. 'Still, I just don't listen when they talk like that, it's only really a pose and the best fellows never talk like that.'[3] A report from an unidentified Canadian colonel somehow found its way into the Windsor archives. The Prince, it read, 'had been the best force in real Empire building that it was possible for Great Britain to have, because he absolutely won the hearts of the many he came in contact with. As they put it, he was every inch the gentleman and sportsman, so simple, so charming and so genuine . . .'[4] Even allowing for hyperbole, he seems to have made himself uncommonly well liked.

The armistice was signed while the Prince was with the Canadian Corps. 'I feel it can't be more than a marvellous dream and I still feel in a sort of trance,' he told the Queen. 'But I suppose I shall soon wake up to the fact that it all really is true.'[5] It was soon time for him to move on. 'I don't think my month with the Australians will be so pleasant somehow,' the Prince had written, when his love of all things Canadian was at its height. 'These Canadians are so much more English and refined.'[6] His first reaction, indeed, was to find the Australian troops somewhat shy and rough, but 'that's because they live so far from England', he concluded charitably.[7] It did not take him long to decide that he liked them enormously, and they seem to have responded quite as warmly. 'The Prince has won the hearts of the Australians,' General Rawlinson told Wigram. His stay had been an unqualified success; he would be fervently welcomed in Australia; not just because he was Prince of Wales 'but as a personal matter between the soldiers and himself'. The Prince was nervous about his forthcoming visit to General Pershing, Rawlinson went on, 'but it is both right and necessary for him to be with the Americans for a period'.[8]

The Prince had in fact long been anxious to see something of Pershing and the 2nd US Army. In common with most British he had been quick to denounce the 'rotten Americans' who sat back and let the allies do the fighting. 'They said they were "too proud to fight"; I have never heard such rot!! Of course it is their game to keep out of it.'[1] But once they were in the war, his enthusiasm for their efficiency and fighting qualities rapidly grew. They welcomed him rapturously at their headquarters at Coblenz and put twenty thousand men on parade to honour him, making some of them march twenty-five miles for this privilege. The Prince professed mild surprise: 'How far more democratic we really are, and the American discipline is really fearfully strict.'[2] Yet the spirit of the men, the quality of the drill and turnout, the immense vitality and exuberance, impressed him profoundly. 'They are a big power in the world now,' he told his father, 'I might say the next biggest after ourselves, and they are worth while making *real* friends with . . . I'm just crammed full of American ideas just now, and they want me to "go over to them" as soon as possible, which is another item for consideration and one that should not be "pigeonholed".'[3]

His time with the Australians and Americans took him into occupied Germany. He found himself billeted at Bonn in the home of the Kaiser's sister, Vicky, Princess of Schaumburg-Lippe, and was outraged to find photographs of his family displayed in the principal rooms – 'I feel *so* ashamed, however one is consoled by the thought that we've "cut them *right* out" for ever!!' He was still more annoyed when the Princess addressed him as 'dear' and told him that the Germans would have been able to continue the war for several years but for the revolution. Rather grudgingly he admitted that she seemed 'a nice enough woman for a Hun', no doubt because she was 'one third English'.[4]*

He had no doubt that the Germans must be ruthlessly crushed and complained to the King about the 'idiotically mild and lenient treatment of this ——— Hun population. No one,' he claimed, with more justice than usually accompanies such a boast, 'is more against a bullying spirit than I am, as that would only place us on the same level as the Huns . . . But we are not making these Huns feel that they are beaten . . . There is no danger of serious fraternization as, thank goodness, the infantry and in fact all the

---

* *prima facie* a curious proportion, the mathematical basis for which was not explained.

men, still loathe the Huns and despise them. Of course, as regards the women, well all women in the world are made the same way, whether German or Japanese or any race you like, so that isn't fraternization, it's medicinal . . .'[1] The spirit behind these words was neither magnanimous nor far-sighted. It was, however, shared by almost every junior officer, indeed by every soldier, in the allied armies. They read curiously in the light of later charges that he had been pro-German from his childhood and thus an easy convert to Nazi doctrines.

'I just don't know what's happened to me since "this 'ere armistice",' the Prince told Joey Legh in mid-December. 'I'm so mad and restless that I can't sit down to think and write.'[2] Sitting down and thinking was never to be one of his favoured activities, but the end of the war found him exceptionally agitated. He knew that what he was doing was of value, and did not dislike doing it, but at the same time he itched to escape from his military harness and address himself to his real profession. 'I know that there is an enormous amount of work waiting for me in England, that is really why I'm so anxious to return and to "get down to it",' he told his father. Whether he would find the work tolerable once he had embarked on it, he did not know, but it was his future and he had better confront it now than later. He was more than ready for a change: 'This makes the 6th Division I've visited in under a fort-night and it is wearing work.'[3]

He felt qualms about his ability to do the job ahead of him but also believed that he had qualifications lacking in any previous Prince of Wales and, still more, in King George V. There can be few sons in the same line of business as their father who do not from time to time believe that they have a monopoly of prescience and the spirit of progressiveness. The Prince was convinced that his father had failed to come to terms with the realities of the post-war world. In this belief he was fortified by the Queen. 'I sadly fear Papa does not yet realize how many changes this war will have brought about,' his mother wrote apprehensively.[4] She did less than justice to the King, who could hardly have failed to notice the maelstrom which threatened to consume the heartlands of Europe. Bolshevik revolution had triumphed in Russia and was now rampant in Germany. 'It all makes one feel anxious about the future,' wrote the King; 'all this sort of thing is very infectious, although thank God everything seems to be all right in this dear old country.'[1] The Prince was very doubtful whether all was right in Britain, or at least whether all would continue to be right once the euphoria of victory had subsided.

He was certain that he understood the fears and aspirations of his future people far better than his father ever would and at least as well as any from the despised legion of politicians. His years with the Army had given him an opportunity denied to any other prince of getting to know the common man. This knowledge was, in part at least, illusory. He could never shed the prejudices of his caste and generation. When he heard that two of his closest friends had been transferred to the front line, he wrote that he hoped it was not true, 'as we *must* have a few "gentlemen" left after the war . . . I'm afraid that's rather a snobbish thing to say, tho' I mean it, and so I suppose I'm a snob!!!!'[2] He never doubted that, by training as well as breeding, 'gentlemen' were best qualified to run the country.

But unlike many of his contemporaries, he did not believe that the country was *made* for gentlemen. He knew that the men who had fought for Britain deserved more from society than they had enjoyed in the years before the war: better pay, better houses, better education for their children and treatment for their sicknesses. If their rulers failed to provide such treatment then they were not worthy to be rulers, were indeed not worthy of the title of 'gentlemen'. His creed was *simpliste* perhaps, but it was generous and sincerely held. The war had left him a more thoughtful, socially conscious and open-minded man. At the end of May 1919 he received the Freedom of the City of London. Talking of his life as a soldier he told his audience:

> The part I played was, I fear, a very insignificant one, but from one point of view I shall never regret my periods of service overseas. In those four years I mixed with men. In those four years I found my manhood. When I think of the future, and the heavy responsibilities which may fall to my lot, I feel that the experience gained since 1914 will stand me in good stead.[3]

On the whole, it did.

5

L'Éducation Sentimentale

IT IS A TRUTH UNIVERSALLY ACKNOWLEDGED, THAT A single man in possession of a good fortune, must be in want of a wife. When that man is not only in possession of a good fortune but is heir to the throne of Great Britain, the want becomes imperious necessity. From the moment the Prince of Wales advanced into adolescence, the need to find him a suitable wife began to preoccupy the King and Queen, their advisers, and increasingly the Prince himself.

Traditionally, spouses for the royal children were drawn from the courts of Europe, most of which were intricately bound together in a great web of cousinship that was the delight of genealogists and the despair of less well-equipped historians. This avoided not only adulteration of the blood royal but also the embarrassment involved in raising any individual noble family above the others by admitting it to relationship with the throne. When Queen Victoria's daughter, Princess Louise, married the future Duke of Argyll, the precedent was felt by many to be a dangerous one. Certainly such a match would never have done for a likely occupant of the throne. If the Prince of Wales, when young, did not share this view, he kept his doubts to himself. Whether he would have married Princess May* must be uncertain, but that he would in the end have married some European princess is highly probable.

Then came the First World War, and in an instant many of the possible brides were transformed into enemy aliens. An already difficult problem became almost insoluble. 'I hope some day you will find *the* woman who will make you happy!' Queen Mary wrote to her eldest son, 'but I fear this will not be easy as so much will have to be considered.'[1] The Prince was not over-worried by the inevitable delays. Physically slow to mature, he enjoyed the

---

* See pages 43–4.

companionship of women but felt no strong urge to consummate the relationship. 'I hope you are home by now,' he wrote to a Grenadier friend in May 1916, 'and having a jolly good time and are appeasing your sexual hunger, which I more than understand, tho' don't actually experience it myself, strange to say.'[1] With some fellow officers he visited a brothel in Calais and watched naked prostitutes striking a series of what were considered to be erotic attitudes. 'A perfectly filthy and revolting sight,' he called it, 'but interesting for me as it was my first insight into these things!!'[2]

A little later all was changed. Towards the end of 1916 his equerries, Claud Hamilton and Joey Legh, decided that his virginity had been unhealthily protracted, took him to Amiens, gave him an excellent dinner with much wine, and entrusted him to the experienced hands of a French prostitute called Paulette. 'She brushed aside his extraordinary shyness,' recorded Lord Esher, to whom the Prince recounted a censored version of his experience.[3] Paulette herself was permanently attached to an officer of the Royal Flying Corps and only on loan to the Prince for that and a few subsequent evenings, but she did her job with tact and skill. 'A heavenly little woman of the kind,' the Prince described her.[4] From that moment, sex became one of the Prince's most urgent preoccupations. 'Oh! to set eyes on one of the darlings again,' he wrote in anguish from the front in France, 'how one does miss them, and I don't think of anything but women now, tho what's the use?'[5] At Sandringham, in January 1917, they sang in the drawing room after dinner and the Prince then settled down to his crochet work. 'What an occupation for a fellow on leave!!' he complained in his diary. Shooting pheasants was as empty a pastime as patience or crocheting: 'I can't raise much enthusiasm over . . . anything except women!!'[6]

His new pursuit sometimes proved hazardous. In Paris, in July 1917, he spent '3 days bliss' which disturbed him so profoundly that he was quite unable to settle down and write letters for several days afterwards: 'It's fearful what a change in my habits 48 hours of the married life in Paris has wrought.'[7] Unfortunately his inability to write letters did not extend to Maggy, the object of his passions, and when he tried to disentangle himself he found that his emotional effusions were held against him. 'I got a regular stinker from her this evening . . .' he ruefully told Joey Legh. 'Oh!

those bloody letters, and what a fool I was not to take your advice over a year ago!! How I curse myself now, tho' if only I can square this case it will be the last one, as she's the *only* pol I've really written to and the last!! ... I'm afraid she's the £100,000 or nothing type, tho' I must say I'm disappointed and didn't think she'd turn nasty: of course the whole trouble is my letters and she's not burnt one!!'[1] The Prince never lost his touching belief that if one asked a woman to burn a letter, she would infallibly do so. Some of his correspondents seem to have done so, more did not. Maggy, however, proved that he had been right in his first judgment of her; having given her delinquent lover a nasty fright she let the matter drop.

Paulette and Maggy were excellent fun for a night or two. He was long in losing his taste for these diversions and planned to continue them once the war was over. But he did not delude himself that such affairs had anything to do with love, still less with matrimony. Until Mrs Simpson entered and monopolized his life he never found casual sex incompatible with a grand passion; indeed the first seemed sometimes positively to enhance the second. From the age of twenty-two or so until the day he died he was never out of love, occasionally with two women at the same time, far more often obsessively with one.

His first great love, almost certainly unconsummated, was for Marion Coke, wife of Viscount 'Tommy' Coke, heir to the Earl of Leicester. Small and vivacious, fond of much laughter, song and dance, she provided a delectable relief after the sombre splendours of the Palace. At first it was 'Marion is a little dear', always ready for a 'delightful talk'; then she became 'a little darling and I'm afraid I love her'; then, 'Marion is heavenly and I love her more and more'.[2] In 1917, by which time he had discovered that women were not solely for delightful talks, he became more ardent. 'Dear Lady Coke' had long given way to 'Dear Marion', now she became 'My dearest Marion'. ('By the way, *of course* I burn *all* your letters as I'm sure you do mine,' he concluded one such letter,[3] though Marion proved as unreliable as Maggy when it came to this searching test.) 'How can I express to you all I feel about it or thank you for everything?' he asked after his leave in London had proved particularly enjoyable. '*C'est impossible*, tho' you know how much I long to and do in my thoughts. You have been too angelically kind to me for words and have absolutely changed my life; it is *so* wonderful to feel I have someone I can really confide in as you have let me do!! In your own words, "You now have your little M C" absolutely expresses my feelings and it does make *all* the difference as you may imagine.'[1]

The 5th Earl of Leicester told Frances Donaldson that his father had once warned the Prince of Wales not to see so much of his wife.[2] Certainly if Lady Coke had fallen in with the Prince's lunatic scheme to join him and Claud Hamilton in Paris, her husband would have had good cause to complain. She was far too sensible, however. Twelve years older than the Prince, she knew that her role was principally that of confidante and comforter.

When he visited Bombay some years later his equerry, Bruce Ogilvy, noted his failure to flirt with any of the half dozen attractive girls provided to entertain him, and wrote in his diary, 'I think that what he liked was being "Mothered".'[3] 'Liked' is too weak a word, he craved for it, could hardly live without it. That a young man unable to establish a warm relationship with his own mother should seek a substitute elsewhere is so much a psychological cliché as to deserve to be treated with grave suspicion. At the end of the war he had in fact grown close to the Queen. But whether because of deprivation as a child or for some other reason, it was not enough. He looked for maternal qualities in every woman he knew well, and Marion Coke dutifully mothered him. She remained a prominent figure in his life until the advent of Freda Dudley Ward in the spring of 1918 drove all other women temporarily from his mind.

She did not reign alone, however. The Prince of Wales, in the last years of war, came closer to marriage than he was to for another fifteen years. Even with the memory of his Parisian idyll fresh in his mind he wrote in his diary, 'How I long for some leave to see Marion again and P!!!!' Before he left London in May 1917 he bade 'tender farewells' to Lady Coke, and 'fond farewells' to P.[4] P was Portia – Lady Sybil – Cadogan, one of the five daughters of Earl Cadogan. She was unlike most of the women he loved in that she was a large and clumsy girl; handsome rather than pretty, a powerful personality, as enthusiastic a dancer as Marion Coke but with less of her charm and spontaneous gaiety. She was a close friend of and later a maid of honour to Princess Mary and the

Prince first got to know her at Windsor in the spring of 1915. They played golf together and talked endlessly; within a few days he was writing in his diary, 'She was looking more lovely and attractive than ever and we had a delightful talk; I am really smitten now!!'[1] They began to correspond (Portia Cadogan was one of those who seems to have heeded his injunction to burn his letters) and Princess Mary, who was delighted to act as go-between, sent her brother a signed photograph of his beloved. Prince Albert, who seems also to have been attracted by her,[2] lent a hand in the romance as well. 'I am enclosing a letter from the "Angel" Portia . . .' he wrote. 'I am always going to forward her letters on to you now.'[3]

The romance came to a peak early in 1916. While in London in January he contrived to see her most days and nights. On 5 January, after driving half a dozen times round St James's Park and enjoying a protracted farewell at her house, he recorded that he had had 'the best night I have had since the war began'. A fortnight later it was, without qualification, 'the best night I have ever had'. They dined at the Carlton, went to a musical at the Gaiety, and then danced for two hours to the gramophone. 'It was divine, particularly as I'm madly in love with her!! Oh, if only – But I must be careful even in a diary.' A fortnight later again they 'fixed up certain things' and the following night the Prince returned surreptitiously to Portia's house after formally dropping her off at the front door. '*She* let me in and we sat talking till after 1.30. What a joyous 2 hours alone with my "angel". How the time did fly; we talked about every sort of thing; better not to mention what!! . . . What it is to be in love!!'[4]

That matrimony was one of the 'things' discussed cannot be proved but seems more than likely. What happened then is hard to establish. The romance continued in full fury and even at the beginning of 1917 he could still remark that 'it was wonderful to see HER again'. But on that same wonderful night he and Claud Hamilton dropped Portia off at her home at 12.30 and then went on to a party where Marion Coke was awaiting them: 'I took sweet little Marion home and she bid me a tender farewell.'[5] Whether Portia Cadogan took offence at having to share her admirer's affections, whether she despaired of bringing him to the point, or whether she just got bored of him: in June 1917 she abruptly became engaged to the Prince's old friend from Oxford days,

Edward Stanley. The news came as a surprise to everyone, not least her parents, who received a telegram reading 'Engaged to Edward' and at once assumed that they would eventually have a daughter on the throne.[1] The Prince had discussed Portia Cadogan and the possibility of marriage with his mother only a few days before, but nothing had been concluded. The Queen, however, made it clear that nobody was going to bring pressure on him to make an early marriage, still less to someone he did not love. This did something to relieve his disappointment, but: 'How depressed I am,' he wrote in his diary. 'I suppose it's Portia having gone West, for of course that talk with Mama has cheered me up and taken a big weight off my mind.'[2]

The affair had been conducted with remarkable discretion. Godfrey Thomas, who always felt the Prince should not marry a commoner, welcomed Portia's engagement, 'if only for the reason that a lot of people in London were beginning to talk about her and the Prince himself, people I mean who might have been thought to know, not just the usual gossipers'.[3] The 'usual gossipers' never seem to have mentioned Portia Cadogan's name, and the survivors among those 'who might have been thought to know' were often equally in the dark. Many other names, however, were mentioned in connection with the Prince: Claud Hamilton's sister Cynthia; Irene Lawley; Diana Manners; Rachel Cavendish — 'a very pretty girl, and sensible too,' noted George V approvingly;[4] and, most frequently of all, Rosemary Leveson-Gower. There was 'wild excitement' during the Prince of Wales's leave in March 1918, recorded Cynthia Asquith. 'No girl is allowed to leave London . . . and every mother's heart beats high. So far, he dances most with Rosemary and also motors with her in the daytime.'[5]

Rosemary Leveson-Gower was indeed a natural subject for such gossip. Her father had been the 4th Duke of Sutherland; her mother, born Lady Millicent St Clair-Erskine, was one of the great beauties of her generation; she herself was strikingly attractive, charming and, by all accounts, generous and kind as well. There is, however, no evidence in the Prince's diaries or correspondence that he ever thought of her as more than pleasant company. To Lady Coke, perhaps unsurprisingly, he described her without great enthusiasm as 'quite attractive and pretty . . . tho' she is rather spoilt'.[6] In September 1917 he had mentioned to his mother that he had seen her when visiting the Duchess of Sutherland's hospital and had thought her 'attractive tho' very cold'.[1] The Queen took mild alarm, presumably lest her son might view the coldness as a challenge. 'I agree Rosemary is attractive,' she wrote, 'but pray don't think of her, there is a taint in the blood of her mother's family.'[2] Her comment related, presumably, to an alleged strain of madness in the St Clair-Erskine family which was much gossiped about at the time, rather than to the somewhat chequered career of Rosemary's uncle, Lord Rosslyn. 'I didn't mean I was really struck,' the Prince hurriedly protested. 'You need have no fear of my having any designs on her!!'[3] Probably he protested a little too much; he certainly paid Rosemary marked attentions during the first months of 1918. Lady Rosemary does not seem to have been overwhelmed by these enticing prospects. 'What a good thing I never contemplated marrying the Prince of Wales merely for the sake of the glamour,' she wrote to her mother after her own marriage to the future Lord Dudley. Now she had 'got all that as well as Eric'.[4] At all events, any incipient romance was checked when that February he met the first of the two great loves of his life, Freda Dudley Ward.

They met by chance some time in February 1918, when the Prince was at a dance in Belgrave Square and Mrs Dudley Ward, with her escort of the evening, took shelter in the doorway when an air raid warning sounded. The couple were invited in, the Prince was immediately attracted to the interloper and danced with her for the rest of the evening. Next day he wrote to 'Mrs Dudley Ward' to suggest a further meeting. Freda's mother-in-law, with whom she was staying, first assumed that the letter must be for her, then that it referred to her unmarried daughter. She invited the Prince to tea and tried to send Freda out for the occasion, but her well-meaning efforts were thwarted and the happy couple were soon reunited. The association was to last some fifteen years.

Freda – Winifred, to give her the full name by which she was never known – Dudley Ward was small, elegant and exceptionally pretty. Some people underestimated her, but no one seems to have disliked her. She was intelligent and no worse educated than most British ladies of the time, funny, lively, a passionate and

94

accomplished dancer, a good golfer and tennis player. A strong personality, she contrived to appear feminine and frail; Cynthia Asquith's somewhat contemptuous description, 'a pretty little fluff',[1] was a complete misjudgment of a woman whose independence of mind was no less striking than her tact and discretion.

A few weeks younger than the Prince of Wales, she was of bourgeois stock; her father, Colonel Charles Birkin, was a prosperous lace-manufacturer from Nottingham. When only nineteen she married William Dudley Ward, 'Duddie', a Liberal member of parliament and kinsman of the Earl of Dudley. Dudley Ward was sixteen years older than his wife; no doubt he had loved Freda when he married her but by 1918 the couple led largely separate lives. An affair between his wife and the heir to the throne, provided it was conducted with due decorum, would have seemed to him acceptable, even commendable. He could be confident that, with Freda in charge of the liaison, it would never be less than decorous.

Though the Prince quickly made it obvious that he was overwhelmingly attracted by Freda, the relationship had little chance to burgeon until he came back to London early in 1919. For the next four years or so it was all-consuming. No letters survive from this early period but the Prince had a compulsive need to pour out his heart on paper and in 1921 and 1922 he was writing to her at least once a day whenever they were separated, and often when they were not. One day in August 1922 he wrote to her at 9 a.m., noon, 6 p.m. and 11.30 p.m., also fitting in a long telephone call just before dinner. The first surviving letter is dated 18 November 1920. 'Fredie darling, beloved *à moi*,' it read, 'I feel *ever, ever* so much better since our little talk on the phone this evening, sweetheart; you just can't think what a huge comfort it was to *your* little David just to hear your divine little voice again which I wanted to hear so much this morning. I'm terribly lonely tonight my Fredie darling and it maddens me to be away from *TOI*; it seems all wrong somehow when we love each other as we do.' At 2 a.m., before he went to bed, he dashed off another brief note: 'I must tell you once again how far more crazily and madly and overwhelmingly I love you love you my Fredie darling, and how utterly down and out I am tonight at the thought of not seeing you for 12 bloody days.'[2]

These letters strike the notes which would become familiar

to anyone who studied the correspondence in full: genuine and passionate devotion marred by a strident self-pity that bores and sometimes repels. In almost every letter he bemoans his uniquely unhappy lot: the miseries of being Prince of Wales, trapped in a routine that was wearisome and futile, surrounded by hostile relations and treacherous servants, starved of the company of the one person who could have made him happy. It is indeed an unhappy condition to be in love with a married woman, and still more so when there seems no possible way by which the situation can be improved; but it must have taken all Freda Dudley Ward's resolution to provide the constant consolation and reassurance that was demanded by her lover. Endlessly he poured out to her his fears and woes. 'Fredie darling, I love you love you now beyond all understanding and all I can say is bless you, bless you, for being so sweet and divine and tender and *sympathique* to your David last night and for saving him, *mon amour*. And you know that the truth is I was on the verge of a mental disaster or whatever you like to call it . . . that might have been permanent.'[1] He knew that his insatiable demands for reassurance were unreasonably taxing and apologized constantly for his weakness – 'You have made me feel so terribly badly as regards my foul grousing and unpardonable glooms'[2] – but he could no more have cut off the flow of desolation than he could have ended the relationship.

Freda Dudley Ward, as nobody else was able to do before the advent of Mrs Simpson, gave him the strength he needed. She alone could cheer him up when he was in the blackest depression, could cajole or bully him back to the path of duty. Without her he could manage, but at a fearful cost to his nerves and to conspicuously less good effect. When on his foreign tours, he constantly inveighed against the cruel fate that separated them and agonized over the strain of keeping going without her support. His tone was sometimes hysterical, but essentially he wrote no more than the truth.

She was an excellent influence on him. She made him drink and smoke less – though herself a chain smoker; she encouraged him to do what he was best at; she laughed him out of his occasional absurdities. She fostered his genuine concern for the injustices of society and tried, to less good effect, to broaden his intellectual horizons. Once she gave him a copy of *Wuthering Heights* to read.

'Who is this woman Bront?' he asked dubiously.[1] She told him home truths in a way nobody else did, yet never forfeited his total confidence. 'Self-pity is a most degrading thing,' he wrote, 'and you've driven all mine right away and about time too. I know I'm hopelessly spoilt and therefore discontented . . . I'm so grateful to you for showing me myself . . . and it's the first time I had a look at "the brute" for months!! But now I can see how utterly ridiculous and futile he is, and I'll try and reform him a bit in Canada.' And then a great cry of pain: 'If only I didn't feel so lonely nowadays.'[2]

Great though her influence was, she was reticent in using it and never did so to her own advantage. The Prince's Comptroller, Sydney Greville, once reported a scare over the Prince 'rushing off to appoint a nominee of Mrs Dudley Ward' as equerry,[3] but there is no other suggestion that she interfered in the running of the royal household. On the contrary, all the Prince's staff liked her and welcomed her; 'one of the best friends he ever had in his life,' Bruce Ogilvy described her.[4]

As she was to discover herself in due course, there was only room for one great love in the Prince's life. Any previous claimant to the title was ruthlessly discarded. Portia Stanley appeared at a shooting party at Sandringham. 'I stood no rot from her,' reported the Prince. 'She only stood with me at *one* drive and that was because she asked to and it was tricky to say NO. I loathe that woman, and it maddens me her showing herself in here like this.'[5] He was fiercely jealous of any rival. Freda's admirer of long standing was Lord Pembroke's cousin, Michael Herbert. The Prince was in torment whenever he knew that the two were likely to meet. She wrote to him from Lady Desborough's home to report that, though Herbert was in the house party, she had seen little of him. 'Good! good! and more! more!' applauded the Prince. 'I do love to hear that and I bet he tried hard enough to get you alone and he must have been furious too!! I'm *so so* glad and happy darling.'[6] In return he constantly assured her that he found all other women dull and unattractive, and she professed to be upset if he seemed to favour one or other of them. She wrote crossly when he was seen at the Grafton Galleries with Edwina Mountbatten. 'I'm sorry if I annoyed you . . .' he wrote penitently, 'though I hate your putting it that Edwina *took* me. Darling, no bloody woman takes me anywhere and it was Dickie who suggested it and I couldn't see any harm . . . But I'm sorry my sweetheart, though please don't think that I'm led around by other women.'[1] In these first hectic years, indeed, to all effects there *was* no other woman. His intimates continued to hope otherwise. In Canada at the end of 1919 Claud Hamilton believed he might propose to the lady who was subsequently to marry Joey Legh – 'if only "it" would happen, it would be the most wonderful thing in the world and save the British Empire'.[2] But such hopes were illusory. When he visited Kyoto during his tour of Japan the geishas wanted to take the rings off his hand. He let them remove the signet ring 'but *naturally* not *yours* my sweetheart and it took me quite a time to assure them that I wasn't engaged!! If only they knew how *very heavily married* I am, darling angel.'[3]

He found in Freda Dudley Ward's home the family life that was lacking – or that he convinced himself was lacking – at court. He loved her two daughters, and would call in to see them even when their mother was away. 'The babies were in marvellous shape,' he wrote after one such visit, 'and I can never tell you what they didn't do to me, from binding me up on the floor with ribbands and pulling my hair etc etc. I do adore those divine little girls of yours, sweetheart, and love playing with 2 wee editions of Fredie!!'[4] They for their part treated him as a much-loved uncle and pined for his visits. Towards the end of the Second World War the younger daughter, Angela Laycock, wrote to him: 'It is so many years since I last saw you that I suppose I can no longer start my letters "Darling Little Prince" though that is how I should like to begin . . . You can't imagine how much I miss you still, after all this time. You see, my childhood is so full of *happy, happy* memories and you are bound up in all of them.'[5]

His own siblings abetted the romance. Princess Mary forwarded the letters which he wrote to Freda almost every day from France, slipping out to post them when her French governess had her back turned.[6] Prince Albert kept the home fires burning when his brother was on tour: 'She is miserable now without you and feels quite lost . . . I will look after Freda for you to the best of my ability.'[7]

Not surprisingly, the King and Queen were less enthusiastic about their son's liaison. The king had never met Mrs Dudley Ward and considered her social background made her inappropriate as a friend for his eldest son, let alone anything more intimate. Though time modified his attitude, his first assumption was that she was a pernicious influence and should be cut out of the Prince's life. 'Papa seems to think that anything you do which he doesn't like has been influenced by Fredie,' warned Prince Albert. 'This of course is due to the great popularity which you have everywhere, and Papa is merely jealous.'[1] The Queen was quick to indignation if she thought that her son was allowing his mistress to distract him from the course of duty. On one occasion he asked if he might miss a court function. Queen Mary knew that he wanted instead to go to a dance which Freda Dudley Ward was attending. 'I was aghast when I read your letter,' she wrote. 'It would be *very rude* to us were you not to come tonight.' 'A pretty hot letter!!' was the Prince's rueful comment when he passed it on to Mrs Dudley Ward.[2] Such rebukes did not shake his affection for the Queen. 'My mother is sweet to me and so sensible,' he told Freda; 'there's really no rot about her although she is a martinette. But that is her upbringing and no fault of hers, and she really is a wonderful woman.'[3] But inevitably this new, all-important association eroded the relationship which had been built up between mother and son. 'Curious David does not confide in you any more,' commented the King in 1922. 'I suppose he only does so to her.'[4]

What evidence there is suggests that, for the first eighteen months or so of their affair, Freda Dudley Ward cared as deeply for the Prince as he for her. It could not endure at such intensity. Mrs Dudley Ward needed someone who was more regularly in her life than the itinerant Prince, whose friendship posed less social problems, who was more sophisticated and less doting. He was made miserable when, in the summer of 1920, Freda tried to cool down his ardour and to put the relationship on to a new, more platonic basis. 'So you have heard from Fredie at last,' the recently created Duke of York wrote to him. 'It must have depressed you and worried you a good deal, I know, but whatever she says I know you will listen to.'[5]

Michael Herbert remained a threat. For a time Mrs Dudley Ward kept her two admirers in uneasy balance; each grudgingly acquiescing in the claims of the other. Then in 1922, when the Prince was in the Far East, there was talk of divorce. 'What I can't get at is when you intend to divorce Duddie, my beloved,' wrote the puzzled Prince. 'Will it all be going on when I return or do you intend to wait till we can discuss it all, or what? Also, are you going to divorce him or is he going to divorce you?' The thought that disturbed him most was that, once free, Freda might marry Herbert or somebody else. 'I can't bear the thought that our lives should have to be in any way different to what they've been for the last 4 years.' If the divorce was to go through, then it would obviously be essential that he keep well out of the limelight: '. . . if I'm in the way *for the present* you will tell me, won't you? . . . I'm making the very biggest sacrifice that I'll ever make in my whole life by writing to you what I am tonight my sweet Freda, and I'm crying a bit, though as I love you love you I do want so to help you too. It is *so so* terribly hard and cruel to be away from you at a time of crisis.'[1]

Talk of a divorce blew over and by the time he had reached Japan he had reassured himself that their love affair would survive unimpaired. He wrote from Kyoto to tell her 'how I've missed you and pined for TOI my precious beloved, and how I'm always wanting TOI and yearning for you!! And I know from your letters that you've felt the same, Fredie, and the fact that both still feel as mad as we ever did is a real test, isn't it, darling angel?'[2] He deluded himself. She was devoted to him, loyal to him, but she no longer loved him madly. When he got back to England later that year, it was to find that the reputation of her children was advanced as a reason for their seeing less of each other. Reluctantly he accepted the excuse: 'We are indeed a hunted and pathetic little couple, aren't we, Fredie, but nobody can stop us loving each other.'[3]

The unhappiness and frustration caused by Freda Dudley Ward's coolness towards him drove him to seek solace in drink, night clubs and the ostentatious pursuit of other women. Many of the accounts of the Prince of Wales misbehaving in public stem from this period. In the spring of 1923 it seems to have come to a head. Freda must have stated bluntly that their relationship could never be what it had been and that he would have to content himself with friendship. 'I'm at last beginning to realize what I've lost through going quite quite mad . . . in April,' he wrote despairingly, 'though I suppose it's too late now . . . Oh! Fredie – I just don't understand a thing about life except that it's all d—d hard and foul and cruel, and I'm so depressed and puzzled about it all.'[1]

To solace his woes he indulged in a brief fling with Audrey Coats, a girl who as Audrey James had played havoc with a wide swathe of London society. Mr Coats, however, was evidently less complaisant than Mr Dudley Ward. 'Never have I had such an exciting week as this,' the Prince told Freda from a house party at Drummond Castle, in which the Coatses were among the guests, 'and the air is electric and it's all too tricky for words. I'm quite exhausted and shall be lucky if I escape without the hell of a row . . .' But though he found Mrs Coats attractive and enjoyed his affair with her, he was being entirely sincere when he told his true love: 'I'm *not* madly in love and never will be again, and she'll never mean a fraction to me of what you do.'[2] There were to be many such meaner beauties of the night but the moon of Freda Dudley Ward reigned supreme, and was to continue to do so until all other luminaries were dimmed by the solar splendour of Mrs Simpson.

Freda was sometimes painfully honest in her efforts to keep the Prince at bay. 'I can't help hating and loathing the fact that you are in love with somebody else and it was a *big blow* when you told me the other day,' he wrote to her. 'It's a horrid thought for me that I really mean nothing whatever to you now, though you mean the hell of a lot to me, bless you.'[3] He did, of course, mean a great deal to her, and was to do so for many years. He for his part continued to treat her as confidante and friend; she remained the lodestar of his life, he reported back to her faithfully after every new amatory or other escapade. To the outside world – or at least those parts of the outside world which were near enough to the inside to know of Mrs Dudley Ward's existence – they remained inextricably linked. In 1927 Churchill travelled in the same train as they to Nottingham – 'It was quite pathetic to see the Prince and Freda. His love is so obvious and undisguisable'; the following year Brian Howard refused to let his seaside house to the Prince – 'He'd only break all the furniture to pieces playing Blind Man's Buff with Mrs Dudley Ward'; a year later again the Prince's equerry, John Aird, was relieved to find that his employer wanted to leave Epsom as soon as the Derby was over. Then Freda Dudley Ward appeared on the scene. 'The result being that we now waited to see the next race and in consequence the car was blocked all the way back.'[1]

Though the Prince's devotion to Mrs Dudley Ward continued unabated throughout the 1920s and well into the next decade, it was for him in some ways an unfulfilling, even sterile relationship. He craved total mutual devotion and dependence; deprived of it, he thrashed about aimlessly, causing pain to many in so doing and most notably to himself. The relationship was not close enough to satisfy him, yet it was too close to permit any more permanent liaison. While Mrs Dudley Ward reigned, there could be no Princess of Wales. In 1922 he described to Freda his feelings towards her younger sister Vera: 'I love Verie a tiny bit for herself, though more because she is your sister and still more because *you* love her so!! You will remember our discussing her as a possible wife for me, darling, but each day longer that I live, the more certain I am that I'll *never never ever* love anyone else again. And I would *never* marry any woman I *liked* unless I *loved* her!!'[2] Seven years later nothing had changed. 'I know our two lives aren't absolutely satisfactory and I'm afraid they won't ever be now, but I do know this, my angel: that I *love* you too much to ever be able to love anybody else ever again. I'm always comparing and they can't any of them compare and I'm so glad. I lost my head once over a crazy physical attraction. Look at the result. Just made a fool of myself, that's all. Nothing left of it but nausea.'[3]

One page survives from a reproachful letter written to him by one of the women with whom he tried to solace the pain of Freda Dudley Ward's inaccessibility. 'I only hope,' the page concludes, 'that as you love her so much, Freda will marry you and make you very happy.'[4] The words were presumably ironic; the writer must have known that the idea of marriage with the Prince of Wales never entered the head of Mrs Dudley Ward. How far it entered the head of the Prince is harder to decide. He said often that Freda was the solitary woman whom he could marry; yet the only person who stated positively that he had proposed to her and been rejected was Lord Brownlow.[5] Brownlow knew the Prince well but it is curious that there is no reference to any such *démarche* in the Prince's many surviving letters. The implication in his correspondence, indeed, is that he had never contemplated any such possibility. His lament was always that he had not known her before

1913, the year of her marriage;[1] once she had become Mrs Dudley Ward she had put herself for ever out of his reach.

If he had known her before 1913 he would have been too immature to pay her any serious attention. It is tempting to speculate, however, on what would have happened if Dudley Ward had died in battle and Freda, when he met her in 1918, had been not an estranged wife but a decorously merry widow. Could he and would he have married her, and if so, what difference would it have made?

The fact that she was a commoner would have created difficulties but would not have made the match impossible. As late as 1932 the Prince of Wales told his father that he had never realized he might be allowed to marry 'a suitable well-born English girl'. No one had ever suggested the possibility to him before, he said, 'There was only one lady he had ever wished to marry and that was Mrs Dudley Ward – and he would still like to marry her. But the King said he didn't think that would do.'[2] The Prince's ignorance is extraordinary; the matter had constantly been debated over the previous fifteen years. All the evidence suggests that if he did not know that he might be allowed to marry a British commoner it was because he had not asked. And if he did not ask, it was because he did not wish to know; he was determined not to marry anyone except Freda and preferred to keep in his mind this half-imaginary barrier in the way of matrimony. In fact as early as 1917 George V recorded that he had told the Privy Council his children would be allowed to marry into British families: 'It was quite a historical occasion.'[3] The fact that Edward was Prince of Wales would have made the King more cautious about the suitability of any candidate, but nothing was said to indicate that the eldest son was to be treated differently from his siblings. The objection to Rosemary Leveson-Gower had been not that she was a commoner but that there was 'a taint in the blood'.* If the Prince did not know this then he wilfully blinded himself to reality.

A widowed Mrs Dudley Ward would certainly not have seemed suitable to the King and Queen. There would have been strong opposition, possibly too strong to overcome. For one thing the previous marriage, with the problems it would have posed, such

---

* See page 94 above.

as semi-royal stepchildren, would have been a serious obstacle. For another, a lace-manufacturer's daughter, however respectable, would not have seemed the right sort of match for a British prince, let alone the heir to the throne. But beneath his testiness George V was a kindly and susceptible man, sincerely anxious that his son should find happiness and security. There was at least a chance that the obstinacy of the Prince and the charms of Mrs Dudley Ward would in the end have worn down his resistance. Queen Freda would have seemed a surprising concept to the British people, but so great was the popularity of the Prince of Wales in the years after the war that public opinion would undoubtedly have supported him. It could have happened.

It is also possible to argue that though it *could*, it *would not* have happened. The Prince, it has been said, loved Freda Dudley Ward just because she was inaccessible. If she had been free to marry him, he would not have wanted to marry her. Whether he was aware of it or not, the argument goes, he was resolved never to marry; by falling in love with a married woman he was providing himself with an alibi against having to marry anyone else. He was temperamentally unable to accept such a commitment, or perhaps he sought to leave open a route by which he might one day escape the throne.

It is impossible to prove the contrary; where motives are in question it must always be a matter for surmise. The theory, however, does not seem to be supported by what facts there are. He had once been anxious to marry Portia Cadogan; when the time came he was resolved to marry Mrs Simpson; everything he said or did indicated that he would have liked nothing better than to make Freda Dudley Ward his wife. Far from seeking to avoid commitments he sought them with relentless fervour. The lesson to be learnt from the last thirty-five years of his life is surely that, though he might not have been particularly happy as a married man, he was far unhappier as a bachelor.

And if he had been allowed to marry Freda Dudley Ward, or Portia Cadogan, or any other strong woman whom he could have loved; if, like his luckier brother, he had found his own version of Elizabeth Bowes Lyon; would it have made any difference? Might he have become, to use the *simpliste* but by no means valueless terminology of *1066 and All That*, a 'good king'? One has, of course, not the remotest idea. All that can be said with certainty is that in 1919 the potential was there: the charm, the good will, the enthusiasm, the readiness to learn, the enquiring mind. So too, of course, were the corroding weaknesses; but with the support and encouragement of the right wife the weaknesses might have been overcome and potential become reality. At the least, the reign of King Edward VIII would have taken a very different course.

6

The Role of the Prince

══════

ON'T THINK YOU CAN ACT LIKE OTHER PEOPLE, THE King warned his son at the end of the war. 'You must always remember your position and who you are.' But, the Prince asked himself, 'who exactly was I?'[1] He was a man apart, that much was clear, and he loathed it. He did what he could to mitigate his isolation, to treat others and to be treated himself as if he were a normal human being; but though a normal human being was what he was, he would never win acceptance of the fact. Even by those who knew him best he was treated with gingerly deference, as a freak with a touch of the divine, an improbably animated refugee from Madame Tussaud's. His jokes would be greeted with sycophantic fervour by those who were amazed a prince could joke at all; his peccadilloes were met with extravagant censure by those who did not believe a prince should be vulnerable to the weaknesses of the flesh. Part at least of the sympathy he felt towards Americans came from his conviction – rarely justified – that they would not view him with the curious compound of reverence and resentment that the average Briton adopts towards its monarchy.

That veteran courtier Fritz Ponsonby placed all the Prince's qualms firmly into focus when he remonstrated with him for making himself too accessible. 'The Monarchy must always retain an element of mystery,' he maintained. 'A Prince should not show himself too much. The Monarchy must remain on a pedestal.' The Prince flatly disagreed. The last place he wished to be was on a pedestal, he wanted to be down among the people, getting to know them and letting them know him.[2] There was more truth in both points of view than either party was ready to concede. But the argument was anyway academic. Every time the Prince of Wales tried to descend from his pedestal the British people put him back again. Wherever he went, whatever he did, he was walled around by deferential affection, a barrier imperceptible sometimes but inexorably setting him apart. Even when he first went out with the Pytchley hunt, six stalwart followers were secretly deputed to escort him and to ensure that he returned unharmed.[1] If he could not be treated as an equal on the hunting field, where a man is traditionally worth no more than his courage, his prowess as a rider and the quality of his horse, then where could he hope to find the sort of acceptance that he craved?

To be isolated was bad enough, to be isolated in inactivity was insupportable. The designated successor to the leadership of some great company or institution will be fully occupied with the specialist duties that fall to him while he is waiting to take over. The heir to some great estate, even in 1919, could busy himself in whatever career he chose until the title and the land became his. The Prince had no specialist duties, yet the tasks that were imposed upon him effectively prevented him pursuing any serious career. His life was divided between furious bouts of what he described as 'princing' – opening hospitals, addressing dinners, receiving addresses, smiling, smiling, smiling – and tracts of emptiness which it was up to him to fill as best he could. Geddes, the British Ambassador in Washington, suggested that the Prince would make an ideal Governor General of Canada.[2] The King insisted that he was needed nearer home. The Queen said that he must 'learn how to govern'.[3] Yet little indeed was done to teach him. He was denied access to all but a limited range of state papers, never encouraged to talk to politicians or civil servants. He told Lady Airlie that he realized he must work to keep his job, but was given no work and was not even sure he had a job.[4]

In the middle of the nineteenth century Bagehot had written perceptively of what was now the Prince's problem: 'Whatever is most attractive, whatever is most seductive, has always been offered to the Prince of Wales of the day, and always will be. It is not rational to expect the best virtue where temptation is applied in the most trying form at the frailest time of human life.'[5] The Prince had done no more than taste the flavour of the fleshpots before the war, there had followed four years of dour privation, now everything was his for the taking. If his life had developed as had been expected in 1914 he would have had time to adjust to the heady and dangerous delights of liberty. As it was, he was almost entirely inexperienced. In 1921 he told Freda Dudley Ward that he had been reading Max Beerbohm's essay on King George IV.[1] 'I've found a sentence in it that I think must be amazingly suitable and applicable to *me* and somewhat an apology for my doings and behaviour . . . "He was indeed still a child, for royalties not being ever brought into contact with the realities of life, remain young far longer than other people." No one realizes how desperately true that is in my case [more] than I do.'[2] When he surveyed the monstrous banquet of pleasures which the world laid in front of him, and the unsubstantial restraints placed upon his capacity to gratify himself, he might have been inclined to cry with Clive that he stood astonished at his own moderation.

'I think David ought to return home before *very* long,' wrote Queen Mary to the King three weeks after the armistice, 'as he must help us in these difficult days.'[3] In a letter that must have chilled the Prince's heart, Lord Stamfordham sketched out the sort of help that was in question. The King had decreed he should take over the Presidency of the King Edward VII's Hospital Fund. 'Then there is the Royal College of Music. The University of Wales is the most pressing as the King really constitutionally ought *not* to be the Chancellor. Then Your Royal Highness is to be elected a Trustee of the British Museum.'[4] And so the dismal catalogue went on.

The first essential was to find him a private secretary. Lord Cromer, a former diplomat and banker turned courtier, was the Prince's original choice, but the King ruled that he could not be spared from his present duties. Next to be canvassed was a former journalist and much-decorated officer in the Brigade of Guards, Edward Grigg, who seemed to accord admirably with Stamford-ham's prescription: 'someone with brains, with some Colonial knowledge: a facile pen – a nice fellow . . .'[5] Grigg, however, hankered after a career less restricted than he would find in royal service. Eventually the job went to Godfrey Thomas, whose diplomatic career had already been interrupted by the Prince's demands on his time. In his diary the Prince described Thomas as a 'topper' and a 'ripper' and he wrote to him as 'my greatest friend and the one man I can trust and who really understands me'.[6] It was perhaps a feeling that the two men were too close to each other that led the King to question the wisdom of the appointment. The Prince stuck to his guns. Thomas was '*very* able, full of tact, and popular with everyone . . . in addition to never hesitating to point out or tell me of any failings he may think I am guilty of'.[1] It proved a good choice. A stronger personality than Thomas might possibly have curbed some of the Prince's excesses, but more probably the two men would have quarrelled and greater mischief been done than good. Thomas served his master with loyalty and devotion until the abdication.

With a private secretary came an independent household. The Prince insisted that, at twenty-five, he could no longer live under his parents' roof. 'I must be free to live my own life,' he told Lady Airlie.[2] The King took the line that the roof of Buckingham Palace was quite large enough for two – or twenty for that matter – but he grudgingly gave way and in July 1919 the Prince moved into York House, not so much a house in fact as a fragment of the great complex of St James's Palace, which grew or shrank according to the needs and pretensions of the occupant. It was not ideal, few good rooms and those north-facing, dark, antiquated, but it suited the new owner's needs and gave him the privacy and independence he so much desired.

And so, in his new premises, he set up in business as Prince of Wales. Lloyd George still presided over a coalition government elected with a large majority at the end of 1918, but though his personal prestige was high the overwhelming Conservative preponderance in the alliance meant that his position was far less strong than it seemed. The Prince's views at the time of the election were much as might have been expected from a serving officer: 'One dreads to think of the Labour people returning a greater number of members . . . and then all these crazy women candidates; however Lloyd George seems to be all right just now, tho' one can't trust him a yard.' Wigram had been sending him the Scotland Yard reports on the state of opinion among the working classes and he read them with alarm: 'I'm afraid I'm always a pessimist but the situation looks pretty black just now, tho' it's not half as black as it will be in a year's time, perhaps less than that.'[3] The problems were going to start when the soldiers were demobilized and expected employment and a decent standard of living. Only radical action could avert disaster: 'Oh! we've got funny, or, rather, serious times before us, but they've got to be faced and in the right and proper way and to hell with precedents!! They won't wash nowadays!!'[1] He agreed wholeheartedly with his mother when she rejoiced at the defeat of the more extreme socialists in the general election and concluded her letter: 'If only the Coalition Govt will now hurry up and get the much needed reforms (which the working classes need) passed, they can take the wind out of the sails of the extremists, and I trust they will be wise enough to realize it.'[2]

He returned to a Britain that was riven by class antipathies and violent industrial disputes. 'One can't help seeing the work people's point of view,' he told the Queen, 'and in a way it's only human nature to get as much as one can out of one's employer.'[3] He soon found that he sympathized with Lloyd George and the more radical wing of the government and resented the intransigent callousness of the hard-faced men who had done well out of the war. 'I look on [Lloyd George] as the only possible man living to be PM and feel that if he goes a Labour govt is bound to come in. I have the greatest confidence in him now, tho' I didn't use to!!'[4] That the accession to power of a Labour government would be an evil seemed as obvious to him as it did to 99 per cent of the upper classes, but that the injustices of society required drastic redress and that, if nobody else would do it, it would have to be done by the socialists, seemed quite as evident. 'It is a very sad and depressing thought that there are so many desperately sad and sordid homes this Christmas,' he wrote in 1921, 'destitute men (thousands of them ex-service men) and consequently still more starving women and children.'[5] Such sentiments are easily voiced, but less easily acted on. The Prince of Wales was no crusader and was disinclined to concern himself with any problem which was not thrust forcibly on his attention. But the unemployment and destitution among so large a part of the population were thrust on his attention, and the issues preoccupied him for many years.

In June 1919 he made the first of the provincial tours which were to be so conspicuous a feature of his public life and were to give him a deeper understanding of British industry and working men than any monarch or heir to the throne had enjoyed before him. He spent four days in south Wales, was taken through the least salubrious slums, and in his speeches laboured constantly 'the welfare of our ex-service men and the improvement of housing conditions, both of which I have very much at heart'. He went down Cymmr pit in the Rhondda Valley and found chalked on a wall a thousand feet down: 'Welcome to our soldier Prince. Long may he live.' He borrowed a piece of chalk and wrote below the slogan: 'Thank you. Edward, Prince.'[1]

Until his Commonwealth tours were behind him he was not to be put to the task of doing something practical to implement his sincere but vague benevolence. He did, however, manage to fit other provincial visits into the gaps between his voyages abroad. Glasgow, traditionally the most republican and fiercely left-wing of British cities, was a tough assignment. The first day he met with boos or sullen silence, but his patent good will, humility and charm gradually prevailed. 'It's with the greatest possible relief and gratitude to the people of Glasgow that I can tell you that I'm more welcome here now than I was yesterday,' he wrote proudly to Freda Dudley Ward. 'I've driven miles through the streets of this vast city today and the people . . . have been divine to me and were very kind and enthusiastic. Even the men cheered and far more took off their caps than yesterday and there were only ½ dozen boos.' Next day was even better; 'a large crowd gave me a marvellous send off tonight. To TOI, and TOI only, I say that I do feel I've been able to do just a little good propaganda up there and given Communism a knock.' But he did not delude himself that the royal touch could miraculously cure economic ills: 'I'm afraid the effect of my visit won't last very long. Things have gone too far, darling, on the Clyde and I take a very gloomy view of the whole situation.'[2]

In Cardiff three months later he was flabbergasted by the warmth of his reception. 'They've all been divine to me today,' he told Freda, 'and I've seen hundreds of ex-service men and they were the nicest of the lot. Christ only knows why, for they are all having a real bad time and one is so terribly sorry for them.'[3] One of his problems was that the local dignitaries sought to swaddle him in pompous formalities, while his preoccupation was to meet and be seen by as many people as possible. In Lancashire in 1921, for example: 'Old Lord Derby has organized this tour marvellously, and I'm able to put in an occasional human touch or stunt of my own, so that I think it's going well, though I'm afraid my ultra-democratic spirit has annoyed him a few times.' He had his own way over the programme: 'No waste of time, such as laying foundation stones and opening things, it was all just driving through miles and miles of crowded streets and stopping at groups of ex-service men and schoolchildren.' But, as he found still more markedly on his tours abroad, the strain of constantly giving himself to the people, exuding warmth and enthusiastic interest for eight or nine hours on end, was sometimes cripplingly oppressive: 'I'm down to bedrock, my angel, and Christ only knows how I'm going to scrape through the next 2 days.'[1]

Painfully, he acquired the art of public speaking. Churchill appointed himself his coach. Don't be ashamed to read a speech, he wrote, but in that case 'do it quite openly, reading it very slowly and deliberately'. Of course it was better to memorize a text or talk from notes. To accommodate the notes, he advised, take a tumbler, put a finger bowl on top of it, put a plate on top of that, and then arrange the notes on top of the plate, 'but one has to be very careful not to knock it all over, as once happened to me'. This advice was given before a banquet for the allied leaders in July 1919. Whether the Prince followed Churchill's somewhat alarming system is uncertain. He memorized the speech, however, and evidently delivered it well. 'You are absolutely right to take trouble about these things,' wrote Churchill approvingly. 'With perseverance you might speak as well as anybody in the land, and naturally and gracefully besides.'[2] The Prince never learned to speak as well as that but he mastered the technique of seeming sincere and spontaneous: 'He talks very simply,' wrote Frances Stevenson, Lloyd George's personal secretary and future wife, 'just like a schoolboy – saying little things that come into his head as he goes along, and then coming back again to the prepared speech. He charms everyone.'[3] But he never enjoyed making speeches. On another occasion Frances Stevenson congratulated him on his success. 'He told me he would never get used to speaking in public – he was far too nervous. "My trouble is that I have not a ready pen," he said. "I find it so difficult even to prepare a speech . . ." He is a dear thing, with beautiful eyes, but such a boy.'[4]

The vast estates of the Duchy of Cornwall in London and the West Country gave him a chance to do something practical to help the unemployed and the homeless. He invested a large amount of money in new machinery for the Cornish tin mines, set up a farming concern run on cooperative lines and planted 250 acres of forest on the eastern side of Dartmoor. In London he regularly visited his estates in Kennington and the areas of the borough which he owned were conspicuously better furnished with houses than the parts for which the Council was responsible. At a public meeting the Mayor tried to blame his Council's shortcomings on the policies of the Duchy. 'Thereupon the whole Labour party who were in the hall rose and practically hissed the Mayor off the platform.' The socialist leader in the borough later told Sydney Greville that the Prince, after the interview which he had given them, could do anything he liked with the Labour Party.[1]

His public life directly after the war was not restricted to the University of Wales, the Royal College of Music and the other pressing calls on his time that Stamfordham had enumerated. 'Other men might be chained to their desks,' he wrote wryly in his memoirs. 'I was metaphorically chained to the banquet table.'[2] A typical day in July 1919 saw him receiving Indian army and navy officers, attending a meeting of the Duchy Council, visiting the Australian YMCA, spending the evening at the Royal College of Music, moving on to a boxing display and ending up at the Embassy night club. In March he was initiated by the Duke of Connaught into the Household Brigade Lodge of the Freemasons. For once it seemed he might be spared a speech, since replies to toasts were traditionally limited to five words, 'Worshipful Master, I thank you,' but the rule was waived for the heir to the throne and the Prince had to hold forth about his 'ardent desire to do his utmost to promote the principles of duty, loyalty and benevolence, on which Freemasonry rested'.[3] Closer to his heart was his appointment the following year to be Honorary Colonel of the newly formed Welsh Guards. For one who was often to claim that this was the office which meant more to him than any other, his initial reaction was, however, hardly ecstatic. 'Of course it is inevitable and is only right I suppose and I more than appreciate the honour etc. etc.!!' he wrote to a friend. 'But once a Grenadier always a Grenadier!!'[4]

But such diversions were no more than aperitifs to the daunting meal that was to come. It was Lloyd George who first conceived the idea that the Prince should embark on a series of tours around the Empire, ostensibly to visit the soldiers he had met during the war in Europe and the Middle East and to thank their governments and peoples for all they had contributed to the final victory. Lloyd George knew that demands for reform in the structure of the Empire, pent up during the years of fighting, would now be vigorously put forward. Difficult and probably acrimonious negotiations were inevitable. Anything that could be done to ensure that they were conducted in a spirit of unity, and against a background of harmony, would be of the greatest value. Otherwise the strains might prove too great and the Empire disintegrate. 'The appearance of the popular Prince of Wales,' Lloyd George maintained, 'might do more to calm the discord than half a dozen solemn Imperial Conferences.'[1]

The King was not convinced that his son's apparition would thus magically still the tempest, but he felt that at least it would be a useful stage in the education of a future monarch. Canada had asked first for a visit from the Prince, so Canada would start the series, the other Dominions and parts of the Empire would follow in the next few years. It was a prospect that exhilarated and alarmed the Prince. He longed to travel, but though he had no concept yet of how gruelling his tours would be, he knew well that they would be no joy ride. He would be constantly on parade, scrutinized in every detail of his behaviour, blamed if he were too solemn or too frivolous, criticized for his formality, rebuked for his informality. 'Your visits to the Dominions will be made or marred according as you do and *say* the right thing,' Lord Stamfordham sternly warned him. 'The Throne is the pivot upon which the Empire will more than ever hinge. Its strength and stability will depend entirely on its occupant.'[2] The Prince found it troublesome enough always to do and say the right thing in the restricted periods during which he was on duty in the United Kingdom; to have to do so for months at a time under the microscope that is trained upon a royal visitor would test him unreasonably hard. It was with grave qualms that he sailed from Portsmouth on 5 August 1919, on his way to the New World.

7

The First Tours

T HE PRINCE'S HAPPINESS, ALMOST HIS SURVIVAL, ON
his gargantuan tours depended as much as anything on
the people who accompanied him. For the trip to Canada
Stamfordham recommended a man who, like Thomas and Legh,
was to serve him until his reign was over. Admiral Halsey – 'the
Old Salt' as he was derisively but affectionately nicknamed – was
something of a Hansell; sound, honourable, humourless, unimaginative. He was 'the ideal Chief of Staff', the Prince told his mother,
'and I know we are going to be a very happy family'. Needless to
say they were not; friction in such a party was almost inevitable,
and became completely so when Halsey was matched by a political
adviser with unspecified responsibilities, the energetic and somewhat impatient Edward Grigg. Grigg, by family background as
well as predilection, was destined to devote the greater part of
his life to the service of the British Empire. He was 'a very exceptional man', the Prince went on, 'so clever and able and he has
such splendidly broad-minded and far seeing ideas, a great
imperialist . . .'[1] He was all that, but also assertive, suffered fools
badly, and considered Halsey something of a fool. The prospects
for harmony were not bright.

In a memorandum which Grigg prepared for the Colonial Secretary, Milner, he observed that the main object of the Prince's
visit was 'to create an atmosphere. He will do this largely by
natural tact and charm.' But he would have to overcome the
feeling in North America that the monarchy was no more than an
'interesting feudal anachronism'. His speeches should emphasize
his 'appreciation of the political institutions of the Empire and of
the very vital place which the Crown takes as the nodus of the
whole web. That line is, I think, good for the Canadian as well as
the American market.' Lloyd George minuted dubiously: 'There
must be nothing that would look in USA like a challenge to

republican institutions'; an indication of the many tightropes the Prince was going to be required to walk over the next few years as he teetered between America and Canada; Westminster and Dominion governments; federal capital and state capitals; French Canadian and Anglo-Canadian; Boer and *rooinek*.[1]

When he left Portsmouth, however, the Prince was looking not forward to such problems but backward towards Mrs Dudley Ward. At one point he had tried to persuade her to accompany him to Canada, or at least to meet him there. She had taken the possibility seriously enough to consult Piers Legh's fiancée about it, but had wisely decided to stay behind.[2] The Prince was disconsolate and only began to regain his spirits when the battle cruiser, HMS *Renown*, arrived at St John's and the demands of the tour left less time for brooding.

'No enthusiastic mob – seems a dead place on the whole,' commented Sub-Lieutenant Hutchinson gloomily. 'Went ashore, but the only thing they seem to sell here is ice-cream.'[3] He failed to note the Prince's favourite feature of his arrival, the triumphal arch composed largely of drums of cod-liver oil and festooned with the carcasses of dried codfish.[4] Nor was the Prince disturbed by the relatively meagre crowds, proudly describing his 'rapturous reception' to the King: 'The fact that my first day in the Dominion was a success has given me confidence for the future.'[5] What gave him greatest confidence was that he was performing well in public. Godfrey Thomas, who was also in the party, told the Queen, 'I cannot describe . . . how well the Prince is speaking.' The Canadian Prime Minister, Sir Robert Bordern, had been 'immensely struck and talked of nothing else after the St John visit'.[6]

The Prince was less struck by Sir Robert Bordern. 'Quite pleasant, but rather a dull old stick,' he described him to the Queen.[7] Sometimes the Prime Minister was worse than that. When the Prince was about to make the most important speech of his Canadian visit, Bordern noted that he was nervous and distrait: 'I endeavoured to divert his attention by recounting some amusing anecdotes, but he quite frequently consulted his notes.' In spite of his no doubt well-intentioned sabotage, the speech, Bordern concluded, was 'admirable in every way'.[8]

The Prince's next important stop, Quebec, introduced him to what he had been told would prove the greatest impediment to a successful tour, the hostility between anglophone and francophone Canada. Expecting the worst, he was pleasantly surprised. 'They are a curious people and very touchy, but they seemed quite pleased and certainly gave me a good welcome,' he wrote of the French Canadians to the King.[1]

In Montreal, speaking half in French and half in English, he claimed that the union of the two races was more than a matter of political convenience, 'it was, and will always remain, an example of the highest political wisdom'.[2] The French Canadians, an anonymous lady assured the King, likened the Prince to 'L'Enfant Jésus'.[3] One may doubt whether many French Canadians spotted the similarity but the Prince went down well with a public disposed to be critical and captious.

It was Toronto which offered the most turbulent welcome. The Prince's stay there, Thomas told the Queen, 'were the most extraordinary days I have ever seen'. Things began relatively quietly, enthusiasm mounted by the hour, and the scenes when he drove through the city on his final day made Thomas think 'that half the people had taken leave of their senses'.[4] To the Prince it was overwhelming. For the first time he tasted the heady, dangerous wine of mass adulation. 'The most wonderful days of my life,' he described them, '. . . amazingly marvellous. People seemed to go quite mad.'[5] An unidentified lady in Toronto wrote to a friend in England and at third hand her letter came to the Queen. 'He has won all hearts, and the demonstration here was *personal love* for him,' wrote the lady. She had been to hear him speak: 'He was very boyishly shy and very pink, but the dearest, sweetest and most bewitching creature. He really looked as if he were going to cry and bit his lip, but imagine, he faced a crowd of 50,000 people, who rose of course and yelled and screamed and cheered, never was there such a greeting. He spoke beautifully and to the point and looked sweet, his lovely complexion and blue eyes are the admiration of everyone.'[6]

There was a physical price to pay for this glorification, beyond the exhaustion that followed a day among the crowds. He was jostled and buffeted, his right hand so bruised by constant shaking that he had to use his left. The King saw photographs of his son being mobbed and deprecated the loss of dignity. 'It isn't my fault,' protested the Prince. 'You just can't think how enthusiastic the

117

crowds have been, and they just go mad and one is powerless!!'[1] Grigg described 'his happy way of making crowds no less than individuals feel that he meets them half way. It is always quite obvious somehow that the huge masses of people who have thronged his movements everywhere feel that his heart goes out to them as much as theirs to him, and the effect is (I use the word literally) indescribable.'[2]

By the time that the Prince had visited all the main centres of the east, he was close to collapse. 'HRH really does work very very hard,' Halsey reported. What tired him most were visits to hospitals, 'especially as he talks to practically every soldier who is bedridden, and his sympathy with them is so genuine that of course he finds it extremely hard to go on for any length of time'.[3] Some at least of his exhaustion was brought on by his refusal to rest when he had a chance. As he grew more tired, so he would insist on staying up later and later, talking, smoking, feverishly restless. No one else could have stood the strain so wonderfully, said Thomas, 'but he could give himself much more chance if he would only be sensible and occasionally sit down in a chair or go to bed at a normal hour'.[4] The strain was not eased by interminable official banquets without even a solitary glass of wine to ease his nerves or dull the pain of other people's orating. The Prince deplored prohibition, not just because of the personal inconvenience it caused him, but as being 'the very worst form of class legislation'. There was plenty of liquor to be had, but only for those who were prepared to pay the exorbitant prices. 'It's the women's vote which is the trouble, otherwise prohibition couldn't last.'[5] On those occasions when liquor was available, things were bad in a different way. Thomas described a dinner at Calgary where he knew things were beginning to warm up when a Justice of the Supreme Court tottered to his feet and sang 'Another little drink couldn't do us any harm'. 'It is a very remarkable thing now that the country has gone dry, the appalling effect of liquor on everybody when they manage to get some.'[6]

The Prince would certainly have preferred an orgy like the one in Calgary to the more formal functions of eastern Canada. He thought the Governor General, the Duke of Devonshire, though in a 'hopelessly narrow groove', was at least 'a d—d good fellow and has no side', but the Duchess was 'hopelessly pompous . . .

she plays the "Queen stunt" far more than Mama would, and that doesn't go down on this side'.[1] The Duke gallantly did his best to be one of the boys, but found the effort uncongenial. 'There is a good deal of regard for what is called "a real sport",' he told Stamfordham. 'It is an odious term. After I had been to a hockey match I was described as "a real sport in spite of his white hair".'[2] The Prince, he recognized, was 'a real sport' *par excellence*; he refrained from criticism but contrived to leave the impression that he felt the performance hardly becoming the heir to the throne.

It was with some relief that the battered and enervated Prince escaped from all this to the space and relative tranquillity of the west. 'I came to Canada as a Canadian in mind and spirit,' he declared in Calgary, 'I am now rapidly becoming a Westerner.'[3] He was impressed by the immense potential of the prairies and saw the west as the 'country of the future . . . It is up to the Empire and particularly to the UK to see that its population is British and not alien!!'[4] He told his mother that he would love to work on a ranch for a few months – 'That's a real life.'[5] Such wishes are habitually voiced by those who know there is no risk that they will become reality, but the Prince did something to forward his ambition when for £10,000 or so he bought a small ranch in Alberta. The King was doubtful about the purchase as an investment and feared too that his son would be under pressure to do the same when he visited the other Dominions.[6] He left it to the Prince to decide, however, and he went ahead – to the great pleasure of the Canadians. In spite of the King's fears, there is no record of the Prince being asked to buy a farm in the Australian outback or the South African *platteland*.

In all his major speeches, the Prince hammered home his creed that he was not primarily a Briton and only secondarily a Canadian: 'On the contrary, I regard myself as belonging to Great Britain and to Canada in exactly the same way.'[7] This was not just rhetoric reserved for public consumption. He told the Queen that the royal family must keep closely in touch with Canada and pay regular visits. '*We* belong to Canada and the other dominions just as much as we do to the UK.'[8] The King warned him that if he called himself a Canadian in Canada then he would have to be an Australian in Australia and a New Zealander in New Zealand. And why not? asked the Prince. 'Of course in India there would be no question of it as I happen to have been born a white man and not a native.'[1]

'I do like all these Canadians so much,' the Prince wrote after a few weeks. 'They are charming and so kind and hospitable if one takes them the right way and if they take to you, and the latter means success or total failure.'[2] No one can doubt that the Canadians *had* taken to him and that his first tour abroad had been not merely a success but a triumph. 'It almost takes one's breath away,' a Canadian wrote to Grigg. 'It is not mere loyalty to the Crown, but the expression of a deep, spontaneous affection for the young man who is heir to the oldest throne in the world . . . The Prince has something to offer that can come from no other human being. He symbolizes the unity of the whole Empire, and does it with the joyousness and courage that belongs to youth.'[3] Even courtiers as loyal as Stamfordham admitted that George V offended by his constant carping at the Prince and decrying of his accomplishments. Sometimes the complaint was justified but on this occasion his praise could hardly have been more generous. 'I offer you my warmest congratulations on the splendid success of your tour,' he wrote in mid-October, 'which is due in a great measure to your own personality and the wonderful way you have played up. It makes me very proud of you.'[4]

'When I go down to the United States next week,' said the Prince on his way back through Toronto, 'I shall regard myself as going there not only as . . . a Britisher, but also as a Canadian.'[5] He almost missed going in any capacity. The King had been against the visit from the start – mainly, believed the Prince, because of his anti-American views.[6] When the President, Woodrow Wilson, fell seriously ill, King George V at once insisted that the tour must be called off.[7] The Prince, supported strongly by Grigg, felt that the cancellation of the visit would give the Americans the impression that he had leapt at any excuse not to go: 'I realize the spirit in which the American public has welcomed the proposed visit too highly not to regard any such possibility with deep dislike.'[8] The King held to his view, but left the matter to the government to decide, and the Foreign Secretary felt the visit should take place.[9] The Prince went to Washington and dutifully visited the President on his sickbed. He also managed to attend a dance or two which Grigg had arranged: 'He holds very strongly that he can influence American feeling even better by dancing with Senators' daughters than by talking to Senators, and I am sure he is right.'[1]

There was still greater doubt whether the tour should be extended to New York. Godfrey Thomas felt that the risk of a hostile reception from the Irish more than outweighed any possible advantage, and the King fully shared his doubts.[2] The Prince, though, was determined to go, the American Ambassador in London supported him, and the Cabinet concluded that 'a good deal of the magnificent results to be expected from the visit might be thrown away' if it seemed he was avoiding contact with 'the real American people'.[3] The American press then published stories announcing that the Prince was planning to stay at notoriously opulent Newport, with the still more notoriously opulent Mrs Vanderbilt, and that lavish entertainments were being planned. The Secretary of the Interior took the rumours seriously enough to raise the matter with the British Ambassador, and the Acting Counsellor urged that the Prince should steer clear of the Newport crowd which was synonymous with 'all that is most extravagant and frivolous in American life'.[4] 'There never was the faintest intention of the Prince going to Newport,' Stamfordham reassured the Counsellor. 'It was a pity that the American press almost exceeded itself in concocting absolutely fabulous stories of what HRH was going to do and of the different young women that were to be submitted to his choice as his future wife!! It is difficult to conceive how newspapers can give way to such vulgarity.'[5] The Prince nevertheless contrived to see something of New York's young women; at least one ball was given in his honour and he never returned to the ship before two or three in the morning.[6]

New York gave him the same almost hysterical welcome as he had received in Toronto. 'It was not crowd psychology that swept him into instant popularity but the subtle something that is personality,' wrote the *New York World*.[7] Whether New York's love would matter in the long run, was a difficult question to answer. Edward Grey, then British Ambassador on a special mission in Washington, believed it would. 'It has done more good than any number of political speeches,' he reported to the Foreign Office. 'His Royal Highness has created in New York a feeling of personal affection so strong that, though it may have no direct influence on politics, it must do something to create kindly feeling in New York itself.'[1] British Ambassadors must be expected to laud the prowess of their future monarch; M. Jusserand, the French Ambassador, had no such axe to grind. '*Son succès a été complet auprès des gens les plus divers,*' he wrote to the Quai d'Orsay, '*les Anglais n'ont jamais rien fait qui ait pu si utilement servir à effacer les anciennes animosités.*'[2] Sub-Lieutenant Hutchinson was amazed when he saw the size of the crowd that assembled to see the Prince depart. 'The Yanks seem quite enthusiastic about him,' he wrote in his diary, a laconic understatement that did not conceal the immense pride the crew of *Renown* took in the Prince's triumph.[3]

The Prince was to spend only three months in England before he set off on his next, still longer, tour to Australia. He was exhausted and flat after his efforts, and distraught at the thought that he would so soon be separated again from Freda Dudley Ward. The last straw was that he found himself expected to sacrifice three weeks of this precious interval to stay with his parents at Sandringham. On Christmas Day 1919 he wrote in desperation to Godfrey Thomas:

> A sort of hopelessly lost feeling has come over me and I think I'm going kind of mad!! . . . I'm simply not capable of even thinking, let alone make a decision or settle anything!! I've never felt like this in my life before, and I'm rather worried about it and feel incapable of pulling myself together . . . How I loathe my job now and all this press 'puffed' empty '*succès*'. I feel I'm through with it and long and long to die . . . You'll probably think from this that I ought to be in a mad house already, tho' this isn't necessary yet: I'm still quite sane and very much in earnest, but I don't know for how much longer!! Of course I'm going to make a gt effort to pull myself together, and it may only be that I never realized how *brain* weary I returned from the 'Other Side' . . . But my brain has gone and I can hardly think any more . . . What you must think of me, and you and all the staff have been and are working so desperately hard for me . . . How can I even try to thank you, my dear Godfrey?[4]

The First Tours

Thomas had received many such *cris du coeur* in the past, but this struck him as worryingly unbalanced. He replied with a dose of robust common sense. The Prince was not destined for a mad house, but he would find himself in a nursing home if he did not change his idiotic train of life. 'It is inconceivable to me that anyone who has got such sound, if perhaps somewhat exaggerated ideas about health from the point of view of exercise ... should be so utterly insane and unreasonable about the elementary rules of health as regards other things. How you survived Canada I cannot imagine ... You are highly strung and nervy to begin with. You never allowed yourself a moment's rest the whole time. You sat up every night, often quite unnecessarily, till godless hours ... You smoked far too much and you drink a great deal too much whiskey.' Only a change of heart would 'stop you being thoroughly bloody minded, irritable and impossible when you start for Australia (a nice prospect for your Staff) and [you] will crack up by the time you reach the Panama Canal'. He would do better if he sometimes let off steam 'and got cross and irritable instead of *pathetic*'. Of course his was bound to be 'a more or less bloody life, but give it a chance. It's certainly a life worth fighting through, not one to chuck away.'[1]

This letter, which the Prince described as 'marvellous', and the enforced tranquillity of Sandringham, together worked wonders. 'I'm feeling a new and completely sane man,' he told Thomas. 'I promise to take things easily and not make a B F of myself any more.'[2] Rest, and the attentions of those who cared for him, almost always sufficed to rescue the Prince from the blackest of his depressions. But Thomas recognized his extreme fragility and was alarmed by it; under the stresses of the Australian tour, with Freda Dudley Ward ten thousand miles away, might he not crack more seriously, perhaps even irrecoverably? It was a distant but daunting menace.

Back in London, the Prince first tried to defer the tour by three weeks on the plea that *Renown* could not be ready in time – an argument which the Under Secretary at the Colonial Office, Leo Amery, disposed of with alacrity[3] – and then engaged in a wrangle with Amery and the Prime Minister over the composition of his staff. Halsey, said Amery, was incompetent to handle the most important aspects of the tour, he was 'difficult to deal with, indifferent to political considerations and indeed incapable of appreciating them. He upset the Press badly on the Canadian tour.'[1] The Prince liked Halsey and had serious reservations about Grigg, whom Amery wanted to put in charge: 'We are not in any way kindred spirits and for this reason I do not regard his presence on my staff [as being] of any value whatsoever.'[2] He argued that, since his was not a political tour, there was no need for it to be managed by an expert in politics. 'Its consequences are of the highest political importance both to the Throne and the Empire,' retorted Lloyd George. Grigg must have complete control over the programme and relations with the press.[3] In the end the Prince and the Prime Minister met in Downing Street, with Stamfordham, Halsey and Grigg to act as referee and seconds. 'If you are one day to be a constitutional King,' said Lloyd George, 'you must first be a constitutional Prince of Wales.'[4] The Prince swallowed his medicine, but it did not make him any the more cheerful about the prospects for the tour.

One other important change was made to the staff which had accompanied him to Canada. The Prince's young cousin, Louis Mountbatten, was added; in theory as Flag Lieutenant to Halsey, in practice as companion and confidant to the Prince. 'Such a charming boy, and he cheers me up,' the Prince told the Queen.[5] Cheering up the Prince was, indeed, Mountbatten's main function. He got some idea of what was in store for him when he found his cousin in tears just before the formal departure. 'Have you ever seen a Post Captain cry?' the Prince asked. Mountbatten admitted that he had not. 'Well, you'd better get used to it, you may see it again.'[6] But few except his intimates realized the strain that he was under. He dined with the Asquiths in January. 'The Prince has excellent manners, and has come on immensely in ease and savoir faire,' wrote his host. 'He talked quite amusingly of his experiences in America, and I think is not sorry to be off again in March, even to so dismal a goal as Australia.'[7]

And so the pompous ritual of departure was enacted once again, the Prince forlorn among the beribboned dignitaries – 'In a little tight naval uniform which clung close to his figure he did not look above 15,' wrote Curzon, 'quite a pathetic little person.'[8] Mountbatten was quickly set to his principal duty. 'Poor chap, with all these hundreds of people round him he's as lonely and homesick as he can be and is at present HATING this trip!' he told his mother. 'He says he'll cheer up later. But then he is very, very badly smitten, I think.'[1] Of those aboard, only Mountbatten understood the extent of his gloom; the Prince joined in the traditional shipboard romps with good will, and gave every appearance of enjoying himself as he inadvertently flooded Halsey's cabin with a power hose. The hose was too powerful for Grigg's peace of mind: 'I had visions of HRH, who does not weigh much in a state of nature, being projected into the Atlantic by a sudden jet of salt water.'[2]

The *Renown* travelled by the Panama Canal, with stops in the West Indies on the way. In Barbados he found the inhabitants disturbed by rumours that some of the islands were to be sold to the United States. 'I need hardly say that the King's subjects are not for sale to other governments,' the Prince reassured them loftily. 'Their destiny as free men is in their own hands.'[3] At Bridgetown the Governor's lady had prepared an immense ball of flowers which was supposed to disintegrate and shower the Prince with blossoms as he passed. Fortunately she lost her nerve and pulled the string too soon; the ball, welded into a congealed mass, fell heavily into the road and would have reduced the Prince to pulp if released at the proper time.[4]

It soon became obvious that the Prince was not going to allow his pining for Mrs Dudley Ward to deprive him of all diversions. At a ball in Balboa he danced almost exclusively with a particularly pretty girl, who turned out to be the daughter of the local storekeeper – 'and a very good thing too,' commented Grigg, 'but the local dignitaries felt mournful that their more patrician daughters had not been preferred.'[5] Swimming at midnight, Sub-Lieutenant Hutchinson approached a raft crewed by three nubile American girls. 'Is that you, Teddy?' one enquired. Hutchinson denied the charge but boarded the raft nevertheless, to be joined a few minutes later by the Prince of Wales. They returned to *Renown* at 2 a.m. and tiptoed to the Prince's cabin for a whisky. 'Don't wake the baby,' whispered the Prince, pointing to Halsey's adjoining cabin.[6] There was much junketing at San Diego, including a Mayoral Ball. Among those present was an American air force officer, Earl Winfield Spencer, and his wife Wallis. No doubt gatherings of this kind were enjoyed by the locals, wrote Halsey disdainfully to the

King, 'but one has to be extremely careful at these sorts of places where one meets all sorts of conditions of people'.[1]

The Australian Prime Minister, William Hughes, had originally insisted that the Prince must visit Australia before New Zealand, even though the opposite would obviously have been more sensible: 'To ask the poor Prince to imagine glorious Alpine views in a howling blizzard, and to spend days tossing about in Antarctic gales looking for noble fjords hidden in rain and mist, is really a little too much,' wrote Amery.[2] Lloyd George agreed, and Australia was told that it would have to wait its turn. The visit to New Zealand had been envisaged as an important but relatively relaxed rehearsal for the main task ahead. The authorities of both Dominions had been told that the Prince wanted no ceremonies before 10 a.m., three half-days a week for recuperation, and at least one large public reception in every city to allow him to meet the people.[3] However, when the representatives of the two governments joined the ship at Suva it was found that they had ignored their instructions. Programmes of impossible complexity and arduousness had been prepared – 'I do not believe any human being could go through with all that was proposed,' wrote Halsey.[4] He and Grigg set to work and managed to cut back the Australian programme to something physically possible, but it was too late to do more than nibble at the edges of what had been planned for New Zealand. 'I cannot understand the Governor General having passed it,' Godfrey Thomas told the Queen, 'unless the object was to break the Prince down and make it impossible for him to do justice to himself in Australia.'[5]

Lord Liverpool, the Governor General in question, was to be held responsible for almost everything that went wrong in New Zealand. 'A pompous, interfering ass who has been dogging not only my own footsteps but also never leaves the Admiral and Grigg alone,' the Prince described him to his father. 'He rubs everybody up the wrong way and . . . is most unpopular throughout the dominion.'[6] The Prince was habitually quick to denounce British governors, ambassadors, or others in positions of authority, but on this occasion Halsey, Grigg and Thomas all echoed his views. Liverpool could hardly be blamed for the railway strike which threatened to disrupt the visit, but even this, Grigg complained, he handled with notable incompetence, behaving 'one minute as if the end of the world had come, the next as if there was nothing to worry about'.[1] The strike had been fomented by a group of Sinn Fein supporters who dominated the union executive. Fortunately for the royal party the most prominent of the Irishmen found the strain too much and suffered a nervous breakdown. Without his leadership the strike collapsed. Grigg's preoccupation had been to keep the Prince out of the dispute, whether he were presented as taking the side of the management or the strikers. He succeeded, though the Prince could not resist one bland remark in a speech in Wellington: 'Somehow or other the trains were not running very well last week, but mine could not have run better.'[2]

In spite of the taxing programme, the tour of New Zealand went extremely well. Neither the nature of the people nor the size of the population made possible the sort of mass hysteria the Prince had witnessed in Toronto or New York, but his reception was never less than enthusiastic. He remained downcast, however. Grigg found him reading, 'with an air of profound dejection', an article in the Wanganui newspaper which referred to him as 'the coping stone of Imperial federation'. 'I never saw a coping stone in worse condition,' Grigg commented drily.[3]

New Zealand might have its striking railwaymen, but Australia traditionally possessed the most left-wing and militant working class in the British Empire. The Prime Minister had broken with most of his Labour colleagues in 1916 to form a national government, and his action had caused as much bitterness among those who felt themselves deserted as Ramsay MacDonald was to experience in Britain ten years later. The Prince had to step gingerly between these rancorous groups. But this was not the only Australian problem which required diplomatic handling. The federal and state governments were perpetually at loggerheads; the relationship between the state Governors and the Governor General was little more harmonious. The Prince found himself a particularly savoury bone of contention between the warring elements; anything he did to please one was certain to offend another. 'One Governor suggests that the destiny of the Empire depends on HRH spending three extra days in his State,' wrote the Governor General, Munro-Ferguson. 'Another deprecates the Prince enjoying a kangaroo hunt . . . and the masterful little Prime Minister has decided views on all questions and never forgets he is the supreme authority.'[1]

Any fears that the Australians might receive the Prince with less exuberance than he had found elsewhere were quickly dispelled. 'I can't begin to tell you how amazingly enthusiastic the Melbourne people are,' he told his mother, 'and they've kept it up ever since I landed and it's really frightfully touching, and I do appreciate it all so much. It beats anywhere in Canada.'[2] Always it was the ex-service men who were to the fore; even when he was in the comparative safety of a car he might find himself plucked from the back seat and 'tossed cheerfully about the streets' by the excited 'diggers'.[3] It was gratifying, it was exhilarating, but it was also alarming. One drive to the Town Hall, scheduled to take five minutes, lasted an hour. The folded hood was torn off the back of the car and the running boards trampled away by a crowd determined to get near its Prince.[4] To see him from close quarters was desirable, to touch him best of all; he was prodded, patted, slapped on the back, shaken by the hand, so that by the end of each day his body was covered with bruises and his hands swollen and aching. The Prince had worked like a slave, Halsey told the King, and had been totally successful. 'On every hand I hear most wonderful things as a result, such as people who, before his arrival, refused to have anything to do with his reception or allow their children to take part in the various functions, completely coming round and being, if possible, more enthusiastic than any of the others.'[5]

Such experiences were as emotionally draining as they were physically demanding. When coming on top of the endless formal banquets, receptions, parades, receiving of addresses, hospital visits, balls and relentless speechifying, it is small wonder that the Prince should have been worn out by the time he had finished at Melbourne. Things were a little easier when he left the great city centres and travelled by train thousands of miles across the Australian plains, but even there he could rarely relax for long since at every suggestion of a station scores or hundreds of locals would gather, some of them having travelled thirty or forty miles by cart to see the Prince pass. They could not be disappointed. When he occasionally failed to appear, as at Gilgandra, he was 'counted out' by the indignant crowd, who chanted from one to ten and ended with a resounding 'OUT!', a traditional Australian way of registering disapproval. On the return journey he made sure to present himself and the forgiving inhabitants counted him in again.[1]

He never slept well in a train and the lack of sleep added to his cumulative exhaustion. His morale was not improved when the royal train was derailed in the depths of Western Australia. The only casualties were the Prince's doctor, who cut his leg, and the pride of the Minister of Works, who was trapped in the lavatory, but if the accident had occurred a hundred yards further on, where the embankment was steeper, it could have been far more serious. The Prince preserved admirable sang-froid; as he clambered from the wreckage he remarked cheerfully: 'Well, anyway, at last we have done something which was not on the official programme.'[2] But though his entourage thought that he was unscathed by the incident, he admitted to his mother that he had been badly shaken: 'I live so much on my nerves nowadays that they get very easily upset and I just loathe a train now and have "the wind up me" the whole time!!'[3]

Brisbane was the city the Prince most dreaded visiting, for Queensland was 'bolshie or rather full of Sinn Feiners and the Labour premier is a hot Irish RC'.[4] In the event, not a red flag was to be seen and the crowds were as welcoming as any in Australia. The Acting Premier, who at one point had threatened to boycott the visit, became almost embarrassingly fond of his visitor and in his determination to say goodbye chartered a special aircraft to pursue the Prince to the frontier and, missing him there, continued the chase many miles into New South Wales.[5] For Grigg, the most memorable feature of the stay at Brisbane was the Shakespearean Ball, at which a gentleman dressed as Shakespeare presented a series of his characters to the Prince: 'It was a very mixed show, and Shakespeare himself became somewhat confused at times, introducing Othello as Julius Caesar until corrected by the indignant Moor in question.'[6] It is unlikely that the Prince would have been much the wiser if Othello had been presented as Ancient Pistol or one of the witches from *Macbeth*.

Adelaide should have been something of a rest cure, since the programme was less onerous than elsewhere and the Governor's wife, Lady Weigall, was a woman of common sense and great kindness as well as a close friend of Freda Dudley Ward. 'It cheered him up no end,' Godfrey Thomas wrote thirty years later, 'to have found in Australia someone with whom he could talk freely about his lady-love.'[1] Lady Weigall mothered and cosseted him, at a time when he craved for such treatment; when he left Adelaide he wrote to thank her for having done so much to boost the morale of 'a very worn out little boy, who really was beginning to think the whole show too big for him and too much to go thro with'.[2] But though the therapy was effective she undid much of the good by encouraging him to stay up every night until 3 or 4 a.m. cooking buttered eggs in her boudoir.[3] The Prince left Adelaide more cheerful but little more rested than he had been on his arrival.

As a result he teetered permanently on the edge of extreme depression. 'I feel fit enough,' he told Philip Sassoon in early August, 'but mentally I'm *absolutely* worn out. Thank God it's all over bar the shouting now as I really don't think I could carry on much longer without the top of my head *cracking like an egg* and making a mad house my only possible [word omitted] for the remainder of my natural life.'[4] In such a state of mind, trials which normally he would have borne lightly seemed intolerably burdensome, pleasures became pains, inoffensive companions were categorized as the lowest of the low. He had hardly seen a pretty woman yet, he told Sassoon, they were 'a hen-faced crowd and make me tired'.[5] He confused cause and effect; it was because he was tired that they seemed hen-faced. Similarly, the journalists who accompanied the party were not 'virulent scum', 'absolutely spoilt' and 'bloody rude to my staff';[6] they were, as he would have agreed when in sounder mind, professionals doing a difficult job with considerable competence – and on the whole giving a most favourable account of all his doings.

Certainly they were sympathetic when, in mid-July, the Prince had something close to a complete breakdown. He lost his voice, rambled off the point in speeches, appeared wan and disconsolate even to those who did not know him well. 'Renewed sign of nerve strain . . . very disturbing,' cabled *The Times* correspondent; 'Use utmost influence to save Prince continuance of the terrible strain imposed by many months of public appearances,' the *Morning Post* representative urged his editor. 'Situation at any moment may become serious . . . He is game to the backbone, but there are limits within sight.'[1] His staff were at one point so alarmed that they insisted the programme be postponed by a week, allowing the Prince a chance to recuperate.

Such messages, suspiciously similar in phrasing, may have been inspired as part of an orchestrated campaign to change the dates of the Prince's next tour abroad. One of the most pressing causes of his gloom was the knowledge that he would hardly be back in Britain again before he had to set out on an even longer tour of India and Japan. His separation from Freda Dudley Ward would have lasted nearly a year. Even before he left for Australia he had suggested to Lloyd George that Prince Albert should replace him on the Indian tour. The King was displeased when he heard that the matter had been discussed in Downing Street before his son had raised it with him; Frances Stevenson noted with some amusement that he treated Lloyd George coldly at the station when the Prince departed.[2] The Prince was mainly alarmed lest he be 'unconsciously drawn into a conflict between "monarch and premier". Of course that's the last thing I want as it w'd probably end in a row between father and son.'[3] The question was temporarily dropped.

When reports began to come in of the strain the Prince was under, the King was unsympathetic. 'Papa naturally said it was all your fault doing too much,' wrote Prince Albert, or as he had recently become, the Duke of York, 'but he doesn't understand how difficult things are now.'[4] Grigg and Halsey also argued the perils of sticking to the original schedule – 'The Prince . . . is only a human being and not a machine,' wrote Halsey, 'and he cannot continue at high pitch indefinitely.'[5] The King began to feel alarm. From Adelaide Weigall wrote to say that the Prince was 'weary in mind and body'. Milner saw the letter and told Lloyd George that he had not mentioned it at court 'because I happen to know that the King is very touchy about the Prince's possibly not going to India'. His own view was that unless the Prince were given a decent rest at home before his next tour, 'we shall have a disaster'.[6] Lloyd George braved the wrath of the King and found that his opposition had already crumbled. At the end of July, to his immense relief, the Prince was told that his visit to India was postponed until the autumn of 1921.

The King made it plain he expected a quid pro quo. In the period between the tours the Prince should lead a 'strictly normal life', rest, more food, more sleep, less exercise; otherwise 'you will give cause to numbers of people who are disappointed, to say that the plea of health is not genuine'.[1] To this not unreasonable condition the Prince responded with an indignation which showed how overwrought he must have been. 'The lecture you gave me in your last letter made me rather sad,' he told his father. His health was perfectly good, the strain was only mental. 'You may find it very difficult to see my point of view, perhaps you never will, but such is my case.' What he needed was a normal life, but not the normality that the King envisaged; his life must include much sport and exercise, 'and after a month or two lots of work, which every man should have!!'[2] To Philip Sassoon he ranted about his father's 'foul' letter. 'It's odd how inhuman a lot of people (and big people) are, and I haven't much use for them.' The King was determined to treat him like an invalid but 'You know just as well as I do that invalids don't go down with the British public, there's no room for them nowadays so forget them!! *Nobody* is going to make me play the invalid!!'[3]

The Prince reacted with the same intemperance to relatively mild rebukes from home. The King deplored a photograph of his son and Mountbatten in a swimming pool – 'You might as well be photographed *naked*, no doubt it would please the public.' He objected to the wearing of a turned-down collar in white uniform with a black tie, 'anything more unsmart I never saw'.[4] 'His father's letters might be the letters of a Director of some business to his Assistant,' commented Mountbatten.[5] The remark was not wholly unjustified, George V did find it hard to communicate affection. But the affection was there, and the Prince must have known it was. Nor did the letters contain only criticism. Three weeks before Mountbatten made his comment, the King had written to say how the Queen and he rejoiced 'at the splendid success of your tour and the way in which you have won all hearts by your hard work and your own personality. I must say we are very proud of you. You are doing untold good for the Empire.'[6]

Not everything went to plan on the tour, nor was the Prince's behaviour always impeccable. He caused offence to several ladies of eminence by preferring to dance with the prettier of the – evidently not so hen-faced – Australian girls. He upset one family who had taken endless pains to prepare for his reception by brusquely cancelling a visit at the last moment on the flimsy pretext that the roads were impassable.[1] He sometimes looked bored at the stuffier public performances or snapped angrily at slow or incompetent servants. But these were minor blemishes on an otherwise almost flawless performance. The visit had been a tumultuous success.

There had been moments when his staff had doubted whether he could carry it through. Grigg told Lord Cromer what an immense relief it was to have reached the end of the Australian programme: 'HRH has done splendidly from first to last, though working hard against the collar for the better part of the time.'[2] Any minor complaints were forgotten in the paean of praise that greeted the accomplishment of his mission. More important than the views of his own staff were the feelings of the Australians. Billy Hughes, the Prime Minister, had been determined not to be impressed by any mere princeling. The fact that the princeling was English was an additional reason for suspicion. Yet he had succumbed totally to his visitor's charm and simplicity. His valedictory letter to the Prince of Wales might be ascribed to politeness, if almost on the same day he had not spoken to Grigg 'most touchingly of the Prince'.[3] There is no reason to doubt that he meant what he wrote:

> When you first came amongst us we welcomed you as a Prince who is one day to be our King; but we part from you as a dear friend who has won our affections and whom we love. Your visit has provoked demonstrations that in their spontaneous enthusiasm are unique in our history.
>
> The Australian people see in you all that our glorious Empire stands for, that deathless spirit of liberty, of progress, that distinguishes it from all other Empires, ancient or modern . . .
>
> Come back to us, Prince, as soon and as often as you can.[4]

8

India

'I AM DELIGHTED AT THE PROSPECT OF AN UNINTER-
rupted twelve months in the Old Country,' declared the Prince
of Wales at a Guildhall luncheon shortly after his return from
Australia; '– a treat I have not had for several years.'[1] His parents'
view was that he should now have a badly needed rest, 'free from
functions and photographers' and occupied by 'ordinary country
pursuits'.[2] The Prince was delighted to dispense with functions and
photographers and by no means averse to country pursuits – with
the emphasis on hunting and steeplechasing; but nothing was going
to make him go early to bed, or away from London if that was
where Freda Dudley Ward was to be found. In fact his freedom
from functions proved illusory; the Guildhall luncheon was only
one of many such occasions. It was also typical in that it involved
an acrimonious exchange with the King, who wanted his son to
drive to the City in cocked hat and scarlet tunic. The Prince argued
that, with fifteen thousand men still unemployed, this was the
wrong moment for a display of military pomp.[3] He carried his
point. Lloyd George was due to speak at the same occasion. Grigg
noted that his draft speech contained no reference to the King and,
knowing how sensitive things were between father and son, urged
that one be included: 'As the happiness of the Prince does depend
a great deal on keeping all well between the King and him, I feel
you will forgive this reminder.'[4]

This year at home was an unhappy one for the Prince's relationship with his father. It was tolerable in London, where they met
only occasionally, but cooped up in Balmoral or Sandringham and
cut off from Mrs Dudley Ward the Prince found the court routine
more than he could endure. 'It's all terribly irksome and it's such
a gloomy atmosphere.'[5] There was an explosion at Balmoral in
October 1921. 'I've turned Bolshie tonight,' he told Freda, 'as
H M has been the absolute limit, snubbing me and finding fault

sarcastically on every possible occasion. It really isn't fair, darling, particularly as I've been playing up to him all I can since I arrived.'[1] The Prince's doubts about the forthcoming tour of India provided an extra cause for wrangling between the two. Once the Prince threatened to ask Lloyd George whether he really felt the visit essential. 'I don't care whether the Prime Minister wants you to go or not,' retorted the King. '*I* wish you to go and you are going.'[2]

The Prince was not alone in wondering whether his visit was necessary or desirable. India was in disarray. The Montagu-Chelmsford Report, which had reiterated that the aim of the British government was to establish India as an independent democracy within the Empire, had signally failed to convince the Indian National Congress Party that British intentions were honourable. The unrest that followed led to the introduction of trial without jury for those accused of political crimes, and, in April 1919, to the massacre at Amritsar. Peaceful non-cooperation was Gandhi's formula for India's dealings with the British, but non-violence frequently led to violence, and Congress's decision to boycott the Prince's visit carried with it the threat of disorder and much personal risk for the visitor. Almost all the provincial governors, led by the experienced Lord Willingdon, concluded that the tour was unwise,[3] while from a different point of view the private secretary to the Maharaja of Dewas, E. M. Forster, felt that to the educated Indian 'this ill-omened visit does seem an impertinence. You can't solve real, complicated and ancient troubles by sending out a good-tempered boy; besides, this naive slap-on-the-back method, though the very thing for our colonies, scarcely goes down in the East.'[4] Indeed, almost the only champion of the tour was Lord Reading, who was unshakeable in his conviction that the visit would pass off well, serve British interests in India and, above all, consolidate Britain's relationship with the Indian princes. Since Reading was the Viceroy and Montagu, the Secretary of State for India, was his faithful ally, planning for the tour continued.

Montagu's original idea, indeed, had been that the functions of executive ruler and Viceroy should be divided and the Prince himself serve for a few months as Viceroy.[5] Lloyd George vetoed the idea, no doubt to the Prince's considerable relief.[6] But the project that survived seemed little better. 'How I'm loathing and hating the thought of India . . .' he told his mother. 'But as I have

135

to go, I must try and make the most of it.'[1] Till the last moment
he hoped that something would turn up to prevent the tour. 'I'm
afraid the trouble in India seems to be subsiding,' he wrote to
Freda, 'and that there isn't a chance of it stopping my going, damn
it.'[2] Against the wishes of most members of his staff, he insisted
that Louis Mountbatten should once more be in the party – 'to
look after my private and personal comfort and do small and
unimportant jobs for me,' as he explained to Godfrey Thomas.[3]
Thomas was not pleased, nor was Lord Cromer, who was to
perform in India the part played by Grigg in Australia. 'We all
deplore his inclusion in the Staff,' Cromer wrote to another colleague, Colonel Worgan. The Prince had ruled that Mountbatten
was always to have a room, however small, near his own. 'You
need have no scruples about a very literal interpretation of the
Prince's own words "however small",' instructed Cromer grimly.[4]
The real significance of the appointment lay in the light it threw
on the Prince's alienation from his regular staff. He told Grigg that
he wanted Mountbatten to come along since 'he now has *no* friends
on his own staff except perhaps Legh'. 'I gather that Halsey is no
longer a friend!!' commented Stamfordham.[5] In fact the Prince was
still close to Godfrey Thomas as well as Legh, and fond of a new
recruit, Bruce Ogilvy, but in his black mood as he prepared to
leave he could see nothing but enemies around him.

The Prince was convinced that the style which had worked so
triumphantly in Canada and Australia would serve in India as well.
If he was only allowed to be himself, then he could get through to
the people and win their hearts. He was appalled by the dense
thickets of ceremony with which the authorities seemed determined
to hedge him round. Even before he landed, he told Mrs Dudley
Ward, he was convinced 'that all the official rot and pompousness
is overdone and is quite unnecessary'. He was determined to break
it down, 'even though I'll risk getting into trouble with the officials
and powers that be'.[6] And it was not just the stuffy British officials
who were at fault; the semi-independent Indian princes were
equally out of touch with the real people, 'their ceremonies are so
irritating and ridiculous'.[7]

The King was quite as certain that the sort of informality

136

which had been so successful in the white Dominions would prove disastrous in India.[1] Stamfordham rubbed in the argument – 'I have impressed upon him the absolute necessity for a maintenance of strict dignity on all official occasions'[2] – and Cromer battled valiantly to hold the line, complaining ruefully to Wigram that 'it is not always easy to get HRH to adjust his mind as to what is suitable to certain occasions'.[3] The old brigade was not wholly wrong. The Prince's style did give offence to many British and a few Indians, some of them of real importance. But he won many more friends by his behaviour. Professor Rushbrook Williams, Director of Public Information at the time and official historian of the visit, told Frances Donaldson many years later that he 'never knew an Indian who had met HRH who was not charmed by him – he was human, informal and genuinely interested in them. Again and again I heard the remark: "If only all you Europeans were like him!" . . . Above all, he *wanted* to meet and get to know Indians.'[4]

Professor Williams gives the Prince credit for more enthusiasm towards the Indians than in fact existed. As usual it was the serving soldiers and ex-service men who most appealed to him.[5] He was quite as colour conscious as any of the British rulers of India; when Mountbatten reported a conversation with Mrs Besant in which that formidable lady revealed that the Prince was a reincarnation of Akbar, his cousin was disgruntled at the idea of having been a 'black man' in a previous life.[6] He had no doubt that the Indians and Burmese were wholly incompetent to run their own affairs and would be lost without the benevolent supervision of their colonial masters.[7]

And yet he did do his best, often in spite of the authorities, to get through to them. 'I want to know you and I want you to know me,' was a personal note that he grafted on to the formal message from the King Emperor which he delivered in Bombay. At Poona he horrified officials by walking around the stands after laying the foundation stone so that people could see him. They rose to their feet and cheered themselves hoarse.[8] In Lucknow he went to see four thousand poor being fed. 'I insisted on walking about amongst them despite the ruses of the officials and police to prevent me stopping and getting out of the car. I feel that I'm one up on them all for once!'[9] He learned enough Hindi to exchange a few words with the many thousands of military pensioners whom he inspected: 'It's worth it every time, as these Indians do appreciate it and it makes it far more interesting for me too. And it's a heart-breaking job going round these poor devils, many of them maimed and limbless, whose govt pensions are hopelessly inadequate and for whom I can do so little.'[1] And when the Indians were there and he was allowed to move among them, he could work the same magic as in Canada or Australia. At a People's Fair near Delhi he was mobbed by five or six thousand natives who surged round him, reported the military commander, General Rawlinson, 'cheering him to the echo, salaaming and almost worshipping him. He was perfectly delighted . . .'[2]

The Prince believed that the police were overdoing his protection and cutting him off from the people who were ready to acclaim him. 'Surely they can trust me not to make a BF of myself and do anything idiotic?' he enquired indignantly of Freda Dudley Ward. The police always retorted that they were doing no more than they did for the Viceroy – 'All I say is "God help the Viceroy"!!' Everyone was working loyally and diligently but, 'alas they are working in the wrong way and completely preventing this tour being of the slightest use as far as the natives are concerned, which is after all the real reason for my coming'.[3]

But it was not primarily the British authorities who thwarted his efforts to get through to the Indians; Gandhi and the Congress Party ensured that the crowds were rarely there to succumb to his blandishments. He was disappointed and dismayed when, in Allahabad, less than a thousand Indians were on the streets out of a total of 120,000 – 'we go from cold to frost,' commented Halsey.[4] He was infuriated when, at Benares, the university authorities tried to cover up for a student boycott by filling the empty seats 'with high school boys, boy scouts and Europeans; I suppose they hoped I would never get to hear . . . what a BF they had made of me'.[5] He was outraged when the Chief Commissioner of the North West Frontier Province, Sir John Maffey, took alarm at threats to assassinate the Prince and redirected his procession through the back streets of Peshawar. Convinced that everyone would believe him a coward, he returned to Government House in what Mountbatten described as 'the blackest rage I ever hope to see him in'.[6] The Prince described the incident to Mrs Dudley Ward as 'the worst thing that has happened to me in India', and blamed himself for not overruling Maffey – 'but then you know I'm not very good in a crisis, Fredie darling, and do lose my head all too easily'.[1] Maffey, in a different sense, would have lost his head if he had stuck to the original plan and the Prince had been murdered. The police can hardly be blamed for their vigilance. There was real danger; the Prince's staff knew of at least two cases in which people had been offered more than a thousand rupees to throw a bomb at the royal visitor.[2]

The Prince had no sympathy for the independence movement and blamed Edwin Montagu for fomenting it. His letters home are filled with denunciations of 'that despicable man' who had 'given in and pandered to the natives'. Naturally the Indians wanted more, 'which they can't possibly have so long as we maintain the policy of governing and running India'. The result was 'hopeless unrest' and growing support for Gandhi: 'It's all very disgusting and very depressing.'[3] He rejoiced when Gandhi was arrested and Montagu resigned, but feared it was too late. Montagu's reforms had so far changed the atmosphere in India that 'most Englishmen of Indian experience are dissuading their sons or any good fellow from coming out'. As a result the standards in the Indian Civil Service were slipping, 'and, as you know, the natives are the quickest to size up a white man and can always recognize a gent, or anyway a "nature's gent" which is even better'.[4] Given what he saw as the incipient collapse of British rule in India, he felt that his own presence was a mere palliative, as irrelevant as applying a piece of sticking plaster to a gaping and mortal wound. His visit was unwanted by the Indians and of doubtful value to the British. His speeches, which were written for him by a member of the Indian Civil Service attached to his staff, struck Piers Legh as 'really lamentable . . . claptrap of the worst description'.[5] The Prince read them conscientiously but loathed them. The men who composed them, he considered, were 'bureaucratic and behind the times. They can't help it, poor brutes, as the Indian Govt is the same.'[6]

By mid-December he was in such despair that he contemplated abandoning the tour. He wrote to the Viceroy, bemoaning the fact that he was achieving nothing, meeting almost no Indians, strengthening support for the independence movement rather than diminishing it, causing the expenditure of vast sums of money to no good end.[1] The letter exudes pessimism, but his true frame of mind is portrayed more vividly in the letter he wrote to Freda Dudley Ward a few days later:

> My beloved, I couldn't be more gloomy or depressed than I am tonight, and I'm oh! so desperately sad and lonely and missing and oh! wanting you and wanting oh! so badly my precious little Fredie!! I naturally want you most when I'm up against it all as I am now, sweetheart, as I do love you love you so, and although I loathe Xmas as a festival, yet it does somehow suggest happiness, and it's so ironical everyone wishing me a happy Xmas . . . Surely they must know that I can't possibly *ever* be in the teeniest way happy when I'm away from my Fredie?[2]

This was his blackest moment of the tour. Reading's robust reassurance that the visit was of immense importance and was 'doing real good – infinitely more than you think',[3] came at a moment when the crowds had been responding more enthusiastically and the Prince's morale was in some measure restored. The Viceroy reported in February that the Prince 'really does feel that his trip has done and is going good'.[4] He overstated his case. The Prince really did feel, and continued to feel, that the trip had been, on the whole, a futile enterprise. But he was ready to accept that *some* Indians had been favourably impressed, *some* British heartened. He even began to feel a modest measure of pride in his achievements.

As in Australia, physical exhaustion contributed to his depression. He slept badly during the interminable journeys by train, stayed up too late, ate too little, drank and smoked too much, as always overdid the exercise. 'HRH's present method of life,' reported his doctor, 'is such as may involve a complete breakdown of his whole nervous system.'[5] One trouble was that, deprived of Freda Dudley Ward's companionship, he got very little fun out of the tour. Confronted by the great archaeological finds at Taxila, he remarked gloomily to Lady Birdwood: 'This place ought never to have been dug up.'[6] The famous Buddha's tooth at Kandy in Ceylon 'isn't a tooth at all, merely a sordid, dirty piece of bone. Then there was a ghastly procession of elephants which included native dancing and hideous noises, which was really native music.'[7]

Almost the only exception was the Taj Mahal. After the statutory visit by moonlight he told Queen Mary that it had 'gripped me and I shall never forget what I've seen tonight'. He even paid a second visit – 'a contingency,' Thomas remarked, 'against which I should have betted heavily'.[1]

'One of the tragic things about this Tour,' wrote Lord Cromer, 'is that HRH is not really keen on big-game shooting or shooting of any kind.'[2] Tragic is perhaps too strong a word, but to the Indian princes, who invested shooting with an almost mystic significance, the Prince's indifference seemed inexplicable. In Nepal fortunes were squandered in setting up a big-game camp; the Prince preferred to wander around with a shotgun looking for jungle fowl, or better still, to exercise his polo pony in a nearby clearing. It was a great disappointment to the Maharaja, Piers Legh told his father. It was a great disappointment to Legh too. 'Everything is sacrificed to polo, which the Prince is mad about,' he wrote resentfully. 'We consequently don't get as much shooting as we should.'[3] Polo, pig-sticking and steeplechasing were indeed the Prince's greatest pleasures in India. Yet even on the polo ground he could not escape from his role: in Jodhpur the young players had been told to treat him gently and only on his insistence did they relax and ride roughly against him; in Mandalay his team won a competition, 'though it's become such a farce this cup business as somehow it's always arranged that I should win . . . and I do loathe it!!'[4]

His morale was not improved by periodic carping from Buckingham Palace. George V was disconcerted to see photographs of the Prince wearing blue overalls with white tunic – 'A most extraordinarily ugly uniform . . . The regulations ought never to have been altered without my approval.'[5] He felt 'little short of despair' when he read that, at Lucknow, the Prince had taken over the drums in the band playing at a dance at Government House – 'What will the natives think of the Heir Apparent assuming such a role?' asked a shocked Lord Stamfordham.[6] The band was playing in a gallery, invisible to the dancers, answered Cromer. The journalist who reported the news had been grossly indiscreet. 'I have spoken to HRH about this and he quite understands the point.'[7]

'The whole crux is whether the Prince of Wales makes the

Indians feel he *likes* them,' Lord Riddell told Cromer. 'They are extraordinarily sensitive and they know intuitively, past belief.'[1] The Prince did not like them; least of all did he like those to whom he came closest, the Indian rulers. He disapproved of the pomposity and lavishness of their way of life; their propensity to ape all the most unattractive features of European civilization; their determination to ingratiate themselves with the son of the King Emperor. In Nepal tigers were paraded before him so that it was almost impossible for him to miss them; in Mysore the Maharaja let him win at squash. After this last offence he raged vengefully against those ignoble potentates and cannot have left the Maharaja himself in much doubt about his feelings.[2]

Since the Prince at the time was suffering from insomnia, indigestion and what he described as 'smoker's heart', his bile is perhaps explicable. His staff should have been able to jolly him out of such excesses. Unfortunately only Mountbatten was close enough to him to understand his moods, and Mountbatten was preoccupied with his own courtship of Edwina Ashley. The Prince luxuriated in his sense of isolation. His staff, he told Freda Dudley Ward, was 'the finest ground possible for foul and bloody gossip and scandal!! . . . They do their utmost to make life hell for me instead of helping me.'[3] Before the tour was over Halsey offered his resignation on the grounds that he felt he had lost the Prince's confidence. 'How right he is, isn't he, my precious angel, though I said it was all rot . . . He knows better now than to say a word to me about TOI or anything private as he knows I would fire him on the spot.'[4] Already the Prince's reluctance to allow even the most trusted members of his staff to talk to him about what he considered his private life was becoming more marked. Godfrey Thomas no longer dared speak with the freedom he had enjoyed in the past, Claud Hamilton was to lose his job when he trespassed on forbidden territory. The Prince's attitude, strengthened to the point of paranoia, was to make it impossible for those who worked for him to do their duty properly in the years before the abdication.

His alienation from his regular staff became more complete when Captain Edward 'Fruity' Metcalfe was recruited to look after the Prince's polo and other equine diversions. Metcalfe was charming and impecunious; an Irishman who had won a good MC in the war and held important posts in three princely states. He was 'very nice and irresponsible', Thomas told the Queen.[1] Halsey was still more censorious: 'Metcalfe is not *at all* a good thing for HRH,' he wrote. 'He is an excellent fellow, always cheery and full of fun, but far, far too weak and hopelessly irresponsible. He is a *wild, wild* Irishman and' – crowning horror – 'no one knows anything about his family.'[2] The Prince was seduced by his charm, his friendliness and his endearing habit of treating his new employer as an ordinary human being: 'He always referred to me as "The Little Man". People were sometimes shocked by the familiarity of his attitude towards me.'[3] He became the nearest approach the Prince ever had to an intimate male friend. 'Honestly, and you must know it by now,' the Prince wrote to him a year or so after they first met, 'I miss you terribly when you are away, and . . . I'm ever so grateful to you for being the marvellous friend to me you always have been.'[4] Against his dulcet blandishments the stern voice of duty as enunciated by Halsey or Thomas seemed still less appealing. His coming placed a barrier between the Prince and those who should have been closest to him.

This catalogue of lamentations may make it sound as if the tour of India had been a total disaster. This would not be true. In the first port of call, Bombay, he achieved something close to triumph. The Viceroy rhapsodized about his 'wonderful success'. 'It represents solid truth,' he told Montagu, 'when I tell you that the Prince did receive a splendid reception . . . and by his unaffected manner and simple heartiness and friendliness to the people, won his way right into their hearts.'[5] The Governor, Sir George Lloyd, told Cromer that the success was due 'entirely to the chief actor, whose personality is amazing and whose gift of keen appreciation of every situation in a flash, of the perfect word to say and the perfect way to say it in, struck me tremendously'.[6] Even the Prince, always first to doubt his own capabilities, told Freda Dudley Ward that he would have been driven mad by the tedium of the official receptions 'except for the fact that I am having a real success here, my beloved, and I think I've managed to *get* these natives'.[7]

Gandhi's campaign ensured that he was not usually so successful, but the Congress Party did not achieve as much as it had hoped. In Delhi, in particular, all went well for the visitor. 'I feel as if I had lived a life time these last two days,' Lady Reading told her family. 'Such processing of troops, booming of guns, Royal salutes

. . . acres of red carpet, hundreds of scarlet coats, thousands of decorations.' The Vicereine did not realize it, but she was describing everything her visitor most disliked. Still, 'the Prince was splendid and played up nobly'.[1] By this stage in the tour, Reading believed that the Prince was much more satisfied with his visit and taking a real interest in India. 'I . . . am glad to find that he is willing to take trouble to understand the difficulties of the situation here. He has, undoubtedly, shrewd perceptions and is not misled by the outward glamour . . .'[2] He was not misled, either, by the Viceroy's accomplished line in flattery. Proposing the royal visitor's health at a banquet in Delhi, Reading ascribed every conceivable virtue to the Prince and spoke of the tour as if it had transformed the future of India. 'You just can't think how much that man has deteriorated,' commented the Prince.[3]

Yet the Viceroy was not just being sycophantic. It was no smooth-tongued statesman, but the police officer attached to the Prince, Mr Stead, who said that he had at first been opposed to the tour but by the time it had finished he was convinced he had been wrong. 'It had gone infinitely better than he had thought possible, and . . . the good that it had done was incalculable.'[4] A question was put down in the House of Commons suggesting that the Prince should have conferred on him the title of 'Prince of India'. The King opposed the idea and it was dropped.[5] If he had not done so, his son would have proved even more reluctant. But the idea was not altogether foolish.

The rest of the trip, though longer than the Prince wished, was less taxing. For one thing, he did not have to cope with a hostile independence movement; for another, he was on the way home. He had badly wanted to visit China. 'It does seem very hard,' he told the King, 'that when one has come all this long way to the Far East . . . I shouldn't be able to go to Pekin, Shanghai, and other places of interest, all *far* more interesting than Japan, and the Chinks are much nicer people too.'[6] The Foreign Secretary, Curzon, vetoed the idea however, and the Prince got no nearer than Hong Kong.

His determination not to find Japan interesting lasted throughout his stay there. The Ambassador, Sir Charles Eliot, noted with regret that he showed no curiosity in the institutions or government of the country and seemed bored by any discussion of the issues of the moment – 'I think that really he was mentally fatigued and that his mind and nerves had not recovered from the strain of his journey in India.'[1] Eliot also realized how dull everything must appear on a royal tour: 'Princes must think that red carpets and flags are a kind of vegetation that grows everywhere like grass or trees. It certainly makes all places look the same, and the welcome organized by the police was also monotonous.'[2] But even allowing for the bland and homogenized aspect of the country which was offered him – royalty's equivalent of the tourist proceeding from Hilton Hotel to Hilton Hotel – the Prince does seem to have been over-ready to transmute Japanese gold to lead. Even the famed scenery he despised: 'I don't take much interest in it at any time and none at all sans TOI,' he told Freda Dudley Ward, 'and having been to Lake Louise and the Canadian Rockies with Scotland thrown in, I can't ever hope to see anything better.'[3]

His indifference to the charms of Japan did not blind him to the fact that the Japanese were 'a very great power in the World and their navy and their infantry is amazingly efficient'.[4] He told the King that the Japanese navy was copied from the British, the army from the Germans and the press from the Americans. 'And how wise they are from the viewpoint of a young nation, which can *never* hope to emulate ourselves, but who are rapidly, if they haven't done it already, coming up to the level of a continental power!! And I should add the Yanks!!'[5]

This greatness, he considered, had been achieved in spite of rather than because of the imperial family. The Prince surveyed his hosts with bilious disapproval. The Emperor he never met, since he was insane and confined to his palace; with the Empress conversation was conducted through an interpreter and confined exclusively to the weather and the cherry blossom.[6] In the absence of the Emperor, he was entertained most frequently by the young Prince Regent, Hirohito, who would try to talk French though he had no understanding of the language. The journalists tried to depict the two young princes as bosom friends but Eliot reported 'the idea that he felt any real friendship for the Prince Regent is a pure myth, though perhaps the latter felt a sort of timid affection for him'.[7]

145

'My God, one has to be careful what one says unless one can be *quite quite* sure one is alone,' the Prince told Freda Dudley Ward.[1] He managed generally to keep his feelings under control. He 'got on excellent terms with all those with whom he could converse,' wrote Thomas, 'and generally gave the impression that Tokyo was the one place he had set out from England to see'.[2] Eliot clearly felt him hypercritical, yet admitted 'he never failed in charm and courtesy when brought face to face with any Japanese'.[3] He was equally successful with the press. Incensed by the plethora of restrictions imposed upon them by the Japanese authorities, the journalists accompanying the tour decided in future to boycott it. The Prince called them together and talked them round. One correspondent who had been most active in advocating a press boycott 'rose and said that after hearing HRH's remarks he had entirely changed his views. He was now in favour of giving a full and favourable account of the Prince's doings.'[4]

The Japanese courtiers were much struck by the way the Prince mixed informally with mere commoners. There was debate as to whether Hirohito should do the same and tremendous excitement was caused when the Prince Regent was observed personally to thank the landlord of the hotel where the Prince of Wales was staying at Hakone. So very condescending a gesture was unprecedented in the history of the imperial family. Eliot noted how the Prince's presence breathed life into the atrophied court, 'even the Empress became slightly skittish'.[5]

Informality could, however, become indiscretion. The Prince forgot his own remarks about the keen hearing of the Japanese, and though he kept his opinion of his hosts to himself, he aired his views on other subjects with disconcerting freedom. Lord Reading, he told Eliot, was clever but not at all the man to be Viceroy. Aware of the attentiveness of those around him, the Ambassador had to beg the Prince to remember that many Japanese spoke English.[6] He was apt too to change plans at the last moment or cancel expeditions for which elaborate and expensive arrangements had been made. When called to order by the senior members of his staff he would be penitent for a while, but soon transgressed again. Eliot remembered one occasion aboard *Renown* when he and Halsey together tried to persuade the Prince to mend his ways. 'HRH was sitting in a large high-backed chair close to the wall and as the sermon proceeded gradually wriggled upwards until he squatted on the top of the back and from that elevation regarded his two elderly monitors with a most impish and incredulous smile.'[1]

Eliot and Halsey might note his imperfections, a few of his hosts might have suffered from his whims and unpunctuality, but to the vast majority of the Japanese who encountered him or followed his doings he seemed little short of perfection. Piers Legh told his father that the Prince had 'made as great an impression here as he had ever done before. His reception everywhere has been nothing short of marvellous, and he has apparently completely captured the country by storm. People who live here say they have never seen anything to compare with it. I know it is going to do an enormous amount of good here.'[2] In spite of his reservations about some aspects of the Prince's behaviour, Sir Charles Eliot would not have dissented from that opinion.

And so it was home again at last. 'How splendidly HRH has done – a true Ambassador of Empire,' Sir Reginald Wingate wrote to Cromer. 'I do hope the Public will now let him take a rest and holiday from these endless functions which must be terribly wearing.'[3]

9

'The Ambassador of Empire'

THE PRINCE OF WALES GOT BACK FROM THE FAR East in July 1922. It was not until April 1925 that he completed his imperial tours with a visit to South Africa. Between those dates, however, he twice visited Canada and once the United States. The second of those two voyages was to prove something of a turning point in his life.

'I always feel that I have a right to call myself a Canadian because I am, in a small way, a rancher,' he told the Canadian Club at the end of 1922.[1] To the Prince the ranch was more than just a plaything, as her dairy was to Marie Antoinette; it was the only piece of land which he actually owned himself and it represented reality in a world which he found increasingly artificial. He corresponded regularly with the ranch manager, took an intelligent interest in the building up of the stock and prided himself in particular on the excellence of his shorthorns. When he visited Canada in the autumn of 1923 it was above all to inspect his ranch and spend some weeks there.

He could not escape without some junketing in the great cities. 'The Prince gets here on Tuesday,' Ernest Hemingway told Ezra Pound from Toronto. 'Prince Charming, the Ambassador of Empire, the fair haired bugger.'[2] There was an awful sameness about the ceremonies, so much so that when a provincial mayor lost a page of his speech and yammered helplessly after: 'Not only do we welcome Your Royal Highness as the representative of His Majesty the King, but we . . .', the Prince obligingly completed the hallowed phrase, 'also welcome you for yourself'.[3] But some events were unscripted. In Quebec he danced all night with an attractive woman, only to discover next morning that she was a journalist from New York. 'I was had for a mug,' he told Freda Dudley Ward, 'but she was quite nice about it and said she wouldn't say too much despite the fact that she had got off with me. I think she's a sport.'[1] She was, but the Prince was to discover a year later that not all journalists were equally sporting.

There were no journalists on the ranch, and the general public, or what little there was of it in rural Alberta, left the Prince in peace. He threw himself with zest into his role as rancher, riding around the fences of his four thousand acres, inspecting the stock, ordering new equipment. 'I've even helped to muck out the cow house,' he told the King, 'and I chop and saw up wood and I can assure you that it's very hard work indeed.'[2] His staff were delighted to see him so contented and harmlessly employed, though less enthusiastic about the nature of their occupations – 'Our conversation is largely of sheep-dips, shorthorns and stallions,' Godfrey Thomas reported gloomily.[3] Nor did the Prince pretend that it *was* more than a temporary role: 'It's a fine healthy life and a real rest for the brain . . . But of course one couldn't stick it for very long.'[4]

It had been an honour and a joy to entertain him, wrote the Governor General, Lord Byng of Vimy, and the thought that the Prince planned to come again the following year filled him 'with the pleasantest anticipations'.[5] He might have revised his views a year later. In mid-1924 the Prince announced he would visit his ranch again in the autumn, stopping in New York for a few days to watch the international polo. In the event he spent nearly three weeks in New York and less than a week on the ranch. The King had originally wanted Halsey to go on the tour, but the Prince insisted that on a holiday of this kind the Admiral would be superfluous.[6] He told his mother that Halsey's illness prevented him joining the tour, but the Admiral assured the King that he was perfectly fit. 'What a pity the dear boy should invent a story like that simply because he didn't want to take him and tell you a regular untruth,' the King commented to Queen Mary.[7] Instead, the Prince was accompanied by Metcalfe and a new recruit to the household, Brigadier G. F. Trotter, known to everyone as 'G'. Trotter was 'a wonderful friend and so understanding and sound too', the Prince told Godfrey Thomas. 'Thank God I didn't bring the Admiral. He would have sent me dippy on the voyage, let alone in the States.'[8] 'Sound' was the last word to describe Trotter. He was, said Bruce Ogilvy, 'a right old rip', an amiable roué whose function was to facilitate the Prince's pursuit of pleasure.[9] Everybody liked him; nobody, except perhaps the Prince, trusted him.

149

He and Metcalfe together acted as siren voices leading their master on to ever more perilous rocks. The only voice in the party suggesting that the Prince would do well to plug his ears to their dulcet chorus, or at least bind himself to the mast, was that of the assistant private secretary, Alan 'Tommy' Lascelles – and Lascelles, as the British Ambassador, Esmé Howard, told the King, was 'excellent in every way but ... too young to have any great authority'.[1]

Long before the visit began there had been suggestions that all would not go easily. Having set up the Prince as an immaculate hero in 1919, the American press was more than ready to redress the balance. In the intervening years the papers had been filled with gossip, linking his name with various women of the *demi-monde* and, more convincingly, with Mrs Dudley Ward. 'Quite regardless of the looseness of its own sexual standards,' wrote the British Ambassador to Curzon in 1922, 'this country loves to be shocked and pained by what it is pleased to regard as the peculiar licentiousness of Princes, and the Prince was so successful on his visit here that he has naturally made our enemies desirous of showing that he is not what he was thought to be.' In 1919 society women had gushed about the Prince as a 'charming boy', now he had sunk, or perhaps graduated, to the status of 'a gay young man'.[2] Some at least of the journalists who accompanied him when he sailed to New York in the *Berengaria* seemed intent on reducing him yet further to 'reckless libertine'. 'These Yank pressmen are b—s,' the Prince told Thomas. '... one does resent their d—d spying so and they get so tight!! It seems a mean shame having them around when one is on a holiday trip.'[3]

Unfortunately he gave them plenty of material to work with; beginning with his departure, when he boarded the liner at 2.30 a.m. and kept everybody up awaiting him: 'a most undignified proceeding,' the King dubbed it, 'and then refusing to come on deck or see anyone until she sailed, although thousands of people had come to the docks to see him off, was very rude.'[4] Once arrived, he took up residence in the palatial home of Mr James Burden and settled down to divert himself in the intervals of watching polo. There was no shortage of hostesses eager to oblige him; his visit, wrote the columnist Cholly Knickerbocker, became an endurance test, 'with the bank balances of the refulgent chieftains of the Long Island set pitted against His Royal Highness's health . . . Never before in the history of metropolitan society has any visitor to these shores been so persistently and so extravagantly fêted.'[1] Over-excited newspaper reports did more than justice to the Prince's train of life and were forwarded to Buckingham Palace for gloomy perusal.

Nor was it only journalists. An English businessman, unnamed but described by the Prime Minister's private secretary as 'an important source in America', wrote to Downing Street to complain that Metcalfe had arranged for the Prince to be entertained by 'social outcasts and parvenus' like Cosden, the oil speculator, and Fleishman, the yeast king. He had insulted one eminent hostess by asking that the Dolly Sisters – 'notorious little Jewish actresses who have never been received anywhere' – should be invited to a ball given in his honour, and by failing to attend himself when his request was refused. Twice he had been so drunk in public that he had had to be taken home. The impression he gave 'was that of a desperately unhappy, wilful, dissipated boy without much brain, who could be very charming when he chose, but who was always seeking to avoid the duties of his position'.[2] The businessman was probably Frederick Cunliffe-Owen, who wrote in very similar terms to Lord Stamfordham and was described by the British Ambassador as 'a tiresome busy-body who cuts no ice'.[3] Thomas was shown his letter and replied in fury that it was 'a tissue of malicious and probably deliberate falsehoods'. Metcalfe had made no arrangements for the visit; the Prince had hardly met Fleishman; he had only made a brief appearance at Cosden's dance because Mountbatten and the organizer of the British polo team, Lord Wimborne, had asked him to; he had not even known the Dolly Sisters were in New York. The writer of the letter had clearly been affronted because he had himself not been invited to some party.[4]

Certainly the charges were grossly exaggerated, but the Prince's hectic hedonism caused some concern to Tommy Lascelles.

[Troubles are beginning,] he told Thomas we hadn't been in the house two hours before a new comet blazed across our sky and Honey's wagon was firmly hitched to it. Since then we haven't seen much of him. The comet, unluckily, is not in the best Long Island constellation; the lorgnettes of the other

151

stars are already fixed on its activities with strong disapproval, and it is of course only a question of time for the telescopes of Hearst to pick it up . . .

How do you, I wonder, fight against the influence of comets on these occasions? I feel quite powerless. As you know, I've always kept as far away as possible from that side of his life, which is certainly no concern of a private secy *pur et simple*, and only happens to be your concern because, apart from being a p.s., you are also a close friend and adviser of many years standing. But there must come moments . . . when the private pursuits of comets mess up the ordinary public highway which it is quite definitely the business of the private secy to keep straight and tidy.[1]

There is no evidence that the Hearst press detected this particular comet, but they made merry with the misfortunes of Metcalfe, who contrived to leave his wallet, containing several letters from the Prince, in the flat of a New York prostitute. 'Damned old fool,' commented Lascelles, 'but it is impossible to be really angry with him, and tho the incident might do the Prince very serious harm, we have all rocked with laughter over it.'[2] Though nobody tried to involve the Prince directly, his name was inevitably linked with the resultant scandal – 'Hard on me,' he wrote wistfully to Thomas, ''cos I was on my best behaviour all the time and avoided the demi-monde like the plague till it became boring.'[3] The press did full justice too to the Prince's decidedly lax church attendance; journalists who had probably themselves not been to a service for years wagged their heads sadly over this delinquency. The whole visit, concluded Stamfordham, 'has been characterized as one continuous form of recreation and amusement, not altogether devoid of frivolity and with a certain lack of dignity'.[4]

The Prince would not have rebutted the charges too vigorously; he enjoyed frivolity and attached little weight to dignity. He could justifiably have complained that Stamfordham and the King concentrated on the few bad press reports and ignored the more numerous good ones. Colonel Oscar Solbert, the White House aide attached to the party to help over liaison with the newspapers, concluded that: 'The general press, particularly outside of New York City, was extremely pro-Prince and was based largely upon the human interest of a young man of his position who was so democratic, so unaffected and so humanly spontaneous.' The Prince, he believed, had a hold upon public opinion such as 'no other person has either in or out of our country today'.[1] The Prince told his father that the American press worked on different lines to the British and that their sensational stories were forgotten by the following day. 'The newspaper men hunted me a good deal the first week,' he wrote, 'but after that only at intervals and the press was never very nasty and if they were a bit indiscreet sometimes it was more in the nature of ragging me than anything else – they rag everybody, particularly a prince.'[2]

Things went better after an informal tea party was arranged for seven or eight of the leading editors. Tommy Lascelles admitted that he had been 'in a muck sweat, feeling rather like Guy Faux', before the party started, but it had been a 'howling success'. 'It was amusing to see how every one of them, even the two Hearst editors, succumbed to him completely after 5 minutes talk.'[3] Thenceforward the press said relatively little about his nocturnal revelries and gave reasonable, if at times slightly sardonic, coverage to the items of 'serious' sightseeing which the Prince fitted in towards the end of his visit – the offices of the New York Times, a telephone exchange, a school, the Museum of Natural History. More daringly he visited Chicago, where the huge German and Irish colonies were expected to ensure a hostile reception – 'I have never seen a more hearty welcome given to the Prince in any one of the various big towns in England to which I have been with him,' Lascelles told Queen Mary. 'During the whole day, I never saw or heard a single sign of unfriendliness.'[4]

Though the King and Queen grumbled at the publicity given to their son's activities – they were, said Stamfordham, 'to say the least of it concerned'[5] – they were on the whole restrained in their letters to the Prince. Queen Mary permitted herself one barb: 'So after all you are only spending a week on your Ranch, what a pity when I thought that was the raison d'être for your going out.'[6] The stay at the ranch was in fact something of a disaster. The party arrived under leaden skies with sleet beating against the cars to find the fires smoking and the one living room uninhabitable.[7] Next day the sun came out and the spirits of most of the party rose, but not those of the Prince. 'I had the flu and fever the whole time,'[1] he told Thomas, and he remained resolutely gloomy until the time came to move on to Vancouver. There he and General Trotter restored themselves by staying out every night until 6 a.m. The Prince's behaviour, though perhaps lacking the gravitas desired by his father, was impeccable compared with that of the Lieutenant-Governor, who at the end of a ball at Government House announced to his guest of honour that he was 'as full as a bloody goat' and then tumbled flat on his face, destroying a china vessel in his fall.[2]

The Prince stayed at Ottawa on the return journey. Mackenzie King's diary describes a row between the Prince and the Governor General, Byng. The Prince was said to have compromised himself with a married woman at a ball in Byng's residence, Rideau Hall. Next night he announced that he was going to dance at the Country Club. Byng insisted he must come back when the dance ended and not visit any private house. Instead, he went to the home of his new conquest and did not return until breakfast. Furious, Byng said he should never visit Canada again so long as he was Governor General.[3] The story is not substantiated by any reference in George V's papers, even though John Buchan, future Lord Tweedsmuir, was apparently deputed to take the news to Buckingham Palace. Nor did Lascelles refer to the incident, although he wrote an otherwise singularly communicative letter to Legh the day after the dance at the Country Club.[4] The Prince could anyway not have visited Canada again before Byng's retirement in 1926, but when this took place the two men exchanged almost fulsomely friendly letters. Mackenzie King would hardly have made up his conversation with Byng, nor Byng himself been guilty of invention, but it is at least possible that more was made of the affair than it deserved. The King was quite concerned enough without additional causes. He studied a programme of the Canadian visit and gloomily underlined all the dances. 'Not very wise to go ball dancing on *Sunday*,' he wrote in a minute to Stamfordham.[5]

'Of course, New York was his undoing,' was the judgment of Gray Phillips, who was later to be very close to the Prince.[6] This seems to be a considerable overstatement. Tommy Lascelles, who was to become one of the Prince's sternest critics, wrote enthusiastically when the party reached Winnipeg that the Prince was 'the most wonderful travelling companion and we have the greatest fun together. And I am finding out that he is a much bigger character than I ever expected. From the idiotic Press dope that has appeared during the last 3 weeks you might think that he had done nothing but jazz and ride and flirt . . . Don't believe it. He certainly enjoyed himself to the top of his bent, sat up late, and did everything with that super-energy which is merely natural to him . . . though any hint that he did anything whatever . . . of which he need be the least ashamed, is utterly false.' He had, concluded Lascelles, 'in his own little way, done as much good to the Brit. Emp. as the Baldwin debt-settlement'.[1] The statesman and historian, H. A. L. Fisher, was still more emphatic; the Prince of Wales, he maintained, had proved to the American people 'that a Monarchy is compatible with a democratic State and that the heir to the Monarchy can be as democratic as anyone. I am convinced that this is a great gain.'[2] Even the British Ambassador, who had criticized several aspects of the Prince's conduct, concluded that it was nonsense to say lasting damage had been done. The impression left, he said, was that the Prince was 'a kindly, simple, unaffected good fellow and a "good sport" – not perhaps over-serious – but then the "people" do not love a "highbrow"'.[3] Some even found him serious. Given the role *The Times* was to play ten years later, it is interesting to find that the man with whom the Prince 'talked American and English politics vehemently till midnight' on the return journey across the Atlantic was that journal's recently reappointed editor, Geoffrey Dawson.[4]

The importance of the 1924 visit to America was not, as Cunliffe-Owen and a few others suggested, that it demonstrated the Prince's licentiousness or irresponsibility. What it did demonstrate, however, was the existence of an irreconcilable difference between the Prince and his advisers, which was to prove ever more significant over the next decade. The Prince believed that he had a right to a private life; that what he did with it was his own affair; that if he performed his public duties properly, no one had any business to complain about the rest. His advisers held that there was no such thing as a private life for the heir to the throne, or that if there were it had to be conducted in such cloistered secrecy as to be invisible to the general public. Whenever he could be seen, he was on duty. It was a hard doctrine, and it was one the Prince of Wales was never to accept.

*

155

In January 1925 Princess Alice, Countess of Athlone, wife of the Governor General of South Africa, Queen Mary's sister-in-law, and herself a granddaughter of Queen Victoria, wrote to the Queen to pass on some compliments she had heard about the Prince in America. She was sure they would be welcome, she said, 'because I know how disappointed you were at the time. I hope David will enjoy his time out here, tho' the programme seems to me a very exhausting one, and he will not find any amusement socially I fear.'[1] The Prince of Wales's visit to South Africa had originally been planned for 1924 but was deferred because of a general election. The pro-British government of General Smuts was defeated by General Hertzog's Nationalists, and there were doubts about how well the new rulers, the core of whose support consisted of intransigent Boer farmers, would receive their royal visitor. The Prince's brief was to do what he could to raise the morale of the British element of the population, and, still more important, to reconcile English and Afrikaner, with the Crown as a symbol of South African unity.

The Prince had wanted Metcalfe to accompany him, but was talked out of the idea. With Trotter also absent and Halsey back in charge there was a more businesslike air about the party than had been the case with the recent North American visits. The Prince was on duty and showed his recognition of the fact by inspecting the engine rooms of HMS *Repulse* three times on the way out, always choosing a particularly hot day and lingering lengthily in the less salubrious compartments.[2] Halsey reported that he was keeping himself very much to himself and complaining of being bored, but that he was 'in better spirits than I have ever known before when leaving on a tour, and he really has been absolutely splendid'.[3]

There were calls on The Gambia, the Gold Coast and Nigeria on the way south, though the last had to be curtailed because of plague. In The Gambia he caused some confusion by the simplicity of his dress; 'He no wear feather in for him hat,' complained one local, comparing him unfavourably with the Governor General.[4] The chronicles of those deputed to report the tour abound in such picturesque saws – some genuine, others no doubt conceived in the fertile minds of authors anxious to make their books more entertaining: 'I lookum proper. He catch young face, old eyes,' was a remark ascribed to a Nigerian soldier, while an up-country chieftain contributed: 'A fine boy too much. He open his face plenty to us. He make fine palaver.'[1] The heat was appalling, the humidity gross, everyone except the Prince had violent diarrhoea: 'HRH has seen all there is to be seen, and done all he can do, and done it jolly well,' wrote Halsey. 'He has been in the most marvellous form . . . just like he used to be in the old days.'[2]

He carried on as he had begun. As if to emphasize that when he had a job of work to do he would do it to the best of his ability, he gave even the most censorious journalist no cause to find fault on the South African tour. His finest hour came forty-eight hours after his arrival in Cape Town, when he spoke at a dinner for both Houses of Parliament. His speech followed predictable lines – the throne, he stressed, stood for 'a heritage of common aims and ideals shared equally by all sections, parties and nations within that Empire'; unity for the common good was the heart of his message.[3] It was drafted by Thomas and Bede Clifford, Athlone's political secretary, but the Prince had worked over it himself: 'It was characteristic of his sure appreciation of public sentiment,' wrote Clifford, 'that when the speech appeared in the Press next day the headlines and many of the sub-headings were made up from the passages HRH had personally composed.'[4] But to his audience the most sensational element of his speech was the fact that he concluded with a few sentences in Afrikaans. In South Africa in 1925 it was almost unheard of for an Englishman to speak a word of Afrikaans. His effort did more to convince the Dutch that he was *their* Prince as well than would have been achieved by any number of pious platitudes. His words 'brought the house down', reported Thomas, 'and after the actual dinner broke up he was taken charge of by a body of the younger Nationalist members, who sang old Dutch folksongs, and the evening ended with members of Parliament chatting together, who owing to party bitterness had not spoken to one another for years'.[5] The younger Nationalists might have been less enthusiastic if they had read the Prince's letter to his mother, in which he described their language as 'a patois composed of Dutch, English and Malay, and such bad Dutch that Afrikaans is barely understood in Holland. Of course it's a farce and no use commercially . . . and they'll get over it.'[6]

After this performance, the word went out throughout the Union that the Prince was a good fellow who deserved a warm reception. 'The Boers like me to ride into their towns at the head of their commandos, for which performance they generally provide a monstrous stallion with flowing mane and tail,' the Prince told Lascelles. 'You would laugh if you could see me.'[1] At Bloemfontein he rode in at the head of a commando two thousand strong, alongside 'General' Conroy, who had fought for the Boers and in the rebellion during the First World War.[2] That same day he visited the memorial to the 27,000 Boer women and children who died during the Boer War: 'A very bitter reminder really that English and Dutch cannot and will not ever hit it off out here . . . I do believe that my official tour is helping a bit to tone down this racial feeling, and I'm making a dead set at the Dutch to get in with them.'[3] Nobody of any sense, least of all the Prince, imagined that the bitter prejudices of generations could be expunged overnight, but as Godfrey Thomas remarked, 'they *have* discovered one thing, that they and the British section . . . were able to sit on the same platform with a common object – welcoming the P of Wales – and it is a long time since they have done that'.[4]

It was an uphill struggle, for the Prince privately considered the Boers 'a sticky, slow, dull, narrow-minded and unattractive race'.[5] It was noteworthy how he was preoccupied solely by the relationship between the two white races; the rights of the blacks scarcely occurred to him, or indeed to anybody else in public life. The Prince was racially prejudiced, probably even beyond the norm for his generation. In Sierra Leone, on the journey out, he was disconcerted to find black guests at a dance – 'tho' I've flatly refused to dance with black women! That's too much!!' In the cathedral next day he was still more upset to receive the sacrament from a black priest; for a moment he hesitated, but then decided, as he told his mother, that he 'couldn't very well hurry back from the altar at the last moment'.[6] In South Africa Bantu, Coloureds, Indians, Malays gave him a tumultuous welcome, and he was touched by it, but he could not conceive the crowds as composed of individuals to whom he could relate. At the best, they seemed picturesque, or perhaps figures of fun, as when Chief Khama at Serowe paraded an army dressed in discarded British uniforms including those of Field Marshals and Admirals of the Fleet: 'The

Prince of Wales,' wrote Clifford, 'was probably the first and only British King who will ever be able to boast of being conducted to the Kgotla (native parliament) by a mounted escort wearing kilts.'[1] On the one occasion when he delivered a major speech to a black audience – of Zulus and Xhosas at King William's Town – he warned them solemnly against any tendency to mistrust those in authority.[2]

It was 'the most heart-breaking, the most soul-less programme I have ever undertaken', Thomas told the Queen. The Prince had 'worked like a slave'.[3] Dudley North, another veteran of earlier tours, complained that there was no fun to be had: 'It is all work and very uninteresting work at that. The dances and evening entertainments so far have been dreadful. There simply isn't a nice-looking woman in the whole of the Union.'[4] To a dog-breeder friend, Millicent Howard, the Prince bemoaned the amount of travel between the various appointments. The tour was 'more boring and monotonous than strenuous, and I prefer the latter 'cos it keeps you going better'.[5] (In the same letter he wrote wistfully: 'I wish I knew something about Alsacians [sic]. One of my many troubles in life is that I don't know a thing about anything! I have to be so very promiscuous in my interests.') There was too little polo, too little golf, too little dancing. When offered bowls as a possible diversion he exclaimed scornfully: 'Bowls! When I play a game I like to hit something; yes, I want to have a swipe at something.'[6] When he contrived to get a game of golf with the Bishop of Bloemfontein he played abominably: 'However . . . he exercised the most praiseworthy restraint and, barring a few mild "damns" and "blasts", there was nothing to which the Bish could take exception.'[7]

Yet his morale remained resolutely high. 'I'm so heartily sick of being cheered and yelled and shrieked at, it almost hurts some-times,' he complained to Princess Alice,[8] but nobody would have suspected it to look at him. He delighted the press correspondents travelling on the royal train by regularly inviting them in for drinks and a sing-song; he would play the ukulele and Thomas a small harmonium.[9] 'I wonder what there is in that young man which attracts one so to him,' speculated the Minister of Defence, one of the more fervent Labour members in Hertzog's coalition.[10] 'HRH kept going far better than any of us,' Thomas told Wigram. 'He took an infinity of trouble throughout, never really lost his good spirits.'[1] Nor was there a trace of scandal on which the journalists could swoop. 'He has behaved himself like the first gentleman in the land, which he is,' reported Lord Athlone.[2]

It helped, of course, that there was little in the way of temptation. Thomas ascribed the Prince's immaculate good conduct to the fact that he had now adjusted himself to his relatively detached relationship with Freda Dudley Ward and that there were no distracting influences like Mountbatten, Trotter or Metcalfe to lure him from the paths of righteousness.[3] To Metcalfe he boasted proudly: 'I'm keeping the deadly booze well under this trip and the cigs too, so that I really am d—d fit considering. No drinks before 6.0 and only 2 cigs before ten. It was a strain at first but it's easy now.'[4] He still searched for any excuse to postpone going to bed; 'But one mustn't find fault with him,' wrote Legh resignedly, 'because he really has been perfectly marvellous.'[5]

The King wrote to congratulate him on his great success. 'It has certainly been the most strenuous, the most exacting and the most difficult of all your tours. I am astonished that you have been able to have carried through without getting too stale or bored ... I hear from all sides the enormous trouble you took to please people, and there is no doubt you gave pleasure to many thousands of people and your visit has done an enormous amount of good.'[6] In the six years that he had worked with him, Halsey said, he had never known the Prince so genuinely pleased as he was by this message – 'that letter has done *far* more good than the King or anyone else can imagine'.[7] The King's patent pride in his son's achievements, and the Prince's pleasure at his father's praise, show how much latent good will still survived in the relationship. If either of them had been able to demonstrate face to face the warmth and affection that still sometimes permeated their correspondence, then the history of the British monarchy might have been different.

The tour of South Africa was the Prince of Wales's apotheosis. There were to be many good moments over the next ten years, but never again was he to display his qualities to such great advantage and over so long a period. It was sad that, worn out as he was and longing to be home, he had to append a postscript to the visit and cross the Atlantic to South America.

The tour was formally designated as a return of the visit recently paid by the Argentine President to London, but was really intended to drum up trade in a part of the world where the Americans had largely taken over what had traditionally been a British market. The Prince decided to learn a little Spanish for the occasion, found it gratifyingly easy, and talked it with enthusiasm. Henceforth he was never to miss a chance to air his German and Spanish, showing an equally marked reluctance to embark on French. 'I'm picking up a little Spanish and tango as well . . .' he told his mother from Buenos Aires, '– and neither are very difficult.'[1] His reception was spectacular, in Buenos Aires particularly where hundreds of thousands of Argentines crammed the streets, shouting '*Viva el Principe*' and clouds of doves, with their wing tips dyed red, white and blue, were released from the tops of the highest buildings.[2]

But though to the more remote elements of the public all seemed highly successful, in fact things did not go well. A combination of Latin exuberance and the fatigue caused by the South African tour almost overwhelmed the Prince. 'I absolutely cannot compete with it all, or be natural or cheerful, when they won't treat me like a human being,' he admitted to his mother.[3] He had not made a very good impression, Godfrey Thomas told his wife, 'simply, poor thing, because he has been looking tired and bored all last week, with these interminable pompous functions, and they expect a "smiling Prince". I don't know what he has to smile about.'[4] Wherever he went, whatever he did, he was besieged by a multitude of well-intentioned but oppressive hangers-on. When he paid a 'private' visit to an estate some thirty miles from Buenos Aires, sixty-six car loads of officials, police, newspapermen and assorted dignitaries took the road in his wake. 'I can laugh now,' he told the Queen after a couple of days recuperating on the Uruguay river, 'but *entre nous* I was as near a mental crash on Saty night when I left Buenos Aires as doesn't matter. I felt crushed by it all.'[5] Halsey was so alarmed by his condition that he was on the point of calling off the rest of the tour and returning home. The Prince's rapid recovery when given a little time by himself encouraged Halsey to carry on, but he still cabled the British Ambassador in Chile, the last country to be visited, insisting that the programme must be cut down.[1] The tour was completed, but the Prince was noticeably the worse for wear. An American officer who saw him during the visit described how: 'Talking to people he hung his head, mumbled, tugged at his cuffs or toyed with his necktie or his fly. He smoked cigarettes incessantly, with nervous little gasps. He was boredom personified – restless, impatient to be away.'[2]

And so, on 16 October 1925, the Prince returned home after completing the last of his great international tours. There was to be much travelling in the future, but nothing on the scale of these arduous peregrinations. In the course of them he had visited forty-five different countries and colonies and travelled 150,000 miles. Since the war he had spent thirty months abroad; since the beginning of 1915 less than a third of his life had been passed in Britain. It was high time he learned to know his country, and his country him.

10

'Half Child, Half Genius'

=======

AT THE END OF 1920 ALAN LASCELLES JOINED THE
Prince of Wales's staff as assistant private secretary. 'He
won me completely,' he wrote after their first meeting. 'He
is the most attractive man I've ever met.'[1] Eight years later Lascelles
resignèd, a disillusioned man who was henceforth to be among the
harshest critics of his former master. Though it is far from being
the whole story, the Prince's relationship with Tommy Lascelles
epitomizes his evolution over these eight years.

It was Lascelles's contention that the Prince never grew up. 'For
some hereditary or physiological reason,' he told Godfrey Thomas,
'his mental and spiritual growth stopped dead in his adolescence,
thereby affecting his whole consequent behaviour.'[2] Stanley Baldwin made the same point: 'He is an abnormal being, half child,
half genius . . . It is almost as though two or three cells in his brain
had remained entirely undeveloped while the rest of him is a mature
man.'[3] To be childlike is in many ways attractive. The Prince never
lost his enthusiasm, his curiosity, his freshness of outlook, his
open-mindedness. But the word also carries with it connotations
of volatility, irresponsibility, self-indulgence, an inability to establish a mature relationship with another adult. With all these the
Prince can fairly be charged. At one moment urbane, charming,
putting men of far greater intellectual distinction at ease, he could
at the next be gauche and nervous. 'He seemed to be quite as
frightened of me as I was of him, although he was seven years
older than me, and fidgeted his way through dinner,' wrote Helen
Hardinge, wife of King George V's assistant private secretary.[4]

His restlessness and inability to concentrate was the despair of
his staff. John Aird was recruited as equerry more or less at the
time Lascelles resigned. 'He had a most curious mentality . . .' he
wrote in his diary. 'His mind is so active that unless nature eases
it off he will have many moments of great depression.'[5] That

163

activity of mind leads to depression is something that many psychiatrists would dispute, but the Prince did suffer from bouts of depression so cruel as to be virtually incapacitating. Mountbatten described how the fits would come upon him like a flash and 'he'd shut himself in his cabin for days, alone, face drawn, eyes brooding'.[1] He wrote to Freda Dudley Ward to apologize for his behaviour the night before: 'But I just couldn't help it; the *black, black*, mist came down and enveloped me irrevocably . . . and it wasn't any good making an effort to cheer up.'[2]

Writing of the ecstatic reception the Prince had received in Canada, Lord Rosebery hoped that he would not become spoilt, 'for such adulation might turn the head of anyone'.[3] No young man could be so fawned upon and indulged as was the Prince without beginning to feel that everything was his as of right. He did expect special treatment, assume that hostesses would meet his every whim, treat any personable woman as a likely prey. Feeling tired after a long day of visits and inspections he cried off a ball at Lord Revelstoke's house at two hours' notice – forgivable, no doubt, but inconsiderate given the trouble to which his host had gone.[4] He telegraphed at the last minute to cancel his attendance at a ball in Fife because of court mourning for the Duchess of Albany. 'It is felt that he is stretching family etiquette too far,' wrote Lord Crawford. 'It is a pity that the impression grows prevalent that he shows ill-concealed boredom with his public engagements.'[5] When his chauffeur refused to take a short cut by driving the wrong way down a one-way street there was an 'awful scene . . . the Prince jumped about in the car with rage'.[6] Yet though he took his privileges for granted, he never came to believe that he himself was anything extraordinary. He did not have a conceited idea in his head, wrote Aird.[7] He was 'terribly modest about himself', noted Robert Bruce Lockhart, author and editor of the Londoner's Diary column in the *Evening Standard*. 'He has an inferiority complex.'[8] Certainly he seemed to find pleasure in abusing himself. 'If only the British public really knew what a weak, powerless misery their press-made national hero was,' he told Freda Dudley Ward, 'they would have a nasty shock and be not only disappointed but d—d angry too.'[9]

'Don't . . . imagine that we weren't with it when we were younger,' he said in an interview when he was an old man. 'In fact

I was so much with it that that was one of the big criticisms that was levelled against me by the older generation.'[1] He rejected the exaggerated formality of court life and the pompous trivialities which plagued his appearances in public – a very proper urge to modernize and cut out unnecessary frills, would say his admirers; a refusal to take the minimum of trouble to conform to the rules of his profession, was the opinion of his critics. Both were right and both wrong. No one could reasonably complain when he asked the Duke of Sutherland not to lay on any elaborate junketings for a weekend at Sutton Place – 'Don't make it all too formal as I do hate all that sort of thing so much';[2] yet when he visited Magdalen College he should have consented to dine at High Table given that (or, perhaps, in spite of the fact that) the Archbishop of York was there as well.[3] When in the mood he could go through the ritual hoops with grace and good will. Aird felt sorry for him as he stood for over an hour at a levee bowing to passers-by, yet 'he looked extremely well and impressive'.[4] His sense of propriety could be unexpectedly strong, particularly when the victims of the First World War were in some way concerned. He was dismayed when the King proposed that the Prime Minister should unveil the memorial to the dead of the British Empire in Westminster Abbey. 'I do suggest that it's absolutely a stunt for *you* or, if you can't make it, for me as second best,' he remonstrated with his father. 'It's absolutely not a stunt for the P.M. with all the Dominion Premiers present . . . I hate worrying you in this way, but I really do feel it's important.'[5]

He found the demands of security as bad as if not worse than those of ceremony. A proposal that plain-clothes police should follow him around affronted his passionate desire for privacy. In August 1922 there was a scare over an IRA murder plot. 'Winston is first on the list to be murdered . . . and your poor little parpee is the second!!' he told Freda Dudley Ward.[6] Halsey discussed the problem with the Home Secretary, Edward Shortt, and agreed to various additional precautions. The Prince indignantly disavowed them. 'Please issue no further orders . . . as regards my so-called . . . protection,' he wrote to Shortt. 'I will not stand for having a car following me.' He absolved Shortt from all responsibility. 'So please don't worry any more. If anybody wanted to kill me all the CID in the world won't stop him.'[7] The Home Secretary could hardly stop worrying about a threat to assassinate the heir to the throne; in the end the Prince compromised and grudgingly stayed away from London during the most dangerous period.

In everything he tried to distance himself from the more traditional manifestations of the Establishment. He became known as something of a sartorial innovator, but almost always his departures from the accepted style were in the direction of simplicity and comfort – a dinner jacket instead of a tail coat, soft white collars, the abandonment of gloves for dancing. When he did introduce something more extravagant – loud check suits, two-toned shoes – it was usually done to annoy his father. His excesses sometimes dismayed his more conventional brother. 'We ought to conform to what he does, really,' the Duke of York wrote dubiously to Lord Londonderry, 'but this is often difficult knowing that he is in the wrong.'[1] He took trouble over his clothes but did not like to waste time with them; his valet, Crisp, estimated that he could undress, take a bath, and be on the way downstairs in tails and Garter star within three minutes. Similarly, he took great pains over the decoration of York House but the style he affected – chintzes, light panelling – was notably unregal. Aird disapproved. 'The hall and staircase have just been scraped and look very moderate. The Secretary's room is quite decent . . . upstairs the Equerry's room is like a French brothel only there are no ladies.'[2] His mother proved more enthusiastic – 'really very nice and in good taste,' she commented[3] – but wished he had reserved his efforts for Marlborough House. His parents wished fervently to see him installed in that draughty mausoleum; the Prince regarded it with a horror almost equal to that which he felt for Buckingham Palace and resolutely refused to move.

He could be touchingly considerate and appreciative of his staff. Once at Balmoral he found himself deprived of a private secretary. 'It's very good for me,' he told Lascelles. 'I open *everything* and so am getting a pretty good insight of all the drudgery and toiling that you and Godfrey do for me and for which I may not appear grateful. But I am I can assure you.'[4] But he did not have the gift of running a happy ship. Trotter, Legh and Halsey all vied for his favours, and squabbled over who was responsible for the small quantity of work that there was to do. 'No one likes going away for fear the other supplants him,' wrote Aird. Trotter had the most influence with the Prince but Godfrey Thomas did all the work that mattered, 'which I should say for the sake of the work was a good thing'.[1]

Aird's first impression, to some extent corrected when he went on tour, was that the Prince's reputation for being a hard worker was a myth. He rarely rose before eleven, played squash or golf for much of the day, and spent part at least of most nights in the Embassy Club or the Grafton Galleries.[2] But his capacity to work hard and play hard when he had to remained phenomenal. After an early start and a gruelling day of official visits at Nottingham, Aird dropped the Prince at 7.45 p.m. at a block of flats. He heard him come back to York House at 4.30 the following morning. 'What energy!!'[3] Though he drank little or no alcohol during the day, from the early evening onwards his intake was considerable. He had a strong head, but not strong enough. Many sightings of a noticeably intoxicated Prince of Wales were recorded, some exaggerated, some not. He wrote to Mrs Dudley Ward in contrition from Biarritz in 1926: 'I know I'm not leading a life to be very proud of here, though not very bad really, and it's hard to keep out of casinos and all the rottenness they involve. Still, I'm not being *very* bad.'[4]

Such excesses did nothing to impair his almost absurdly youthful looks or his public image. Duff Cooper saw him at the State Opening of Parliament in 1924, 'looking most like a fairy prince, his pink face and golden hair rising out of ermine, beautiful as an angel'.[5] Beatrice Webb thought him like a hero of one of Shaw's plays: 'Was it the Dauphin in *St Joan* or King Magnus in *The Apple Cart?*'[6] One photograph showed him 'in naval uniform . . . glancing upwards with a radiantly happy smile'.[7] It was reproduced on innumerable chocolate or biscuit boxes, turned into hundreds of thousands of postcards, adorned the window ledges of countless housemaids, nestled in the blotters of a whole generation of susceptible schoolgirls. It was the image of Prince Charming, and it made its subject sick.

He did not want to be a fairy prince, that was certain, but did he want to be a prince at all? It was a question he never ceased to ask himself. He was not pretending to be overworked, he told Godfrey Thomas in the spring of 1927:

167

It's just the *chronic state* of being the P of W – of which I'm
so heartily and genuinely fed up. It's just so nerve-racking and
distracting sometimes, Godfrey, that I could really go mad,
and that wouldn't be suitable, would it? . . . I can put up with
a certain amount of contact with officials and newspapers on
official trips, when one is obviously on the job. It's when they
get in on my private life and trips that I want to pull out a
gun and kill . . . I've got a lot older lately and don't look for
excitement the way I used to. And I believe I'm more serious
and conscientious over the less artificial side of my stunting
than I was. But I have to go through with too many artificial
'bulls'. I suppose some of it is inevitable, still I rebel against
it and I find it tricky.[1]

Again and again in his private letters the same refrain occurs: he
was not cut out to be Prince of Wales.

But did he seriously contemplate a future in which he would not
be King? Chips Channon, a shrewd observer, believed in 1925 that
he 'would not raise a finger to save his future sceptre' and quoted
the Prince's intimate friends as saying he would be happy to
renounce the succession.[2] Lord Strathmore, father-in-law to the
Duke of York, is said to have predicted that he would never succeed
to the throne.[3] Yet there is no evidence from the Prince's own
writings or quoted conversations that he felt more than a general-
ized distaste for the appurtenances of his job. What he wanted
was to be Prince, and eventually King, without the pomp and
circumstance which traditionally enveloped the holders of these
offices. As Prince he knew he could never do more than alleviate
the burden of his life, as King he believed he would be able to
rewrite the rules, to create a new, streamlined monarchy which
would allow him the privacy and the liberty that he desired. A time
was to come when even this would not be enough, but in the 1920s
it seemed to offer the prospect of a tolerable existence. He must
from time to time have played with the idea of a retreat from the
succession, but it was no more than idle dreaming. He had been
born to be King, he had been trained to be King, and King he
would one day be.

*

Every year, however, it became more clear that his concept of that office differed alarmingly from that of his father. Given the personalities of the two men, it was inevitable that the differences should result in mutual suspicion and sometimes even rancorous dislike. 'There *must* be a happier condition of affairs between the King and his eldest son,' Stamfordham wrote despairingly to Thomas. It was quite wrong to think the King did not appreciate the Prince's achievements on his tours abroad, on the contrary he was 'grateful for and proud of his son's remarkable, nay unique performance'. The trouble was that the King found it hard to show his appreciation, and the Prince was quick to take offence at what he saw as a deliberate slight. If only the two men could be brought to see the affection and respect which each one held for the other, then all would be well.[1] Stamfordham's conviction that the King rejoiced in his son's successes was not supported by other members of the family. The Duke of York, in particular, remained critical of his father's motives. Only a few weeks before Stamfordham's letter to Thomas he had told his brother: 'His great complaint against you, of course, is due to jealousy . . . He knows too well what a success you have been . . . and I must tell you that at times his jealousy is quite apparent.'[2]

Family Christmases can be a test for even the most affectionate relations, Christmas at York Cottage was a feast of acrimony. The King, the Prince told Freda Dudley Ward in December 1922, was 'as sour and costive as could be because Henry and I arrived late for dinner. How I longed to tell him that it's d—d nice of us to come at all and that we couldn't loathe it more.'[3] No doubt the King was unnecessarily irritable, equally his sons knew how unpunctuality upset him and might have taken the trouble to arrive on time. Inevitably things got worse. 'An atmosphere of restriction, killjoy pompousness, mystery, artificiality and the most complete and utter boredom,' the Prince represented it a few days later. 'And all that doesn't half describe how ghastly it is.'[4]

Even the loyal Stamfordham admitted that the King was too censorious, and that it was difficult for the Prince always to 'do what was right'.[5] There was no need for George V to take his son to task for wearing a kilt jacket of too light a grey for church; nor did he have to reprimand him in front of guests when he appeared at tea still in his shooting clothes, or instruct him not to appear at balls in future unless he was wearing gloves.[6] But equally it was not necessary for the Prince always to keep his father in the dark about his plans, or to treat it as a joke when he mistakenly shot a presentation red deer from Alberta which was kept as a pet in the grounds of Balmoral.[1] Could not the Prince, pleaded Stamfordham, 'just be a little tactful, as HM does if I may say so need a little management'?[2] At times the atmosphere improved: in 1923 the Prince reported 'a friendly but heart-to-heart talk with HM . . . which has cleared the air';[3] in 1928 George V told the Queen, 'I have had several talks with David, all quite satisfactory, and I have got on capitally with him';[4] but the very fact that these instances were five years apart and were presented as something remarkable, shows how frosty the relationship usually was.

'I'm not going to be wet-nursed or interfered with any more,' the Prince had announced defiantly in 1920. 'I ought to have put down the barrage ages ago, but as I haven't it's got to be done now. And what is more, I've got to win and come out on top or it'll be the end of me.'[5] Despite this somewhat melodramatic announcement, it was a long-drawn guerrilla campaign that the Prince waged rather than open battle. The one person who could have worked on both parties for the better was the Queen, but with the advent of Freda Dudley Ward she had forfeited most of her influence over her son. The Prince lost confidence in his mother's readiness to help when she failed to talk to George V about the possible marriage of their daughter Mary. 'I'm so annoyed with her that I haven't been near her for over a week,' he told Lady Airlie. 'You know how I always used to sit with her for half an hour before dinner, but I've given that up now.'[6] Lady Airlie besought him to accept the fact of his mother's love for her children and make allowances for her difficulties in expressing it, but had as little success as Lord Esher did with the Queen – 'I asked her did she never go and sit on his bed and have a chat with him as mother and boy, and she said she could not do it.'[7] On minor issues she could sometimes smooth the way, as when she forestalled a likely row over some rooms formerly occupied by Princess Marie-Louise which the Prince had appropriated without permission – 'I am thankful I spoke of it or there would have been a rumpus'[8] – but on the central issues she felt there was no contribution that she could make.

The marriage of Princess Mary to Lord Lascelles, the future Earl of Harewood, had removed one source of irritation between father and son. The Prince had long felt that his sister was a victim of the King's craving for a well-ordered and secluded life. He was in India when the news of her engagement reached him and was delighted. 'I only hope it isn't too much arranged,' he told Freda Dudley Ward. 'It really is marvellous, isn't it, my beloved, to think that that poor girl is going to be free and let out of Buckhouse prison. Of course Lascelles is too old for her and not attractive, is he, my darling? But anyway he's rich, and I'm afraid that is a very important thing for poor Mary. I hope to God he'll make her happy, as she does deserve that if anyone does.'[1] He could not be back in time for the wedding, a deprivation which he faced with equanimity. 'I have an inordinate dislike for weddings . . .' he told the Queen. 'I always feel so sorry for the couple concerned.'[2]

The Duke of York remained the Prince's closest ally among his siblings. 'There is a dreadful blank in my life directly you leave on one of your tours,' the Duke wrote,[3] and again when trouble threatened, 'I am not going to let you fight your battles alone with the family.'[4] But though the Duke remained devoted, the Prince, absorbed by his relationship with Mrs Dudley Ward and impatient of his brother's slower wits and more phlegmatic nature, grew distant from his sibling. The two men were very different, and as they grew older it began to become apparent that the younger son was in spirit much closer to his father. 'You have always been so sensible and easy to work with,' wrote the King to his second son, 'and you have always been [so] ready to listen to any advice and to agree with my opinions about people and things, that I feel that we have always got on very well together (very different to dear David).'[5] The Duke of York was not unconscious of this growing rapport. When the Prince came back from the Far East his brother told the Queen that he was sure the old atmosphere of trust and intimacy could be restored. 'We must all *help* him to get him back to our way of thinking.'[6] It would not have been 'our' way even a year before.

At the beginning of 1923 the Duke of York became engaged to Elizabeth Bowes Lyon. His brother had been sceptical whether he would ever bring it off. 'Little Elizabeth Lyon, the future Duchess of York, *I don't think* . . .' he had referred to her some time before.[7] At one point the papers announced that she was to marry the Prince of Wales and drove the Palace into issuing an official denial.[1] They had got the wrong prince, and the putative fiancé was delighted when the true facts of the engagement became known. He had no such reservations as he had felt over the marriage of Princess Mary. '*Splendid* news about Bertie and Elizabeth . . . She is a very sweet girl . . . I am delighted,' he wrote to his mother.[2] He grew even more fond of her with the years. She was 'the one bright spot' at Buckingham Palace, he told Diana Cooper. 'They all love her and the King is in a good temper whenever she is there.'[3] He spent a few days at her Scottish home, Glamis Castle: 'I'm so fond of Elizabeth, she is too sweet for words and she was the life and soul of the party.'[4]

The new Duchess reciprocated his affection and took his part in the family rows. Though she herself found the King easy to get on with, she realized how different it must be for a son. From a holiday in Africa she wrote to tell him:

> I know now your feelings of relief and freedom when you get away from England on your own – away from the petty little annoyances and restrictions that drive one crazy . . . I hate the thought of coming home – no, I love coming home, but I hate being always under the eye of a narrow-minded autocrat . . . Dear David, I hope your affairs are going well, and that neither your heart nor your staff are giving you cause for worry. Those two seem to give you most trouble in life, and also of course you are *very*, very naughty, but delicious.[5]

In the same year Prince George rallied to the common cause. He was going to stand up to the King when he got back, he wrote from the Fleet in the Far East; 'and have no more being told off without answering back. I'm sure it's the only way . . . as he's so impossible.'[6]

In April 1926 the Yorks had a daughter. 'I'd have voted *for a boy myself*!!' the Prince told Piers Legh, 'but they all seem very pleased and very well so I guess it's *muy bien*.'[7] The fact that his brother had produced a child to some extent relieved the pressure on him to marry and provide an heir to the throne. A son would have been even better, but that no doubt would happen in due course. Yet he knew he could never escape the conviction of his parents and his people that his own marriage had been too long deferred, and that it was his duty to maintain the dynasty. At various times his name had been linked with a bevy of European princesses, most conspicuously the daughter of the Queen of Italy. Gossip about the match reached such a point that Lloyd George took advice on the reaction of British Roman Catholics to the possibility. He was told that, if the Princess renounced her religion to marry the Prince, no Catholic would appear at court. Without such a renunciation, the marriage, of course, could never take place. 'So that is off,' wrote Frances Stevenson. Not that it had been on anyway. 'The Prince himself is not the least inclined to marry,' she went on, 'and is very obstinate on the point.'[1] In Tokyo he had made it clear to Embassy staff that he was not in love with the Italian Princess, and that he would only marry for love.[2] This did not curb newspaper speculation. In 1927 the King of Spain forbade his daughter Beatrice to visit London because of rumours linking her with the Prince,[3] while American journalists at intervals married him off to at least nine continental princesses, least probably Princess Eudoxia of Bulgaria, thirty-nine years old, hefty and a musician.[4]

In 1920 Lloyd George is said to have told the King that the country would not tolerate the Prince marrying a foreign princess.[5] A few years later J. H. Thomas, the trade union leader, declared that the Labour Party would not tolerate the Prince marrying anyone else: 'Of course a Cavendish would have done but there are now none left.'[6] Confronted with such divergent counsels the Prince might reasonably have concluded that any marriage would be worse than none. In fact he professed himself ready in principle though reluctant in practice. 'I'm getting quite an old bachelor now and a more confirmed one each year,' he told Mountbatten in 1924, 'tho' I suppose I'll have to take the fatal plunge one of these days, tho' I'll put it off as long as I can, 'cos it'll destroy me.'[7] When Godfrey Thomas married later the same year, he wrote: 'It must be . . . rather frightening, I'd say. Such a big change in one's old bachelor life, tho' I guess it's all right if you love.'[8]

When in South Africa in 1925 he talked to the Athlones with unusual freedom. He admitted that he was lonely but stressed that 'in his position he could not make a mistake and must find someone who would be both agreeable to him and suitable for the duties she would be called upon to perform'.[9] What he dreaded most of all was overt pressure from the King. 'Any pushing of his marriage by George would be *absolutely* fatal and will drive him into a most obstinate course,' Princess Alice told the Queen. 'You will just have to stop George about that.' She was certain he was 'ripe for being married and he is evidently turning it over in his mind'.[1] He may have been turning it over, but it is hard to believe that he took the possibility seriously, if for no other reason than that he still felt himself committed to Freda Dudley Ward. He wrote to her when she was in Paris with her current admirer, the American socialite and polo player, Rodman Wanamaker: 'My God – it's so damned silly that you and I aren't married, my angel. I absolutely know that you'd be far happier with me now than with any bloody Pappapacker. Their kind may be all right for an affair but I guess that's about all . . . Anyway, we love each other, nothing can change that, can it?'[2] Something was to change it, but in the meantime any potential bride had to be weighed in the balance against Mrs Dudley Ward and was invariably found wanting. The King restrained himself from proffering any advice on the subject, but though his reticence may have saved a few unnecessary quarrels it can have made little difference on the essential issue. Neither his speech nor his silence would sensibly have affected his son's determination.

He made more impression on other issues. The role of Fruity Metcalfe in the Prince's life was a subject of frequent and acrimonious debate. When the Prince got back from his Far Eastern tour Metcalfe was still in attendance: 'The two are inseparable and all the Prince's staff and his family are furious about it,' noted Frances Stevenson.[3] The Prince was devoted to his new friend. When he went to Balmoral in the autumn of 1922 he wrote to say how much he loathed having to 'leave you behind the first time in nearly a year . . . I'm not going to write a soppy letter though I *insist* on your driving out of your silly old head any ideas or thoughts of returning to India when your year's leave is up . . . I'm just not letting you go back to that godforsaken country and life and insist on you staying with me (officially) to run my stables etc, but actually to . . . well, to carry on being what you've always been to me and are now, my greatest man friend.'[4]

It did not take the King long to conclude that Metcalfe was a thoroughly pernicious influence. 'He has been given the credit for encouraging His Royal Highness in his escapades,' wrote Wigram; in his drinking, in his night club excursions, worst of all in his reckless riding in point-to-points and steeplechases.[1] George V told his son that Metcalfe must go, the Prince fought tenaciously to retain his friend. 'Had a talk with D on getting home about Metcalfe. I found him very obstinate,' noted the King gloomily in his diary.[2] The climax came when the Prince wanted to include Metcalfe in his party for South Africa in 1925. After much argument he was satisfied that too many people would be offended if he stuck to his guns and that anyway Metcalfe's career would be damaged beyond repair if he stayed longer away from the Army. Regretfully he gave way. He tried to get Metcalfe transferred to a cavalry regiment in England, but the powers that be were able to thwart this project. Metcalfe must return to India. Before he was due to leave, however, he became engaged to Lord Curzon's daughter Alexandra. 'I'm awfully glad that Fruity has at last pulled it off, and now that he is fixed up I feel less bad about having had to give him the push,' the Prince told Lascelles.[3] The two men were not going to remain separated for very long.

Metcalfe's standing in the eyes of the King was above all affected by his association with another cause of conflict between father and son – the Prince's riding. It was ironic that the recreation which the King had forced upon his reluctant son before the First World War should now give rise to so much disagreement. Riding had become one of the Prince's greatest pleasures: 'All his thoughts and passions seemed centred on the horse,' wrote Wigram.[4] The King at first had no objection to what could have been a harmless obsession. He loved riding himself, and whenever they were together at Windsor he would lead his sons and other guests in a stately progress through the park. He disliked being passed, so the Prince and the Duke of York would drop behind, make a great circle, jumping everything they met, cross the royal path too far ahead to be seen and end up dutifully behind their father.[5] The King no doubt knew what was happening but preferred not to notice.

He equally made no attempt to interfere with the Prince's hunting. Addressing a dinner of the Farmers' Union at Leicester, the Prince referred to hunting as 'the best and healthiest of sports'.[6] He no doubt tailored his sentiments to his audience, but he still spoke from the heart. He first patronized the Duke of Beaufort's hunt but moved on to Leicestershire after two years, according to Bruce Ogilvy because the 9th Duke objected vociferously to the Prince's over-riding hounds and the Duchess had designs upon him for her daughter.[1] Installed at Melton Mowbray, he began to hunt with the Quorn, the Cottesmore and the Belvoir. For him hunting was competitive and intensely exciting. 'I'll hunt flat out just as long as I still want to jump fences in front of other people,' he told Metcalfe. 'The moment I don't, I'll stop.'[2] He won a reputation for courage, determination and a fair measure of skill. Guy Paget, for a book he was writing, canvassed thirty or so of the best men across country in the shires, huntsmen included, on the riders they most admired. The Prince was on every list of those who 'took their own line, rode as a sportsman should, and always got to the end of the hunt'.[3] 'He was a real sportsman,' wrote Paget, 'taking the rough with the smooth, scorning all privileges, and ever ready to take his turn at the chores of the hunting field . . . He was as brave as a lion, and bore pain without a sign.'[4] From time to time he got into trouble, but Paget did not believe he took more falls than any other bold rider: 'He is such a good thruster in the hunting field that he is bound to come to grief,' wrote Wigram, '. . . everyone says that he goes very well but just lacks judgment and takes too many risks.'[5]

Such risks the King could accept, with resignation if not equanimity. It was a different matter when it came to riding in point-to-points. The Prince was a better than competent rider, with horses of high quality, but when he was racing his recklessness pushed him into hazards beyond the technical ability of himself or his horse. He claimed that he took no more risks and fell no more frequently than other riders of his calibre, but the daemon which drove him on was exposed in an unhappy letter he wrote to Freda Dudley Ward in 1923: 'Thank God I've got 2 races tomorrow as I must do something desperate, which is just what race-riding gives one.'[6] By the time he wrote these words, the King was already urging him to abandon the dangerous sport. 'He *must* be tactfully informed that I'm *not* going to promise never to ride in pt to pts again,' the Prince told Thomas, 'I'm sorry but I'm obstinate.'[7] He was always obstinate, but rarely tactful. The King's indignation mounted as his son broke his collar bone, blacked his eyes, and suffered concussion with what seemed alarming regularity: 'It is too bad that he should continue to ride in these steeplechases,' he wrote to the Queen. 'I have asked him not to on many occasions.'[1] The Prime Minister, Ramsay MacDonald, was recruited to the campaign. 'Pray do not put me down as an interfering person who having no zest in life himself wishes to knock it out of others,' he wrote. But would the Prince please not take unnecessary risks? 'No one in these days can do more good than you, sir, to your people and, through them, to the world, and were a serious mishap to come upon you, who could take your place?'[2] All such appeals were ignored; it was to be several years later and only after the almost fatal illness of his father, that the Prince renounced his hazardous hobby.

The air provided some of the same excitement, though without the fierce competitive thrill. After his visits to Australia and New Zealand he predicted that Britain would soon possess 'a great air organization on the same lines as our mercantile marine' and looked forward to the day when he would be able to do a Dominion tour without recourse to slow-moving ships.[3] It was several years before he was allowed even to tour Britain by air, but by the end of 1927 the King had grudgingly agreed that the Prince could use a plane in exceptional cases when a tight schedule made it essential. The exception soon became the norm. The following year a personal pilot was appointed and the Prince darted happily from appointment to appointment around the country. By mid-1929 he was grumbling about the intolerable delays whenever the weather or other circumstances forced him to use the train.[4] Once in the air, he was always for pushing on, however dire the weather forecast. On one occasion he insisted that his plane must take him from Castle Bromwich to Cardiff, even though there were storms ahead. The pilot disappeared, then came back and led the puzzled Prince to a telephone. Down the line boomed the voice of the legendary father of the Royal Air Force, Air Marshal Trenchard. 'Good morning, Group Captain. I am giving you an order. You are not to fly on to Cardiff.'[5]

To sit behind a pilot did not satisfy the Prince for long. 'I've bought a Moth, and flying is my latest craze,' he told Lascelles in October 1929.[6] It was not for another six months, however, that his father agreed he could learn to fly, and a year later he was still refused permission to fly solo. The Prince was very depressed, noted Aird; 'It struck me as almost sad that he should get upset over such a childish and small thing.'[1] It was not small or childish to the Prince, but another illustration of the fact that he was swaddled always in a cocoon of protective restrictions, never allowed to behave like a man. In the end he made an illicit solo flight, with only a mechanic and his pilot, Squadron-Leader Don, watching apprehensively from below. 'He was as excited as a Cranwell cadet,' said Don.[2] The Prince had been enormously impressed when Lindbergh made his first trans-Atlantic flight in 1927 – 'Chaps who make those kind of stunts make me feel sillier than I already do.'[3] He had no illusions that he was a second Lindbergh but he felt a little less silly after his solo flight.

The magazine *Air* said that the Prince's example had done as much as any other single factor to popularize air travel in Great Britain.[4] The devotees of golf might have said as much about their pastime. His passion was slow to mature. 'I hate golf,' he had told the King in 1922, when he was trying to escape from some ceremonial occasion at St Andrews.[5] A few years later, however, and he was 'crazy keen', boasting to Joey Legh that he had 'some kind of a permanent swing now' and at least knew what he was doing wrong.[6] He used to take a cottage in Sandwich Bay, which served the double purpose of being near three championship golf courses and the holiday home of Mrs Dudley Ward. He never became as good as he wanted to but by 1929 he was well above the average, beating Bruce Lockhart level at three and two when in previous years he had been given a handicap and had still lost: 'He now plays really well and hits the ball as far as anyone.'[7]

He did not show the same tenacity in intellectual pursuits. He virtually never read a book, and if he went to the theatre at all chose musicals or the lightest of comedies. At the Academy Dinner in 1923 he held forth eloquently about the importance of the arts – 'We have only to turn the pages of history to realize that a nation's art is the mirror of its inner mind' – but it was not he who had turned the pages; the voice was the Prince's voice, but the hands were the hands of Tommy Lascelles.[8] In 1930 he joined the board of the National Gallery. Lord Crawford, who had a low opinion of him, wrote with some contempt of his first attendance: 'He fairly amazed us. About halfway through our proceedings, which happened to be extremely important, he got bored and began to smoke . . . The cigarettes . . . enlivened the Prince and he began to talk to his neighbours, Sassoon and D'Abernon . . . Sassoon . . . with his raucous Syrian voice and his acute desire to "honour the King" chattered away – and between them the two made business practically impossible . . . So far as I could make out, the chatter was chiefly about racing and society.'[1] Lord Lee was the chairman. 'Poor Arthur Lee is in despair,' wrote Crawford after a later meeting,[2] but in his own account Lee said that he at first thought the appointment 'foolish and flunkeyish' but later changed his mind. The Prince, he wrote, showed real interest and set great store by his membership.[3]

Whether Lee or Crawford was more nearly right, all the pundits agreed that the Prince was singularly ignorant. 'Is this by one of the painters they call a Primitive?' he enquired, when a picture by Hieronymus Bosch was being discussed.[4] 'What does a picture cost?' he asked Kenneth Clark.[5] The latter question, at least, sounds improbably naive; the Prince may have been ignorant but he was no fool. Clark's low opinion of the Prince as art critic must be set against Godfrey Thomas's equally extreme judgment that, as a guide to the Kunsthistorisches Museum in Vienna he was 'as good as any professional'.[6] The truth lies somewhere between the two. The Prince did not enjoy looking at works of art and had little knowledge of them, but he had a quick mind, a retentive memory, and could put up a tolerable show of enthusiasm if he felt in the mood. He rarely did, and would have retorted if taxed with this delinquency that a Prince of Wales could only concentrate on a limited range of things, and that the artistic affairs of the nation did not rate high in his scale of priorities. What ranked higher must be the subject of a separate chapter.

11

'A Steady Decline'

I T CANNOT BE PRETENDED THAT THE PRINCE'S NOR-
mal working day was arduous. Even if Aird's portrait of a
leisurely rise at eleven, followed by squash or golf and ending
up at a night club, was far from typical, he frequently had only
one or two official appointments in a day and his 'stunts' were
relatively infrequent. A week picked at random in November 1923
has him acting as pall-bearer at Bonar Law's funeral on Monday,
receiving Smuts and dining with the Overseas League on Tuesday,
spending a day of official visits in Winchester on Wednesday,
lunching with the Child Emigration Society on Thursday and
receiving a group of Indian dignitaries followed by the opening of
Chatham House on Friday. Weekends were usually sacrosanct,
though in this week the annual armistice ceremony at the Cenotaph
took place on Sunday. Even this gentle routine was not conducted
without protest – Bonar Law's funeral deprived him of a day's
hunting. In fairness it must be said that these were only the public
engagements, the Prince wrote many letters and interested himself
in a variety of matters which would not figure in the official
calendar. On Tuesday, for instance, he spent an hour discussing
the affairs of the Duchy of Cornwall and had a long meeting with
Lascelles and Thomas about a forthcoming visit to the north. But
there was still plenty of time left over for whatever private diversions he chose to pursue.

What should not be forgotten, however, is that he could have
done a great deal less. Beyond the few formal obligations which
his position in the state imposed upon him it was entirely up to
him how he spent his time. If he had chosen to devote himself
exclusively to his own entertainment, his staff would have
grumbled to each other and the King might from time to time have
issued some remonstrance, but nobody could have done anything
about it. In fact he devoted much time and energy to the causes

which he had at heart, and used his very considerable influence to good effect on their behalf.

'I can never speak too strongly or too often of the great debt that the Empire owes to its soldiers and sailors who fought and won the Great War,' he had declared at the Mansion House in 1919. 'I want all ex-service men in every part of the Empire, and particularly in the Old Country, to remember me as an old comrade-in-arms, one who wants them always to look on him as a comrade-in-spirit.'[1] The ex-service men must have, he was convinced, if not a land fit for heroes, then at least a tolerable existence. That meant, above all, guaranteeing them a house to live in and a job to do. It should also mean education for their children, proper hospital treatment and all the desirable appurtenances of life in the twentieth century, but though he dutifully visited schools and hospitals, they were not his prime concern. Unemployment and housing were and remained the focus of his most serious efforts.

Many of the servicemen who returned after the First World War found no job waiting for them and little prospect of one in the future. 1.2 per cent of the work force had been unemployed in 1913; in 1920 the comparable figure was 9.8 per cent. Things were gradually to improve before fresh disaster struck the economies of the world in 1929, but wherever he went in the British Isles the Prince was confronted by evidence that his old comrades were suffering grievously, in body as well as mind. What he could do beyond the utterance of consoling bromides was the problem that exercised him most. Early in 1921 Sir Robert Horne, President of the Board of Trade and future Chancellor of the Exchequer, lunched with him. 'I'm going to have it out with him about the unemployment,' the Prince wrote stoutly to his mother.[2] But though he could occasionally let off steam to ministers, he was conscious of the limitations of his knowledge as well as of his power. Esher taxed him with being unduly modest: 'You certainly know quite as much as anybody else knows, and that is next to nothing.'[3] But the Prince had no vestige of economic lore and a deep lack of confidence when it came to embarking on arguments with those whom he believed to be better qualified. All he could do was plead with the employers to be as expansive as they could and himself support well-intentioned institutions like the National

Relief Fund: 'The Prince of Wales,' wrote Sir George Arthur, 'in addition to his fine work in inaugurating the Fund, seems to have stumped up nearly £4000 for wages of the clerical staff.'[1] In time the National Council of Social Service was to provide a framework in which he could fit his activities, but it was not until the 1930s that this organization began to have any noticeable effect.

On housing, equally, he would show endless interest, make encouraging noises, take every opportunity to visit slum areas and to deplore the things he saw, yet he had no effective power. 'I don't think there would be much discontent if only the people were housed properly,' the Queen wrote to him in 1930.[2] The Prince agreed. He did at least set a good example by rehousing the more shabbily accommodated of the Duchy's tenants in London, and bringing farm workers' houses on his estates in the West Country up to an acceptable standard, but this was little enough. A Prince of Wales need not inevitably be bound by such restrictions. If he had been a different man, more pertinacious, more able to concentrate, better qualified to master a brief and chair a committee, he might have made a more positive contribution to the housing and employment of the nation's poor. He could have provided the public voice which the expert, however well-meaning, can so rarely find for himself; he could have goaded the great landlords and employers, city councils, the government itself, into taking steps to mitigate what he saw as being a national scandal. But neither by education nor by temperament did he have it in him. As it was, his periodic outbursts were taken as evidence of amiable eccentricity which could safely be ignored. His good will was boundless, his stamina and diligence less impressive.

Where he showed to best advantage was in the tours he undertook of the industrial north and the other great centres of population. 'I'm all for touring the provinces and visiting industries a lot and not getting tied down to a lot of useless pompous dinners and engagements in London,' he told Thomas.[3] The concept was admirable, but he found that dinners were quite as useless and pompous in the provinces, and that the emotional demands of a great crowd in Glasgow or Newcastle were as taxing as any in Melbourne or Toronto. On the eve of a five-day tour of Yorkshire he confessed to his mother that he was dreading the prospect; 'it is all such a terrible strain nowadays and it wears one to a shred'.[1] Yet wherever he went he received a spectacular welcome. In 1926 he went to Birmingham with the young Conservative member of parliament Victor Cazalet. For five miles into the city centre crowds massed along the route: 'It is amazing how popular he is,' wrote Cazalet, 'even the ordinary workmen come out and cheer lustily, and of course the women worship him. What an asset such a Prince is!'[2]

By hard work he had turned himself into a more than competent speaker, having the greater part of his speeches prepared by Lascelles or Thomas but adding remarks of his own – 'usually very shrewd' said Bruce Ogilvy.[3] On a journey to Cardiff to unveil a war memorial he asked Lloyd George for a phrase in Welsh to round off his speech. Lloyd George suggested: 'They will never be forgotten as long as the breeze blows over their grave.' The Prince was delighted. 'He pronounced it very well at the ceremony and it produced a tumult of cheering.'[4] Lord Rosebery said of him that his quality could be seen in his public speaking: 'He is a charmer. But he is more. I tell you . . . he will yet rive the bonnet of all you professional orators.'[5]

His radicalism and disapproval of social injustice were real enough, but he was still to the right politically. He rejoiced at the overwhelming victory of Baldwin's Conservatives in 1924, on the grounds that it 'must mean a little peace and a settled year or two anyway'.[6] But though he was perhaps exaggeratedly conscious of the threat of communism, he did not, as many Tories did, lump all socialists and communists in a common revolutionary bloc. The King and the Prince of Wales, J. H. Thomas once declared, 'knew their people . . . they recognized that patriotism, love of Empire, service, and duty were not the gift or monopoly of a class or creed'.[7] In a conversation in the autumn of 1925 the Prince praised the Labour leaders for knowing their own people in a way no Conservative could hope to do. 'I think the Labour people give me of their best,' he went on, 'and recognize that I am trying to understand their difficulties.'[8]

His support for the Conservative Party was in large part based on the affection and admiration he felt for the Prime Minister, Stanley Baldwin. His letters in the mid-1920s are filled with laudatory references: 'I've got great faith in Baldwin's human personality and soundness'; 'What a charming man, I like him so much'; 'He's absolutely straight and fair with no axe to grind or political stunts to pull.'[1] Their intimacy was engineered by Godfrey Thomas and Baldwin's secretary, Ronald Waterhouse, who set up a series of informal meetings at which everything and anything was held to be on the agenda. Both men enjoyed their talks and felt that they were of mutual benefit.[2] By the time foreign competition impelled the pit-owners to try to impose harsher terms of employment on the coal-miners and the resultant imbroglio led to the General Strike of 1926, the Prince's letters to the Prime Minister were couched in terms which Baldwin's biographers described as demonstrating 'affection, at times near veneration'.[3]

Whatever his reservations about the social and economic policies which had led the British working man to turn upon the government, the Prince was in no doubt that the General Strike was a threat to the realm which had to be resisted. He went out with the police, lent his car and chauffeur to transport the *British Gazette* to Wales, and resented the fact that he could do nothing directly himself to combat the communist agitators whom he believed to be behind the trouble.[4] He put forward a proposal for a provincial tour but met with the response that, while many 'would applaud the energy and public spiritedness of the enterprise', it would pose serious security problems and would inevitably involve him in striking political attitudes and 'taking sides'.[5] But though he had no doubt where his loyalties lay, he did not see the issue as one of right and wrong, white and black. It had been 'an amazing and wonderful week', he told Fruity Metcalfe, 'but disastrous at the same time as victorious'.[6] He welcomed the conciliatory tone of Baldwin's broadcast to the nation in May 1926 – 'It's *wonderful* and will help a lot, I'm sure'[7] – and was strongly opposed to any measure that smacked of vengeance on those who had led the strike.

The Prince's letter of congratulation was received by Baldwin within half an hour of the broadcast. Next day the Prime Minister showed it to Tom Jones, his confidant and deputy secretary of the Cabinet. 'The PM was obviously much moved at receiving so promptly so cordial a message,' wrote Jones.[8] William Bridgeman, the First Lord of the Admiralty, later told the Prince how near to complete breakdown Baldwin had come; 'I found that the words of sympathy he had received from you had done more to keep him up than anything else during those two or three days of terrific anxiety.'[1]

As the Depression began to bite and unemployment rose dramatically, the Prince's tours of the industrial areas inevitably took on a political connotation. One of the most controversial was to the coal-mining areas of Durham and Northumberland early in 1929. Before he started Baldwin rather nervously asked him under whose auspices he was making the visit. The Prince replied that it had been suggested by Sir Alexander Leith, a pillar of the Conservative Party. Baldwin expressed great relief. 'I was somewhat puzzled as to the precise difference between Conservative and Socialist humanitarianism,' the Prince noted drily.[2] He was accompanied on his tour only by Godfrey Thomas and Noel Curtis-Bennett, then in charge of the Coalfields' Distress Organization, and he deserted the well-trodden ways to visit some of the smaller mining villages and call on the miners in their homes. He wrote to Baldwin on the return journey: 'One really does have to see the conditions of housing, squalor and distress which exist to have any idea of what they have been "sticking", many of them ever since the war, and the most striking impression that I retain is their amazing bravery and friendliness despite the ghastly times they are existing through.' The most pathetic thing, he concluded, was that they 'weren't at all complaining, seemed glad to see one, and only told of their troubles when asked'.[3]

The tour, he believed, had done something to cheer the benighted. Curtis-Bennett went further; a tremendous success, he called it, 'indeed from a human sympathy point of view it was probably the most remarkable event of recent years. His Royal Highness's energy, enthusiasm and above all sincerity won all hearts and there can be no doubt that his visit brought a ray of happiness and hope to thousands of our unfortunate countrymen.'[4] Lord Londonderry, immensely rich coalmine-owner and member of Baldwin's government, saw things differently. The visit had been 'very unfortunate from every point of view'. The Prince's remarks about the 'appalling' or 'perfectly damnable' conditions had won most undesirable publicity. He had been hoodwinked by carefully contrived evidence of misery and destitution and had formed a 'thoroughly stage managed point of view'. The miners would undoubtedly benefit by the Prince's remarks when they next sought 'further to exploit the community'.[1]

There can be no doubt that the Prince's sympathy for the victims of the Depression was as sincere as Curtis-Bennett suggested. His cousin, Prince Christopher of Greece, said that he came back from the north looking tired and depressed. 'I can't get those poor fellows out of my mind,' he said. 'It's terrible to see the despair in their eyes.'[2] To the South African, Thomas Boydell, he fulminated about the unemployment and 'hellish' housing conditions: 'It was obvious he was deeply conscious of the social and economic wrongs, and resented them with every fibre of his body.'[3] How long the impression lingered, and how much he did once back in London to follow up these generous impulses, are harder to establish. Probably not much. But Lord Londonderry's indignation shows that the Prince's comments caused some alarm among the pit-owners and strengthened the hands of the miners. This alone was enough to justify the visit. And though the hopes which Curtis-Bennett said had been kindled in the hearts of the miners might not have been realized, surely it was better that they should believe someone in high places was concerned about their plight than that they should feel themselves totally neglected? The government had reason to feel grateful to him for having reminded people that all authority was not oppressive and all the rich were not indifferent to their woes.

It is sometimes said that Baldwin was discomfited by the success the Prince enjoyed on trips like these and tried to curb his freedom to tour the country. There is no evidence that he did so, or that he thought the views of men like Londonderry anything but self-interested and short-sighted. His opinion of the Prince was still extremely favourable. The friendship between Prime Minister and Prince was at its warmest before and during the tour of Canada in 1927. The ostensible object of the visit was to open the International Peace Bridge over the Niagara River between the United States and Canada. Baldwin came along because he thought it was high time a British prime minister visited Canada and also, no doubt, because he wanted to get to know his future King better than their occasional meetings in London permitted. The programme began with five hectic days of junketing in the cities of the east – 'a frightful week of princing,' the Prince described it to Freda

Dudley Ward, with endless ceremonies by day and hospitality by night. '"Burning the candle", etc, and I'm too old to make it now.'[1] To his father he complained about the interminable speeches; 'Of course the Canadian politicians love them. A speech to them is like a good day's shooting to you.'[2] The premier, Mackenzie King, was particularly long-winded. 'He's the limit and altogether very tricky and I can't take to him at all,' the Prince told Thomas, though after a long conversation after dinner in Ottawa he did admit that King became 'less – well, bloody is the only word that comes to hand'.[3]

Tommy Lascelles, who was in attendance, had started off in a mood of considerable irritation with his employer, 'as a stage-manager might feel if his Hamlet persisted in breaking off the play and balancing the furniture on the end of his nose'. He was particularly put out when the Prince dropped what Lascelles felt was the key sentence from a speech in Ottawa and substituted a funny story, 'not an unsuitable one for, say, the Commercial Travellers' Festival Banquet, but utterly out of place at the Govt of Canada's ceremonial board'.[4] After that things went better, however, and at his farewell dinner in Montreal, Lascelles reported, he 'spoke better than I ever remember hearing him do – with no hesitation, with conviction and with weight and gravity'.[5] And even when he had been misbehaving, Lascelles wrote ruefully, 'damn him, he is so affectionate to me that I find it terribly hard to nourish vipers in my weak bosom'.[6]

The Prince himself seems to have been sublimely unaware that he had caused Lascelles any anguish. 'Princing,' he told Freda Dudley Ward, was much easier abroad: 'Guess it's because one isn't hit up with a lot of old-fashioned and boring people and conventions. One feels somehow that people are so much more genuine out of England.'[7] (The comment was echoed three years later by John Aird when the Prince spoke particularly well at the Spanish Club. 'He seemed very happy, which I notice is always the case when he is with foreigners. He seems much more at ease with them than with the British.'[8])

The actual ceremony on the Peace Bridge got off to an unfortunate start since the Prince, through no fault of his own, kept the American Vice President waiting for two hours. To increase the tension still further, Sacco and Vanzetti, the left-wing agitators, were due to be executed the following day for a crime which many believed they did not commit, and the Americans were in a panic because of threats that the Vice President would be assassinated by way of retaliation. 'To emphasize the fact that we king-ridden Britons had really reached the land of the brave and the free,' wrote Lascelles, 'quantities of policemen, armed to the teeth, did a ceaseless ladies' chain through the crowd all the time the ceremony was in progress.'[1] Their pains were rewarded, Vice President and Prince were unmolested, the tape was cut, and the bridge duly opened.

The Prince and the Baldwins then set off westwards, travelling together as far as Alberta. In his memoirs the Prince was to claim that on this trip he first detected in Baldwin signs of the arrogance and John Bullish nature which were to become so much more apparent to him when he was King. There are no traces of this revelation in his letters of the period. To the Queen he reported that the Baldwins had been 'most charming travelling companions . . . The PM has been absolutely wonderful . . .'[2] 'Absolutely marvellous,' he wrote to Godfrey Thomas. The Prime Minister had made 'some d—d good speeches . . . Mrs B has been wonderful too . . . A very nice family indeed and I'm glad to have got to know them.'[3] Baldwin reciprocated this approval. The warmth of the Prince's welcome had been a revelation, he wrote, the popular enthusiasm was extraordinary. 'The Prince of Wales was at his best and it was a real pleasure to be with him.'[4]

It is hard to equate this feast of mutual congratulation with the response that Lascelles claimed to have received when he took advantage of a tête-à-tête with Baldwin to pour out his doubts about the development of the Prince and the future of the monarchy. He summarized his feelings in a letter to Godfrey Thomas: 'The cold fact remains that, as Joey and I both agree, it would be a real disaster if, by any ill chance, he was called on to accede to the throne now and that neither of us see any prospect of his fitting himself any better, as time goes on, for what is, ultimately, his job in life, and ours – ie making a good, or at any rate, a safe king.'[5]

When he expounded this thesis to Baldwin, the Prime Minister is supposed to have appeared unsurprised, and to have given the impression that he had suspected it all already. If true, he kept his suspicions to himself; certainly nothing he said at this stage to the

Prince gave any indication that he did not look forward to the next reign with sunny confidence.

Lascelles was the most rigidly high-principled of the Prince's household. Himself a man of total integrity, he despised any shortcomings in lesser mortals. He attached the greatest importance to intellectual ability, and condemned sloppy thinking and judgments swayed by prejudice or sentiment. Though himself in fact one of the most emotional of men, he abhorred and feared it as the basis of activity in others. He saw humanity in black and white. Once he had extravagantly admired the Prince; now that he was disillusioned he found it hard to believe that the qualities he had applauded were all still there. His perception of his employer's weaknesses increasingly blotted out any objective assessment of pros and cons. It was inevitable that the two men could not continue to work harmoniously together. A tour of Africa the following year brought about their separation.

The Prince had long wanted to go on safari in East Africa, more to observe the game than to destroy it, since as Lascelles warned Edward Grigg, political adviser to the royal tours of Canada and Australia and now Governor of Kenya, he was 'definitely bored by shooting and fishing'.[1] Amery, the Colonial Secretary, pleaded with him to give as much notice as possible: 'His own preference would be to dash off without notice.'[2] The Prince agreed, but refused to be tied down to an inflexible schedule on what he insisted was primarily a holiday trip. Lascelles urged Grigg to humour this wish. The Prince throve on the improvised and the unexpected, wilted when trapped into a formal ritual: 'I can say with perfect truth that I have never seen the P do such good work, or play his part with greater advantage to himself and the Brit. Emp. than on those occasions when he had no set programme and has himself fixed up a plan of campaign with the man on the spot.' There was also nothing to be done, he said, about the Prince's refusal to bring dress uniform: full dress meant pomp and formality, formality would ensure that he did not do his best, 'and his best is such a good best, that my own belief is that it outweighs the harm done by abrogating that outward regality to which we have all been accustomed in his predecessors'.[3]

The plan was for the Prince and Prince Henry to travel out together in September 1928, to pursue their separate safaris, then to join up and, if the rains permitted, continue overland to South Africa where they would spend Christmas with the Athlones. The two Princes diligently studied Swahili on the way out – 'and are rather boring about it,' commented Lady Grigg resignedly after their arrival[1] – and enjoyed a preview of the seamier side of Kenyan life through the presence on board of Gladys, Lady Delamere. The Prince admitted to Freda Dudley Ward that he saw a lot of Lady Delamere, 'but only *faute de mieux* . . . I guess she's a bit keen but as I just couldn't be less she has to be content with a little dancing for exercise.'[2] He protested too much or too early; Gladdy Delamere was to play a conspicuous part in his sojourn in Nairobi.

Kenya was consumed by excitement at the Prince's arrival. The ballroom at Government House was hurriedly completed, the roads round Nairobi were put in order, the shops burgeoned with new hats and dresses. 'The English are completely crazy over their royal family,' commented the writer Isak Dinesen – Baroness Blixen – in surprise, but soon she was as crazy as anyone. 'The Prince is really absolutely charming, and I am so much in love with him that it hurts.' He invited himself to a native dance at Isak Dinesen's farm, spoke Swahili to the chiefs, and had an electrifying effect upon the natives.[3] John Arthur, who had worked with the natives in Kenya for more than twenty years, told Grigg that his protégés were overwhelmed by the Prince's 'humility and his approachableness'. When the rain came and he turned up his collar like any other mortal they collapsed with astonishment. He aroused a spirit of 'loyalty and real affection' for what had been a remote institution. 'It seems to me an absolutely vital change, fraught with infinite prospects for good.'[4]

All this Lascelles could applaud, but he found it hard to condone the more frivolous side of the visit, revelry by night and high jinks at that mecca of the more social settlers, the Muthaiga Club. 'The Prince never likes going to bed before 3 a.m. I *do* wish I was in England,' he remarked plaintively to Lady Grigg.[5] Lady Delamere was at the centre of the merry-making, throwing herself at the Prince and, in the view of most beholders, making a considerable impression. At supper at the Muthaiga Club she bombarded him with pieces of bread, incidentally giving Isak Dinesen a black eye with a misdirected volley, and finished up by rushing at him, overturning his chair and rolling him around on the floor. 'I do not find that kind of thing in the least amusing,' commented Isak Dinesen.[1] Lady Grigg did not find that the Prince improved on acquaintance. By the time the visit to Nairobi was over, she was describing him as 'the most unpleasant and uncivil guest I have ever had in my house'. Yet only a few days before she had written of his 'sweetness and charm. I simply adore the Prince,' and when they next met she was to describe him as 'a perfect host and so sweet'.[2] It is striking how often those who condemned the Prince at one moment for frivolity or licentiousness, forgave him the next for his humility, his sweetness of nature, his eagerness to make amends.

The Prince told Freda Dudley Ward that he did not enjoy his stay in Nairobi, which he portrayed somewhat disingenuously as an unbroken series of 'official stunts' such as dinner and garden parties.[3] He never felt at ease with Grigg, though he sympathized with his problems, caught as he was between the Colonial Office, who believed that in the long run Kenya should be ruled by its black inhabitants, and the white settlers, who felt still more emphatically that it should not. The Prince took the part of the settlers: 'Why should they who have been pioneers in Kenya for 30 years, who have taught the natives everything they know, and who know them far better than any official ever could, why should they submit to a policy of equal rights with the natives and Indians which would change their position of "bwana" or master out here to that of merely the white section of the population?' It was India over again; Montagu had ruined the proudest jewel in the imperial crown, now the Colonial Office, egged on by 'labour and other political influences', was moving on the lesser targets.[4]

The safari proper began in mid-November, with the great white hunter, Denys Finch Hatton, in charge of the operation. 'We have been fairly good here – fairly,' was Lascelles's final judgment on the visit to Nairobi.[5] At Malisa the Prince shot an elephant and thought it poor sport, easy and unexciting. He revised his view a few days later when a one-tusked elephant, which he had previously scorned as a target, erupted from the forest and charged the party. The Prince and Lascelles politely debated which of them should have the privilege of shooting the elephant, until it came to within about twenty feet, at which point Peter Pearson, of the Uganda Game Department, pushed the Prince into the comparative safety of a thorn bush and the professionals in the party opened fire. The elephant veered away when only eight feet from its enemies. 'Does that often happen?' asked the shaken Prince. 'No, sir,' replied Pearson irascibly. 'We don't usually go assing about arguing who is going to shoot the elephant!'[1]

The holiday was dramatically disrupted when 'G' Trotter suffered an almost lethal heart attack. The party was on the Upper Nile at the time and for a day he lay below in his cabin, on the fringes of death, with the doctor twice giving him up as lost and, in Lascelles's words, 'the Prince crying like a frightened child on deck'.[2] 'I nearly went mad,' the Prince told Freda Dudley Ward. '. . . it's been just one of the very longest days of my life and it would have been so ghastly if he had died.'[3] Trotter survived, but clearly could not continue the trip beyond Kampala. Lascelles stayed with him until he could be loaded aboard a ship for England; 'The Prince would have stayed too, but they have prepared this elaborate camp for him and the Governor was terribly anxious that he should not miss it, so we made him go.'[4] This was only the first of the misfortunes which overtook the expedition. On 27 November 1928, when the Prince was beginning to think of joining up with his brother and heading for South Africa, a cypher telegram from Baldwin informed him that the King was dangerously ill. 'We hope that all may go well,' cabled the Prime Minister, 'but if not, and you have made no attempt to return, it will profoundly shock public opinion.'[5] Lascelles later recorded the scene in vivid detail, and though his description may have owed something to the animosity that he increasingly felt towards his former master, the story has the ring of truth. 'I don't believe a word of it,' was the Prince's first reaction. 'It's just some election dodge of old Baldwin's.' Lascelles lost his temper: 'Sir, the King of England is dying, and if that means nothing to you, it means a great deal to us.' The Prince looked at him, went out without a word, and spent the remainder of the evening in the successful seduction of the wife of a local British official. 'He told me so himself next morning,' wrote Lascelles.[6] According to another account, the Prince explained to a friend who expressed some surprise at his behaviour that this was the best thing to do after suffering a shock.[7]

He *had* suffered a shock, and coming on top of Trotter's near death, it threw him totally off balance. He was not and never would be callous, but the death of the King would have meant not only the loss of a father but also his abrupt accession to the throne. The prospect was a dreadful one. The Duke of York told him of 'a lovely story going about' that the reason for his hurried return home was his fear that 'I am going to bag the Throne in your absence!!!! Just like the Middle Ages.'[1] The Prince was in no mood to be amused. He barely made sense in the first few days after the news reached him. Once he had accepted that his father's life was really in danger, he wanted to return by air but was talked out of what would have been a decidedly hazardous enterprise. Instead he rushed to Dar-es-Salaam where a cruiser picked him up. The heavy luggage had gone on to South Africa, so he was still in his safari clothes when he arrived at Brindisi. Godfrey Thomas met him with something more suitable to wear and Mussolini's special train hastened him on to England. At Brindisi he was also handed a letter from the Princess Royal rejoicing at his return: 'You don't realize what a help it is to Mama as she says she feels rather lost without being able to consult Papa and was so anxious to have you back.'[2] And at Folkestone the Prime Minister told him that the King was weak and his life still in danger, even if he survived the Prince would have to shoulder much of the burden of monarchy in the coming year. He was thirty-four years old. Shades of the prison house had at last closed upon him.

From Uganda, in October, Lascelles had written that the Prince had not been doing at all badly but 'I am thoroughly and permanently out of sympathy with him ... His personal charm has vanished irretrievably so far as I am concerned, and I always feel as if I were working, not for the next King of England, but for the son of the latest American millionaire.'[3] He could endure the work in London, he remarked a fortnight later, but he found the tours intolerable. And there was no reason to hope that these would diminish in number: 'Only two things keep him at home now — riding races and F.W. Both those sheet anchors may part any moment; hunting, as opposed to pt to pts has already faded out of the picture, and he himself admits that F.W. won't last for ever.'[4] Shortly after their return to England Lascelles resigned. He profited by the occasion to tell the Prince exactly what he thought of him and his way of life. The Prince, wrote Lascelles, 'heard me with scarcely an interruption, and when we parted, said, "Well, good-night Tommy, and thank you for the talk. I suppose the fact of the matter is that I'm quite the wrong sort of person to be Prince of Wales" – wh was so pathetically true that it almost melted me.' The Prince gave Lascelles a car as a leaving present, invited him to stay with him at his country house and treated him thereafter with his usual friendliness.[1]

Lascelles was not the only member of the household to feel dissatisfaction and distress. Thomas told him that he too was planning to resign: 'My reasons are obviously the same as yours. I have for some time past ceased to do my job to my own satisfaction.'[2] Halsey announced that he would go too: 'Going out into Society is getting more and more difficult as one gets attacked on all sides about HRH's shortcomings and general way of behaviour, and I have now become a professional liar.'[3] But neither Thomas nor Halsey did resign. Partly, no doubt, this was because they were older men than Lascelles and would have found it harder to get another job. Even more, though, it was because they were still devoted to the Prince and believed that, when the time came, his good qualities would come to the fore and his weaknesses fall away. Lascelles could not feel loyalty towards an employer whom he did not thoroughly respect; Thomas and Halsey, Piers Legh too, could criticize and complain yet retain their allegiance towards and affection for their maverick master.

Thomas summed up the problem when he told Lascelles that, 'HRH, knowing so little English history, alas, will always go on believing that, provided he carries out his public duties to the satisfaction of the Press and the man in the street, his private life is entirely his own concern. I'm terribly sorry for him, but unless someone can succeed in disabusing him of this *idée fixe*, I see nothing but disaster ahead.'[4] In a memorandum that he wrote at this time he said that he thought 'HRH's high watermark had been in about 1922, since when he had shown a steady decline, with a sharper drop in the last two years'.[5] Sadly Stamfordham agreed that the Prince's stock had fallen, 'not only among the Victorians, the old frumps like myself, but even the young and frivolous, to say nothing of the upper classes: ... even the Eastenders and the Labour Party'. He longed, he said, to see the Prince 'get into touch with a wider circle . . . remember his grandfather who *never* let go dignity, not be bored with state functions and all the "outward and visible" signs of monarchy'.[1]

The criticisms of the courtiers must be seen in perspective. Whatever Stamfordham may have believed, there is precious little reason to think that the Eastenders or the Labour Party, or for that matter the middle classes or the country gentry, felt that the stock of the Prince had fallen. Gossip about his drinking or his love affairs was confined to a small section of London society; complaints about his informality or his indifference to tradition were heard only from an old-fashioned and perhaps blinkered elite. But the circle of those who felt the Prince to be less than perfect widened by the day; and those who were losing faith in him were the very people with whom he would have to work in the forthcoming years. Their disapproval augured ill for the next reign.

12

The Last Years as Prince

===

THE PRINCE OF WALES IS SAID ONCE TO HAVE EXPRES-
sed approval of the Nepali system of government, under
which the Crown Prince took over the reins of power as
soon as he was mature, the old monarch being relegated to formal
duties.[1] In 1929, with his father incapacitated, he found that
Katmandu had come to London. He was a member of the Council
of State, he received Foreign Office telegrams though not Cabinet
minutes, he took over all the visible functions of the King. Even
when his father had recovered sufficiently to return to Windsor the
Prince was still thrust to the forefront. It was he who stood
beside the Queen when the American Ambassador, General Dawes,
outraged protocol by appearing at court in trousers rather than
knee breeches – a misdemeanour which the Prince found singularly
easy to forgive. It was he who had to receive the Russian Ambassador when the King refused to be in the same room as a representative of the murderers of his cousin.[2] When the *New York World*
made much of this story, the Foreign Office dismissed it as mischievous and false; the Prince they said had received *all* foreign representatives presenting their credentials in 1929. To Bruce Lockhart,
however, the Prince confirmed that his father had indeed balked
at this unsavoury task; he himself had been quite content to take
it on since he had hardly known the Tsar and accepted the Soviet
government as an inescapable reality.[3]

By the beginning of 1930 the King's recovery was so complete
that the Prince was able to resume his interrupted safari. The trip
differed from its predecessor in that for much of it his current
favourite, Lady Furness, was in attendance – Lord Furness, too,
but inconspicuously. The Prince was always happier when all his
attentions could be concentrated on one object – promiscuity
distracted but never satisfied him. On safari 'the Prince's tent was
always on one end of the line and mine next to his, and we

196

shared a fire', Thelma Furness wrote in her memoirs;[1] a convenient arrangement which would not have appealed to Tommy Lascelles.

Lady Furness was on a cross-country drive with the Prince when he collapsed and had almost to be carried to his train. There he was found to have a dangerously high temperature and malaria was diagnosed. The Prince had objected strongly to having a personal physician in attendance on safari, but fortunately for him an eminent Nairobi doctor had been sent along by Grigg disguised as a chauffeur.[2] When he got back to Nairobi he was still feverish and semi-conscious but his recovery was rapid and he was soon well enough to be exigent about his food – prunes and dates were all he would eat – and to devour all the picture papers that Lady Grigg could procure for him.[3] Stamfordham wrote to Grigg to congratulate him on the Prince's wonderful recovery: 'It was very gratifying to read what you said of the niceness and charm which the Prince displayed.'[4] Either Grigg had larded truth with tactfulness or the Governor and his Lady were not as one; in her diary Lady Grigg noted: 'I see his charm but I think he is ungracious and terribly self-centred.'[5]

The more the Prince travelled, the less inclined he felt to return home and settle down to 'princing'. He wrote to Freda Dudley Ward from the Upper Nile, feeling '*sunk*, and inferiority complex worse than usual'. He was dreading the return to London and 'all the silly stunting, and I'm getting too old now for all that silly artificial nonsense. The older I get, the bigger fool I'm made to look, and God knows that's not difficult.'[6]

As always, his failure to get on with his father was an important factor in his malaise. Towards the end of 1928 things had gone better. The Prince 'is closer to his Father and Mother in every way than he has been – probably since he was a child', Halsey told Wigram.[7] Halsey went too far, but the Prince surprised himself by the warmth he felt towards his father when he returned from Africa to find him 'a little, shrunken old man with a white beard; the shock was so great that I cried'.[8] Baldwin reported that the doctors tried to bar the Prince from what they feared would be the King's deathbed, but he ignored them. 'The old King, who had for nearly a week been practically unconscious, just opened half an eye, looked up at him and said: "Damn you, what the devil are you doing here?" And from that moment he turned the corner.'[9] The scene might have echoes of the dying Henry IV's confrontation with Prince Hal, but George V knew only too well that his eldest son was not hankering after the crown. The first half of 1929 showed a real rapprochement between father and son, as the Prince took on many of the burdens of monarchy. He even gave up riding in point-to-points. But as the King grew stronger, so the frail reconciliation crumbled. The Prince made little attempt to disguise the situation. When he visited Ealing Studios to see a film being made he regretfully left early on the grounds that he had to call on his father at Buckingham Palace. Basil Dean remembered that the prospect seemed to make him irritable and nervous. 'From his remarks it was clear that relations between them did not run smoothly.'[1] Sometimes the Prince set out to annoy and too easily succeeded, more often he gave offence inadvertently. A typical example was the King's first Christmas message to the nation in 1932. The Prince, who had heard the broadcast rehearsed several times already, disappeared into the garden when the moment came. 'I confess I was rather hurt that you should have gone out to play golf just when I made my short broadcast,' complained the King.[2]

In March 1932 George V had what was for him an extraordinarily long and intimate conversation with his son. He told the Prince that he was still worshipped by the public but that this would not survive the gradual revelation of his private life, in particular his liaison with Lady Furness. He asked his son whether he was really happy and whether he did not wish to have someone to whom he could turn for sympathy and true affection. How could he face the loneliness of the throne without a Queen with whom he could share it? The Prince admitted he was not happy but said the only woman he had ever wanted to marry was Freda Dudley Ward. It was in the course of this conversation that the King asked whether his son had considered marrying 'a suitable well-born English girl', and the Prince replied that he had never supposed it would be possible. Next day the Prince told Halsey that he had had 'a very satisfactory interview' with his father. He thought the King 'was a bit old-fashioned, and rather resented HM's remarks on his personal friends. Otherwise HRH generally admitted that the King's criticism of his behaviour was fair comment.'[3]

Two years later Thomas announced hopefully that the King was

'going to take some action with HRH, which would be excellent
... It can't do any harm but might do good.'[1] Nothing came of
it, however, and this conversation in 1932 seems to have been the
last attempt the King made seriously to influence his son, or to talk
him into marriage. There were suggestions that Princess Ingrid of
Sweden might be a suitable bride, but though the Swedish King
personally liked the idea it was never seriously contemplated in
York House, or even Buckingham Palace.[2] Mountbatten, he said at
the Prince's behest, prepared a list of seventeen European princesses
who were theoretically possible, ranging in age down to the
fifteen-year-old Thyra of Mecklenburg-Schwerin, but such ritual
gestures were made increasingly without conviction. No one who
knew the Prince of Wales at all well believed by the mid-1930s
that it was possible he would ever marry.

The King retreated into resigned despair. The records abound
of his dire prognostications. 'After I am dead the boy will ruin
himself within twelve months,' he is supposed to have said to
Baldwin – the boy then being forty.[3] 'What use is it, when I know
my son is going to let it down,' he retorted to Archbishop Lang,
who had congratulated him on the high standing of the monarchy.[4]
'My eldest son will never succeed me. He will abdicate,' he told
the courtier Ulick Alexander.[5] And finally, and most bitter, when
within a few weeks of his death: 'I pray to God my eldest son will
never marry and have children, and that nothing will come between
Bertie and Lilibet and the throne.'[6] Such remarks may have been
embellished by the hearer, or not have reflected the King's considered views, but there can be no doubt that in the closing years
of his reign he viewed the prospects of his successor with the utmost
pessimism. Not all the Prince's retinue would have agreed with
Lascelles that the pessimism was well justified. His equerry, John
Aird, for one, believed that the King was ill-informed about his
son's real nature and activities and that his concerns were for the
most part illusory. 'I have been told that HRH's behaviour is killing
the King,' he wrote in his diary. 'If so I am very sorry, but feel that
it is not probable and quite unnecessary.' The trouble, he felt, lay
with the courtiers, the staff at York House not excepted, who
eagerly retailed to the King 'all the nasty gossip, which is very
wrong of them and does no good'.[7]

As his brothers did what he had failed to do and married, so the

Prince drifted away from them. The pattern of his life was not
suited to the domesticity of the royal Princes. The inimitable
Crawfie – Marion Crawford, who had been governess to the
Princesses since 1932 – described in her book about the royal
children how he would regularly visit the Yorks and romp in the
children's nursery after tea, but in fact he saw the Duke of York
with increasing rareness and never penetrated to the nursery. Freda
Dudley Ward's two daughters were far more like nieces to him
than the Princesses Elizabeth and Margaret Rose. Prince Henry he
rarely saw; when the future Duke of Gloucester became engaged
in 1935 he did no more than express mild surprise that he could
not remember having ever met his fiancée. 'I am glad for Harry
and hope they will be very happy,' was the limit of his fraternal
rapture.[1]

Prince George was both the closest to him and gave him by far
the most cause for concern. After he left the Navy Prince George
took up residence in York House. Intelligent, artistic and disastrously ready to sample any delight that might be laid in front of
him, he quickly proved ill-equipped to look after himself in the
jungle of London society. He was a constant source of anxiety to
his parents, and one of the reasons why the Prince of Wales got
on better with them in 1928 and 1929 was their shared anxiety
about his brother. The trouble came to a head when Prince George
fell into the clutches of an attractive American called Kiki Preston
who introduced him to drugs. For several months the Prince tried
to persuade both parties to break it off, then intervened heavily in
the summer of 1929. Somehow he forced Mrs Preston to leave the
country and to write to Prince George saying that she would
henceforth live permanently abroad. As for his brother, he more
or less incarcerated him in the country and personally took charge
of his recuperation. He told Freda Dudley Ward how exhausting
he found the work of 'doctor, gaoler and detective combined', but
he was getting used to it. 'I know I shouldn't feel bitter and
disappointed that my holiday with you has gone West and on the
contrary should only be too delighted that the cure is going so
well.'[2] A month or so later he was still unable to fix up a meeting
with her, 'but the cure has reached rather a tricky and critical stage
and it may be that I'll be needed this next fortnight'. To soothe his
nerves, he told her, he had taken up needlework, which he did

while sitting in Prince George's sickroom: 'It would make you laugh and maybe cry a little too.'[1]

By the end of 1929 the worst was over and in mid-January 1930 the Prince was able to tell the King that he felt happier about the future: 'It really is a terrible and terrifying thing to happen to anyone, and far worse to one's brother.'[2] In South Africa he discussed the case with his aunt Alice. 'He really has given me an enormous amount of trouble and anxiety and I worry over him all the time, even while I'm away ... The old saying "Boys will be boys" is all right until you get too old and should have known the form better.'[3] A few weeks later he received a 'long, pathetic and repentant' letter from Prince George, but though every word in it was obviously sincere, he still had doubts about how permanent the cure was going to prove.[4] He was right; in 1932 Prince George ran into Kiki Preston while in Cannes and had to be removed almost by force. 'I was sorry for HRH as he took it so much to heart ...' wrote Aird. 'I was very much impressed with the way he handled the situation.'[5]

His brother's troubles undoubtedly caused the Prince real and lasting pain but he would have been superhuman if he had not felt a tremor of satisfaction when he told his mother how sad it was that somebody who possessed as much charm and intelligence as Prince George should be 'such a bad "picker", both as regards friends and the company he keeps. He seems to lack all sense of knowing what is so obviously the wrong thing to do.'[6] For one who had so often been criticized for his selection of friends and his talent for doing the wrong thing, it must have been agreeable to be so conspicuously enrolled among the angels. The patience, the determination and the self-sacrifice that he showed in caring for his brother were of the highest order. Getting Prince George off drugs, wrote Bruce Ogilvy, was 'a very good mark for the Prince, as I am sure he was largely responsible'.[7] On this at least the King was equally approving: 'Looking after him all those months must have been a great strain on you, and I think it was wonderful all you did for him.'[8]

In 1934 Princess Marina of Greece became engaged to Prince George. She had been a friend of Freda Dudley Ward, who had once suggested she might make a suitable wife for the Prince of Wales. The Prince liked her and appreciated her beauty, but was no more disposed to marry her than any other continental princess. He was startled when the engagement was announced. 'Brother George was quick on the job, wasn't he?' he commented to Godfrey Thomas. 'So d—d quick that one wonders how long it will last. You know my views on "Royal Marriages", so that unless they really are fond of each other I'm sorry for both. However, marriage of some kind was the only hope for him, giving him some responsibility and a home of his own.'[1] The wedding took place in Westminster Abbey, preceded by a Greek Orthodox service. At the latter the Prince of Wales caused a mild furore when he not only absent-mindedly pulled out a cigarette but lit it on a candle held by a priest.[2] It did not take him long to conclude that his doubts were uncalled for. The Duke and Duchess of Kent, as they had now become, really were fond of each other. They became his closest friends and allies in the royal family and regular visitors at his homes.

The home to which they came most often was Fort Belvedere. This castellated folly – 'a child's idea of a fort,' Diana Cooper called it[3] – lay on the edge of Windsor Great Park above Virginia Water. The Prince had asked his father for the use of it in 1929. 'What could you possibly want that queer old place for?' asked the King. 'Those damn weekends, I suppose.'[4] It was more than that, it was a home, the first home he had ever had, the house he always said he loved more than any other material thing. With the help and advice of Freda Dudley Ward he redesigned the interior, put in extra bedrooms and bathrooms, built a swimming pool and a tennis court. But it was the garden and surrounding grounds that gave him the greatest joy. Inheriting a jungle of rhododendrons, laurels and scrubby birches, he set to work to carve great vistas and to open up the house. Whenever he had a spare hour he would plunge into the undergrowth. At lunch time, if there were no guests and sometimes if there were, the footman would bring him out an apple and a cup of tea. He would whistle to indicate his arrival, the Prince would whistle back, and eventually the two would stumble across each other. He would keep at his pursuit until the last moment and would then rush in, stripping as he advanced through the house, his shirt in the hall, his trousers in the doorway, until he arrived naked by the bath. Any guest was recruited to help in the work. 'Prince of Wales has gone mad on gardening,' noted Bruce Lockhart in his diary. 'Taken to it 100 per cent like golf. Prince George wanted to bring Marina down. Prince of Wales put him off several times. At last agreed grudgingly, if George would bring a scythe. George had to cut grass all afternoon.'[1]

For the Prince it was the antithesis of Windsor Castle, of all that was formal or pompous. He flew from the tower not the Prince of Wales's standard but the flag of the Duchy of Cornwall. Responsibilities and dignity fell away when he was there. Once a consignment of gramophone records was delivered, labelled unbreakable. Determined to test this boast to the uttermost he and the Duke of York took them on to the terrace and began to throw them around like discuses. Then the game was transferred indoors and only stopped when a particularly treasured lamp was broken.[2] Meals were — by the standards of palace life — informal, clothes even more so. There was dancing after dinner, or sometimes not too taxing paper games. 'Frank Estimations' was briefly a favourite. In this game each person gave himself points out of ten for certain qualities, while the other players did the same and handed in their lists anonymously. The marks were then compared. On one occasion the Prince gave himself three for sex appeal against a popular verdict of four; six for good looks against eight; five for charm against eight; and ten for sincerity against a mere three and a half. He was indignant at this judgment. 'Sincerity is the most important qualification I think I have,' he expostulated.[3]

Secluded in the woods as it was, Fort Belvedere was an ideal site at which to practise the bagpipes. He had first learned to play this fearsome instrument at Oxford, had neglected it since, but now took it up with redoubled fervour. On a trip in the Mediterranean he even conceived a slow march, which he kept in his head and played to George V's piper, Henry Forsyth. Forsyth set it down as music and the Prince's career as composer attained its apotheosis when the pipes of the Scots Guards played 'Mallorca' at the Derby Day dinner in 1935.[4] Not all his guests appreciated his prowess. When asked how he liked the pipes, Thomas Beecham replied candidly: 'Not much, and then only on the other side of a mountain.' His punishment was to be subjected to a barrage of music from his host and Piper Fletcher.[1] His other musical speciality was the ukulele, on which he would strum away for hours. Once Godfrey Thomas brought his schoolboy son Michael to Fort Belvedere. Michael was exiled to the kitchen for supper. The Prince heard he was there, came downstairs, and sat on the table playing the ukulele while Michael ate.

The performance says more for his good nature than his musical appreciation. His contretemps with Rubinstein at Lady Colefax's dinner illustrates both his limitations in this field and the problems of the biographer. Kenneth Clark records how the Prince, when Rubinstein was persuaded to play Chopin's Barcarolle after dinner, was upset because he had expected the intermezzo from *The Tales of Hoffman*. When Rubinstein embarked on a Chopin Prelude at 10.15 p.m., the Prince rose to leave. The situation was only saved by Noël Coward, who took over the piano. Rubinstein left in dudgeon, escorted by Clark who murmured polite nothings about the philistinism of the British.[2] Harold Nicolson tells much the same story, but puts the time of the Prince's attempted departure at a more respectable 12.30 a.m. and has Rubinstein embarking on his fourth piece.[3] Bruce Lockhart maintains that the Prince looked bored but made no attempt to leave.[4] Finally Rubinstein himself says that the Prince was an old friend with whom he had spent several uproarious evenings at the Embassy Club. It was a standing joke between them that the first time Rubinstein had played the piano at York House, a leg had broken and the instrument collapsed in ruins. He knew perfectly well that the Prince cared nothing for classical music and liked him none the less well because of it. The Prince had not, as Clark recorded, reproached Rubinstein with playing the wrong Barcarolle, but had not noticed the difference. Rubinstein had been amused but not in the least offended.[5]

If the problems of a biographer are so complex over an incident as trivial as the above, how much worse it is when it comes to deciding what an individual really thought about serious political or social issues. Not only does every witness tell a different story but the principal character himself will almost certainly prove fluctuating in his views and unclear in his own mind as to what at any given moment those views might be. The Prince of Wales's opinions on international affairs were slow to take shape and not conspicuously consistent or coherent when they had done so. Before 1930 or thereabouts, he took no special interest in the world outside the Empire. Bruce Lockhart remembers him in 1926 sitting up until two and talking about Russia and Central Europe, but the chances are that he was determined to sit up until two and had to talk about *something*.[1] But it was during this period that he shed the prejudices that had dominated him at the end of the First World War. Germany ceased to be the hated enemy, perhaps, in part, due to the influence of the Dudley Ward family who regularly took their holidays there and were fond of the people and the country. France ceased to be the favoured ally, as the memory of wartime comradeship faded. 'The Franco-German situation looks mighty bad, doesn't it?' he wrote to his father in 1923. 'The French really are impossible people, and so impetuous.'[2] By the end of the 1920s his thinking was dominated by sharp fear of the communist threat from Russia, sympathy for Germany in its economic and political woes, and doubts about the good judgment of the French. It was his fear of the communists and doubts about the French that combined to make him view the future of Germany first with apprehension and then with hope.

The 1930s show him taking a more informed interest in foreign affairs. Harold Nicolson met him at dinner and discussed 'America and diplomacy . . . He knows an astonishing amount about it all. "What can I do?" he says. "They will only say, 'Here's that bloody Prince of Wales butting in.'"'[3] Duff Cooper was amused when the Prince began to interrogate an American shooting friend, Harry Brown, about the latest decision of the Supreme Court. Brown had to admit 'that neither he, nor, so far as he was aware, any of his friends at Palm Beach had ever heard of the Supreme Court'.[4] But the Prince's interest was selective and depended on whom he had happened to meet or where he had been. In 1935 he put forward a project for a tour by yacht of the resort ports of Italy. 'I fear you don't read the newspapers much,' wrote his father, 'otherwise you would know that our relations with Italy at the moment are distinctly strained about Abyssinia.'[5] The Prince in fact did know quite a lot about British relations with Italy, and had considerable sympathy with the Italian position, but he saw no reason why what he regarded as the mismanagement of the Foreign Office should disturb his holiday plans.

Increasingly his belief that communism posed the most important threat to the future of Europe coloured all his other convictions. Count Mensdorff, a former Austrian Ambassador in London and exceptionally well-informed about British affairs, called on him in November 1933 and was amazed how much sympathy the Prince expressed for the Nazi Party in Germany – 'Of course it is the only thing to do,' he said, 'we will have to come to it, as we are in great danger from the Communists too.' Mensdorff got the impression that the Prince had given little thought to the realities of National Socialism, or to the likely future for such a regime.[1] But this did not stop him defending it publicly. About the same time he told Louis Ferdinand of Prussia that Germany's internal affairs were its own business and added 'that dictators were very popular these days and that we might want one in England before long'.[2]

It is important to put such remarks in the context of their times. The Prince saw the balance of power in Europe as lying between a degenerate and enfeebled France and a virile and resurgent Germany. He admired the achievements of National Socialism in the fields closest to his heart, of housing for the workers and of unemployment. He ignored, or paid little attention to, the thuggery and brutal authoritarianism which were the hallmarks of the regime. He was mildly anti-Semitic, in the manner of so many of his class and generation, but would never have condoned persecution, still less genocide. He believed the horror stories which were beginning to filter out of Germany to be at the best exaggerated and more often propaganda, based on communist disinformation. In all this he shared the views of a large proportion, possibly a majority, of senior Conservatives, and was far more moderate than some. He was encouraged in his attitude by some who within a few years were themselves to be the victims of German aggression. The future King Olav of Norway in December 1935 wrote to him deploring the fact that France had 'double-crossed the whole of the League and us all', and said that the only hope for a secure Europe was 'a close relationship between England and Germany'.[3]

A visit that he paid to Austria early in 1935 shows him in a different light. Walford Selby, the British Ambassador, thought that his presence gave support to the Austrians at a time when they were under much pressure from Hitler.[1] Selby was perhaps professionally bound to think things like that. But the left-wing journalist G. E. R. Gedye praised the way the Prince insisted on visiting the model workers' houses which were the legacy of the previous government and refused to go to the Rathaus. 'Rathaus?' he exclaimed, when his barber at the Hotel Bristol expressed surprise at this, 'Good God no! What on earth would my workers think of me in London if I went to that place which the Fascists took away from the Socialists?' According to Gedye, 'Soon all underground Socialist Vienna was seething with admiration for the Prince.'[2] If this was indeed the case, then their seething was far from justified; but if one is going to view this sort of story with scepticism, it is only fair to be equally sceptical about accounts which make the Prince out to be a crypto-Fascist and a would-be Jew-baiter.

The German government certainly attached great, perhaps exaggerated importance to his attitude. To have support in high places in London was one of their objectives, to find it in the man who must soon occupy the highest office in the realm was an unlooked-for bonus. Successive German Ambassadors were instructed to cultivate him; National Socialist sympathizers among his German relations were despatched with messages of good will from the Nazi leaders; the Duke of Brunswick was even asked to arrange a marriage between his seventeen-year-old daughter Frederica and the Prince. The Duke pleaded that the difference of ages was too great, and in the end she became Queen of Greece.[3] There was no shortage of reports from the German Embassy to convince Hitler that the Prince was a useful ally. In April 1935 the Ambassador, Leopold von Hoesch, described him as being critical of the Foreign Office's one-sided attitude on German affairs and said that he 'once again showed his complete understanding of Germany's position and aspirations'.[4] In June of the same year Wigram told the King that Ribbentrop, Hitler's principal adviser on foreign affairs, had met the Prince at a party given by Lady Cunard. Subsequently Ribbentrop telegraphed Berlin to report that the Prince had once again showed complete sympathy with Germany's aspirations. 'After all, he is half a German,' he added in explanation.[1] 'I cannot believe there is any truth in this,' Wigram told the King, but in fact he took the story seriously and he was probably not wrong to do so. In congenial surroundings the Prince was capable of startling indiscretions, and on most issues of international policy he felt that there was much right on the German side. He would have preferred it if there had been no Anschluss, if the Germans had not so overtly menaced Czechoslovakia, if they had been more restrained in their demands for the return of their colonies, but on all these issues he condoned German behaviour and encouraged the forces of compromise.

He made no attempt to conceal his views. At dinner at Lady Colefax's in mid-1935 there was a long discussion of foreign policy. Brendan Bracken was 'very anti-German and warlike'; Bruce Lockhart 'rather anti-French and our own foreign policy'; the Prince 'came out very strong for friendship with Germany: never heard him talk so definitely about any subject before'. After this episode Bruce Lockhart was accused of influencing the Prince in favour of the Germans. 'Quite untrue,' he wrote in his diary. 'The Prince of Wales had been playing about with this pro-German idea long before our conversation.'[2] There was much pro-German sentiment in Britain, reported the American Ambassador: 'The Prince of Wales has become the German protagonist.'[3]

It was the German dream that the Prince might not only influence his fellow countrymen in favour of their position, but that he might one day intervene more directly in the machinery of government and himself shape British foreign policy. Though his information was admitted to be only at third hand, the German Ambassador in Washington reported the Prince as saying that he did not share his father's view that it was the King's duty meekly to follow the Cabinet's bidding. 'On the contrary, he felt it to be his duty to intervene if the Cabinet were to plan a policy which in his view was detrimental to British interests.'[4] This too is not implausible, though it is unlikely that the Prince had given any thought to what he meant by 'intervene'. Certainly he believed in strong government, and saw no reason why a monarch should not play a part in it. In Germany he felt the threat of communism had become so desperate that strong government was essential. In Britain it was as yet only desirable, but the need was growing every day. In May 1934 the Home Secretary buttonholed the Prince and told him how anxious he was about the fascist Blackshirt movement. Aird was in attendance. 'Talking to HRH on the way back we agreed that, without knowing much about them, we both thought it quite a good movement except for Mosley.'[1]

The Prince's views led him into conflict with the government in June 1935, when he addressed the British Legion and proposed that a group of its members should visit Germany: 'I feel there would be no more suitable body . . . of men to stretch forth the hand of friendship to the Germans than we ex-Servicemen.' This proposal was greeted with loud cheers, said *The Times*;[2] the cheers were muted in the Foreign Office. The Prince claimed that the text had been cleared in advance through the Legion's President, Sir Frederick Maurice; the Permanent Under Secretary at the Foreign Office, Vansittart, denied that there had been any consultation.[3] The Cabinet considered the matter a week later and were told that the Prince's remarks had been ill-received in Paris and had complicated the Anglo-German naval conversations that were then going on. They concluded that the Prime Minister or Foreign Secretary should have been consulted. As a special exception it was agreed that the King could show the Cabinet conclusions to his son.[4]

The Prince was genuinely taken aback by the uproar. He told Hoesch that he had not wished 'to get involved in the maelstrom of political events but had only expressed, entirely on his own initiative, an idea which had seemed to him right and useful'.[5] The British public was largely unaware of the contretemps, but if they had known about it most people would probably have thought that he had done well. The delight with which the proposal was received by the Nazi leadership should, however, have suggested to him that he had handed them a propaganda weapon. Prince Henry of Reuss spoke for Hitler when he congratulated the Prince on his bold initiative: 'All of us know perfectly well that You in Your exposed position would never have taken a step which would not have been felt deeply by Yourself . . . That's good sport!'[6] The British Legion party was welcomed effusively in Germany, their visit including, according to a refugee, a visit to the concentration camp at Dachau during which the inmates were herded underground and their places taken by SS guards dressed up as contented and well-fed prisoners. The visitors sent back telegrams to George

V and the Prince, rejoicing in their 'overwhelmingly friendly reception'.[1]

Almost immediately the Prince was in trouble again for a speech he made at Berkhamsted Boys School, in which he praised members of the Officers' Training Corps for their excellent results in shooting. 'It is always a mystery to me,' he said, 'that a certain number of misguided people – I will even go so far as to call them cranks – should feel that the only way in which they can express the feeling we all have of abhorrence of war . . . is by discouraging, and if they are in authority prohibiting, any form of healthy discipline and training.'[2] The rearmament lobby, led by Churchill, who had deplored the British Legion speech, found nothing to criticize on this occasion; it was George Lansbury, the pacifist and socialist, who denounced it and said OTCs and all other paramilitary organizations should be abolished.[3]

Four considerations above all shaped the Prince's thinking over this period. The first was that war was a prospect so horrible that almost any sacrifice was justified to avoid it. Alfred Munnings tells how the Prince once noticed in his studio a bronze statuette of an exhausted infantryman. He looked at it in silence, then said 'Poor b—!', and asked to buy it and meet the artist.[4] The horror of the trenches, made all the more horrible by the fact that he had not been allowed to participate in it himself, always haunted him and dominated his mind whenever the risk of war seemed imminent. Second, he believed that the greatest safeguard against war was to remain strong oneself; on issues of rearmament he was at one with Churchill. Third, he felt Russia and international communism to be a greater threat to the future of Britain than fascism. And fourth, he was convinced that many of the claims of Germany, and for that matter of Italy, were justified, and that to satisfy them was not ignoble appeasement but a sensible acceptance of political realities.

The Italian invasion of Abyssinia in 1935 illustrated his attitude. He believed that Italian pretensions were not unreasonable, and that it was anyway folly to alienate Mussolini over an issue on which he considered the British were virtually powerless to intervene. He deplored the fact that the Foreign Secretary, Samuel Hoare, was driven into resignation because of the deal he had struck with the French Foreign Minister Pierre Laval, which in effect gave Mussolini a free hand in Abyssinia. He attended the debate in the House of Commons at which Hoare made his resignation speech, and openly declared that he did not believe the imposition of sanctions on Italy could possibly achieve the intended aim. In this he once again reflected the opinion of a substantial section of the Conservative Party and must have been close to the private views of the Prime Minister and of his successor, Neville Chamberlain. It has been said that he did more than express approval of Hoare's manoeuvrings. Fanciful accounts, based on the insubstantial testimony of Laval's son-in-law René de Chambrun, allege that he flew to Paris in December 1935 to confer with Laval about the Abyssinian problem.[1] It is evident from his personal records that it would have been extremely difficult for him to have squeezed in a visit to Paris at this period; if he did so his staff had no knowledge of it – a difficult trick for him to bring off; and it is anyway impossible to imagine what benefit could have been derived either by the Prince or by Laval from such a meeting. The report can safely be ignored. But the Prince did think that Hoare and Laval were right and that the policy of Hoare's successor, Anthony Eden, was ill-conceived and ill-managed.

Outside Europe, the Prince's interest centred on South America, an area which, in common with most British bankers and industrialists, he inexplicably believed was on the verge of an economic breakthrough. He toured the area in 1931, unashamedly with the aim of boosting trade. 'I hope I may be able to help our industries a little,' he told his mother. 'That is my only desire, and if I can get some enjoyment out of it, so much the better.'[2] Prince George came along and the two busily brushed up their Spanish on the way out. Aird marvelled at the way the Prince would complain bitterly about trifling impositions and yet work hard at something really troublesome, like learning a foreign language. He found a Spanish doctor on board and persuaded him to act as tutor, a role in which, Aird suggests, his efforts were seconded by an attractive Peruvian girl.[3] The results were excellent; the Prince was already a competent Spanish speaker and quickly attained considerable fluency. He was proud of his prowess and in future never missed a chance to air his talent; Owen Morshead reported him taking a party of Argentine students round Windsor Castle, 'talking in courageous and as it appeared to me adequately correct Spanish – at any rate it was faultlessly fluent'.[1]

The tour illustrated vividly the sort of pressures to which the Prince was subject on such occasions and the way in which he increasingly succumbed to them. It can be followed through the reports of the American diplomats along the route, who expressed themselves with a freedom that to their British colleagues would have smacked of *lèse-majesté*. All went swimmingly in his first stop, Peru. The American military attaché said that he made an excellent impression – 'He was democratic and anxious to go out of his way to show small kindnesses to the poor' – while the Ambassador praised his unsparing readiness to do all that was asked of him and marvelled at the amount he could drink while still preserving his dignity.[2] In Chile the naval attaché reported that he created a tremendous amount of good will 'by his willingness and desire to meet people'. He 'made a very good impression', confirmed the Ambassador. 'He is endeavouring to subordinate himself to the task in hand, and he knuckles under and does quite a good job' – 'quite', presumably, in the American sense and thus implying greater enthusiasm than would be deduced from the English usage. The Ambassador added a manuscript postscript on the Prince's 'extra-curricular activities; baccarat, roulette, double whiskey sodas and ladies with pasts were his favourites'.[3]

By Argentina the pace was beginning to tell. His informality, so successful when he was at his best, was less well received when he turned up at important functions two hours late, in the wrong dress and noticeably the worse for wear. He gave offence to many people who considered themselves important and some who really were. But nevertheless the American Ambassador concluded: 'The Prince of Wales is still Britain's great salesman, his cordial, carefree democratic manner wins even those who would go out of their way to criticize him, and it is because of his personality that we believe that Great Britain as a whole has gained by his visit here.'[4]

In Uruguay the scales had dipped the other way: 'I regret to observe that His Royal Highness . . . appeared to be deeply tired, rather uninterested, and to have unfortunately lost a great deal of the personal charm which was so long the most engaging of his many delightful qualities.'[5] Rio de Janeiro was disaster: the Princes insisted on meeting the wrong people, were rude and casual, invariably late for engagements. 'Neither their suite nor the British Ambassador appeared to have any control over them, and their conduct was marked by a desire to gratify their personalities rather than to conform to the rules which usually guide distinguished foreigners.'[1] Finally in Sao Paolo, with the end in sight, he pulled himself together. His visit 'aroused great enthusiasm among everyone and the British are intensely proud of the two Princes and with reason, for they have won the good will of everyone with whom they have been in contact'. But the Ambassador noted with some amusement that, though the Prince urged everyone to buy British, he himself smoked Camels, used a Kodak camera, rode in a Lincoln and went to see an American film.[2]

Even at his worst, the Prince could do good work when the need was greatest. After his sojourn in Buenos Aires, Aird remarked that he did not know whether the British Ambassador 'felt most relief at our departure or apprehension at the social consequences'. Yet at the opening of the British Empire Trade Exhibition, which was at the heart of his visit, 'HRH put up a wonderful performance, making two speeches, one in English and the other in Spanish'. His speech to the Chamber of Commerce that evening was 'one of the best I've ever heard him make, quite natural, obviously his own ideas and criticisms which were very good to my mind'.[3] In Argentina he worked vigorously to promote the sales of British aircraft, flying everywhere in his own De Havilland Puss Moth, and ensuring orders for several of these at least; 'and more will follow if I can get my way in London'.[4] In a Senate Committee enquiry in Washington into the munitions industry, Mr Driggs referred to the Prince's visit to Argentina. 'He is their best salesman, they say, and creates good will, and it is a gesture of the royal family interesting itself in British business.'[5]

It was said of the Prince of Wales – and sometimes fairly – that he would be quick to take promising initiatives, but equally quick to abandon them when the going got rough or tedious. In the case of Latin America at least the charge was unfounded. He made a sustained if largely fruitless effort to persuade British manufacturers that the prospects for profitable trade were there but were being lost through inertia and complacency. He urged the Foreign Office and British news agencies to do more to improve the coverage of British affairs in South American newspapers. He sponsored the visit of a group of Oxford undergraduates to Argentina, and encouraged the popular historian, Philip Guedalla, to set up the Ibero-American Institute, under whose auspices the 'Prince of Wales's Scholarships' were established to send postgraduate Argentine students to Oxford.[1] When a high-powered Argentine mission visited Britain in 1933, the Prince urged his father to make a fuss of them: 'You know how much I hate any extra official receptions . . . but I really do feel that it is worthwhile in this case.'[2] He himself met them on arrival; gave a dinner for them; went to two other dinners given in their honour; got them invited to the Duke of Portland's home, Welbeck Abbey, for the weekend and joined the house party; and had two or three of the delegation to stay at his own country house the following weekend.

Though ministers may from time to time have wished that the Prince would be more discreet, their views on foreign affairs were for the most part very similar to his. It is doubtful whether Ramsay MacDonald or Baldwin, Simon or Chamberlain, would have seen anything to criticize in his assessment of the threat of communism, of a renascent Germany and of an unstable France. He ardently supported the National Government formed in September 1931. 'You were so right in realizing that the financial position of Great Britain had gone beyond the realm of party politics and politicians and their platforms,' he told the King. His only fear was that the rump of the socialist party would fall into the hands of extremists: 'We must hope that it will not be anybody too violent or ignorant of what the nation – not the TUC – needs just now.'[3] The government valued his support. When Britain went off the gold standard the Prince lunched with MacDonald at Chequers. 'I thought it would be advantageous if he stayed a day or two in London before proceeding to Balmoral,' wrote the Prime Minister. 'I considered that that would have a good effect on the country.'[4]

But though his sympathies were with the old guard, the Prince tried to keep his lines open to other politicians, who might think differently on foreign affairs but whose views on internal policies were often more in line with his own. Anthony Eden, who was to take Hoare's place as Foreign Secretary after the latter's resignation, had a long talk with him in November 1934. 'South America was his favourite topic,' he noted in his diary. On domestic politics, 'he shows a shrewd appreciation of men and matters and is probably more receptive than the King. Very friendly and I liked him'.[1] Churchill too, though the Prince increasingly doubted his judgment, remained an ally. The Prince was one of the 140 or so friends who clubbed together in 1932 to buy Churchill a motor car as a celebration of his recovery after an accident in New York.[2]

Harold Nicolson saw him as a 'very right wing' figure. When Nicolson described himself as 'an evolutionary socialist', the Prince appeared horrified.[3] Yet when he diverged from the policies of the National Government it was increasingly over social issues. In April 1934 he told the American Ambassador, Robert Bingham, that there had to be a 'change in conditions here, and a correction of social injustice among the English people which would relieve poverty and distress; that this must come and that it would come either wisely, constructively and conservatively, which would save the country, or it would come violently, which would destroy it . . .' What Britain needed, he said, was leadership of the kind Roosevelt was giving to the United States.[4] He was always strikingly open to opinions that to most Conservative politicians would have seemed revolutionary and seditious. He summoned the firebrand Clydesider David Kirkwood for a conversation, dismissing Kirkwood's plea that he had no proper clothes with the brisk retort: 'It is you, not your clothes, that I want to talk to.' Kirkwood harangued him as if at a public meeting: 'But the Prince of Wales egged me on.' Kirkwood talked for fifty minutes, and at the end of their meeting, 'I felt, as I feel when I see an expert engineer at work, that I had been in the presence of a man who had a big job to do, and is earnest, and determined to do his job well.'[5]

Unemployment, which reached epidemic proportions in the early 1930s, remained the Prince's principal concern. Towards the end of 1927 he had become Patron of the National Council of Social Service; a somewhat amorphous organization which was intended to organize the plethora of voluntary organizations into some sort of loose federation, so as to eliminate muddle and duplication. He recognized that neither he nor the Council could do much to alleviate the economic malaise that was the root cause of unemployment, but believed there was still a great deal to be done by encouraging job creation and organizing social centres in the depressed areas. Addressing the National Council in January 1932 he called upon the whole country 'to accept the challenge of unemployment as a national opportunity for voluntary social service, to undertake such services in the spirit of the good neighbour and, refusing to be paralysed by the size of the problem, to break it up into little pieces'. The response was overwhelming, more than seven hundred schemes were put forward to the Council in the course of 1932, many foolish but others practical and useful.[1] One scheme which he personally introduced involved the employment of extra men in Windsor Great Park. Sufficient funds were raised to keep twenty-four men in work for four months at least. 'This is being done in a lot of places, which is a very useful and helpful social activity,' he told the Queen.[2]

In the three or four years during which unemployment was at its worst, the Prince made extensive tours of Tyneside, the Midlands, Lancashire, Yorkshire, Scotland and Wales. He visited hundreds of working men's clubs and schemes for the unemployed, seeking out the most sordid slums and inviting himself into the most miserable hovels. Occasionally, though rarely, he was angrily rebuffed, more often he was met by sullen apathy. The experience disturbed him, he was used to an enthusiastic welcome. He knew that the hope which he sought to rekindle in his hearers was faint and often illusory; 'But I had the feeling that empty as was my mission, my appearance among them was in large measure appreciated and taken as a sign that the Monarchy had not forsaken them in their misfortunes.'[3] George Haynes, the General Secretary of the Council, remembered vividly his 'way of approach; his transparent interest and concern, and the immense regard people had for him. He had a charisma in those days which was unique.'[4]

Housing remained another of his concerns. The few shining examples of new working-class accommodation which he saw on his tours around the country convinced him that far more could be done. He invited Ramsay MacDonald and Chamberlain to dinner at York House with a dozen or so of those who were grappling with the problem; not much may have been gained but at least the Prime Minister and Chancellor were left in no doubt about the force of people's feelings on the subject. He was struck by American ideas for mass-produced, low-rent housing, and raised the necessary financing for a development of this kind on his Kennington estates. Unfortunately part of the land involved belonged to the London County Council, and the project foundered on the reluctance of the bureaucrats to countenance an experiment that might have proved unsuccessful but was surely worth a try.

So far as one can tell, the setting up of a Silver Trust Fund to commemorate the Jubilee of 1935, which would be dedicated to the support of existing youth organizations and the encouragement of new ones, was entirely the Prince's initiative. He proceeded cautiously: 'Before inaugurating the Fund I am going to assure myself that it will be an idea favourable to all political views,' he told his father, 'that is essential or it would not be national in character.'[1] The Cabinet gave the scheme their blessing and Lord Lieutenants and Mayors were summoned to a grand council in St James's Palace. The appeal got off to a good start, reported Wigram,[2] and promised to develop into something as long lasting as the King Edward VII Hospital Fund, but the idea ran out of steam when the Prince succeeded to the throne and other, more urgent considerations occupied his mind. More long lasting if on a more modest scale were the Feathers Clubs, centres providing some of the amenities of social life for the unemployed and, by extension, for many lower paid workers. The clubs were inspired by the Prince and turned into reality by Freda Dudley Ward; in their heyday eight branches flourished and the movement survives today. The Prince took a genuine interest in their progress and visited them often and with a minimum of formality. Each time a new one opened he would give Freda a tiny version of the Prince of Wales's feathers in sapphires, rubies and diamonds to add to a gold bracelet which she often wore.[3]

Somebody will find reason to criticize any member of the royal family who expresses an opinion or hopes to get things done; mute inactivity is the sole recipe for safety. This Prince was neither mute nor inactive and he suffered accordingly. DeLisle Burns, a Reader in Citizenship at the University of Glasgow, complained that the Prince devoted disproportionate attention to the unemployed; what he should do was honour the employed.[4] Burns was not alone in thinking that the Prince was unduly preoccupied with the unfortunate and the underprivileged, and indifferent to those who were generating the nation's wealth. Even the generally loyal Aird commented that the Prince had spoken well when addressing a sales managers' conference but wished that he would devote less of his energies to attacking employers, 'who must be getting rather tired of being told what their faults are'.[1] Another common line of attack was that he was stealing other people's ideas or trespassing on their territory. When he tried to install a clothing depot for the relief of the destitute in a disused house on his Kennington estates, he met with sharp recriminations from those who were pursuing a similar idea elsewhere – 'I can't help feeling it must be one of those petty cases of jealousy which occur amongst those who occupy themselves with "good works",' he wrote sourly.[2]

Complaints of this kind do little more than confirm that the Prince was doing useful work. One cannot say the same about the strictures which were increasingly often heard, complaining that he was becoming more wilful and idiosyncratic in his ways, insistent that everything should be done in the way he wanted it, yet inconsistent and sometimes unreasonable in his demands. At a dinner of the Camden Society he rejected *hors d'oeuvre*, soup and fish, settled for a pair of cutlets and a salad, insisted on Perrier water, changed his mind and drank champagne, rejected the salad, and finally ordered another of a more arcane variety which arrived when everybody else was on their pudding. 'I found him excellent company,' said Lord Crawford, 'talking with freedom and good humour, but on the whole too visibly engrossed in the menu: why, for instance, should he keep sending away the toast in order to get a new and very hot supply?'[3] Aird, who was to attend him at the Lord Mayor's reception, was telephoned at eight and told he was expected to dine *à deux* with the Prince before they set out, arrived half an hour later to find the Prince had already forgotten he was coming, and witnessed a ceremony of salad dressing so exotic that it put him in mind of life at the court of the mad King Ludwig of Bavaria. The Prince sent away the cheese savoury and almost did the same with the beef. He told Aird he had a chef coming in to help with dinner the following night, then a few minutes later expressed surprise that Aird knew about this intention. 'I have never seen HRH so odd before,' wrote Aird, and again a few months later, 'Personally I think HRH is going mad, and going mad faster each quarter.'[4]

The Last Years as Prince

Eccentricity as harmless as this, probably embellished in the telling, signifies little, but Aird went on, '. . . he is running a very bad show as his Staff (Admiral and Godfrey) are very unhappy and I fancy he is displeased with them. It is a most gloomy show in every way to work with, so if HRH can't get a small show like his staff running well and happily, it does not look good for the future.' Halsey and Thomas were indeed very unhappy, because they found their job increasingly impossible to perform with any credit, or even without scandal. Stories of the Prince's misbehaviour in 1934 and 1935 are so plentiful that it is only a question of deciding which to select: Sister Toddie of the Royal Infirmary complaining bitterly about his behaviour during a visit to her hospital – 'he had looked bored the whole time and had taken no interest whatsoever . . . He was in a savage temper and did not co-operate at all.' When the Superintendent's little dog jumped up, he kicked it;[1] Lloyd George back from Caernarvon – 'The Prince made a bad impression, evidently disliking the ceremonies he attended, and being unpunctual and ungracious in his appearances';[2] the Prince arriving late and after the King and Queen at the party he himself gave in their honour at the time of the Jubilee, noticeably distrait if not actually intoxicated.[3] From such accounts the picture emerges of a moody and irresponsible egoist, wholly involved in his own personal problems, unable or unwilling to carry out even the minimum of the duties associated with the role.

And yet for every such instance one can find two in which the Prince is praised: Mary Shiffer, stillroom maid at the Hyde Park Hotel, testifying to his charm (if also to his frequent tipsiness) – 'If he'd stayed there would never have been a republic in Ireland. He was worried about the poor. Always';[4] Hamar Greenwood at the Iron and Steel Federation Dinner delighting Aird by referring to the great role Aird's grandfather had played in the industry. Aird wrote to thank him: 'I want to make it clear,' Greenwood replied, 'that it was HRH who prompted me . . . it was a fine example of his thoughtfulness';[5] Hensley Henson, Bishop of Durham, dining with the Prince on one of the tours of depressed areas, praising his 'irrepressible boyishness' and 'unusual tactfulness' – 'He likes popularity and seeks it. Since, however, he seeks it by the most honourable method in the world, ie public service, he deserves the popularity he wins ... He is genuinely kind and unaffected.'[1]

This is the side of the Prince of Wales that most people saw, and for every Sister Toddie from the Royal Infirmary there were many more ready to swear that he was the most chivalrous, the most generous, the most compassionate, the best of men. Halsey and Thomas, however, had to live with the reality and to endure the unpunctuality and indifference to business. They tended, perhaps, to take for granted the many occasions that the Prince did his duty; they suffered agonizingly when he fell down on the job. Godfrey Thomas, who was closest to him and who had been his friend for more than twenty years, was the most embittered. 'I've wasted hours and hours sitting here till late at night in the hope of seeing you,' he wrote angrily in July 1935. 'I don't mind a bit working out of office hours if there's any certainty of catching you, however late, but I can't go on like this. You come up nowadays on such rare occasions, which means it's always such a rush. You are practically inaccessible on the telephone and seem to resent it if one has anything to consult you about. I hate you being a laughing stock, but even your friends laugh behind your back when you make one of your speeches on "business efficiency" and "up-to-date methods". They say you are the most unbusinesslike person in the world ... And they only know half.'[2] The letter exists only in draft. Possibly it was never sent. If it had been, the Prince would have been genuinely upset, not in the least resentful, resolved to do better in future. But he would not have mended his ways for long.

At the beginning of 1936 Halsey, in consultation with Wigram, drew up a Grand Remonstrance which he proposed Baldwin, MacDonald and Simon should lay before the Prince. His private life, Halsey said, had become his only life. It could not go on like that. The fate of the monarchy and the Empire depended on his carrying on the old traditions. The King's health was being undermined by his worry over his son's future. The Prince's excesses were becoming the subject of common discussion and he was setting a bad example to the people over whom he would one day rule. 'The value of the work done by HRH from 1918 to 1925, both in this country and in the Dominions, and also in foreign countries, had been incalculable, but during the last 6 or 7 years, entirely on account of his private life which had devalued his public life, it is beginning to be realized that he is not likely to be a fitting monarch.'[1]

Before ministers could consider the propriety of such a *démarche*, George V was dead and the Prince had become King. Probably their intervention would have made no difference anyway. 'I can't help feeling that he is too old now to follow Prince Hal's example and change his entire way of life,' Thomas had written the previous year. 'If he had a wife I believe he could pull it off, but as things are I am afraid I am a pessimist.'[2]

It was not so much his not having a wife which was at the root of the trouble, as his having a mistress. His relationship with women, in the last two years his relationship with Mrs Simpson, dominated his private life – and as Halsey said, that private life had now become his only life.

13

Mrs Simpson

'FOR TEN YEARS BEFORE HE MET MRS SIMPSON,' wrote Lascelles, the Prince of Wales 'was continuously in the throes of one shattering and absorbing love affair after another (not to mention a number of street-corner affairs)'.[1] To follow these fleeting romances in any detail would be difficult and unprofitable. None was of real importance to the Prince. As late as 1931 he was still telling Freda Dudley Ward: 'I love and adore *only you* really my darling.'[2] For another three years he turned to her for advice and comfort and treated her home as an extension of his own. But as he moved into early middle age he began to hanker for a relationship that would fulfil his sexual needs and yet offer something nearer permanence; he looked for someone who would be more than a temporary mistress, though still less than a wife.

For a time he thought he had found her in Thelma Furness. Lady Furness was one of the Morgan sisters, twin daughters of an American consul. Her sister Gloria married the immensely rich Reginald Vanderbilt. Thelma first eloped at the age of sixteen with a roué twice her age, divorced him, and then married the even more elderly Lord Furness, scion of the shipping family. 'Duke' Furness was irascible and earthy, something of an oaf; his young wife was exquisitely pretty, glossy, elegant, good-natured and relentlessly frivolous. She had tired of her husband and was ripe for an affair by the time she met the Prince, who was dutifully awarding rosettes to prize-winning cows at the Leicester Fair. 'The Prince of Wales . . . has been going great guns with Lady Furness,' wrote Bruce Lockhart in Bayonne in September 1931. 'Lord Furness is miserable about it.'[3] By then the affair had been spoken of for a year or more and Lord Furness's misery did not prevent him finding distractions in other directions.

It was a pleasant and undemanding relationship. Thelma Furness was quite content to take things as she found them and had no wish to reform the Prince or to appropriate him exclusively: 'We talked a great deal, but mostly about trivialities,' she wrote in her memoirs. 'The Prince was not a man for abstract ideas or ponderous thought . . .'[1] Almost the only time she caused a furore was when she took the Prince to Lourdes and he knelt as a priest went by carrying the Blessed Sacrament. Indignant Protestants wrote to protest at photographs of the heir to the British throne 'kneeling in the mud at a Catholic ceremony'.[2] But though she did little positive harm, her hedonism and indifference to any consideration that did not bear directly on her comforts encouraged the Prince in traits that were already too well pronounced. Freda Dudley Ward had curbed his selfishness and self-indulgence, Thelma Furness encouraged them. In Paris after the trip to South America Aird went out to the airport, waited several hours for the Prince, then got a message that the flight would have to be postponed till the next day. Returning to the hotel Aird found that the two Princes, after visiting the Queen of Spain, 'had joined Lady Furness, got rather tight and arrived too late to get across in daylight, a bad show . . . as they were to stay at Windsor with Their Majesties'.[3] Mrs Dudley Ward would never have abetted such delinquency. The Duchess of Sutherland and Lord Rosslyn found him 'more irresponsible than he was. They blame Lady Furness, who has a bad influence on him. Freda, at any rate, kept him under restraint.'[4] To Chips Channon she was the woman who 'first "modernized" him and Americanized him, making him over-democratic, casual and a little common. Hers is the true blame for this drama.'[5]*

This judgment attaches too much significance to an essentially minor figure. But though the true blame could not fairly be assigned to Thelma Furness, she was the unwitting agent who set the drama rolling. It was she who, early in 1931, first introduced the Prince of Wales to Mrs Simpson.

The career and personality of Wallis Simpson have been the subject of so much speculation, so much lurid and unbridled fantasy, that it seems ungenerous to the reader to resort to established truth. If

* I am indebted to Robert Rhodes James for confirming that this woman, whose name was left blank in the published diaries, was in fact Lady Furness.

all the books and articles on the theme can be believed, she was illegitimate; she was both a lesbian and a nymphomaniac; she was a spy for the Nazis and probably the KGB; she was Ribbentrop's mistress and had a child by Count Ciano; she learnt her sexual techniques in the brothels of Hong Kong, or was it perhaps Shanghai? It is notoriously almost impossible to prove that something did *not* happen, but the evidence for all these charges seems, to say the least, unlikely to hold up in court. A typical example is the 'China Dossier', a report allegedly commissioned by Stanley Baldwin for George V which explored the iniquities of the then Wallis Spencer during her time in the Far East. As with all the best ghosts, everyone had a friend who had a friend who had read the dossier, yet no one seems actually to have read it himself. It is inconceivable that the King would have asked for such a report and supremely unlikely that Baldwin would have done so. No copy or reference to a copy exists in any official archive. Unless the document unexpectedly emerges it can safely be forgotten.

To stick, then, to prosaic and verifiable truth. Wallis Warfield was born on 19 June 1896, two years after the Prince of Wales. Both the Warfields and her mother's family, the Montagues, were of distinguished Southern stock and Wallis was brought up as one of the Baltimore aristocracy. She was, however, a poor relation; her father, Teakle Warfield, had little money and died of tuberculosis when his daughter was only five months old. Teakle's widow existed on the charity of relations, eked out by what she made from letting rooms in her apartment. Wallis was brought up in a world in which her friends and relations had nicer clothes than she did, lived in bigger houses, took for granted as the necessities of life what to her seemed almost unimaginable luxuries. 'Here was the root of her ambition,' wrote Michael Bloch perceptively, '– a desire to avenge early struggles, to prove herself in the eyes of rich and snobbish cousins, to restore herself to a social and material level which, in her heart, she felt to be rightfully hers.'[1]

She had little natural beauty to help her in her battle. 'Nobody ever called me beautiful or even pretty,' she wrote in her memoirs. '. . . My jaw was clearly too big and too pointed to be classic. My hair was straight when the laws of compensation might at least have provided curls.'[2] Her assets were fine eyes, a radiant complexion, an excellent figure and a sense of style which was refined with time but apparent from the moment she first took responsibility for her own appearance. Cecil Beaton found her 'alluring. Her skin . . . was incredibly bright and smooth like the inside of a shell, her hair as sleek as only the Chinese women know how to make it . . . I like her surprised eyebrows when she laughs and her face has great gaiety.'[1]

She was no more an intellectual than she was a beauty. She rarely read books, cared little for painting and nothing for music. She was quick-witted and enjoyed a retentive memory but as a schoolgirl neither excelled in class nor wished to do so. Her main preoccupation from an early age was boys, and to attract them she had wit, blazing vitality, a capacity for total concentration on her interlocutor of the moment, a shrewd perception of masculine weaknesses and an understanding of how to exploit them to her advantage. In society she was ruthless and voracious, the fact that a boy belonged to some other girl was a challenge to secure him for herself. One of her oldest friends and admirers, Herman Rogers, is quoted as saying that she was the most selfish woman he had ever known – 'Even men she didn't want, she didn't want anyone else to have.'[2]

In 1936 Nancy Dugdale, the wife of Baldwin's parliamentary private secretary, showed a sheet of Wallis's handwriting to the German graphologist Fräulein Gusti Oesterreicher, who spoke no English and could have had no inkling who the writer might be. Miss Oesterreicher's report described Wallis as being:

A woman with a strong male inclination in the sense of activity, vitality and initiative, she *must* dominate, she *must* have authority, and without sufficient scope for her powers can become disagreeable . . . In the pursuit of her aim she can be most inconsiderate, and can hurt, but on the whole she is not without some instincts of nobility and generosity . . . She is ambitious and demands above all that her undertakings should be noticed and valued. In the physical sense of the word sadistic, cold, overbearing, vain.[3]

It is a harsh verdict, but it reflects some credit on the science of graphology.

Her main preoccupation was to get away from Baltimore, and she snapped up the first remotely eligible husband who came her way. The marriage proved disastrous. 'Win' Spencer was a handsome naval officer who seemed to have a promising career ahead of him, but he proved to be a moody and sometimes violent alcoholic. How far a more sympathetic wife could have helped him is another matter – Wallis was not kind to failures – but as it was the marriage soon became intolerable. Wallis left him, lived alone in Washington for six years during which she had at least one flagrant love affair with an Argentine diplomat, briefly rejoined her husband in the Far East, left him again but spent another year in China before she returned home in 1925 and sued for divorce.

It had been a rackety ten years, and when she remarried it was for respectability. Ernest Simpson worked in the family shipping business. He had an English father and an American mother, preferring the social pretensions of the former. He had served briefly in the Coldstream Guards, an all-important association in his eyes, and valued highly such connections in high places as he could muster. He was diligent, ponderous, uninspired. For Wallis he meant security; what she meant to him is harder to say, but undoubtedly he loved her. They married in July 1928 and settled down in a rented house in London to live the life of a prosperous upper-middle-class couple with social aspirations slightly, though by no means absurdly, beyond their purse. Wallis was a highly competent manager and quickly established herself as a hostess who gave her guests excellent food and drink and, more important, made sure they enjoyed themselves and left in the belief that they had been appreciated. Their friends were mainly Americans in London, among them Benjamin Thaw, the First Secretary at the US Embassy, who was married to another of the Morgan sisters. It was through Thaw that she came to know and – in so far as she could be on affectionate terms with another woman – to make a friend of Thaw's sister-in-law, Thelma Furness.

Lady Furness's claim to have introduced Wallis Simpson to the Prince of Wales is not undisputed. Mountbatten insisted that the first meeting took place at his brother's house, Lynden Manor. Lord Milford Haven, presumably to oblige the Prince who was staying nearby, invited Thelma Furness for the weekend. She brought the Simpsons with her. The Prince duly came over to lunch and seemed wholly unimpressed by Wallis's charms. Within a few weeks, however, she had somehow 'reached a position where they went to bed. From that moment he lost all sense of reason.'[1] The dates, at least, are wrong. The gap between first meeting and the start of the affair proper was far longer than a few weeks. It seems certain that they first met at Lady Furness's country house, Burrough Court, near Melton Mowbray, on 10 January 1931, when the Thaws fell ill and the Simpsons were asked to stand in at a weekend house party.[2] But it is true that Wallis made little impression at their first meeting. Lady Kimberley, who was dining with the Furnesses, says that Wallis was sitting opposite the Prince at dinner. Suddenly she leant forward and said, 'Sir, do you think me very like Rita Kruger?' (a woman whom the Prince had courted in New York). 'Good God! No!' said the Prince, and turned back to his neighbour.[3]

Wallis was delighted to have met the Prince and hoped that she would see more of him in the future. The most exalted London hostesses found the company he kept a little louche, but they were none the less gratified when he graced their assemblies with his presence. He was not merely at, he *was* the pinnacle of society. To be accepted as one of his circle of friends would be for Mrs Simpson an achievement as glorious as she could well imagine. 'Probably we will never hear or see any of them again, however,' she wrote resignedly to her aunt and most faithful correspondent, Mrs Bessie Merryman.[4] It was May 1931 before they did meet again; mid-January 1932 before the Prince dined at their flat in Bryanston Court – he stayed till 4 a.m. – and the end of that month before they spent a weekend at Fort Belvedere. By 3 May 1933 she had passed several more weekends at the Fort and the last two nights dancing with the Prince at the Embassy Club, but, she told Aunt Bessie, 'Thelma is still the Princess of Wales'.[5] For the first time, however, the possibility that this shadowy title might become hers was forming in her mind.

The coast was soon clear. In January 1934 Thelma Furness sailed to the United States. In her memoirs she describes how she asked Wallis to 'look after him while I'm away. See that he doesn't get into any mischief.'[6] If she was genuinely anxious to keep the Prince to herself she played her cards singularly badly. First she left the field open to somebody whom she must have realized was potentially a dangerous rival, then on the way back from New York she conducted a flamboyant flirtation with that celebrated rake, Aly Khan. The news of this escapade stilled any pangs of conscience the Prince might have felt. She went to Fort Belvedere for the weekend soon after her return, but the atmosphere was uncomfortable, the Prince distant and at pains to avoid any intimate conversation. At dinner she noticed that the Prince and Wallis were having private jokes together; when the Prince picked up a piece of salad Wallis playfully slapped his hand. Thelma looked disapproving. 'Wallis looked straight at me. And then and there I knew the "reason" was Wallis . . . I knew then she had looked after him exceedingly well. That one cold, defiant glance had told me the entire story.'[1] Next day she left the Fort and the Prince of Wales's life.

It did not take long before those who knew the Prince well realized that this was not just a casual affair, that Mrs Simpson was there to stay. She established her authority with unrelenting thoroughness. She would not make the same mistake as Thelma Furness. Any rival must be eliminated. For several months Freda Dudley Ward had been wholly preoccupied by the illness of her elder daughter. In mid-1934, with the crisis behind her, she began to pick up the threads of her life and telephoned York House. With extreme embarrassment the operator told her that she had been instructed not to put her through to the Prince. The brutality of this ending to an intimate friendship of sixteen years cannot be condoned; it can only be explained by the assumption that Mrs Simpson had told the Prince it must be either her or Mrs Dudley Ward, and the Prince had lacked the courage to break this news to the victim. Wallis herself denied this, claiming that she had tried to ensure the Prince at least kept in touch with Freda Dudley Ward's children.[2] Whatever she may have said, she can have intended one thing only, the relationship must end.

The Prince cut out of his life not merely Freda, but also the two daughters who had been so close to him. When Angela married a soldier, Robert Laycock, the Prince did not attend the wedding or even send a token present. He had never kept the letters of women before he met Wallis, so it is not surprising that virtually no trace of Mrs Dudley Ward's existence survives among his papers, or even his vast collection of photographs. One scrap of evidence is to be found, however. In 1944 Angela Laycock took advantage of the fact that her husband had to write to the Duke on official business to include an affectionate letter of her own.[1] The Duke of Windsor did not answer it but he kept it among his records. Perhaps the fact meant nothing, but it is possible to imagine in such a gesture some degree of nostalgia for the past.

John Aird was at the weekend party that saw Lady Furness's final retreat, but had no suspicion what was happening. The Prince, he said, could not have been nicer or more charming but 'his friends of his own selection are awful and one of the worst examples was there, a couple called Simson [sic], she is an American 150 per cent and HRH seems to like her a bit extra; he is a very unattractive and common Englishman . . . They seem terrible at first and this feeling does not decrease as one sees them more often, although basically, I think, they are quite nice . . .'[2] By the following weekend his eyes were beginning to open. Halsey had told him that he thought Lady Furness had been dismissed and Aird concluded he must be right 'as Wallace Simson [sic sic!] seems to do all the things *she* used to except the cigar lighting'. He continued to find the Simpsons uncongenial bores; 'he seems full of general information like a Whitaker, while she pretends to have taste in decoration and food – maybe the *first*, but certainly not the second'.[3]

She did indeed do all the things that Lady Furness had done, and more besides. She made herself felt in every aspect of life at Fort Belvedere; 'she ploughed it up,' in the phrase of one of the staff. A footman brought in by Thelma Furness was quickly dismissed, the cook soon followed. She infuriated the staff by visiting the kitchen at 2 or 3 a.m. and cooking bacon and eggs, leaving 'the hell of a mess' behind her. She was not actively rude, but hostile and assertive.[4] The Prince's valet, Jack Crisp, even claimed that she would go round the Fort breaking the tips of the pencils so that the staff would have to sharpen them – a somewhat far-fetched charge which perhaps says more about the paranoia she induced among the servants than her actual behaviour.[5]

'If Ernest raises any objections to the situation I shall give the Prince up at once,' Wallis told Aunt Bessie in May.[6] It is clear that she then, and for many months to come, saw her relationship with the Prince as being an enjoyable extra, with her marriage as the bedrock of her life. So far as possible she included her husband in all her royal engagements and she sedulously maintained that all three were the best of friends. Nor was she being untruthful: the Prince at this stage was perfectly happy to endure the presence of Ernest Simpson while Simpson, snobbishly reverent of all things royal, basked contentedly in the reflected glory of his wife's conquest.

The first time Simpson was significantly absent was in August 1934, when the Prince took a party to Biarritz and then for a cruise in Lord Moyne's yacht, the *Rosaura*. Aird was responsible for organizing the holiday. It started badly with two days of continuous rain and the Prince suffering from a surfeit of langoustines and being sick at his table in the Café de Paris. Wallis complained that she was not being introduced to all the English notables whom she felt sure were to be found at Biarritz. 'I think she would complain more if she was,' commented Aird drily. 'I feel that she is not basically a bad sort of tough girl out to get what she can, but unless she is much cleverer than I think, she does not quite know how to work it so as to cash in best.'[1] At this stage Aird thought he detected signs that the Prince was tiring of his liaison and seeking ways to escape from it; by mid-August he had revised his views. 'Behaviour in public excellent, in private awful and most embarrassing for others,' he wrote. The Prince 'has lost all confidence in himself and follows W around like a dog'.[2]

On the whole Aird at this stage thought Wallis's influence was beneficial; she made the Prince dress better, and except for introducing him to Old Fashioned cocktails, kept his drinking down. He revised his opinion when the party took to sea. A storm blew up. Wallis was never good when confronted by physical danger and the Prince seems to have been infected by her fear. 'He was really frightened, and in my opinion is a coward at heart,' wrote Aird.[3] His previous record shows him, on the contrary, to have been physically intrepid. Yet Aird was partly right. Formerly the Prince had delighted in flying in small aircraft and had always been the one who wanted to push on in bad conditions; once Wallis came on the scene he seemed to lose all confidence in aeroplanes as a means of transport. It is a striking illustration of her influence over him.

This holiday inspired the first reference in the press to the Prince's new romance. *Time*, in September, referred to the fun that 'Edward of Wales [was] having at Cannes last week with beautiful Mrs Wallace Simpson'.[1] Aird still saw no danger; at the end of the holiday he concluded 'she does not seem to have any illusions about the situation and definitely does not want to do anything that will lose her husband'.[2] But there could be no doubt about the ever-increasing importance the Prince attached to the relationship. 'I have had the best holiday in my life,' he told Godfrey Thomas.[3]

Up till now Mrs Simpson's existence had been tacitly ignored by the King and Queen. In November 1934, however, the Prince included Mrs Simpson's name in a list of people he wanted invited to an evening party in Buckingham Palace in honour of the Duke of Kent's wedding. The King scratched her out. According to Wigram the Prince nevertheless introduced her surreptitiously into the Palace; Cromer says that it was the Duke of Kent who reinstated her on the list.[4] At all events she was present, ostentatiously squired by the Prince. Christopher of Greece was taken up to meet her and asked who she was. An American, the Prince answered; 'Then he smiled. "She's wonderful," he added. The two words told me everything.'[5] He introduced Wallis to his mother, 'and would have done to HM if he had not been cut off,' wrote Aird.[6] The King was outraged. 'That woman in my own house!' he stormed to Mensdorff. At least Mrs Dudley Ward had come from a better class. As for the Prince: 'He has not a single friend who is a gentleman.' When Mensdorff pleaded that the Prince had many qualities, the King replied: 'Yes, certainly. That is the pity. If he were a fool we would not mind.'[7] He gave orders to the Lord Chamberlain that Mrs Simpson was not to be invited to any Silver Jubilee function nor to the Royal Enclosure at Ascot.[8]

The Prince's staff became seriously alarmed when in February 1935 he set off on another expedition with Wallis in the party and no husband in sight. This time it was a skiing holiday in Kitzbühel. 'People will not remain silent for ever,' Halsey wrote apprehensively.[9] Bruce Ogilvy took Aird's place. He was asked to bring along another man and chose his Scottish neighbour and old friend Andrew Lyall. Lyall, however, was an enthusiastic skier; Wallis, after her first tentative foray on to the slopes had ended in disaster, decided the sport was not for her. Ogilvy had to find another man to entertain her, and from the few available unwisely chose the extremely handsome James Dugdale.[1] Wallis took a fancy to him and insisted on sitting next to him at every meal; the Prince fretted miserably; Dugdale, finding the situation impossible, began to skulk in his room all day. When Ogilvy tried to tip the waiter more than the obligatory 10 per cent, Wallis spotted what he was doing and at once objected; and most of the presents which had been brought along for presentation to local dignitaries remained in their cases because she saw no reason for their distribution. It was not a relaxing holiday.[2] It was, however, popular with the Austrians who interpreted the presence of the heir to the British throne as an encouragement to them in their efforts to resist the pressure of Nazi Germany.[3]

It was this holiday which convinced Wigram that enough was enough. He called on the Prince at the Fort and tried to convey to him how worried the King was about his private life. 'The Prince said that he was astonished that anyone could take offence about his personal friends. Mrs Simpson was a charming, cultivated woman.'[4] Halsey had pressed Wigram to make this *démarche* and was convinced that good must come of it – 'I *do* believe that you have given him a good shake,' he wrote, but Thomas knew his employer better. He doubted if the Prince was at all shaken, he told Wigram; on the contrary, he was planning a holiday with Wallis in Italy for the spring.[5] Aird, too, had no illusions. The result of the protest was nil, he wrote, 'and the devotion of HRH if possible greater'. Two rooms at the Fort had been turned into one for Wallis's benefit, presumably to obviate the risk that, when the house was full, the dressing room adjoining her bedroom might be occupied and access thus impeded.[6] Trotter had joined in the chorus of disapproval and been equally unsuccessful in persuading the Prince to change his course. More optimistic than Thomas, however, he believed that the Prince knew 'in his inmost heart' that he was behaving badly. We must be patient, he told Thomas: 'I am sure his eyes will be opened to the folly he is making of himself, and when he does come for help and sympathy, I am sure you will respond as I know I shall.'[7]

Halsey had previously urged the King to support the efforts of his courtiers, but George V refused to speak directly to his son, saying that he had tried to remonstrate with him about Lady Furness and had achieved nothing. 'He went as far as to say that he was beginning to think it would almost be better if the POW abdicated, but of course that was a course which would be bound to cause trouble.'[1] His ban on Mrs Simpson's appearance at court did, however, lead to a confrontation with his son. First the Prince tackled Cromer, the Lord Chamberlain, and having made no progress with him, asked the King direct that the Simpsons should be invited to the Court Ball. The King said he could not invite his son's mistress on such an occasion. The Prince swore that she was not his mistress, the King accepted his word and said that she could come; 'I think this is all for the best,' wrote Aird in his diary, 'but it is rather a shock to think of the Prince of Wales lying on his oath, which a lot of people who know think he has.'[2]

The Prince always maintained that he had never slept with Mrs Simpson before his marriage, and sued for libel an author who referred to her as his mistress. Few of those who were closest to him believed his word. After the Prince's talk with the King, Wigram wrote that 'Halsey and the staff were horrified at the audacity of the statements of HRH. Apart from actually seeing HRH and Mrs S in bed together, they had positive proof that HRH lived with her.'[3] Aird saw him emerge early in the morning 'with his upper lip all red!! So that's that and no mistake.'[4] Alan Lascelles said that he would find it as easy to believe in the innocence of their relationship as in 'a herd of unicorns grazing in Hyde Park and a shoal of mermaids swimming in the Serpentine'.[5] Yet no one knows what happens behind a bedroom door except those who are inside. It is perfectly possible, and indeed not out of keeping with what is known of Mrs Simpson's character, that the Prince had been kept at bay and that, technically at least, he was telling the truth when he promised the King that Mrs Simpson was not his mistress. The question can never be resolved but the King at least was convinced by Wigram that his son had lied. Wallis went to the Court Ball, danced only once with the Prince, and behaved impeccably; but when, after supper, the King left, Aird noted that 'HRH went as far as the private door but got no remark from HM, not even "goodnight"'.[6]

The rest of the royal family shared the King's dismay. The Duchess of York openly said that she would not meet Mrs Simpson, though in fact they encountered each other on several occasions and Aird was amused to see them in the same room when the

Prince gave a party at Fort Belvedere.[1] William Teeling, the author and traveller, was dining with the Yorks at the Dorchester when the Prince and Wallis arrived in another party – 'After one dance the Yorks decided to leave and our party broke up.'[2] The Duke of Kent was better disposed towards his brother's affair, but it was widely said that his wife too was reluctant to meet somebody whom she considered a dangerous adventuress. Meanwhile the relationship became more and more widely known. Lady Constance Gaskell 'talked of the terrible way the Prince of Wales carries on'; Miss Bigge, Stamfordham's daughter, ruled that his behaviour was 'deplorable and wretched';[3] Lord and Lady Stanley were said to 'loathe the Prince of Wales's attitude'.[4] These were the voices of the Establishment; many others could have been found who saw little or nothing wrong in the Prince's conduct. But the Establishment was a powerful force, and once on the move could be hard to resist.

No one doubted that the Prince's holiday in 1935 would again include Mrs Simpson. Thomas felt that, if they had to be together, it was best it should be outside England. His concern was that they should not travel out together: 'He has drawn so much attention to it on previous occasions abroad by taking her out with him, passing her and her luggage through Customs under his laissez-passer.'[5] George V agreed, and made this a condition of his sanctioning the trip.[6] At one point the Prince announced that he planned to tour the Italian coastal resorts; since tension over Italy's invasion of Abyssinia was then extreme the King consulted Hoare about the 'silly yachting trip David wants to make in the Mediterranean', and then quashed the idea.[7]

Aird was back in attendance and was disconcerted when, on arrival at Cannes, the Prince rushed to the house they had rented and himself arranged the rooms, giving the best bedroom to his equerry and apportioning himself 'a rotten little room next to W'. An hour later the decision was reversed, 'at whose suggestion I do not know'.[8] Aird noticed that Ernest Simpson was mentioned less often than the year before and then only in a disparaging way.[9] But he persisted in his conviction that all would come right in the end: 'I feel she is getting tired of the pace and having secured the cash will chuck her hand in,' he wrote hopefully in his diary.[10]

The pace continued to quicken, and Wallis's hand was far from being chucked in. Some time in the summer 'G' Trotter wrote to the Prince, criticizing the transfer of his loyalties from Thelma to Wallis – 'very stupid and impudent,' Aird considered Trotter's behaviour. '. . . after all, there is nothing to choose between the women, both are tough girls, and if one can't treat tough girls like this, what is the point of tough girls?'[1] The Prince did not respond, but brooded on the offence, and when Trotter reverted to the matter shortly before Christmas he found himself summarily dismissed. The Prince refused even to shake hands with him. Aird thought the dismissal justified, if only because Trotter had most evidently not been up to the job over the last year or two, 'but the manner in which it would appear HRH did it is unpardonable . . . especially in view of G's age and what G has done for and with him'.[2] Thomas gloomily speculated that he might be the next to get into Mrs Simpson's bad books and meet the same fate: 'I steer completely clear of her, but HRH knows only too well what I think of the whole business, and one day I may blurt out more than I've already said and produce a crisis.'[3]

New Year's Eve found them at Melton for a fancy dress ball: the Prince, Wallis and, for once, Ernest, all dressed as pirates, which since the theme of the ball was '1066 and Before That' seemed doubtfully appropriate. The Prince was in notably good spirits and did not appear in the least put out at being confronted by some of Freda Dudley Ward's closest friends and both her daughters – 'I do not think he noticed any women there except Wallis,' recorded Aird.[4] But though the Prince was unaware of it, a Freda faction – and indeed a Thelma faction – had formed, who criticized his fickleness as vociferously as any of the starchier figures who deplored illicit liaisons of whatever kind. Harold Nicolson went with him to the theatre a fortnight later. 'I have an uneasy feeling that Mrs S . . . is getting him out of touch with the sort of person he ought to frequent,' he wrote in his diary. 'Yet the Dudley Ward row prevents all that, and I fear that her supporters are better than us, although Lady Furness's supporters are worse than us.'[5]

Within a few days of this diary entry being made the King was on his deathbed. The next time that Nicolson met his theatre companion he would be on the throne.

*

No holds were barred when the gossips of the period or the friskier biographers of a later age sought to analyse the appeal that Wallis Simpson held for the Prince of Wales. Wigram believed she was, to all intents and purposes, a witch. Lady Cynthia Colville discussed with the psychologist Dr William Brown the theory that Mrs Simpson had hypnotized the Prince. Brown did not dismiss it out of hand but thought it more likely that the Prince's sex life had hitherto been 'difficult, unsatisfactory and a constant source of inward misery' to him. Mrs Simpson had dispelled these difficulties – by arcane arts studied in a Far Eastern brothel, say the more fanciful – and so appeared 'in the guise of a wonderful saviour', who easily obtained undue ascendancy over her victim. Lady Cynthia hastened to impart these speculations to Queen Mary.[1] Wigram read her letter, and nodded his head sadly over the infinite frailties to which the human heart was subject. Dr Brown's thesis confirmed what he had long suspected, that the Prince 'had a weak spot in his mental equipment which Mrs S by foul and unfair means has exploited for her own advantage. As long as HRH is under this spell it would be useless to try to get him to go to a doctor to dispel this evil influence. She has him too tight in her grasp and is like a vampire.'[2]

Lady Furness is among others who advanced the theory that the Prince was sexually deficient and that only Wallis found the means of releasing him from his inhibitions.[3] Bruce Ogilvy, who lacked Lady Furness's specialized knowledge of the subject but, not being a woman scorned, has a greater claim to objectivity, took the same view.[4] The trouble with the theory is that, far from finding sex difficult, unsatisfactory or a constant source of inward misery, the Prince appeared to rate it among his greatest pleasures. The hectic abandon with which he pursued women during the interwar years is surely hard to reconcile with the vision of an inhibited and bungling lover? Any man may accept humiliation once or twice; to court it time and time again would be conduct hard to comprehend. That Wallis Simpson provoked in him profound sexual excitement is self-evident. That such excitement may have had some kind of sadomasochistic trimmings is possible, even likely. That she introduced him to a brave new world which had previously been closed to him is, to say the least, not proven. We shall anyway never know: what Yeats called 'the foul rag-and-bone shop of the heart' is mercifully padlocked against even the most prying and prurient of biographers.

Nor does it greatly matter. Wallis Simpson's sexual allure might have gained the Prince's attention, quickened his interest, engaged his passionate commitment, but it could not have retained him for a lifetime. Until the day he died his eyes would follow her around the room; if she went out he would grow anxious and would shortly find a reason for following her; at the dinner table he would be always craning forward to hear what she was saying; at a party he would watch her, to see if there was some service he could render. Total devotion it certainly was, slavish devotion some would say, but he found contentment in it.

It was her personality, not her appearance or her sexual techniques, which captivated him. She gave him something that he had never found before and which he now realized he needed desperately. All his adult life he had been surrounded by deferential courtiers and fawning hostesses. Halsey and Thomas were honourable men, who were ready to tell him when they felt he was doing wrong, but they did so with profound respect, respect for the office if not always for the man. Wallis respected neither office nor man, and made it abundantly plain that this was so. No Englishwoman, however assertive, however independent, however little wedded to the cause of monarchy, could have done the same. Wallis was harsh, dominating, often abominably rude. She treated the Prince at the best like a child who needed keeping in order, at the worst with contempt. He invited it and begged for more. When the weekend guests at Fort Belvedere had departed, she would taunt and berate him until he was reduced to tears.[1] 'She completely dominates every situation in which he is present,' remarked Victor Cazalet.[2]

Nor did he ever weary of this sensation. At a dinner party in Paris after the war, the Duke of Windsor unthinkingly asked the butler to give the chauffeur a message about his needs the following day. The Duchess, who missed nothing that happened at her table, raised her hands high in the air and brought them down with a crash that set the plates and glasses rattling. A horrified hush fell on the company. 'Never,' hissed the Duchess, 'never again will you give orders in my house!' Realizing that she had gone a little far, she then turned to her neighbour and explained, 'You see, the

Duke is in charge of everything that happens outside the house, and I on the inside.' Far from resenting this somewhat cavalier treatment, the Duke cringed and for the next ten minutes muttered incoherent apologies.[1] Ulick Alexander, a courtier who was perhaps more devoted to the Prince of Wales than any other in the inner circle, described him as being possessed by 'the sexual perversion of self abasement'.[2] A psychiatrist would perhaps venture some explanation based on his relationship with his mother or bullying by his nanny. Whatever the origins, now he was a man of forty the facts were clear: he was frightened by Wallis Simpson, enjoyed being frightened by her, and accepted her lightest word as law. He loved her; it was perhaps a peculiar kind of love, but it was love all the same.

Whether she loved him is another, more difficult question. Certainly she exploited him. She was a mean and acquisitive woman: cheerfully accepting a present of £50 from a friend with an invitation to a royal reception provided as a recompense, buying her clothes half-price at Mainbocher's in Paris and making the Prince fly them back duty free in his private aircraft.[3] The author Mrs Belloc Lowndes exclaimed with surprise that a woman as well dressed as Mrs Simpson should wear such garish costume jewellery. The other women present, all in the Simpson circle, 'screeched with laughter, exclaiming that all the jewels were real, that the then Prince of Wales had given her fifty thousand pounds' worth at Christmas, following it up with sixty thousand pounds' worth of jewels a week later at the New Year'.[4] The figures seem high, but not out of all contact with reality; certainly the Prince several times drew more than £10,000 from the Duchy accounts, apparently to finance purchases of jewellery. Nor was it just presents of jewels. In July 1935 Halsey admitted to the King that Mrs Simpson was receiving 'a very handsome income' from the Prince: 'I also told HM that in my opinion Mrs S and her husband were hand in glove in getting all they could out of HRH.'[5] Aird, at about the same time, put the sum at £6000 a year and recorded that 'W looks like succeeding to get some more money out of him'.[6]

But it is possible to exploit someone and still to love them. Bruce Ogilvy's opinion is that she was at first dazzled by the royal glamour, then genuinely attracted by his charm.[7] She never matched his consuming passion, but for some months at least he was all-important to her. By the time he succeeded to the throne, however, the man and his worldly position had long been separated in her mind. Duff Cooper talked lengthily to her and concluded, 'she is a nice woman and a sensible woman – but she is hard as nails and she doesn't love him'.[1] She was touched by his devotion to her, felt protective towards him, but it was no more than that. She was loyal to him, however, and by her own lights good-natured. She wanted him to be happy, and knew that she could make him happy as nobody else could. What would happen to him when he became King she did not know, but of one thing she was sure: she was not going willingly to relinquish her hold on his affections.

14

Accession

═══

O N 16 JANUARY 1936 THE PRINCE WAS SHOOTING IN
Windsor Great Park, 'in the highest spirits,' said Duff
Cooper, who was a guest.[1] A message was brought to him
from his mother: the King was ill, he was breathless, had no energy,
and was very sleepy during the day. He was in no immediate
danger, but it would be a good thing if the Prince were to invite
himself to Sandringham for the weekend.[2] The Prince was there the
following morning, to find his father half unconscious. Bronchial
catarrh had affected an already weakened heart, he was visibly
sinking and seemed unlikely to rally. On Saturday night the Prince
wrote to Mrs Simpson to tell her that all hope for his father had
been abandoned. 'You are all and everything I have in life and WE
must hold each other so tight,' he concluded. 'It will all work out
right for us.'[3]

On Sunday the 19th the Prince drove to London to break it to
the Prime Minister that his father had no more than a few days to
live. Baldwin told Chamberlain next day that he had been pleased
by his visitor's attitude and 'evident sense of his responsibilities'.[4]
The occasion was an emotional one; as he was leaving Mrs Baldwin
said, 'We have faith in you,' and he pressed her hand in gratitude.
But the Prime Minister had his reservations. 'It is a tragedy that he
is not married,' he told Tom Jones. 'He had been to see Mrs S
before he came to see me. She has a flat now. The subject is never
mentioned between us. Nor is there any man who can handle
him.'[5]

Back at Sandringham a Council of State had been set up to fill
the role of the dying monarch; the Queen and her four sons were
its members and they passed the few hours of its existence in coping
with the backlog of papers that needed the King's attention. At tea
time on 20 January, recorded the Archbishop of Canterbury,
Cosmo Lang, 'The Queen was still amazingly calm and strong, the

Prince of Wales full of vitality and talk, and touchingly attentive to the Queen.'[1] There were only a few hours more to wait. At five minutes to midnight the King died. Queen Mary's first act was to take her eldest son's hand and kiss it. The Duke of Kent, who was standing next to her, followed her example. Like it or not, for better or worse, Edward had become King.

His grief seemed to some extravagant. 'The Prince of Wales became hysterical, cried loudly, and kept on embracing the Queen,' Wigram remembered.[2] His emotion was 'frantic and unreasonable', wrote Helen Hardinge. 'In its outward manifestation, it far exceeded that of his mother and his three brothers, although they had loved King George V at least as much as he had . . . While he demanded attention for his own feelings, he seemed completely unaware of those of others.'[3] The death of a close relation takes people in different ways, some slip into almost catatonic shock, others — perhaps more fortunate — can let out their grief in noisy lamentation. The new King was of the latter school. It was natural for him to bruit his sorrow abroad, as natural as it was for his mother to take refuge in cool restraint. Even when he was most alienated from his father he had craved for his approval; that approval now could never be won. Instead he was thrust into that position of vertiginous eminence which he had always dreaded. He had had forty years in which to prepare himself for the moment when he became King, but when it happened it came with all the shock of the unexpected and the unknown. He was unsettled, he was frightened, and he was very much alone.

Since the reign of Edward VII the clocks at Sandringham had always been kept half an hour fast. The new King had barely left his father's deathbed before he ordered that they should be put back to the proper time. 'I wonder what other customs will be put back also,' pondered Lang apprehensively.[4] This act has been much criticized as being at the best insensitive, at the worst symbolizing a brutal rejection of his father's standards. Helen Hardinge called it 'a jarring descent to the trivial' which caused much distress to the old courtiers and retainers,[5] while Virginia Woolf imagined it to be the revenge of a man who had been 'daily so insulted by the King that he was determined immediately to expunge his memory'.[6] The haste was indeed maladroit; Edward VIII would have done better to leave the reform for a few days, if only to avoid reactions like those of Mrs Woolf. But in no way was it a gesture of defiance aimed at his family, or calculated to shock his mother. On the contrary the Duke of York professed himself delighted to hear what had been done and Queen Mary volunteered that she had 'always loathed' the eccentric system of Sandringham time.[1]

'King Edward VIII,' announced Baldwin rotundly in the House of Commons, 'brings to the altar of public service a personality richly endowed with the experience of public affairs, with the fruits of travel and universal good will. He has the secret of youth in the prime of age. He has a wider and more intimate knowledge of all classes of his subjects . . . than any of his predecessors.'[2] The first reaction to the accession of the new monarch was generally to join with Baldwin in praise of his qualities and his qualifications. 'He starts with the great advantage of having visited every part of the Empire and of being personally known by all its inhabitants,' wrote the Duke of Connaught. 'He is too *very well* known by most of the people of the Kingdom and to be [sic] very popular with them.'[3] Clement Attlee, leader of the Labour Party, referred approvingly to his charm and 'genuine solicitude for the unemployed'.[4] The new King did, indeed, seem formidably well equipped for his new task. He was a better speaker than his father, quicker-witted, with incomparably greater charm. 'He knows an enormous amount of general knowledge, never forgets names, knows statistics and really has the mind of the average man *par excellence*,' wrote Cecil Beaton[5] – and the mind of the average man *par excellence* was exactly what was needed by a constitutional monarch in the twentieth century. Paul Gore Booth, a young diplomat recently posted to Vienna, was struck the following year by his 'extraordinary range of knowledge, experience and interest', though detecting slight inaccuracies on any subject with which Gore Booth was particularly acquainted.[6] His memory was agreed by all to be truly royal – 'remarkable,' said Esher, 'astonishing,' Helen Hardinge, 'prodigious,' his secretary Dina Hood.[7] If a committee had been set up to devise a pattern for a modern monarch, it would have ended up with something very similar to what the country had now acquired.

Accession

George V was no democrat, Wigram wrote to the new Governor General in Australia; he 'felt his people wanted him to keep up the state of a King . . . Now we have another type of King. One of the new generation, a product of the war. No King could have a better start than King Edward. He is well known and the whole Empire is solid behind him. He is keenly interested in social problems and the working classes. There may be diversity of gifts but I am sure there is the same spirit.'[1] Anyone who knew Wigram would have detected the note of pious hope in that panegyric. He was not alone in his doubts. Baldwin freely admitted to those he knew well, and some he did not, his uncertainty about the future.[2] 'My heart goes out to the Prince of Wales tonight,' wrote Channon, as George V lay dying, 'as he will mind so terribly being King. His loneliness, his seclusion, his isolation will be almost more than his highly strung and unimaginative nature can bear.'[3]

In the little circle that made up informed London, there were rumours that Edward VIII would renounce the throne, or at least that he had only accepted it with reluctance. Alan Don, the Archbishop's principal adviser at Lambeth Palace, was told that the new King was to turn Roman Catholic as the easiest means to escape from his unwelcome task: 'This was told me by a Diocesan Bishop who had just been talking to an ex-Cabinet Minister.'[4] Diocesan Bishop or not, Don rightly dismissed such prattle; but it is harder categorically to gainsay the belief of Alan Lascelles that the Prince had been caught napping by the King's death and that given a few months more he would have opted out of the line of succession and retired into private life with Mrs Simpson. Once he had told Lascelles that he was keeping the Canadian ranch so as to have somewhere to which he could retire. 'You mean for a holiday, Sir?' asked Lascelles. 'No, I mean for good.'[5] Hardinge was equally certain that another six months would have seen the Prince out of the line of succession.[6]

One cannot ignore the opinion of men so close to the throne, nor can it ever be proved that they were wrong. The Prince of Wales must from time to time have contemplated the delights of a life free from pomp and the demands of duty, and played with the idea of escaping from the gilded prison of the Palace. In many ways he dreaded the prospect of the succession and would have postponed it as long as he could. Yet in the last resort it was his life, it was what he had been born for. To deny it was to deny his destiny. The time was to come when he would find the throne intolerable, but it was to take a stimulus far sharper than any which he experienced in January 1936 to drive him into abdication. What he hoped for when he acceded was that he would be able to run the monarchy in his own way, to preserve his privacy and his freedom of action, to live his own life within the walls of formality and tradition that encompassed him. He wanted to have his cake and eat it too; to be the King and yet retain the freedom of an ordinary mortal. Only when that proved impossible did abdication seem to him the sole remaining move that he could make.

For the moment he could still hope. He was borne along by the adulation and the heady scent of glory that encompasses any new incumbent of a throne. He had enough sense of history, enough pride in his ancestry and his country, to feel his spirit rise within him at Winston Churchill's dedication of himself to his new King and his 'heartfelt wishes that a reign which has been so nobly begun may be blessed with peace and true glory; and that in the long swing of events Your Majesty's name will shine in history as the bravest and best beloved of all the sovereigns who have worn the island Crown'.[1]

The morning after George V's death the King and the Duke of York flew to London – the first time that a British monarch had travelled in an aeroplane. 'David very brave and helpful, for he has a difficult task before him,' wrote Queen Mary in her diary.[2] An early ordeal to face was the Accession Privy Council. More than a hundred of the country's foremost dignitaries gathered at St James's Palace to witness Edward VIII's first public appearance. He was 'solemn, grave, sad and dignified', reported Duff Cooper.[3] It was an occasion on which *not* to have been all those things would have called for comment, but the calm confidence of his bearing impressed everyone. His short speech produced more mixed reactions. Cooper thought it excellent and told Mrs Simpson so. She responded by repeating it word for word. 'Apparently he had spent a very long time composing it – walking up and down the room and dictating it to her. But it had been his own idea.'[4] 'Happily-phrased,' Amery thought it, even if Edward VIII had been defeated by the word 'entituled' and after one or two shots plumped for 'instituted'.[1]* But to the more censorious Neville Chamberlain, the King looked nervous and uncomfortable. His speech 'did not contain anything original or striking and made but little impression'.[2]

The proclamation of the new King by Garter King of Arms at St James's Palace followed the next morning. Edward VIII arranged for Mrs Simpson to view the ceremony from a convenient window, then at the last minute decided to break with precedent by watching himself proclaimed and hurried across to join her. It was an unobtrusive gesture, but Diana Cooper spotted the two standing together at the window and mentioned it to her husband. 'This is just the kind of thing that I hope so much he won't do,' wrote Duff in his diary. 'It causes so much criticism and does so much harm.'[3] Walking away from the scene of the proclamation, Wallis Simpson mentioned to Godfrey Thomas that it had brought home to her how very different the King's life was in future going to be.[4] Almost the only man who did not accept the truth of this was Edward VIII himself; if his life did not remain essentially the same it was not going to be for want of trying on his part.

Back at Sandringham George V's body was carried on a gun carriage to the railway station three miles away, with the royal brothers and the late King's shooting pony, Jock, walking behind. For four days the body was to lie in state in Westminster Hall while more than a million mourners filed past. It was as the cortège wound through the streets from King's Cross to Westminster that the Maltese cross fell from the top of the Imperial Crown, which was resting on the coffin, and had to be surreptitiously retrieved by the Sergeant-Major of the Grenadier escort. Many people later claimed to have found something sinister in this widely reported accident, but for the most part their dire prognostications remained unuttered until the reign had prematurely ended. It was only a few days after the event, however, that Godfrey Thomas wrote: 'I am not superstitious but it confirms me in my conviction that he is not fitted to be King and that his reign will end in disaster. Increased responsibility may work a miracle but I don't think he will last very long. One could prop up the facade for a Prince of Wales –

---

* A mysterious comment, since the King's address as published contained neither word.

not so easy for a King.'[1] That Edward VIII's oldest friend and secretary for nearly twenty years could write in such terms within a few days of the accession was an augury for the future far more ominous than a few jewels tumbling into the gutter.

The King is usually credited with proposing that he and his three brothers, late one night, should replace the officers of the Household troops who normally stood guard around the catafalque and themselves take on the vigil. It was entirely his own idea, wrote Helen Hardinge, 'and it showed how priceless his imagination could have been to his country . . . It was to us then an act typical of the new King at his best, and a hopeful indication for the future.'[2] Praise was not often lavished on Edward VIII from this quarter and it seems churlish to seek to diminish it, but according to Lord Stair, who at that time was Adjutant of the Scots Guards, it was the Duke of York who conceived the idea and promised to put it to the King.[3] Whoever first thought of it, however, Edward VIII espoused it enthusiastically, as something that was both an excellent piece of public relations and a gesture of genuine respect and affection for a departed father. Nothing was said about the plan in advance, lest it should be cheapened by publicity; Edward VIII gave Aird another reason, he was afraid that if the news leaked out, 'King Carol of Romania might have come and insisted on standing on top of the coffin'.[4]

Once more the coffin took to the streets for its last journey to Windsor. Lady Ravensdale said the King 'marched badly and looked bored',[5] but no one else seems to have seen anything amiss. Many years later he recalled that it was one of the only occasions in his life when he had felt absolutely alone. The worst moment came when the procession was rounding Marble Arch and the police cordon broke. The crowd swept towards the gun carriage and for a moment he thought that the coffin was about to be thrown to the ground while he stood by helplessly. So vivid was his recollection of the incident that when King George VI was buried he announced his intention of visiting every police checkpoint along the route to ensure that the same thing did not happen again.[6]

The harmony within the royal family that followed the death of the King did not survive for long. On 22 January George V's will was read at Sandringham. Some £¾ million went to each of the royal Dukes and the Princess Royal; nothing was left to the eldest son. Only Queen Mary, the King and Wigram were present when the royal solicitor, Sir Bernard Halsey-Bircham, delivered this news – news, one suspects, only to Edward VIII. 'Where do I come in?' he asked. Wigram tried to explain that George V had assumed that he, as Prince of Wales, would have built up a substantial fortune out of the revenues of the Duchy of Cornwall and had no need of any more. King Edward VII had similarly left nothing to *his* eldest son. The King was unconvinced. His anguish must have been heightened by the fact that it was only a few days since he had released his father's estate from a loan of almost £90,000 made from the Duchy of Cornwall revenues in 1915 to enable the King to purchase additional land at Sandringham.[1] He kept on saying: 'My brothers and sister have got large sums, but I have been left out.'[2]

Alan Lascelles met the King as he left the room after the reading of the will, 'striding down the passage with a face blacker than any thunderstorm'. He went straight to his room and for a long time remained secluded there, speaking on the telephone. Lascelles was convinced that up to this moment the King had intended to renounce the throne almost immediately but that now, encouraged by Mrs Simpson, he decided to stay on and extract whatever additional fortune he could out of it.[3] Lascelles by 1936 was by no means disposed to give the benefit of any doubt to his former employer. Probably he attributed to the King clear-cut designs which in fact had hardly begun to form. But his father's will had come as a painful shock to Edward VIII, a shock not diminished by the fact that he had already accumulated great wealth and could expect to do as much again out of savings from the Civil List and the Privy Purse. He had believed, and must have promised Mrs Simpson, that another huge fortune would soon be theirs; it was not to be, and the disappointment he felt for himself was a hundred times worse because it would distress and anger the woman he loved.

Among all the thousands of people who wrote to Edward VIII to commiserate with him on his father's death, only one, Diana Cooper, referred directly to Wallis Simpson: 'Wallis . . . is and always will be the most wonderful friend and help to me,' he wrote in his reply. 'She gives me the courage to carry on.'[4] The day before he wrote this letter Baldwin had sent for Duff Cooper to say how disturbed he was about the affair. 'If she were what I call a respectable whore, I wouldn't mind,' he said, a description which Cooper took to mean 'somebody whom the King occasionally saw in secret but didn't spend his whole time with'. Baldwin's hope seemed to have been that Duff Cooper would talk to Mrs Simpson and persuade her to leave the country, for a time at any rate. 'I shall certainly do nothing of the kind,' wrote Cooper in his diary. He knew that it would achieve nothing except to poison his relationship with the new King.[1] But still scarcely anybody believed that this was more than an embarrassing entanglement which might give rise to a public scandal but would not drag on too long. Time, in the end, would solve the problem; he would grow bored with her and seek a younger substitute. The worst that Lord Crawford could contemplate was that, if he were too openly criticized, he might 'do something fatuous by talking of abdication: he has done so *en famille* before now'. That he might do more than talk of abdication seemed inconceivable; Crawford pinned his hopes on the influence of Queen Mary and, even more, on the King's own fickleness.[2]

The affair was still far from being a public scandal. Only a handful of people in the British Isles had even heard of Mrs Simpson, and of these few believed she would present an insuperable problem. Tom Jones voiced a hope that many cherished when he wondered 'whether it is going to be a case of the Prince in Shakespeare's Henry IV and the King in Henry V'.[3] Lord Harewood made the same point, claiming that Edward VIII would prove himself a better and wiser monarch than Henry V.[4] The analogy between Mrs Simpson and Falstaff was far-fetched and flimsy and none of those who worked most closely with the King believed that he would banish her as Henry V had banished the fat knight. The most that they hoped was that he would continue to keep her in hugger-mugger and not flaunt her in the full light of day. Their hopes were soon to be eroded.

15

'The Most Modernistic Man in England'

——

IT IS TODAY GENERALLY ACCEPTED THAT WHILE A monograph on X's foreign policy or Y's parliamentary career can be of interest and value, a biography proper must delve into the private life as well as the public and seek to relate one to the other. Usually the two are handled in isolation, the private life being dealt with in a separate chapter which provides a background and an explanation for the narrative of public events that is to come. In the case of Edward VIII this is impossible. Paradoxically, it was his determination to keep the two apart that forces the biographer to treat them together. 'He would be available for public business and public occasions when he was wanted,' he told Walter Monckton, 'but his private life was to be his own.'[1] His family, his courtiers, and in the last resort his subjects, knew this could never be. 'La royauté est un rôle. Les souverains doivent toujours être en scène,' Napoleon told Caulaincourt. Because Edward VIII would never accept this harsh but immutable law, his private life swelled in importance until in the end it fused completely with the public and brought his reign to an end.

This still seemed an almost inconceivable contingency when the Archbishop of Canterbury, Cosmo Lang, called on the King a week after his accession. Lang had been much esteemed by George V, and in his conservatism, his caution, his formality, his slightly unctuous but well-meaning concern for the new King's moral welfare, he symbolized everything Edward VIII most disliked and distrusted about the old establishment. Given this, the interview could hardly have been easy. Lang admitted that he had often discussed the Prince with George V but claimed that he had always tried to put his conduct in the best light possible. 'He did not seem to resent this frankness,' was Lang's judgment; 'Hiding my resentment, I turned the conversation in the direction of my new responsibilities as head of the Church,' was the King's comment.[1] On this subject things went no better; 'It was clear that he knows little and, I fear, cares little about the Church and its affairs,' wrote Lang, adding, however, that he had been impressed by his 'alertness and obvious eagerness to know and to learn'. The King was impressed only by the Archbishop's smug censoriousness. Given how large his obligations as head of the Church were to bulk over the next twelve months, it is a pity that Lang was not a man with whom he found himself able to communicate. If Archbishop Temple had been at Lambeth in 1936 then it is at least possible that things would have turned out differently. As it was, Lang and the King scarcely met. Baldwin told his niece Monica that once when he was waiting to see the King, the Duke of Kent came into the room and announced that his brother was 'damning the whole root and stock of the Episcopacy. He has just shooed the Archbishop of Canterbury out of the house.'[2]

His attitude towards the Archbishop was only part of his systematic rejection of the values of an older generation. Ormsby-Gore, the Colonial Secretary, noticed how ready he was to talk to the younger ministers but, 'with the old men like Ramsay MacDonald he shuts up like an oyster. He is all out for youth and the "common people"; he hates Society and the conventions of Court life.'[3] This was in many ways commendable, but it meant that the older statesmen and courtiers were brutally thrust into the wings, while there were not young men around with the experience and authority to take their place. Ray Atherton, at the American Embassy, noted how much offence the King gave to those who should have been his most senior advisers 'by failing to give due weight to their opinions and by a lack of consideration'. Even the Prime Minister on one occasion was kept waiting for an hour and twenty minutes.[4]

'I am better known to you as the Prince of Wales,' said the King in a St David's Day broadcast. 'I am still that same man.' The sentence was interpolated by him in a draft speech prepared by Lascelles. As Prince of Wales he prided himself on having been progressive, innovative, open to new ideas and to new influences. As King he meant to be the same. At a dinner party where he had been talking with some pride of his old-fashioned and 'outspokenly suburban' rock garden, Emerald Cunard turned to him and told him he was the most modernistic man in England. 'The King blinks his fair eye-lashes and says with the utmost simplicity: "No, Emerald, I am not a modernist, since I am not a highbrow. All I try to do is to move with the times."'[1] His 'modest ambition', as he expressed it in his memoirs, 'was to broaden the base of the monarchy . . . : to make it a little more responsive to the changed circumstances of my times'.[2] Courtiers, both by training and by disposition, tend to be opposed to change; and anyone who had served in the school of King George V was likely to be doubly so. It was certain that, even if his ambitions had been as moderate as he professed, Edward VIII would have found himself viewed with suspicion and some resentment in Buckingham Palace. The doubts of the courtiers were fortified by the inflexible conservatism of Queen Mary. In 1901, after Queen Victoria's death, the Duchess of York, as she then was, had deplored the changes at court initiated by King Edward VII: 'It is always better to do such things very piano and with much reflection,' she had written.[3] If she had thought this when young, how much more she would see the need for caution after twenty-five years as Queen, during which her always firm ideas had set into immutable rigidity. Even if there had been no Mrs Simpson, a clash between the King and the Establishment was inevitable. It would be unjust to the King to assume that this clash was between a self-centred and maverick monarch and his wise old counsellors. There were many ways in which those counsellors and the system which they operated needed to be brought up to date, many fossilized rules of earlier reigns which could advantageously be disposed of. Edward VIII recognized that he would be offending vested interests and injuring people who felt that they deserved better of him, but he was a strong proponent of the view that omelettes are only made by breaking eggs. Besides, 'I think it might have helped the Establishment too,' he said wistfully many years later. 'I think it might have revived the thinking of the Establishment.'[4]

Edward VIII's revolution was more a matter of presentation than of reality. H. G. Wells saw him as a gadfly reformer, spreading terror among the conventional and the traditionally minded: 'He flies about in aeroplanes, arrives unexpectedly and looks at things, instead of travelling in a special train . . . He betrays the possession of a highly modernized mind by his every act, he is unceremonious,

251

he is unconventional, and he asks the most disconcerting questions about social conditions . . .'[1] William Temple, Archbishop of York, wrote to thank him for 'the constant understanding and sympathy which Your Majesty has shown towards the working people of the country, especially the miners and the unemployed'.[2] Such accolades might lead one to believe that an active and pros-elytizing radical now occupied the throne. The contrary was true. Edward VIII did have an enquiring mind, was disinclined to accept dogma as invariably correct, grew impatient if told that something could not be done because it had never been done before, but he had no wish to disturb the existing social structure or to do more than mitigate its worst injustices. Nor did he wish to revolutionize the workings of the court. 'It is clear that he means to make no real break in tradition,' wrote Leo Amery shortly after the ac-cession.[3] He would have said as much six months later. Edward VIII himself said that the only two innovations of his reign were the setting up of the King's Flight, for royal transport by air, and the provision that the Yeomen of the Guard need not wear a beard unless they wanted to.[4]

But where he did try to change the rituals prescribed by his father, he found that he ran into a wall of opposition, no more permeable because it was deferential and obviously well inten-tioned. When he walked the few hundred yards from the Palace to the office of the Duchy of Cornwall, reports soon filtered back of the dismay felt by certain of his subjects. 'We can't have the King doing this kind of thing,' said one prominent Conservative. 'The Monarchy must remain aloof.'[5] He tried to abolish the system by which certain traders were given Royal Warrants and allowed to display the Royal Arms, but the civil servant involved, Sir Austin Strutt, played for time, eventually conceded that the Warrant might be phased out over twenty years, put the file in the pending tray and destroyed it with relief after the abdication.[6]

The King had his modest victories. He opposed the Archbishop's plans for redevelopment around Westminster Abbey as a memorial to George V, urging that a scheme to create playing fields all over the country would be more appropriate.[7] He insisted that his left – and as he saw it more pleasing – profile should appear on coins and postage stamps, and ignored the protests of the Master of the Mint, who maintained that monarchs always alternated from side to side and that in his reign it was the turn of the right.[1] He ruled that the twenty privileged bodies who had the right to present loyal addresses to a new sovereign – Oxford University, the Bank of England, the Royal Society . . . – should parade *en masse* and receive one common reply.[2] A few dignitaries were upset but on the whole the innovation was accepted gratefully: he made a most excellent impression, reported the Archbishop; while the Duke of York's private secretary, Louis Greig, told Thomas, 'The speech was of course quite excellent, but it was the way in which it was delivered that moved everybody . . . It was the first time I had seen HM in public since he came to the throne . . . and it was a really magnificent thing.'[3]

A battle which he lost, indeed which he barely fought, was over his move from York House to Buckingham Palace. He still found the Palace gloomy and oppressive and would far rather have used it only as offices and for state occasions, but he realized that the opinions of his advisers on the subject were too passionate to be brushed aside. Wigram told John Reith, the Director General of the BBC, that, if the King did not make the move, 'that would be the beginning of the end of the British Empire, as Buckingham Palace was the centre of it'.[4] Wigram's view seems unduly alarmist, but Queen Mary was no less emphatic that the monarch must occupy his proper residence and busied herself with her own move down the Mall to Marlborough House. In this he complied with the demands of tradition, but it proved harder to persuade him to attend church with any regularity. He missed a Sunday, did better the following week, then missed two Sundays in a row, and by May 1936 was only going when his presence was essential because of some official role he had to play.

India provided another source of conflict with his advisers. Despite his reservations about the fitness of the Indians to manage their own affairs, and the dislike of the Montagu reforms which he had shown on his visit as Prince of Wales, he seems to have been more liberal in his views than most of his ministers. In March 1936 he tried to insert in the text of a broadcast a sentence about the realization of Indian aspirations, which would in effect have conceded Dominion status. Sir John Simon had it removed, but only after much argument. 'All goes to show,' wrote Lord Crawford gloomily, 'that we have to deal with a very opinionated man who probably feels much more resentment than anybody knows at the restraints and restrictions which have surrounded him hitherto.'[1] Edward VIII was indeed opinionated, but not all those opinions were heretical or crass.

His attitude, however, does not seem to have been based on any profound consideration of the subject. When Linlithgow took leave before he assumed office as Viceroy, he asked the King whether he would like to be sent regular reports. 'Only when you have to,' replied the King. 'They will probably bump you off anyway!'[2] The distaste with which he recalled his own visit in 1921 became evident when he was told there was a general expectation that he would visit India in the winter of 1937 for a Coronation Durbar. He greeted the proposal with a marked lack of enthusiasm.[3] When the Secretary of State for India, Lord Zetland, reverted to the idea, the King suggested that the Duke of York could take his place, or even the Duke of Kent. Linlithgow deplored these suggestions; the Indians would be bitterly disappointed if anyone other than the King Emperor presided and only his august presence would avert the danger of disorder.[4] Talk of disorder at once stirred the King's darkest suspicions. This suggestion that his visit might not be well received produced a shift in his position. He now accepted that if anyone went it would have to be him but insisted 'he could not contemplate holding a bazaar with applauding troops, police and officials, with a sprinkling of the public carefully selected inside the ring and a disdainful and angry mob outside it'. His qualms put Zetland in an awkward position. 'For some reason or other His Majesty will not face a decision,' he wrote crossly.[5] It was late October before the King relented and gave Zetland permission to state that he would definitely attend a Durbar in India, though even then he would not commit himself to a date or the duration of the visit.[6] Given what he must by then have known to be the uncertainty of his future his reticence is hardly surprising; long before the time had come to prepare a programme he had left the throne.

The part of his royal responsibilities which he took most seriously was his role as head of the armed services. He was a re-armer at a time when Baldwin was reluctant to devote any considerable resources to such an enterprise, but he was not possessed by Churchill's burning sense of urgency and he caused the government no embarrassment by talking out of turn. His concern for the future of the services was, however, constant and energetic. The Navy was closest to his heart. 'He was keenly interested in the new programme of construction,' wrote Samuel Hoare, now back in the government as First Lord of the Admiralty. 'Even the smallest details of naval administration he liked to discuss with me, and his knowledge of the fleet's personnel was altogether exceptional.'[1] This knowledge he owed in part at least to his energetic cousin and naval ADC, Louis Mountbatten, who was constantly enlisting his aid in a wide range of good works, from the return of the Fleet Air Arm to the Royal Navy to the removal of a statue of King George IV from Trafalgar Square to make way for memorials to Jellicoe and Beatty.[2] But though Hoare had no doubt that the Navy was Edward VIII's favourite service, the Chief of the Imperial General Staff, Sir Cyril Deverell, knew otherwise. Duff Cooper saw him immediately after he had had an audience with the King. Usually notably taciturn, on this occasion 'his tongue was loosened and his eyes were dancing. He told me . . . he had been impressed by His Majesty's obvious love of the Army and his interest in it. "The interview," he said, "was really inspiring."'[3]

After the abdication the Duke of Windsor wrote to King George VI to urge him not to let his courtiers wear him to the bone and at all costs to maintain the privacy of his weekends at his country house, Royal Lodge. 'Don't ever give them up as they are one's only defence against the strangle grip of Buckingham Palace and its officials!! How they would hate that remark!!'[4] They would have too, but they would not have been surprised, for it was painfully obvious by the time his reign had run a few weeks that he regarded his closest advisers as enemies to be kept at bay and if necessary deceived. The litmus test of their loyalty was whether they approved, or at least condoned, his liaison with Wallis Simpson. Silence was tolerated, overt criticism earned immediate dismissal. Thomas was silent, and though Edward VIII had little doubt about his real views, he needed him too much to invite a confrontation. Halsey was less reticent and had told the King, when he was still Prince of Wales, that his affair was damaging both his reputation and the country. Shortly after the accession he was told that there would be no place for him under the new regime. To Alec Hardinge this showed black ingratitude towards a man 'who had given up a great career in the Navy and been Head of his Household for twenty years, whose only crime was that he would not condone an intrigue which 98 per cent of the country were shortly to condemn'.[1] Halsey was sixty-three and the King had lost confidence in him: it does not seem unreasonable to have retired him at the start of the new reign. But it is harder to forgive the rancorous nature of his dismissal and the grudging award of a pension: 'This trait in HM's character of no sign of gratitude for past work is a very nasty one,' wrote Aird.[2] Edward VIII was capable of great generosity and extravagant loyalty, but in 1936 all generosity and loyalty was pledged to Mrs Simpson, nothing was left over for old friends and servants. Aird, and the King's comrade since 1917, Joey Legh, were similarly denied his confidence.[3] Ulick Alexander was the only courtier of whose loyalty he seemed wholly confident. George Crichton was removed so as to make room for Alexander as Comptroller. 'He had no grudge against Crichton,' wrote Alexander; 'he never had a grudge against anyone except on account of his amours. Now if Crichton had had to refuse a ticket for Mrs Simpson to attend some function – snap: that would have been the end of him.'[4]

The monarch has at the best of times a lonely task; a bachelor monarch is doubly unfortunate; while a bachelor monarch who has no affection for or confidence in those with whom he must work every day is uniquely desolate. Edward VIII had always been inclined to doubt the loyalty of those who worked for him, even though they had given him little cause to do so. Mrs Simpson, consciously or unconsciously, had exaggerated this tendency, had fed his fears and suggested new grounds for suspicion. The consequence was his virtual alienation from his own court; Buckingham Palace was enemy territory, Fort Belvedere the only redoubt where he could feel totally secure. It could hardly have been a more unpromising background to what promised anyway to be a difficult reign.

The crucial appointment, the man with whom it was all important that the King should work closely, was the private secretary. It is difficult to overstate the importance of this functionary in the working of a constitutional monarchy. He is not only the sovereign's eyes and ears, he is responsible for interpreting the sovereign to the government and the government to the sovereign. He must be ready to offer informed advice on any one of the myriad subjects which may erupt into crisis from one day to another, to act as a buffer between his employer and the outside world and to know who should have access to the presence, which paper should be read and which dealt with in some outer office. If all goes well he will not be noticed; if anything goes wrong it is his fault. If there was to be any chance of Edward VIII's reign unfolding without some fearsome constitutional calamity, the right man had to be found, and found quickly, for this vital slot.

King Edward VIII had inherited Lord Wigram from his father and tradition demanded that he should keep him on for six months or so to ensure a smooth transition from one reign to the next. This he was ready to do, but no more than that. Wigram, like Halsey, was sixty-three years old and had served King George V with total devotion and loyalty for thirty years. The new King wanted a man of his own generation and one who was not steeped in the traditions of the old regime. Horace Wilson, Baldwin's personal adviser, states that Wigram became increasingly unhappy and 'quite early in the new reign came to the conclusion that he could not carry on'.[1] This no doubt is true, but it is equally true that he would not have been asked to do so.

The only man who had any chance of filling the post to the King's satisfaction and yet doing a decent job was Godfrey Thomas. Thomas was not as close to Edward VIII as he had used to be – Mrs Simpson left no room for such intimacy – but he had avoided any overt quarrel and was still classified as one who was essentially on the right side. He was offered the post but refused it, saying that he did not feel he was right for it and that, anyway, he needed a rest. In fact he had had enough; he was prepared to soldier on as number two but someone else must bear the brunt. As Wigram's successor he recommended King George V's assistant private secretary, Alec Hardinge. Hardinge had served sixteen years with George V and thus might seem open to the same objections as Lord Wigram, but at least he was younger, having been born in the same year as the new King. *Faute de mieux* King Edward VIII accepted him.

It would have been difficult to make a more unfortunate appointment. Hardinge was intelligent, hard-working, competent and totally honourable, but temperamentally there was no possibility that he would achieve a working relationship with the King. Aird thought it a bad choice 'as Alec seems to be so very narrow-minded', while Horace Wilson, whose sympathies were on almost every issue against the King, held Hardinge's intentions to be excellent but his execution of them lamentable: 'His feelings seem to have led him to make remarks that were to say the least of it tactless and some of them were said to have been retailed to the King.'[1] Alan Lascelles, who worked with Hardinge more closely than anyone, admired his great administrative and executive talents but felt that these barely compensated for 'his complete inability to establish friendly, or even civil, relations with his fellow men'.[2] Patience, sympathy and an understanding of man's frailties were essential in Edward VIII's private secretary; Hardinge, among his colleagues, though not his family and friends, was felt to be an irascible and rigid martinet. It was typical of his dealings with the King that, when he had excellent reason to protest about an arbitrary cut in his pay, he did so not face to face and with some effort to reach an understanding but in an impersonal note of bleak incivility. When the King showed himself offended, Hardinge wrote in some surprise to say that he had thought he had so worded his letter 'that I should not cause you the slightest annoyance'.[3] It is a measure of his unsuitability for his task that he undoubtedly believed what he said to be true.

Alan Lascelles was also taken on from King George V's household. Having left the Prince of Wales's employment with some ill-feeling eight years before, Lascelles fully expected to find himself looking for a job outside the royal service, but Edward VIII bore him no grudge and respected his abilities. The crucial point was that he had left before the advent of Wallis Simpson; so long as he was prepared to accept the existence of that liaison, the King would have no quarrel with him. In fact, he succeeded in establishing a relationship of cautious cordiality with Mrs Simpson: 'Tommy Lascelles has fallen under W's control almost completely,' noted Aird with some amusement.[4] Cromer, the Lord Chamberlain, was another official of the old court who was asked to stay on. He had some doubts, for he knew 'that war was in effect declared against the old gang', but decided that his duty was to retain his post.[5] Cromer intervened to save Louis Greig from dismissal as a Gentleman Usher, pleading that he was generally felt to have done valuable work for the royal family. The King grudgingly agreed. His reply illustrates well the mounting paranoia with which he viewed the world around him: Greig had been 'very disloyal'; 'You tell me that Louis Greig is supposed to have been helpful to the Royal Family. This hardly includes myself, because far too often gossip of a destructive nature reaches my ears from that source.'[1]

It was in part at least the King's fault that the atmosphere at court was strained and unhappy. Charles Lambe, a young naval officer who was appointed equerry in July 1936 as a result of being Louis Mountbatten's closest friend, was at once unfavourably impressed. 'A great deal of whispering and secrecy,' he noted. 'One courtier always bleating, a centre of discontent ... Another – *ancien régime* – outraged, pompous and ineffectual.' The organization seemed inadequate; there was no Chief of Staff to ensure that all ran smoothly. 'Consequently the good old atmosphere of competition for the King's Ear prevailed, as it must always have done in history.'[2]

The unpleasantly tense relationship between the King and his staff was exacerbated by the ferocious economy drive which he now instituted. Instances abound of his generosity as a young man: he was said to give a £5 note to anyone who opened a gate for him when out hunting; he several times came to the financial rescue of friends of Freda Dudley Ward; when Bruce Ogilvy left his employment he offered to pay his debts and gave him a substantial cheque as a wedding present.[3] He was capable of similar liberality all his life; when his old servant Frederick Finch wrote to say that he had been ill and had had financial problems, he at once replied: 'What a pity you didn't let us know instead of selling some of your things. Anyway, I enclose check in the amount of £100, which I hope will pay for the doctor's bills.'[4] But during his last years as Prince of Wales he was noticeably more cautious about laying out his money, and once King he became obsessed by the need to cut down every expense and realize every asset. Lascelles thought that, in small things, he had shown 'signs of minginess' for several years but that 'what really started him on the economy stunt was his father's will'.[5]

It is impossible not to connect King Edward VIII's growing parsimony with the influence of Mrs Simpson. For her, money and material possessions were of inestimable importance; she hungered for them and greeted every new acquisition as an incentive to grasp for more. Wigram had heard that the King had put over £250,000 in a trust for Mrs Simpson out of the accumulated Duchy of Cornwall revenues. This was supposed to be invested in Britain but a close friend of Ernest Simpson said that a large sum had also been remitted to the United States.[1] Hardinge noted with some alarm that during discussions of the new Civil List the King laid special stress on the provision to be made for a Queen: 'It was on this aspect that he concentrated far more than any other.'[2] But no accession of fortune, real or hypothetical, could appease her craving for security. She urged the King to economize in every way. An early example, which gave an unpleasant shock to the humbler of his employees, affected the presents which were handed out to the household at Christmas time. When Freda Dudley Ward or Thelma Furness had been responsible for these they had been lavish and tailored to the tastes of each recipient. In 1935, when Wallis Simpson took over, they were cut to a meagre sum in cash.[3] But the real campaign began a month or two after the accession. There was plenty of room for economies; under King George V the royal households had been run on lavish and wasteful lines. By the end of April the Financial Secretary, Sir Ralph Harwood, was able to report that the cost of food had been cut from £45,000 a year to £13,500. But the situation was different when it came to the wages of the staff. Harwood made himself unpopular with the King by insisting that it was 'a false economy to pay poor wages' and that, even if lower wages were paid to new recruits, it would be unjust to slash the salaries of those who were already in royal employ. Furthermore, the new Civil List allowed for the recent increase in wages: 'It would be rather in the nature of a breach of faith to reduce the wages and then utilize the surplus specifically granted for these high wages for what might be termed private purposes.'[4]

The King was undiscomfited by this broadside. No opportunity was to be missed to reduce outgoings. Drink allowances were lowered and livery compensation discontinued, costing the lower paid staff some £20 a year and, in Harwood's view, making it inevitable that some of them would have to move 'into slummish quarters'.[5] Told that a 'Groom' would be travelling on the box of the royal car, the King asked, and asked again, what else the groom did. 'I feel sure it is economy,' wrote Aird, 'and that HM felt he had found a superfluous man.'[1] The cost of the royal aeroplane and pilot was transferred to the Air Ministry: 'Nevertheless,' noted Hardinge, 'on several occasions during the summer it was used to bring ladies over from Paris, and for the importation of goods for Mrs Simpson, on which duty should have been paid.'[2]

In June Harwood threatened to resign. There was no need for these economies, he argued. There would be a surplus of £50,000 on the Civil List, which added to the Duchy revenues would produce a Privy Purse income of £212,000 – 'a sum greatly exceeding His Late Majesty's income notwithstanding the large economies which it is known are being made in the private Estates'. In order to make this huge income even huger, the King would 'exchange a contented and willing staff for one which will be unhappy and seething with discontent . . . Your Majesty has several times mentioned to me that Your Majesty does not wish to be regarded as a "pincher", but . . . this very term, accompanied by even more objectionable suggestions, is being freely used with reference to Your Majesty.'[3] The King heavily underlined the last sentence in red, but it made no difference to his behaviour.

It was not only Buckingham Palace and Windsor which were affected by the economy drive. In his memoirs the Duke of Windsor described Sandringham as a 'voracious white elephant'[4] and he horrified the Queen by telling her he considered it a 'hobby' which could not be allowed to cost the £50,000 a year or so required to keep it going. The Duke of York and Lord Radnor were despatched to find ways of running the place more cheaply. The *Daily Telegraph* announced that as a result the staff was to be more than halved, 'most offensive and quite untrue,' the Duke protested,[5] though the real recommendation – that one hundred out of the four hundred employees should be made redundant[6] – was drastic enough. It did not satisfy the King, however. He made plans to sell Flitcham and Anmer, two of the largest of the adjoining farms, and the contract was actually drawn up and awaiting final signature at the time of the abdication. The purchaser sportingly renounced his claim; 'I have stopped the sale of Anmer,' King George VI told his mother with some satisfaction.[7] He had stopped more than that; the King told his agent that he proposed to sell two other farms as well. It is true that the farms involved were those bought by King George V with money borrowed from the Prince of Wales's Duchy income,* but few doubted that in the end the main house would have been dispensed with.[1]

Balmoral was subjected to the same treatment, but this time the King delegated nothing to his brother. 'He arranged it all with the official people up there,' wrote the Duke of York. 'I never saw him alone for an instant . . . I do hope he will realize that he must go slow, as he does not know anything or anybody . . . I do think it such a pity that David will never listen to anybody.'[2] The Duke tried to mitigate the effects by taking over a couple of grouse moors and employing some of the personnel made redundant by his brother, but he knew the damage could not easily be repaired.[3]

Sandringham and Balmoral were the private property of Edward VIII. He associated them with some of the most boring and unhappy periods of his life. In his view it was generous on his part not to dispose of them altogether, to expect him to continue to run them at a loss was asking too much. He had a valid point, but if he had not been so obsessed with the need for economy and so preoccupied with his own personal affairs, he would have handled the business with greater consideration for those who would inevitably be hurt and financially injured by his behaviour. He paid only one visit to Sandringham and then was come and gone before most of the staff had even glimpsed him. 'I wish it had been longer,' wrote his aunt, Queen Maud of Norway, who spent much of her time at Appleton House on the estate. 'Poor old Walker was so disappointed not to see him and had tears in his eyes.'[4] His sensitivity towards the feelings of his fellow men, hitherto so marked a feature of his character, had deserted him. At Windsor, after much persuasion, he at last consented to go round the gardens and glass houses. The particular pride of the gardener was the peach house, at that time a mass of blossom, promising a record crop of peaches. The King made no comment as he surveyed the luxuriant flowers; then, at the end of his tour, told the gardener to cut the blossoms and send them to Mrs Simpson and one or two other ladies. 'Caligula himself,' wrote Ulick Alexander, 'can never have done anything more wanton.'[5]

It seemed he had resolved that nothing was sacred, anything

---

* See page 247 above.

262

which could be turned into cash should be so sacrificed. In 1910 Edward VII had agreed that the estates of those dying intestate and heirless in the Duchy of Lancaster should be placed in a 'Bono Vacantia' fund; the income to be paid to the monarch, the principal retained against possible future claims. George V continued the practice. Claims were rare and by 1936 the fund amounted to £38,000. Edward VIII decided to reduce it to £1000 and apply the rest to his own purposes. Wigram felt that this was unjust, both to Edward VIII's eventual successor and to the heirs of King George V. He consulted the Chancellor of the Duchy of Lancaster, who considered that the King was within his legal rights. Legal or not, Wigram had no doubt that King Edward VIII was behaving in a way which his predecessors would rightly have deplored.[1]

The general public saw nothing of what was going on; indeed to all but a handful of courtiers or their near associates the new King seemed to be carrying out his duties with grace and due decorum. He was indeed playing much of his part with considerable distinction. The Earl of Athlone dined at Buckingham Palace when the King entertained those who had come to his father's funeral: 'I must say that David was wonderful as a host,' he told Princess Louise. 'He spoke German and French and was at ease with his guests.'[2] He was sometimes loath to take on a duty which tradition assigned to him, but equally likely to accept another which he could well have avoided. He attended the Maundy Service at Westminster Abbey where alms were distributed to those in need and 'played his part with great good will', wrote Alan Don. 'It was his liking for the poor which brought him to the service . . . how delighted the old people must have been.'[3]

In July he presented colours to three battalions of the Guards in Hyde Park and addressed the troops in a speech which he had drafted himself and sent to Winston Churchill for embellishment. He chose to stress the horrors of war: 'Humanity cries out for peace and the assurance of peace, and you will find in peace opportunities of duty and service as noble as any.' As he rode back towards Constitution Hill a man in the crowd pulled out a gun. A policeman grappled with him and the gun was thrown on to the road at the feet of the King's horse. Seeing a metal object flying towards him, the King assumed it was a bomb and braced himself for the explosion. 'I have held the opinion that HM is a coward . . .' wrote Aird, who remembered his behaviour when at sea with Mrs Simpson in a Mediterranean gale, 'but after today I must reconsider my opinion and give HM the fullest marks for not looking round, even when it happened. The King rode on in complete calm, not even quickening his horse's pace.'[1] As soon as he got back to the Palace he wrote to congratulate the GOC on the success of the parade. 'We have to thank the Almighty for two things: firstly that it did not rain, and secondly that the man in the brown suit's gun did not go off!!'[2]

The man in the brown suit was Jerome Bannigan, alias George McMahon, an Irish journalist with a grudge against the Home Secretary, John Simon. Probably he intended no more than a demonstration, but his mental instability was such that he might have done anything, the gun was loaded,[3] and the King had every reason to think that he had only a few seconds to live. Two years later a fanciful news story said that the Duke of Windsor had been giving financial help to McMahon after the latter's release from prison. 'He is about the last man I would help,' commented the Duke. His reason was not that he had been put in fear of his life but that 'McMahon got all the front page and the headlines and nobody read my speech'.[4]

His public appearances rarely fell below this high standard. Philip Guedalla was at the first dinner the King gave in Buckingham Palace after he moved across from York House. The guest of honour was the Argentine Foreign Minister, Dr Carlos Lamas, who was over to negotiate a new trade agreement. The other guests – ministers, bankers, ambassadors – were hardly the ingredients for a merry evening but the King was indefatigable, chattering away in Spanish and treating Dr Lamas with flattering courtesy. Towards the end of the evening a kilted piper vehemently played 'Mallorca' – '*mi composición*,' said the King proudly. He 'managed the entire occasion effortlessly and with admirable effect', wrote Guedalla; and could claim some little part of the credit when the trade agreement was signed a month later.[5]

The State Opening of Parliament in November was of interest as being the first occasion several people referred to the American accent which was increasingly replacing the Cockney that had in the past tinged his speech. 'The King looked like a boy of eighteen and did it well,' wrote Harold Nicolson. 'He referred to the "Amurrican Government" and ended "And moy the blessing of Almoighty God rest upon your deliberoitions".'[1] The Chicago-born Chips Channon thought he looked 'a young, happy Prince Charming . . . not nervous, not fidgety, but serenely dignified', but recognized a familiar American flavour in the way he said 'prog-ress' and 'rowts' instead of 'roots'.[2] Lord Crawford was more censorious. 'His pronunciation is poor – one might say bad,' he commented severely: 'the inflection on the letter R in America was noticeable and Route pronounced "Ro-ut" as though it were a composite word.'[3]

The Coronation should have been King Edward VIII's apotheosis. Archbishop Lang called on him to discuss the service and told Don that he was relieved to find that the King was prepared to follow the ritual as laid down for the last two Coronations: 'Cosmo Cantuar had feared that he might want to cut out some of the more ancient and picturesque features.'[4] Lang in fact agreed to omit the sermon and the litany. Though he said nothing about it at the time he claimed subsequently to have been struck by the way the King urged the Duke of York to follow the book of the service with him and himself took little interest in the discussion: 'I wonder whether even then he had in the back of his mind some thought that the Coronation might not be his, but his brother's.'[5] Helen Hardinge drew the same sort of deduction from the fact that the Duke of York regularly attended meetings of the committee set up to arrange the ceremony.[6] There is no reason to read too much into the King's behaviour. He found any sort of religious service tedious, and one conducted with as much antique ritual as the Coronation would have seemed to him uniquely burdensome. Added to that the fact that he personally disliked the Archbishop, and the surprise is that he attended even one meeting on the subject. In fact the Duke of York was Chairman of the Coronation Commission and attended the very rare meetings of the Coronation Committee of the Privy Council, but was rarely present at meetings of the Coronation Joint Committee, which was presided over by the Duke of Norfolk and which did all the work.[7]

*

265

The plea for peace which he had made to the Brigade of Guards was echoed only ten days later when the King went to Vimy Ridge in France to inaugurate the memorial to the Canadian dead of the First World War. Vimy had been the site of one of the bloodiest of battles and the spectacle of the fields and woods where twenty years before there had been such fearful carnage reminded the King vividly of the hell of war and the need to avoid it at almost any cost. This consideration, more than any other, coloured his thinking about British foreign policy and the line to take over the swelling crisis on the continent of Europe.

The only other principle which influenced him to a comparable extent was his belief that communism presented the greatest threat to the peace and stability of Europe. When Marshal Mannerheim, who represented Finland at the funeral of King George V, remarked that whatever one might think of the Nazi Party they had at least done Western civilization a good turn by destroying the Communist Party in Germany, the King agreed. Edward VIII said that he hoped for a reconciliation between the Western Powers and Germany, though he added doubtfully: 'But it is difficult to approach Germany because it can only be done together with France.'[1]

By January 1936 Hitler's National Socialist Party was firmly installed in Germany. The 'economic miracle' followed by rearmament had brought full employment and a measure of prosperity to every class. Hitler was bracing himself for his first great international gamble, the invasion of the demilitarized Rhineland in defiance of the Locarno Pact. Edward VIII in his memoirs described himself as finding Hitler a 'somewhat ridiculous figure' but as admiring the German people and sympathizing with many of their aspirations.[2] This is disingenuous; if he did indeed find Hitler somewhat ridiculous he never seems to have mentioned it at the time. Whether the reoccupation of the Rhineland was one of the aspirations with which he sympathized is not revealed, but his conduct suggests that at least he did not take it tragically.

On the day of the accession the German Ambassador, Leopold von Hoesch, wrote to Berlin to report on the new monarch. Edward VIII, he said, was distinguished by sincerity of mind and warmth of heart. He was closer to the people than his father, deeply interested in social questions and in large part personally responsible for the improved housing conditions which the government had reluctantly brought about. He enjoyed unparalleled popularity. Of more immediate interest to Berlin, he 'feels warm sympathy for Germany'. He would have to proceed with caution, said Hoesch, but 'I am convinced that his friendly attitude towards Germany might in time come to exercise a certain amount of influence on the shaping of British foreign policy. At any rate, we should be able to rely upon having on the British throne a ruler who is not lacking in understanding for Germany and in the desire to see good relations established between Germany and Britain.'[1]

Von Hoesch was a professional diplomat, experienced and cautious, and with no liking for the new regime in Germany. There was nothing in his description of the King's attitude towards Germany to which Edward VIII could have taken exception, nor, incidentally, which could not have been applied to Chamberlain or Halifax, Hoare or Simon. The Nazi leadership preferred the more sensational reports of the Duke of Saxe-Coburg, who called on the new King when he was in London for George V's funeral. King Edward VIII, he recorded, saw a German–British alliance as 'an urgent necessity and a guiding principle for British foreign policy'; not an alliance against France but preferably including her. He thought Hoesch 'oily', and a bad representative of the Third Reich, and said he would prefer a good National Socialist like Ribbentrop. The Duke asked whether it would be useful if Hitler and Baldwin were to meet. 'Who is King here?' Edward VIII is supposed to have demanded. 'Baldwin or I? I myself wish to talk to Hitler, and will do so here or in Germany. Tell him that please.' The King, the Duke concluded, 'is resolved to concentrate the business of government on himself. For England, not too easy. The general political situation, especially the situation of England herself, will perhaps give him a chance.'[2]

It is inconceivable that the King would have expressed himself with quite such freedom or such folly; the Duke of Saxe-Coburg was notoriously unreliable as a witness.* But though he could hardly have put himself forward as the architect of British foreign

* On 8 Jan 1963 the present Lord Norwich wrote to *The Times* to point out that Coburg's account of his conversation with Duff Cooper was grotesquely at variance with Cooper's known views. It was clear, Lord Norwich temperately remarked, that Coburg had 'little gift for accurate reporting. After all, anyone who could think that he had been at Eton with the Earl of Avon, with my father [Duff Cooper] and with Neville Chamberlain (who was 28 years older than Lord Avon and never went there at all) could think anything.'

policy, his intention when he became King was certainly to play a more active role than his father would ever have permitted himself. He had, too, a strong authoritarian streak which made him better disposed than most of his fellow countrymen to the conduct of affairs in Germany. Duff Cooper remembers him, shortly before the abdication, asking why the government did not exercise closer control over the BBC. Cooper explained the measure of its independence. 'I'll change that,' said the King. 'It will be the last thing I do before I go.'[1]

Whatever the scale of the King's pretensions, or the reality of his influence, there is no doubt that the German leadership took it seriously. Ribbentrop, in particular, told Prince Kyril of Bulgaria that he was convinced Edward VIII was 'a kind of English National Socialist, with strong concern for the social problems of his country and warm sympathy for an understanding with Germany'. Only the Foreign Office and other similarly sinister centres of anti-German feeling had frustrated the King's wish to bring about an agreement.[2] Sir Orme Sargent of the Foreign Office at the end of 1936 recorded a conversation in which he was told of Ribbentrop's belief that the real reason for the abdication was neither moral nor constitutional but political: 'Mr Baldwin's real motive was . . . to defeat those Germanophile forces which had been working through Mrs Simpson and the late King with the object of reversing the present British policy and bringing about an Anglo-German entente.' Hitler also was said to be very distressed by the abdication, 'since he had looked upon the late King as a man after his own heart and one who understood the *Führer-prinzip* and was ready to introduce it into this country'.[3] At the time the Foreign Office were incredulous that Ribbentrop and Hitler could really be so misguided; only with the publication of the official German documents did it become clear that this in fact reflected the official view. In December 1936 the German Ambassador was personally instructed by Hitler to do all he could to prevent the abdication since this would 'weaken the moral power of the Crown, and so assist the undermining influence of communism in the Empire'.[4]

The King, the American Ambassador told Roosevelt, was 'surrounded by a pro-German cabal'.[5] Studying the guest lists for Fort Belvedere or the records of those whom he met regularly, it is hard to see whom the Ambassador had in mind. Most of the *habitués*

were socialites without a political thought in their heads or employees of the American government. The only political figure who
appeared at Fort Belvedere with any regularity was the francophile
Duff Cooper. Probably most of the people whom the King saw
frequently would have shared his feeling that there was a lot to be
said for the German point of view and that everything possible
should be done to reach an understanding between the two
countries, but if the word 'cabal' implied some element of considered planning, or at least discussion, then it was wide of the
mark.

'Many people here suspected that Mrs Simpson was actually in
German pay,' the Ambassador went on. 'I think this is unlikely . . .'
But though not in German pay, he considered, she was wittingly
or unwittingly a tool of German policy. He was not alone in this
view. The Danish Ambassador maintained that the worst thing
about Mrs Simpson was that she 'tried to mix herself up in politics.
She endeavoured in every way to single out the German Embassy
and to have everything German preferred at Court . . . Under the
influence of these surroundings the King, at times, made statements
which tended to show that his sympathies were coloured by nazism
and fascism.'[1] Not all his Scandinavian colleagues would have
agreed with him; the Swedish Ambassador, for instance, felt that
Mrs Simpson's influence on the King was 'calming and beneficial';[2]
but the historian John Wheeler-Bennett told Blanche Dugdale that
he was 'convinced that Ribbentrop *used* Mrs Simpson'.[3] The idea
that she was a paid agent of the Nazi government can safely be
dismissed – Baldwin told Osbert Sitwell that her dossier disclosed
nothing 'except that she was a paid agent of the Hearst Press'[4] –
but she was flattered by the attentions lavished on her by Ribbentrop and other German dignitaries and anyway shared the views
of the King about the merits of the National Socialist system and
the decadence of the French. Politics, still less political philosophy,
meant little to her. When told of the hopes Ribbentrop and others
were supposed to have pinned on her ability to influence the King,
Vansittart commented: 'It seems almost incredible that serious
people should have believed that the projected marriage would
result in the establishment of the *Führer-prinzip* in England and in
thus ensuring the German hold over foreign policy. But there it is;
and the fact is incontestable.'[5]

In March 1936 the German Army entered the Rhineland. Today it is generally agreed that prompt intervention by the French, with British support, would have driven the Germans into ignominious retreat and brought down Hitler's government. At the time armed opposition to the German move was advocated only by Churchill and a handful of his supporters, branded as warmongers by the government. Baldwin and Chamberlain were resolved not to risk war over an issue which they felt to be of secondary importance and in which they anyway had some sympathy for Germany's point of view, if not her actions. In this the King fully supported them.

The Germans believed his role to have been far more significant. Fritz Hesse, a press attaché in the German Embassy, claims to have been listening on a second telephone when the King rang von Hoesch. 'Is that Leo?' the King asked. 'David speaking. I sent for the Prime Minister and gave him a piece of my mind. I told the old so-and-so that I would abdicate if he made war. There was a frightful scene. But you needn't worry. There won't be a war.' Hoesch then danced round the room with joy. 'I've done it. I've outwitted them all. There won't be a war ... It's magnificent! I must inform Berlin immediately.'[1] Dr Stutterheim of the *Berliner Tageblatt* reported that the King was taking an extraordinarily active part, had summoned several ministers, and argued to all of them that there must be no war: 'In view of the tremendous influence possessed by the King, and his immense energy, due importance must be attached to this where Germany is concerned.'[2] Von Hoesch himself eschewed the more fantastical elements of Hesse's account and said only that he had had 'indirect contact' with the court, but the essential message was the same: 'The directive given to the Government from there is to the effect that, no matter how the details of the affair are dealt with, complications of a serious nature are in no circumstances to be allowed to develop.'[3]

It is astonishing that a diplomat of von Hoesch's experience could have written of a 'directive' being issued from the court to the government on a major issue of foreign policy. The King in fact saw Baldwin, Duff Cooper and Hore-Belisha while the Rhineland crisis was in progress. The appointments had all been made well in advance, but it would be surprising if the most pressing question of the hour had not been among matters discussed. With Baldwin, at least, he would have found unanimity of outlook; for that reason alone the conversation as reported by Hesse is nonsensical. With the other two he would have found more to argue about; though a majority of the Cabinet were close to sharing his views, Cooper and Hore-Belisha were more determined in their opposition to German expansionism. But what is incontrovertible is that, if he had differed from the Prime Minister, his views would have been listened to with respect but would not have been treated as a factor of serious importance when the policy was finally decided. The German military attaché was wiser than his Ambassador when he wrote: 'A warning must be given against building solely on the attitude of the monarch.'[1] He could have put it much more forcibly and still have been correct.

There seems little doubt that one of the reasons Hitler sent Ribbentrop to London as Ambassador was his belief that Ribbentrop enjoyed a special relationship with the King and Mrs Simpson. At the presentation of letters King Edward VIII was 'most affable, enquired after the Führer and repeated clearly that he desired good Anglo-German relations'. But it never got much further than that: 'A real conversation with the King . . . never materialized,' noted Ribbentrop sorrowfully; 'something unforeseen always intervened.'[2] He attributed his failure to the machinations of a germanophobic Foreign Office. In fact the explanation was simpler. In the last two or three months of his reign, the King was far too preoccupied with his personal business to give much thought to foreign affairs.

He was consistent in his belief that the dictators should be conciliated, and also that nothing should be done to drive Mussolini into Hitler's arms. When Haile Selassie, the Emperor of Abyssinia who had been driven from his country by Italian troops, sought refuge in England, he argued that he should not be admitted. The Foreign Secretary, Anthony Eden, said that Haile Selassie could go where he wanted.[3] It was suggested that it would be a popular move if the Emperor were received at Buckingham Palace. 'Popular with whom?' asked the King. 'Certainly not with the Italians!'[4] He proposed as a compromise that the Duke of Gloucester, who had attended the Coronation in Addis Ababa, should pay an informal call on the Emperor in his hotel. 'Oddly enough the idea . . .

occurred to me too a few days ago,' wrote Queen Mary. 'This is an excellent way out of the difficulty.'[1]

The visit of Haile Selassie was not the only subject on which the King differed from Eden. He did not believe that the League of Nations made any useful contribution to world peace – a will-o'-the wisp, he called it[2] – and deplored any attempt to bolster its strength. Channon defended Eden to the King on the grounds that he was an idealist. 'Heaven spare us from idealists,' said Edward VIII. 'They cause all the trouble.'[3] But he did not pin all his hopes on the conciliation of the dictators. He asked Norman Davis, who had come to London for King George V's funeral, when the United States and Britain could 'get definitely together ... the only hope for us and the world was to stand together'.[4] He believed that Germany did not want war, and that German aspirations could be conceded without war being necessary, but though he was thus deluded, he believed also that rearmament, a united Empire, and a strong Anglo-American alliance were necessary to counterbalance the increasing power of the fascist countries on the continent.

Reviewing his position in 1946 the King reflected that he had believed then, and still believed, that 'clever diplomacy, as opposed to Eden's policy, could have avoided the second clash with Germany. Maybe I was what they used to call "an appeaser", but I believe that time will prove the wisdom of my thinking.'[5] Few would agree with him today, but the opinion was sincerely held and shared by many, if not most informed Englishmen in 1936. Nor did he allow his convictions to blind him to other points of view or lead him to quarrel with old friends. In the summer Duff Cooper made a characteristically bellicose speech in France, pledging unanimity in the face of the fascist threat. He came back to a chilly reception from his fellow ministers. Next day he met the King at dinner. 'As he approached me I saw that his face was heavy with displeasure. I expected a rebuke and I think he was preparing one, but suddenly the frown fled, giving way to his delightful smile as he laughed and said: "Well, Duff, you certainly have done it this time."'[6]

16

The King and Mrs Simpson

K ING EDWARD VIII BEGAN THE NEW REIGN WITH AN
impressive display of zeal, scouring his official red boxes
in search of interesting matter, reading and initialling everything, dutifully discussing a variety of subjects with his private
secretaries.[1] Even if there had been no Mrs Simpson to distract
him, his enthusiasm would not have lasted. However protective
his staff may be, a King is deluged with official documents, and
Edward VIII cheerfully admitted that he never had much zest for
paper work.[2] Within a few weeks the complaints began. The King
insisted that Cabinet papers must go to him first, said Wigram, but
then left his boxes unopened, or the papers no more than glanced
at – by the time they got back to the private secretary it was too
late for any action.[3] While in his possession they were handled
carelessly, said Hardinge, no responsible person was put in charge
of them, it was sometimes weeks before they reappeared. 'Who
among the "exotic circle" had had access to them in the meantime
can only be a matter for conjecture. At any rate, the possibilities
were serious enough to create alarm among those who were aware
of the pro-German leanings of the clique.'[4] On one occasion Martin
– 'Mike' – Scanlon, the air attaché at the American Embassy, was
staying at Fort Belvedere. On leaving he was surprised to be handed
the official boxes and asked to drop them off at Buckingham
Palace. 'I had a feeling that Hardinge did not approve of the King's
practice of confiding state papers to the care of an American
intelligence officer.'[5]

Scanlon was at least an official in the employ of a government
which, if not an ally, was felt to have its heart in the right place.
Hardinge's fears about other members of the 'exotic circle' were not
confined to him alone. In February 1936 Wigram was summoned to
Baldwin's room in the House of Commons. He found Warren
Fisher, Maurice Hankey and Vansittart, as imposing a trio of civil

service mandarins as could readily be imagined, awaiting him. 'From all the evidence available,' he recorded, 'the King is discussing all problems with Mrs Simpson and showing her State Papers.' Vansittart put in that agents of the French and Swiss in London had reported to their governments 'that Mrs Simpson is one of the key points in this country as the King discusses everything with her. The Foreign Secretary is very anxious lest the FO Cypher may be compromised, as Mrs S is said to be in the pocket of the German Ambassador.' The civil servants urged Baldwin to take some action about this, but 'he was afraid to move and preferred the line of least resistance'. Wigram himself told the King how much concern was felt in Whitehall over the safety of secret documents in his possession. 'HM assured me he was very careful, and read them going down to the Fort in his car. As HM leaves about 3 a.m. in his car, I did not feel there was much light to read!'[1]

There is no reason to suppose that any German or ardent Nazi sympathizer ever visited Fort Belvedere, and there was nothing found in the German archives after the war to indicate that Mrs Simpson, or anybody else, passed on to the German government information gleaned from papers in the King's keeping. Though Hankey and Vansittart had reason for disquiet, it was almost certainly a mare's nest that they were investigating. What was still more certain, however, was that the King grew increasingly lax over official engagements, and less and less punctual in his habits. He decided at the last minute not to attend a Garden Society dinner. 'One hears these stories of engagements being chucked or of outrageous examples of tardiness,' complained Lord Crawford. 'He doesn't yet realize how much trouble is taken on his behalf nor what inconvenience is caused by his forgetfulness and vacillation.' Someone had remarked to him in the House of Lords that afternoon that the King would be blackballed for any decent London club.[2] Cromer was so indignant when he was kept waiting for two hours and then told that the King could not see him at all that day that he threatened resignation. He could not do his job properly, he protested, if he was not able to see the King from time to time.[3] Edward VIII seemed increasingly reluctant to do the sort of odd job which can only be done by a King and which can do so much to ease matters for his ministers and officials. He refused to see King Carol of Romania, even though the Foreign Office urged him to on the ground that pro-German tendencies in that country made it particularly important to keep Carol well-disposed to Britain.[1] He was equally disobliging about Prince Paul, the Regent of Yugoslavia, whom he spoke to politely enough during a visit to England but failed to invite to anything. 'Prince Paul is head of a friendly state,' Eden told Harold Nicolson, 'and it is almost an insult to ignore him. If the King is so selfish and unconventional about a real friend like Prince Paul, how will the Government ever induce him to do his duty when some President of a Baltic State comes to London?'[2]

'He appeared to be entirely ignorant of the powers of a constitutional sovereign, and of the lines on which the King's business should be carried on,' Hardinge wrote after the abdication. 'In fact, in its transaction, his unpunctuality, inconsequence, lack of consideration and self-conceit created every possible difficulty for those who served him. Not only did he give proof of a desire to change merely for the sake of changing, but a dislike, amounting almost to hatred, of the regular methods of his Father, was painfully apparent, nor could he see that this regularity was less a choice than a necessity for the proper discharge of his duties.'[3]

Hardinge's diatribe was written by a man who disliked the King, in the mood of bitterness that followed the ending of his reign, but it is hard to find anyone closely associated with King Edward VIII who did not grow more and more critical as the months passed. Wigram was so concerned about his behaviour that he called on the Lord Chancellor and told him, 'I did not think the King was normal, and this view was shared by my colleagues at Buckingham Palace. He might any day develop into a George III, and it was imperative to pass the Regency Bill as soon as possible, so that if necessary he could be certified.'[4]

If to be obsessively in love is to be mad, then Wigram was not altogether wrong. The King's natural untidiness and unpunctuality were exaggerated a hundredfold by his devotion to Mrs Simpson. If he cancelled a dinner at the last moment the chances were that she had expressed a wish to see him; if he was two hours late for Lord Cromer it was almost certain he had been visiting her. Nothing mattered to him so much as the gratification of her wishes and the performance of her instructions. She herself believed that her effect on him was beneficial. 'I am implored on all sides not to leave him as he is so dependent on me and I am considered to be a *good* influence, believe it or not,' she told Aunt Bessie.[1] Margot Oxford was on one of the sides to which Mrs Simpson referred. 'I am an excellent judge of character,' she told Lord Cromer firmly, 'and think Mrs S's influence is a *good* one. I have had several *very* private talks with her – one about his going to Church, one about his drinking more than is good for his health . . . and have always found her trustworthy and discreet.'[2] Even those who most resented her baleful presence admitted that she was in some ways good for him; Queen Mary herself is said to have remarked that her worst fears for her son had always related to his drinking. 'She has been a sane influence in that respect. And that is important.'[3] And some of those who found his passion most ill-advised conceded that it was touching in its depth and its sincerity. Victor Cazalet watched them at dinner together. 'Every few minutes he gazes at her and a happiness and radiance fill his countenance such as make you have a lump in your throat.'[4] Baldwin told John Reith that he had come into the room while Edward VIII was talking to Mrs Simpson on the telephone: 'The King's face was as if he had seen a vision; he walked about in ecstasy saying "She is the most wonderful woman in the world".'[5]

She was not the most wonderful woman in the world. Nor was she the fiend incarnate envisaged by Wigram or Halsey. Her letters written at the time suggest that she was a shallow and greedy woman, delighting in the reflected glory of the throne but with no very clear idea of what she wanted or how she was going to get it. She told her aunt Bessie in February that it was a tragedy the King would not marry some convenient Duke's daughter.[6] This was surely disingenuous – it would not have suited her at all if the King had taken a wife who would inevitably have displaced her from some of her most cherished redoubts – but it does suggest that at that time she had barely contemplated the idea that she might marry Edward VIII herself. From time to time she jokingly referred to the possibility that she might be Queen, but always with the implication that it was something too absurd to contemplate. Perhaps she sought to conceal her real intentions, but it seems more probable that she was telling the truth. She later repeatedly told Lady Monckton that she had never envisaged the likely course of events: 'It came upon me with devastating force that I did not know England very well, and the English not at all.'[1] At the beginning of the new reign she was riding with the tide and relishing every minute of it, without giving too much thought to what lay ahead for herself and the King.

Edward VIII was giving thought to little else. He later told Monckton that he had made up his mind to marry Mrs Simpson as early as 1934, and that from that time onwards his mind never wavered. He would have made his intentions clear to his father had the King lived a little longer.[2] There is no reason to doubt the first part of his statement; he had no reason to try to deceive Monckton once the deed was done, though he kept him in the dark until November 1936. Edward VIII had always been secretive, and he was convinced, quite rightly, that any open admission of his intentions would provoke violent efforts to thwart them on the part of courtiers, ministers and his family. He kept his own counsel; extraordinary though it may seem, all the evidence suggests that even Mrs Simpson was given no inkling of his real wishes until his reign was some way advanced. Whether he would ever have plucked up his courage to tell King George V is more doubtful. He had plenty of opportunities in 1935 and missed them all; there is no reason to believe that he would have been more forthright in 1936. Probably things would have drifted on; it took the growing incompatibility of his love for Mrs Simpson and his role as King as envisaged by his advisers to drive him into decisive action.

Helen Hardinge first conceived the idea that marriage was on the cards after a dinner at which Mrs Simpson was present at Windsor on 28 March. She claims that, when she discussed it with her husband and other courtiers, it was dismissed as 'too wild to even be considered'.[3] Either her husband thought it better to keep her in ignorance or he omitted to discuss the matter with his senior colleagues. More than six weeks before, Wigram had consulted the Lord Chancellor 'about the Marriage Laws of a Sovereign, so that I could have a ready answer if HM suddenly said he was going to marry Mrs S'. He imagined the answer would be that, if he were to do so, the King must abdicate, which he expected would put an end to any matrimonial aspirations: 'HM likes this King business too much.'[4] A week later he complained to Baldwin that 'some of his younger Ministers' – presumably he had Duff Cooper particularly in mind – were doing mischief by staying with the King and encouraging Mrs Simpson: 'Neither HM nor Mrs S were normal, and were inclined to think that such a marriage would be accepted by the people.'[1] On 27 February Aird noted in his diary that Wigram seemed 'obsessed with the idea that HM wants to marry her, which in my opinion is absurd, even if Ernest consented I doubt W wishing to'.[2]

Wigram had first been alerted to the possibility by a former Lord Mayor of London, Sir Maurice Jenks. Jenks had been drawn into the drama the previous year when the Prince of Wales had asked him to secure the admission of Ernest Simpson to the Masonic lodge over which he presided. Jenks agreed but ran into opposition from certain fellow Masons who said they would not accept a candidate on the recommendation of his wife's lover. Jenks reported this to the Prince, who replied indignantly that he was not and had not been Mrs Simpson's lover. On this basis Simpson was admitted but only after much hesitation. According to Godfrey Thomas, the initiation meeting was 'a humiliating fiasco. Hardly any of the outside bigwigs invited came. The story now goes throughout the City that HRH has violated his Masonic oath, that E.S. wishes to be a Mason for business reasons, and that HRH to keep him quiet about Mrs S was more or less blackmailed into sponsoring him.'[3]

In early February 1936 Jenks arrived at 10 Downing Street and poured out the next chapter of the story to a startled Prime Minister. Simpson had been to see him and had announced that the King wanted to marry his wife; what action did Jenks recommend? Baldwin sent for Wigram, whose first reaction was to burst out laughing. 'However, we talked the situation over and came to the conclusion it was blackmail. Unfortunately Mr S was a British subject, and it would be difficult to deport him.'[4] They might have reached a different conclusion if they had heard the testimony of Bernard Rickatson-Hatt, the editor-in-chief of Reuters, who had accompanied Simpson to York House. According to Rickatson-Hatt, Simpson had directly challenged the King and asked him what his intentions were. The King rose from his chair and answered: 'Do you really think that I would be crowned without Wallis at my side?'[5] If correctly quoted the words were momentous as being the first definite indication that the King believed he would be able to marry Wallis and make her his Queen.

Jenks next called on Wigram. He dismissed the blackmail theory, insisting Simpson was an honourable man who was above all anxious to make sure that his wife and the King were not involved in scandal. What was a loyal subject to do? Wigram sent word to Simpson that he should remember his marriage vows and hold on to his wife at all costs. 'I urged Sir Maurice that he should impress on Mr S that the duty of the latter was to cart his wife back to the USA.'[1] The message was duly transmitted and Simpson promised to do his best. He made it clear, however, that he did not think he had much chance – anyway until after his wife's aunt Bessie had visited London in March. It was during her visit that the crucial decision about the marriage was likely to be taken.[2]

Wigram pleaded with the Prime Minister to intervene but met with bland assurances that problems of this kind were best solved by ignoring them; in time they were almost sure to go away. Halsey had made a similar approach a month before and done no better. 'I don't say he would have done any good then,' he told Aird, 'but it was worth trying.'[3]

Baldwin was not the only dignitary who showed himself reluctant to intervene with the King. The Archbishop was all for the Prime Minister doing his duty but when Wigram suggested he might say something himself he declared that he 'was *persona non grata* with the King and could not help'.[4] Lang told the Bishop of Pretoria that he repeatedly tried to point out to the King the error of his ways, but it was made clear to him that advice on such a subject would be accepted from no one except the Prime Minister. The Canadian Prime Minister, Mackenzie King, had every right to speak his mind and told Malcolm MacDonald that he had done so forcibly, but it transpired he had done no more than tell the King how much he was admired in Canada and how important it was that the prestige of the Crown should not be impaired. If the King gained any impression from this somewhat opaque *démarche* it was that he should be encouraged to pursue his plans.[5]

Meanwhile Mrs Simpson established herself more and more overtly as the shadow queen of King Edward VIII's private life. She spent almost every weekend at Fort Belvedere, rarely accompanied by her husband, and played the part of hostess with enthusiasm and considerable ability. 'Wallis must not get too bossy,' remarked Diana Cooper after a weekend at the Fort in

February. It was admirable that she should encourage the King to read his papers and master the main points in them, but less desirable that she should lecture him on the subject at the dinner table.[1] Osborne, the butler, told Ulick Alexander in March that he was very unhappy: 'Mrs S had got her knife into him, and he felt that he was doomed. O said that things were very unsatisfactory, and that after a night at the Fort with Mrs S the King was absolutely limp and a rag.' Osborne reported that he had picked up a label in Mrs Simpson's writing which had evidently been attached to some present given to the King. It read 'To our marriage'.[2]

The company over which she presided was not particularly distinguished, either in wit or in achievement. It consisted, wrote Michael Bloch, who analysed the guest books with care, of 'an innocuous, if fairly jolly, collection of courtiers and diplomats, American men of affairs and English Society, garnished with a sprinkling of statesmen, soldiers and sailors'.[3] The statesmen, soldiers and sailors were sprinkled thinly indeed, but the gatherings were never less than respectable; there was a touch of raffishness perhaps about a few of the *habitués*, but nothing calculated to cause real distress at Lambeth Palace or in Downing Street. The entertainment was equally undramatic: a lot of golf and gardening; bathing in summer; fairly heavy drinking, though no more than in most English country houses; occasional cards or roulette for modest stakes; dancing to a gramophone. The high spot of the weekend usually came when the King put on his bonnet, picked up his bagpipes, and paraded around the dining room playing 'Over the Sea to Skye' or his own 'Mallorca' – 'It's clever to have chosen the pipes as one's show-off,' commented Diana Cooper, 'for which of us can detect mistakes, or know good from bad artistry?'[4] Such humdrum goings-on proved insufficiently sensational to satisfy various commentators who should have known better. The company was perhaps not worthy of the King of England, yet how could Osbert Sitwell describe the King's friends as 'the riff-raff of two continents . . . the rootless spawn of New York, Cracow, Antwerp and the Mile End road'?[5] There may have been a dearth of intellectual conversation or political discussion, but how could Baldwin's parliamentary private secretary, William Dugdale, have referred blithely to the 'orgies there used to be when

Mrs Simpson did the "danse du ventre", and other un-English performances of an unsavoury nature'?[1]

In May 1936 the Prime Minister and his wife were invited to dine at York House, where the King was still ensconced. The other guests were eminently suitable for such an occasion: the Mountbattens, the Wigrams, the Chatfields, the Lindberghs. Only Lady Cunard and the Simpsons struck a discordant note. It was the last time Ernest Simpson accompanied his wife on an outing at court. When the King told Mrs Simpson he wanted her to be at the dinner, he went on: 'It's got to be done. Sooner or later my Prime Minister must meet my future wife.'[2] Baldwin had no idea of the significance of the meeting; he admitted to some surprise at seeing Mrs Simpson at one end of the table, but at least her husband was there as well.[3] Others reacted more violently. Lady Astor said that only the best Virginian families should be asked to court, and that the effect in the United States would be deplorable.[4] To Reith, the announcement in the Court Circular that Lady Cunard and the Simpsons had attended the dinner was the worst news that *The Times* had carried for many years. 'It is too horrible and it is serious and sad beyond calculation.' Two days later the King made the Victorian Order open to women in all grades. 'Will the first GCVOs (female) be Lady Cunard and Mrs Simpson?' asked Reith bitterly.[5]

At the beginning of July the King sent Cromer a list of the people he wanted invited to an afternoon reception. The names were not supposed to be in order of precedence, but the Lord Chamberlain may still have been put out to find the Simpsons at the head and the Duke of Sutherland, the Earl of Sefton and the Earl of Dudley following behind.[6] The inclusion of Ernest Simpson was a formality; by the beginning of July he had moved out to his club, though it was not until late October that Wallis Simpson was installed in a house rented for her by the King in Regent's Park. Ramsay MacDonald spoke angrily about the King's 'appalling obstinacy' in sending Wallis Simpson to Ascot in a royal carriage and featuring her in Court Circulars. It would not have mattered if she had been a widow, he told Harold Nicolson: 'The people of this country do not mind fornication but they loathe adultery.'[7]

The name of Mrs Simpson still meant nothing to anyone outside a tiny circle of informed Londoners. The circle was to expand, when the King's summer holiday made headlines throughout Europe and the United States. His original intention had been to take a villa near Cannes. Aird was sent off to find something suitable; he was now better off, the King told him, 'so could afford to spend a little, but must still be careful'.[1] The British Ambassador in Paris instantly applauded the idea, then took alarm at the political instability in the area caused by the Civil War in Spain, and advised against it. 'I really am very annoyed with the FO for having messed up my holiday in this stupid manner,' wrote the King to his mother. 'You and I could have told them that the Riviera was no place for me to go this summer a whole month ago!!'[2] Aird wanted to offer the owner of the villa £1000 as compensation for the cancelled lease. The King agreed, then consulted Mrs Simpson and reduced the amount to £100.[3]

The King now decided to charter a yacht. His first idea was to borrow the Duke of Westminster's but Mrs Simpson vetoed this as insufficiently comfortable. Aird then inspected Lady Yule's yacht, the *Nahlin*, and found it nice enough, though 'furnished rather like a Calais whore-shop'.[4] Lady Yule was ready to charge no charter fee, only expenses, but even so Aird calculated that the yacht would cost the King £6000 or more and the whole holiday about £10,000 – say £250,000 at current prices.[5] All the books were removed from the yacht's library on the no doubt justified grounds that they would not be wanted and that an extra bedroom was more useful, and a plentiful supply of golf balls was stowed aboard for the King to drive into the sea.[6] The guests varied from stage to stage but included Duff and Diana Cooper, Lord Sefton, Helen Fitzgerald, a few other old friends, and Thomas, Aird and Lascelles from the household: 'Outwardly as respectable as a boatload of archdeacons,' commented Lascelles. 'But the fact re- mains that the two chief passengers (the King and the Earl) were cohabiting with other men's wives.'[7]

The image of the *Nahlin* cruise which has been imprinted on the public mind is of the King, his mistress and a group of disreputable hangers-on carousing around the eastern Mediterranean, in- variably under-dressed, usually drunk, shocking the local inhabi- tants and causing any Englishman who met them to hang his head in shame. There is a smattering of truth in this caricature, but it is far indeed from being a fair picture of what was on the whole a harmless and sometimes modestly useful escapade.

Though planned as a holiday, and treated as such, the royal progress did yield valuable political dividends. The reports of American diplomats are as usual likely to be more objective and less obsequious than those of the British. From Belgrade the American Minister reported that the visit had had a good effect on Britain's relationship with Yugoslavia and the other nations of the area. The King, however, was clearly there to enjoy himself and 'the political consideration was an afterthought, albeit an important one'.[1] His colleague in Athens considered the visit had 'done much to re-establish any British prestige which may have been lost last spring. The conditions under which it was made favoured its delicacy and its effectiveness.'[2] From Ankara came the report that: 'The Italian press . . . sees in the visit a step towards the setting up of a new combination in the Eastern Mediterranean directed against Italy. There have been rumours that the USSR was not overly pleased at the royal visit, on the theory, apparently, that it might lead to a loosening of the ties, sentimental and otherwise, which bind that country and Turkey.'[3] In Sofia the press devoted columns to Edward VIII's three-hour visit to King Boris and 'voiced their praise of the democratic spirit he displayed'.[4]

The fact that American diplomats took the tour seriously does not prove that it was serious, but the King's performance in Turkey at least deserves some credit. It was the first visit in history by a British king and the first by any European sovereign since the Kaiser's forty years before. Atatürk, the absolute ruler of Turkey, met Edward VIII when he landed and drove with him to the British Embassy in an open car (a fact remarkable in itself since Atatürk normally favoured an armour-plated limousine). After dinner the King returned to the *Nahlin* and stood on the bridge for an hour and a half acknowledging the applause from the fleet of illuminated boats that circled round him. Like all the best spontaneous demonstrations it was carefully orchestrated – the ferry from the Galata bridge to Therapia was made to circle the *Nahlin* for five hours with its indignant passengers aboard and ended up at its starting place – but the enthusiasm of the crowds was unmistakably sincere.[5] 'Psychologically, it transformed the attitude of the Turkish people towards Britain, to whom they had grown used, from the outbreak of the First World War, as an enemy,' wrote Lord Kinross, the biographer of Atatürk. It was 'an exercise in cordial diplomacy to rank with the foreign excursions of his grandfather, King Edward VII'.[1]

As to Atatürk himself, the British Ambassador, Percy Loraine, reported that the Turkish ruler was greatly interested in and impressed by his visitor. 'The King has an extraordinarily happy manner and a way of putting everyone at their ease, and I could see that Atatürk felt at once his uncommon charm and appreciated his simplicity and directness.'[2] That is the sort of thing Ambassadors tend to say, but to Lascelles, who Loraine knew was highly critical of his employer, he insisted that the King had made a great impression on Atatürk and that this sort of informal trip was far more effective than a state visit, with all its protocol and pompous paraphernalia.[3] To set against this, Atatürk, having noted how obviously enslaved by Mrs Simpson the King was, is said to have remarked that he would lose his throne because of her.[4]

The fact that the King was travelling with a woman who was everywhere considered to be his mistress attracted much attention. John Balfour, at the British Legation in Belgrade, was not best pleased when a Romanian colleague remarked that when *his* King travelled abroad, he left his mistress behind.[5] In Vienna Victor Cazalet was shocked to find the names of the Duke of Lancaster (traditional travelling alias of British monarchs) and Mrs Simpson posted up in the porter's lodge for all to see.[6] Nor was everyone gratified by the King's habit of peeling off his shirt, even when under the eyes of a startled crowd, or of wandering around the streets of some Adriatic town with a bottle of lemonade in his hand. To some such behaviour was charmingly informal, to others it was deplorably undignified. Aird was one of the latter. When, in Athens, the King insisted on dining with Lord Dudley at a sleazy restaurant and then went on to the flat of a 'Levantine Englishman called Reiss',* Aird sulked on board and blew up when the King got back. 'I . . . told HM that much as I liked him as a man I could not despise him more as a King, and that I thought I had better go home tomorrow, as feeling as I did I feared that I would only spoil the rest of his holiday. HM took it very well but of course pulled in W, who to my surprise on the whole sided with me.'[7]

Sir Sydney Waterlow, the British Ambassador in Athens, sup-

---

* Probably, in fact, an Anglo-Greek shipowner called Billy Rees.

plemented his official despatch with a private letter to Hardinge. The tour, he said, had been a great success, and the Greeks, usually the most malicious of people, had showed nothing but delight at the fact that the King spent some time with them and the obvious pleasure he had derived from his visit. But he still felt a sense of depression 'made up partly of uneasiness as to the *ultimate* results on our prestige abroad if the King should persist in being surrounded on his travels by Mrs S and other people of little or no standing . . . and partly of the effect produced on me by the atmosphere of the jaunt, which was of an almost unbelievable vapidity, quite without any taint of raffishness indeed, but equally with no dignity and no spark of intelligent interest in anything seen or heard'. The King's character, he believed, was unformed and fluid, 'almost a case of arrested development – with great possibilities for good, which may be lost unless some strong, sympathetic and humanly understanding influence can be brought to bear, which, without imposing itself, would canalize the energy now running to waste in a restless pleasure hunt (he is obviously, and pathetically, worried, anxious, preoccupied, all the time) . . . There is something appealing about him – something really charming and good, with such good intention . . . all of which makes me anxious that he should be helped.'

At the root of his restlessness, Waterlow thought, was an 'unsatisfied craving for domesticity' and it was to this craving that Mrs Simpson was a response, 'and, I think, a serious response'. And yet her most marked characteristics were 'perpetual restlessness and a vacuum as complete as that of the prairie or small town from which it originally derives. What can be hoped from mating restlessness with restlessness, vacuum with vacuum?' Mrs Simpson, then, must be the wrong woman for the King. But still Waterlow was uncertain. He had taken to her, he could understand why the King had so fallen for her. In the end he wondered 'whether this union, however queer and generally unsuitable and embarrassing for the state, may not in the long run turn out to be more in harmony with the spirit of the new age than anything that wisdom could have contrived'.[1]

This somewhat unexpected conclusion would not have appealed to Diana Cooper, who after ten days afloat with Mrs Simpson found that she wore badly, 'her commonness and her Becky Sharpness irritate'. After they got back from a visit to the King of Greece, the King went down on his hands and knees to rescue a corner of her dress which had caught under the chair. She stared at him coldly: '"Well, that's the *maust* extraordinary performance I've ever seen," and then she started to criticize his meanness, the way he had talked to Mrs Jones [the King of Greece's English mistress], his attitude to the other King. Diana Cooper left the room in protest. "The truth is, Wallis is bored stiff with the King."'[1]

After abandoning the yacht, the last stop of the holiday was at Vienna. Edward VIII visited the President and the Chancellor, von Schuschnigg, but the American Ambassador said that nobody was inclined to attach political importance to the visit, though 'he is believed to have obtained a good grasp of the present Austrian situation'.[2] While in Vienna he went with Aird to the clinic of the celebrated ear specialist, Dr Neumann, where they both had their ears tested and were found to be not in the least deaf.[3] The point is worth mentioning, because the legend has grown up that Dr Neumann was a sex therapist who, at Mrs Simpson's behest, performed some arcane operation on the King.

And so it was the train to Zurich and a flight back to England. Talking to Aird while they were in Vienna, Lascelles vouchsafed 'he could not be better pleased with HM's behaviour as compared to past trips'.[4] The reason, no doubt, was that the King was entirely fulfilled by Mrs Simpson and so felt no need for the restless womanizing which, in Lascelles's eyes, had marred their earlier excursions. The judgment, however, coming as it did from a man who was harshly critical of the King, is worth bearing in mind when the supposed iniquities of the *Nahlin* trip are considered. The most immediate result of a holiday that was enjoyable and useful, if also somewhat indecorous, was that the names of Mrs Simpson and the King were now firmly linked in the newspapers of the world outside Britain. Within Britain not a word was said. Even within the royal family not a word was said – to the King at least. 'David got back from abroad looking very well and came to dine with me and we had a nice talk,' Queen Mary wrote in her diary on 14 September. But they talked about nothing except the details of his sightseeing and the weather he had enjoyed.[5]

*

The King and Mrs Simpson

Traditionally the royal summer ended with a few weeks at Balmoral, and though the King cut the visit to less than a fortnight he did not defy precedent altogether. According to one account, his private secretaries on the *Nahlin* produced letters of invitation for his signature to all the dignitaries who had attended in the past: the Prime Minister, the Archbishop, the Moderator of the Church of Scotland.[1] The King scrapped the lot, inviting instead 'a number of friends to whom I was indebted for hospitality over the years'.[2] But it seemed at one moment as if the most important guest would be missing. While the party was still in Vienna, Aird had noted in his diary: 'Heard today that W is to be at Balmoral. Thank God I shall not be there.'[3] On the way she stopped off in Paris. She fell ill, and spent some days in bed at the Hôtel Meurice, studying with mounting horror the American press coverage of the *Nahlin* cruise. On 16 September she concluded that the affair was becoming too much for her and wrote to the King to tell him that she proposed to return to Ernest Simpson. 'I am sure you and I would only create disaster together . . .' she wrote. 'I want you to be happy. I feel sure that I can't make you so, and I honestly don't think you can me.'[4] Whether or not she was totally sincere in this renunciation; whether or not, indeed, Ernest Simpson would have welcomed her back if she had offered to return; the effect of her letter on the King was dramatic. He telephoned her at once, according to Lascelles threatening to cut his throat if she did not come to him in Scotland.[5] She came, with Herman and Katherine Rogers as her escorts.

On 24 September the Court Circular announced that Mrs Simpson had arrived at Balmoral. 'Everyone now knows of Mrs Simpson and talks freely of her,' commented Alan Don.[6] 'Everyone' was still only a handful of the well-informed but the note of disapproval was growing more marked. Winston Churchill, who had taken the line that the King could do what he liked with his private life, told Monckton that he 'deprecated strongly Mrs Simpson going to such a highly official place upon which the eyes of Scotland were concentrated'.[7] There were bitter complaints that the King had installed his mistress in the room hitherto reserved for Queen Mary, an unjust accusation, though what he actually did was little better in the eyes of the more traditional retainers: 'He put her in what has always been the best spare bedroom,' wrote Lascelles, '*but* he refused to occupy the King's room himself, and put himself

287

into what is, in effect, the dressing-room of her suite.'[1] To his mother the King wrote cheerfully that the weather was fine and the house most comfortable; 'only a few more baths will have to be added for another year'.[2]

'I could never believe that any place could change so much and have such a different atmosphere,' wrote the Duke of Kent after he left the Castle. 'It was all so comfortable and everyone seemed so happy – it really was fun.'[3] A man is not under oath in his bread-and-butter letters, but the comment still reads oddly in view of the uniformly bad press which the Balmoral holiday was later to receive. The Duke of Connaught told Princess Louise that he was very distressed at the party staying at the Castle: 'What a pity. I wonder what the Scotch people thought of it.'[4] Probably not much, but whatever resentment there might have been was fanned on 23 September when the King sent the Yorks to open a new hospital in Aberdeen and himself drove to the same city to meet Mrs Simpson off the train. 'I do wish that David could have done it,' the Duchess of York wrote sadly, 'as they have all worked so hard for so long, and it will be one of the best in Scotland, and it would have given such enormous pleasure to the countryside.'[5]

The King's defence was that he had long ago told the Lord Provost of Aberdeen that he would not be able to open the hospital because the court was still in mourning. It seemed curious to his subjects that he should be able to disport himself in the Mediterranean while in mourning, yet not visit a hospital, and that his brother should somehow be exempt from rules which applied so strictly to the monarch. Even if his behaviour can be justified on grounds of protocol, it was to say the least tactless to visit Aberdeen for his own purposes on the same day. The Aberdeen newspaper featured two photographs side by side: one of the Yorks opening the hospital, the other with the caption, 'His Majesty in Aberdeen. Surprise visit in car to meet guests.' 'This has done him more harm than anything else and has lost him Scotland,' wrote Thomas in his diary; melodramatically, perhaps, but not without some justice.[6]

That he made such a blunder is indicative both of his consuming desire to see Mrs Simpson again as soon as possible and also of the strain which he was under. His preoccupation with the future of his relationship with Wallis was increasingly making it impossible for him to judge any situation objectively or to take any account of the feelings of others. Anne Lindbergh met him at a dinner party and found 'his face is drawn, lean and terribly sad ... That boy's face drawn tight into the responsibilities of age. Very sad to look at. One feels either he is prematurely old for his looks or else still nostalgically young for his age.'[1] He was irascible and easily upset. At another dinner party he was absurdly put out and sulked all evening when he claimed to have met one of the guests before and was told he had not. 'It seemed absurd that he should have allowed himself to be so upset by so trivial a mishap in his briefing,' wrote a fellow guest, John Boyd-Carpenter, a young barrister and future member of parliament, 'it was in retrospect an indication of the nervous condition which showed itself in the abdication crisis.'[2] Even though things had not yet reached a point of crisis, he seemed to sense that difficulties were building up. A week after his return from Balmoral he was asked to approve the name of *King Edward VIII* for a new battleship. He scratched it out and substituted *Prince of Wales*.[3]

The strain was exaggerated by his growing alienation from his brothers. At first he had tried conscientiously to keep the Duke of York briefed on affairs of state, insisting that he should be shown as many official papers as possible.[4] But the same did not extend to his personal affairs, and as these absorbed his full attention, so the brothers grew apart. He rarely saw the King, the Duke of York told his mother, and when he did the conversation never turned to the subject which was at the forefront of both their minds. 'It is all so worrying and I feel we all live a life of conjecture; never knowing what will happen tomorrow.'[5] The distress which this caused the royal family is movingly shown by a letter which the Duchess of York wrote to Queen Mary from Scotland a few days after the King and his party had left Balmoral. The weather had been wonderful, she wrote, and the flowers too:

But there has also been a great sadness and sense of loss for us and all the people. It will never be quite the same for us ... David does not seem to possess the faculty of making others feel *wanted*. It is very sad, and I feel that the whole difficulty is a certain person. I do not feel that I *can* make advances to her and ask her to our house, as I imagine would be liked, and this fact is bound to make relations a little difficult. However, luckily, Bertie is quite outside all that, and I am sure that it is very important for him to steer clear of those very difficult questions. The whole situation is complicated and *horrible*, and I feel so unhappy about it sometimes, so you must forgive me, darling Mama, for letting myself go so indiscreetly. There is nobody that I can talk to, as ever since I have married I have made a strict rule never to discuss anything of Family matters with my own relations – nor would they wish it, but it leaves so few people to let off steam to occasionally.

. . . Has anything transpired about Xmas? Can we all spend it together? Do suggest it to David as he loves and admires you and I am sure would arrange what you wish.[1]

Things were little happier with the rest of the family. On one of the few occasions that the Gloucesters visited Fort Belvedere the Duchess was noticed to be 'most nervous and fidgety'.[2] The Duke of Kent was even worse, since Mrs Simpson used him as a weapon to provoke the King into displays of jealousy. Kent told Dugdale that, at Balmoral, she did this to such good purpose that by the end of dinner 'the King was beaten into a frenzy of jealousy and desire'.[3] Once when Baldwin was waiting to see the King the Duke of Kent stormed in. 'He's besotted by the woman,' he exclaimed. 'One can't get a word of sense out of him.'[4] Yet until the crisis was in its dying throes, none of the royal brothers could bring himself to believe that the affair would end in abdication; somehow, the King would come to his senses, Mrs Simpson would vanish from the scene, all would be well.

The same was true of Queen Mary. 'I am so pleased to hear that you and dear David can talk over everything together,' wrote Queen Maud of Norway in April 1936, 'he is devoted to you and you can both help each other.'[5] It is difficult to imagine what Queen Maud can have heard to create this delusion. The King and his mother had hardly a single serious discussion between the accession and the abdication and the letters they exchanged were few and far between and confined to trivialities. In February Queen Mary told Lady Airlie that she could not say anything to the King about Mrs Simpson because she did not want to interfere in his private life and also because he was the most obstinate of her sons. 'To oppose him over doing anything is only to make him more determined to do it. At present he is utterly infatuated, but my great hope is that violent infatuations usually wear off.'[1] She still cherished that hope when the King left Balmoral, but it was to become less substantial every day.

Lascelles claimed that as early as February 1936 he had been warned by Legh 'that plans were already afoot to liquidate Simpson (matrimonially speaking) and to set the crown upon the leopardess's head'.[2] It must have been about this time that Ernest Simpson realized how seriously his marriage was in danger, though it was not until July that he moved out, installed himself with his current woman friend, Mary Raffray, and left the field to the King. Some people claimed that he had received a handsome quid pro quo for this complaisant conduct, but there is no evidence to support the charge and it seems more likely that he was actuated by reluctance to let a humiliating situation drag on further, a wish that his wife should be happy, and a genuinely patriotic if somewhat misguided deference towards his King. The picture of Ernest Simpson that emerges is of a man who was unattractive, dull and inclined to lechery, but above all anxious to conduct himself publicly in a manner he felt befitting an English gentleman. Even as late as September, Mrs Simpson was telling the King that she had 'the deepest affection and respect' for Ernest, and felt secure with him in a way she never had with anyone else.[3]

By then, however, she was far down the road towards divorce. Monckton had told Churchill as early as 7 July that the possibility of a divorce was now being openly discussed and that Simpson would not oppose it. Churchill was horrified and begged Monckton to stop proceedings which were likely to lead to open scandal.[4] Monckton would have liked to, but could bring little influence to bear on Mrs Simpson and was comforted to some extent by her repeated assurances that she had no intention of marrying the King. Monckton put Mrs Simpson in contact with the solicitor Theodore Goddard.[5] The ritual act of adultery which the husband was required to commit if an unopposed divorce were to be granted had taken place at Bray, and Goddard therefore tried to get the divorce proceedings taken at the Assizes at nearby Reading. It so happened, however, that no divorces were being taken that season at Reading, so Goddard had the case transferred to the next convenient Assizes, which happened to be at Ipswich. The choice of this somewhat remote venue seems to have been entirely fortuitous and not made from any desire to transact the proceedings in hugger-mugger; if secrecy had been the object, Goddard would hardly have retained England's most celebrated and flamboyant barrister, Norman Birkett, to appear for Mrs Simpson.[1]

The news of what was in the wind spread panic in Whitehall. Neville Chamberlain, on 17 October, told his sister that Baldwin had planned to stay on as Prime Minister until the Coronation, though doing little if any work: 'However, that may not pan out as he thinks, for tomorrow morning he will hear that a certain lady . . . intends on *Friday next* to begin proceedings for the purpose of obtaining a divorce from her husband. S.B. will be informed that the most alarming consequences would or might ensue and that it is his duty to stop it. What effect that will have on his health remains to be seen,' added Chamberlain with mild *Schadenfreude*.[2] Horace Wilson was sent posting down to Chequers a few days later to tell Baldwin he *must* now intervene to stop the divorce. Hoare added to the dismay within the Cabinet by returning from a shooting party at Sandringham with the opinion that King Edward VIII was 'contemplating a morganatic marriage if the lady is free'[3] – an early mention of a possibility that was to bulk much larger in the ensuing weeks. It was the only time Edward VIII acted as host at Sandringham. When he arrived and the Royal Standard was hoisted on Sandringham church the flag pole snapped; a carpenter worked through the night to mend it and thus deprived the attendant journalists of a spectacle which would doubtless have joined the accident to the Imperial Crown in popular mythology as a sinister portent of impending doom.[4]

Reluctantly Baldwin accepted that he could no longer put off the unwanted confrontation. On 20 October he met the King at Fort Belvedere. His son Oliver gave Harold Nicolson a curious account of the interview, in which he has probably muddled elements of several meetings. Tired from the drive in his unpleasant little car, and in considerable pain from arthritis, the Prime Minister first asked for a whisky and soda. Having got it he raised his glass and said: 'Well, Sir, whatever happens, my Mrs and I wish you every happiness from the depths of our souls.' At this the King burst into tears, and Baldwin began to cry too. 'What a strange conversation-piece, those two blubbering together on a sofa,' commented Nicolson.[1] After this unpromising start, the two men got down to business. Baldwin told the King that his correspondence about the relationship with Mrs Simpson was growing larger every day and a tide of public outrage was beginning to flood in. Could not the affair be conducted more discreetly? 'The lady is my friend and I do not wish to let her in by the back door,' answered the King with dignity. Then could not he put off the divorce? 'That is the lady's private business'; a disingenuous but unanswerable reply. Then at least could not Mrs Simpson leave the country for six months? To this the King made no answer.[2]

Baldwin found the King 'stiff and in the toils'.[3] He felt he had conducted himself with some aplomb at this interview, but according to Chamberlain the King spoke of it 'with good-natured amusement and some very near say that it is of no use to repeat the warning unless it is given by the C of E, for whom, they say, HM has a wholesome respect'.[4]* The Archbishop of Canterbury offered, with some diffidence, to intervene if it would be useful. Baldwin replied that his line with the King had been to sympathize with his need for domestic happiness but to insist that 'if Mrs Simpson was to supply his need she must be kept in the background'. Lang reasonably felt that this was hardly a point of view which he could advocate, whereupon Baldwin 'realized my difficulty in intervening . . . and agreed it would be better to leave the matter in his hands'. The Archbishop concluded that he might find a chance to put in a word with the King when going over the Coronation service.[5]

But though the imminent divorce seemed certain to increase the risk of public scandal, still few people believed that the King would marry Mrs Simpson. To this illusion the two principal protagonists contributed vigorously. When Theodore Goddard spoke of a possible marriage to Mrs Simpson, she blazed out at him: 'What do you take me for? Do you think I would allow such a thing? I would never think of it . . . Some day I shall just fade out . . .'[6] Monckton, the King's closest adviser, was similarly kept in the dark until the

---

* Presumably Chamberlain was referring to the Chancellor of the Exchequer (i.e., himself) rather than the Church of England. The King disliked both but certainly had more respect for the former.

divorce case had been heard and a decree nisi granted.[1] In the light of such assurances the Cabinet remained optimistic. On 31 October Chamberlain noted that he was greatly reassured by all he heard about the 'attitude of *both* parties . . . I am told that Mrs S is likely soon to be paying a six weeks visit to the Riviera'.[2] The King and Mrs Simpson had, of course, excellent reasons for propagating the view that they had no thought of matrimony; if the judge who heard the divorce proceedings had been given any reason to believe that the plaintiff was already involved with another man then, according to the law as it stood at that time, the case would have collapsed.

The divorce was heard on 27 October. The judge disliked the whole proceedings and made it plain that he did so, but the evidence which Mr Simpson had obligingly provided, that he had spent a night at a hotel with another woman, was watertight as far as it went. A decree nisi was granted; a divorce, that is to say, but only a provisional one. The decree absolute, after which remarriage would be possible, had to wait six months and would not be granted if in the meantime any proof had come to light of collusion between the couple seeking the divorce or of misconduct by the innocent party. Ipswich was thronged with journalists for the occasion, but though the British pressmen present busily filed their stories, only the most emasculated versions appeared in next day's papers. The longest report was carried by the *News Chronicle* and that did no more than mention that Mrs Simpson 'had been well known in social circles in London for several years'.[3]

The restraint of the British press was indeed one of the most remarkable features of this strange affair. On 16 October Beaverbrook had called at Buckingham Palace – 'name your time,' the King had said, which had led the press lord to think that his presence must be badly wanted. It was; Edward VIII asked him to ensure that only the briefest facts about the Simpson divorce appeared in the newspapers. He put his case with 'considerable cogency and force', said Beaverbrook; his main point being that otherwise Mrs Simpson would be traduced in the press for no fault of her own but because she was a friend of the King.[4] Edward VIII did not state categorically that he had no intention of marrying Mrs Simpson, but he implied it strongly; the divorce, he maintained, was simply to allow her to escape from a marriage that had become intolerable. It was on this understanding that Beaverbrook persuaded the other British newspaper proprietors to maintain silence about the affair, and also made somewhat desultory efforts to do the same by the continental papers. 'The sole purpose of this application to you,' he told Jean Prouvost, director of *France-Midi* and *France-Soir*, 'is to escape as far as possible the publication of unjustifiable gossip concerning the King.'[1]

So far as the American press was concerned, the cat was already far out of the bag. The divorce was covered in lurid detail and the *New York American* for one announced categorically on 26 October that a marriage between Mrs Simpson and the King of England would follow eight months later. Lady Cynthia Colville reported from Canada to Queen Mary that the whole front page of many American papers had been occupied by the news. Most of the comment was friendly enough; the principal feature being 'naive admiration for the King's democratic and unworldly character in thus choosing his own friends'. The Americans, not surprisingly, took it for granted that the British were at least as cognizant of the affair as the citizens of other countries: 'One quite nice American ... casually told me how astounded he had been, travelling with an English MP ... to find that the Englishman had never even heard of Mrs Simpson.'[2]

The Canadian press observed the same self-denying ordinance as the British, but there was no stopping the gossip flowing across the border from the United States. Lord Tweedsmuir, the Governor General, was asked about Canadian reactions and described them as having at first been incredulity and indignation at the lies of the American press. As it slowly dawned on the Canadians that a large part of the rumours, at least, was true, their mood turned to irritation, shock and genuine alarm. There was, said Tweedsmuir, particular sensitivity about anything which touched on the King: 'He is really idolized here. Canada feels that he is, in a special sense, her own possession. It is wonderful how strong this personal affection is in all classes, from guides and trappers and prospectors and small farmers up to commercial and political leaders. Any smirching of their idol is felt as almost a personal loss.' The sentiment was even stronger among the young, who felt personal intimacy with the monarch. 'Like all devotees they are unwilling to believe that any clay can enter the composition of their god.

And if they are compelled to admit this there will be a most unfortunate reaction.'[1]

On 26 October, Dawson of *The Times* took to Hardinge a letter which he had received from a Briton in New Jersey signing himself 'Britannicus'. The writer claimed that the prevailing American opinion was that 'the foundations of the British throne are undermined, its moral authority, its honour and its dignity cast into the dustbin. To put the matter bluntly, George V was an invaluable asset to British prestige abroad; Edward VIII has proved himself an incalculable liability.'[2] The evidence of the American press suggests that this was nonsense: a few of the more socially traditional elements might have been repelled by what they felt to be a *mésalliance*, and there would no doubt have been some dismay over Mrs Simpson's two previous marriages among the inhabitants of the bible belt, but the tone of most press comment was extravagantly friendly. Britannicus wrote what Dawson and Hardinge wanted to hear, however, and the editor asserted gloomily that it could only be a matter of a few weeks, perhaps far less, before the British people learnt what was going on and rose in outrage. Hardinge was so struck by the cogency of the letter that he told Dawson he was sure it would make the 'desired impression' on the King. If it made any impression at all it was not perceptible.[3]

The circle of the informed was growing every day. At the end of October John Reith was told that Coronation insurance risks had risen from 4 to 21 per cent in two and a half months. 'This is all due to the wretched Simpson affair and it is most significant.'[4] Ten days later a question was asked about the Coronation in the House of Commons. John McGovern, an Independent Labour Party member from Glasgow, jumped up and shouted, 'Why bother, in view of the gambling at Lloyds that there will not be one?' There were roars of 'Shame! Shame!' but McGovern, unabashed, called out, 'Yes, Mrs Simpson.'[5] It was the first time the name had been heard in the House of Commons, indeed, the first time that there had been a reference to the affair in any public forum in the British Isles. *Hansard* dutifully made no mention of the exchange, but McGovern's intervention introduced a new and final phase of the protracted story.

17

The Last Weeks

NTIL THE VERY END OF KING EDWARD VIII'S REIGN
he could, when the circumstances were right, play the
royal role with outstanding skill and gusto. On 11
November he went with the First Lord, Hoare, to spend two
days with the Home Fleet at Portland. Away from what seemed
to him his enemies at court and in Whitehall, visiting the service
which was still closest to his heart, he relaxed, enjoyed himself,
and gave vast pleasure to the sailors in so doing. Hoare wrote
of 'his surpassing talent for inspiring enthusiasm and managing
great crowds'. At a smoking concert on HMS *Courageous* he
announced that he was going to see what was going on at the
other end of the hall. He pushed his way through and 'started
community singing to the accompaniment of a seaman's mouth
organ. When he came back to the platform, he made an
impromptu speech that brought the house down ... Here,
indeed, was the Prince Charming, who could win the hearts of
all sorts and conditions of men and women.'[1]

Prince Charming returned to Fort Belvedere, riding on a wave
of euphoria, to find awaiting him a letter from his private secretary,
Alec Hardinge. It warned him, in terms that to Hardinge seemed
measured and sympathetic and to the King brutally offensive, that
the government were growing alarmed at his relationship with Mrs
Simpson, that an approach would shortly be made to him which
– if rejected – might lead to the government's resignation, and that
the silence of the press could not last much longer and would
probably break within the next few days. Hardinge ended with a
plea that Mrs Simpson should leave the country without any delay.[2]

As a conscientious private secretary it was Hardinge's duty to
tell the King what was going on. The pity was that the news had
to come from a man whom the King disliked and distrusted. If
Godfrey Thomas had been in Hardinge's shoes he would have

insisted on telling the King face to face and would have spoken as a proven friend of many years' standing. It might not have made any difference in the long run, but at least the private secretary might have remained at the King's side during the coming crisis. As it was, the King's reaction was to refuse to have anything more to do with Hardinge, whom he assumed to be Baldwin's agent: 'Who could have told Alec Hardinge all this but the Prime Minister?' he asked Beaverbrook.[1] Hardinge was hurt; his letter had not been intended as an ultimatum, he protested, but a friendly warning.[2] He told Baldwin that he had heard no reaction of any kind: 'This is rather what I anticipated, but it does not necessarily mean that the warning has been ignored.'[3]

Hardinge had written when he did because he had been told two affidavits alleging collusion in Mrs Simpson's divorce proceedings were in the process of being filed. If these seemed to provide a prima facie case requiring investigation, the King's Proctor would be bound to reopen the case and the King's alleged misconduct with Mrs Simpson might be cited as grounds for annulment of the divorce.[4] The possibility was widely mooted. 'Will the King's Proctor intervene?' asked Ramsay MacDonald. 'It will be a scandal if he does not.' Hardinge said nothing of this to the King, but if Edward VIII was ignorant of the risk, his eyes were opened a few days later when Walter Monckton, the old friend and barrister who had been appointed Attorney General to the Duchy of Cornwall and in effect was to play the role that should have been Hardinge's in the coming crisis, wrote to warn him that a temporary separation from Mrs Simpson would be the most prudent course. Nothing must be done to support the cause of those who wanted to upset the divorce and thus make it impossible for the King and Mrs Simpson eventually to marry. It would be difficult if not impossible to interfere with the progress of the divorce if the King remained on his throne and was thus immune from involvement in the legal proceedings. To be sure that he could marry Mrs Simpson, therefore, the King could not afford to abdicate; yet it was to become increasingly obvious over the next few weeks that abdication was the price he would have to pay if a marriage were to be possible.[5] In any case, the danger of the divorce being upset should be minimized as far as possible. Though urging prudence Monckton did not at that stage take the threat very seriously. Nor did the Home Secretary, who considered the prospect of any private person intervening as being remote in the extreme.[1]

Hardinge's letter persuaded the King that he could no longer remain inactive while events unrolled around him. On 16 November he asked the Prime Minister to call on him at Buckingham Palace. If he had not done so, the Prime Minister would soon have taken a similar initiative. Three days before he had presided over a conclave of senior ministers – Ramsay MacDonald, Simon, Runciman, Chamberlain and Halifax. Chamberlain had prepared two drafts for their consideration: a letter of formal advice to the King urging a rapid end to the liaison, and an informal letter telling the King of the first document's existence and stating that, if it were presented and ignored, the government would resign.[2] Baldwin sensibly pointed out that if the fact that the government had adopted so minatory an approach became generally known, it would put the public on the King's side. He ensured that the drafts were buried with as little debate as possible. But he could defer action no longer; MacDonald caught the sense of the meeting when he wrote in his diary: 'Agreed that the scandal should be ended and HM brought right up against it.'[3]

When Baldwin was given the opportunity to bring the King right up against it, the two men unsurprisingly left somewhat different accounts of their meeting. Baldwin told the Cabinet that the King had stated his definite intention of marrying Mrs Simpson. 'You are right about public opinion in this country, so I shall go,' he stated, adding plaintively that nobody minded if he had a mistress but they seemed to draw the line at a wife.[4] Edward VIII in his account agreed that he did state his intention to marry and to abdicate if necessary, but went on to insist that this would be because of the attitude of the government, not because he believed it was really the will of the people – a subject about which he was satisfied he knew quite as much as Baldwin.[5] The effect at any rate was the same: Helen Hardinge, overwhelmed by the secrecy of the information, wrote in her diary in French so as to baffle any spy, 'Le Premier Ministre a vu le roi ce soir. C'est fini – le Souverain va partir.'[6] She was premature in her conclusion, but Baldwin would not have disputed the essential correctness of her judgment. He told his colleagues that he doubted whether he had made any impression on the King; with this part of his presentation Edward VIII would undoubtedly have concurred.

The only two people in the Cabinet whom Edward VIII felt were truly his friends were Hoare and Duff Cooper. With Baldwin's approval he saw them both. Hoare admitted 'that I was more nervous of the meeting than I had been even of my first encounter with Gandhi' (an analogy that must have startled the Duke of Windsor if he read Hoare's memoirs when they came out in 1954).[1] The King said that he had little expectation of finding Hoare a champion but had hoped that he might be at least an advocate for his cause.[2] Hoare, however, was not to be drawn into such an exposed position. He insisted that the country would be solidly behind Baldwin in his opposition to the match, and when the King doubted this, added that the Empire would not stand for it. From this, he told Chamberlain, the King did not dissent.[3] In his own notes of the meeting he added: 'Decision irrevocable,' and then, more revealingly, 'No single middle-aged man willingly stays in a tomb.'[4]

Duff Cooper was predictably more stalwart, though to judge from the account written in his diary immediately after the conversation, not quite so 'encouraging and optimistic' as the King imagined.[5] Edward VIII began by saying that his father's position and popularity had depended on his happy married life and that he had concluded that it would be the same with him; he could not be a successful monarch except with a wife whom he loved. Cooper pointed out that the blame for the catastrophe if it occurred would fall on Mrs Simpson – a suggestion which shook the King, who said it 'would be very unfair' – and followed this up by painting a lurid picture of the existence of an ex-monarch, citing Alfonso of Spain as an example. 'Oh, I shan't be like Alfonso,' expostulated the King. 'He was kicked out. I shall go of my own accord.' But what will you do? asked Cooper. 'Oh, you know me, Duff. I'm always busy. I shall find plenty to do.' Cooper relented; with time, he suggested, it might be possible to have both throne and wife. If Wallis went abroad, remained there for a year or so, anyway until the Coronation was safely over, then the country might grow reconciled to the idea. The King was not impressed by the proposal. 'He said he would not like to go through a solemn ceremony like the coronation without being perfectly frank with the country . . . "Mind you," he went on, "if I can stay and marry, Wallis is going to be Queen or nothing." If he had the thought of a morganatic marriage, he had evidently dismissed it from his mind.' Cooper's parting shot was to remark how shocked the country would be if the King married a twice-divorced woman. 'He winced at the word "twice" and said that the first marriage hadn't really counted. What, if anything, he meant by that, I didn't enquire.'[1]

Two days later Cooper took Mrs Simpson aside after dinner and tried to impress on her the importance of leaving the country. 'She said he would not hear of it, and that if she went he would follow her.'[2] Cooper believed that, on the contrary, if she went, there was at least a chance he would forget her, and used to claim that this was the thinking behind the advice he gave to the King. Wigram was less charitable about Duff Cooper's motives. Edward VIII, he wrote, had seen Hoare and Cooper, 'two careerists whom HM has been cultivating, probably with the object of having them on his side, should such a crisis occur'. Hoare, however, 'is a man of religion, and reports say he took a firm line with HM'.[3] About Cooper, clearly, he was less confident.

Briefly, the crisis was shelved while the King toured the mining villages of south Wales. As with his visit to the Fleet a week before, the occasion brought out the best in him: he was indefatigable, endlessly interested, sympathetic without being mawkish, bringing into the lives of the unemployed and destitute a ray of hope and the conviction that one person in high places at least cared about their plight. 'The Welsh visit went extremely well,' Hardinge told Baldwin; relieved no doubt to have something on which he could report favourably about his employer. 'The reception was everywhere splendid and there was no discordant note.'[4] Ministers were less pleased. 'These escapades should be limited,' MacDonald wrote in his diary. 'They are an invasion into the field of politics and should be watched constitutionally.'[5] The visit is best remembered for the King's remark when confronted by one scene of particularly dismal urban squalor: 'Something must be done.'* That he did in fact care, and was genuinely moved by what he saw,

---

* William Deedes in the *Daily Telegraph Magazine* of 17 March 1989 quotes evidence that the King was referring to the recently closed Dowlais steelworks and in fact said: 'These steelworks brought the men hope. Something must be done to see that they stay here – working.'

is incontestable: the visit had been 'very strenuous and heart-rending', he told his mother, 'but the spirit of these poor people is marvellous'.[1] That other matters swept the memory from his mind is no less obvious. But when he got back to London he was still full of it, and held forth endlessly on all he had seen at a dinner party the same night. He blamed the communists as much as the government for what had gone wrong; 'agitation and bolshevism' above all had ruined the chances of south Wales.[2]

A flurry of rumours, the most extravagant attributed, probably unfairly, to the Minister of Transport, Leslie Hore-Belisha, now circulated in London. The King had been given three weeks in which to renounce Mrs Simpson or face the resignation of his government. He had taken up the challenge, proposed to speed up the Simpson divorce, marry Mrs Simpson at Windsor, appeal to the nation. Winston Churchill had agreed to form a new 'royalist' government. The King, wrote Channon darkly, 'is going the dictator way'.[3] MacDonald was equally alarmed: 'The danger is that a new Govt might get hold of the Executive and act as dictators. A person like Churchill might well put his hand to that job!'[4] Monckton was sufficiently put out by such stories to write to Baldwin assuring him that the King's position was unchanged. 'He will not do anything precipitate or selfish, saving *il gran rifiuto*.'[5] But it was soon apparent that the King was having second thoughts about the need for his abdication. Baldwin told Lang that this arose from the 'evidence of his popularity' he had encountered while on his Welsh tour. 'On his return he seemed to waver.'[6] Certainly the enthusiasm of the Welsh crowds had bolstered his confidence, but there was a more immediate cause for his change of mood. The idea of a morganatic marriage – that Mrs Simpson might be his wife but not his Queen – which he had told Duff Cooper was out of the question, had been revived and suddenly seemed less impossible.

It is surprising that he had not harboured the idea before. Three weeks earlier, Harold Nicolson had referred to 'very serious rumours' that the King would marry Mrs Simpson and create her Duchess of Edinburgh.[7] Neville Chamberlain had heard the reports and taken comfort from Warren Fisher's dogmatic assertion that 'any woman whom the King marries is *ipso facto* Queen Consort . . . This makes a morganatic marriage, which I thought a danger-

1. Princes Albert and Edward bathing at Cowes in 1901.

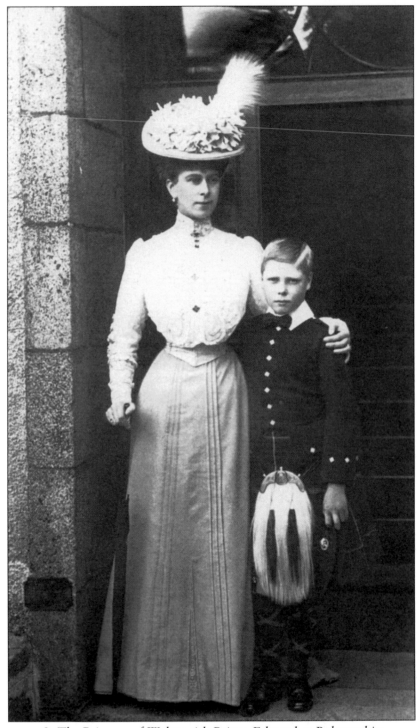

2. The Princess of Wales with Prince Edward at Balmoral in about 1906.

3. *The Prince of Wales at the time of his investiture: 'The incarnation of all the Fairy Princes who have ever been imagined.'*

4. Punting at Oxford in 1913.

5. *The Prince leading his company of the Grenadier Guards on a route march in 1914.*

6. *Looking even younger, as supernumerary ensign with the King's Guard at Buckingham Palace.*

7. Portia Cadogan, on the right, boating on the Thames with Princess Mary.

8. The Prince standing between Rosemary Leveson-Gower (on his left) and Diana Capel at the Duchess of Sutherland's hospital in France.

9. The Prince as 'Chief Morning Star' at Banff in September, 1919.

10. Freda Dudley Ward with her two daughters.

11. *Taking a jump successfully and . . .*

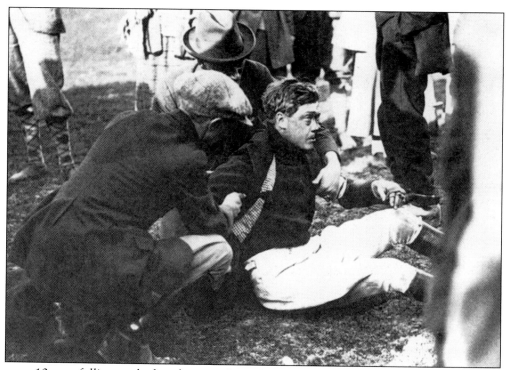

12. *. . . falling at the last fence at the Arborfield Cross point-to-point in 1924.*

13. With Fruity Metcalfe, Audrey Coates and Prince George at Drummond Castle – 'Never have I had such an exciting week as this!'

14. With the Duchess of York and the cairn terrier, Cora.

15. Skiing with Prince George.

16. Mrs Simpson, photographed by Dorothy Wilding.

17. *The snapshot of the Duke which the Duchess always kept beside her bed.*

18. An after-wedding photograph – the names written in by Lady Alexandra Metcalfe.

*19. The Duke and Duchess being greeted by Josef Terboven, the Gauleiter of Essen,
during their visit to Germany in October 1937.*

20. *A group of dignitaries in Nassau. Harold Christie is directly behind the Duke and Gray Phillips behind him.*

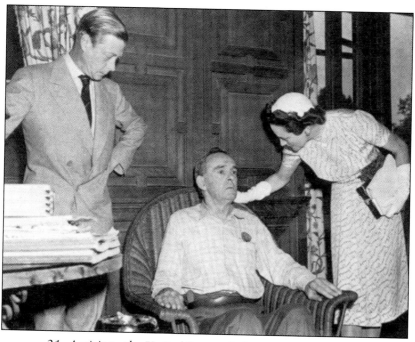

21. *A visit to the United Seamen's Service in May, 1943.*

22. The Duke in dressing gown and with cairn terrier, photographed by the duchess whose shadow is visible on the gravel beside him.

ous possibility, out of the question.'[1] King Edward VIII had probably rejected the idea as being unworthy of Mrs Simpson. During his visit to Wales, however, the press magnate, Esmond Harmsworth – acting, Leo Amery believed, on Churchill's inspiration[2] – had taken Mrs Simpson to lunch at Claridges and put the possibility to her. She was doubtful but did not rule it out, and her cautious acquiescence induced the King to reconsider a solution which would give him the companionship he craved while allowing him to retain the throne.

Precisely what the King's attitude was towards the proposal is hard to establish. Both Lord Beaverbrook and Ulick Alexander quote him as saying, 'I always thought I would get away with a morganatic marriage'[3] – Beaverbrook, however, probably basing himself on Alexander's testimony. The word 'always' begs a lot of questions but suggests an acceptance of the idea pre-dating his return from Wales. On the other hand, he told the lawyer William Jowitt many years later that morganatic marriage was something to which he would never have assented.[4] Probably the truth is that he had played with the idea over many months, but only espoused it when all else failed; Mrs Simpson reported him as saying: 'I'll try anything in the spot I'm in now.'[5]

The more he thought of it, the more it appealed to him. By the time he saw the Prime Minister again on 25 November it had become a preferred solution. 'He wanted Mrs Simpson to be a Duchess,' Baldwin complained to a colleague, 'not to be royal, but less than royal, but rather better than the ordinary Duchess.'[6] It was not inconceivable; the Liberal politician Lord Lothian for one thought it a possible compromise, though difficult to sell to the middle classes or the Empire.[7] Baldwin, however, found it repugnant. The mere fact that it was advocated by Harmsworth was enough to make him disapprove it: 'a disgustingly conceited fellow and yet curiously timid at heart,' he described the press magnate, while his paper, the *Daily Mail*, Baldwin told the King, was 'the worst judge in England of what the people were thinking'.[8] 'Is this the sort of thing I've stood for in public life?' the Prime Minister asked Thomas Jones,[9] while he told the King that public opinion would not tolerate it. 'I believe many people would be sorry to see me go,' said the King wistfully. Baldwin agreed, but insisted that they would not be willing to see him stay on the terms proposed.

Duff Cooper tried to persuade the Prime Minister that the idea was at least worth consideration, but found him adamant that neither the House of Commons nor the Dominions would accept it.[1] At all costs Baldwin wanted to avoid an open clash between the monarch and his ministers. He told King Edward VIII of the words of a Clydeside MP: 'I see we are going to have a fascist King, are we?'[2]

Once the proposal for a morganatic marriage was on the board, however, it had to be formally disposed of. Baldwin buried it with all due ceremony. Even before his meeting with the King he had sounded out the opposition. He called in Archibald Sinclair for the Liberals and Attlee for Labour and asked what their reactions would be if the King refused to give way and the government resigned. He felt certain that Sinclair would promise to back the government but was less sure about Attlee. There was a strong emotional attachment among socialists to Edward VIII, because of his stand on poverty and the unemployed, and many, like Francis Williams, editor of the *Daily Herald*, were at first inclined to say, '"Good luck to the King", and let him marry whoever he pleases.'[3] Attlee, however, unhesitatingly told the Prime Minister that the Labour voters would have no objection to an American marriage as such, but would not accept Mrs Simpson or a morganatic marriage. He found that he had correctly gauged his party's attitude. 'Despite the sympathy felt for the King and the affection which his visits to the depressed areas had created, the Party – with the exception of the intelligentsia, who can be trusted to take the wrong view on any subject – were in agreement with the views I had expressed.'[4] 'Our people won't 'ave it,' said Ernest Bevin bluntly,[5] while Walter Citrine more rotundly told Baldwin that he was 'undoubtedly interpreting the minds of people in the Labour movement'.[6]

Fortified by this support, Baldwin on 27 November raised the matter in the Cabinet. The morganatic marriage found not a single champion, Chamberlain being the most vociferous opponent: if it were accepted, he had written in his diary two days before, it 'wd only be the prelude to the further step of making Mrs S Queen with full rights'.[7] Even Duff Cooper accepted that it was no solution, he contented himself with pleading for a year's delay on the grounds that 'when the wrong people wanted to marry one another the best expedient was usually to persuade them to wait a year'.[1] He reinforced his argument with the claim that the King 'might destroy himself if by her action or ours he could not marry her'.[2] He got no support – the situation had gone too far. The bogeyman who was invoked frequently during the meeting was Winston Churchill. When Baldwin had asked him whether he would take the same line as Attlee and Sinclair, he answered cautiously that 'though his attitude was a little different, he would certainly support the Government'.[3] But could he be trusted? If the government resigned in direct confrontation with the King, would Churchill resist the temptation to take up the gauntlet and endeavour to form an alternative ministry? If this happened, wrote the Secretary of State for India, Lord Zetland, 'there would be a grave risk of the country being divided into two camps – for and against the King. This would clearly be fraught with danger of the most formidable kind.'[4]

It was time to bring in the Dominions. Beaverbrook, who had hurried back from the United States at the King's behest, claimed to know that the telegrams requesting the opinions of the Dominion governments on the choice between abdication and a morganatic marriage had been phrased by Baldwin in such terms as to make it inevitable that they would opt for abdication. By allowing Baldwin to consult first the Cabinet and then the Dominions on such a basis, the King had deprived himself of any freedom of action. He would now be faced by the brutal choice between accepting the advice that would be given him or leaving the throne. Beaverbrook urged the King to have the telegrams recalled, but it was too late for that.[5] In fact the drafts had been prepared by the Secretary of State for the Dominions, Malcolm MacDonald, and his Permanent Under Secretary,[6] but they were undoubtedly couched in terms which expected a negative reply. After explaining the morganatic proposal the draft included the sentence: 'I feel convinced that neither the Parliament nor the great majority of the public here should or would accept such a plan.' To this the Cabinet made their position unequivocally clear by adding, 'any more than they would accept the proposal that Mrs Simpson should become Queen'.[7]

The responses were predictable. The Australians were the most decided. The Prime Minister cabled that: 'There would be outspoken hostility to His Majesty's proposed wife becoming Queen, while any proposal that she should become Consort and not Queen . . . would not be approved by my Government.'[1] The High Commissioner told Baldwin that he had been so distressed by events that he and his wife would probably have refused to attend the Coronation, to let things drag on would be disastrous, abdication was the only solution.[2] There is always some doubt how far such lofty sentiments reflect the true feelings of the man in the street. It is worth quoting the despatch sent to Washington from the American mission in Canberra after abdication had become inevitable: 'Australian opinion was virtually a unit in holding that no other solution was possible without weakening the ties of Empire . . . The Australian outlook on life is distinctly middle-class, and on morals is distinctly Victorian.'[3] From Sydney the American Consul reported that 'with the exception of the Radical Labor Group' all elements considered abdication to be the proper solution.[4]

The Canadians were less forthright. Mackenzie King stated that they would prefer abdication to Mrs Simpson becoming Queen or Consort, but went on: 'Were it believed King's abdication was something imposed by his Ministers . . . and not a step voluntarily proposed by His Majesty himself for reasons of State, the whole matter would I believe be very differently regarded.' If he *did* abdicate, the Prime Minister believed, his action 'would win for him if that were possible an even greater measure of affection and influence than . . . he at present enjoys'.[5] But for the two divorces, he told the US minister, 'marriage to a woman of Mrs Simpson's strong character and good influence on the King would have been well received'.[6] A sidewalk poll in Ottawa showed that 75 per cent of the women thought the King should renounce Mrs Simpson, but 65 per cent of the men wanted him to marry as he pleased.[7] On 8 December Baldwin asked Mackenzie King whether he could quote him as saying that Canadian public opinion had been seriously perturbed by the affair. King refused: 'While anxious to be helpful, Canada and he would be put in a wholly wrong light if impression was conveyed that . . . Canadian opinion had been a determining factor in the situation.'[8]

South Africa was categoric. Abdication was the lesser of two evils: it will be a great shock, cabled Hertzog, but 'marriage under the circumstances will prove a permanent wound'.[1] There was no trace of any disposition on the part of the public to accept Mrs Simpson, reported the American Minister.[2] The Prime Minister of New Zealand was less emphatic. Mrs Simpson as Queen was impossible, but as for a morganatic marriage: 'The great affection felt in New Zealand for His Majesty and the desire of the people in this country for his happiness inspire the thought that some such arrangement might be possible.'[3] The Governor General hurriedly stepped in to curb what seemed to him undue sentimentality. It was due, he explained, to the King's inspiring personality and the great popularity he had won on his visit in 1920. 'I pointed out to Mr Savage the great and insuperable difficulties which may arise from [the morganatic marriage] and added that a violent revulsion of feeling may and probably will take place.'[4] For Ireland de Valera took a detached attitude; at first saying that, since divorce was a recognized institution in England, he supposed that a morganatic marriage was the solution. Since his object was avowedly to secure the removal of all reference to the King from the Irish constitution and he anyway later came down in favour of abdication, his attitude did not affect matters one way or the other.[5]

There was some but not much comfort here for the King; certainly Baldwin had grounds for contending that the Dominions would not accept Mrs Simpson either as Queen or as morganatic consort. Meanwhile the pace of events was quickening in London. Though the press still reported nothing, the numbers of those in the know multiplied by the day. Mrs Simpson began to receive poison pen letters, some threatening her with violence, and a stone was thrown through her windows. Churchill claimed that this had been organized by Beaverbrook, who wanted to get Mrs Simpson out of London. Beaverbrook denied it, but – according to Churchill – admitted that possibly someone from the *Daily Express* might have been involved.[6] Never the most physically courageous of women, Mrs Simpson moved to Fort Belvedere, with Aunt Bessie as chaperone. For the royal servants, wrote Helen Hardinge sourly, this at least had the advantage that they were no longer required to ferry champagne and other delicacies from the Palace to Regent's Park. 'They had undertaken this task with a certain amount of bitterness, their employer having cut off their traditional beer-money a short time previously.'[7]

She left just in time. A few days later the house was beset by a booing, stone-throwing mob and police had to be drafted in.[1] At last the silence of the press had broken. It was a miracle it had not happened before. For weeks Dawson of *The Times* had had a leading article set up demanding that the King make some reply to the calumnies published about him in newspapers overseas.[2] The Archbishop had received sackfuls of letters, and was finding it ever harder to restrain the clergy, who wanted to denounce their erring monarch from their pulpits.[3] The floodgates were, in fact, opened by a cleric, A. W. F. Blunt, the Bishop of Bradford, who had been much struck by the fact that a businessman a few weeks before had complained that it was all very well to say that he ought to take a religious view of the Coronation but what was the point 'when the principal actor in it has no use for that sort of thing himself?' Blunt claimed that he had thereupon written a sermon on the theme of the King's duties as head of the Church of England, heard of the Simpson affair a few days before he was due to preach it, wondered whether to change his words but decided that they could not possibly be misinterpreted.[4] The Archbishop did not accept these protestations. 'Why can't he hold his tongue?' he snapped. 'If he only knew all that I know . . .'[5]

The press had no doubt that they knew what the Bishop meant and treated his sermon as the starting pistol in a race to produce the most sensational reports. The *Mail* and *Express* spoke up for the King but did not commit themselves on exactly what course they were advocating, the more sober and non-conformist *News Chronicle* was surprisingly the only major daily newspaper overtly to support a morganatic marriage. The King did his sums, and calculated that the papers supporting him had a readership of some 12.5 million, while those ranged against him could boast only 8.5 million.[6] 'The *Express, Mail* . . . *Mirror* etc., have eclipsed themselves in sentimentality to such an extent as to be ridiculous,' wrote Thomas Jones loftily.[7] Lady Houston in the *Saturday Review* was ridiculous in another way: 'Primed with instructions from Russia – to get rid of the King – Mr Baldwin has had a busy week – backwards and forwards – backwards and forwards – several times a day to hold a pistol to the head of the King, crying, "Do my will – or – abdicate".'[8] Sadly, Low's cartoon was censored: three portraits on a wall – Mr Spencer, Mr Simpson and Edward

VIII – labelled 'The Wallace Collection'.[1] Kingsley Martin in the *New Statesman* supported the morganatic marriage. He had almost scooped the whole of Fleet Street with an article on the constitutional issue which the King had seen, approved, and then asked to be postponed by a week in case its publication damaged the chances of a settlement. By that time it had been overtaken by events.[2]

The paper that the King feared most was *The Times*, both because of its national and international standing and because he regarded its editor, Dawson, as an arch enemy. Beaverbrook accused Dawson of being more responsible than anyone else for driving Edward VIII to abdication, he achieved it 'by methods many would condemn', and 'he pursued his quest with a vigour that seemed more like venom'.[3] This was characteristically extravagant, but Dawson certainly played a role more prominent than that of any other newspaper editor; he saw Baldwin frequently and Hardinge showed him a draft of his letter to the King before finally sending it. But though *The Times* made it very clear that it supported the government, it argued its case with reasonable restraint. On 2 December the King heard that *The Times* was about to come out with a fierce attack on Mrs Simpson and asked Baldwin to get it stopped. Baldwin protested that he could not control the press but told Dawson of the request. Dawson sent the Prime Minister a proof of his leading article to read to the King; it proved to be innocuous.[4] What was less innocuous was the letter which *The Times* published in its first edition on 8 December, drawing attention to some alarmingly apt lines from Racine's *Bérénice*, in which Titus puts his glory before his mistress and denies that he would ever be:

> . . . so vile a thing
> Tied to thy train – a hopeless, throneless King,
> Loathesome to men below, to gods above,
> A sad example of the sleights of Love.[5]

The letter was cut out of subsequent editions, but was in the version that caught up with Mrs Simpson in the south of France.

The hurricane of publicity that had now burst about the King and Mrs Simpson convinced him that it was essential to get her out of the country. She decided to join Katherine and Herman

Rogers at their villa near Cannes. An old friend, Lord Brownlow, was asked to escort her and agreed without demur. He arrived at Fort Belvedere in time for dinner on 3 December to find the King 'rather pathetic, tired, overwrought, and evidently dreading Wallis's departure, almost like a small boy being left behind at school for the first time'. Dinner was a brief and melancholy feast: 'Wallis deeply oppressed, the King nervous and, as ever, over-attentive to all of us, such as mixing the salad, pouring out the soda-water, and lighting cigarettes for all of us.'After dinner the King took Brownlow aside to thank him and to urge him to take all possible care of his precious cargo – doubly precious, since Brownlow discovered once they were *en route* that Mrs Simpson was travelling with much of her jewellery; worth, he estimated, £100,000.[1]

When the moment came to leave, Mrs Simpson walked through the King's bedroom on to the lawn without saying goodbye to any of the staff. 'Well, that's the end of that,' one of the footmen said to the butler, Osborne. 'Don't be too sure,' Osborne replied. 'We'll keep our fingers crossed.'[2] Brownlow and Mrs Simpson clambered into the car and the King said goodbye. According to Brownlow, 'he leant across to her to get one last touch of her hand – there were tears in his eyes and on his cheeks, and his voice was shaking. "Wherever you reach tonight, no matter what time, telephone me. Bless you, my darling!"'[3] Brownlow wrote his account the following day, so probably his version of the King's last words is more accurate than the Duchess's: 'I don't know how it's all going to end. It will be some time before we can be together again. You must wait for me no matter how long it takes. I shall never give you up.'[4] But whether the King uttered these words or not, they were certainly what he thought.

18

Abdication

O NLY EIGHT DAYS SEPARATED MRS SIMPSON'S DE-
parture from the abdication, but to the chief protagonist
it must have seemed a lifetime of tribulation. In the case
of Wallis Simpson, to be out of sight was not to be out of mind,
nor even out of touch. Her exile was punctuated by a series of
anguished telephone calls as she was harried across France by the
press and then skulked in the Rogers's small and gloomy villa.
Each conversation left the King emotionally exhausted, yet the
absence of a call drove him into a frenzy of anxiety. 'Those
telephone calls, with a bad line, at a long distance, will never be
forgotten by any of us,' wrote Monckton, who was in almost
constant attendance at the Fort, with Ulick Alexander and the
King's solicitor, George Allen.[1]

At first the burden of the calls was that whatever happened the
King should not abdicate. Edward Peacock, who as the King's
principal financial adviser saw a lot of him at this period and was
more nearly in his confidence than anyone except Monckton and
Allen, claims that Mrs Simpson insisted Edward VIII should fight
for his rights and that his popularity would carry him through.[2] If
she took this line at first she soon changed her tune. The horrors
of the flight through France, the blandishments of Perry Brownlow,
the abuse and hostility to which she found herself subjected if ever
she ventured outside the villa, convinced her that her present
situation was intolerable. On 6 December she arrived in Cannes
and the following day issued a statement for the press in which
she claimed she was anxious to avoid any action which might do
harm to the King or his throne, and stated her readiness 'to
withdraw forthwith from a situation that has been rendered both
unhappy and untenable'.[3] Before releasing it she read it over the
phone to the King; he welcomed it as being likely to deflect some

311

of the animosity now directed against her, but made it clear that in no way would it affect his handling of the crisis.

To the government it seemed that the statement opened new possibilities. Mrs Simpson's solicitor, Theodore Goddard, was summoned to Downing Street, where he was seen first by Horace Wilson, then by Baldwin. Wilson later recorded that 'what Mr Goddard was really saying was, in effect, what price could be paid to Mrs Simpson for clearing out?'[1] This interpretation of the interview was passed on to Chamberlain, who noted in his diary that 'it is evident she is an entirely unscrupulous woman who is not in love with the King but is exploiting him for her own purposes. She has already ruined him in money and jewels and it is thought that she can be squared when she realizes that she has lost the game.'[2] If Goddard in fact gave that impression it must have been unwittingly; certainly he made no attempt to find out from Mrs Simpson whether she had a price and, if so, what it was. He did, however, agree that Wilson's statement that there was little prospect of the government giving the King any sort of financial grant after his abdication was a factor which Mrs Simpson would think relevant. Dugdale, who was with the Prime Minister that evening, thought Goddard 'a typical tough type of hard-working solicitor'. He was very obviously ill at ease in such rarefied circles, 'like an uneasy bull having walked into the farmer's sitting room instead of his own stable'. His opening remark was: 'I hope you won't think me a Bolshie, Sir.' Baldwin asked why on earth he should. 'During the interview,' Dugdale considered, 'Mr Baldwin was obviously more preoccupied in thinking over Mr Goddard's strange introductory remarks, and the possible thoughts that provoked them, than what Mr Goddard was actually talking about.'[3]

Baldwin urged Goddard to go to Cannes to find out exactly what Mrs Simpson's intentions might be, and placed an official aircraft at his disposal. In his memoirs the Duke of Windsor recollected that he had expressly forbidden Goddard to go to see Mrs Simpson.[4] Goddard's partner, Bertram Ogle, denied that any such veto was imposed, at the most an expression of mild disapproval was received by way of Monckton.[5] Goddard, anyway, decided that his duty to his client and his country made the journey essential. It was much misinterpreted. As he had never flown before and had a weak heart he decided to take his doctor with him. It was at once assumed by the more prurient-minded that the doctor was a gynaecologist, summoned by Mrs Simpson: 'This is foolish and most unfortunate,' wrote Chips Channon sternly.[1] Another speculation was that Goddard was sent out to recapture Queen Alexandra's emeralds, which the King had given to Mrs Simpson, and that he returned with his pockets stuffed with jewels. 'If the tale be true were the things brought back for restitution or to be put safely into Wally's bank?' enquired Lord Crawford.[2] Ogle categorically denies that any such duty was imposed on his partner; Lord Brownlow, who was present at the meeting with Goddard and who had already commented on Mrs Simpson's jewellery, makes no mention of such a transaction; and anyway, though the King had some very valuable old jewels reset for Mrs Simpson, it has never been possible to identify any as having been specifically handed down from Queen Alexandra. It seems that Goddard did no more than any solicitor would have done in such circumstances, lay the facts before his client and accept her instructions; even though the fact that he proposed to charge the British government five hundred guineas for his trouble shows how far his visit was considered official.[3]

In his own record of the interview Goddard states that he told her something of the feelings aroused in Britain and questioned whether it was wise for her to contemplate marriage: 'After a long talk she definitely said she was quite prepared to give him up, but did say that wherever she went the King would follow her.'[4] Goddard told Dugdale that he had found her 'in a most terrified state of nerves, complete capitulation and willingness to do anything'.[5] A statement was prepared, dated 9 December and countersigned by Brownlow and Goddard, in which she offered to withdraw the divorce petition.[6] Armed with this, Goddard returned, his triumph muted by the knowledge that it would be worthless if the King remained entrenched in his position.

Goddard believed that his client was sincere in her protestations, that she would in fact have felt relief if the King had acquiesced in her wish to call the whole thing off.[7] Monckton was equally convinced that she meant what she said.[8] Brownlow, on the other hand, who saw more of her at the time than anyone else, insisted that he 'had no belief in the statement',[9] though it is not entirely clear whether he was referring to the sincerity of Mrs Simpson's words, or their likely efficacy. Hardinge was quite as certain that she only signed the statement in the conviction that it would be repudiated by the King: 'It could not be anything but bogus.'[1] The Prime Minister, not surprisingly, preferred the opinion of Hardinge, but it is hard to accept that he had the right to be quite so categoric when he assured the Dominions' Prime Ministers that the statement was no more than an 'attempt to swing public opinion in her favour'.[2] It seems more likely that Mrs Simpson was so bemused and battered by events that she herself hardly knew what she wanted except to be ten thousand miles away and out of touch with everyone in England. But she also knew that, however many thousand miles might separate them, the King would have followed her. King Edward VIII's attitude was unwavering throughout the crisis. He was determined to marry Mrs Simpson the moment that she was free, and to tell the world that this was his intention. Peacock heard that Harmsworth had turned up at Cannes and urged Mrs Simpson to persuade the King to give her up, on the private understanding that they would go back on their promise and marry later on. She put this suggestion to the King. 'Certainly not,' he replied. 'If we did that we ought both to be hanged.'[3]

Meanwhile in London the return of Max Beaverbrook moved the action a stage further towards a final dénouement. Randolph Churchill claimed that, when asked why he had chosen to play so prominent a part in the abdication crisis, Beaverbrook replied succinctly, 'To bugger Baldwin!'[4] That was certainly a part of it, but there is probably as much truth in the explanation he gave himself at the time, that he wanted to help the King because he thought his cause was just.[5] His role, as he saw it, was to stiffen the sinews of the King and to rally support for him. In both tasks he foresaw difficulties. In the first he feared he would be ham-strung by what seemed to him the curious reluctance of the King to challenge his government and bring down the pillars of the consti-tutional temple upon his own and his people's heads. In the second, he saw the main opposition to the marriage as being religious. It followed that the divorced and the free-thinkers should support the King, but here the argument broke down, for whatever their real feelings, the divorced were all trying to become respectable while the free-thinkers disliked the monarchy.[1] He did his best, however; in so far as there was a motive force behind the creation of a King's party it was provided by Max Beaverbrook.

When he called on the King at Fort Belvedere he found him chain-smoking and holding a handkerchief to his head 'as if to ease some hidden pressure or pain'.[2] There are many other testimonies to the strain under which Edward VIII was labouring at this time. His attitude created 'real doubts about his sanity', wrote Leo Amery;[3] he was under great mental pressure, said Piers Legh, 'his outbursts on being asked some obvious questions plainly indicated an unbalanced and thoroughly abnormal frame of mind'.[4] The American Ambassador reported that for some days the King had been in 'an exhausted and nervous mental state'.[5] Helen Hardinge even claimed that the King was sleeping with a loaded pistol under his pillow – whether to turn on himself or a possible intruder was not revealed.[6] The story is not impossible, but Walter Monckton, who slept at Fort Belvedere the last eight nights, denied that it was true.[7]

The King had now evolved a new plan of action. First he would broadcast to the nation, stating his intention to marry Mrs Simpson but stressing that neither she nor he would insist that she should be Queen. Then he would withdraw temporarily to some foreign country so as to give people time to make up their minds. If he were called back he would be happy to resume his reign with Mrs Simpson as his consort; if not, then he would accept the will of the people and abdicate. He told Brownlow of this plan just before the departure of Mrs Simpson and insisted that it was not abdication, he was 'going to Switzerland to let things simmer down'. Brownlow later noted this as being 'the first and the last important lie of our friendship', but in fact it was an exact statement of what the King proposed at the time.[8] Piers Legh was instructed to book rooms at the Dolder Hotel in Zurich while Ulick Alexander went to Coutts' bank to secure a letter of credit for £5000. The account was overdrawn but no difficulties were made.[9] Lord Swinton, the Minister for Air, informed Baldwin in some alarm that two private aircraft had been chartered in the King's name to fly to Zurich and were waiting at Hendon. Baldwin said that they would not be needed.[10]

315

The plan had foundered on the King's wish to broadcast to the nation before he departed. He told Baldwin about this intention on 3 December; he was 'frantically keen', said the Prime Minister. Baldwin promised he would put the proposal to the Cabinet, but made it clear he felt it would be constitutionally improper. The King could speak only the words of his ministers. 'You want me to go, don't you,' the King challenged him. Baldwin admitted that, in the circumstances, he saw no alternative.[1] Next day the Cabinet supported the Prime Minister. The King's proposed text was 'a plausible and blatant attempt to get the country and Empire to throw over his ministers', concluded MacDonald.[2] One alarmist minister suggested that the King might get hold of John Reith, Director General of the BBC, and broadcast in spite of the government's opposition. Baldwin, who knew his Reith, said that this was not a serious risk. Everyone agreed that the urgency was great and the crisis must not be allowed to drag on indefinitely.[3]

The King did obtain one concession from Baldwin – which the Prime Minister later considered to be his first blunder[4] – that he could consult Winston Churchill about his future course of action. A few days before, Churchill had harangued Duff Cooper on the subject. 'What crime had the King committed?' he asked. 'Had we not sworn allegiance to him? Were we not bound by that oath? Was he to be condemned unheard? Was he seeking to do anything that was not permitted to the meanest of his subjects?'[5] The royalist rhetoric was sincere enough, but Churchill was as anxious as anyone to stop the King marrying Mrs Simpson. A few days after the abdication he told Mrs Belloc Lowndes that women played only a transient part in Edward VIII's life. 'He falls constantly in and out of love. His present attachment will follow the course of all the others.'[6] His judgment was dramatically wrong but it explains his wish that any final decision should be deferred as long as possible.

Churchill dined at Fort Belvedere on 4 December. He found the King 'most gay and debonair' for the first quarter of an hour, but soon it became obvious that 'the personal strain he had been so long under, and which was now at its climax, had exhausted him to a most painful degree'. He was 'down to the last extremity of endurance'. The King was emphatic that he had not abdicated, nor even used the word to the Prime Minister. Churchill urged him on no account to leave the country, and, still more important, to see a doctor as soon as possible. He insisted that there could be no need to worry about time: let him ask for as long as he wanted to make up his mind, 'there is no force in this country which would or could deny it you'. Play for time, he urged, time may resolve all your difficulties.[1] The King listened with interest but told Peacock that, though Churchill had been very amusing, he was quite wrong in what he proposed – 'Such a course would be inexcusable.'[2] It was a point of view that Churchill deplored but admired. The King considered, Churchill told Boothby, 'that it would not be honourable to play for time when his fundamental resolve was unchanged, and as he declared, unchangeable. It was certainly this very strict point of honour which cost him his Crown.'[3]

The desperation of the King touched Churchill deeply. At lunch with Margesson, the Chief Whip, he was on the edge of tears the whole time and in the House of Commons he talked loudly of 'the twisting, crooked tricks of the Government'.[4] He wrote to Baldwin stressing the King's mental turmoil and saying 'it would be most cruel and wrong to extort a decision from him in his present state'.[5] Baldwin was unimpressed. He told the Cabinet next day that there was no truth in Churchill's assertion that the King's health was seriously impaired. He 'had never known the King more cool, clear minded, understanding every point and arguing the different issues better'.[6] Nevertheless, Churchill was sufficiently encouraged by the reactions of the various ministers to whom he talked to send the King an ebullient message assuring him that no pistol would be held to his head. A final decision could be deferred till February or March, he believed. Meanwhile there had been: 'Good advances on all fronts giving prospects of gaining good positions and assembling large forces behind them.'[7]

The Cabinet, meeting exceptionally on a Sunday, was not concerned primarily with the King's health. A point that was increasingly obsessing the King was that he might lay down his throne in order to marry Mrs Simpson and then find that the divorce was blocked and his sacrifice in vain. At lunch with Horace Wilson and Dugdale, Monckton said that, if the King was forced to wait five months for his marriage without the certainty that it would be possible in the end, he 'might well go off his head or take to drink'.[8] As a corollary to the Abdication Bill, could there not be a second bill making Mrs Simpson's divorce immediate? Wilson accepted that the request was not unreasonable, and when Baldwin saw Edward VIII on 5 December he said that he foresaw trouble with some members of the Cabinet but that personally he felt it fair. Whether, as the King maintained, Baldwin also said that he would resign if he did not get it accepted is an open question; at the least he promised to champion it vigorously, and this he did.[1]

Next morning Baldwin first saw Chamberlain and Simon. Simon thought it a shocking precedent – 'What would the non-conformists say?' Chamberlain agreed: 'It would be considered an unholy bargain to get the King to abdicate.' If, however, when the Abdication Bill was passed, the Prime Minister could say that the government felt the uncertainty over the divorce imposed an intolerably cruel strain on the King and that they were considering legislation to speed it up, the second bill could be introduced in two or three days and the appearance of a bargain avoided.[2] This was devious enough to satisfy even Simon, and Baldwin faced a special meeting of senior ministers that afternoon with some confidence. The accelerated divorce, he said, was 'the only solution for which it might be possible for him to be responsible'. The King was making a tremendous sacrifice and was entitled to ask for something in return. But Duff Cooper, Edward VIII's only real friend in the government, brushed Chamberlain's sophistry aside. How could they, he asked, refuse to pass special legislation for a morganatic marriage which would enable the King to stay, yet introduce a bill to legalize adultery so as to expedite his departure?[3] Chamberlain and Simon largely retracted their agreement of that morning and only Hoare was left to argue that he could not see that it was a matter of principle: the choice was between a ramp now or in five months.[4]

The Cabinet then adjourned while Baldwin went to see Queen Mary. On the way he met Lang and put the case to him. As always ready to see at least three sides to any question, Lang first expressed surprise at and dislike of the proposal, then paused to appreciate its advantages, and ended up doubting its constitutional propriety.[5] Back in Cabinet, Baldwin accepted that the large majority was against him. Monckton was summoned to be given the bad news. He said that in that case the King would need more time to decide his position. Baldwin said that the matter must be settled before

Christmas, whereupon Chamberlain remarked that the Christmas trade had already suffered.[1]

'I have felt all day that the tide is turning against the Government, and is more pro-King,' wrote Channon on Sunday, 6 December.[2] That weekend marked the high water mark of the royalist party, in so far as such a movement could be said to exist when given no overt encouragement by the King. Margesson told Baldwin that some forty Tory members would probably support the King,[3] less than a tenth of the total parliamentary party but still a formidable nucleus which could rapidly expand if public opinion seemed to be moving that way. Channon put the figure even higher: 'Belisha is a secret Cavalier and there are many in the Cabinet,' he wrote, 'Duff Cooper is one, Sam Hoare is another.'[4] Lord Cottenham had chosen Churchill's royalist government for him: Duff Cooper and Sassoon were to take the Exchequer and the Air Ministry, and Hoare and W. S. Morrison could be counted on.[5] Outside the Houses of Parliament, Lang agreed with the Moderator of the Evangelical Free Churches that the mass of the people would support the government, but 'a large proportion, especially of the young to whom the King was a popular hero ... felt a strong sympathy with him'.[6] Anthony Cox, who wrote literate detective stories under the alias of Francis Iles, was told by military friends of 'a conspiracy by certain young hotheads, junior captains in particular, to take up arms against the Government and for the King'.[7] At the other end of the spectrum General Sir Ian Hamilton told Baldwin that 'there would be an ex-service men's revolution if the King abdicated'.[8]

None of this adds up to much, but it does show that feelings were running high and by no means entirely against the King. Lady Houston was mercifully untypical of any section of British society but she voiced the feelings of many when she urged: 'Be of good cheer, Sir – the Country are *with You* ... Sir, I am *sure* you are conquering. I have outside my windows a flying banner – "The King's happiness comes first", and last night a lot of young people stood and cheered it and sang "For He's a Jolly Good Fellow!" They *love* you, my King. Do not desert them.'[9] Less romantically, Lloyd George in Jamaica announced: 'If the little fellow marries her, I shall back him.' He telegraphed to his son and daughter: 'Hope you are not going to join the Mrs Grundy harriers who are hunting the King from the throne.'[1] Ribbentrop announced confidently that if the Abdication Bill were forced through there would be rioting in the streets and the King's party would restore Edward VIII to the throne;[2] Margot Oxford agreed that there would be revolution and in a letter to the King went on to predict that 'all our enemies, Germany, Italy and Russia, would triumph. No one can take your place. You will rise to a pinnacle of fame unknown before to *any* King of England.'[3]

If the King ever read the effusions of Lady Houston or Lady Oxford, he would have paid little attention to them. He had more than enough solid evidence, however, to convince him there was sufficient support for him in the country to make things thoroughly difficult for the government. How much that support would in fact have amounted to was never put to the test, because the King had no intention of giving it the encouragement it needed if it was to mobilize and multiply. If he had to go, he would go quietly. An old friend and senior civil servant, Colin Davidson, wrote to congratulate him on his 'obvious and inflexible determination not to encourage a "King's party". It was within your power to create civil war and chaos.'[4] Lord Halifax, who on the central issue felt that the King was wholly in the wrong, paid tribute to his behaviour. When he came to London from the Fort large crowds cheered him outside Buckingham Palace and in Downing Street; when Baldwin came to the door to see him off he was roundly booed. Such demonstrations could easily have been encouraged, wrote Halifax, instead 'he never came up to London again'.[5] 'You ran dead straight at me;' was Baldwin's verdict. 'You maintained your own dignity throughout; you did nothing to embarrass your successor . . .'[6] To his biographer, G. M. Young, Baldwin summed it up: 'Whoever writes about the Abdication must give the King his due. He could not have behaved better than he did.'[7]

But though there was evidence enough of a strong royalist tendency in the country, awaiting the call to spring to arms, there is more to show that the weight of public opinion was behind the government. The weekend of 5–6 December produced a dramatic evolution of feeling in the House of Commons. The always wraith-like King's party almost entirely disappeared. Churchill found himself isolated from his most faithful followers: Boothby thought his stand a deplorable dissipation of energies and influence that were desperately needed for other purposes;[1] Macmillan reassured the Prime Minister that, while he might disagree with him on social, foreign and economic problems, 'you are dealing with eternal verities here, from which no deviation is possible without disaster'.[2] The working classes, where the King might have been expected to find most of his support, proved resolutely hostile: reports came flooding in, wrote Francis Williams, 'from the East End of London and from industrial areas in the Midlands and North and in South Wales that the general mass of middle-class and working-class readers of the *Herald* were deeply upset that a woman who had been twice through the divorce courts might become Queen'.[3] Reports of provincial working-class opinion were remarkable for 'penetration, common sense and outraged feeling', wrote a relieved MacDonald in his diary.[4] In Islington Harold Nicolson addressed an audience of four hundred, of whom only a handful would join in singing the national anthem.[5] The American Consul in Plymouth reported that feeling against the King had hardened every day: it was nothing to do with Mrs Simpson's nationality, but 'people here consider that the proceedings leading up to the second divorce were too much of a farce for them to endure'.[6] Contemporary polling techniques could perhaps have established the way in which public opinion evolved in the ten days before the abdication; for the government the critical factor was that the members of the House of Commons returned on Monday, 7 December, convinced, in Amery's words, that 'the country as a whole was getting progressively more shocked at the idea that the King could hesitate between his duty to the Throne and his affection for a second-rate woman'.[7]

Perhaps as marked was the feeling that the affair must not be allowed to drag on. Enough damage had already been done. Sylvia French, from 14 East 60th Street, New York, had her own particular axe to grind but she spoke in essence for many millions when she cabled: 'Dear King, I wish you could come to a decision regarding Mrs Simpson as my stocks fluctuate with every report.'[8] With such a mood prevailing there was no hope that the new compromise Churchill had hatched over the weekend – that the King would agree not to marry except with his ministers' consent, and the matter be left pending – would prove acceptable to anyone, least of all the King.[1] Nor did Churchill fare any better when he pleaded in the House of Commons for further delay and a pledge that no final decision would be made without reference to the House. He was howled down with a ferocity that amazed and horrified him. 'You have delivered a blow to the King ... far harder than any that Baldwin ever conceived of,' Boothby accused him bitterly. 'You have reduced the number of potential supporters to the minimum possible – I should think about seven in all.'[2] G. M. Young congratulated Baldwin on his prescience in foreseeing how opinion in the House would evolve. 'I have always believed in the weekend,' replied Baldwin. 'But how they do it, I don't know. I suppose they talk to the station master.'[3]

On Tuesday, 8 December, Baldwin paid his last visit to Fort Belvedere. He went, he told a friend, determined to help the King wrestle with himself, if necessary all through the night.[4] For this purpose, he came armed with a suitcase, a precaution which cast the King into even deeper alarm and despondency than he was in already. Peacock, knowing how close the King was to complete collapse, offered to remove Baldwin for dinner to his home nearby. The King refused: 'I could not let the Prime Minister, who has been so kind as to come here to help me, leave without dinner. He must stay.' He finally agreed that Peacock should do all he could to ensure Baldwin left soon after dinner, but even then 'he was urgent that I should not do so unless I was quite sure that it would not hurt the Prime Minister's feelings'.[5] In fact it was clear before they even sat down to dinner that the two men had long ago exhausted all they had to say to each other; only a radical change of heart on the part of the King would have affected the position and that, it was quickly obvious, was not forthcoming. In spite of his fatigue, the King, wrote the Duke of York, 'was the life and soul of the party, telling the PM things I am sure he had never heard before about unemployment centres etc ... I whispered to Walter Monckton, "and this is the man we are going to lose". One couldn't, nobody could believe it.'[6] Baldwin was on his way home shortly after dinner. 'This is making history,' he remarked to Dugdale with some satisfaction. 'This is what I like.'[7]

At Cabinet next day Baldwin reported on his conversation and said that it would be useless to do any more. Hoare insisted that the ministers should send one more plea to the King to reconsider.[1] The message was rushed to Fort Belvedere and the reply returned almost before the messenger had had time to take a cup of tea. 'His Majesty has given the matter his further consideration,' Edward VIII wrote in his own hand, 'but regrets that he is unable to alter his decision.'[2] The fact of abdication was now accepted by everyone concerned. It remained only to work out the remaining details.

There were many questions relating to finance and the King's future status which had to be resolved. In all of them the rest of the royal family, in particular the man who would have the crown thrust upon him, the Duke of York, were intimately involved. It is remarkable how little communication the King had had with his closest relations in the months and weeks before the abdication – something he explained by saying that, as the issue was a constitutional one, he had thought it best to confine his negotiations to the government.[3] It was not till after he had told the Prime Minister of his plan to marry Mrs Simpson that he braced himself to break the news to Queen Mary. He dined at Marlborough House on 16 November. It must have been a macabre feast. The presence of the Duchess of Gloucester kept conversation at dinner to small talk about racehorses and repainting Buckingham Palace, and it was only after she had mumbled some excuse and fled, that the King told his mother and sister, the Princess Royal, what he had in mind. They were sympathetic but it was then, to use the King's words, that: 'The word "duty" fell between us.'[4] To Queen Mary there could be no doubt that Mrs Simpson was unfit to ascend the throne and therefore unfit to be her son's wife. The only course was for him to renounce her, or at the very least, to keep her cloistered. King Edward VIII's happiness was neither here nor there, or perhaps more correctly it was both, for the only true happiness lay in doing one's duty. Not merely would she not give her blessing to such a match, she would refuse to receive the woman whom she regarded, and in her heart always would regard, as her son's mistress. 'As your mother I must send you a letter of true sympathy on the difficult position in which you are placed,' she wrote after their conversation. 'I have been thinking so much of you all day, hoping you are making a wise decision for your future.'[1] Further than that she could not go.

It was indicative of the King's mood at the time, swinging between wild elation and blackest gloom, that he interpreted this letter as actively encouraging. 'I feel so happy and relieved to have at last been able to tell you my wonderful secret,' he wrote in reply; 'a dream which I have for so long been praying might one day come true ... God bless you darling Mama for all your sweetness and understanding.' Two years later Queen Mary showed the letter to Wigram with the dry comment: 'I cannot think why my eldest son speaks of my "sweetness" to him during that awful time, because I thought I was extremely outspoken and tried to express my displeasure, but I suppose he never listened to what I said.'[2] By then, however, many things had gone wrong and much bitterness had built up; she would have expressed herself more gently in 1936.

The King now saw each of his brothers in turn to tell them his story: Gloucester, he wrote in his memoirs, 'appeared little moved'; Kent was 'genuinely upset'; York was characteristically unable to express his innermost feelings.[3] A few days later, however, the future King wrote to say, 'I do *so* long for you to be happy with the one person you adore. I, of all people, should understand your own personal feelings at this time ... I do realize all your great difficulties and I feel sure that whatever you decide to do will be in the best interests of this Country and Empire.'[4] He ended with a plea that he should be allowed to come to see the King next day. His letter was backed up by a letter from the Duchess of York which illustrates, perhaps better than any other document, the turmoil of emotions in which the royal family were floundering at this time.

Darling David. *Please* read this. Please be kind to Bertie when you see him, because he loves you, and minds terribly all that happens to you. I wish that you could realize how loyal and true he is to you, and you have no idea how hard it has been for him lately. I *know* that he is fonder of you than anybody else, and as his wife I must write to tell you this. I am terrified for him – so DO help him, and *for God's sake* don't tell him that I have written. We both uphold you always. We want you to be happy more than anything else, but it's awfully difficult for Bertie to say what he thinks, you know how shy he is – so do help him.[1]

In a letter to Queen Mary written at about the same time, the Duchess of York confided how 'every day I pray to God that he will see reason, and not abandon his people'.[2] The King knew only too well that this was what his relations were praying, he had no intention of seeing what they regarded as 'reason', and he was resolved to spare himself and them useless pain by arguing the matter with them. Godfrey Thomas complained to the Duke of York that he had been shut out of all discussion of the King's relationship with Mrs Simpson. 'That is what we all have, myself included, and I feel it very much,' replied the Duke. 'I have tried to broach the subject many times this year but he has always turned a deaf ear to it. If the worst happens and I have to take over, you can be assured that I will do my best to clear up the inevitable mess, if the whole fabric does not crumble under the shock and strain of it all.'[3] It was not till 7 December, when the die was irrevocably cast, that the Duke managed to have a proper talk with his brother. 'The awful and ghastly suspense of waiting was over,' he recorded. The Duke went to the Fort at 7 p.m., went home for dinner and returned later. 'I felt that once having got there I was not going to leave. As he is my eldest brother I had to be there to help him in his hour of need.'[4]

An hour of need was one thing, a lifetime of need another. It was the financial arrangements for the King's future that did more than anything else to poison the atmosphere between the future Duke of Windsor and his family. Godfrey Thomas stated the problem concisely in his diary: 'Will Mrs S, who is really not in love with him, be prepared to face life as Mrs Edward Windsor, or even the Duchess of Sussex, on an income of £12,000 a year, which Ulick Alexander says is all that he will have if he packed up and departed as a private individual?'[5] But he also mis-stated the problem, and in his mis-statement lay the seeds of appalling discord. An income of £12,000 a year would suggest capital of some £300,000 – well over £7,000,000 at today's values – substantial enough but not adequate to sustain a former King of Great Britain in the style to which he was accustomed, or even the style in which his former subjects would wish him to exist.

In fact Alexander, who as Keeper of the Privy Purse was in a position to find out as much about Edward VIII's finances as anyone except perhaps Peacock, later put the King's total fortune at £1.1 million.[1] This figure did not include the Canadian property. Samuel Hoare also put the total at £1.1m but states that a proportion had been settled on Mrs Simpson.[2] Michael Bloch, in his most reliable editing of the later correspondence between the Duke and Duchess of Windsor, puts the settlement at £300,000 and the King's fortune at £800,000.[3]

Nevertheless, when the King and the Duke of York met at Fort Belvedere with their legal advisers on 10 December to discuss financial arrangements, the King 'made an impassioned speech, pointing out how badly off he would be'. He 'distinctly told his brother that . . . he did not think he had £5000 a year'.[4] In a later record, Wigram recorded that the King had claimed only to have £90,000 as his total fortune.[5] In view of this, he regretfully insisted that the terms of his father's will should be strictly observed and his life interest in Sandringham and Balmoral treated as absolutely his, to dispose of as he thought best. Whether he cited a similar figure when he spoke to Churchill is uncertain, but he certainly left him in no doubt that he was so poor that he could not possibly survive without some sort of subsidy from the government or the new King.

There are plenty of mitigating circumstances to plead on Edward VIII's behalf. He was physically at the end of his tether, having hardly slept for a week and eaten only the most inadequate meals. He was distraught at his separation from Mrs Simpson and felt himself desperately alone, suspecting that even his closest counsellors – Monckton, Peacock, Alexander – disapproved of his plans and would have been glad to see them thwarted. He was tormented by the thought that at the end the divorce might be refused and his sacrifice prove to have been in vain. The pain that he was causing his mother and his brothers weighed heavily upon him. He was constantly harassed by telephone calls from the south of France, in which threats of renunciation were mingled with demands that he should stick up for his rights and extract every halfpenny of advantage from the situation.[1] He was agonized by the fear that he would let Wallis down, secure for her less than she deserved, earn her contempt. Under such pressure, it is hardly surprising that he clutched at any straw which he thought might help him improve his bargaining position.

Nevertheless, he told a lie for reasons of self-interest, and this cannot be condoned. It was a foolish lie. If he had thought straight, if he had thought at all, he must have known that even if the Duke of York did not already know his brother's financial situation, he would be bound soon to find out. The lie was pointless, told in blind panic. It was an exceedingly dangerous lie. Even if it gained him temporary financial advantage, the risks involved in being found out were far greater than any possible benefit. By telling it, the King alienated the two men on whose good will he was to rely most heavily: his brother and Winston Churchill. On 10 March of the following year King George VI reminded the Duke of Windsor that he had insisted that if he received no grant from London he would be very badly off. 'Your recent letter does not dispute that you told me so, and I believed it,' the King continued. He had now learned the truth about his brother's fortune. 'You were under great strain and I am not seeking to reproach you or anyone. But the fact remains that I was completely misled.'[2] He did reproach him all the same, the basis of trust had been destroyed between them. Churchill at first refused to believe that he had been tricked, but finally told Ulick Alexander he was convinced: 'And that,' wrote Alexander, 'occasioned the rift between Winston and the Duke – when Winston discovered that the latter had double-crossed him.'[3]

It was a suicidal lie, and could only be explained by the traditional charity of the coroner recording a verdict of suicide – that the deceased took his own life while the balance of his mind was disturbed. At Windsor on 10 December 1936, King Edward VIII, the balance of his mind being disturbed, made the worst mistake of his life. He was to suffer the consequences until the day he died.

At first the government seemed well disposed towards the idea of granting the ex-King an allowance to help him maintain an appropriate train of life. Monckton was sure that, if he had decided to go even a few days earlier, a wave of sentiment in his favour would have ensured a generous provision.[4] Hardinge suggested

£25,000 a year. Chamberlain and Simon, however, hesitated to commit themselves and urged caution on the Prime Minister. Peacock saw Baldwin and Chamberlain and asked how long it was felt the King should stay away from Britain after his abdication. Two years, suggested Baldwin. 'They were both very cordial, but guarded about finance.'[1] Away from the chilly restraint of the Chancellor, Baldwin was more disposed to be generous. At the last dinner at Fort Belvedere, Dugdale had been briefed to stop his master making any rash commitment. Unfortunately Baldwin was rather deaf, and when Dugdale tried to make his point unobtrusively, he replied loudly: 'What did you say? What money?' The point having finally been made, he protested: 'But you can't let him starve.' No promise was made, however. Later that evening Mrs Simpson telephoned. Dugdale was in the room: 'He was heard to tell her he would get less than he hoped for, which caused a harsh-voiced twang of rich American invective from Cannes.'[2]

The meeting at Fort Belvedere therefore took place amidst uncertainty whether the King would be provided for by the government. Nor was it known whether the life or freehold interest in Balmoral passed to the Crown under Scottish law. 'The discussions tended to become heated, as sentiment and legal fact were getting rather mixed, so I intervened,' recorded Peacock. '. . . I removed the technicalities which were perplexing the Duke and stated directly and simply what I thought would be his desire.'[3] The essentials of the agreement were that the King would sell his life interest in Sandringham and, if appropriate, Balmoral for a sum to be agreed, and would waive any claim to the royal heirlooms. The price agreed for the two estates would not be paid over, but instead the new King would grant his brother £25,000 a year if no similar provision was made by parliament from the Civil List. The only qualification to this was that the new King would not be responsible for making such a grant if the reason for parliament's refusal to do so itself was 'His Majesty's conduct from this date'. The promise, in other words, was conditional on the King not alienating parliament by his behaviour. The new King would take over Edward VIII's responsibility for pensions at present shared by the four brothers.[4] 'Wigram was present at a terrible lawyer interview which terminated quietly and harmoniously,' recorded the Duke of York. 'E. R. Peacock was a very great help.'[5]

Harmony had equally reigned when Peacock and Monckton had called on the Duke of York the previous day to secure his assent to the King retaining royal rank after the abdication. Another point which Peacock made and the Duke apparently accepted was that 'if and when he [the King] was allowed to come to England he should have the Fort to live in. The Duke of York authorized Monckton to tell this to the King.'[1] This part of the agreement foundered in the storms that followed the abdication; a fact that was to cause especial chagrin to Edward VIII.

Since he had broken the news to his mother in mid-November, Edward VIII had barely seen Queen Mary. The following day Baldwin had called on her. 'This is a nice kettle of fish, isn't it?' she said, a remark which so struck the Prime Minister that he repeated it at once to Dugdale.[2] Since then she had watched helplessly as the kettle boiled. On 3 December she wrote to her eldest son: 'This news in the papers is very upsetting, especially as I have not seen you for ten days. I would much like to see you, won't you look in some time today?'[3] It was another few days before he could resolve himself to face what he knew would be a painful interview and he was very obviously under severe strain when he finally did so. Queen Mary, wrote a close confidant, 'made a last attempt to induce him to give up Mrs S for the country's sake – he had stormed and raged and shouted like a man demented'.[4] King Edward VIII himself denies that his mother made any attempt to change his mind;[5] the cause of his fury was probably more her refusal ever to receive Mrs Simpson. She had, she told Lady Airlie, promised King George V before he died that she would never do so,[6] but no deathbed undertaking was needed to fortify her inflexible resolve. The day after Edward VIII left the country she wrote to thank Baldwin for all the 'kindness and patience' he had shown the King and to express her grief at 'the failure of my Son in not carrying on the duties and responsibilities of the Sovereign of our great Empire'. George V and she had worked always to instil a sense of duty and tradition in their children; 'that one of them failed is very painful to me'.[7]

One victim of the crisis who was little thought of at the time was Ernest Simpson. On 7 December he sent a message to Wigram via the faithful Jenks to say how distressed he was at the course of events. He was prepared, he said, 'to come forward and say that

329

the divorce was entirely a collusion between HM, himself and Mrs S
. . . he felt he could squash the divorce by turning King's evidence'.
Wigram was horrified by the thought that the apple cart might be
upset at this late stage: if the King could not marry Mrs Simpson,
he said, he would certainly live with her and the crisis would be
indefinitely protracted.[1] Simpson assented: three days later, on the
eve of the abdication, he wrote to the King what must surely be
one of the most generous – if curious – letters ever sent by a
cuckolded husband to his usurper:

> My heart is too full for utterance tonight. What the ordeal of
> the past weeks have meant to you I well know, and I want
> you to know that my deepest and most loyal feelings have
> been with you throughout. That you may find an abundance
> of happiness in the days that lie before you is my earnest hope
> and prayer.
>
> For the last time, Sir, let me subscribe myself your devoted
> subject, but always your loving friend and obedient servant.[2]

The King must have received this letter at almost the same time
as his brothers arrived at Fort Belvedere to sign the Instrument of
Abdication. Monckton had brought the draft at 1 a.m. the morning
of 10 December. The Duke of York arrived at 9.30 a.m., Gloucester
a few minutes later, Kent at 10, the King remarking with a laugh:
'George *would* be late.'[3] Immediately the signing began. Edward
VIII declared his 'irrevocable determination to renounce the throne
for Myself and for My descendants'. That afternoon Baldwin was
to set out the sad story to the House of Commons and Edward
VIII insisted that, as a private individual, he had at last the right
himself to speak directly to the nation. Having read the Prime
Minister's speech, Queen Mary tried to dissuade him. Baldwin had
spoken in 'a wonderfully dignified manner', she wrote. What more
was there to say? 'You are very tired after all the strain you have
been and are going through, and surely you might spare yourself
that extra strain and emotion?'[4] Probably nothing would have
changed the King's resolve; as it was he was incensed by Baldwin's
failure to include in his speech a reference which the King had
requested to the fact that Mrs Simpson had done all she could to
dissuade him from abdicating. He was resolved that he, at least,
would put the record straight.

Abdication

The King's decision precipitated a debate, which till then had not seemed very urgent, about what he was to be called. A meeting of ministers had concluded that he would be entitled to the title of His Royal Highness, and that he would probably take precedence over the Dukes of Gloucester and Kent but not the Princesses Elizabeth and Margaret. The Prime Minister was asked to sort out the point with the new King.[1] Not surprisingly he deferred the matter. Now it was made pressing by the fact that Sir John Reith would have to call the ex-monarch something when he introduced him before the broadcast. Reith's own suggestion was 'Mr Edward Windsor'. The matter was referred to the new King, who disposed of it with the lapidary common sense that was to be the hallmark of his reign. He couldn't be Mr anything, the King pointed out, because as the son of a Duke he would be Lord Edward Windsor. If he were given no other title, he would, in theory, be able to stand for the House of Commons. Was this really what was wanted? He must be created a Royal Duke.[2] He told his brother he would create him Duke of Windsor; Edward VIII spoke it aloud, liked it, and it was settled.[3] Reith was told he should introduce the former King as 'His Royal Highness, Prince Edward'.

The broadcast was to be from Windsor Castle. Reith chatted for a few minutes about Spain and other subjects; he had thought it right, he later explained, 'to behave as if nothing untoward or specially unusual was happening'[4] – quite an undertaking in the circumstances. The signal was given and the former King began to speak. He declared his allegiance to the new monarch, and his sense of duty towards his country and the Empire, and then continued with the sentence which is the best remembered of anything he said in his whole life: 'You must believe me when I tell you that I have found it impossible to carry the heavy burden of responsibility and to discharge my duty as King as I would wish to do, without the help and support of the woman I love.' The decision to abdicate, he said, was his alone; he had taken it in the knowledge that his brother, 'with his long training in the public affairs of this country and with his fine qualities', was well qualified to take his place: 'And he has one matchless blessing, enjoyed by so many of you and not bestowed on me – a happy home with his wife and children.' After that it only remained to pay due tribute to Queen Mary, Mr Baldwin and all others concerned and to embark on his peroration:

> I now quit altogether public affairs, and I lay down my burden. It may be some time before I return to my native land, but I shall always follow the fortunes of the British race and Empire with profound interest, and if at any time in the future I can be found of service to His Majesty in a private station I shall not fail.
>
> And now we all have a new King. I wish him, and you, his people, happiness and prosperity with all my heart. God bless you all. God Save the King.

It was Edward VIII's speech, drafted with some help from Monckton and embellished but not substantially changed by Winston Churchill. He began nervously, noted Monckton, but gathered confidence, and ended almost with a shout. When it was finished, he stood up, put an arm on Monckton's shoulder, and said: 'Walter, it is a far better thing I go to.'[1]

For the most part the speech was well received. 'A triumph of natural and sincere eloquence,' Beaverbrook described it. 'It won back the people's good will.'[2] Even Lang found it had 'some real pathos', though he objected to the reference to the new King's good fortune in enjoying a wife and family — 'as if he might not at any time have honestly possessed this happiness if he had chosen'.[3] Helen Hardinge wept herself, but said everyone else found it vulgar,[4] while Lady Ravensdale considered it 'hot-making and melodramatic'.[5] In the pubs and middle- or working-class homes no such squeamishness was felt; the atmosphere was more often similar to that reported from San Francisco. A restaurant had been cleared and fitted with chairs to accommodate those who wanted to hear the speech. 'The place was crowded out, everyone weeping, and they all stood up and sang "God Save the King" at the end!'[6] Amery recorded in his diary that Brownlow's 'description of Mrs S moaning and sobbing while King E gave his farewell broadcast was quite harrowing'.[7] But the account that, in a chilling way, rings most true, is that of Chips Channon, who was dining with the Stanleys. 'It was a manly, sincere farewell,' he judged. 'There was a stillness in the Stanleys' room. I wept, and I murmured a prayer for he who had once been King Edward VIII. Then we played bridge.'[1]

For Britain too there was time for a brief tear and then it was back to the bridge table. With startling speed the memories of the former King were brushed under the carpet and eyes were turned towards the future. At Windsor things took a little longer to settle down. After the broadcast the ex-King went back to Royal Lodge to take leave of his family. Queen Mary, wrote Monckton, was 'mute and immoveable and very royal'.[2] Considerately, she had left off her mourning for the evening so as not to cast further gloom on an already melancholy occasion. The Duchess of York, now the Queen, was in bed at home with a high temperature. She wrote to say how sad she was not to have been there 'as I wanted so much to see you before you go, and say "God Bless You" from my heart. We are all overcome with misery, and can only pray that you will find happiness in your new life. I often think of the old days and how you helped Bertie and me in the first years of our marriage. I shall always mention you in my prayers.'[3] He said goodbye to his eldest brother last. 'When David and I said goodbye we kissed, parted as freemasons and he bowed to me as his King,' wrote George VI.[4] In another account George VI protested when his brother bowed to him. 'It's all right, old man,' said the ex-King. 'I must step off with the right foot from the first.'[5]

For the ex-King, one of the saddest features of his departure was the refusal of his former servants to accompany him. Fred Smith, who had been with him since 1908, angrily expostulated: 'Your name's mud. M.U.D.!' 'Oh, Frederick, please don't say that. We've known each other for so long,' was Edward VIII's reply. When Alfred Amos refused to accompany him into exile, he said that he quite understood and asked him to work for him when he returned to England.[6] Crisp, his valet, refused to come because he didn't want to leave his wife. Edward VIII fixed up for him to work with George VI. The junior piper was asked to come instead. He said that his parents would be shocked.[7] Edward VIII affected to be indifferent, even amused, but he was deeply hurt. He wrote to his mother hoping that all his old employees could somehow be fitted in: '. . . they are reliable and trustworthy people despite their amazing disloyalty to me by not one of [them] offering to come away with me for a week or two as valet. I neither know nor care their reasons but I can never forget how they let me down when I most needed them.'[1]

HMS *Fury* had been provided to take the Duke as far as France. The Captain, Cecil Howe, had had hurriedly to borrow linen, crockery and glasses from the royal yacht and, at Piers Legh's insistence, had smuggled aboard a surgeon-commander 'in case the ex-King's state of mental stress should cause him to require any medical attention while at sea'.[2] In fact Howe found nothing out of the ordinary about the Duke's behaviour,[3] while the Commander-in-Chief, William Fisher, thought that he looked as if he had passed through a very trying experience, 'but his manner betrayed no weariness, his voice had animation and my general feeling was one of relief that he was so normal'. He insisted that the Flag Officers should come to his cabin for a celebratory drink. When Fisher said his final farewell, the Duke replied, 'Oh, it's not goodbye . . .'[4]

Fury sailed at 2 a.m. The plan had been for her to lie off Bembridge for a few hours so as to allow the Duke to get some sleep. He insisted on sitting up, however, drinking brandy and going over the events of the last few weeks with the exhausted Legh and Alexander. At 3.30 Legh, in desperation, sought out the Captain and begged him to come down and engage the Duke in conversation, so that the others might get some sleep.[5] The Duke was still sending wireless messages of farewell and thanks when *Fury* reached French territorial waters and the wireless had to be closed down. He ordered the ship to sea again and continued with his task.[6]

Back in England Monckton motored back to London to catch a little sleep before he paid a final visit to Fort Belvedere to tidy up. The only objects he found it necessary to dispose of were a piece of paper beside the Duke's bed on which Mrs Simpson's private telephone number was written and, in the room that had been occupied by Mrs Simpson, a biography of George IV's more-or-less morganatic wife, Mrs Fitzherbert.[7] In the back of the car as he drove away from Portsmouth he wrote a short letter to Queen Mary:

During the journey he talked quietly of old times and places well remembered by both of us, but above all he talked of

Abdication

You – how grand you were and how sweet to him and especially at the last when he wanted it most. (You will recognize the words as his.)

There is, and I think there always will be, a greatness and a glory about him. Even his faults and follies are great. And he will, I feel sure, never lend himself to any such dangerous courses as some, not unreasonably, fear. He has shown that he cares for unity: and he felt deeply the unity of the Family with him last night.[1]

19

Exile

T HE SIX MONTHS BETWEEN HIS DEPARTURE FROM Britain and his marriage to Mrs Simpson were the unhappiest of the Duke of Windsor's life. To abandon totally what one has for forty years been taught to believe is sacred and immutable must be for anyone a traumatic experience. For the Duke it was made doubly destructive by the fact that he was bored and lonely, those two corrosive elements that can destroy happiness as surely as any tragic accident. 'I can never describe to you, darling Mama, the complete and utter loneliness of these endless months of separation from Wallis . . .' he wrote to Queen Mary. 'It really is a nightmare and so much worse than I ever expected.'[1] He was as ill-equipped as any grown man could have been to grapple with these new and fearful pressures; pressures the worse because they were accompanied by the disappearance of all those mundane and practical compulsions which beset an active monarch. His intellectual resources he had never cultivated; he had been sustained by a hectic routine of duties and pleasures and total dependence on one adored human being. Now the routine had been abolished, and the human being was far away. Lascelles judged him harshly but there was some truth in his assertion that the Duke was 'like the child in the fairy story who was given everything in the world, but they forgot the soul. He has no spiritual or aesthetic side at all. He did not know beauty when he saw it . . . He cared for nothing in nature.'[2]

Cut off from his roots, he almost visibly withered. He clung pathetically to those few relics of his most precious relationship which he had managed to carry with him into exile. Brownlow described him as sleeping in a room which was almost entirely bare except for several large photographs of Mrs Simpson: 'No bibelots, nothing personal at all except a little yellow pillow on his bed that once was hers.'[3] There was no shortage of people to talk

336

to, but there was only one person to whom he wanted to talk. He had never found intimacy easy – perhaps no Prince of Wales could – and now it had become impossible. 'So much has been written and said of the bad influence of his "intimates",' wrote Brownlow. 'So far as I know he had *none*! . . . and he told me in Vienna that he was proud of this fact as being a Kingly virtue – but if friendship and an open heart are vices, what hope is there for a man in trouble?'[1] When the Archbishop attacked Edward VIII's circle of friends, Malcolm Bullock, a Conservative member of parliament and son-in-law of Lord Derby, exclaimed: 'The late King had no friends.' 'It's terribly true,' reflected Channon, 'only Fruity Metcalfe with his checks and his brogue. No other man friend did the King ever have.'[2]

His only solace was interminable telephone calls – after three months the bill was over £800 – which often left him more distracted than when he had begun. For the rest, he had endless time in which to brood, to imagine slights where none had been intended, to build up minor grievances into intolerable misfortunes. It is impossible to read the letters which he wrote before he rejoined Mrs Simpson without sensing the bleak and anguished desolation that lay behind them. They were written by a man who had not merely lost all sense of proportion but who was – in the most literal sense possible of that most metaphorical phrase – out of his mind.

To those who saw the Duke casually none of this was evident; most accounts stress his cheerfulness and freedom from apparent strain. Indeed, things at first did not go badly. His original idea had been to take up the reservation in the Zurich hotel which had been made by Legh a week before, but Mrs Simpson and Brownlow joined in protesting that the former King of England could not retire to a hostelry, however respectable. They jointly concocted the plan that he should borrow from Baron Eugene de Rothschild his country house, Schloss Enzesfeld, near Vienna. He had visited the house briefly during his stay in Austria in September, and had had a cold at the time. Brownlow now telephoned to ask whether 'his young brother David, the one who had the bad cold last time' could come to stay.[3] Kitty Rothschild cracked this simple code, and said she would be honoured and delighted. Mrs Simpson wrote to thank her: 'Dear Kitty – be kind to him. He is honest and good and really worthy of affection. They simply haven't understood.'[1]

Walford Selby, the British Ambassador, met him at the station and was relieved to find him 'looking less tired than I had expected after the terrific strain through which he must have passed'. The platform had been cleared but the Duke insisted that the dozens of journalists and photographers who had made the journey from all over Europe should be allowed to approach him. Then it was off to the Schloss; an ideal site, Selby thought, among remote woods in the foothills of the mountains, with large and secluded grounds and plenty of scope for golf and skiing within a few miles.[2] It had only two flaws, in fact: it was not Fort Belvedere and Wallis Simpson was far away.

It would never have been much of an idyll, but what little chance there was of the Duke finding tranquillity at Schloss Enzesfeld was quickly dispelled. The first blow was struck by the Archbishop of Canterbury. 'My heart aches for the "Duke of Windsor",' Lang wrote directly after the abdication, 'remembering his childhood, his boyhood, his days at Oxford, the rich promise of his service as Prince of Wales – all ruined by his disastrous liking for vulgar society, and by his infatuation for this Mrs Simpson.' Presumably the Duke would now go through 'some form of marriage' with his mistress. 'Then either his better self will be destroyed, or if it survives and he longs again for his old interests and occupations he may try to return . . . Either prospect is dark.'[3] The Archbishop elected to demonstrate his aching heart by an address on the BBC in which he attributed the King's failure to carry out his responsibilities to a 'craving for private happiness', and denounced the 'vulgar society' which had led him down this primrose path.[4] Baldwin, Reith, Lord Salisbury and Queen Mary predictably wrote to congratulate him on this effort, but of the 250 letters Lang received within the first day or two, most were abusive and many violently so.[5] Churchill wrote to tell the Duke that there had been a storm of anger raised against Lang for his unchivalrous references to the late reign: 'Even those who were very hostile to your standpoint turned round and salved their feelings by censuring the Archbishop.'[6]

The Duke was outraged. 'The strain here is pretty great as you can imagine,' Piers Legh told Thomas, 'and the Archbishop's outburst hasn't helped.' Legh proposed to stick it out till the end of the year, when he hoped that Thomas, Alexander, or the naval equerry Charles Lambe, would relieve him. Lang's address, he reported, had caused much comment in Vienna and left the '*haute noblesse*' wondering whether the Duke should still be treated as a member of the royal family.[1] Monckton, alarmed by the rumblings of indignation from Schloss Enzesfeld, urged Lascelles to get the King to do all he could to forestall such fulminations in the future. So far he had managed to stop the Duke making any public statement but at any time he might insist upon 'rushing to the defence of those who have tried to help him'.[2] The King needed no such warning, the night after the broadcast he had to endure a 'tirade which went on endlessly' from his brother on the subject.[3]

Not to be outdone, the Archbishop of York now chose to include a passage on the abdication in his diocesan letter. 'I was considerably annoyed to see that my brother of York, after an interval of more than a week, had seen fit to publish his own remarks about poor King Edward,' wrote Lang, with slightly belated squeamishness.[4] George VI was thoroughly put out; he felt that his brother had given certain undertakings and that the other side of the bargain was not being kept. To show his feelings he proposed to include in his New Year's Day message a reference to 'a brother whose brilliant qualities gave promise of another historic reign – a reign cut short in circumstances upon which, from their very sadness, none of us would wish to dwell'. Evil-minded persons, remarked Lascelles blandly, might detect in this a veiled rebuke to the Archbishops, 'but I think their minds would have to be very evil to do that!'[5]

Even more disturbing to the Duke was the proposal to withdraw British police protection from Mrs Simpson. John Simon had a point when he asked how he was supposed to justify in the House of Commons the expenditure of public funds for this purpose, and Baldwin another when he argued that the presence of British policemen achieved little and annoyed the French, but Mrs Simpson was convinced she was about to be a target for the vengeance of royalist fanatics and she communicated these fears to the Duke colourfully and at length. Legh believed that the withdrawal of police protection would 'drive HRH mad quicker than anything else' and added that in that case he would not be responsible for what might happen.[1] He said as much to the Prime Minister when he got back to London. 'I imagine that he thought the Duke might go to join her,' noted Baldwin; a thought alarming enough to ensure that the police were retained for the time being.[2]

The arrival of Fruity Metcalfe in January 1937 did something to relieve the tension at Schloss Enzesfeld. He was not allowed to bring his wife, however, on the somewhat unlikely grounds that it might be mentioned in the papers if he did. The Duke made it clear he wanted no woman around the Schloss.[3] The true reason for this became clear to Metcalfe early in February when Mrs Simpson berated the Duke for having an affair with his hostess, Kitty Rothschild – 'This is d—d funny, but I can tell you it was no joke last night.'[4] Mrs Simpson's nerves were every bit as frayed as those of the Duke, and she found some relief in nagging him ruthlessly over the telephone. 'I feel so sorry for him, he never seems able to do what she considers the right thing,' commented Metcalfe, and again a week later: 'God, that woman's a bitch, she'll play hell with him before long.'[5]

Meanwhile hundreds of letters a day poured in, most of them hostile, some viciously so, in particular in their attacks on Mrs Simpson. The majority were intercepted by the staff but the Duke saw some and was aghast: all his life he had been fawned on and flattered, suddenly to find himself execrated was a painful experience. The press was even worse. 'The papers (the bad ones) are too horrible and so mischievous about David,' the Queen wrote to Queen Mary. 'He doesn't realize that they are doing so much harm I feel sure, and thinks that Beaverbrook and Rothermere are "on his side" and worth cultivating.'[6] To the royal family in London it seemed as if the Duke was deliberately fomenting publicity so as to advertise his grievances; to the Duke it was equally obvious that 'those in power' were using the press to boost the monarchy at his expense.[7] In fact the press needed no encouragement from either party to report or invent scandalous titbits about the story which had done so much to boost their circulation. To the Duke, however, it all seemed part of the giant conspiracy which had driven him from the throne and now sought to extinguish him altogether. He was, reported Legh, generally in good spirits, but 'I cannot pretend that he is in a normal state of mind, and on occasions he becomes most excited and causes me much anxiety'.[1] 'I do hope David's nerves will stand the strain of waiting so long,' wrote George VI apprehensively.[2]

Not all the mail was hostile. Lloyd George sent Christmas greetings from a former minister 'who holds you in as high esteem as ever, regards you with deep and loyal affection [and] deplores the shabby and stupid treatment accorded to you'.[3] Lloyd George's championship of Edward VIII had earned him a bulging post bag, nearly all supporting his stand. The most common theme was that of a Mr Hawkins who said he would be loyal to George VI but 'our hearts will be with that great socialist Edward', while another correspondent said the late King's two greatest enemies had been 'Finance and Moscow'; finance because he supported the poor and unemployed, Moscow because he was 'the most formidable obstacle to Communism in the country'.[4] Fortified by such messages, Lloyd George contemplated a campaign in favour of the ex-King. 'Nothing would suit me better than to have a damn good fight at the end of my days . . . I will make such a stink that the Coronation won't count for very much.'[5]

He got no encouragement from the Duke. Nor did Mr Gordon of Brighton when he wrote to propose the setting up of a 'King's Party' which would make public its support for the former monarch. 'The suggestions do not commend themselves to His Royal Highness,' replied a private secretary coolly.[6] Nor did many other similar proposals. In the dying weeks of his reign he had refrained from any action that might embarrass his successor, and he did not intend to change his ways now that he was in exile. The furthest he would go was to welcome the setting up of an informal committee, which met at the Marlborough Club under the aegis of Godfrey Thomas with Monckton and Philip Guedalla among the members, to consider how best to counter the attacks of the press.[7]

The many accounts that survive of this period show how effectively he disguised his depression from the outside world. Mensdorff dined at the Schloss just before Christmas and was made to watch old films about the Emperor Franz Joseph's jubilee; he found the Duke 'well and in fairly good spirits'.[8] Queen Marie of Romania met him a month later at the British Legation: 'He was looking well and . . . seemed less jumpy than he used to be –

but he does look rather sad.'[1] Another month again and Amery lunched with him. He was 'in great spirits ... He shows no outward sign of strain, and it may be that he really doesn't care.'[2] Aird, who spent February in the Schloss, found the Duke rather pathetically looking at his official diary of the previous year. He had just been to a dinner for Anglo-American businessmen and Aird noticed that he seemed to welcome the chance to attend such 'tawdry but worthy shows'. He was much more at ease with the Americans present than with the British; a fact Aird somewhat chauvinistically explained as being because 'HRH naturally likes common people, perhaps because he feels assured he is superior to them. He now uses frequently some terrible common slang such as "good egg".'[3] It must have been at this same dinner that the young English journalist Douglas Reed was presented to the Duke. All the other Englishmen had been asked what school they had been to, and Reed, who had left school at thirteen, was awaiting with some relish the chance to answer. Years of experience warned the Duke, however: 'What paper do you represent?' he asked.[4]

In the first two or three weeks he found it particularly hard to find any occupation. He consoled himself, said Legh, by 'playing the jazz drums very loud and long to a gramophone record; he also drank quite a lot of brandy, and performed his celebrated imitation of Winston Churchill trying to persuade him not to abdicate: "Sir, we must fight ..."'[5] By the time Metcalfe had arrived, the household had settled into a routine of golf, skiing or shopping in Vienna by day, poker and conversation until 4 a.m. by night. Metcalfe found the Duke's energy as phenomenal as ever, and was perpetually exhausted, but 'never have I found him easier or more charming, he is at his very best, and quite in his old form. I must say I am devoted to him.'[6] Every time Metcalfe settled down late at night to write to his wife, the Duke would come to his room to talk over old times and the wonders of Mrs Simpson. 'It's very pathetic. Never have I seen a man more madly in love.'[7] Food at dinner was cooked by the French chef and was delicious, but breakfast was in the English style; Charles Lambe had to arrange for Fortnum and Mason to send out kippers and six pots of Oxford marmalade.[8]

Walford Selby told Aird that it had been difficult to explain to the Austrian aristocracy why the Duke was staying with a Jew.[9]

Exile

The point does not seem to have caused the Duke any concern; indeed, one somewhat unconvincing report states that he told the Baron he planned to write a book in defence of the persecuted Jews.[1] Kitty Rothschild, however, got on his nerves; helpfulness itself, but always saying she was just about to go and never doing so. Mrs Simpson effectively poisoned the atmosphere between them, and when the Baroness finally did leave, the Duke was on the telephone to Cannes and failed even to say goodbye.[2] 'I feel she will be a dangerous enemy for HRH to have made, especially as he must be in the wrong,' wrote Aird.[3] In fact she remained a good friend, always maintaining that the Duke had been a perfect guest and denying gossip that he had left unpaid a large bill for the telephone.[4]

At the end of March he moved on to the Landhaus Appesbach, near St Wolfgang. 'Gosh, I bet you were glad when you went down that drive for the last time,' wrote Metcalfe, a remark that suggests life at Schloss Enzesfeld had become oppressive in the previous few weeks. He would probably have found life equally gloomy anywhere else, however, and he cannot have been cheered by Metcalfe's report on a visit to Fort Belvedere: the daffodils were out, and the tulips well advanced – 'I went into the house, but it looked so sad, all empty, that I did not stay long.'[5] Life, in fact, was much the same at Appesbach as it had been at Enzesfeld. The only difference was that hiking had taken the place of skiing; 'and I think on the whole you would dislike the hiking most,' the Duke told Aird.[6]

Before this he had received his first royal visitors. Early in February his sister, the Princess Royal, arrived with her husband, Lord Harewood. 'Although they both try their best they do not add to life,' judged Aird, but even so they were 'better than nothing'.[7] It was not an easy visit and made no easier by a malicious story in the *Daily Mirror* about the financial negotiations then going on between the Duke and the royal family. Mrs Simpson rang up in high indignation: 'I tried to calm him,' Harewood told the King, 'but I expect she gave him Hell down the telephone.' 'I have a feeling that David has told her that she will be received by his family with open arms as soon as they are married,' Harewood went on, 'and that his whole future will be jeopardized if she thinks this is not so. I am therefore very much afraid of intimate conversation.'[1] The last sentence contradicts Aird's belief that the main purpose of the visit was to break to the Duke the news that Mrs Simpson would not be received by the royal family even after she had become Duchess of Windsor.[2] If this unpleasant message was delivered, it must have been so sugar-coated that the Duke did not fully take it in.

He was still less likely to get unpalatable truths from the Duke of Kent, who visited him three weeks later. It had at first been proposed that Kent should come in early January, but King George VI vetoed the proposal on the grounds that at last the newspaper interest in the abdication had died down and a visit at this time would make it front-page news again. 'It is too soon after what has happened to take any risks in this way, and we both want David's future life settled in April. The best chance for him to marry Mrs Simpson is by lying low.'[3] The Duke could not accept this explanation. The King, he believed, had been coerced by his advisers into banning something which might result in favourable publicity for the former monarch. 'How can I possibly think otherwise,' he asked his mother, 'or not feel that having got me "down" certain forces who have done their best to achieve this, wish to keep me there.' It was the first reference to the 'great conspiracy' theory which was increasingly to dominate his thoughts. So far the royal family themselves were deemed innocent: 'While not blaming Bertie in any way for the inspiration or the operation of this plan I do feel that he could assert himself a bit more on my behalf . . . I know that he and I could not be on better terms as brothers and that he is watching out for my interests in England in every way he can.'[4]

If he had known rather more about the threats to the divorce proceedings he would have been more tolerant of his brother's apparent timidity. Even before the abdication a solicitor's clerk called Francis Stephenson had served an affidavit on the King's Proctor alleging that the Simpson divorce was founded on collusion and that the decree should therefore not be made absolute. 'It is by no means certain that she will get her divorce,' wrote Neville Chamberlain; 'in fact the probabilities are the other way.'[5] The King's Proctor summoned Stephenson, who said that he was working on his own initiative and based his belief in Edward VIII's adultery with Mrs Simpson 'on rumours he had heard from friends in America on the Stock Exchange'. He had also heard from the same source that Simpson had been paid £100,000 or perhaps £150,000 to let his wife divorce him. The Proctor politely suggested that this could hardly be called conclusive, whereupon Stephenson agreed and abandoned his attempt.[1]

A more serious threat was that of Anthony Cox, who took an obsessive interest in the abdication. Where Stephenson's driving force seems to have been 'Justice must be done', Cox was more concerned that 'The King must be saved from himself'. He began vigorous investigations to prove that the King had committed adultery with Mrs Simpson and found several promising leads but no evidence that would stand up in court.[2] When he in turn appeared before the King's Proctor, the best he could offer was witnesses from a hotel in Budapest who would be prepared to come to London to give evidence provided they were paid £300–£600 each. The Proctor said that no funds were available for such a purpose, nor would it be proper to pay witnesses to give evidence.[3] Mr Cox then too disappeared from the scene.

The King's Proctor, however, felt bound to launch his own investigation. On the issue of collusion, he concluded that the suit had clearly been an arranged one but that there was no evidence to prove this. On adultery, he concentrated on the crew of two yachts, the *Nahlin* and the *Rosaura*. The evidence he secured was reminiscent of another famous divorce case in 1820. '*Non mi recordo*' had been the refrain of Queen Caroline's steward, Majocci; 'I ain't seen nothing,' was the prudent response of all the stewards. One serving in *Rosaura* had thought it odd that they should have adjoining cabins but saw nothing to suggest 'Mrs Simpson was other than a respectable lady'; his counterpart in the *Nahlin*, after careful observation, did no more than conclude that she was 'a personal friend of the King'.[4] With some relief the King's Proctor decided that there were no grounds on which the decree absolute could be refused, but the Attorney General did not give a final ruling on the point until March 1937. At any moment before that there was a real risk of the question being reopened, with results that could have been painful for the Duke.

He said nothing to indicate that the threat was weighing on his mind, but it can never have been wholly forgotten. There were other, more immediate issues to cause him chagrin. He had left

England in such haste that many questions about his future status had not been considered; one by one they were decided, and usually, as he saw it, against his interests. He had assumed, for instance, that since the Duke of York had been his personal ADC when he was King, he would fulfil the same role now the positions were reversed. Harewood wrote to disabuse him. King George VI, he said, took the view that 'it would be looked upon as a slight to you to put you straight into his service thus'. He could not step directly from the throne into the position of a younger son. 'The truth is that such an appointment would be treated as a joke, and neither you nor Bertie want to be looked on in that light.'[1] The logic of Harewood's letter does not seem compelling. It left the Duke 'very upset', wrote Metcalfe. 'He said just now: "Well, I suppose I have no standing of any kind now – I used to be a Field Marshal and an Admiral of the Fleet – but now I'm nothing!!"'[2]

A still unkinder cut came from the Welsh Guards. The King knew that his brother was anxious to retain the Colonelcy of the regiment, and put the question to General Sergison-Brooke, saying that he would like this to be done if it were acceptable to the officers. Sergison-Brooke took soundings and reported that the senior officers did not want the Duke, they felt he had let them down.[3] This was broken to the Duke as tactfully as possible, but he wrote to Queen Mary to say that he was 'hurt and disappointed that they seem to be anxious to have the vacancy of Colonel filled at once and don't seem to care to wait until such time as it would be considered suitable to reappoint me. However, this is only one of many small hurts that have been coming from various quarters lately.'[4] Colonel Beckwith-Smith wrote to assure him how much every Welsh Guardsman, past or present, regretted that he could not continue as their Colonel.[5] The message was no doubt kindly meant but it fed the Duke's suspicions that it was not the Guards' officers who were to blame but that nefarious clique of courtiers whom his brother seemed so reluctant to call to order.

He had also taken it for granted that he would remain a member of the Privy Council. The Law Officers' Department, however, concluded that he had no automatic right to resume his place and, furthermore, that in abdicating he had obviated the constitutional tradition by which close relations of the sovereign were usually

Exile

Privy Councillors.[1] The question was put into the pending tray where it mouldered until the time was long past for any such gesture of trust or friendship. Not everything was lost, however. Mrs Simpson was nervous lest they removed his Garter – 'That is what they did to Beauchamp and people of that sort.'[2]* One of George VI's first acts, however, had been to reappoint his brother as a Royal Knight on 12 December; some doubted whether the reappointment had been necessary, but everyone accepted that it settled the matter for ever.

Almost as insulting as rebuffs of this kind were the offers of employment that flowed in, particularly from the United States. From Detroit came an invitation to open the Zorine Springs nudist colony; he was pressed to become mayor of Chippewa Falls, Wisconsin; the Orpheum Theatre, Los Angeles, offered him and his 'lovely lady' a million dollars and a Hollywood mansion to star in a 'stupendous historical film'. At least the 'peaceful little city of Orlando, nestling among half a hundred lakes in the picturesque citrus heart of Florida' offered nothing except 'a haven of happiness'. Since their letter was addressed to 'Mr Edward Windsor, Balmoral Castle, London', it is perhaps surprising it was received at all.[3]

The Duke had left Windsor on a wave of emotional good will. In the first few weeks of exile he suffered various unpleasant shocks but he assumed that, in so far as anyone was responsible for them, it was those whom he had identified as his enemies: Hardinge and Lascelles, who were now respectively private secretary and deputy private secretary to George VI, from within the court; Baldwin, Lang and Dawson from outside it. His attitude was set out in a long letter which he wrote to the King in mid-January.

> The events of December are past history and you and I have now only the future to look forward to. You have your life as King and you know how hard I have tried to make your succession as easy as possible. And I will throughout your reign (which I hope will be a long and grand one) . . . do all

---

* Lord Beauchamp was hounded from the country as the result of a homosexual scandal; Mrs Simpson seems to have been pointing out the self-evident fact that the Duke's case was very different.

in my power to help and support you . . . For me the future is different. For the first time in my life I shall be very happy – that is, when Wallis and I can get married. Until then it is difficult for both of us . . . and you and the family can help us so much by giving us your support just now and creating a dignified background for our marriage and our married life . . . you and you alone can dispel . . . any of the doubts and rumours that are abroad to the effect that you and Mama disapprove of us and that anyone who does stick to us as friends will have a bad mark against them in your 'book' . . . I doubt your ever having heard that such gossip and rumour are being spread indiscriminately. But believe me, they are, Bertie, and it hurts like the dickens. Of course a great deal of the bunk is levelled at Wallis and I can't take it because you must always think of Wallis and myself as *one* from henceforth . . . and anything said or aimed against her hits me a thousand times harder. So that anything you can do towards putting a stop to all the detrimental bunk will be making it more dignified for our future, and for our sakes let it be known that on the contrary by giving us 'the cold shoulder' or spreading false rumours, people would be getting in wrong with you . . . After all, Wallis and I have committed no crime. All we ask is our married happiness, and then we hope to be of use and service to you and the community later on. I know that you want to help as you've told me so all along, but it's some of the government and the court and other officials who are against us . . . Oh! Bertie, a lot of people are kicking us for the moment and you can stop it all. Please do so quickly for our sakes . . . You can and you must do that.[1]

George VI did want to help but he did also disapprove of the marriage to Mrs Simpson. Left to himself he would probably have gone further than in fact he did to support his brother, but Queen Mary was rigid in her insistence that nothing should be said or done to suggest the royal family condoned the relationship or were prepared to accept Mrs Simpson – married to the Duke or not – as one of them. In this attitude she was supported by her daughter-in-law, the Queen, and abetted by the courtiers. The latter worked diligently to stiffen the King, who they feared might otherwise succumb to his generous instincts and do more than they felt to be prudent in championship of his predecessor. The first few months after the abdication show a melancholy pattern of eroding good will between the royal brothers, with the Duke, isolated, forlorn and increasingly embittered, swinging rapidly from protestations of eternal friendship to the blackest hostility.

For the first few weeks George VI was bombarded by telephone calls as his brother expounded his needs, poured out his woes, or held forth on the various problems of kingship on which he felt his views would be of interest. George VI, a slow thinker and, thanks to his stammer, a still slower speaker, contributed little to these conversations and found them increasingly arduous. 'I had a good long talk with Bertie last evening and was able to ask him to think over a few domestic points as regards myself,' the Duke told his mother.[1] To the King the talk was more long than good. What to his brother was a vitally important link with the outside world, to the King became a dreaded imposition. His increasing impatience was shown towards the end of January when he refused to speak to the Duke before 6.45 p.m. next day as he was too busy. 'It was pathetic to see HRH's face,' wrote Metcalfe. 'He couldn't believe it! He's been so used to having everything done as he wishes.'[2] Urged on by his staff, who felt that the strain on him was too great and who anyway disliked the King receiving advice through other channels than their own, he finally struck. According to Monckton it was he who was entrusted with the delicate task of cutting off the fusillade of calls.[3] The Duke recorded two other versions of what happened. In one it was the King himself who said the telephoning had to stop. 'Are you serious?' asked the Duke. 'Yes, I'm sorry to say I am.'[4] In the other Ulick Alexander telephoned from Sandringham to explain that the conversations made the King nervous. In either case the result was the same. 'Our relations as brothers were, as far as I am concerned, severed,' the Duke later told his brother.[5] The statement was over-dramatic, but there is no doubt that from that moment the Duke ceased to look upon the King as a champion and began to suspect that he must be numbered with his enemies.

But it was financial matters that first put a serious strain on the relationship. When the Duke left England the new King had pledged himself to pay £25,000 a year to his brother if the government did not take on the burden. This promise had been made, however, in the belief that the Duke would otherwise be reduced to relative penury. As it became more clear that this was not the case, the King's advisers urged him to declare the agreement null. Any hope that the government would settle the issue by themselves giving the former King a pension was quickly quashed. Chamberlain told Peacock, even before the abdication, that it was most unlikely and would depend on the acquiescence of the opposition. That acquiescence was not forthcoming.[1] Pierson Dixon, then a young diplomat in Ankara, returned to London in February 1937 to find that opinion in the House of Commons and Whitehall had moved solidly against the Duke and few could be found to support the principle of a pension.[2] Indeed, so strong did feelings run that when those concerned met in Warren Fisher's office on 10 February it was said that, if it became known that the King had himself promised his brother £25,000 a year, there would be a move to cut the Civil List by a similar amount. At the same meeting Allen stated that the Duke had deposited £800,000 abroad, though a large part of it was under the control of Mrs Simpson. Fisher said that an extra £80,000 would shortly be due to the Duke as a result of the balances from the Civil List and the Duchies of Cornwall and Lancaster.[3]

The *Daily Mirror* now came out with the story about the financial agreement which had so upset the Duke.* To him it seemed a typical example of the failure of the authorities in London to protect him, even perhaps of their active wish to harm him. To his brother it seemed more likely that the story had been fed to the *Mirror* by someone who wished to bring pressure on him to honour the agreement – the someone being probably Mrs Simpson. Neither judgment was fair; it is only too easy to understand why both seemed convincing at the time. The King wrote to say how unfortunate the timing was, when the Civil List was about to be debated. 'There seems to be a strong feeling in the House of Commons that the Country shall not provide for you directly or indirectly,' he wrote, adding, 'You see, I think they are still a little sore with you for having given up being King.' It was essential that he should know exactly how the Duke stood financially, 'I understood from

---

* See page 343 above.

you when I signed the paper at the Fort that you were going to be very badly off.'[1]

To the Duke it seemed as if his brother was trying to wriggle out of a moral if not legal obligation. The £25,000 had not been calculated on the basis of his personal fortune, why should that now be taken into account? If it was related to anything it was to a fair rent for Sandringham and Balmoral. 'It would be a grave mistake, if the private means of any member of the Royal Family were to be disclosed at the Select Committee and . . . it would only embarrass you and your advisers if I were to put you in the position of being able to answer questions on this subject.' He stuck to his assertion that he was badly off, 'which I am, considering the position I shall have to maintain and what I have given up'. 'I have kept my side of the bargain,' he concluded, 'and I am sure you will keep yours.'[2]

George VI accepted that in the end the £25,000, or at least the greater part of it after certain deductions, would have to be paid, but he declined to be hurried. When the Select Committee considered the Civil Estimates, he had to be able to tell them that he had made no binding commitment to pay a pension to his brother: 'You know that I don't want to let you down, but . . . I do want you to give me a free hand . . . A new agreement will, of course, have to be arranged legally as soon as the Civil List is passed.'[3] The trouble was that the Duke was no longer certain that the King did not intend to let him down. The unfortunate Monckton, trying to retain the confidence of both parties, found that increasingly each one doubted the other's good intentions and that the Duke in particular was convinced that he was being cheated.

When the Select Committee began to discuss the Civil List, the fact that the Duke of Windsor's name was not included struck some of its members as being unfair if not unacceptable. Churchill knew too much of the background to press any such demand, but he told the Chancellor, Chamberlain, that he must be satisfied that the Duke was going to get his £25,000 a year from one source or another.[4] The discussion dragged on, but early in April Churchill returned to the charge: 'The best solution would surely be that the King should honour his signature about the £25,000 a year, and that the Duke of Windsor should intimate to you that he does not desire to make any request for provision in the Civil List?' he wrote to Chamberlain. Otherwise someone was bound to mention the extent of the Duke's fortune and the Labour Party would argue that, if savings on such a scale could be made, the Civil List could certainly be cut.[1] In some alarm Chamberlain posted off to see the King. In his record of the meeting Wigram wrote that the Chancellor was authorized to tell Churchill that King George VI and his brother were on friendly terms, 'and that HM would look after his brother'.[2] In his diary Chamberlain merely remarked that the Fort Belvedere agreement struck him as 'vague and contradictory' and needing replacement by 'something more specific and carefully prepared. I hope the King will take steps to set about this soon.'[3] Wigram, evidently uncertain how explicit Chamberlain would be, himself went round to see Churchill and told him he could be sure that the King would not let his brother down. Churchill accepted the assurance. 'I therefore hope and trust that all will be well,' he told the Duke.[4]

In the end it was, but there was much bargaining to come and it was 1938 before the agreement was fully worked out. The haggling generated much ill-feeling, but alone could never have accounted for the embittered hatred for his family which the Duke conceived as the day of his marriage grew closer. Until the last moment the Duke shut his eyes to the fundamental refusal of his closest relations to accept, to tolerate even, his future wife. His chagrin was all the more fierce when at last he was forced to acknowledge it.

Mrs Simpson had foreseen their attitude long before. At the end of 1936 she was already expressing her concern about the lack of support the family was likely to give the wedding: 'After all, we have done nothing wrong so why be treated that way?'[5] In every direction, it seemed to her, the Windsors were to be traduced and let down, and she had no doubt that she was the principal target. Even when she tried to get her wax effigy removed from Madame Tussaud's – 'It really is too indecent and so awful to be there' – she could achieve nothing. She could only object, she was told, if so placed as to bring her into hatred, ridicule or contempt, for instance in the Chamber of Horrors. As it was she was grouped with Voltaire, Marie-Antoinette and Joan of Arc; curious companions, perhaps, but giving her no grounds for protest.[6]

It was her belief that the Queen – the Duchess of York, as she always referred to her – was their most inveterate enemy. Channon, on the other hand, was convinced that it was Queen Mary who was most hostile to any recognition of the marriage. He maintained that she hated Wallis Simpson 'to the point of hysteria'; when Lord Queenborough asked her when the Duke of Windsor would return to England she was said to have replied: 'Not until he comes to my funeral.'[1] If the remark had been reported to the Duke, he would have known that his mother could never have thought, still less spoken, such a thing; but he could not comprehend that her love for him was complemented by rigid opposition to his marriage. He told her she was the only member of the family he could fully trust: 'Your letters to me are so sweet and sympathetic that I hope when the time comes you will extend all those feelings you have for me to Wallis. It is no longer a matter for approval or disapproval. I left with dignity, and now Wallis and I are going to live our life together with dignity.'[2] Queen Mary did not reply directly to his implicit question; 'I assure you we are all out to help you in every way we can,' she wrote, 'knowing only too well what a dreadfully difficult time you are going through.'[3]

The help that was all important to him was over his relationship with Mrs Simpson, first and foremost over his wedding. It is difficult to overestimate the significance that he attached to the ceremony. He had, as he saw it, been fortunate enough to win this love of a woman of transcendent quality, fit to grace any position on earth. He had failed her. Instead of the throne which she deserved; instead, at least, of a position of honour in his own country, he had inflicted upon her the hounding of the world's press and ignominious imprisonment in a villa in the south of France. The rest of his life was to be dedicated to making up to her for this betrayal. The first and most significant opportunity would be their wedding.

According to the Duke of Connaught the Duke originally believed that Queen Mary herself would be prepared to come to France for his marriage.[4] It seems almost impossible that he could so have misjudged his mother's sense of propriety, but he was encouraged by his cousin Louis Mountbatten to believe that the King and the other royal Dukes were likely guests: 'I succeeded in fixing a date for your wedding that suited Bertie, George etc,' wrote Mountbatten, but then 'other people stepped in' and the atmosphere changed dramatically.[1] Whether Mountbatten was indulging his characteristically ebullient optimism, or the King really was at one time thinking of attending the wedding, is uncertain; anyway, when Monckton made an approach to Wigram in early April, all illusions were quickly dispelled. Queen Mary had apparently remarked casually that it would be 'rather nice' if there were some sort of religious service; Monckton seized on this to suggest that a royal chaplain should officiate and at least the Dukes of Kent and Gloucester be present. Wigram was outraged. He wrote to Lang to say that to agree to such a request would be to hammer 'a firm nail in the coffin of monarchy'. 'Excuse this outburst,' he said, 'but my religious feelings are really hurt by such monstrous suggestions.' He and Hardinge were 'hand in glove', and they were telling the King that he could shelter behind Baldwin and the Dominion Prime Ministers: 'I am sure they would never advise HM to allow any of his family to be present at such a mock ceremony.'[2]

Whether, left to themselves, ministers would have wished to express any strong views on the issue, is doubtful. Once consulted, however, it was inevitable what their advice would be. Chamberlain and Simon were both emphatic that no member of the family should be present. If any did attend, wrote Simon, it would be taken as proof that they were 'accepting the future Duchess *for all purposes* into the Royal Family'. This would have unfortunate implications: 'If, for example, it is desired to discourage return to this country, absence from the wedding would be indicative of a desire to maintain a certain aloofness.'[3] Baldwin claimed that he had not been directly consulted but told Brownlow that 'he would be anxious regarding public opinion and Press comment' if any of the Princes attended.[4]

King George VI did not need much persuading; quite apart from Simon's subtler arguments he shared Wigram's revulsion from the thought of a member of the family attending a service which would not be accepted by the Church of England. But he dreaded the painful task of telling his brother. 'I have been preparing draft after draft of what I should say and how to put it, so that the news should not hurt his feelings too much,' he told Queen Mary. 'It has been such a worry to me all this time, as he is bound to be very upset about it.'[5] The final version was despatched on 11

Exile

April 1937. He could not do as the Duke wished, he wrote:

> I can't treat this as just a private family matter, however much
> I want to. I am afraid it will not be possible for Harry and
> George or any of the family to come out to your wedding. I
> simply hate having to tell you this; but you must realize that
> in spite of the affection which of course there still is towards
> you personally, the vast majority of people in this country are
> undoubtedly as strongly as ever opposed to a marriage which
> caused a King of England to renounce the throne. You know
> that none of us in the family liked it, and were any of them
> now, after a few months' interval, to come out and, so to
> speak, help you get married, I know that it would be regarded
> by everybody as condoning all that has happened; it would
> place us all in an impossibly false position and would be
> harmful to the Monarchy . . . This is a matter where I can't
> act like a private person and I have had to get advice from
> Ministers . . . Do understand how much I loathe having to do
> this, but with your knowledge of the world, you will appreciate
> the fact that I cannot do anything else.[1]

He was not surprised to hear the King loathed writing this letter,
the Duke replied bitterly. 'I will never understand how you could
ever have allowed yourself to be influenced by the present Government and the Church of England in their continual campaign
against me.' After this insult he felt that he would never wish to
set foot in Britain again. All that remained was to arrange his
marriage in the most dignified way possible. 'I appreciate your
frankness, and there is nothing more for me to say, except that I
shall always be sorry to remember that you did not have the
courage to give me the same support at the start of my new life,
that I so whole-heartedly gave to you at the beginning of yours.'[2]

After this hammer blow, the Duke found little comfort in
Mountbatten's assurance that he had not 'quite given up all hope
yet' that he might be able to attend the wedding,[3] or the protestations of the Duke of Kent: 'You have always been a wonderful
friend to me and you know (I hope) my great affection and regard
for you, and so I am very *sincerely* sad at not being with you on
June 3.'[4] But there was worse besides. The newspapers were abuzz
with speculation about who would be allowed to attend, and

after some anguished pother those courtiers who had been invited decided that they would not put the King in the position of having to grant or refuse permission, but would decline without more ado. 'I am terribly sorry that, largely owing to this damned press, things have developed over here in this way,' wrote Thomas apologetically.[1] Aird, who had already written to accept, heard what was going on and hurriedly recalled his letter. He would not be able to get away from his course at Sheerness, he explained to the Duke, adding in his diary: 'Feel a slight shit at leaving HRH to be married with only the Metcalfes and Walter Monckton at the ceremony.'[2] In fact another old friend, Hugh Lloyd Thomas, had no difficulty in getting permission to attend in a personal capacity, although he was Minister in the Embassy in Paris.[3] Walford Selby, from Vienna, was advised not to go, but his wife was allowed to make the journey.[4]

Lord Brownlow was asked early in May by the Bishop of Lincoln whether he would be going to the wedding. He said he had not yet been invited but supposed he would. The Bishop then said that, as Lord Lieutenant of Lincolnshire, Brownlow could not possibly countenance this masquerade, and that if he did go there would be 'a storm of criticism, censure and hostility' which would force him to resign. Brownlow told this to Harry Crookshank, the Minister of Mines, who disconcerted him by agreeing with the Bishop. To attend the wedding, Crookshank argued, would only 'provoke a further unpleasant and squalid controversy around the Duke of Windsor'. Brownlow duly received his invitation and wrote to the King to ask his wishes. He got no reply, asked Ulick Alexander what was happening, and was told that the courtiers had refused the invitation themselves on their own initiative.[5] Brownlow withdrew his letter, whereupon Hardinge wrote to say: 'His Majesty is grateful to you for your consideration in not asking for a decision from him in the matter to which your letter referred.'[6] In fact the King told Monckton that, while he did not want to rule on the question, he would have liked Brownlow to have attended the wedding and was disappointed when he heard of his refusal.[7] Brownlow cabled to the Duke: 'Fear considerable difficulties here. Letter follows', to which the Duke replied coolly, 'Quite understand. No point in writing.'[8]

The letter followed nonetheless, written 'unwillingly and in a state of considerable embarrassment'. Brownlow realized, he said, that many of his friends would accuse him of ratting, but felt that this was the lesser evil.[1] The Duke did not reply. 'Ratting' was indeed an accusation flung at several of those who refused the invitation by those who were fortunate enough not to receive one. No one emerges with great credit from this episode except for Lloyd Thomas, who made it clear he would attend the ceremony whether given permission or not, and the Duke, who met these humiliating rebuffs with stoical dignity.

The dignity soon ran out. From the time of the abdication the Duke had been nervous about the status of his wife after they eventually married. Monckton urged him not to press the point, advice to which he reluctantly conceded.[2] He was not the only one to speculate. Would Mrs Simpson automatically become a Royal Highness? asked the Duke of Connaught. 'How awful that would be.'[3] In mid-April, after being told that the royal family would not be present at the wedding, the Duke of Windsor wrote to George VI to say: 'Although Wallis's royal title comes automatically with marriage in our case, I hope you will spare us the last and only remaining embarrassment, by having it announced that she will be styled "Her Royal Highness" . . . You know how essential this is for the protocol of foreign countries.'[4]

If he had really felt certain that the royal title came automatically upon marriage he would hardly have placed so much emphasis on the need for the King to pronounce it formally. He would have done better to continue to take it for granted and not invite rejection, but he cared much too much about the issue to accept a situation in which there would be any ambiguity. When Mrs Simpson wrote to say that Queen Mary wished to deny her 'the extra chic' of being styled HRH, she added that it was 'the only thing to bring me back in the eyes of the world'.[5] The Duke accepted this, and by admitting the possibility that it might be denied, he made it probable that it would be. The officers of the law, however, took some convincing that there was any basis on which the title could be refused his wife.

Wigram put the question to Granville Ram, of the Office of the Parliamentary Council, in mid-January 1937. Would Mrs Simpson automatically become HRH on marrying the Duke of Windsor? 'The King is certainly of the opinion that such a title requires his consent.'[1] Ram's reply was categoric. The question had been settled by the statement in *The Times* of 28 April 1923 that 'in accordance with the general settled rule, that a wife takes the status of her husband, Lady Elizabeth Bowes Lyon on her marriage has become Her Royal Highness the Duchess of York'.[2] But things were quite different then, protested Wigram: 'as the Duke of Windsor does not come under the Royal Marriages Act, perhaps the Home Secretary might see fit to advise another course'.[3] Ram replied that he could see no difference between the two marriages in point of law. 'The title seems to me to follow, not from the King's consent, but from the validity of the marriage . . . I sincerely hope that the Home Secretary's ingenious mind may find some way of reaching a more satisfactory conclusion, but for the life of me, I cannot see how ever he will achieve it.'[4]

Wigram now appealed to Simon, admitting that the case was not a strong one but that 'HM hopes you will find some way to avoid this title being conferred'.[5] At first Simon saw no way of obliging, except by depriving the Duke himself of the title of HRH: 'I should not have thought it possible . . . to have put the Duke in one position and his wife in another.'[6] But he was not known as Sir John Snake for nothing. On 5 April he drew up a memorandum which argued that the title of HRH should be applied only to members of the royal family who were *within* the line of succession. 'Why should ladies curtsey to a Duchess who cannot possibly be Queen?'[7] Maurice Gwyer, also of the Parliamentary Council, was not impressed. 'I should have thought myself that an attempt to deprive the Duke's wife of the title of HRH would have the most disastrous results,' he told Wigram. 'I have no doubt at all that it would be popularly regarded as an attempt to strike at the Duke through his wife, and resented accordingly . . . It would be impossible to imagine a more public or deadly slight.'[8]

Simon wavered. Would it not be best to let sleeping dogs lie, he asked, and allow Mrs Simpson to assume the title automatically? Wigram had no doubts about the answer. The marriage was not likely to last a long time, he argued; if all the Duke's wives were to become HRH and bear their titles away with them as a choice fragment of the alimony, then what would become of the monarchy?[9] This conviction, that the marriage would not last long, seems to have been an important factor in shaping the views of the royal family. King George VI saw the issue with characteristic clarity, even if a fine indifference to the law. The question was, he told Baldwin: 'Is she a fit and proper person to become a Royal Highness after what she has done in this country; and would the country understand it if she became one automatically on marriage? ... I and my family and Queen Mary all feel that it would be a great mistake to acknowledge Mrs Simpson as a suitable person to become Royal. The Monarchy has been degraded quite enough already.'[1]

Chamberlain and Baldwin were initially as hesitant as Simon while Warren Fisher and Horace Wilson opposed the proposal: 'Theirs was a sentimental point of view that the working classes would think that The King was kicking his brother when down,' explained Wigram.[2] But eventually everyone was cajoled into line. Even Gwyer agreed that the 'vulgar press propaganda and photographs issued by the Duke of Windsor's press department' had so far forfeited public sympathy that there would be no resentment at the decision.[3] The legal justification was minimal, but they would get away with it, seems to have been the resigned conclusion of the law officers of the Crown. Curiously enough, the most robust support for the King's position came from Winston Churchill, who told Wigram that any government to be found in England would advise against creating the Duchess HRH. 'The fact that such an issue was still being proposed would certainly be an obstacle to the Duke's wishes in other respects.'[4]

It remained to break the news to the Duke. Monckton was asked to prepare the way by warning him of the likely outcome of the legal wrangle. 'The Duke was at first rather excited, but afterwards asked Walter Monckton to see The King and tell him how much he would resent it,' Hardinge noted.[5] The King's letter followed. The first draft laid heavy stress on the fact that the Duke, not being in the line of succession himself, had no right to be styled HRH, and that the only way this privilege could be retained was by issuing Letters Patent specifically limiting it to him alone.[6] 'The King evidently found it a great relief to be able to tell his brother that so far from taking anything away, what he had done was to give him a title from which he would otherwise have been debarred,' noted Chamberlain, with what one must suppose was a touch of irony.[7] King George VI evidently felt on reflection that this was not a point he wished to labour, the final version of his letter was considerably shorter.

'This is a nice wedding present,' was the Duke's bitter comment when the letter was handed over.[1] His immediate reaction was to renounce his own right to style himself HRH, but Monckton and Mrs Simpson between them convinced him that to do so would achieve nothing except to give satisfaction to his enemies. For the moment he contented himself with firing back a rejoinder claiming that he was HRH by right, not Letters Patent, and that he considered the new Letters to have no validity.[2] But this insult to his wife, as he saw it, rankled in his mind throughout the ceremony and honeymoon and finally led to an outburst of rage which destroyed whatever relationship survived between him and his family in England.

The first salvo was fired at Queen Mary a week before the wedding. He began his letter 'Dear Mama', then relented and changed 'Dear' to 'Darling'. But that was the last concession. Her letters to him, he said, read as if they were written 'to a young man who is stopping for a while in a foreign country in order to learn the language'. That was disheartening enough, but his brother's behaviour left him 'definitely disgusted' . . .

> And to be quite frank, many things that I have heard of your attitude do not encourage me. You are more than right in your supposition that I am happy now. And I can further assure you that for the first time in my life I am happy and can honestly say that I look forward to the future.
>
> Thank you for your good wishes, but it saddens me that the present conditions do not make me feel that they ring very true.
>
> Your disappointed son. David.[3]

After brooding for a few weeks the Duke struck vengefully again. His mother had not even bothered to send a wedding present, he complained. 'I was bitterly hurt and disappointed that you virtually ignored the most important event of my life.' George VI had consistently humiliated him ever since the abdication, he claimed. The King had tried to shelter from the charge that he had insulted the Duke in the eyes of the world by pretending that he had acted only on the advice of his government, 'a sorry enough show of weakness', but there was ample evidence that 'this humiliating policy is not only the policy of the present government, but is also Bertie's personal attitude towards myself, and further, I regret to say, your attitude and that of the whole of my family. You must realize by this time, that as there is a limit to what one's feelings can endure, this most unjust and uncalled for treatment can have had but one important result; my complete estrangement from all of you.'[1]

Queen Mary showed the letter to the King, who wrote to say how much pain it had caused her. The Duke could not really believe that his family wanted to humiliate him. Everything the King had done had been '*absolutely* necessary for the sake of the country'. The Duke did not realize what a shock he had given to the monarchy: 'How do you think I liked taking on a rocking throne, and trying to make it steady again? It has not been a pleasant job, and it is not finished yet.' Let them now forget what had happened and work together for the future, 'and if you do want to let yourself go, do write to me and not Mama, as it makes her absolutely miserable'.[2]

The Duke was beyond the power of dulcet phrases, and found in his brother's letter only fresh reason for indignation. He picked up the statement that he had made his mother miserable. 'Have you ever stopped to think how unhappy I have been made by the family's treatment of me?' he asked. He listed all his grievances, including the award of a Coronation medal when none was offered to his wife, and went on:

> I do not agree with your description of the throne as 'tottering'. I know it has not been easy for the Monarchy to adjust itself to the trend of the times, and I do not think that even my most vindictive enemies would deny that I have done a great deal to preserve the system, over which you now preside . . . I have always felt that one of the sources of power of the Monarchy in Great Britain has been the fact that we were a united family, with no public discords and working together as one for the welfare of our people. What other motive had I in abdicating except a patriotic one, and to avoid a conflict between the Crown and the Government? As you knew when I left in December, that I was going to marry Wallis, it would

have been far better had you expressed your personal opinion of this marriage to me privately at that time, rather than publicly later.[1]

Overtures from other members of the family were rebuffed with equal harshness. A wedding present of a Fabergé box was returned to the Duke of Kent with the sharp retort: 'The only boxes I happen to be collecting now are those that can be delivered on the ears.'[2] Nor did a cable of congratulations win a kinder response. He did not doubt the sincerity of the Kents' good wishes, wrote the Duke, but they were 'not at all in tune with the attitude that has been taken by Mama, by Bertie, and by the rest of the family'. Nor had the Duke of Kent done anything to show he wished to follow a different line. 'I tell you, here and now, that I will never forgive or forget the lead Bertie has given you all in your behaviour to me ever since I left England.'[3] In the summer of 1937 there was no doubt in the Duke's mind that his family had betrayed him and that he had done with them for ever.

Meanwhile the decree absolute had at last come through on 3 May 1937. 'I am into the last week now, thank God, and I am too excited to know whether I am coming or going,' the Duke wrote to Thomas a few days earlier.[4] He was going, and on 4 May he went. The Orient Express was stopped forty-five kilometres from Paris so as to avoid the press and the Duke continued his journey unmolested to join Mrs Simpson at the Château de Candé in Touraine. Candé was a renaissance castle which had been transformed by its multi-millionaire owner, Charles Bedaux, into a miracle of modern comforts with a pipe-organ costing $40,000, a $15,000 telephone system, avant-garde American plumbing and the vault transformed into a bar. Bedaux had made his fortune and won the hatred of organized labour by inventing the time-and-motion study and showing big business around the world how to apply it. He was an important figure in the United States but was anxious to establish closer links with the leadership in Germany and was looked at askance by the intelligence services of France and Britain.[5] The Duke was blindly unaware of this, as indeed was King GeorgeVI, who thought that a castle in Touraine sounded a far more suitable place for his brother's marriage than a villa near Cannes. When Bedaux, who was a friend of Herman Rogers, offered his château for the wedding it was accepted with alacrity. Bedaux's only condition was that it should be stated publicly that the Duke and Mrs Simpson were there as his guests, 'for I am a hard-working business man and in these critical times, if the erroneous thought were to penetrate the public that we rented Candé for the purpose intended, it would be sure to have a disastrous effect on my business career'.[1]

The Duke's hope of getting a royal chaplain to perform the wedding service had been rapidly shattered by his brother. His second choice, the Rev. Martin Andrews whose parish was in the Duchy of Cornwall, regretfully refused on the grounds that 'it would be letting the church down, and as long as I hold office in the church I must keep the rules, however cruel they may seem'.[2] Though after the ceremony a bevy of clergymen protested how pleased they would have been to conduct the service if only they had been invited, at the time it proved difficult to find anyone prepared to defy the church hierarchy by giving a religious marriage to a divorced person with a husband, let alone two husbands, living. At one time the only candidate seemed to be the Rev. Rolfe Davies, who rested his claim on the fact that 'The late Sir John Williams, who was Physician Accoucheur in 1894, was a first cousin of my father's'.[3] Then the Rev. J. A. Jardine, a turbulent priest from Darlington, offered his services. Lang described him as 'a seeker of notoriety, a Kensitite at heart'. How, the Archbishop enquired, could a man who had been King of England a few months before have 'so far lost his dignity as to ask a man of this sort to celebrate his marriage?'[4] The Duke's answer might have been that he did so because the Church of England made it impossible for a man of any other sort to play the part. In fact both he and Monckton thought that Jardine seemed a decent and straightforward man; it was only when he embarked on a lecture tour in the United States to delight audiences with the inside story of the Windsor wedding that they began to wonder if they had chosen well.

Fruity Metcalfe was best man, to replace the royal 'supporters' the Duke had expected. Metcalfe and his wife, the Bedaux, Walter Monckton, Aunt Bessie Merryman, Lady Selby, George Allen, the young equerry Dudley Forwood and Herman and Katherine Rogers made up the total congregation at the wedding. Outside, more than two hundred journalists including Winston Churchill's son Randolph (who in fact was more often inside than outside) vied for what scraps of news might emanate from the château. Cecil Beaton arrived the day before the ceremony to take the photographs; he hoped to be asked to stay for the wedding, but invitation came there none. He talked late into the night with Mrs Simpson and decided she 'not only has individuality and personality, but *is* a personality – a strong force. I find she is intelligent within her vast limitations . . . She has obviously a tremendous admiration for the Duke and considers him one of the greatest brains . . . of our times. She admires his character, his vitality and is determined to love him, though I feel she is not in love with him.'[1]

A bogus renaissance chest adorned with plump caryatids was hauled out to provide an altar. 'The Duke, like a little boy home from school for the holidays, in staccato tones would exclaim: "Marvellous – that's marvellous – couldn't be better – but put it further back – put it here – there – no, a little more this way" – and completely lacking in self-consciousness he would get down on hands and knees to tuck in the carpet under the altar.' The caryatids were swathed in a coffee-coloured table cloth from Budapest which the indignant lady's maid had to unpack from one of Mrs Simpson's trunks. Constance Spry and her minions swamped the room in an avalanche of flowers. Beaton then photographed the Duke. 'His expression, though intent, was essentially sad, tragic eyes belied by impertinent tilt of nose. He has common hands – like a little mechanic – weather-beaten and rather scaly and one thumb-nail is disfigured. His hair at forty-five [in fact he was almost forty-three] is as golden and thick as it was at sixteen. His eyes, fiercely blue, do not seem to focus properly – are bleary in spite of their brightness and one is much brighter than another.'[2]

For reasons best known to herself Mrs Simpson had on 8 May changed her name by deed poll to Wallis Warfield. On 3 June Queen Mary wrote in her diary: 'Alas! the wedding day in France of David and Mrs Warfield . . . We all telegraphed to him.'[3]

After the service Walter Monckton took the new Duchess aside and told her that she was deeply disliked in England because she had been responsible for the King abandoning his throne: 'If she made him, and kept him, happy all his days, all that would change; but if he were unhappy nothing would be too bad for her.' She received this somewhat direful prophecy simply and kindly, recorded Monckton, just saying: 'Walter, don't you think I have thought of all that? I think I can make him happy.'[1]

20

Married Life

I T IS TODAY TAKEN FOR GRANTED THAT ANY ABLE-bodied man in his mid-forties will wish to be actively at work. Even in 1937 the concept of the idle rich was more dishonoured in the breach than the observance. Many of those who had and needed no paid employment were to some extent involved in the management of their estates; even those who were not were kept on the move by a routine of hunting, shooting, fishing and the delights of the London season. All this the Duke of Windsor had forfeited. It was not merely Othello's occupation gone, but Bertie Wooster deprived of the Drones' Club. In time he was to construct a new framework for his existence but at first he had nothing but the Duchess and infinite leisure to brood upon his grievances. It was not enough; either for him or for his unfortunate wife, who had to bear the burden of his restless idleness.

He never admitted that life was less than perfect, so far at least as his marriage was concerned. There were those who said that the Duke had given up so much for love that he could not afford even to admit the possibility that he had made a mistake. Speaking of his daughter Sarah, married against his will to the comedian, Vic Oliver, Winston Churchill said grimly: 'Like the ill-starred Duke of Windsor, she has done what she liked and now she has to like what she has done.'[1] Yet it was Churchill too who, two years later, found the Windsors 'entirely happy and as much in love with each other as ever'.[2] Monckton professed himself baffled by the Duke's devotion – 'He could understand Helen of Troy but he could not understand this. She had a nice figure and was well preserved, but what was there so wonderful in her?'[3] – but that the devotion was undiminished by time he accepted absolutely. 'He . . . is obviously intensely in love with his wife,' William Bullitt, the American Ambassador in France, told his President.[4]

But he still had to think of something to do. After breaking the journey for a day in Venice, the married couple took their honeymoon at Wasserleonburg, a castle in Carinthia belonging to a cousin of Lord Dudley's, Count Paul Munster. 'We are passing a very pleasant and peaceful summer here,' the Duke told Godfrey Thomas, '. . . there is plenty of relaxation in the shape of mountain-climbing, fishing, golf, tennis and then sun-bathing and the swimming pool for one when one feels lazy.' It was near enough to Salzburg for a trip to hear *Fidelio* and to Venice for an occasional day's bathing in the sea.[1] Monckton visited them in August and found them 'both really well and happy'. He urged them to find somewhere in the area where they could settle, temporarily at least, and where the Duke could scythe his own grass rather than somebody else's: 'it is going to be difficult to keep his time occupied, but she is genuinely trying to help – and though it is early days, I was honestly impressed and feel happier about them than I expected'. The Duke's principal worry at that moment seemed to be a letter from McMahon – 'the fellow who threw a revolver at him in the Park' – protesting his loyalty and suggesting the Duke might like to give him a helping hand. Monckton urged the Duke not to reply.[2]

From Wasserleonburg they moved on to Budapest and Vienna and then back to France, where they were to make their home until the war. Within a few days of their return on 28 September, they had their first visit from a British minister. 'I don't believe in deserting friends,' Hore-Belisha told Liddell Hart,[3] and without wasting time consulting his colleagues, he called on the ex-King at the Hôtel Meurice. Nothing much was said, but the contact with official London was immensely important to the Duke. Until they took a house in Versailles in February 1938, the Meurice was their regular base when they were in Paris. Then, at the end of 1938, they leased a house in the Boulevard Suchet near the Bois de Boulogne: a solid, respectable mansion in Louis XVI style, with an imposing marble staircase and salons suitable for entertaining on the grandest scale. 'Although we naturally do not publish the names of the guests we have been inviting to our private dinner parties,' the Duke told Rickatson-Hatt, who was acting as his unofficial publicity agent, 'a list of them would be found to include Ambassadors, Ministers, *Hommes des Lettres*, and an ex-Prime

Minister of France. It might be useful to allude to this when reporting our move to the South.'[1] In fact, according to the Duke's secretary, Dina Hood, they entertained rarely, eschewed night clubs, casinos or race meetings, dined only with close friends and 'led as peaceful and unobtrusive a life as it was possible for them to do'.[2]

'The South' was La Cröe, a substantial white villa set in twelve acres of land in Antibes a few miles from Cannes. It had been built seven years before by a British newspaper proprietor, Sir Pomeroy Burton, who had carved a swimming pool from the rocks and installed a dining room to seat twenty-four, a swan-shaped bath and various other appurtenances of gracious living. Herman and Katherine Rogers lived nearby, as well as Somerset Maugham, and Maxine Elliott with whom Churchill habitually stayed. Thelma Furness caused a slight stir by taking a villa in the vicinity: 'It is a little silly of her,' commented the Windsors' old friend, Martin Scanlon, '. . . but I suppose she has the right to do as she pleases.'[3] All the Duke's favourite possessions from Fort Belvedere and York House were sent to La Cröe, the Duchess redecorated vigorously, it became a home.

It also had overtones of a palace. Churchill was amused to find 'everything extremely well done and dignified. Red liveries, and the little man himself dressed up to the nines in the Balmoral tartan with dagger and jabot, etc. When you think that you could hardly get him to put on a black tie and short coat when he was P of W, one sees the change in the point of view.'[4] There were sixteen servants, including two chauffeurs, an English butler and a French chef. When Dina Hood took dictation she was expected to stand, for as much as an hour at a time.[5]

The Windsors dined with Maxine Elliott in January 1938 when Churchill was staying there. Lloyd George came over too. 'You have a strange party tonight, my dear,' commented Churchill. 'It consists entirely of *ci-devant*. Ex-kings, ex-prime-ministers, ex-po-liticians. It is like Voltaire.' The writer, Vincent Sheean, was a fellow guest. He said that the Duke dominated the conversation, which was 'lively, well-informed and sensible throughout'. There was a passionate discussion about the welfare of the Welsh coal-miners, in which the Duke held forth on their needs and the harshness of their existence. Sheean felt that he 'wished to see them clean, healthy and contented, as you might wish your horses or dogs to be; to him they were not men and brothers'.[1]

Later that same year Harold Nicolson was staying with Somerset Maugham when the Windsors came to dinner. The Duke entered with his 'swinging naval gait, plucking at his bow tie'. They were late and he excused himself: '"Her Royal Highness couldn't drag herself away." He had said it. The three words fell into the circle like three stones into a pool. Her (gasp) Royal (shudder) Highness (and not one eye dared to meet another).' Nicolson had a long talk with the Duchess and formed the impression that she both wished and intended to return to England. 'I don't want to spend all my life in exile,' she told him.[2] Two days later the visit was returned. Nicolson noticed the large red and white tent surmounted by the Prince of Wales's feathers in which the guests undressed before bathing, the flag similarly bearing the Prince's feathers flying above the house, the Garter banner of the Prince hanging in the hall. '"When Oi became King," he said, "they had to toik it down as there was no Prince of Woiles. So I did not see whoy Oi shouldn't have it here!" I saw why. But he didn't. It is his insensitiveness to such things which brought on all the trouble.' The food was elaborate: melon with tomato ice in it, eggs with crab sauce, chicken with avocado pear salad, a pudding which only Queen Alexandra knew how to make, fruits. The Duke ate nothing but waited patiently for his cup of tea at five o'clock.[3] In spite of this abstinence, Nicolson thought he looked 'epileptic – a brick red face against which his fair hair and eyelashes look artificial'.[4]

The other guests were Lord Sefton and the Buists, *habitués* of Fort Belvedere and for that matter participants in the *Nahlin* cruise. Though the Duke might congratulate himself on entertaining ambassadors and former prime ministers, it was old cronies who composed his regular court. The press announced that he had invited a British workman with his family to spend Christmas 1938 with them because he was anxious to spend a holiday 'in the company of one of the ordinary people of his country'. The Duke not unreasonably remarked that the holiday would be thoroughly uncomfortable for host and guest alike. Apart from the butler, the nearest approach to a British workman in the house that Christmas was Lord Brownlow.[5]

When Nicolson told the Duke that he was going back to London the next day 'his eye twitched in pain'.[1] Raymond Mortimer, staying with Maugham on another occasion, described the Duke as 'wretched and sad . . . he wanted to know what was going on in England'.[2] The Duke was not wretched, for most of the time he was, in fact, in high spirits and without regrets. But he was homesick. Like his father, he did not like foreigners – except the Americans, who did not count. In spite of his record of long holidays abroad, he felt that Britain was the only place to live. It is interesting to note as he became older how he grew into his father's prejudices and mannerisms, even to the short temper and rather brutal humour from which he had himself often suffered. Dudley Forwood, who had come to the Duke from the Embassy in Vienna, was roundly abused when he made a muddle over the cars. When he bowed for the first time he was told: 'You look like a randy duck, now do it properly.' One of the Duke's favourite jokes was provided by a roll of lavatory paper which, when pulled, played 'God Save The King'. The Duke would lurk outside the lavatory door and bellow 'Stand to attention!' when the unsuspecting guest pulled at the paper.[3]

The Lindberghs dined with the Windsors in Paris early in 1939. They found the Duke obsessed with the danger of courting a Russian alliance, though he darted at such speed from one subject to another that any coherent conversation was impossible. 'He seemed to me under a strain,' wrote Anne Lindbergh, 'like a man struggling with some problem, distractedly talking from habit – genuinely nice feelings and sometimes *extremely* apt perceptive comments flashing out of this confusion and disorder. Hamlet, I kept thinking.' He explained that they had to be in Paris because so many people came from London to see them and they could not all be expected to go to the south of France. From this the Lindberghs deduced that nobody came to see them.[4] The deduction might have been a fair one in 1937 but was no longer so in 1939. Monckton had decided that, if the Duke could not visit London, then it was important that London should visit him. Some, like Philip Sassoon, had to be shamed into going; others, like Duff Cooper, were more than ready. Halifax made the journey, Baldwin said he was too old to travel but sent a Christmas card. 'I didn't want an old friendship to die in my hands,' he told Monckton. 'Of course she will look over his shoulder and say "That old b—!" (or whatever may be the Baltimore equivalent) "pitch it on the fire!" '[1] In November 1938 Chamberlain, now Prime Minister, called on the Duke in Paris. The visit had no particular significance, said Halifax's private secretary, Oliver Harvey,[2] but to the Duke it possessed great importance, for it gave him a chance to raise the subject that was always near the top of his mind, the moment of his return to England.

If only because it would expose him to heavy taxation the Duke had always known that he was unlikely to be able to live permanently in England. He told the actress Lilli Palmer that the country where he really wanted to make his home was the United States, but that his wife disliked it, so they had compromised on France.[3] But equally he had never envisaged a future in which long periods each year would not be spent in Britain. Churchill encouraged him in this belief. The Attorney General had declared formally that there could be no obstacle to the Duke's return, he wrote, 'so I earnestly hope that it will not be many months before I have the honour to pay my respects to you at the Fort'.[4] It was for Fort Belvedere that the Duke above all felt nostalgia, so it must have caused him a special pang when an anonymous correspondent wrote to tell him that all was desolation, the swimming pool full of leaves, weeds growing between the pavings: 'The King has said he is going to let the house and grounds go to ruins so bad that you will not be able to live in it again. I think this is wicked.'[5]

No one disputed that he would eventually be free to return whenever he wanted, the question was one of timing. It is difficult to work out exactly where everyone stood on this issue because the word 'return' was used promiscuously to refer to fleeting visits, longer stays or permanent residence. When Monckton told the King in August 1937 that 'they are not considering the possibility of a return within 5 years',[6] it seems improbable that he meant the Duke had accepted that he should not set foot in England during that period, yet this was certainly what the King hoped would be the case. The royal family were resolved to keep the Windsors out of the country for as long as possible. They knew the Duke still had a vociferous group of supporters who would agitate on his behalf if given the opportunity provided by his presence in England, they knew too that this would inevitably provoke counter-demonstrations, aimed particularly at the Duchess. Whether the Duke was acclaimed or the Duchess reviled, it would create controversy and redound to the discredit of the monarchy. The only safe solution was to defer their return until public interest had died down and a visit could be treated as part of the normal course of things. By this means, too, the unpleasant moment of confrontation was postponed when it would become finally obvious to everyone that the Duchess of Windsor was not to be received at Buckingham Palace or Marlborough House.

The Duke's friends and advisers saw the point of this. Monckton urged a long residence abroad, Brownlow recommended that he should postpone return for as long as possible: 'A premature or ill-timed visit might well leave a scar of sorrow and disappointment you might find difficulty in removing from your memory.'[1] The King spared no pains to ensure that his ministers took the same point of view. When Chamberlain, Inskip and Hoare stayed at Balmoral in September 1937, George VI told them that Beaverbrook was trying to get the Duke back to England. 'I told all 3 of my Ministers that I did not wish to be let down, and that after all ... I did step into the breach and that I was not the culprit for what happened. I am sure they all 3 understood and are very much alive to the fact that David cannot come back here. I have been worried about all this for ages but ... I really do think they do see how important it is to prevent any untoward and premature return.'[2]

The word 'premature' begged a multitude of questions. By the end of 1937 the Duke was sufficiently impatient to demand that a definite date be fixed after which he would be free to visit England. He wrote to Chamberlain, angrily repudiating any suggestion that the allowance he was to receive from the King should be linked to his promise not to return without the specific approval of the government; 'I should have thought that my record as Prince of Wales and as King was sufficient to convince anyone that I am a man of my word and that there was no necessity to impose financial sanctions on me.' He had told the King already that he would give warning in advance as to when he was coming, that he 'would scrupulously avoid doing anything which might in any way cause embarrassment to him or the Government', and that he had at present no thought of living in Britain. What more could reasonably be asked of him?[1] The Prime Minister's reply was conciliatory, but promised little in the way of settling the Duke's grievance.[2]

There the matter was allowed to rest until August 1938, when the Duke renewed battle. He had now been away for twenty months, he reminded Chamberlain, and 'I need hardly tell you as an Englishman how distasteful voluntary residence in a foreign country without a defined object can be'. He had only stayed away so as to allow his brother to establish himself on the throne. That had surely now been achieved, and he proposed to pay a short visit to England in November.[3] The Prime Minister received this letter just before he went to Balmoral where Walter Monckton was also invited. Monckton told the Duke that Chamberlain's long-term object was to see him treated as a younger brother who would relieve George VI of some of his royal functions. The King, though thinking November was still too early for a first visit, did not seem fundamentally opposed to the Prime Minister's view. The Queen, however, felt quite plainly 'that it was undesirable to give the Duke any effective sphere of work. I felt then, as always, that she naturally thought she must be on her guard because the Duke of Windsor ... was an attractive, vital creature who might be the rallying point for any who might be critical of the new King.'[4]

After the Balmoral conference King George VI wrote to his brother to say that he would never oppose a visit on personal grounds, but that the question of the national interest was one for the government. Every month that went by lessened the chance of any hostile demonstration that might mar the Duke's visit, and therefore 'I agree with the Prime Minister that the spring or early summer of next year would be a better moment'.[5] Whether the King agreed with the Prime Minister or, more probably, the Prime Minister with the King, the two men presented a united front. Chamberlain told the Duke that he too felt the first half of 1939 would be a better time for a successful visit, and would give a chance for public opinion to be prepared.[6] The Duke had no doubt where the responsibility for the decision rested and told Monckton that he could not bring himself to write to the King on the subject.[7] To Chamberlain he suggested a visit in March or April 1939. He agreed public opinion should be prepared: 'So much has been unofficially written and said to poison the minds of British people against us, that a carefully and judiciously planned publicity to counteract this would not only help to undo a great wrong done to us, but would also avoid the danger to which you refer, that of would-be mischief-makers exploiting our first visit ... for sensational purposes.'[1]

The news that the Windsors might soon be visiting Britain inevitably stirred up all those who felt themselves passionately involved one way or the other. The great majority of the letters the Duke received welcomed the prospect but there was plenty of hostile comment too, including menacing messages such as that of S. Game from Kensington to the Duchess: 'If you value your health, don't ... There are hundreds of us in Great Britain who have never forgiven you for ruining the life of that unhappy little Ex-King of England.'[2] Other loyal friends like Colin Davidson confirmed that the threat of unpleasantness at least, if not of violence, was a real one – there would be hostile crowds and rotten eggs might be thrown.[3] Lord Harewood took an even stronger line: the Prime Minister did not realize how much opposition there would be; 'If you do come this spring I fear it will be the last time for many years.'[4] The Police Commissioner said that there would certainly be trouble in the streets, though he was confident he could control it.[5] A Special Branch report on the projected visit concluded that the communists would probably sit on the fence but that the fascists would undoubtedly mount demonstrations in the Duke's favour: 'The Fascists, although outwardly proclaiming loyalty to King George VI, have made no real secret of their support for the Duke of Windsor.'[6]

When he forwarded a bunch of threatening letters to Scotland Yard the Duke told the Duke of Gloucester that he foresaw 'this negligible quantity of anonymous "tripe" being used both by Bertie and the Government, in an attempt to dissuade us from our projected visit to England in the Spring'.[7] When Chamberlain, who had taken over as Prime Minister in May 1937, called on him in Paris in November of the following year, he had made it clear that there was more substance for their fears than the Duke suspected. Of the letters received in Downing Street, 90 per cent had been hostile to the Windsors' visit. Queen Mary had received a spate of letters on the same lines. The resentment and bitterness aroused at the time of the abdication had not died away as soon as Chamberlain had hoped and expected. Rather nervously he suggested the Duke might like to pay his first visit without the Duchess, who would be the main target for popular hostility. 'No, I certainly could not do that,' the Duke replied; 'married people ought not to be divided.'[1] Told of this, King George VI urged the Prime Minister to insist that the visit be postponed: 'I think you know that neither the Queen nor Queen Mary have any desire to meet the Duchess of Windsor, and therefore any visit made for the purpose of introducing her to the Royal Family obviously becomes impossible.'[2] Chamberlain obliged but made it plain to Monckton that he was not just responding to pressure from the King, he had genuinely been taken aback by the strength of popular feeling against the Duchess, and the criticism which his visit to the Duke in Paris had provoked.[3]

Gloomily the Duke accepted a further short postponement. The only controversy over his visit, he complained, would arise if the royal family refused to receive his wife. 'I must therefore tell you frankly,' he wrote to Chamberlain, 'that I will never allow this attitude on their part to be used as a reason for keeping me out of my country.'[4] The King for his part was equally emphatic that there should be no question of a visit in 1939: 'Public opinion won't stand it, and they would be wise to drop the matter entirely for some years.'[5] Monckton, as usual, was left trying to reconcile the irreconcilable. He urged the King to leave some hope alive of a visit being possible in the not-too-distant future. 'To put the matter at its lowest, I find it increasingly difficult to keep him quiet and not outwardly complaining and yet indefinitely away.'[6]

Viewed from fifty years on it is hard to say whether the King's fears were justified. A Gallup poll conducted early in 1939 showed that 61 per cent of the population wanted the Windsors to return, 16 per cent were against, 23 per cent did not know. Polling techniques were primitive before the war, but the result at least suggests that overt hostility would have been confined to a small minority. The fact that, when the Windsors *did* return, there were no public manifestations of any kind, proves little; in September 1939 the British people had other matters on their mind. On the whole it seems likely that passions ran less deep than the authorities imagined; there would only have been vigorous demonstrations for or against the Windsors if certain individuals or groups had worked to bring them about. There were plenty of individuals and at least one group that might have done so, however; the King's gloomy forebodings were perhaps exaggerated but by no means chimerical. The test was never made; the problem was swept away on the tide of a European war.

There were plenty of other problems. A book called *Coronation Commentary* by Geoffrey Dennis was generally sympathetic to the Duke but unwisely referred to Mrs Simpson as having been his mistress and suggested he had drunk too much in the weeks before the abdication. In April 1937 the Duke sued for libel, urged on by Churchill: 'These people require a lesson and the only thing they appreciate is being made to pay.'[1] Monckton was determined to keep the case out of court if he possibly could – the thought of the Duke in the witness box being cross-examined on his relationship with Mrs Simpson was too horrible to contemplate – but to his dismay found the Duke full of fight, convinced he could get damages of £5000 or even £10,000.[2] It was another example of the '"loopiness" of our friend in Austria', wrote Hardinge. 'Does he realize the amount of muck that they can rake up about him?'[3] The rest of the royal family agreed with Hardinge and Monckton that a court case must be avoided: 'We cannot afford any more scandals and insinuations,' wrote the Queen.[4] The case did come to court, but the Lord Chief Justice, Hewart, was so obviously on the Duke's side – the libels, he said, were so gross that a jury might have considered them 'almost to invite a thoroughly efficient horse-whipping' – that the defendants hurriedly settled for costs and substantial damages.

The Duke considered that the book should never have appeared and unreasonably blamed his family for having done nothing to help. It was yet one more scrap of tinder to add to the furious fires of his resentment. But it was the long-drawn-out wrangle over money which contributed most to his sense of embittered alienation from his family. As early as April 1937 the lines of a new understanding to replace the Fort Belvedere agreement had begun to emerge. The annual payment from the King would be £20,000 rather than the £25,000 originally proposed, to take account of several pensions for which the Duke continued to be responsible (this was later raised to £21,000, but the King refused to agree that the amount should increase as the pensioners died – 'My pension list has to go on and I shall have to pay it alone,' he expostulated).[1] To account for part of this Balmoral and Sandringham were to be valued and the equivalent sum placed in 3½ per cent War Loan or some other investment, the income from which was paid to foreign residents free of tax. The Duke was thereby guaranteed a tax-free income in perpetuity: the difference between this amount and £21,000 would be provided by the King and would cease at his death.[2] To the King this was clearly to the Duke's benefit; he would have a guaranteed income for life while under the previous agreement it would all have ended if George VI predeceased him – 'a very fair clean-cut proposition,' the King described it to Queen Mary. 'It is a much better one than the original.'[3] To the Duke it was equally obvious that he was being cheated out of the £4000 for pensions, which at the very least should diminish as the years went by, and he questioned whether it had ever been envisaged that the allowance should end on the death of his brother.

The valuation of Sandringham and Balmoral provided fresh reason for acrimony. The government valuers came up with figures of £146,000 and £90,000 respectively.[4] The Duke insisted on an independent valuation.[5] Knight, Frank and Rutley valued Sandringham at £200,000.[6] The final total was £289,853, which invested in War Loan produced £10,144.[7] George VI contributed a further £11,000 odd. The Duke told Allen that his treatment throughout the negotiations had been so insulting that he felt neither grateful nor appreciative: 'I can merely express satisfaction.'[8]

But the feature which most distressed the Duke was the attempt to link the payment of the voluntary allowance to his promise not to return without the consent of the government. According to Harold Farrer, the royal solicitor, this somewhat mean proviso had been the brain child of Chamberlain and Simon; King George VI had opposed it because he thought it would give offence to his brother. Anyway, the Duke had already given his word that he would not return without prior agreement and that was good enough for the King.[9] Monckton took the same line, and recorded that he himself had carried to the Duke of York just before the abdication an assurance from Edward VIII that he would not return to England without the new King's consent.[1] It seemed as if Chamberlain's proposal would encounter the united opposition of the royal brothers, but unfortunately the Duke now contrived to obfuscate the issue. When Monckton repeated to the Duke the assurance that he had given Chamberlain and the King, the Duke at first merely remarked that 'he was a man of his word', then later denied that he had given any explicit promise of the kind Monckton had recollected. Nor would he make it now, least of all as a quid pro quo for a financial settlement which anyway gave him less than his due. The most he would undertake was that he would always give warning of his intention to return, and would scrupulously avoid causing embarrassment to King and government.[2] The King in turn now stiffened his position. If the Duke thus repudiated his undertaking not to return without permission, then it must after all form part of the financial settlement: 'The whole question of the Duke's return to this country is not a personal one for HM,' wrote Farrer, 'but is one that concerns the State.'[3] In the end the Duke conceded the principle but lost little in practice. Ground rules were drawn up as to the circumstances in which the government might advise against the Duke's return – in particular, if it was likely to lead to public disorder – and only if the Duke then defied their advice could the financial sanctions be invoked.[4]

Both sides were left feeling that the other had behaved disgracefully. A family squabble over money is always unattractive and the fact that one party is a King and the other an ex-King makes it no more edifying. The chances of obtaining a quick and friendly settlement had been jeopardized from the start by the Duke's misleading statement of his own financial situation, and each fresh twist of the plot had made it more certain that the final solution would leave everyone with the conviction that they had been misused. It would be pointless to apportion the blame: the Duke was in the weaker position and so perhaps might have been treated with greater generosity, but it is not hard to understand the forces that impelled the King and his ministers to drive a hard bargain with the former monarch. It was a miserable story, and it did not augur well for the Duke's future relationship with his family.

It was no fault of Monckton that the gulf became so wide. He laboured heroically to put each party's behaviour in the best possible light to the other, to avoid conflict where it was possible and soften it where it was not. 'I hope Your Majesty will not think me impertinent if I suggest for Your Majesty's consideration whether You could possibly write a short personal note saying that You were pleased to hear how well and happy they *both* were,' he put forward in August 1937, and when the King obliged, wrote again to say how good the effects had been. With patience and forbearance, he said, he was sure that friendly relations could be restored, a task which he would always regard as his 'main job in life'.[1]

But olive branches could prove cankered. The Duke and Duchess of Kent, in the autumn of 1937, went to stay with Prince Paul of Yugoslavia at Brdo, only a few hours from the Windsors at Wasserleonburg. Kent wrote to his brother to say how much he would like to visit him for a night or two.[2] When they spoke on the telephone, it became clear that the Duchess of Kent would not be coming too. The Duke of Windsor pressed for an explanation and soon extracted what he described as the 'incredible information' that it had been arranged with Queen Mary and the Queen that 'the Duchess of Kent should not meet my Duchess'.[3] Queen Mary had been emphatic that, since the Duchess of Kent was a foreigner by birth, it would be quite wrong for her to be the first female member of the family to call on her new sister-in-law.[4] The Duke of Windsor's outrage when told of this was such that his youngest brother hastened back to the King for fresh instructions. The King thought it was most desirable that Kent should visit his brother even if the price were that his wife accompanied him; the Duke of Windsor would be likely to speak to him with a freedom he would not show even with Monckton and it must be useful if he were given a chance to let off steam. 'I do hope your visit will not be too difficult for Marina and you,' he wrote, 'especially for her, but I do feel it will do good.'[5] To his mother he rather apprehensively admitted that he had ruled that the Duke of Kent 'had better take Marina with him, as it would help matters all round'.[6] The Duke of Windsor was told that both the Kents would after all be coming and was left triumphant over 'a definite change of policy . . . not that we cared one way or the other'.[7]

His triumph was short-lived. You can take a Duchess to the

water, but you cannot make her drink. 'Marina has no wish to go
to see David at all,' the King regretfully conceded.[1] Nor was Queen
Mary any more complaisant. As soon as she heard of the King's
instructions to the Kents she urged that they be rescinded.[2] The
King gave in, though telling his mother, 'Some time later I am sure
we shall have to have some liaison with David other than through
members of the legal profession or of the household.'[3] The next
thing that the Duke of Windsor heard was that the Kents would
after all not be coming, with limp excuses 'that they would not be
back in time' from a yachting trip.[4] His rage was redoubled. He
believed that Queen Mary was most to blame and wrote to her in
terms which made obvious his own raw pain:

> I unfortunately know from George that you and Elizabeth
> instigated the somewhat sordid and much publicized episode
> of the failure of the Kents to visit us ... I am at a loss to
> know how to write to you, and further to see how any form
> of correspondence can give pleasure to either of us under these
> circumstances ... It is a great sorrow and disappointment to
> me to have my mother thus cast out her eldest son.[5]

The fact that the episode was 'much publicized' was blamed by
Hardinge – in this case, at least, unfairly – on the 'systematic
propaganda' of the Windsors.[6] He told the King that his brother
was trying to stir up trouble. Once again, both parties were left
with a sense of grievance.

It was not till November 1938 that King George VI got his way
and members of the royal family exchanged a visit with the
Windsors. The Gloucesters stopped in Paris on the way back from
safari in Kenya. The visit, according to the Duchess of Gloucester,
was asked for by Chamberlain as a means of testing the water. At
the back of his mind he had the possibility that the Duke of
Windsor might be given some role in public life in the next year
or two.[7] The visit got off to an unhappy start when the King,
at Hardinge's suggestion, urged his brother to avoid any press
publicity.[8] 'I must say that I am surprised that you should express
anxiety lest *I* should inform the Press of their visit beforehand,'
the Duke replied indignantly. If only the Kents had paid their visit
the year before there would anyway have been no newspaper
interest to contend with.[9] To Monckton he wrote of the 'quite

stupid and rather impertinent suggestion' that he was a publicity seeker,[1] a protestation that would have been more convincing if he had not on occasion pulled a variety of strings to ensure that his activities were portrayed in a favourable light.

Colin Davidson, who was in somewhat nervous attendance for the visit, had expected embarrassed silence from the Gloucesters and a string of grumbles from the Windsors. In fact everyone was on their best behaviour and scarcely a bitter word was said. 'The Duchess of Windsor could not have been nicer and did everything to make things go.'[2] But from the Windsors' point of view the consequences of the visit were unfortunate. The Duke of Gloucester received more than a hundred letters which protested at the meeting, some of them 'extremely rude', and only one in favour. 'All our friends are pleased that we met,' he told his brother,[3] but it was not the reactions of the friends of the Gloucesters that interested the government. Chamberlain was further convinced that it would be premature to bring the Windsors back to England.

The Duke's resentment over his wife not being styled HRH was temporarily in abeyance. Partly at least this was to the credit of Colin Davidson, who refused to bow to the Duchess and repeatedly urged the Duke not to refer to her as HRH himself. 'Every time they heard in England that he was doing it, the reconciliation and the arrangements for his return were probably retarded.'[4] At dinner with the American Ambassador early in 1939, Anne Lindbergh found it generally agreed that no curtsey was necessary. A year before, it was said, 'he minded terribly, but this year he doesn't care'.[5] He cared quite as much as ever, but he had reluctantly agreed that reticence in the short term might prove more profitable in the long.

In May 1937 the King asked the Foreign Office to prepare guidance for Ambassadors on the way they should treat the Windsors. Eden's proposal was that the couple should be considered as members of the royal family on holiday.[6] Hardinge's reply emphasized that the King's representatives should have no hand in arranging official interviews and must not 'countenance their participation in any official ceremonies'. They might be entertained privately but never asked to stay.[7] In September Selby telegraphed from Vienna to say that the Duke wanted to call on the President, who would certainly be delighted to receive him. He assumed he should fix it up and himself accompany the Duke. Hardinge replied in dismay to say he should do neither. 'As the Duke of Windsor is no longer in the line of succession to the Throne, he has no claim to official status, and this applies with much greater force to the Duchess.'[1] In January 1938 it was Phipps from Paris who wanted to invite the Windsors to a reception for 1200 guests being given after a dinner for the President. This time it was Lascelles who replied that, as the function was an official one, it would be inappropriate to invite the Windsors.[2] No doubt such decisions could be justified in terms of protocol but the situation was not one for which any precedent existed, and it is hard not to feel that a less doctrinaire approach could have been adopted without undue risk to the monarchy.

In the spring of 1938 King George VI and Queen Elizabeth paid a state visit to Paris. The Duke first read of this plan in the press, a fact which caused him some chagrin. He at once instructed Monckton to try to ensure that the King and Queen called on the Windsors during their visit. He hoped that he and his wife would be invited to some official receptions.[3] Monckton did his best, but found the atmosphere poisoned by the letters the Duke had written after the abortive visit by the Kents, and by gossip from the south of France over offensive remarks the Windsors were said to have made about the royal family.[4] 'State visit a most unsuitable moment for meeting,' the King minuted. 'Great publicity (which is wanted by him) in both countries and in World would raise storm over here. Official invitation would help their position in French society. Recent reports show that no woman in Paris wishes to meet her. Their behaviour has not been polite to us ... Much better for them to go away while visit is on.'[5] It shows how far the relationship between the brothers had deteriorated that the belief that an official invitation would help the Windsors' position in French society seemed a reason for not issuing one.

The Duke agreed to go quietly, but insisted that his position in Paris would become impossible if they were not invited to the Embassy for some sort of formal reception before the royal visit.[6] The King spoke to Halifax, who had replaced Eden as Foreign Secretary, and Phipps was told to give a large dinner party, with ministers invited and decorations worn if the Duke so wished it.[7] George VI's only stipulation was that the occasion should not be publicized. The Duke, however, took the opposite view. He wrote to Rickatson-Hatt of Reuters to give the news, promising a list of the guests when it was available: 'I attach great importance to this occasion being properly reported in Great Britain on the day following.'[1] When he found the details of his party placarded across the pages of the *Daily Telegraph* Phipps was dismayed. He traced the leak to the Duke's equerry, Dudley Forwood, and informed the Palace accordingly.[2] The Duke professed great amusement at the annoyance shown by Buckingham Palace – 'not the King's of course, but that of the same old Palace enemies'.[3] That oldest of Palace enemies, Hardinge, heard Monckton was on his way to visit the Windsors and urged him 'to rub in the great success of the Paris visit both at home and abroad – especially *her* [the Queen's] personal triumph in Paris. That will get home, I think!'[4]

The affair of King George V's memorial illustrates still more vividly how minor failures of tact or consideration could quickly be blown up into monstrous grievances. The Duke had agreed to split with his mother the cost of Reid Dick's statue which was to be installed in St George's, Windsor. He asked that, when the unveiling took place, the fact that he had thus contributed should be made public.[5] Queen Mary replied that, while there would be no formal unveiling, the Duke's participation in the enterprise would of course be mentioned in any announcement.[6] In due course Claud Hamilton told the Duke that the statue would soon be put in place and that a short statement would then be issued, naming the donors.[7] Three weeks later Ulick Alexander telephoned the Duke and gave him the exact date.[8] The Duke first maintained that he had never been told when the ceremony was to take place and then, when Alexander reminded him of their conversation, refused to accept that this 'casual reference' to the date could be taken as constituting 'formal notification of this ceremony, particularly as you made no mention of the message as coming from my brother'.[9] He expostulated that there had been no mention of his contribution to the cost of the statue as had been promised, and then, when Queen Mary said that there had been an announcement in *The Times*, claimed that, as *The Times* had 'a very limited circulation', it was obvious the royal family had not wanted the British public to know that he was one of the donors.[10] Finally, stung by his mother's comment that the King had asked Hardinge to tell the Duke what was planned, he burst out:

> Your letter of March twentieth is extremely illuminating, although I greatly regret that it should have taken so sacred an occasion to disclose so much that is unpleasant, and to destroy the last vestige of feeling I had left for you all as a family.
>
> It was of course obvious that neither you nor Bertie could notify me yourselves of the ceremony . . . You, by your final refusal to receive Walter Monckton last month . . . have made further normal correspondence between us impossible . . .[1]

The matter could have been handled better by Buckingham Palace: if the Duke was not to be invited to the erection of a monument to his father then at least the King or Queen Mary should have written personally to him about it. His reaction, however, was out of all proportion to the offence. On this, as on so many other issues concerning his family, he was determined to believe himself grossly misused, and was incapable of thinking straight. Even in 1939 he did himself grave harm by striking such an attitude, harm that was to become almost irreparable a year later when his country was at war.

To list all the other issues, most of them trifling, which added to his sense of alienation from his family, would be as fruitless as it would be unedifying. Even when they were not directly involved – as on the occasion when the American Ambassador in London, Joseph Kennedy, told his wife not to call on the Windsors – the Duke believed that the Palace was ultimately to blame. 'Things have come to a pretty pass, when we have to take a snub from an ex-newsboy,' he told Monckton,[2] but he believed that the 'ex-newsboy' took his line from the court. At the heart of all his grievances lay the royal family's refusal to accept the Duchess of Windsor. The Duke could never convince himself that this was not some temporary aberration which would suddenly pass away; each time the offence was renewed he felt the same sense of anguished shock. His mother's attitude was set out with chilling clarity in July 1938 in answer to a plea that she should write frankly about her feelings. She reminded her son of the extreme misery she had felt at the time of the abdication and of his refusal to listen to her arguments, and went on:

I do not think you have ever realized the shock which the attitude you took up caused your family and the whole Nation. It seemed inconceivable to those who had made such sacrifices during the war that you, as their King, refused a lesser sacrifice. While sympathizing with your distress of mind at the time, I fail to see that your marriage has altered the point of view which we all took up, or that it is possible for you both to come to England for a long time to come. Naturally I am very sorry not to see you, as my feelings to you as your Mother remain the same, and our being parted and the cause of it grieves me beyond words. After all, all my life I have put my Country before anything else, and I simply cannot change now. The feeling about your marriage is far deeper and wider than you seem to realize, and your return to England would only mean division and controversy.[1]

Even this implacable reaffirmation did not seem conclusive to the Duke. Within a few months Walter Monckton was sent to Queen Mary to ask whether she would receive the Duchess when the Windsors came to London. The answer was an uncompromising no. 'Though I completely understand the decision,' Monckton told King George VI, 'it naturally did not go very well with the Duke.'[2]

21

The Duke in Germany

═══

O F ALL THE DUKE OF WINDSOR'S ACTIVITIES IN
the years between the abdication and the war, it is his visit
to Germany in October 1937 which is the best remembered. The image lingers, as from a flickering newsreel, of his shy
smile as he shook hands with the Führer, of the half-sketched and
aborted fascist salute, of glowing words in praise of workers'
housing and the miracle of full employment. Such images, superim-
posed on what we know today of the vileness of the Nazi regime
and the inevitability of war, create a picture of a man condoning
atrocities and giving comfort to Britain's enemies. In fact, when
the Duke visited Germany, most members of the Conservative
government would have agreed with him that Britain could live
with German aspirations, that war was not inevitable, and that
Soviet Russia posed at least as great a threat to national security.
His tour was ill-timed and ill-advised, but it was not a crime.

A failure to take advice was indeed at the heart of the Duke's
problems. Six months earlier Brownlow had passed on a message
from Baldwin, warning that 'prolonged visits or close contacts in
Fascist countries would be unwise' because they would alienate
left-wing opinion and make his return to England more difficult.[1]
Since then there had been little contact with British ministers and
when the Duke did encounter one he was careful not to raise the
issue, knowing that what he would hear would be unwelcome.
Chamberlain would have advised against the tour, but not from
hostility to Germany. He would have felt that the Duke's proper
course was to lie low, to withdraw from public life as he had
promised in his abdication speech, to shun the headlines. A visit
to the United States would have seemed equally unwise. The Duke
wanted no such counsel, so asked no question. Instead he relied
for advice on Charles Bedaux, the millionaire efficiency expert who
had lent the Windsors his château for their wedding and now

presented his bill; gift-wrapped so subtly as to be most appealing to the Duke but still calculated to cost its recipient very dear.

Bedaux had substantial business interests in Germany which had been imperilled by the hostility of the present regime. He was working his way back to favour and was anxious to do anything he could to ingratiate himself still further. To organize a visit by the Duke of Windsor would earn him much credit in Berlin; the Germans could be trusted to extract the maximum propaganda advantage from the Duke's presence, and they would be enabled to keep close links with a man whom they believed could one day still be of great use to them. Bedaux also genuinely believed that there was urgent need for a third force that would stand aloof from the great power blocs and provide an impetus towards peace. His ideas were vague, but of one thing he was sure; in any such movement both the Duke of Windsor and Charles Bedaux should play a prominent role.

The Duke shared both the fatuity and the basic benevolence of this vision; he believed that he had a part to play in reconciling Britain and Germany and that his contribution could be as valuable as it would have been if he had remained on the throne, perhaps even more so. The ostensible object of his visit, in which he was genuinely interested, was to study the housing and working conditions of the German labour force. He was convinced that the Nazi government had done wonders in improving the lot of the working classes, and he wanted to know how, and whether, the same techniques could work in Britain. But beyond this, he felt that he should improve his knowledge of and acquaintanceship with the German leaders, so that one day he could use his influence to good purpose. The time might come, he felt, when only he could avert a war.

There was another, less altruistic reason for his readiness to fall in with Bedaux's plan. After twenty years of grumbling about the pressures of public life, he found his isolation from it irksome. He wanted to step back for a while into the centre of the stage. Still more, he wanted to be there with his wife beside him. He wanted to prove to the Duchess that, even though she had not married a King, she was at least the wife of someone who commanded the respect of a major power. He could never do that in Britain and, following the lead of his family in London, the French aristocracy and ruling class treated him with cautious restraint. In Germany at least he could be sure of a proper welcome and, more significantly, so could the Duchess. Philip Guedalla noticed that he did not like to hear unfavourable comment about Germany: 'One feels that he has ties of family hard to break.'[1] It is doubtful whether the ties of family counted for much; for the Duke Germany was contented, prosperous, self-disciplined, and eager to welcome an ex-monarch with the deference to which he had once been used but now had to live without.

The visit to Germany was to be balanced by a similar tour of the United States, again centred on study of workers' housing and conditions. In the case of Germany Bedaux effected the introduction and then stepped discreetly aside; in America he hoped to play a more prominent role, personally conducting the Duke around the industrial concerns where his efficiency methods had been adopted. It seemed to the Duke an unexceptionable proposal which would save him both money and effort. He was soon to revise his ideas.

The first word of the intended visits came to London from Washington, where Victor Mallet at the British Embassy commented in mid-September that if the Duke were to arrive 'all the old bally-hoo' would be revived. At the time of the abdication Edward VIII's solicitude for the Welsh miners and the supposed indignation of Baldwin's government at his outspokenness had been much featured in the American press. His plan to research the life of the American working man would inevitably revive the story.[2] Hardinge sourly minuted: 'After the experience of the South Wales miners last year, the so-called investigations into the life of the American working-man are not likely to have much effect in this country.'[3] The King anxiously asked Monckton whether he thought the rumours true. 'I don't think it wise,' he remarked.[4] Nor did Monckton. He planned to tell the Duke as much, and when a projected visit to Paris was cancelled at short notice, guessed that it was because his ex-monarch had set his heart on making the trip and did not want to hear any advice against it.[5]

The first official notification the British government received was a letter from the Duke to the British Ambassador in Berlin, Nevile Henderson. 'Although our two weeks tour is being organized under the auspices of the Reich, it will naturally be of a purely private nature,' wrote the Duke.[1] Vansittart was put out that the Foreign Office should have been given no advance warning: 'The direct approach to our missions, without our knowledge, is hardly fair.'[2] The Duke felt that the Foreign Office had made no effort to keep in touch with him, so why should he consult them? The demands of courtesy had been satisfied by a letter to the British Ambassador. Henderson – himself as well-disposed towards the Germans as was the Duke – replied that he would be on leave at the time; an alibi which was genuine but must have caused him some relief. His personal view, though, was that the visit could well be useful: 'There is much in the legislation of the Nazi government which is worthy of study, though our Labour MPs did not like it when I said so in a speech some months ago.'[3]

On 3 October came the first public declaration: the Windsors, read a statement issued to the press in Paris, would shortly be visiting Germany and the United States 'for the purpose of studying housing and working conditions'. Wigram seethed with indignation. It was a most arrogant and undignified announcement, he told King George VI; it implied that the Duke was the sole champion of the working classes and that if they would get him back to Britain he would look after them. It was a 'dangerous, semi-political move'.[4] There was nothing in the text of the statement which overtly supported Wigram's interpretation, but Monckton also believed that it implied the Duke hoped to acquire knowledge which might one day be of use to him in his work in Britain. Even if the statement had been more tactfully phrased, Monckton would still have deplored the enterprise. He believed it was wrong for the Duke to embark on 'public (and advertised) political work' so soon after he had announced his intention of retiring to a private station.[5]

Meanwhile in Germany plans were being made to ensure that the Duke saw what the authorities wanted him to see and that his favourable reactions were given ample publicity. He had asked to meet the Führer, and Hitler who, as his adjutant Captain Wiedemann put it, had 'always had a certain weakness for the Duke of Windsor', willingly consented. The Nazi leaders were lined up to play their part in the welcome and Dr Robert Ley, head of the Labour Front, was detailed to act as cicerone (an unfortunate choice, since he was a drunken and brutal boor, but probably inevitable given the nature of the visit). Hitler insisted that all the planning should be done in strict secrecy, nothing should be made public until the Duke had notified the British Ambassador and the King in London.[1]

The more King George VI heard of his brother's plans, the more dismayed he became. 'A bombshell and a bad one,' he described the news to Monckton.[2] He resented the fact that he had been given no notice of the tour and was emphatic that no official support should be given to it. 'The world is in a very troubled state . . .' he told Queen Mary, 'and David seems to loom ever larger on the horizon.'[3] Oliver Harvey, Eden's private secretary, discussed with Hardinge what the Embassy in Berlin should do. He assumed that someone from the staff should be at the station when the Duke arrived, but Hardinge 'was inclined to doubt whether even this courtesy should be shown, lest it might appear as giving a British official nature to the tour'.[4] Ogilvie Forbes, the chargé d'affaires in Henderson's absence, protested at this. 'It will be extremely embarrassing and painful for me if I am instructed to ignore His Royal Highness's presence, for this will not be understood here. Moreover, I am rather under an obligation to His Royal Highness.'[5] He won his point, a junior member of staff was sent to the station, and Ogilvie Forbes himself later called on the Duke at his hotel. He contrived to make it abundantly clear that he disliked his instructions and several years later the Duke remembered with appreciation the way he had turned what might have been 'a somewhat cold interview' into 'a very pleasant evening. I am afraid that it was a series of similar gauche blunders committed by the Foreign Office that is greatly responsible for the appalling mess the world is in today.'[6]

Phipps in Paris passed back to London reports that Ribbentrop was exultant about the forthcoming visit: 'Ribbentrop believes that HRH will some day have a great influence over the British working man and that every effort will be made . . . to make HRH even more pro-German than he is already supposed in Germany to be.'[7] The Ambassador warned the Duke that the Germans were masters in the art of propaganda and would be quick to turn to their advantage anything he said or did. The Duke replied that he was well aware of this, would be on his guard and would make no speeches.[8] On the whole he seems to have stuck by these good intentions, though Ogilvie Forbes reported that the German government were making the most of their visitor.[1] The Duke probably committed himself further than was wise, but the Germans did not hesitate to put into his mouth statements of an effusiveness which he could hardly have intended. As a prime example of his gullibility his critics usually quote a speech he was supposed to have made in which he declared that, in all his travels, he had never seen an achievement so great as that brought about in social conditions by the German government: 'It . . . is a miracle; one can only begin to understand it when one realizes that behind it is one man and one will!' The thoughts may have been his but their expression in public was not. The words quoted were not spoken by the Duke but were an interpretation of his reactions rendered by Dr Ley at a meeting of the Labour Front in Leipzig some days after the Duke's departure.[2] Writing to Lindsay in Washington the Duke merely remarked temperately that the visit was proving most interesting and that he was being given every facility to study housing conditions.[3]

All the evidence suggests, however, that he thoroughly enjoyed his time in Germany. He was conspicuously cheerful throughout the tour. According to the *Daily Express*, the Duke visited a beerhall in Munich, drank three pints of beer, put on a false moustache, joined in a sing-song, and made an impromptu speech saying how much he liked the city.[4] There are no other recorded instances of such unbridled merriment, but all went very well. The local authorities had been instructed that the Duchess was always to be referred to as Her Royal Highness; a courtesy which by itself would have been enough to make their visitors look kindly on the inhabitants of the inner ring of Dante's *Inferno*, let alone the German people. He must have been flattered too by the eagerness of the Nazi leaders to fête him. They dined with Hess, whose wife Ilse remembered the Duchess as 'a lovely, charming, warm and clever woman with a heart of gold and an affection for her husband that she made not the slightest attempt to conceal'. The Duke's abdication, Frau Hess considered, had been brought about by 'his own sound attitudes on social issues and his pro-German inclinations'.[5] Göring said much the same thing to his wife before the Windsors dined with them. The German government, he told her, had earnestly hoped to see Edward VIII remain on the throne.

'The natural opposition between British and German policy . . . could,' said Göring, 'easily be set aside with the aid of such a man as the Duke.'[1] The two men played happily with the toy railway set up for Göring's nephew, and the aeroplane which flew across the room on a wire scattering wooden bombs on the trains below.[2] More sinister was the map on the wall, on which Austria figured as part of Germany. The Duke questioned this and was told it was inevitable that the Austrians would soon decide to throw in their lot with their neighbour.[3]

The high spot of the tour was a call on Hitler at his mountain redoubt of Berchtesgaden. Hitler was conspicuously affable, though he mildly irritated the Duke by insisting on using an interpreter rather than speaking directly to him in German.[4] According to the interpreter, Hitler seemed to take it for granted that the Duke sympathized with the ideology and the practices of the Third Reich, but the Duke kept off politics and said nothing which could have justified the Führer's assumption.[5] After they left, the Duchess, who had not been present at the interview, asked what Hitler had talked about. 'What he's trying to do for Germany and to combat Bolshevism,' said the Duke. 'And what did he say about Bolshevism?' 'He's against it,' replied the Duke briefly.[6]

From the Duke's point of view, the most dangerous consequence of his visit was that it confirmed the Germans in their belief that he was an advocate of their cause and could still be of great use to them. Albert Duckwitz, the well-informed Counsellor at the German Embassy in Copenhagen, told his American colleague that the Duke had 'exhibited a special sympathy and understanding of Germany'. He represented 'a section of liberalism' in England that had always been friendly towards Germany and was becoming still more so. 'The Duke of Windsor is by no means finished in his work.'[7] Bruce Lockhart reported to the Foreign Office that the Germans were still convinced that the Duke would 'come back as a social-equalizing King –' and inaugurate an 'English form of Fascism and alliance with Germany'.[8] It was an illusion which was to have embarrassing results before too long.

Apart from this, the worst that can be said about the German visit is that the Duke closed his eyes to most of what he did not wish to see, and allowed himself to be paraded as an admirer of the economic miracle and as tacitly condoning the brutal side of

the social experiment. 'He did not understand half of what he saw
or what was said to him,' commented the youthful Nigel Law, the
whole visit was 'lacking in dignity'.[1] Yet it was no covert fascist
but Winston Churchill who, briefed by his son Randolph who had
accompanied the tour, wrote to congratulate the Duke on its
success. There had been loud cheering in the cinemas when news-
reels of the Duke's tour were shown. 'I was rather afraid beforehand
that your tour in Germany would offend the great numbers of
anti-Nazis in this country, many of whom are your friends and
admirers, but I must admit that it does not seem to have had that
effect, and I am so glad it all passed off with so much distinction
and success.'[2] When there was criticism, as by Herbert Morrison
in the left-wing magazine *Forward*,[3] it related mainly to the fact
that the Duke was pushing himself forward into the public view,
not that he chose to do so in Nazi Germany.

'The American journey,' Churchill went on, 'I feel sure will be
prosperous, and you will get a reception from that vast public
which no Englishman has ever had before.' The second leg of the
Windsors' pilgrimage caused even greater pother at court than had
the first. Lindsay, the British Ambassador, wrote from Washington
to say that he felt he should accommodate the visitors, present
them at the White House and 'at the least give them a large
Belshazzar'.[4]* The ever vigilant Hardinge hurriedly intervened;
Lindsay should do nothing of the sort, at the most he might tell
the White House that he believed the Duke wanted an interview
and leave it to them to follow the matter up if they so wished.[5]
Lindsay was horrified and, being in England, was summoned to
Balmoral for a conference on the subject. He was confronted by
the King and Queen, Hardinge and Lascelles, and for three hours
argued that to cold-shoulder the Duke would stir up sentiment on
his behalf in the United States and damage the reputation of the
British monarchy. The three men were obdurate. The Duke was
behaving abominably, he was trying to stage a comeback, his
friends and advisers were semi-Nazis. The Queen took a different
line. 'While the men spoke in terms of indignation, she spoke in
terms of acute pain and distress, ingenuously expressed and deeply
felt. She too is not a great intellect but she has any amount of

---

* From Belshazzar's Feast (*Daniel* 5). Hardly a propitious phrase given the ill tidings conveyed at that
uncomfortable banquet.

intelligence du coeur ... In all she said there was far more grief than indignation and it was all tempered by affection for "David". "He's so changed now, and he used to be so kind to us." She was backing up all that the men said, but protesting against anything that seemed vindictive ... And with all her charity she had not a word to say for "that woman".[1]

The final decision was that Lindsay should give a medium-sized dinner party for the Windsors but not accompany the Duke to the White House. It would be best, the Ambassador was told, if the President merely asked the Windsors to tea.[2] Encouraged by a report from the American Ambassador in Paris however, to the effect that the Duke was in excellent form, drinking almost nothing, deeply in love, and genuinely interested in workers' living conditions,[3] Roosevelt was not prepared to be so discourteous. He accepted the tea party, but refused to receive the Duke without the Ambassador being in attendance. Lindsay sympathized with him. 'The Palace secretaries are extremist,' he wrote, 'the Foreign Office still more so. All are seeing ghosts and phantoms everywhere.'[4] The President would probably have had his way if events had not made the question academic.

It was becoming every day more clear that Churchill's cheerful prophecy about the American tour was going badly wrong. William Shirer, an American journalist who reported the Duke's visit to Germany, was one of the first to see the danger. 'A curious thing for the Duke to do, to come to Germany, where the labour unions have been smashed, just before he goes to America,' he wrote from Munich. 'He has been badly advised.'[5] On 23 October the *New York Times* took up the tune; the Duke's visit to Germany had aided the regime and shown him to be a firm friend of national socialism. The reaction of the American press as a whole had been hostile, a friend warned the Duke. Most reports implied that he was 'in complete sympathy with the German National Socialist movement. The present regime in Germany is unpopular in the United States, and in the large industrial cities feeling runs very high.'[6]

The visit to Germany might have been forgiven if the Duke's programme in the United States had been in different hands. Bedaux, however, was anathema to organized labour in America. A Special Branch report on him said that the application of his methods nearly always led to increased production and lower costs, but also to strikes and disputes. If the Duke allowed his name to be associated with that of Bedaux he would quickly lose his popularity among the working classes.[1] The American chargé in Berlin claimed that Bedaux was running the Duke, and probably paying his expenses for the tour of the United States (as, indeed, to a large extent he was). Bedaux intended to make the Duke the standard bearer for his movement to bring about world peace through labour reconciliation.[2] An American diplomat in Paris went still further and suggested that Bedaux was trying to build up the Duke's reputation as 'a great and sincere friend of the working man', with a view to his eventual restoration to the throne.[3]

As reports filtered back from America that the labour unions were beginning to express themselves publicly against his visit, the Duke took alarm. At a dinner of the Anglo-American Press Association in Paris on 27 October he stressed that he would be going to the United States as 'a completely independent observer, without political considerations of any sort or kind, and entirely on my own initiative'.[4] It was too late. A week later Lindsay was reporting that public opinion was hardening: 'Ridicule has increasingly been thrown on a project which has not been regarded as seriously possible in the circumstances in which it would be carried out. Language about Duchess has been unfriendly. But most of all his prospects have been damaged by association with Bedaux . . .' The Ambassador had now concluded that the tour could only reflect discredit on the Duke and had better be abandoned.[5] The longshoremen in New York threatened to boycott the Duke's ship; Jewish organizations made noises of disapproval; the Baltimore Federation of Labor passed a resolution deploring the Duke's association with Bedaux and Nazi Germany and rather unkindly deprecating a visit by the Duchess who, 'while resident here in no way showed the slightest concern nor sympathy for the problems of labor or the poor and needy'.[6]

Lindsay, who had at first expected to be embarrassed by the triumphant success of the tour, by the time it was cancelled feared that it would be 'such a ghastly failure as to be a disaster in the opposite direction'. He drew some consolation from the fact that Bedaux was the principal target of the critics, the Duchess next most vulnerable while the Duke was only abused by association.[1] This would have been scant comfort to the Duke, who could have endured a certain amount of unfavourable publicity himself but shrank from exposing his wife to anything so unpleasant. By now he was agitatedly consulting anyone whose opinion seemed of value. Bedaux was sending alarmed telegrams from New York urging that the visit be cancelled; Lindsay refused to give formal advice but contrived nonetheless to make his opinion crystal clear. William Bullitt, the American Ambassador in Paris, continued to maintain that the visit should take place, but his was a lonely voice. It is said that the Duke was finally persuaded to abandon the tour when he tried to telephone Bullitt, by mistake got through to Phipps, was advised strongly to remain in Europe, and assumed in some surprise that Bullitt had changed his mind. This seems hardly likely, though Phipps if asked would certainly have taken such a line; Monckton believed that the decisive voice belonged to a New York solicitor who worked closely with the Duke's lawyer, Allen.[2] Whatever the immediate cause, the Duke called off the trip; *The Times* on 6 November carrying his statement, in which he once more denied that he was 'allied to any industrial system' or 'for or against any particular political or racial doctrine'.

The Duchess wrote to Bedaux's wife to regret that 'our lovely innocent trip should have met with so disastrous an end'.[3] Inevitably the Duke blamed Bedaux for the debacle, though he held back from any direct reproach, and said he hoped they could meet again when the press furore had died down.[4] If only he had known how unpopular Bedaux's methods were in the United States, he would never have contemplated making the visit under such auspices, he told a friend in Washington.[5] He should have known and could have found out if he had asked the right people, but he had set his heart on making the trip and did not wish to expose himself to any voices of caution or discouragement. The Duchess told Monckton that they blamed nobody but themselves, a piece of humility from which Monckton drew some comfort: 'It is all to the good if their confidence in their unaided judgment and in that of those whom alone they have consulted in this matter is shaken.'[6] Hardinge derived special satisfaction from the fact that most of the criticism had come from the left: 'These expressions of opinion from the different wings of the Labour party, as whose champion the Duke, apparently, would still like to pose, should have a very salutary effect, and prove the death knell of the "slumming party" with all its insincerity and ballyhoo.'[1]

Roosevelt was more sympathetic. He told Lindsay that it would not upset him if the visit were never put on again but he still thought it might pass off all right if properly sponsored.[2] To the Duke he sent a personal message, saying how sincerely sorry he was that 'certain factors' had prevented the tour, but hoping that it would soon take place.[3] He showed his letter to the Under Secretary of State at the State Department: 'I think the letter you have drafted could not be nicer,' was the comment, 'and I think it will be helpful in hastening the obliteration of recent occurrences.'[4]

It was to take a long time to obliterate the memory, and the Duke never ceased to feel that he had been misunderstood and misused. He was despondent and uncertain how best he could retrieve the situation. A curious and somewhat shadowy story dates from this period. William Tyrrell, a former British Ambassador in Paris, was staying with Phipps at the very end of 1937 and told a member of the Embassy staff that he had seen the text of an interview a journalist from the *Daily Herald* had had with the Duke of Windsor. In this the Duke was supposed to have said that 'if the Labour party wished, and were in a position to offer it, he would be prepared to be President of the English Republic'. Tyrrell persuaded the editor to suppress the interview.[5] The Duke's words come to us as recorded by an unknown journalist, read by Tyrrell, related by Tyrrell to an unknown diplomat and finally passed on to Phipps. The game of Chinese Whispers is not a satisfactory basis on which to build a history. But the Duke's despair was so pronounced and his rancour towards his family so embittered, that it is not inconceivable he said something of the kind. Exactly what he meant by such words, whether indeed he had considered them carefully or at all, it is impossible to decide. Given the newspaper for which the interview was given, it is probable that the statement came in answer to a question designed to produce that very response. It need not be taken too seriously. But it should not be ignored.

He was, however, quite as ardent an appeaser as Chamberlain or any member of his government. When the Germans were threatening Czechoslovakia and the crisis was at its most dangerous, he contemplated a visit to Germany to offer his services as a mediator and to 'expostulate with Hitler'.[1] His friends argued that any such visit would be disastrous for his reputation in Britain and might 'revive the legend of his Nazi sympathies'.[2] Probably he would have allowed himself to be discouraged, though he genuinely believed he could offer a useful contribution and was tempted by the thought of making so dramatic a return to the centre of the world's stage. Fortunately he was anyway pre-empted by Chamberlain, who himself flew to Munich to see Hitler. It was a gesture that appealed strongly to the Duke. 'It was a bold step to take,' he told the Prime Minister, 'but if I may say so, one after my own heart, as I have always believed in personal contact as the best policy in "a tight corner". It would not surprise me if there were, amongst your colleagues, some who debated the wisdom of such dramatic last-hour tactics, but you followed the dictates of your conscience in the same fearless way in which you have faced up to all the complex phases of foreign politics that have confronted you in the last year.'[3] (On this at least he and the King were agreed. King George VI wrote to offer Chamberlain his 'most heartfelt congratulations'. He had earned 'the lasting gratitude of his fellow countrymen'.[4]) To Monckton he described Chamberlain's intervention as a stroke of genius: 'I really cannot understand our old friend Winston Churchill's attitude, which is hardly worthy of the brilliant and experienced politician that he is.'[5]

He was more than ever convinced that war was unacceptable as a means of settling disputes, that Russia was a more dangerous enemy than Germany, and that if there had to be a war, it should be between the Germans and the Russians. 'Another world war would see the Democracies go down with the Totalitarian States, and Victory go only to Communism,' he told Bruce Lockhart.[6] In May 1939 he was offered a chance to address the world on the theme of peace when the National Broadcasting Company of America invited him to broadcast to the United States from Verdun after a visit to the battlefield. His speech was short, eloquent, uncontroversial and written entirely by himself. For two and a half years, he said, he had kept out of public affairs and he proposed to go on doing so; he spoke for no one but himself, 'as a soldier of the last war, whose most earnest prayer is that such a cruel and destructive madness shall never again overtake mankind'. No one wanted war, yet the world seemed to be drifting inexorably towards it. He appealed to all statesmen to 'act as good citizens of the world and not only as good Frenchmen, Italians, Germans, Americans or Britons'. One way to help avert war would be to eschew all harmful propaganda: 'I personally deplore, for example, the use of such terms as "encirclement" and "aggression". They can only arouse just those dangerous political passions that it should be the aim of us all to subdue.'[1]

The flaw in this argument is that, whatever term might be used to describe it, 'aggression' is what in fact the Germans were displaying in their foreign policy, and Hitler was not going to be diverted from his plans by a few well-intentioned words. To many who heard the broadcast, however, it seemed the voice of sanity and to offer some hope to an increasingly distracted world. Letters of appreciation flooded in; not only from the United States but from France, Holland and Poland – in all which countries the speech had been relayed – and from Britain – where the BBC had appealed to Hardinge for advice and had then decided not to carry the broadcast. There was also criticism; not so much of the content of the speech as of its timing and the fact that it had been delivered at all. His decision to broadcast was to be regretted, wrote the *Express*. He should have left such matters to the King.[2] By ill luck a visit the King and Queen were to pay to the United States had been rearranged so that they were actually at sea *en route* to New York when the broadcast was made. The Duke took the line that it was too late for him to cancel the arrangements. 'What a fool he is and how badly advised; and everyone is furious he should have done it just after you left,' wrote the Duke of Kent to King George VI. 'If he had mentioned you in it, it wouldn't have been so bad, and why he broadcast such a peace talk only to America, where they have no intention of fighting, I don't know.'[3]

The short answer to the Duke of Kent's question was that nobody else had offered him the chance or was likely to do so – least of all the British. It was hardly the Duke of Windsor's fault if the BBC refused to let the British people hear his words. He believed that he had something of real significance to say and that, coming from him, it might be listened to. He was perhaps naive, but at least he was trying to do something positive to avert war. Hardinge found 'the idea that it can possibly do the slightest good simply ludicrous'.[1] One may wonder whether it is better to act, and run the risk of being ludicrous, or to remain inactive, and accept supinely whatever blows fate has to offer.

However great the risks might be, the Duke continued to believe that war would never happen. Even on 1 September 1939, when *The Times* correspondent in Nice phoned him to report that the Germans had invaded Poland, he commented impatiently: 'Oh! Just another sensational report.'[2] But his optimism was not so blind that he did not plan for the worst. At the time of Munich he argued that, since the British government were responsible for him and the Duchess having to live abroad, they must also accept responsibility for getting them and their possessions out of France if need arose.[3] In August 1939 he appealed to Chamberlain to let him know what was going on, so that he could plan for any eventuality.[4] Monckton for his part badgered Horace Wilson to make plans for the Windsors' repatriation in case of war. On 26 August he wrote to suggest that the Duke gave some thought to the type of public work he might undertake in such an event: 'It would, I feel, assist very much in the eyes of the public if you came back to do some specific task which you had offered to do in the emergency.'[5] Before the Duke could reply, war had begun.

On 24 August 1939 a woman styling herself 'Mother of four children' wrote to the Duke from Yorkshire: 'I am making a desperate appeal to you, on behalf of the children of all nations concerned, to use your influence in the cause of peace. As no member of any government can possibly now appeal to Hitler, I beg of you, as a private individual and lover of humanity, to fly to Germany and have a personal interview with him before it is too late.'[6] It was already too late, but the day after he read this letter the Duke telegraphed Hitler: 'Remembering your courtesy and our meeting two years ago, I address to you my entirely personal, simple though very earnest appeal for your utmost influence towards a peaceful solution of the present problems.'[7] The message had hardly been despatched before the prefect of Nice, warned by the Post Office, telephoned to ask whether the Duke was indeed the 'Edward Hertzog von Windsor' whose telegram had just gone off. If so, he wished to express his deep appreciation and gratitude. Hitler's reply was predictable, the only surprise was that he found time to send one: 'You may be sure that my attitude towards

England is the same as ever . . . It depends upon England, however, whether my wishes for the future development of Anglo-German relations materialize.'[1] The Duke expected no more, but he was satisfied that, however futile it might be, this last plea for peace was one that he had to make.

22

Second World War

O N 3 SEPTEMBER 1939 THE WINDSORS WERE BATH-
ing at their house at Antibes. The Duke was told that
the British Ambassador was on the telephone from Paris.
Ten minutes later he came back. 'Great Britain has just declared
war on Germany,' he announced. 'I'm afraid in the end this may
open the way for world Communism.' Then he dived into the
pool.[1]

Though he felt until the day he died that the war could and
should have been avoided, he had no doubt that now it had begun
he must do anything he could to help the British cause. A few days
before, Monckton had asked Horace Wilson what the government
would do to help the Windsors return to Britain, and had been left
in little doubt that the Duke would have to manage as best he
could for himself.[2] When the crisis came, however, more generous
counsels prevailed. George VI ordered that a plane should be sent
to the south of France to pick up the Duke and Duchess. Now it
was the Duke's turn to hang back. When Monckton telephoned
with the good news, he was asked where they were to stay in
England. Monckton replied that, as Fruity Metcalfe was with them
in France, his wife Lady Alexandra had suggested they come to
the Metcalfes' house in Sussex. The Duke then said 'that unless his
brother was ready to have him and his wife to one of their own
houses they would not return to England and I understood him to
say (though I did not hear this well) that people would have to
know why he was not coming'. He would still like the plane,
however, for the use of Metcalfe and his private secretary.[3]

When the Duke and Duchess reported to Metcalfe what they
had done, he was appalled. 'You have just behaved as two spoiled
children,' he told them. 'You *only* think of yourselves. You don't
realize that there is at this moment a war going on, that women
and children are being bombed and killed while *you* talk of your

PRIDE.' Of course the government would not send a plane just for him and the secretary; if by some miracle it did still turn up the Windsors should get straight into it and count themselves lucky. The Duke accepted this diatribe meekly, and next morning he and his wife appeared at 8 a.m. fully dressed, announcing that they had talked it over and were now ready to return without prior conditions. Possibly, as much as pride and anger, the Duchess's fear of flying had contributed to their first decision: 'The lady here is in a panic,' Metcalfe reported, 'the worst fear I've ever seen or heard of – all on account of the aeroplane journey, talks of jumping out, etc.'[1]

Metcalfe was right and the aeroplane did not turn up, though Monckton flew out a few days later with the news of the jobs that would be offered the Duke when he eventually did return. The King had agonized over this problem, and had concluded that the best solution was a civilian post under the Regional Commissioner for Wales: 'They would both stay in Wales,' he told Queen Mary.[2] On second thoughts he concluded that the Duke would be better out of the country and suggested that he might be found some job with the British Military Mission which was shortly to leave for Paris. This would involve the Duke temporarily at least forgoing the honorary rank of Field Marshal, which was still his, but the sacrifice was one he had already said he would be ready to make. Ironside, the Chief of the Imperial General Staff, argued in some dismay that any such job would mean that the Duke must have access to the secret plans of the French. These would inevitably be made known to the Duchess, who was not to be trusted. The King did not dispute Ironside's assessment of the Duchess but said that the really secret information could be kept from the Duke.[3] The offer of an aeroplane for the return journey was renewed, but the Duke – presumably at his wife's urging – sent Monckton back with a plea that a destroyer should be provided instead.[4] With Churchill back at the Admiralty, what had previously been considered impossible suddenly became easy. Louis Mountbatten in his destroyer HMS *Kelly* was sent to Cherbourg to meet them, with Randolph Churchill, resplendent in the uniform of the 4th Hussars marred only by upside-down spurs, in attendance on behalf of his father.

The royal family awaited their return with trepidation. 'What

are we going to do about Mrs S?' the Queen asked Queen Mary –
'Mrs S' as a designation being a little hard on someone who had
been Duchess of Windsor for more than two years. 'Personally I
do not wish to receive her, tho' it must depend on circumstances;
what do you feel about it, Mama?'[1] Queen Mary's response does
not survive, but it is not hard to imagine that she would have
dismissed the idea that the Duchess should be received at court
with quite as much conviction and considerably more emphasis
than her daughter-in-law had displayed. The Duke of Kent fully
shared his mother's view. 'I've seen no reference to David in the
papers,' he wrote a few days after the Windsors left the south of
France. 'Perhaps they've had too much of *importance* to write
about.'[2]

The Duke was as aware as anyone of the reception that might
be awaiting him. As they entered Portsmouth harbour the Duchess
remembered that he said to her: 'I don't know how this will work
out. War should bring families together, even a Royal Family.
But I don't know.'[3] Any hopes he might have had that a real
reconciliation was possible would have been dashed when he found
only Alexandra Metcalfe, Monckton and the Commander-in-
Chief, Portsmouth, waiting to greet them. There was no member
of the royal family, no courtier, not even a palace car to help with
the luggage. It was a black presage of the future.

The Windsors took up residence with the Metcalfes in Sussex,
spending most of their days at the Metcalfes' house in Wilton Place
in London. On 14 September the Duke called on his brother at
Buckingham Palace. Monckton had agreed with Hardinge that
things would be easier if no women were present, and the Queen
was delighted to be out of London; 'It must have been difficult,
and I'm so glad Elizabeth didn't see him,' wrote the Duke of Kent
sympathetically.[4] The meeting went off all right, 'but it was very
unbrotherly,' reported the King. '. . . He was in a very good mood,
his usual swaggering one, laying down the law about everything.'[5]
As the Duke was leaving the King murmured to Monckton: 'I
think it went all right.' The Duke noticed the exchange and asked
afterwards what his brother had said. Monckton told him, 'and
he said that it had been all right because, on my advice, he had
kept off all contentious subjects'.[6]

One subject they did discuss was the Duke's future employment.

In her memoirs the Duchess of Windsor states that her husband made it clear he would much prefer the job in Wales to a return to France. The King seemed to acquiesce but said he would have to discuss the matter with his ministers.[1] In his own record of the conversation, however, the King says that the Duke was happy to go back to France but wanted first to spend a month in England, during which time he would be attached to the various Home Commands, 'where he could take his wife and flaunt her before the British Army. I told him he would not get a good reception if he did.'[2] Whichever is correct, by the time the Duke called on Hore-Belisha at the War Office the following day, it seems to have been assumed that he would take up the job in France, and discussion turned on his proposed tour of the Army Commands and whether he must give up his Field Marshal's baton. Hore-Belisha, who knew the King would have strong views on the first point at least, played for time and called at the Palace before he gave the Duke his final answer. He found the King much distressed, walking about the room and saying agitatedly that there would be unpleasant scenes if his brother insisted on taking his wife around England with him. He remarked mournfully that all his ancestors had succeeded to the throne after their predecessors had died, but 'Mine is not only alive, but very much so!' The best thing would be for the Duke to proceed at once to Paris.[3]

Hore-Belisha gallantly volunteered to break this as tactfully as possible to the Duke. He did the best he could, pleading somewhat unconvincingly that the job in France was of such importance that a month's delay would imperil the safety of the state, and that visits of inspection around the British Isles by someone so highly placed would risk exposing secret troop movements. It is unlikely that the Duke was convinced by such specious arguments, but he accepted them gracefully. When Martin Scanlon called on him after his first interview with Hore-Belisha he found him 'wreathed in smiles' and talking with evident enthusiasm of his job in France.[4] He can have found little to smile at in the interview he had had the same morning with Chamberlain. The Prime Minister, no doubt with a view to preparing his visitor for the unpleasant news to come, had confined himself to gloomy prognostications about the difficulties ahead. He passed the Duke a bundle of – presumably abusive – letters which he said had been received since the Windsors returned to England; the Duke handed them back unread, saying that he got the same sort of thing himself. That concluded the dialogue.[1]

Lady Alexandra Metcalfe noted in her diary that in fact two to three hundred letters a day were pouring in and that only a handful of these were hostile.[2] Though a visit to the shuttered and weed-infested Fort Belvedere caused a certain gloom, the Duke seems on the whole to have enjoyed his return to England and to have been pleased by his reception. Harold Nicolson met him, looking 'grotesquely young', at lunch with Sybil Colefax. 'I have seldom seen the Duke in such cheerful spirits,' he wrote, 'and it was rather touching to witness their delight at being back in England. There was no false note.' H. G. Wells was also at the luncheon, and Nicolson and Wells left together. 'You must admit that the man has got charm,' said Nicolson. 'Glamour,' amended Wells. 'Charm,' insisted Nicolson; 'Oh very well, have it your own way.'[3]

On 29 September the Duke returned to France. He left his wife at Versailles and arrived the following day at his new headquarters at Vincennes. The Military Mission to which he was attached was under the command of Major General Sir Richard Howard-Vyse, known to everyone as 'the Wombat'. Howard-Vyse was an affable, kindly man, of limited military distinction. Metcalfe, who arrived before the Duke, condemned him as having the tact of 'the ex-heavyweight champion of the world, Mr Carnera', and as being obsessed by the importance of his job and the fact that he was 'the big man . . . who will tell HRH what he is to do and what he is *not* to do'.[4] In claiming this Howard-Vyse was entirely within his rights. A few days before he left England the Duke had written to Ironside, to clarify the position. Although he was technically under the orders of Howard-Vyse, he wrote, he assumed that he would not be put in the position of receiving orders from him which would restrict his movements.[5] Ironside's reply was uncompromising. Howard-Vyse, he pronounced, would 'in no way stop your leave and movements any more than he would any other Major General under his command. But I think you must understand that you cannot be a free-lance in the war area. You have accepted an appointment in His Majesty's Army and must be under the command of your Chief to carry out any orders he may give you. I do not see how it is possible for you to serve under any other conditions.'[1] Whether Ironside cleared the text of this letter with the King in advance is uncertain, but on the day it was despatched George VI told the Duke of Kent: 'David after all these many years does at last come under military discipline and the CIGS will see that he obeys his orders.'[2]

Alexandra Metcalfe predicted trouble; the Duke, she wrote, would think the job too small for him and would get on badly with Howard-Vyse.[3] It at first seemed she had been over-pessimistic. The Duke was determined to make a good impression, while Howard-Vyse, wrote a member of the staff, was a 'most perfect host and there was never any friction between them'.[4] But there was a time-bomb ticking away beneath their relationship which was bound eventually to disrupt if not destroy it. On 22 September Hore-Belisha had asked the Duke of Gloucester, chief liaison officer between the British and French armies, whether his brother should be allowed to visit British units. Gloucester at first said it would be all right for him to call on Corps Headquarters, then changed his mind and told Ironside that he should visit no British formation lower than GHQ.[5] Howard-Vyse, perplexed as to what was intended, appealed to Hardinge for instructions which he could show the Duke.[6] Hardinge confirmed that there would be no objection to occasional visits to the British GHQ but: 'His Majesty presumes that this would only be done for some special purpose, and that he would have instructions to return as soon as his task had been accomplished, and not be allowed to go drifting about at his pleasure among the Units of the Expeditionary Force.'[7] Not surprisingly Howard-Vyse shrank from showing this somewhat brutal directive to the Duke and took the line of least resistance, saying nothing on the subject and hoping that no occasion would arise in which the Duke would 'drift around' among British troops and word get back to London. It was a faint hope, and was duly extinguished a few weeks later.

What the Duke *was* supposed to do, what in fact the Mission was supposed to do, is a matter of some obscurity. In his admirably researched if sometimes partial study *The Duke of Windsor's War*, Michael Bloch has suggested that its real purpose was to spy on the French, who were notoriously reluctant to provide their allies with information about their plans and dispositions.[1] Metcalfe less civilly described the Mission as a group of 'dug-outs from the General down – doing a job of no consequence, a more or less made up job'.[2] However little weight was given to their work in London, the members of the Mission themselves certainly saw it as being an important part of their responsibility to report on the situation of the French. In this work the Duke of Windsor, with his excellent contacts at the highest level and ability to penetrate French headquarters and messes which would be closed to most British visitors, could play a valuable part. Howard-Vyse told Metcalfe he proposed to send the Duke to visit different parts of the French lines and to 'feel the sense of the civil people'. He also mentioned that he would want the Duke to inspect 'the Italian front', a prima facie somewhat surprising assignment which the Duke was to remember a few months later.[3]

The Duke shared Metcalfe's low opinion of the Mission staff. 'They are mostly dug-outs with a sprinkling of . . . pretty slick Regulars,' he told Monckton. 'A quite interesting lot professionally, but I am glad I have decided to mess and be billeted on my own.'[4] The future General Redman remembered him as being 'very much a fellow member of the mess', talking 'simply and freely' and never monopolizing the conversation,[5] but such occasions must have arisen infrequently. When he was not on tour, he was more often to be found in Paris than Vincennes. 'His Nibs is getting gradually more and more dug in at Suchet,' reported Metcalfe early in October,[6] and by the middle of the month he and the Duchess had reopened their house there, with the main rooms closed off and only a skeleton staff employed. They entertained modestly and dined out as often as the reduced social whirl of Paris permitted.

At the beginning of October the Duke took off on the first of his tours. He started with lunch at General Gamelin's headquarters. 'HRH was wonderful . . .' wrote Metcalfe, 'got everything going well and everyone talking and laughing etc. He is really first class at something like this.'[7] Then it was off on an eight-hundred-mile tour of inspection, mainly along those sections of the line which ran from the British sector around Lille to the virtual gap in the defences in the Ardennes mountains. The Duke was impressed by the fortifications he saw the first day but less struck by the defences on the Belgian frontier itself. 'Not so hot, neither the heads, nor the stuff we looked at,' commented Metcalfe, comforting himself with the fact that Belgium lay between the front and Germany. The travel was uncomfortable, they were on the road by 7 a.m., they rarely arrived anywhere before it was time for a late dinner, the Duke enjoyed himself enormously. 'HRH was all through absolutely delightful company,' wrote Metcalfe. He remained in splendid form throughout the tour, except for the uneasy moment when the hotel bills had to be paid – 'Then he was *frightful.*'[1]

Back in Paris he busied himself preparing a report on all he had seen. The four reports which he compiled between early October 1939 and late February 1940 on various sections of the French line[2] have been dismissed as being of insignificant value or, alternatively, entirely the work of the junior officers who travelled with him. Neither charge seems justified. The reports are sensible and well-observed, containing many observations which should have been of interest in London and some serious criticisms of French pre-paredness and morale which were to prove distressingly correct in June 1940. Neither the prose style nor the technical detail suggests that the Duke relied heavily on the help of others; their main value lies not in their elegance nor their profound understanding of military matters, but in the fact that their author had access to parts of the French line which would have been barred to other members of Howard-Vyse's staff.

The first report he sent under cover of a personal letter to Ironside in London. In the letter he said that he had found Howard-Vyse and his staff 'helpful and pleasant to work with' and that he was confident he could continue to do a useful job. In his report he had 'dealt at length . . . with the obvious weaknesses and defects of the French defences along the Belgian frontier'. The French were not digging in and were physically unfit; 'they are determined if possible to give the Germans battle in Belgium. Of course they will burrow like rabbits at the sound of the first shell, but French logic says never dig unless you have to.' He was not impressed by the majority of the French commanders, the best being Georges and Billotte. Gaston Billotte, he believed, was 'a man who might well reach the very top if the war were to last a long time' – or, unhappily, as it fell out, if Billotte was to last a long time; he died in May 1940, cutting short what most people believed could have been a remarkable career and, incidentally, removing a possible rival to de Gaulle.[1] Ironside replied warmly, saying that both the report and the covering letter were most valuable and 'just what we want'; empty courtesy, perhaps, but not wholly undeserved.[2]

The Maginot Line, with its strengths and limitations, psychological as well as physical, was a constant theme of the Duke's reports. Several years after the war a friend told him that, during the advance of the US Third Army across France, General Patton had asked British Intelligence whether the guns of the Maginot Line could be turned round to fire west instead of east. The question was referred to the War Office, who ransacked their archives and 'found that the only adequate report on the Maginot Line had been written by you'. Patton had been given the information he needed. The guns could fire only north and east, the Duke remembered: 'The Maginot Line must have been as useless to the Germans as it was to the French.'[3]

At times the Duke's commentaries were strikingly prescient. The French, he wrote in his final report, were obsessed by the wonders of the Maginot Line. There was no provision for defence in depth, and in the Meuse valley there were virtually no defences at all. 'It is perhaps fortunate the Germans did not attack through Luxembourg and Belgium in November.'[4] But he was by no means always right: Hitler would attack Holland but would not march into Belgium, he assured Ironside, 'because that country will provide him with a buffer state and put Holland out of reach of the Allies by land'.[5] It would be extravagant to claim for the Duke either great strategic acumen or detailed military knowledge; what can fairly be said is that his reports were conscientious, sensible, and well worth studying by those concerned.

Any appreciation of this in Whitehall was marred by one of those silly squabbles which so often arose around the Duke's activities. The incident is worth dwelling on as showing how differently two observers can view the same event. On 18 October the Duke called on Gort and the British GHQ. 'Gort very definitely made me the visiting fireman,' he recalled, 'and had all the Corps and Divisional Commanders and their staffs to meet me as we entered each of their areas. Therefore, when guards were turned out and gave "Royal Salutes" I naturally took them, never doubting for one moment that I was not [sic] expected to do so. Further,

Gloucester was behind with the group of officers in attendance, and the sign of his celebrated high-pitched giggle gave me no indication that these "Royal Salutes" were intended for anyone but myself.'[1] For his part the Duke of Gloucester reported that things began to go wrong when the HQ guard of the 2nd Coldstreams turned out 'and to my horror I saw David taking the salute in spite of the C in C and Dill being present'. The same thing happened at various points along the route. 'The climax of the tour came when . . . he walked along some trenches being dug by the Ulster Rifles and talked to a number of men. Wombat was in despair and at last got the C in C to drag him away. In some ways I blame the C in C for letting him take the salute and for not warning the Corps commanders what to expect . . . Needless to say everybody was very polite to him but one could see nobody was at ease or very pleased.'[2] Gort's Chief of Staff, Henry Pownall, shared Gloucester's view of the incident. The Duke of Windsor was pushing himself forward most indecorously and had outraged the Commander-in-Chief. 'If Master W thinks he can stage a come-back he's mighty wrong.'[3]

The Duke of Kent fanned the flames by writing innocently to the King: 'I see David and Harry went together to look at troops but the former seemed to get all the attention. Was that true?'[4] The King knew that it was true and was determined that it should not recur. Hardinge assured Ironside there were no recriminations: 'His Majesty feels sure that the Duke made everything extremely difficult for all concerned during his recent visit to the Front, and does not blame anyone for the contretemps.' But such visits to the line should be eschewed in future.[5]

Any hope that this storm in a teacup would blow itself out was ended three weeks later when the Duke was due to visit the headquarters of the RAF in France. As King he had been Marshal of the Royal Air Force as well as Field Marshal; since he had now adopted the rank of Major General, it followed, to his mind, that he must also be an Air Vice Marshal. He wrote to ask that his uniform should be altered accordingly.[6] This caused the most fearful furore. Churchill, who mistakenly thought the Duke was planning to appear as a Marshal of the Royal Air Force, reported that the three Service Ministers and their Chiefs of Staff in solemn enclave had decided that only a Major General's uniform was appropriate for him until his period of active service was over.[1]

Meanwhile Howard-Vyse had been finding it ever more difficult to keep the Duke away from British troops without telling him they were out of bounds. The Duke argued that he could not make sensible observations about, for instance, the French system of laying out pill-boxes, unless he had a chance of comparing the British equivalent. 'If he is prevented from coming he will obviously say that he is not being given a chance to do his job properly,' wrote the Duke of Gloucester, continuing rather unexpectedly, 'with, I think, a lot of right on his side.'[2] Eventually the Wombat came clean and told the Duke bluntly about the ruling which restricted his contact with British troops to occasional visits to GHQ. 'His reaction to it was bitter, of course, but not at all surprised, and rather to upbraid me, mildly, for not having been completely free with him from the start.' Howard-Vyse admitted to Hardinge that his hope had been that if he said nothing, the restrictions would eventually be relaxed. 'It is all a great tragedy and depresses me a good deal, especially as he is doing some good work with the French.'[3]

The Duke's private comments about Howard-Vyse were anything but mild; he was 'not intelligent . . . a cracking snob . . . and personally I would never have trusted him a yard, even before this incident'.[4] But the real enemies were in London. His immediate resolve was to fly there to have the matter out with his brother. He telegraphed Monckton to ask him to arrange the necessary interviews,[5] and prepared his notes for what he expected to be a stormy meeting. He planned to reproach the King for his duplicity, to say he would never have accepted the appointment on such terms, to accuse his brother of cowardice – 'On the other hand, maybe you hate me and always have. You have certainly disguised it very well in the past, especially when I was King.'[6] Churchill affected to believe the Duke to be planning his visit so as to enjoy a short holiday, and urged him to postpone it until his leave was due.[7] The Duke responded angrily to Monckton that he only wished to come because: 'The recent exposure of a network of intrigue against me makes my position both impossible and intolerable until I have been able to clear the matter up with my brother.'[8] To Churchill he wrote that the situation was neither new nor surprising, 'being merely fresh evidence of my brother's continued efforts to humiliate me by every means in his and his courtiers' power'.[1] He compounded this last diatribe by addressing a hypothetical censor on the outside of the envelope: 'To whomsoever steams this letter open! I hope you are as edified at the contents of this letter as I am over having to write them.'[2]

He met a brick wall. George VI would not see the Duke unless Ironside was present, Ironside wanted Howard-Vyse there. Howard-Vyse could not be spared from his post. 'The upshot of the matter is,' wrote Monckton, 'that I do not think . . . the King would be willing to discuss the matter with you yet.'[3] The Duke responded yet more indignantly. He might have guessed, he wrote, that his brother would be scared of a tête-à-tête; at least George VI's insistence on having Ironside present meant that he could bring Monckton too – a consolation which was no doubt flattering to his putative second but cannot have given Monckton much pleasure in view of his desperate efforts to avoid embroilment in the row between the royal brothers.[4] Churchill now weighed in with advice to the Duke not to kick against the pricks: 'Having voluntarily resigned the finest Throne in the world . . . it would be natural to treat all minor questions of ceremony and precedence as entirely beneath your interest and your dignity: otherwise one merely gives opportunity for slights from those who are unfriendly.'[5] It was not questions of ceremony and precedence which worried him, retorted the Duke despairingly, it was the ban on his visits to British troops.[6] But he could not ignore Monckton's solemn warning that, if he were to have an open quarrel with the King on the question, 'people would in the vast majority support him because there is a war on and he is who he is'.[7]

It seems to have been Ironside who resolved the question in a way that gave the Duke a measure of satisfaction. The two men met on 19 November. Ironside told Hardinge that he had spoken sternly to the errant Major General and reminded him that he was no more than a liaison officer with no rights of inspection or special privileges,[8] but the Duke himself felt the CIGS had listened to him sympathetically and had agreed that he had been placed in an impossible position. He hoped that Ironside would prevail upon the King as 'he has a forceful personality . . . But we know that the second line of defence in Queen Elizabeth is of Maginot proportions, so that Ironside, like Hitler, may be up against a tougher proposition than he knows.'[1] Hardinge, presumably for the King's signature, prepared a draft letter stating that, if the Duke would not do his duty as a Major General in the same way as the Duke of Gloucester, then he must resign his appointment,[2] but Ironside seems to have persuaded the King to be more generous. A week later Howard-Vyse announced that he had received a letter from Ironside saying there was no objection to the Duke visiting British units for a definite purpose, and with prior approval.[3] 'I have won my point . . .' the Duke told Monckton. 'Still, at the same time, the edge has naturally been taken off the keenness in the job, and I am really only carrying on because it's the one that suits the Duchess and myself the best.'[4]

This altercation over his right to visit British troops contributed to the Duke's soured disillusionment with the conduct of the war. As he saw it, he had thrown himself wholeheartedly into the struggle; his reward had been to meet with a humiliating rebuff. The Duchess egged him on to disassociate himself from a government that sought only to destroy what was left of his reputation; it was 'an amazingly well thought-out piece of cunning propaganda', she told Monckton. The British soldiers in France, little knowing how the Duke was kept away from them, would assume he had no interest in them and would feel resentment accordingly. He would be '"banished from the hearts of the citizens", and by what sly means, for we are like rats in a trap until the end of the war'.[5] Howard-Vyse would hardly have accepted this somewhat tendentious version of events, but he was perceptive enough to realize 'the depth of your feelings about what has passed and the discouragement which it has entailed'. His work, he told the Duke, was of genuine importance, his reports 'extremely valuable', his visits of immeasurable assistance to morale.[6] The Duke was unconvinced. His visits to the Maginot Line at the end of 1939 were noticeably lacking in *élan*. He seemed to take little interest in what was shown him, noted a colonel on the French staff: '*Il posait des questions dans un français hésitant, mais il semblait que cela soit par politesse.*'[7]

It was shortly after this tour that Count Zech, the German Minister to the Netherlands, wrote to Berlin claiming to have a 'line leading to the Duke of Windsor'. The Duke, he said, was disgruntled over the insignificance of his role and had an extremely low opinion of Neville Chamberlain. 'Something like the beginning of a Fronde' was forming about him, which might one day be of significance.[1] Three weeks later he wrote again to pass on gossip apparently derived from the Duke's entourage: even if Germany invaded Belgium the allies would remain in their defensive positions behind the Belgian frontier.[2] Since, as Michael Bloch has pointed out,[3] this was the exact opposite of what the Duke knew to be the truth about allied intentions, the conclusion can only be that Zech's informant was singularly ill-informed or that the Duke was part of an ingenious deception operation. The first seems more likely. But any *habitué* of the Windsors' table would have heard much to comfort those who hoped for a German victory. The Duke was pessimistic both about the allies' ability and their will to wage a war. 'There is no enthusiasm over this war,' he told Herman Rogers after a visit to London: 'A grim and rather sullen determination to make the best of the hopeless mess that successive bad governments have got the British people into, is the atmosphere we left not unwillingly behind us.'[4]

When in London again in January 1940, he encountered Beaverbrook at his most mischievous. Both men agreed that the war should be ended by a peace offer to Germany, and Beaverbrook urged the Duke to 'get out of uniform, come home, and after enlisting powerful City support, stump the country, in which case he predicted that the Duke would have a tremendous success'. Monckton, who was present, drily pointed out that this would mean the Duke would become liable to pay British income tax, and claimed later to have told the errant Major General that Beaverbrook's words were probably treasonable as well. His arguments prevailed, and Beaverbrook's blandishments were dismissed as impracticable if not totally forgotten.[5]

Useful activity could sometimes jolt the Duke out of his despondency. A visit to the French Army at the end of February 1940 was a great success. 'We *really worked*,' reported Metcalfe. 'HRH was *absolutely wonderful* all through. I think he was better on this tour than ever before . . . He *never* got tired and he never was in a bad temper or bad humour and always *interested* in *everything*.'[6] The Duke of Gloucester saw his brother as the tour was starting and found him unusually silent, but 'it is the first time for years I have seen him without that worried look'.[7] Such periods of euphoria were rare, however. One factor which added to his gloom was that he had to some extent lost confidence in Walter Monckton. Monckton was now in charge of the Censorship Bureau, and as such it seemed to the Duke that he was putting the interests of the government before personal loyalties. 'We can sense in our old friend a certain wariness where I am concerned,' he told Guedalla.[1] If Monckton had defected to the enemy, who was left effectively to fight his cause in London? Even in Paris there were only Metcalfe and his comptroller, Gray Phillips, in whom he had complete faith. And from Fruity Metcalfe, his oldest and most loyal friend, he was about to part company.

On 10 May 1940 the Germans invaded the Low Countries; within a few days the French line had been broken; German armies, swarming through the Ardennes and across the Meuse, were threatening Paris. The Duke drove with his wife as far as Biarritz, ensconced her there, and then returned to Paris. 'I would much prefer that HRH did not come back for the present,' Howard-Vyse told Phillips on 20 May. The future of the Mission was uncertain, it might have to move at any moment, its work seemed largely over, 'consequently, and for reasons of personal safety also, there is at the moment nothing which I can ask HRH to do'.[2] Either the Duke never received this message or he decided to ignore it. By 22 May he was back in Paris. He seems to have been given as little to do as Howard-Vyse had prophesied; according to Virginia Cowles he spent hours searching for a map of Holland. Having at last found one he stuck it on the wall, and then realized that, so rapid had been the German advance, maps of Belgium and France were already needed.[3] He fretted desperately at the inactivity, and his separation from the Duchess. 'The futile role I played at the Mission died a natural death with the German offensive,' he told Gray Phillips.[4] Metcalfe, who had no doubt that the Duke's duty was to remain with his unit, wrote to his wife in alarm: 'I am *very* uneasy about him. He might do *anything* – anything *except* the right thing . . . He talks of having done enough! . . . I do not know what will happen. W is like a magnet. It is terrible.'[5] The comments show how little he was now being consulted; Metcalfe evidently did not know that the day before, when lunching at the British

Embassy, the Duke had announced he was returning to Antibes 'to settle the Duchess in'.[1]

The draft of a telegram which Churchill was to send the Duke a few weeks later contained the sentence: 'Already there is a great deal of doubt as to the circumstances in which Your Royal Highness left Paris.'[2] Churchill cut it out. It would have been an injustice to the Duke if he had not done so. Howard-Vyse wrote to Hardinge on 29 May to say that the Duke was now back in the south of France: 'He quite saw my point about there being nothing for him to do here – between you and me he is *not at all* for running into danger – and suggested that he might have a look at the French troops on the Italian front. It is quite a good idea, unless and until Mussolini marches.'[3] The terms of the letter are hardly flattering to the Duke, but they acquit him of the charge of desertion, which has been levelled at him. The letter which the Duke wrote to Howard-Vyse in early June, emphasizing that his departure from Paris had been agreed between them, may perhaps betray a slightly uneasy conscience, but again clears the writer of the main charge, as does Howard-Vyse's affable reply.[4] The Duke left Paris with the approval, indeed to the relief of the Military Mission.

It is less easy to acquit him of the charge of abandoning the faithful Metcalfe with singular ruthlessness. The story as set out by Metcalfe is painfully clear. 'Re my *late* Master,' he told his wife, 'he has run like two rabbits.' His plans must have been made twenty-four hours before, yet he had left without saying a word to Metcalfe or his comptroller, Phillips; he had taken all the cars and left not so much as a bicycle; he had stripped the house of all articles of value: 'After twenty years I am through – *utterly* I despise him . . . He deserted his job in 1936; well, he's deserted his country now, at a time when every office boy and cripple is trying to do *what he can*. It is the *end*.'[5] To the Duke he wrote briefly on 3 June to report that he was leaving that day for England. 'I have had not one word from you, Sir, and so can only surmise that you intend to stay where you are now. I am sorry, Sir, to leave your service, but I feel sure that it is the *only* thing to do.'[6]

To say that the Duke had deserted his country when he had nothing to do in Paris, and had been told to leave by his superior officer, was obviously unfair, but Metcalfe's indignation at himself being left in the lurch is more than understandable. It is not inconceivable that the Duke might have behaved in such a way. It has already been remarked how reluctant he was to receive advice which he suspected was going to be unpalatable. He might have shrunk from a confrontation with the robustly belligerent Metcalfe. And yet the story does not altogether make sense. As Howard-Vyse had ordered him south the main ground for Metcalfe's opposition had been removed. Why then should he shrink from telling Metcalfe what he was doing? Why did Metcalfe not know what had transpired at the Military Mission? Why did he not know what the Duke had said to the Ambassador the day before? Why did he tell his wife that Phillips had not been warned, yet in the same letter add: 'He said to Gray something about coming back later on!!!' There seems to have been a total breakdown of communications between the two men, for which all the blame is not necessarily on one side. The Duke's reply to Metcalfe's letter suggested that it was he who felt he was the injured party. Metcalfe should have resigned before quitting his post, he wrote: 'I believe that is the usual procedure.'[1] To Phillips the Duke wrote that Metcalfe's return to England was obviously the best thing, but that he should have got his employer's permission first: 'However it is a typical Fruity gesture and one would not expect him to behave otherwise.'[2] When the two men met again after the war they renewed their friendship without any recriminations over the past. This suggests, certainly, that Metcalfe was not a man to cherish a grudge, but also, perhaps, that he did not feel the case to have been so unequivocally black and white as it had first appeared to him. The Duke was without doubt preoccupied by what he saw as the urgent need to rejoin his wife, and acted to that end with little consideration for the needs of others, but it does not follow that he behaved with the personal treachery which Metcalfe ascribed to him in the moment of his fiercest rage.

The reunion with the Duchess duly took place. It is important to understand just how much it mattered to both parties in the marriage that they should be together, in a world that seemed otherwise so threatening and hostile. A few months earlier, when the Duke returned from a brief visit to England, Metcalfe remarked how pleased the Windsors were to be together again. 'It is *very true* and deep stuff,' he wrote.[3] It was deep stuff, for the Duke the most deep and true feeling he had ever had in his life, for the

Duchess not so overpowering, but still the only thing to which she could cling in a disintegrating Europe. The Duke knew that at such a time he *had* to be with his wife; it was fortunate for his reputation that Howard-Vyse did not try to keep him in Paris, for no one who knew him well would have staked much money on his obeying such an order.

Together the couple went from Biarritz to La Cröe, where they camped nervously, awaiting the final cataclysm. The Duke made some desultory visits to the French forces on the Italian frontier but most of his time was spent at home. The Windsors were there, entertaining Maurice Chevalier to lunch, when the Italians declared war on France on 10 June. Six days later Pétain became Prime Minister and asked for an armistice. German troops were less than two hundred miles away, with nothing to stop their advance. It was more than time to go. After hectic telephone exchanges with the British Embassy camping in Bordeaux and the Consul Generals at Nice and Marseilles, a plan evolved. Major Dodds, the Consul General at Nice, was about to evacuate his post and drive to Spain. The Duke and his party, which now included Gray Phillips, would join the convoy. By midday on 20 June they reached Perpignan, ten miles from the Spanish border. There they planned to spend the night, but they had hardly reserved rooms before the Mayor in great excitement arrived to report that the entire French government would arrive at any moment, that the town would probably be bombed by the Germans, that the Duke and his entourage must move on.[1] After protracted haggling visas were obtained for the entire party, and at 7 p.m. they crossed into Spain. Wearily they journeyed on; it was midnight before they found temporary refuge in a hotel in Barcelona. The next stage of the Windsors' exile had begun.

23

Spain and Portugal

────

S PAIN WAS FAR FROM BEING AN IDEAL ASYLUM. Under the fascist government of General Franco, who owed much to the Germans and Italians for the help given to the Insurgents during the Civil War, it would have been astonishing if Spain had not favoured the German cause. When France collapsed and the future of Britain seemed insecure, there was a great temptation for Franco to join in the war, seize Gibraltar and close that end of the Mediterranean to British shipping. He hesitated, partly because he had little wish to see Germany all-powerful in Europe, partly because he was determined not to involve his war-shattered country in further fighting unless he was convinced that the pickings would be rich and the risks minimal. He preferred to bide his time, but it was not a comfortable moment for an Englishman to be in Spain.

Among the most uncomfortable was the British Ambassador, whose task it was to convince the Spanish government that the war was not lost, Britain was still a force to be reckoned with, and any aggression on the part of the Spanish would in the long run cost them dear. It was the Duke's good fortune that the man charged with this unappealing task was his old friend Samuel Hoare. Hoare had many enemies in London; Cadogan at the Foreign Office wrote splenetically when he heard of the appointment: 'The quicker we get them out of the country the better. But I'd sooner send them to a penal settlement. He'll be the Quisling of England when Germany conquers us and I'm dead.'[1] But though the architect of the Hoare–Laval pact seemed to many an unfortunate choice for so important a post, he played a weak hand with considerable skill, consolidating such support as the British enjoyed within the Spanish government and countering the efforts of the Germans to cajole or frighten the Spanish into the war. He was disconcerted and not altogether pleased when a telephone call from

Barcelona told him that the Duke of Windsor had entered his bailiwick, but concluded that he must do his best for his unexpected visitor.

He had no choice, anyway. Even in the chaotic crisis engendered by the fall of France, Churchill had found time to remark in Cabinet that steps must be taken to ensure the Duke's safe return.[1] Two days later Eden announced that the Duke had arrived in Barcelona and Churchill ordered that the Ambassador should get in touch to offer him help and hospitality.[2] The King did much the same, though grumbling to his mother that David 'never let anybody know his plans or intentions beforehand'[3] – hardly a fair complaint, since the Duke had discussed his plans with the British Embassy and left with the Consul General. The Duke travelled on to Madrid, where he installed himself at the Ritz. Hoare called on him the same evening.

It cannot have been a cheerful conversation. Hoare was certainly among those who believed that the war, if not lost, was virtually unwinnable, and that a negotiated peace should not be ruled out. With the recollection of France's ignominious defeat still fresh in his mind, and cut off from the belligerent zest of Churchill's Britain, it is not surprising that the Duke held the same view. He was incautious in airing it outside the circle of the British Ambassador. He told a member of the American Embassy staff that 'the most important thing now to be done was to end the war before thousands more were killed or maimed to save the faces of a few politicians'.[4] To think this in June 1940 was forgivable; to say it openly to a representative of a foreign, even if friendly power, was to say the least indiscreet. It is hardly surprising that the British Ambassador had to telegraph London to urge the government to contradict German propaganda saying that Hoare and the Duke were carrying on negotiations for peace.[5] Yet most of the time the Duke conducted himself well. Hoare's final report to Churchill on the Windsors' stay in Madrid concluded that the visit had stimulated German propaganda but had otherwise done good: 'They have both been very discreet and have made a good impression on the Spaniards.'[6] To Halifax he said they had 'behaved admirably' and had made themselves very popular with the Spaniards.[7] They were the star turn at a vast reception at the British Embassy and put up a more than creditable performance: 'So far from making

421

any defeatist remarks, they went out of their way to show their belief in final victory.'[1]

When he reached Madrid the Duke found waiting for him a telegram from Churchill urging him to move on at once to Lisbon, whence a flying boat would take him back to England. Saighton Grange, a country house belonging to the Duke of Westminster, was offered him as a residence. It so happened that the Duke of Kent was at that moment embarking on a visit to Portugal. The Portuguese dictator, Salazar, had already told the British Ambassador, the Duke's old friend from Vienna Walford Selby, that it would be 'inconvenient and undesirable' if the two Dukes were there at the same time.[2] Whether word of this reached the Duke is unclear, but he fully shared Salazar's view; the day after his arrival in Madrid Hoare cabled Churchill to say that the Duke would move to Lisbon as soon as his brother had departed – in a week or so.[3] That the Duke did genuinely wish to avoid what could have been an awkward encounter is obviously the case, that he had other reasons for playing for time was unfortunately soon to be quite as clear.

On 24 June he sent a personal message to Churchill. He was grateful for the offer of a flight back to England, he said, but he could not see what he could do once he got back which would not make his presence 'an embarrassment to all concerned, myself included'. Instead, he suggested, as he was still anxious to serve the Empire, could not 'some useful form of employment with more official backing than I have hitherto received' be found for him somewhere outside the United Kingdom?[4] Churchill replied that it would be best if such matters were discussed *after* the Duke had returned.[5] The Duke now dug in his heels. He could not agree to return, he cabled, until 'everything *has* been considered and I know the result'. He and the Duchess were not prepared once again to find themselves 'regarded by the British public as in a different status to other members of my family'.[6] In a supplementary note to Hoare he explained that he meant by this that he and the Duchess should be received regularly at Buckingham Palace and other royal residences: 'We have no desire to sit in their laps, but THEY must make it publicly clear by whatever means they care to adopt, that this family feud is for once and for all at an end.' What was more, if their return to England involved them in any additional taxation due to their loss of non-resident status, then this must be made good from the Civil List or other public funds.[1] With some apprehension Hoare passed on these demands. 'I could not have put more strongly case for immediate departure but with no result,' he told Churchill.[2] The following day he made the splendidly impracticable suggestion that a command at sea might be the best answer for the Duke's future: 'I feel that you will never have peace and perhaps I shall never get him away unless you can find something for him.'[3]

To lay down conditions in this way, and to badger the Prime Minister over points of protocol, at a moment when Britain, standing alone, seemed faced with imminent invasion and on Churchill's shoulders rested the responsibility for its defence, is conduct that cannot be condoned. To state that something is inexcusable and then to excuse it is a posture not infrequently adopted by the biographer. Without seeking to excuse the Duke, it should be remembered that for the last nine months he had been brooding rancorously on the way he and his wife had been treated on their return to London. Since then had come the fresh and, in his eyes, still more cruel humiliation over his visits to British troops. His sense of proportion, never his strongest quality, had failed him totally, and he saw the wrongs done to him as iniquities rivalling in significance any outrage committed by the Germans. He was prepared to move on to Lisbon, in preparation for a return to England, but until his wrongs had been righted he was not going to take the next and final step. Otherwise he imagined a future in which he and his wife would be compelled to live perpetually as second-class citizens; despised poor relations who were not even accepted as relations; inhabiting a *demi-monde* in which nobody who prided himself on his respectability would dare to tread.

While these exchanges were going on and the Duke was leisurely preparing for the next stage in his journey, a sub-plot was being worked out of which he was almost entirely unaware. In his fascinating *Operation Willi* Michael Bloch has exposed the extraordinary lengths to which the Germans went to keep the Duke of Windsor in Europe, and make use of him as a tool of their policy. The news that he had taken refuge in Spain had caused great excitement in Berlin, particularly in the mind of Ribbentrop. The German Foreign Minister knew that the Duke had been well disposed to Germany before the war, he knew that the Duke thought the war unnecessary, he was soon to hear reports that the Duke was speaking in favour of a negotiated peace: from this it was but a step to imagining the Duke broadcasting to the British people to urge them to see reason and come to terms, or even returning to a German-occupied Britain as a puppet head of state. If this happy dénouement were to be achieved it was essential that the Duke should remain in Spain, a country sympathetic to the Axis cause, where he could constantly be available to the blandishments of German agents or their sympathizers. In Lisbon he would be that much less accessible to persuasion; once back in England or elsewhere in the Empire he would be lost for ever.

On 23 June, with the Duke about to arrive in Madrid, the German Ambassador, von Stohrer, telegraphed Berlin to report the news and request instructions.[1] Ribbentrop replied asking if the Spaniards could detain the Windsors for a couple of weeks while exit visas were being granted.[2] Stohrer saw the Spanish Foreign Minister, Colonel Beigbeder, who promised to do his best.[3] In fact he did little but assure the Duke that the Spanish government would be delighted for him to stay for as long as he wanted and to offer him the Palace of the Caliph at Ronda for a residence. When the Duke called on Beigbeder shortly before he left Madrid he remarked – so Beigbeder told Stohrer and Stohrer Ribbentrop – that he would not return to England unless his wife were recognized as a member of the royal family and he were given a job of influence. He also 'expressed himself . . . in strong terms against Churchill and the war'.[4] When some years later the Duke was shown a copy of Stohrer's despatch he wrote 'Correct' against the first point and 'No' against the second.[5] Stohrer's reliability as a witness is not made more impressive by the fact that in the same despatch he reported the Duke's main reasons for proceeding to Portugal as being to replenish his supplies of money and to meet the Duke of Kent: the first irrelevant, the second the opposite of the truth.

On 2 July, while Ribbentrop considered how to prevent his prey eluding him and decided to have recourse to more drastic measures, the Duke left Madrid. The following day he arrived in Lisbon.

Selby did all he could to make the party welcome. They were installed in the villa of a rich banker, Ricardo Espírito Santo Silva, at Cascais, a few miles outside Lisbon. The house had been recommended by the manager of the Palacio Hotel at Estoril, where the Duke had originally been intended to stay. Selby cheerfully admitted that Espírito Santo was well known for his pro-German sympathies, but said that as the Duke's stay was likely to be only for a few days he had not felt it mattered.[1] In fact Espírito Santo was probably more interested in the social kudos that would arise from the Duke's presence in his house than any possible political dividend, but the Germans must have been grateful to find the Duke installed in the home of one of their supporters.

In spite of Hoare's kind words, the Windsors do not seem to have learned great discretion during their stay in Madrid. On 20 July Herbert Pell, the American Minister, dined at Espírito Santo's house and reported that they were outspoken against the British government. 'Consider their presence in the United States might be disturbing and confusing,' cabled Pell. They spoke of remaining abroad whether Churchill liked it or not 'and desire apparently to make propaganda for peace'.[2] An even odder conversation was recorded, though at second hand, by Marcus Cheke, who was a junior secretary in the British Embassy at the time. According to this the Duke predicted the fall of the Churchill government and its replacement by a Labour government which would negotiate peace with the Germans. The King would abdicate, there would be a virtual revolution, and he (the Duke) would be recalled. Britain would then lead a coalition of France, Spain and Portugal, and Germany would be left free to march on Russia. These ideas, said Cheke's informant, were 'put into the head of HRH by Frenchmen and Spaniards (not Germans with whom he had no contact) who were playing Germany's game'.[3] Hoyningen-Huene, the German Ambassador in Lisbon, told Ribbentrop that the Duke spoke freely in favour of compromise and said that the bombing of England would soon make it ready for peace.[4] (Here too the Duke wrote an indignant 'NO' in the margin when he eventually saw the report.)[5]

Even though one can believe that such reports were dramatized by the hearers, it is obvious that the Duke was speaking wildly and foolishly and must have seemed a dangerous liability to the unfortunate Selby. David Eccles, who was working for the Ministry of Economic Warfare in Lisbon, was more responsible than anyone for keeping official tabs on the conduct of the royal visitor. 'I distrust the Duke of Windsor,' was his first reaction. '. . . I shall watch him at breakfast, lunch and dinner with a critical eye.' After his first lunch at Cascais his suspicions were confirmed. 'I wouldn't give ten shillings for Wallis, she is a poor creature,' he wrote. 'He's pretty fifth-column.' Then he partially relented: 'I am being seduced by the Windsors who have made a dead set at me, and by heaven when they turn their united charm on, it is hard to resist . . . They are the arch beach-combers of the world.'[1]

The extravagance of the Duke's outbursts against the government reflected the progress or lack of it in the embittered arguments that were dragging on about his future. The King was emphatic that his brother must come home before anything could be decided. 'I suspect "she" does not want to come here to be bombed and "she" hates flying,' he told Queen Mary. There could be no question of the family meeting the Duchess.[2] Hardinge encouraged this obduracy. 'It is incredible to haggle in such a way at this time,' he agreed with Churchill. With the King's enthusiastic support, the Prime Minister sent off 'a very stiff telegram',[3] which was awaiting the Duke when he arrived in Lisbon. It reminded him that he was a soldier and that his refusal to obey orders would create a serious situation. 'I most strongly urge immediate compliance with wishes of Government,' Churchill concluded.[4] The Duke's furious response was to draft a reply resigning all his military ranks. Before he could send it, however, an olive branch arrived from London; relieving him of an unpleasant choice between eating his words or sitting out the rest of the war in comfortable ignominy at Ronda.

The idea that the Duke might be found some sort of job overseas had been considered for some time in London. It had at one time been suggested that he could be accommodated on Wavell's staff in Cairo.[5] Then Churchill had a better idea. The Dominions did not want him but could not some colony be found which he could govern? He put it to the King, who 'at once said that "she" would be an obstacle as David's wife'.[6] George VI did not think this ruled out the possibility, however, and Churchill discussed the matter in Cabinet and then ordered the Colonial Secretary, Lord Lloyd, to scour the world for a suitable territory. Dubiously Lloyd suggested the Bahamas: small, reasonably salubrious, and not of much significance. Churchill leapt at the idea, whereupon Lloyd had second thoughts. As Lascelles's brother-in-law he had had ample opportunity over the last decade to hear bad things about the Duke of Windsor; now he decided he would be more dangerous in a colony than at home. He formally placed his objections on record.[1] Churchill brushed them aside. 'Do you think he'll take it?' he asked Lord Beaverbrook, who happened to be there when the telegram was drafted. 'Sure he will, and he'll find it a great relief.' 'Not half as much as his brother will,' replied Churchill.[2]

No one was enthusiastic about the appointment. The Duke must have some sort of job, the King told his mother, 'and though there may be criticism and the Bahamian ladies won't like it,' it was at least better than having him at home.[3] Halifax echoed the thought; a good plan, he conceded, but 'I am sorry for the Bahamas'.[4] The Countess of Athlone could see no virtue in the plan and felt that it proved 'terrible treachery' and 'horrible machinations' were at work at home. 'If David could not be King because of that wife, how can he be the King's representative?' she asked. He would be King himself next, or worse still he might decide to visit the Athlones at Government House in Ottawa. What grounds could they give for refusing to receive the Duchess if he did? 'None! . . . Oh dear, oh dear, the future is going to be more and more difficult. Knowing the nice old-fashioned people of the Bahamas I can picture their distress and the joy of the vulgar drinking Americans who will flock there more than ever.'[5] The Duke of Kent professed to feel that his brother had behaved disgracefully: 'to accept to be Governor of a small place like that is fantastic!'[6] Queen Mary would not even accept that the appointment had been intended. The whole thing, she believed, arose from a misunderstanding between Churchill and the Duke. The Duke had asked if he could be found a house to retire to in the Bahamas, Churchill had got hold of the wrong end of the stick and made him Governor. 'A great mistake to my mind on account of *her*.'[7]

It cannot be said that the offer was accepted more enthusiastically than it was made. The proposal was 'anything but welcomed and was in fact most heart-breaking for both of us', the Duchess told Alexandra Metcalfe.[8] But it was a solution to his problem. It would

427

be a job in the service of his country, and however defeatist he might sometimes have sounded, his patriotism need never have been in question. There was not any real doubt that he would accept the Bahamas; but that did not mean he would not make himself thoroughly difficult while the details of his appointment were being worked out.

There is no news at 10 Downing Street 'apart from the fact that the Duke of Windsor is being cantankerous and maddening', wrote Churchill's secretary, Jock Colville, gloomily in his diary.[1] There were two themes on which the Duke elected to madden the Prime Minister. The first, and least justifiable, was whether he should be allowed to reclaim his soldier servants from active service and take them with him to the Bahamas. When the War Office demurred he sent his comptroller Phillips, who happened to be in London, to see the Prime Minister and explain that it would be a 'serious handicap starting with new valet', and that Piper Alistair Fletcher must be released.[2] It is difficult to decide which was the more frivolous: to seek to remove a young and able-bodied soldier from the Army in wartime, or to pester the Prime Minister on such a matter in July 1940. The Duke, however, had convinced himself that he had been pushed around beyond the limits of endurance, and was determined to make a stand; on what issue it did not really matter. Churchill replied, with commendable restraint, that it was out of the question to release soldiers from the Army for such a purpose. 'Such a step would be viewed with general disapprobation in times like these, and I should ill serve Your Royal Highness by countenancing it.'[3] Lloyd, now evidently once more committed to the Duke's appointment, pleaded that Churchill should relent. He had discussed the matter with Lascelles and Monckton and both stressed that 'HRH had to be treated as a petulant baby, and that there was a by no means remote possibility that he was prepared to force a break on this subject'.[4] Churchill was unmoved. He must have been equally unimpressed by the intercepted telegram from the Duchess of Windsor to Gray Phillips expressing alarm at the government's obstinacy over the soldier servants – 'if treatment persists and obstacles put in way, am afraid of outcome'.[5] Hardinge saw the telegram and commented balefully: 'This is not the first time that the lady has come under suspicion for her anti-British activity, and as long as we never forget the

428

power that she can exert on him in her efforts to avenge herself on this country, we shall be all right.'[1]

Another issue on which the Duke had rather better grounds for complaint simultaneously came to the boil. The Duke had set his heart on travelling to the Bahamas by way of New York, so as to do some shopping and allow his wife to see her doctors. Lord Lothian, the British Ambassador, took alarm: 'If he visits New York there will inevitably be a great deal of publicity, much of which will be of an icy character and which will have a most unfortunate effect at the present juncture.'[2] The Duke had already booked his passage on the SS *Excalibur*, which sailed direct to New York; the Foreign Office offered to pay the shipping line all the costs of diverting the ship to Bermuda, expected to be between $15,000 and $20,000.[3] Suddenly the Duke found his jaunt to New York cancelled. He wrote in rage to Churchill: 'Have been messed about quite long enough and detect in Foreign Office attitude the very same hands at work as in my last job. Strongly urge you to support the arrangements I have made, otherwise will have to reconsider my position.'[4] Always a pragmatist when he had to be, Churchill calculated that something must be conceded. The government could not agree to the Duke going to New York at this period, he telegraphed, 'but I have now succeeded in overcoming War Office objection to departure of Fletcher'.[5] With this partial victory the Duke had to be content.

With the problems resolved and the post formally accepted, messages of good will were exchanged on all sides. Nassau had a lovely climate and a flow of interesting visitors, Churchill reassured the Duke. 'I am sure that Your Royal Highness and the Duchess will lend a distinction and a dignity to the Governorship.'[6] The King too wrote sympathetically. He was so glad his brother had accepted the post, he said: 'Winston and I both saw the difficulty of your coming here, and I am sure you realized it as well. I am afraid you have had a good deal of trouble in arranging the journey . . . I have seen all your telegrams to Winston. Fletcher is returning to you after all. There was a muddle made over him . . . Do please write to me from the Bahamas as to your doings there,' was the King's conclusion; an invitation of which the Duke rarely availed himself.[7]

*

While this acrimonious bickering was going on, the Germans had been working to ensure that the journey never took place. On 11 July Ribbentrop sent instructions to Stohrer stressing the importance of inducing the Duke to return to Spain. Once there, he was to be persuaded, or if necessary compelled, to stay there and to be wooed with promises of a return to the throne after the Churchill clique had been overthrown and peace restored by German arms. Ribbentrop claimed to have proof that the British Secret Service planned to do away with the Duke once they had got him safely to the Bahamas; whether he himself believed this fantasy, or merely thought that it might frighten the Duke if passed back to him by the Spaniards, must remain uncertain.[1] As part of the softening-up operation, the Duchess was allowed to despatch her maid, Jeanne-Marguerite Moulichon, to Paris to collect certain of her mistress's most treasured possessions. Through the Spanish Foreign Ministry the Duke had already requested that his houses in Paris and at Cap d'Antibes should be looked after by the Germans for the duration of the war,[2] now he compounded this already deplorable indiscretion by allowing his wife to send an emissary into the heart of German-occupied France so as to suit their personal convenience. The Germans can hardly be blamed for thinking that he must be in a mood to serve their ends in more important ways. Mademoiselle Moulichon's mission was spun out almost indefinitely, to her own great alarm and discomfort, thus providing another reason why the Windsors should delay their departure from Europe.

As an emissary to persuade the Duke of the benefits of a return to Spain and the perils of a journey to the Bahamas, Don Miguel Primo de Rivera, the amiable but light-weight son of the former dictator, was despatched to Cascais. His efforts, the Duke recollected many years later, were 'distinctly half-hearted . . . I suspect that he realized he was up against a "stone wall" from the outset of his mission'.[3] To judge from Primo de Rivera's account of their meetings, admittedly at third hand as passed on by Don Miguel to the Spanish Minister of the Interior, Serrano Suñer, and thence to Stohrer, the wall was not as stony as all that. The Duke spoke with striking frankness about his lack of enthusiasm for the government in London, described the King as totally stupid 'reichlich töricht' and the Queen as a clever intriguer, appeared enthusiastic about the idea of returning to live in Spain, and said that he was considering making a public declaration of his opposition to present British policy.[1] (The Duke denied that he spoke of making any such public declaration when he saw a copy of Stohrer's report in 1953.)[2] When Primo de Rivera suggested that the Duke of Windsor might one day return to the throne of Britain, the Duke replied that constitutionally this would be impossible. But if Britain lost the war, Don Miguel argued, even the British constitution would not be inviolate. At this 'the Duchess in particular became very thoughtful'.[3]

Meanwhile Ribbentrop decided to reinforce the efforts of his Ambassadors by sending an energetic young SS officer, Walter Schellenberg, to mount an operation to get the Duke back to Spain. In his self-serving yet not unconvincing memoirs, Schellenberg has described how he was summoned by Ribbentrop and told that the Duke was a German sympathizer who needed to be rescued from the grasp of the British Secret Service, by coercion if no other method offered. Schellenberg asked how it would help to coerce the Duke into leaving Portugal if his future usefulness depended on his good will towards Germany. Ribbentrop explained that force would be necessary only insofar as the Duke's hesitation 'might be based on a fear psychosis which forceful action on our part would help him to overcome'. Schellenberg was empowered to offer to deposit fifty million Swiss francs in a Spanish bank account if the Duke would make some statement disassociating himself from official British policy – and there would be more to follow if that proved insufficient.[4]

Schellenberg states that the more he looked into the project, the more convinced he became that it was all based on casual remarks by the Duke which had no real significance. When he got to Lisbon he found that this view was shared by the German Ambassador, Hoyningen-Huene. He did his duty manfully, however; suborned the Portuguese police, placed his own men in the Windsors' household, and tried to foment the Duke's anxiety by hiring ruffians to throw stones at his windows and having a bouquet delivered at the house with a note reading: 'Beware of the machinations of the British Secret Service – a Portuguese friend who has your interests at heart.'[5] An elaborate scheme was worked out, by which the Windsors would leave Lisbon for a shooting holiday on the Portuguese border and then step, or be moved forcibly over the frontier into Spain.[1] Schellenberg also told the Portuguese that a bomb was to be placed in the ship carrying the Duke to the Bahamas, a rumour that was duly passed on to the putative victim and caused much alarm. On 24 July Primo de Rivera applied what was intended to be the final touch to the conspiracy with a letter from Madrid setting out the appalling risks the Windsors were running at the hands of British Secret Service agents, and explaining the plan by which they could escape to Spain. Having thus escaped the clutches of their enemies, the Windsors could settle in Spain in dignified retirement, move on to any other neutral country or, if they wished, proceed to England. According to the emissary who delivered the letter, the Duke read and reread it but made no comment beyond saying that he must think it over.[2]

Enough was known in London about what was going on to cause some alarm. If the Duke changed his mind about the Bahamas and decided to retire to Spain it would, to say the least, cause much embarrassment. Hoare cabled Selby in dismay at rumours that the Duke was coming back to Madrid to launch a peace initiative. 'I much hope you will dissuade HRH from coming here,' he wrote.[3] According to Monckton there was doubt in Whitehall about whether the Duke would take up his post as Governor and, if he did, what his frame of mind would be: 'So I was sent out on what turned out to be another very odd job.'[4] Late in the evening of 28 July Monckton landed at Lisbon. Schellenberg reported that an English minister travelling under the name of Sir Walter Turner Monckstone was said to have arrived but that he was too crafty to be taken in by such an obvious subterfuge: 'It is possible,' he surmised, 'that it concerns a member of the personal police of the reigning King by the name of Camerone.'[5]

Monckton/Monckstone/Camerone found the Duke in a muddled and demoralized condition. He did not believe that the British Secret Service were really plotting his assassination, but who could be sure of anything in these dark days? He was unhappy about the prospect of a return to Spain, yet might it not perhaps be the best course from the point of view of his own long-term future? He felt there was a real risk that the Germans were planning to murder him once he got to the Bahamas, even if it was only so as to throw the blame on the British. How could he be protected from such a menace? He suggested his departure should be postponed by another two or three weeks. Monckton injected some robust common sense into the welter of irresolution and apprehension. What could the possible motive be for an assassination plot? he asked. There was not a shred of evidence that it existed except in the mind of Primo de Rivera and the Germans. If it would help, the Duke could be accompanied on the journey by a Scotland Yard detective. Further delay would only increase whatever risk there might be.[1] At the same time he tried to convince the Duke that Britain was determined to continue the war and believed in the end it would win. Monckton went to Lisbon to tell the Duke 'about the government policy here, which I gather was rather different from his ideas as to what we ought to do', King George VI told Hoare.[2]

Once Monckton had arrived the always slight possibility of the Duke failing to take up his appointment in the Bahamas disappeared altogether. Primo de Rivera made one last effort to persuade him to put off his departure until the facts of the plot against his life had been fully established. Monckton demanded to know what evidence there was that the plot existed. Primo de Rivera said that names and details would be forthcoming in ten or twelve days. Monckton countered that in that case the Windsors would sail as planned. If the plot were a reality there would be time enough to stop them when they reached Bermuda. The Duke was convinced that there would only be the smallest risk in his proceeding, certainly less great than that involved by his remaining in Lisbon. The Windsors sailed at 3 p.m. on 1 August on the *Excalibur*.

The story was not quite over. Two days after their departure Stohrer reported that up to the last moment they had been in two minds as to whether or not to sail. The Duke had told Espírito Santo that he saw in many ways it would have been better for him to have remained in Europe, 'so as to be able to step in at the decisive moment'. He believed, however, that he would still be able to do this from the Bahamas if need arose.[3] A fortnight later Hoyningen-Huene cabled from Lisbon to say that Espírito Santo had received a telegram from the Duke in Bermuda, 'asking him to send a communication as soon as action was advisable'.[4] If Espírito Santo was reported – and reporting – faithfully, then it would suggest the Duke was foreseeing the possibility that Britain might soon be on the verge of defeat, and that the intervention of a mediator acceptable to both sides would then become essential if total destruction were to be avoided. In such a crisis, he might have been such a man. Espírito Santo was not a particularly reliable witness and would have wished to make his reports to the German Ambassador as palatable as possible. The second message is particularly suspect. As Michael Bloch has argued, why should the Duke send from Bermuda a telegram which he must have known would be intercepted by the British and was calculated to arouse the darkest suspicions of the authorities. His behaviour would be odder still, since the message did nothing except confirm an arrangement that, if Espírito Santo is to be believed, had already been agreed at a meeting only two weeks before.[1] Whether there was any message, and if so what it said and what it meant, remains singularly obscure. But even though the details can be questioned and the extent of the Duke's indiscretion minimized, there seems little doubt that he did think Britain was likely to lose the war and that, in such a case, he believed he might have a role to play.

Enough was known about these visions in London to raise grave doubts about the Duke of Windsor's loyalty. Hardinge made notes from an intelligence report: 'Germans expect assistance from Duke and Duchess of Windsor. Latter desiring at any price to become Queen. Germans have been negotiating with her since June 27th. Status quo in England except for undertaking to form anti-Russian alliance. German purpose to form Opposition Government under Duke of Windsor, having first changed public opinion by propaganda. Germans think King George will abdicate during attack on London.'[2] Hardinge was more than ready to believe the worst of his former monarch, and to assume that he would not merely have accepted such a role if it had been offered him by the Germans but would have rejoiced in the disaster to his country which opened the way for him.

Lord Caldecote, the Secretary of State for the Dominions, was no more charitable. When called on by the Prime Minister to prepare a draft to the Commonwealth Prime Ministers announcing the Duke's appointment as Governor of the Bahamas he put forward: 'The activities of the Duke of Windsor on the Continent in recent months have been causing His Majesty and myself grave uneasiness as his inclinations are well known to be pro-Nazi and he may become a centre of intrigue. We regard it as a real danger that he should move freely on the Continent.' Churchill scratched this out and substituted: 'The position of the Duke of Windsor in recent months has been causing His Majesty and His Majesty's Government embarrassment, as though his loyalties are unimpeachable, there is always a backwash of Nazi intrigue which seeks to make trouble about him.'[1] It was Churchill's version that was sent out to the leaders of the Commonwealth, and was sent by Halifax to Roosevelt in a slightly modified form.[2]

Churchill was perhaps too benevolent, but he was nearer the mark than Caldecote. A great many people believed in June and July 1940 that Britain was likely to lose the war. The Duke's fault was that he said so aloud, and not just to his fellow countrymen. He did not do so to Britain's enemies, however; all the evidence is that he had no direct contact with any representative of Germany or Italy, that he believed the Spaniards and Portuguese to whom he spoke supported the British cause, or at least were anxious above all to see peace restored, and that even to these his outbursts were infrequent. One such outburst was too many, and the Duke repeated the offence, but he never consciously aided the enemy cause.

The crucial though hypothetical question is: what would the Duke have done if Germany had invaded and conquered Britain? Would he have joined whatever might be left of Britain's government in exile? Would he have done what he could to secure better terms for his defeated country but remained abroad himself? Or would he have allowed himself to be placed back on the throne as a Nazi puppet? It is unlikely that even the Duke had thought through how he would react in such dire circumstances. All one can do is base a surmise on the flimsy grounds of psychological speculation. Everything that is known of the Duke's character – his obstinacy, his pride, his courage, his conviction that with all their faults the British were the best of peoples – suggests that he would never have played the traitor's part. He may have longed to get his own back on his relations and have deplored the policies of the government, but he had always been and remained a patriot. He could not have allowed himself to rule by favour of the Germans over a sullen and resentful people. The case can so obviously not be proven one way or the other that it is hardly worth lengthy argument: one can only state as a matter of personal conviction that though the Duke of Windsor can fairly from time to time be dubbed defeatist, silly, irresponsible, indiscreet, he never hoped for the downfall of his fellow countrymen and would never have agreed to be imposed upon them by German arms. Ribbentrop deluded himself; the British can count themselves fortunate that the circumstances never arose in which he would have discovered his mistake.

24

The Bahamas

W HEN TOLD THAT THEY HAD BEEN ASKED TO GO to the Bahamas, the Duchess's response was to reach for an atlas. The Duke was better informed, but he had to admit they were one of the few British dependencies in the region that he had never visited. This was unsurprising. The islands stretched in a prolonged straggle from Haiti at one end to Florida at the other, twenty-nine of them with, according to the best authority, 661 cays or sandbanks, and 2387 rocks. Beyond their numbers, there was little in them to engage attention.[1] 'Mediocrity is the word for the Bahamas,' wrote an admittedly embittered former resident. 'The country is mediocre in everything. There are no rivers, fresh-water lakes, mountains. Even from the earliest days the people were mediocre.'[2] Their total area was 5400 square miles, half the size of Wales. In 1940 half the seventy thousand inhabitants were clustered in the capital, Nassau, on New Providence Island; only two other settlements were larger than a village.

From the point of view of the Windsors the posting had a few redeeming features. Except for the high summer, when the heat and humidity were insufferable, the climate was close to idyllic. Nassau was less than two hundred miles from Miami and more than four thousand miles from London. American visitors flocked there for the winter season. There was an adequate if not remarkable golf course. But there was not much more to be said for the islands. In particular, their economy veered between the frail and the disastrous. There had been brief periods of prosperity as conch shells, then tobacco, then pineapples, then sisal and finally sponges had found a profitable market overseas, but always fashion changed or competitors with greater resources undercut the Bahamian producers. The latest period of relative affluence had come when prohibition in the United States had offered the islanders a marvellous opportunity to turn a dishonest penny by smuggling liquor into Florida. That too had passed. By 1938 total exports were worth only £182,000. Unemployment was high, under-employment endemic, especially in the Out Islands, that plethora of tiny settlements outside New Providence where the mainly black population scratched a precarious subsistence from fishing and the soil.

Such economy as there was, was controlled with unscrupulous thoroughness by a group of white traders living in Nassau. Their warehouses and offices clustered along Bay Street, the town's principal thoroughfare, and they were known inevitably as the 'Bay Street Boys'. When tourism from the United States began to flourish, it was these merchants who provided the necessary capital and reaped the profit. Some of the wealth filtered down to the predominantly black population, who lived for the most part in squalid settlements on the outskirts of Nassau, but most of it remained in the hands of the old trading 'aristocracy' – families such as Solomon, Higgs or Sands – or a rumbustious Canadian gold-mining millionaire, Sir Harry Oakes, who with his henchman Harold Christie brought new life to the islands in the years immediately before the war.

Traditionally, the British Governors, arriving from remote corners of the world with little knowledge of the region's problems, and administering the islands with the help of a handful of hard-working Colonial Service officials, had ruled by courtesy of Bay Street. They did their best to stimulate the economy and ensure that the law was administered with justice, but they did nothing to undermine the power of the white oligarchy or to reform the political system by which it was kept permanently in power. The Duke of Windsor's immediate predecessor, Sir Charles Dundas, had been more venturesome. His aim had been to end the Bahamas' dependence on American tourism, which he felt to be precarious and degrading, and instead develop the Out Islands, by encouraging settlers to build up farms and even light industry. He tried to break the power of Bay Street by introducing the secret ballot, a measure which he felt sure would transform the membership of the Legislative Council and thus, in the end, the social structure of the Bahamas. After prolonged and acrimonious argument, the Legislature accepted the secret ballot for a trial period of five years and for New Providence Island only. The price Dundas paid was embittered resistance to any legislation which he tried to introduce into the Council, even when such laws were made necessary by the British war effort. It was not a happy atmosphere for a new Governor to find on his arrival.

The Duke of Windsor was under no illusion that some rich imperial plum had been pulled out for his benefit. 'I naturally do not consider my appointment as one of first importance,' he told Churchill,[1] and whatever excitement he might originally have felt had been dampened by the bickering over his servants and the abortive visit to the United States. But he was still resolved to make the best of it; for all its insignificance it was a job of work, and if he did it well he would confound his enemies. The posting, he told Philip Guedalla, 'may prove to be the first opportunity we have as yet had of really doing something to frustrate their game'.[2] Quite what that something would be, he did not know, but he had no intention of being a fainéant head of state. The role of a Governor was to govern, and govern he would.

Reflecting on the possibility of promoting the Duke to some more important post, the then Colonial Secretary, Oliver Stanley, told Lord Halifax in 1943 that the Governor would have to be prepared 'to take a part in a political fight which is often extremely bitter and unpleasant. I do not think, in the first place, that it is desirable that the brother of the King should be involved in controversy of that kind, and in the second place, I doubt whether a man with his training can really stand the give and take of party political warfare. Nor should I feel sufficient confidence in his judgment and experience when it came to really difficult decisions.'[3] All these considerations applied with equal force in the case of the Bahamas – with greater force indeed; since few colonies could boast political in-fighting as bitter and unpleasant as that to be found in Nassau. The Governor was the chief executive, and the parish pump nature of Bahamian politics ensured that he would be directly and personally responsible for every decision, unable to shelter behind a protective wall of officials to whom he could delegate effective power. It was unlike anything that he had done before, as remote as could be imagined from the role of constitutional monarch who operates only on the advice of his ministers. In the Bahamas he would have advice enough, most of it contradictory, but in effect he would be the ministers.

439

If doubts of this kind disturbed Churchill, he must quickly have convinced himself that they must be suppressed for the greater good, and that anyway it did not matter greatly what happened in the Bahamas. What did worry him was that the Duke might continue to preach the same defeatist doctrines as had been heard in Madrid and Lisbon. One of the messages Monckton brought out to Portugal was that in his new position the Duke would have to be doubly careful what he said.[1] The Prime Minister reinforced the warning with a solemn adjuration. From time to time, he told the Duke, he would find himself having 'to express views about the war and the general situation which are not out of harmony with those of His Majesty's Government. The freedom of conversation which is natural to anyone in an unofficial position, or indeed to a Major General, is not possible in any direct representative of the Crown. Many sharp and unfriendly ears will be pricked up to catch any suggestion that Your Royal Highness takes a view about the war, or about the Germans, or about Hitlerism, which is different from that adopted by the British nation and Parliament.' Stories had been emerging from Lisbon of conversations the Duke had held which could be used to his disadvantage, particularly in the United States, where so many people would be listening with the hope of hearing something of the sort. 'I am so anxious,' concluded Churchill, 'that mischief should not be made which might mar the success which I feel sure will attend your mission.'[2] Given his mood on the eve of his departure from Europe, it is doubtful whether the Duke read this letter with any pleasure, or that he resolved in any way to change his habits. Certainly at dinner on his first night in Bermuda he outraged the Governor by announcing that, if he had been King, there would have been no war.[3]

Even without such solecisms, it is doubtful if the Windsors would have found the atmosphere of Government House, Bermuda, altogether congenial. The Governor, Sir Denis Bernard, was a blimpish figure, who, when he heard of the impending visit, announced 'that he for one would take to his bed if *that* woman came into the house'.[4] A few days earlier he had received a telegram from Lord Lloyd, instructing him that the Duchess was not entitled to a curtsey and should be addressed as Your Grace.[1] The order was punctiliously observed. The Duke can have expected little else, but was sufficiently struck by the uniformity of the reception to enquire what orders had been given. He was shown a copy of Lloyd's telegram and angrily drafted his own response. He had accepted the post in the Bahamas, he said, in the belief that the difficulties involved in his own and the Duchess's official status could be overcome. Lloyd's telegram, however, 'reveals court attitude on this matter and emphasizes impossibility my accepting any post under the Crown. I therefore will not proceed to Nassau to take up my appointment.'[2] Evidently he thought better of this drastic riposte: the telegram was never sent. To the Governor's sister he said that it was all the Queen's fault: 'I don't know whether we will be able to stick it down at Nassau if this sort of thing is going to go on.'[3]

Frank Giles, then a young ADC on Bernard's staff, had expected to be repelled by the Duchess, but instead was dazzled by her: 'She has, to an infinite degree, that really great gift for making you feel that you are the very person whom she has been waiting all her life to meet.' He was struck by her 'watchful, almost maternal devotion' to the Duke, and the way in which she made sure he was punctual for his appointments and devoted sufficient time to preparing his speech for the arrival at Nassau.[4] Gray Phillips thought equally well of her performance in Bermuda. She could not have been more dignified or naturally gracious, he told Monckton. Both of them had worked hard, with excellent results. 'The Duke is a law unto himself with regards to popularity, but I can truthfully assert that the Duchess is running him very close. The Governor ... was rather of the Kitchener of Khartoum type to start with, but ended up eating out of our hands!'[5]

When they arrived in Bermuda, the Special Branch officer who had been sent from London to escort them drew Giles aside and told him that the Windsors were in danger every moment of the day and night and must be constantly guarded.[6] The Duke treated the situation less dramatically but still believed sufficiently in Primo de Rivera's alleged plot to be ill at ease. He was not wholly reassured by a telegram from Monckton, saying that there was no foundation for the rumours and that it was safe for him to proceed,[7] but he had no grounds on which to dispute the conclusion. On

15 August they set out on a Canadian cargo ship, the *Lady Somers*, on the last lap of their journey.

The outgoing Governor, Dundas, was openly irritated at being posted away two years before he had expected. 'I don't know why I should be pushed out to make way for *him*,' he protested.[1] When he presided over the first meeting of the Executive Council after the news became known, it was agreed that 'no very special arrangements' needed to be made for the new Governor's reception.[2] Once Dundas had gone, the occasion began to seem a little more special. Arrival day was declared a public holiday and the waterfront was beflagged.[3] The arrival of a new Governor is always a great occasion in a colony; when the new Governor is also a former King Emperor and protagonist in one of history's most celebrated romances, then expectation verges on hysteria. The appointment seemed to most people astonishing but to be welcomed. Red Bay Billy apostrophized the new Governor in the pages of the *Nassau Daily Tribune*:

> Royal Son of Great Britannia
> And the woman of his choice
> Welcome to these Isles of romance
> Hark! The Tropic's luring voice.
>
> Pulsing hearts of loyal nature
> Heaven borne hymns ascending high
> Kneeling 'fore the Throne of Mercy.
> 'May God bless the Duke!' they cry.[4]

No number of pulsing hearts could have made an arrival at Nassau in 1940 a very imposing occasion, but the Windsors carried it off with style. They 'made a very good impression', the American Consul, John Dye, reported; the Duke's speech was 'short, fluent and well-made'.[5] The impression made on them was less favourable. Their reception was enthusiastic enough but in Nassau in August the summer is at its most oppressive, and under the searing sun the town seemed drab and tawdry. The writer Rosita Forbes referred to 'the curious atmosphere of Nassau, self-irritant as an ingrown toe nail',[6] and it did not take long for this miasma to settle around the new arrivals. The Duke was resolved to make the best of it. 'I think he feels himself in a sort of comic opera,' Phillips

442

told Monckton, 'but on the whole he likes it very well.'[1] The Duchess managed to keep a reasonably good face on it in public, but to her intimates poured out her disappointed bile. 'Where did you stay when you came to this dump and why did you come here?' she asked her aunt Bessie; and then again, 'I hate this place more each day', and again, 'we both hate it, and the locals are petty-minded, the visitors common and uninteresting'.[2]

The shortcomings of Government House were one of the principal reasons for her disenchantment. Dundas had warned his successor that furnishings were threadbare and redecoration badly needed. The house was badly planned and insufferably hot in summer; the accommodation was inadequate and the garden ill cared for.[3] It would not have taken the Duchess long to discover this for herself. The Director of Public Works admitted that the house was not only shabby but riddled with termites, and in need of a major overhaul whoever the new occupant had been.[4] The Legislature had grudgingly authorized £2000 for the work, a sum that was patently insufficient. Work was at once put in hand. 'We found Government House quite uninhabitable,' the Duke told his old friend and predecessor as Governor, Bede Clifford, 'and fled from the place after a week's picnic and sandflies to make room for Frederick van Zeylen [the Director of Public Works] and Mr Sinclair the painter.' A particular grievance was that Dundas had removed the 'E R VIII' cypher from the swimming pool because 'he thought (he wasn't sure mind you) that he was catering to public opinion at the time'. Luckily van Zeylen had kept the tiles, and the Duke was having them put back.[5]

The Duke at once wrote to Lloyd to say that at least an extra £5000 was needed to put the house in order (Lloyd sent the letter to Churchill, who minuted on it 'Comment is needless').[6] Lloyd replied, no doubt with tongue in cheek, that the Duke's 'personal position and popularity' was surely such that he could extract an additional £2000 or so from the Legislature. If £5000 *had* been available from public funds in Britain, then would they not be better spent on buying an extra fighter aircraft?[7] The same idea occurred to the *Daily Tribune*, who hearing that the bill for Government House was now put at £7000, asked whether the money should not be devoted to buying a Hurricane to defend Buckingham Palace (which had just been bombed).[8] The Legislature eventually provided an extra £2000 for structural repairs and the Windsors paid for most of the redecoration: 'Both the Duke and the Duchess put a great deal of their own money into the improvements,' attested van Zeylen.[1]

Whether the money might or might not have been better spent, the citizens of Nassau got a handsome and well-run Government House. The only survivor from the Windsors' domestic staff remembers the Duchess as being excellent to work for: decided, efficient, concerned with every detail of the household, insisting on the highest standards yet never unreasonable, always appearing to take a genuine interest in the servants' welfare.[2] The service was grand without being pompous; at dinner parties the Duke's piper would appear in the floodlit garden and march to and fro playing to the guests. The food and wine were excellent, though the Duke took little of either; René MacColl noticed that his lunch was invariably a plate of stewed fruit and a pot of weak tea, while he 'drank sparingly of alcohol in the evening'.[3] They entertained lavishly, with a reasonable tincture of old acquaintances to alleviate the local worthies. One of the oldest of the acquaintances was Alastair Mackintosh, a friend of the Duke for many years who was now living in Nassau with his two young children. To such a man the Windsors' kindness and hospitality were limitless. His children left to attend school in Canada, and Mackintosh saw them off. 'I loved them very much and felt lonely and unhappy. Driving into my courtyard, I saw a Government House station wagon and the Duke's valet standing beside it. He handed me a note. It said, "The Duke and I know how much you will be missing the children, so please come and stay with us at once." '[4]

One problem was to maintain a style appropriate to a royal Governor without giving censorious journalists too much of a chance to berate them for living in ostentatious luxury while Britain suffered. The Duchess generally had a surer touch than her husband. Etienne Dupuch, the editor of the *Daily Tribune*, wished to do an article about the Windsors' daily life for use in an American magazine. The Duke cooperated, approved the copy and photographs, then decided the Duchess should see it too. She at once vetoed the project. 'I am not questioning the Duchess's judgment,' wrote Dupuch. 'I would say she was right because the pictures showed them living in luxury and security here while

Europe was on fire . . . But why didn't he realise this fact from the start?'[1] The Governor's contribution to public relations, as much for the sake of exercise as to save petrol, was to use a bicycle to go from Government House to their beach hut. An enterprising official produced a tandem and urged the Duke and Duchess to embark together. They obliged, but lost their balance and fell off before the tandem even left the grounds of Government House. The experiment was not repeated.[2]

The problems posed by the Duke's inexperience were compounded by the fact that his most senior officials were also new to the colony. Dundas commended his principal advisers to his successor but regretted that the Colonial Secretary and the Attorney General were not yet *au fait* with Bahamian affairs.[3] Leslie Heape, the Colonial Secretary – playing managing director to the Governor as executive chairman – had arrived only three months before from Grenada; he at least had previous experience of the West Indies and quickly proved himself a thoroughly competent and conscientious if unimaginative administrator. Eric Hallinan, the Attorney General, was a man of greater distinction than Heape, but had been less than a month in the Bahamas and had previously served in the very different environment of Nigeria. With the Chief Justice also a comparatively recent appointment, the only continuity was provided by the Receiver General, Robert Taylor. This was not fair to the Duke, commented the *Daily Tribune*, 'and it is not fair to the colony'.[4]

The Colonial Secretary, the Attorney General and the Receiver General made up the government contingent in the Executive Council, ExCo, the cabinet, or perhaps more accurately the parish council of the Bahamas. They were balanced, or more often confronted, by five local residents, all representatives of the Bay Street interest, though Harold Christie, property developer and close friend of Sir Harry Oakes, had horizons slightly wider than those of his colleagues. Of the other four, effective power rested with Kenneth Solomon, a cunning and unscrupulous lawyer who also held the powerful position of 'Leader for the Government in the House of Assembly'. As such he should have been the Governor's closest ally, and indeed was happy to play that role provided the Governor confined himself exclusively to public relations and feathering the nests of the Bay Street merchants. Walter Moore, a pompous and frequently drunken nonentity, was technically the senior of the unofficial element of ExCo, but in practice left all the important decisions to Solomon.

Not that the decisions were that important save to those immediately involved. At the first meeting over which the Duke presided there was one item of real significance to the islands as a whole when the Council decided that, in view of the uncertain future of the tourist trade, the colony could not afford to lend the British government more than the £250,000 already promised from the Surplus Funds. Other items included a grant of a licence to Father Charles Blesch to practise as an Unqualified Medical Practitioner in the Out Islands, and the refund of import duty paid on a church bell for the Methodist Church on Eleuthera. The Governor undertook to consult Lord Beaverbrook about the possibility of opening a broadcasting station for the West Indies in the Bahamas.[1] This was an unusually meaty agenda. The following week's ExCo decided that Mr Tracy could not practise in the local bar, that Mr Wing Wong might bring his wife and children to the island, and that the Theatre Company should be allowed to put on performances if the Savoy Theatre was available for use.[2] Not everything discussed was as dull as this – the Council at one time or another agreed that the showing of gangster films was an inducement to crime and should be stopped, that Basic English should not be introduced into the colony, that the sentence of death on William Bode should be commuted to life imprisonment – but it was trivial enough; as the *Daily Tribune* remarked, the Duke had neatly reversed Lincoln's career and gone from White House to log cabin.[3]

Two centuries earlier the Executive Council had ceded its power to raise money to the House of Assembly. This least democratic of representative bodies was elected by a small proportion of the population in circumstances that made it inevitable the nominees of Bay Street would be in a majority. It represented, said Morison of the Colonial Office in 1940, nothing but 'the merchant princes of Nassau, is selected in a manner reminiscent of the worst excesses of the unreformed Parliament of this country in the 18th century, and in performance shows itself to be irresponsible, crass or malignant'.[4] It was in this unpromising forum that any reforming initiative launched by the Governor would inevitably founder; in the unlikely event, that is, that it had survived its stormy passage through the Executive Council. Theoretically the Governor had the last word, since he could at any moment suspend the constitution and impose his legislation by direct rule. In practice both Governor and Bay Street knew that this was a solution to which the Colonial Office would have recourse only reluctantly and if all else had failed. Only with endless patience, determination and finesse could a Governor begin to impose his will; even equipped with such virtues the odds were still against him. The money, the Duke ruefully told Guedalla in October 1940, was in the hands 'of the unscrupulous merchants of Bay Street, and they are a very tough nut to crack'.[1]

Five members of the House of Assembly were black. They enjoyed no power. To Bay Street the black population was a source of cheap labour and a captive market; any move to improve its status, whether politically, socially or economically, was dangerous and to be resisted. It would be unfair to accuse the Bay Street merchants of being motivated exclusively by colour prejudice. They were almost equally prejudiced against Jews. At one of his earlier ExCo meetings the Duke reported he had received letters complaining about the attitude of certain hoteliers towards Jewish visitors. He proposed that the Council should disassociate itself from such behaviour. The Council happily consented, on the understanding that they should take no further action in the matter.[2] Jews had always been discriminated against in Bahamian hotels and, so far as Bay Street was concerned, always would be. Anti-Semitism was, however, an optional extra; to be dispensed with if commercial advantage so dictated. Discrimination against the black population was a fundamental part of the structure of Bahamian life.

The less sophisticated of the black Bahamians welcomed the Duke's advent as if he had been sent from heaven to redress their woes. Wild rumours spread around the slums of Nassau in August 1940; the new Governor had personally thrown open the jail doors, he had ordered the statue of Columbus outside Government House to be painted black.[3] Every public utterance was scanned for evidence that he was aware of and sympathetic to their needs. When he spoke on Empire Day, he quoted the line from 'Rule Britannia' – 'Britons never, never shall be slaves'. These were not mere words, he said, 'but a very definite challenge which has been upheld by the bravery and devotion of generations that have gone before'. Probably he meant no more than a general appeal to solidarity in the face of the foe, but to his black listeners the reference to slavery seemed to have a special connotation. Only among the handful of black Bahamians who were qualified to take on the whites in the professions were there doubts about the Duke's status as a champion of black rights. Etienne Dupuch, who as editor of the *Nassau Daily Tribune* was one of the leading spirits in the black movement, wrote that his paper's initial distrust of the Duke arose from a statement he had once made commending the all-white immigration policy of the Australian government.[1] The Duke cordially returned Dupuch's suspicion. The editor was 'a man of the agitator class', he reported. He never lost an opportunity of stirring up racial disharmony. 'It must be remembered that Dupuch is more than half Negro, and due to the peculiar mentality of this Race, they seem unable to rise to prominence without losing their equilibrium.'[2]

That remark betrayed the limits of the Duke's liberalism. He believed that the black man was inevitably inferior to the white and was wholly unfitted to govern. He was ill at ease with them socially and would have found any sort of physical contact repulsive. In this attitude he was abetted by his wife. 'As a Southerner, the Duchess is particularly well adapted to cope with colour problems,' wrote Rosita Forbes, presumably with unconscious irony.[3] Dupuch cites several instances in which the Duke allowed racial prejudice to distort his judgment: his refusal to appoint a well-respected black building contractor as liaison officer between American contractors and Bahamian labour; his objection to an all-black police force.[4] Such instances have the ring of truth. Still less did the Duke feel inclined to defy the social taboos and invite black guests to his home. One of the main reasons he advanced – as Dundas before him had done – against the appointment of a black man to ExCo was that he would expect to be invited to Government House. 'I am well aware that the official colour bar does not exist in the other West Indian Colonies . . .' he wrote to the Colonial Secretary.

The Bahamas, however, which I can well understand from their proximity to the mainland of America, still maintain a very staunch and American attitude towards the coloured problem, and white Bahamians will not allow their wives to sit down to dinner with coloured people. One of the main local arguments against the inclusion of the coloured element into the social life of the Colony is that it would hurt the susceptibilities of the American winter visitors. I personally discard this one with the observation that no one in their right senses would ever be so tactless as to invite coloured people to meet American guests.[1]

There was nothing unusual about such an attitude. As he pointed out, he was reflecting the prejudices of the vast majority of his wife's countrymen, and probably of the British as well. The Colonial Office took a more liberal line, however, and argued that the prejudices of the white Bahamians and American tourists should not be given too much weight 'under modern enlightened conditions'. The Governor – above all *this* Governor – was in a very special position, 'and a lead from you in the Bahamas would be very much appreciated by the coloured people and do much to help towards a more liberal attitude'.[2] The Duke had grave doubts whether a more liberal attitude was in order. It could only encourage demands for radical political reform, perhaps even for self-government. Negroes were ill-equipped to meet the demands of the twentieth-century world, he told Churchill, 'and while these liberal socialistic ideas of freedom and equality, regardless of race and colour, may sound fine theoretically, the forcing of these theories is to my way of thinking, both premature and dangerous so far as the Western Hemisphere is concerned'.[3]

Bay Street would have found nothing to complain about in such sentiments; where the Duke parted company with these myopic merchants was in his belief that, if the black Bahamians were so backward, then they deserved to be educated, fed, housed and generally looked after. The record of the Duke's relationship with ExCo and the House of Assembly shows a consistent and protracted effort on his part to force through reforms that would be beneficial to the black population, against the embittered opposition of those who believed that any change would be to their financial and, in the long run, to their political disadvantage. He told Walter Monckton a few months after his arrival that he was dismayed by the standards of such services as health and housing for all except the rich: 'I have personally rarely seen such slums and squalor as exist in most of the native settlements and many of the Out Islands have no doctor at all.' He accepted that the Bahamas were making a generous contribution to the British war effort: 'At the same time, I am afraid that it will always be a struggle to get Bay Street to devote money to any project that does not directly benefit themselves, and the color [sic] problem is particularly acute and bitter.'[1]

The Bay Street merchants took it for granted that the Duke would be an amiable figurehead who would act as a magnet to American tourists and not interfere in the serious business of misgoverning the islands. He proved instead disconcertingly conscientious. Those who worked under him were surprised to find that he read his papers carefully and pondered them before deciding on his future action: 'I won't let these pinkos push me around,' he minuted on one Colonial Office instruction – not perhaps the response of an enlightened progressive, but equally not what was to be expected from a bored and dilettante idler.[2] He wrote all his own speeches and before delivering one of importance would seclude himself for forty-eight hours till he had got it to his satisfaction: 'And he wrote a good speech, among the finest delivered from the "throne" by a Governor of the country,' wrote the generally hostile Dupuch.[3] John Wilmot, Parliamentary Private Secretary to Hugh Dalton, the Minister of Economic Warfare, reported to his master that the new Governor had buckled zealously to his task and had practically given up drinking: 'The Dook's working very hard,' the Duchess had assured him.[4] Brigadier Daly, who came out to inspect the wartime defence arrangements in the Caribbean, declared the Duke was 'the most capable of the various Colonial Governors he had visited'.[5] John Dye told the Secretary of State in Washington that, though the Duke might have been sent to Nassau to get rid of him, 'he is taking his job seriously and is showing a keen interest in the welfare of the Bahamas'. Every day, reported Dye, he visited some centre of importance to the islands, usually accompanied by the Duchess, who was also active in Red Cross work.[6]

It is notable how often his wife was included in the compliments paid to the Governor. Both were 'doing great work', a friend from

The Bahamas

Nassau told Bede Clifford. 'Really HRH . . . is charming beyond words. He has become really loved by all the people as he takes an interest in the high and the low, and the Duchess is very active in spite of not having been in particularly good health of late.'[1] Privately the Windsors might grumble sourly about the triviality of their task and the squalor of their surroundings, in public they were good-humoured and enthusiastic. The Duke had not been transformed miraculously into a paragon of public-spiritedness and devotion to duty; what he did show was that, to an extent Hardinge and Lascelles would have felt inconceivable, when given a job of work to do and with his wife to support him, he would do it faithfully and with considerable ability.

His first important chance to show his mettle came when he opened the new session of the Legislature at the end of October 1940. He made a courageous speech, stressing his determination to foster local enterprise and to do something about the working conditions (where there was work) and unemployment (where there was none) of the black population. The Bay Street boys, expecting a more *laissez-faire* approach, were disconcerted but not greatly dismayed; flurries of exuberant activity were common in newly arrived Governors and generally came to nothing. John Dye was more impressed. The speech was 'one of the most sensible and businesslike that has been delivered by a local Governor for many years', he told Washington. No Governor before had suggested 'a study of labor in connection with the cost of living'.[2]

But though in the long term something might and indeed had to be done to foster agriculture and light industry in the Bahamas, in 1940 the colony's dependence on American tourism was dangerously complete. 'Lamentable,' the Duke called it. 'This concentration of effort during the four Winter months in Nassau and complete neglect of the fate of the Out Islands was a bad enough policy in time of peace, but with the war . . . this state of affairs is unfortunate to say the least.'[3] For the moment they made the best of it, indeed without the Windsors the best would not have been nearly so good. 'We have patently been Exhibit A,' the Duchess told Monckton, performing for the Bahamas the role that the Tower of London or Changing the Guard played for the British Isles.[4] But with exchange controls and increased taxation in the United States inhibiting the would-be tourists, it was clear that the

451

Windsors' exhibition could not draw the crowds for ever. When the United States entered the war at the end of 1941, it merely applied the *coup de grâce* to what was already a tottering enterprise. Tourism stopped overnight. It was a disaster for the Bahamas. The Duke resolutely saw mitigating features. They had kept all their eggs in one basket for too long, now they would be forced to look elsewhere. In the long run the islands would be the stronger for it. But in the meantime, 'the problem of transition presents many problems, the worst headache of which is, of course, unemployment. The task of finding useful employment for the large percentage of the coloured population, who have suddenly been laid off, is an added and interesting, if difficult, duty for me as Governor.'[1]

In the middle of 1941 the Duke made a determined effort to set about the problems of the poor and the unemployed. He introduced legislation which would have raised the minimum wage, provided an expanded programme of public works, and authorized the importation of agricultural machinery free of duty so as to encourage local farming. Bay Street might not unreasonably have claimed that this placed too large a financial burden on them at a time when they were already under pressure, and have sought to whittle down the effectiveness of the legislation. They scorned such half measures, however. The new proposals were rejected after cursory debate. Kenneth Solomon and the other Bay Street representatives on ExCo were notably lukewarm in championing the projects of the Governor.

Fortunately for the Duke he had recently been provided with a means to strike back at those who frustrated his reforms. Lord Moyne, who had taken Lloyd's place as Colonial Secretary, was a man of notably advanced ideas – far more so indeed than the Duke of Windsor. He believed that in the end black rule must come to the West Indies, and he wished to prepare for it by gradually preparing the blacks for their new role and curbing the power of the white oligarchy. A means towards this end would be to change the composition of the Executive Councils of the various colonies, which were often in the grasp of a self-perpetuating clique of reactionaries who made up a majority of the members and did all they could to block the Governor's reforming zeal. No white oligarchy was more in need of curbing, or more difficult to curb, than that of the Bahamas. Moyne's proposal was that Governors should rarely appoint members to ExCo for a second term and never for a third, thus offering a chance to introduce new blood and change the balance of power within the Councils. If implemented, this would give the Duke the chance to get rid of the useless Moore before the end of 1941, and Solomon early the following year. It was a chance he grasped at. In November he read Lord Moyne's letter to the members of ExCo and announced that neither Moore nor Solomon would be reappointed. Moore, who as well as being old, was crippled with sinus and what the Duke coyly described as 'spells of activity of his right arm',[1] went without too much demur. Solomon was outraged and resigned without waiting for his term in office to expire, resolved to lead the opposition to the Governor's reforms overtly in the Assembly, where formerly he had been content to do so behind the scenes.

Moyne would have liked to see at least one of the deposed members replaced by a black man. The Duke was still convinced that this would be disastrous. Fortunately for him Moyne's Parliamentary Under Secretary, George Hall, visited the Bahamas in the autumn of 1941. Hall was a former miner and one of the socialist members of the coalition government; his views on colour were far less progressive than those of his aristocratic minister. He already had a high opinion of the Duke, gained from his recollections of royal visits to south Wales, and quickly decided that he was also a paragon among Governors.[2] He needed little convincing that the Duke was correct in his view that to appoint a black man to ExCo would precipitate fearful troubles and paralyse the working of government. After personal discussions and various interviews among the Bahamian notabilities, the Duke told Moyne with some satisfaction, Hall 'was, I think, able to get some insight of this Colony's special problems'.[3]

The war, which had done so much to foment the growth of unemployment by the obstacles it placed in the way of tourism, was also to provide at least a partial solution. Long before they entered the war, the Americans showed themselves anxious to construct a chain of bases in the West Indies. The Bahamas provided one of the more eligible sites. The Duke, who believed passionately in the closest possible Anglo-American cooperation, would have championed such a move even if there had been no other advantages. As it was, he saw that the construction and servicing of the bases would prove an invaluable boost to the colony's economy. In the eyes of the British government, indeed, he was too blindly pro-American in his championship of their activities in the area. 'The Duke is rather apt to take a line of his own on these matters,' wrote the Colonial Secretary, when the Governor proposed that Roosevelt should be invited to the Bahamas for the opening of the airfield, 'as he does not appear to be nearly so apprehensive of American infiltration as most of the inhabitants of the West Indies and everyone here.'[1] He now did all he could to forward the project and, being unusual among colonial Governors in that he had the ear of the President of the United States, he wrote to Roosevelt in January 1941 urging that a quick decision be made on the site where the air base was to be constructed.[2] By the time of the Japanese attack on Pearl Harbor, American money was already beginning to pour into the Bahamas. But this would take time to build up and would at the best never provide more than a temporary recourse. The economic weaknesses of the Bahamas called for more fundamental solutions.

At the end of 1941 the Duke set up an Economic Advisory Committee, to investigate all means by which the Bahamas, in particular the Out Islands, could be developed. As in ExCo, the Duke himself took the chair; unlike ExCo the Committee contained black members, in particular the radical editor of the *Daily Tribune*, Etienne Dupuch. Not surprisingly the *Tribune* lauded the new initiative with singular fervour: 'We have maintained that this country needed the leadership of a man who could, by virtue of his position and authority, unify all groups and factions in the Colony in a concerted drive towards a fixed objective. There is only one man in the Colony who could fill this role, and that man is His Royal Highness the Governor.'[3] To claim that the Committee transformed the economic condition of the Bahamas would both exaggerate the ingenuity of this little band of well-intentioned men and underestimate the determination of Bay Street to confound their best endeavours. It did useful work, however, particularly in the encouragement of agriculture in the Out Islands. The Bahamas remained grimly poor, but they would have been poorer still if the Committee had not existed.

One of the Duke's most powerful allies in his efforts to build up the economy of the colony was a Swedish multi-millionaire, Axel

Wenner-Gren. Wenner-Gren was an entrepreneur of outstanding ability, who had built up the great international Elektrolux Company and made himself one of the leading industrialists of his generation. Like many people who are good at making money, he believed that he had the answer to all the world's problems and was constantly propagating naive and impracticable schemes for the resolution of international conflict and the preservation of perpetual peace. It was in this context that the Duke had already come across him. There had been talk before the war of an international organization which would coordinate all the various peace movements, and over which it had been suggested the Duke of Windsor should preside. Wenner-Gren was one of the business tycoons who had expressed himself as ready to finance the enterprise. He had met the Duke briefly in Paris and presumably expounded his ideas, but no record of the meeting survives beyond a brief mention in Wenner-Gren's diary.[1]

It was the Duke's predecessor, Dundas, who had encouraged Wenner-Gren's involvement in the Bahamas. The Swedish millionaire had built himself a stately pleasure-dome on the insalubrious Hog Island, on the edge of Nassau, and undertook great works of drainage and the excavation of canals. In the Out Island of Grand Bahama he set up a crayfish cannery. In the scale of his international enterprises, his activities in the Bahamas were inconsiderable; for the colony they quickly became of the first importance. He and Harry Oakes were the only people who brought substantial sums of foreign capital to the Bahamas.

Shortly before the Duke arrived in Nassau, a letter to Wenner-Gren from a friend in Rio de Janeiro was intercepted by the British censorship. It told him that 'a new and interesting family' would shortly be arriving, 'with which I assume you will at once become very friendly. I have met an old acquaintance who . . . states that family hold sympathetic understanding for totalitarian ideas . . . This should be of great significance for forthcoming development of events.'[2] The significance of this somewhat cryptic message is hard to establish, but to the government in Washington it was additional proof that Wenner-Gren was a German sympathizer, a spy, a dangerous plotter, an enemy to liberty and all good American aspirations. It is impossible to see quite what made the Americans so convinced that Wenner-Gren was thus firmly in the enemy camp.

In July 1940 the Under Secretary, Sumner Welles, told Morgenthau of the US Treasury: 'I haven't got a word of proof, but I have the most violently strong hunch that the man is acting as an agent for the German Government.'[1] Harry Hopkins was equally convinced that Wenner-Gren was 'violently pro-Nazi', with equally little reason for his conviction.[2] Wenner-Gren was supposed to be an intimate friend of Hermann Göring and close to the other Nazi leaders; in fact he met Göring four times, and only briefly, and there is no record of his knowing any of the other leading Nazis. For this misconception he was largely to blame himself, his vanity led him to claim close friendship with the great regardless of their political affiliations. He spoke about himself, with equally slender justification, as an intimate of Roosevelt; a boast which perhaps contributed to the inclusion of his name on a German black list of prohibited traders.[3]

He seems, in fact, to have been committed to no cause except that of peace and, more emphatically, of Axel Wenner-Gren. The Swedish Minister in Washington told Welles that he had known Wenner-Gren for many years and believed him to be very stupid and 'obsessed with an overweening sense of his own importance' but not an Axis agent.[4] The worst that the FBI could find to say of him with any confidence was that he saw himself as a 'high-class middleman' between his contacts on both sides, and a seeker after a negotiated peace.[5] A search of his papers in Nassau after he had been proscribed revealed nothing suspicious.[6] A résumé of the story prepared by the State Department in December 1959 concluded that there was no evidence he had 'indulged in acts prejudicial to the security of the United States'.[7] Yet this lack of evidence did not shake the conviction of influential Americans such as the Assistant Secretary of State, Adolf Berle, and the diplomat George Messersmith, as well as Hopkins and Welles, that he was a dangerous man who must be restrained lest he do grave damage to the allied cause.

The Duke was delighted to find in Nassau a man of international culture, rich enough to provide many of the fruits of gracious living and sharing his general views about the folly of the war and the need to end it as soon as possible. Wenner-Gren's diary abounds in references to their meetings: 'Extremely pleasant and interesting conversation ... He has a good memory and remembers very

456

well our conversation in Paris'; 'Pity that political considerations prevent closer social intercourse. Extremely interesting discussion'; 'Long confidential discussion with Windsor; in many respects we share the same opinions.'[1] When the Windsors had no convenient means of getting to Miami, he put his yacht, the *Southern Cross*, at their disposal – 'Goering's Pal and Windsors,' was the *Daily Mirror*'s headline to announce the event.[2] But as well as being an agreeable addition to Bahamian society, Wenner-Gren was the Duke's trump card in his crusade to vitalize the economy of the Out Islands in the face of the rancorous opposition of Bay Street.

Left to themselves the British government would have welcomed Wenner-Gren's investment in the Bahamas and paid little attention to his views on a negotiated peace, or even to his alleged German sympathies. However, Wenner-Gren's enemies in Washington urged the British Ambassador, by then Lord Halifax, to take some action. The word was passed back and the Colonial Secretary, having studied the American allegations, sent the Duke a cryptic warning that Wenner-Gren was not a suitable companion for a British Governor. The Duke, not unreasonably, asked why. He shared his predecessor's view that the Swede was neutral, well disposed to the allied cause, in addition to being 'a very important and prominent resident of the Bahamas engaged in various development schemes most beneficial to this Colony'.[3] He had no intention of discouraging him unless given much better reasons than so far vouchsafed. Lord Lloyd either thought it too dangerous to pass on the information at his disposal, or saw how flimsy the information was; anyway, for some months the sleeping dog was suffered to lie in uneasy peace.

Then Halifax returned to the charge and passed on the latest allegations of the State Department.[4] Churchill was called in. Wenner-Gren, he warned the Duke, was 'a pro-German International Financier with strong leanings towards appeasement, and suspected of being in communication with the Enemy'.[5] The King had been told of his brother's involvement with the Swedish magnate and wrote to his mother: 'David really can do a lot of harm if he is not careful.'[6] But in the Duke's view it was the British authorities who were doing the harm; victimizing an innocent man and threatening to wreck the Bahamas' most promising economic development. He wrote direct to Halifax to say that he was perplexed by the American suspicions. Could he please be given chapter and verse of what they had against Wenner-Gren?[1] He would try, said Halifax, but it was 'rather a delicate matter'.[2] He had in fact already tried the previous day, and Sumner Welles had admitted 'that I know of nothing specifically against him, but that his associations with high members of the German Government were obviously intimate'.[3]

In the face of this less-than-overwhelming evidence the Duke can hardly be blamed for sticking to his guns. He continued to see and entertain Wenner-Gren until well into the summer of 1941. In the end, however, he was defeated. The American government placed Wenner-Gren on the black list of those to be treated as enemy aliens, the British dutifully if unenthusiastically followed suit. Wenner-Gren wrote to the Duke to express his dismay at what had been to both of them 'a humiliating affair. You are fully aware of my views . . . as I have been utterly frank with you during our conversations, and you must know that there is not and cannot be anything to reproach me for in my attitude towards British and US interests.'[4] All the Duke could do was to try to mitigate the damage done to the Bahamian economy by ensuring that Wenner-Gren's enterprises were allowed to carry on under governmental control.[5] The British Embassy in Stockholm, which had been watching Wenner-Gren's career with interest for many years, were amazed at the American readiness to assume his guilt and to debate only whether he should be shot or hanged; their own view was that he was 'generally disliked and regarded as a pompous ass, but not guilty of any worse offences than extravagance, attempted social climbing and tax dodging'.[6]

The Duke was much criticized for his association with Wenner-Gren, but it is hard not to feel that in this case he — as well as the unfortunate Swede — was misused. On other points he is less easily defended. Given that Mexico had recently appropriated all British oil interests and diplomatic relations had been broken off, it was, to put it mildly, tactless of him to receive the brother of the President of Mexico, Maximinio Camacho, at the request of his friend Harold Christie.[7] Even if he may be forgiven for thinking that the United States should keep out of the war, it was indiscreet, as well as ill-advised, to blurt this out to the anglophile American stockbroker Frazier Jelke. 'Sir, you are certainly not a wishful thinker,' observed Mr Jelke. 'No, I have always been a great realist and it is too late for America to save Democracy in Europe,' the Duke replied. 'She had better save it in America for herself.'[1] To his intimates he was even more disastrously frank. He told Aunt Bessie that, 'The whole of mankind is going to suffer bitterly for the folly of this conflict' and 'I can see no ending to it all, let alone a victorious one'.[2] When Russia entered the war he professed to be delighted but added gloomily that he supposed the British must be prepared eventually to adopt the hammer and sickle as their national emblem.[3]

There were those who thought that he was treasonable as well as defeatist. A report from a representative of the British Secret Service in Lisbon said that the Germans had recently approached Bedaux and asked him to establish whether the Duke of Windsor would be prepared to become King in the event of a German victory. Bedaux declined, but the report contained the transcript of a supposed conversation between Mrs Bedaux and the Duchess, in which the former referred to a talk between Bedaux and the Duke in 1937 and said that the question then discussed was 'very prominent in the minds of certain powers today. We have been asked seriously of the possibility, and we, continuing to believe that both you and ———— are still of the same opinion, have given absolute assurance that it is not only possible but can be counted on. Are we right?' Everything is obscure about this: the timing of the conversation; its precise implications; the relationship between what the Duke might have said in 1937 and what he would have thought in wartime; the response of the Duchess, if there ever was one. What is most interesting, however, is the comment of the Permanent Under Secretary at the Foreign Office, Alec Cadogan: 'The paragraph is certainly capable of the blackest interpretations. But it would be difficult to get a conviction on it.'[4] His remark illustrates vividly what dark suspicions of the Duke and, still more, the Duchess were nourished in the upper reaches of the Establishment, and how unlikely it was that the Windsors, any more than Wenner-Gren, would be given the benefit of the doubt.

The Duchess made her contribution to the sum total of the Windsors' indiscretions. At the end of 1940 the Consul General in New York reported an article by an American journalist in which the Duchess was quoted as asking: 'How can you expect the Duke to live here? I too wish to do our duty. But is there scope here for his great gifts, his inspiration, his long training? I'm only a woman but I'm his wife and I don't believe that in Nassau he's serving the Empire as importantly as he might.' In case Bahamian susceptibilities were insufficiently stirred by these comments, the writer went on to describe Nassau as a 'place of filthy shacks, hidden away where half-naked negroes live in unspeakable poverty and as a place lying sweltering, sweating, stinking'.[1] But the crowning indiscretion came in March 1941 when *Liberty* magazine, shortly followed by the *Sunday Despatch* in London, published an interview between the Duke and an American novelist and broadcaster, Fulton Oursler.[2] Whatever he did or did not say to Mr Oursler – and he claimed to have had many words put into his mouth – the Duke contrived to leave the impression that he saw no hope of a British victory. Nor was there hope of a change of heart in Germany. 'You cannot kill 80m Germans and since they want Hitler, how can you force them into a revolution they don't want?' The only hope was for a Pax Americana: a peace imposed upon a discredited Europe by the New World, which would restore a measure of sanity to international relations. 'The Duke of Windsor has given an interview to a magazine in the USA in which he pretty frankly disclaims all chance of an English victory,' Goebbels is supposed to have commented, adding that they would not use it in their propaganda for fear of discrediting the speaker.[3]

The interview provoked Churchill into a magisterial rebuke. Whatever was meant, he said, the Duke's words would certainly be interpreted as 'defeatist and pro-Nazi, and by implication approving of isolationist aim to keep America out of the war'. Would the Duke in future please seek advice before making public statements of this kind?[4] The Duke responded querulously. He had only seen Oursler on the recommendation of Roosevelt's press secretary; he had been misinterpreted; 'if as your message infers, I am more of a detriment than of assistance to these vital Anglo-American relations, I would rather resign'.[5] A week later he struck back. An article in *Life* had quoted the Queen as referring to the Duchess as 'that woman'. 'I understand that articles about the Royal Family are censored in Britain before release, and this remark is a direct insult to my wife.' His disillusionment with the Establishment in London was now complete: 'I have both enjoyed and valued your friendship in the past,' he told Churchill, 'but after . . . the tone of your recent messages to me here I find it difficult to believe that you are still the friend you used to be.'[1]

But Churchill's objurgations had an effect, or perhaps the progress of the war convinced the Duke that German victory was not inevitable after all. His change of heart is marked in the reports of his meetings with the American President. When Roosevelt met the Duke at the end of 1940 he was dismayed by the gloom which he irradiated and his obvious belief that the United States would shelter in isolationism. When they met again in the autumn of 1941: 'He reported the Duke as being very robust on war and victory and his attitude generally showed a great improvement.'[2] Two months later, with America in the war, he finally put aside the conviction that Britain would one day have to sue for peace as a nation already vanquished, or on the brink of defeat. He continued to believe that insistence on unconditional surrender was a policy certain to complete the damage which the war had already wreaked in Europe, but from the beginning of 1942 what concerned him was the terms the allies should exact, not the terms to which they might have to submit. His new attitude removed the most important of the factors that made him a potential embarrassment to the British royal family and government in his visits to the United States.

461

25

The American Connection

HE CONVERSATIONS WITH PRESIDENT ROOSEVELT did not come about without a protracted battle. The prospect of the Windsors rampaging around the United States appalled the British government for two, contradictory, reasons. According to one scenario he, or more probably she, would speak indiscreetly, behave with impropriety, meet with ridicule or hostility, and generally become a source of embarrassment to the royal family and the nation. According to another he, or less probably she, would charm the American people and their leaders, be fêted and applauded, stimulate comparisons with the King and Queen unfavourable to the latter, and generally become a source of embarrassment to the royal family and the nation. The only acceptable visit to the United States by the Duke would be one that was entirely unobtrusive, and since neither the Duke's temperament nor the interest of the American press made this a probable contingency, the best solution would be to keep him corralled in the territory which he governed.

When Churchill vetoed the Duke's proposal that he should visit the United States on his way out to the Bahamas, he explained that this was because presidential elections were under way; no permanent embargo was intended.[1] From then on a rearguard action was waged to postpone a visit for as long as possible. The government's doubts on the subject were confirmed by a German broadcast stating that the Duke had accepted his job so as to be near Washington and able to work with Roosevelt for a negotiated peace. Monckton gloomily commented that this showed even the discussion of a meeting between the Duke and the President was filled with peril.[2] Roosevelt himself, Mackenzie King told Princess Alice, was as keen as anyone that their meeting should be indefinitely postponed. Yet if the Duke visited the United States it was almost inconceivable that he should not call at the White House.

'What trouble the dear boy continues to give wherever he goes,' commented Princess Alice.[1] In fact he had no sooner arrived in Nassau and taken a horrified look at Government House than he applied for leave to visit his ranch in Canada. Churchill was put out at the proposal that the Duke should abandon his post before he had even properly taken over. He was 'very grieved to hear that you were entertaining such an idea', Monckton wrote. The Prime Minister hoped that, when the people of Britain were suffering so much, the Duke 'would be willing to put up with the discomfort and remain at your post until weather conditions made things less unpleasant'.[2]

'Please stop any nonsense about David's paying a visit to his ranch,' Queen Mary appealed to the Earl of Athlone, now in Ottawa.[3] For the moment the danger seemed remote, but Lothian, the British Ambassador in Washington, unwisely spoke to Roosevelt about a meeting with the Duke and got the answer that the time was not yet quite ripe but that the President planned to see him while visiting the site of the projected American base in the Bahamas. Lord Lloyd wrote crossly that, 'I had just got the Duke, as I thought, clamped down securely in the Bahamas for a while, and now Lothian is stirring up the waters again.'[4] Lloyd, advised presumably by his brother-in-law Lascelles, could always be relied on to take the lead in thwarting whatever the Duke of Windsor might want to do. At his instigation the Foreign Office instructed Lothian to tell the President that they wanted any visit paid by the Duke to Washington to be postponed for as long as possible, and that they hoped Roosevelt would keep clear of the Bahamas for the moment.[5] The Duke for his part was convinced that the Foreign Office were not merely blocking his travel plans but blackening his name as well. 'The persecution of the Windsors goes on relentlessly,' he told Guedalla. 'Lousy publicity' was being diffused in America, 'disgraceful and libellous lies' being spread. It was all part of the same campaign as had used the American press in 1936 to drive him from the throne.[6] 'If Lothian advises that due to the American press he is against a visit to America, where I shall go to visit my family,' the Duchess warned Monckton, 'it does not come from the Americans but from London, and we cannot accept it.'[7]

Roosevelt paid little attention to Lothian's hints and at the end of November told the Ambassador that he would shortly be cruising around the West Indies and looked forward to seeing the Duke while he was in Bahamian waters. By the time this news was received, the Duke had already applied for permission to visit Miami, so as to escort his wife who badly needed the attentions of a dentist. The Foreign Office had not contrived the clash of dates, but they were happy to take advantage of it. Lothian was told to discourage the President from pursuing his intention to meet the Duke, who 'has been left in ignorance of the suggestion'.[1] It seems unlikely that Churchill would have tolerated this slightly squalid piece of deceit if he had known of it; as it was, Colville minuted 'Too late to show the PM' on the copy of the telegram sent to Downing Street.[2] The Duke did not remain in ignorance for long, but his chagrin at being absent from his post when Roosevelt was visiting it was quickly appeased when the President invited him to fly out from Miami to join him for lunch on his ship, the *Tuscaloosa*. He duly did so, and whatever dire consequences the Foreign Office foresaw from such a meeting, nothing much seems to have happened. The Duke was more pessimistic about the progress of the war than seemed suitable to his host; on the other hand, Hopkins told Churchill, he 'spoke very charmingly of the King'.[3]

The visit to Miami too was a 'success from every point of view', according to the British Consul, James Marjoribanks; 'Britain's stock soared with the advent to Miami of our former monarch.'[4] Wenner-Gren, who had put his yacht at the disposal of the Windsors when the regular passenger boat was cancelled at short notice, wrote in his diary of a 'spectacular reception', with tens of thousands of people watching both arrival and departure and hundreds of small boats escorting the yacht to sea when it departed.[5] Indeed, the only feature of the visit which came in for some criticism was that Wenner-Gren had provided the transport and was in attendance, and even this did not attract much attention.

It was while he was in Miami that the Duke learnt of the sudden death of the British Ambassador in Washington. The American press, and indeed the *Nassau Daily Tribune*, assumed that the Duke was likely to be Lothian's successor and that the visit to the *Tuscaloosa* had been made to sort out the details. There was no shortage of advice to the President from those who thought the appointment would be a great contribution to Anglo-American relations: 'Such is the epic quality of the present world struggle,' wrote George Weston, 'that Edward of Windsor might well be more important in Massachusetts Avenue than in Buckingham Palace.'[1] But there were as many to point out the hazards in placing the Windsors in a post of such diplomatic delicacy, and it seems unlikely that the idea of such an appointment was even contemplated in London. The Duke himself can have had few illusions on the subject, though he told an American journalist that he would accept the post if offered it, provided 'I thought it was in the interest of our two countries'[2] – a somewhat disingenuous comment which fuelled the speculation about his likely appointment.

It was instead the Foreign Secretary, Lord Halifax, who was given the job in Washington, and so it fell to Halifax to comment when the Duke asked permission to visit the States in April 1941 to study the Civilian Conservation Corps camps which Roosevelt had set up to help combat unemployment. The new Ambassador regretfully concluded that it would cause less trouble to let the Duke come than to stop him, since to do the latter would encourage those elements in the American press which were prone anyway to see the Windsors as martyrs. His enthusiasm for the visit was rendered still less ardent by the fact that Oursler's article in *Liberty* magazine had only just appeared, and journalists would be eager to lead the Duke into fresh indiscretions. The Duke's arrival, he wrote with some hauteur, would 'inevitably be treated here as a "raree" show', and everything possible would need to be done to keep him away from the press.[3] Churchill, who had been outraged by Oursler's interview, took a more robust line than Halifax and told the Duke bluntly that the visit 'would not be in the public interest nor indeed in your own at present time'.[4] The Duke huffed and puffed indignantly – 'My first six months have been spent doing my utmost to strengthen Anglo-American relations, and I think I have had some success,' he told Churchill[5] – but short of resigning his post he could do nothing save submit. All he could manage was a brief call at Miami to meet his financial adviser, Edward Peacock; during this visit he refused all invitations to private parties on the grounds that his country was at war: 'He seems to have acted with considerable discretion,' commented Eastwood of the Colonial Office.[6] It was July before the Duke finally obtained permission to spend most of the hottest months of August and September on the mainland, and even then the start of the visit had to be postponed to avoid any risk of his meeting the Duke of Kent. The Duke wrote bitterly to Halifax that Kent's presence in America would give the press a chance to 'rehash the sordid story of the feud between my family and myself; a feud which, as you know, is not of my making'. He hoped that his brother would be kept away from Florida: 'Even if there is disunity in high places in Great Britain, it is very important that it be concealed as much as possible from the over-curious American people.'[1]

The Duke had frequently pleaded that he should be sent a press officer, to come between him and persistent journalists and to protect him from mishandling by the likes of Oursler. The best that could be done was to detach René MacColl from the Embassy at Washington for a few days to coach the Duke for the exposure to the press he would inevitably endure when in the United States. 'MacColl arrives next Friday,' the Duchess told Monckton. 'I understand he's very nervous over it all. I believe he thinks HRH is for "appeasement", "negotiated peace", and all the rest of the lies pinned on the Duke.'[2] MacColl for his part was more nervous about the Duchess than the Duke. 'That she dominated the Duke was clear to the least perceptive,' he wrote in his memoirs. 'I have rarely seen an ascendancy established over one partner in a marriage to quite so remarkable a degree.' She made him happy, MacColl believed: 'He seemed to revel in being with the Duchess.' But her approval was essential to him and he sought it constantly. Once in America an American journalist asked him to make the V sign. The Duke started to comply, then caught his wife's eye. 'She shook her head. The Duke dropped his arm.'[3]

MacColl was assigned to the Windsors as public relations officer while they were in the States. His role was not that usually associated with the title: 'The rule seemed to be that the Duke must say as little as possible, must hold no press conferences, give no interviews, make no statements.'[4] MacColl's main problem was coping with unfriendly questions about the amount of luggage with which the Windsors found it necessary to travel. 'Could not the more frivolous side of things be soft-pedalled?' asked the Duke hopefully, but the answer was all too obviously that it could not. The press took inordinate interest in such picturesque if trivial detail. Estimates as to the number of pieces ranged from thirty-five to eighty, seventy-three being the best authenticated figure. He had never intended to say an unkind word about the Windsors, wrote Henry McLamore of the *Washington Star* with unconvincing benevolence, but 'you almost have to question the sanity of a man or woman who would start on a short trip with 58 bags and trunks full of clothing'.[1] Even Lord Halifax observed the phenomenon. The Windsors, he told Alexandra Metcalfe, had behaved 'most sensibly and ordinarily' except for 'their ridiculous amount of luggage of which the papers were so critical ... I was a little outraged at being presented with a bill for £7.10.0 for hire of a lorry to take their luggage to and from the station.'[2]

This superfluity of luggage, together with the costliness and splendour of their suite in the Waldorf Towers – the 'Millionaire Stratosphere', as MacColl called it – and the energy with which the Duchess made up for her year's deprivation from the delights of serious shopping, lent the trip an air of extravagance and self-indulgence. In the House of Commons a Labour member, Alexander Sloan, asked whether the Minister was aware of the bitter criticism in the American press of this 'ostentatious display of jewellery and finery at a period when the people of this country are strictly rationed'. The Minister rather wetly replied that the cuttings in question had not been drawn to his attention,[3] a defence so pusillanimous as to annoy the Duke even more than the original accusation.[4]

In fact, though the Duchess would have done well to exercise more restraint in the style of her travelling, the trip was well conducted and certainly did nothing to ruffle Anglo-American friendship. The Duke saw Roosevelt twice, and the President told Halifax that the visit had gone off well: 'He said that the Duke had been very firm on the question of war and victory and that she had produced a better impression on him than he had expected. I told him I had been through exactly the same experience the only time I had met her.'[5] A large dinner party was given for them at the Embassy; it was 'quite calm', reported Halifax, 'and they both seem to have been very charming to everybody'.[6] At luncheon the Secretary for the Navy and his wife were invited so that the Duke could talk about the Bahamas bases. 'The Duchess's behaviour was completely correct,' Halifax told the King, 'and in one tiny detail I thought she acted with considerable tact by making Mrs Knox go in to luncheon in front of herself.'[1] (The surprise of otherwise sensible people when they found that the Duchess of Windsor did not swear in public or dance drunkenly on the table is one of the more curious features of such reports.)

The visit to the ranch in Canada passed off equally smoothly. The Athlones had been dismayed at the news of the visitation. 'I hate the idea but there is no means of stopping him,' the Governor General told Queen Mary. 'I only hope he will not come here.'[2] The King assured him that he was safe, Churchill was warning the Duke that he could not include Ottawa in his travels, 'as Aunt Alice won't, and cannot from my point of view, receive *her*. How I dislike the perpetual troubles over David ... but it will make him realize, or rather *her*, that they cannot do as they like.'[3] The Canadian crowds were invariably welcoming and large, though not in comparison with the vast throngs which had greeted him as Prince of Wales. Indeed the largest crowds were in Baltimore, where the Duchess fell into the category of 'local girl made good', and the couple were mobbed enthusiastically whenever they appeared in public.

In Washington on their second visit the Duke had a long and important talk with the Ambassador. Halifax reported it to both Churchill and King George VI, in terms that were varied to suit the recipient but did not differ in essentials. To Churchill he said that the Duke felt 'pretty bitter about being marooned in the Bahamas ... I must say it certainly sounds pretty grim. He said that he had done his best to play the game and avoid making difficulties, but that his family had not responded, and he never wanted to see them again ... I should guess that he will want to pay periodic visits to the United States, which personally I think it would be rather cruelty to animals to prevent him doing.'[4] To the King, Halifax laid greater emphasis on his rejoinders to the Duke's protestations that he was monstrously ill-used. He had told the Duke that he underestimated the deep shock caused by his abdication, the effects of which still lingered on. It was too early even to think of living in England. The Duke said he had no intention of doing this unless all the obstacles were removed by his family. But he could not stay for ever in the Bahamas: 'He wondered how long the war would continue, and where they would live after it was finished. He didn't think that France would be much of a place to live in, and thought that the New World would be all right, but it was very expensive! He said that he was very happily married and had got the most wonderful wife . . . He certainly looked very well, and was clearly very happy with her.'[1] The fact of the matter, commented the King, was that the Duke, as a former monarch, could *never* live in England. 'We know this, so does Winston, but we can never tell my brother so in so many words. He has got to realize it for himself.'[2]

The Duke did indeed want to 'pay periodic visits to the United States', but in spite of what he had said to Churchill, Halifax never got used to the idea. One reason was that he was convinced, for no noticeable reason, that the Duke had his eye on the Embassy for himself. When Monckton visited Washington on the way to the Bahamas, Halifax asked him 'to keep his eyes and ears open for signs of whether the Duke was thinking about one day filling my job'.[3] Monckton reported that the Duke seemed terribly bored, though he was 'very popular with the negro population and doing his job very well'. He seemed to have no idea of taking up residence in Massachusetts Avenue, if anything it was some sort of job in Latin America on which he had set his heart.[4] Halifax was unconvinced; a year later he was telling the Colonial Secretary that the Duke, by his frequent visits, was grooming himself for the Embassy: 'I don't think myself that would be a very good plan, although it might indeed be quite a popular appointment with the Americans.'[5] It was not until the middle of 1945 that Halifax conceded the Duke had 'evidently given up the idea of being Ambassador here if he ever had it'.[6]

The criticism of the Windsors' ostentatious extravagance never stopped; some of it was justified, more was not. In August 1944 a Philadelphia engineer called William Harman wrote to the Ambassador to complain about the Windsors' night-clubbing and party-going while allied soldiers were dying in Europe. Halifax passed on the letter to the Duke, who wrote to Harman a dignified and temperate reply pointing out that they had not entered a single night-club since the war began and that the only parties they had been to had been given for military personnel. 'You have been misrepresented and I have been misinformed,' admitted Harman. 'For myself, I want to withdraw what I said.'[7] About the same time an English journalist, Sydney Moseley, received the blast of the Duke's displeasure over newspaper stories reporting that, for her appendicitis operation at the Roosevelt Hospital, the Duchess had reserved ten rooms and the attentions of eight nurses. In fact she had one room and the same nursing as anyone else. The Duke 'was genuinely upset about this . . .' wrote Moseley. 'This was false and unfair.'[1]

A problem which exercised the American Treasury as well as the newspapers was where the money came from for what were obviously highly expensive trips. Much nonsense has been talked about the Duke's finances at this time: that Wenner-Gren held $2.5 million on the Duke's behalf (a report based on the unverified surmise of an unidentified American agent[2]); that Sir Harry Oakes subsidized him from money illicitly transferred to Mexico; even that he was on the payroll of the Mafia. There is no reason to believe anything so picturesque. Substantial sums had been given to the Duchess of Windsor by the Duke while she was still Mrs Simpson and after her marriage, and some of these were invested in the United States. In December 1941 she had two current accounts in the Chase Bank, one at that time containing $9000, the other $29,931.[3] In September 1940 Monckton had pointed out that the Duchess was still an American citizen and thus liable to pay tax on all her income, even though she was not resident in the United States.[4] Whether the American tax-collectors took their share is unknown; even if their exactions had reduced her income to an unacceptably low level, there would still have been no shortage of dollars since J. P. Morgan and Co. had been instructed by the British government to provide any sums that the Duke might require.[5]

The Duke also had dollar securities in his own name. These led to a somewhat acrimonious exchange between Monckton and the Palace. All British citizens were required to declare their holdings in foreign property or securities so that these could be mobilized when exchange ran short. In August 1940 Monckton told Churchill that he thought the Duke would be prepared to comply with this.[6] But when it came to the point the Duke proved reluctant to put at risk what he regarded as his economic lifeline. Peacock asked Ulick Alexander to support an approach to the Prime Minister urging that the Duke should be exempted from the obligation to register his holdings. Alexander refused. 'The King also had a certain amount of money in America, and he at once surrendered it and accepted English money in exchange. I didn't see why the Duke shouldn't do the same.'[1] When the Duke needed to raise French francs to pay the expenses of his household at Cap d'Antibes, the Federal Reserve Bank said they could only provide the exchange with the authorization of the British Embassy. Once again the Treasury came to the rescue, Horace Wilson unenthusiastically approving the transfer of the necessary funds from the Duke's sterling account in London.[2] Whether the Duke was justified in asking for badly needed foreign currency to be applied to such ends, and whether Wilson should have acceded to the request, are matters for individual judgment. It is clear, at least, that there was nothing covert or illegal about the transaction.

The Windsors were in Washington in June 1942, when news began to filter in of violent rioting in Nassau. It did not come wholly as a surprise. Work on the American air base meant not only an inflow of capital and the provision of badly needed employment, but also of foreign foremen and skilled workers who were vastly better paid than the Bahamian labourers. This might have been tolerable, but there was no shortage of mischief makers – communists, and 'men of Central European Jewish descent, who had secured jobs as a pretext for obtaining a deferment of draft from the Army', the Duke dubbed them[3] – who told the Bahamians that the American contractors were ready to pay far higher wages to the locals if the Bahamian government had not imposed restrictions. There was some truth in this – one of the reasons for the Duke's presence in Washington was to negotiate a modestly increased wage for the labour force – but the discrepancy between the two rates of pay would still have remained glaring. A few hotheads demonstrated; the authorities mishandled what could have been a minor disturbance; disaffection spread; all the latent hatred for the selfish white oligarchy overflowed; a mob surged down Bay Street, looting and destroying; the police and the handful of British troops on the island opened fire. The violence died down, only to be renewed next day. To the alarmed administration it seemed as if the forces of law and order might quickly be overwhelmed.

To the Duke the worst danger seemed that the Americans would conclude the Bahamas was no place in which to build a base, and pull out of the operation. He at first tried to persuade the American censors to embargo all news coming from the colony, but it proved to be too late and the attempt was quickly abandoned.[1] Meanwhile, he agreed with the President that a hundred American marines should be flown to the island, ostensibly to protect American installations, in fact to help preserve order.[2] If he had consulted Whitehall before taking such a step there would have been much havering and no guarantee that permission would eventually be given; as it was the marines played an unobtrusive role but the knowledge of their presence gave immeasurable reassurance to the civil authorities. Having taken these steps the Duke borrowed an aircraft from the Secretary to the Navy and himself flew back to Nassau. His presence stiffened the resolve of the authorities to restore order and offered some hope to the black population that their worst grievances would be remedied. It remained to repair the damage and apportion the blame.

On 8 June, a week after the outbreak of the violence, the Governor broadcast to the colony. His address was a nice balance of stern reprimand and sympathetic understanding; he emphasized that further violence would be rigorously repressed, promised free lunches for the workers and his best endeavours to secure an increase in the basic wage, and announced the setting up of an official and independent enquiry to establish the causes of the riots. The speech was remarkable in that it won approval from both the Nassau newspapers, which usually agreed only to differ. The *Guardian* called it 'A speech of high quality . . . it will long be remembered as a model of leadership', while the *Daily Tribune* praised it as 'balanced and firm . . . the result of thorough consideration and careful thought'. Remembering the suspicion, if not animosity with which the *Tribune* had greeted the Duke's arrival, it is remarkable to find it concluding that 'The feature which now stands out above all others is the fact that it was eventually resolved by the dominating personality of one man, His Royal Highness the Governor . . . HRH approached the gigantic problem calmly and efficiently. He held conferences day and night. He acquainted himself with every possible aspect of the question . . . he handled a delicate situation with tact and dignity, resolution and authority.'[3]

The American Connection

The Duke was convinced that, though it was a dispute over wages which had sparked off the trouble, 'sinister racial feelings have been aroused on both sides', and these were the product of the selfish short-sightedness of the Bay Street oligarchy.[1] An official enquiry, presided over by someone from outside the Bahamas, was essential if this was to be established and made public. The Colonial Office doubted whether such a commission was necessary, but the Governor insisted that otherwise Bay Street would set up its own enquiry and put the blame for the trouble on the administration.[2] Whitehall gave way and a retired colonial judge, Sir Alison Russell, was eventually appointed. Bay Street were far from satisfied by the setting up of an enquiry which they foresaw might be critical of their system: to their minds only two questions needed answering – who in the administration was responsible for letting the violence get out of hand, and how soon would they receive compensation for the damage done to their property? They set up their own Select Committee and summoned members of the administration to appear before it. Convinced that the Committee would be hopelessly prejudiced, and encouraged by Walter Monckton who happened to be visiting him, the Duke refused to let his officials give evidence. Kenneth Solomon, for the Assembly, took legal opinion and found an elderly professor of jurisprudence who ruled that the Governor had acted improperly. A legal officer at the Colonial Office concluded that the professor's report was either 'an exceedingly careless piece of work' or 'not a bona fide opinion'. The law officers of the Crown concurred and instructed the Duke to rebuff the protests of the Assembly.[3] The Assembly's Select Committee went ahead undaunted and produced a report which, to no one's surprise, concluded that there were no underlying causes responsible for the riot. 'I consider that the Report is steeped in local politics and I trust, therefore, that its findings will be judged in that light,' wrote the Duke.[4]

'HRH seems to have managed this very well,' minuted Mr Rogers of the Colonial Office. 'An appreciative reply seems called for and I submit a draft (a bit fulsome perhaps).'[5] It cannot have been half as fulsome as the tribute of the Bahamian radical and leader of the black population, Dr Claudius Walker. 'Two years ago when the radiowaves broadcast the news of Your Royal Highness's appointment ... the deaf heard and the dumb spoke, the blind saw and the crippled leapt for joy. Your reputation as a humanitarian and King had preceded you ... You are not just another Governor for one class of people but the Governor for all colours and classes of people.'[1] It is not necessary to take such a rodomontade too seriously, but it would equally be unjust to deny that the Duke had in fact handled the situation well and deserved the plaudits of both the Colonial Office and the black Bahamians.

He returned in triumph to Washington to complete his visit. In theory it was there that agreement had to be won to an improvement in the basic wage, in practice it was the Colonial Office who needed to be convinced. He had recommended an increase of one shilling a day; the Whitehall view was that this was too large for comfort and might have dangerous implications for the rest of the Bahamian labour force, but that the question was ultimately one for the Duke to decide.[2] ExCo considered that sixpence would be sufficient but cabled the Duke in Washington that they too would accept whatever he concluded was best.[3] As soon as he was back in Nassau he broadcast to the island announcing an increase of a shilling a day. 'My endeavours ... met with no little opposition,' he declared – ingeniously giving the impression that it was the Americans, not the British, who had made the difficulties – 'and at one time I feared that I might have to return empty-handed.' The authorities, however, had been persuaded of the justice of the Bahamian cause. More than ever, he was a hero in the eyes of the black people.

The British Army Staff in Washington now curdled the blood of the Colonial Office by predicting further violence, possibly fomented by the Germans, at the time of the forthcoming elections to the Legislative Council. The Duke was unimpressed and rejected any idea that the elections should be postponed.[4] He proved right, but he had barely returned to Nassau before it seemed that he might have underestimated the dangers of the situation. On 29 June 1942 fire devastated the commercial centre of the town. The Duke plunged into the maelstrom and did a useful job helping to bring the blaze under control,[5] then waited apprehensively for a report on the causes of this new disaster. Fortunately, the mischief was traced to an arsonist intending to defraud his insurance company. There was, ExCo concluded with relief, 'no apparent connection with the recent riots'.[6]

The American Connection

Russell's report, when it finally appeared, proved a justification of everything that the Duke had preached for so long. It roundly condemned the Bay Street system; called for a reform of the tax structure, above all for the imposition of an income tax; made recommendations for new labour legislation; and urged the adoption of a secret ballot in the Out Islands as well as New Providence. The Governor was unenthusiastic about the ballot but only took exception to one of Russell's recommendations, the encouragement of birth control; not because he was against it himself, but in recognition of the fact that 'the negroes ignorantly view this beneficial measure as a subtle way of gradually exterminating their race'. One omission also he found regrettable, the failure of the report to consider the issue of racial hostility as a prime cause of the riots. He understood why the commission had shirked the issue but, 'I personally disagree profoundly.' Race was at the heart of the trouble: 'I regret to say that the flame of local race antagonism is still fanned by a certain section of Bay Street . . . and by negro agitators.'[1]

The issue of the secret ballot was to dominate the last two years of the Duke's administration. It was not a matter particularly close to his heart; he doubted whether it would make any noticeable difference to electoral results on the Out Islands, and anyway believed that it was economic and social, not political reform that was urgently needed in the Bahamas. It was the policy of the Colonial Office, and as such he accepted that it was his duty to promote it, but left to himself he would have given it the lowest of priorities. He was not left to himself, however, and by the end of 1942 found himself urged by Whitehall to push the reform forward urgently even at the expense of a confrontation with Bay Street.

It was irritation at what he felt to be ill-informed and misguided pressure which led him in January 1943 to write a long letter to the new Colonial Secretary, Oliver Stanley, in which he set out his views on the main problems facing the Bahamas. Any Governor who sought to achieve greater justice and prosperity for the masses, he maintained, was bound to run foul of Bay Street and its mouthpiece, the House of Assembly. In his case the conflict had been almost continual. Nevertheless, 'although I cannot claim to have achieved a great deal in the two and one-half years of my

Administration, I am at least satisfied that I have started balls rolling in different directions and that my position as Governor is considerably stronger than when I arrived here'. He believed in reform, not revolution. Bay Street was actuated by 'pure avarice and greed', but the black Bahamians were 'a backward people and far more African in their mentality than the casual observer could possibly discern'. It was essential that the white minority should retain political control, 'it would be disastrous for the well-being and economy of the Bahamas should the negroes get the upper hand for a long time to come'. Bay Street must be educated, not roughly coerced or brushed aside. He saw his role as being one of keeping the peace and holding a balance between the 'progressive' Colonial Office and the reactionary white colonists. 'The Constitution of the Bahamas falls between two stools, for it is representative but not responsible and possesses none of the advantages of either self-government as in the British Dominions or Government by an official majority as in the case of the Crown Colonies.'

In this worst of possible worlds, the Executive Council could not rule but could effectively paralyse any activity by the Governor of which it disapproved. The 'low standard of intellect and integrity of the community as a whole' made it inevitable that ExCo would continue to be an obstacle to reform or even reasonable government. There was no body of moderate opinion in the Bahamas: on the one hand the elite consisted of 'a reactionary white group of merchant lawyers', on the other a 'motley collection of lower class whites, high yellows and coloured agitators'.

He ended by reiterating that the black Bahamian was unfit to rule, and that the encouragement of equality of races in the United States, now being pursued by 'certain people in high places in Washington', had dangerous implications for the colony. It was his appreciation of this danger which had led him to adopt policies more conciliatory towards Bay Street than Stanley's Colonial Office officials sometimes approved. An open breach with the House of Assembly would hurt neither the Governor nor the politicians, 'but only the welfare of the masses, which may as a result be denied the necessary legislation to improve social and economic conditions'.[1]

Claudius Walker would hardly have recognized his 'Governor for all colours and classes' in the author of this cautious and conservative epistle, but the Duke would have accepted the title without demur. He was a paternalist, genuinely concerned for the welfare of the black population, and the fact that he found them ill-equipped to manage their own affairs did not affect the reality of his benevolence. He considered that the setting up of the 'Windsor Training Farm' in a previously derelict corner of New Providence, or the establishment of an Out Island Department in Nassau, did far more for the black Bahamian population than the secret ballot or the appointment of a black man to ExCo could ever do. Another proposal to which he attached particular importance was the Bahamas Labour Scheme, by which several thousand unemployed Bahamians were shipped under contract to Florida where farm labour was desperately needed. The Colonial Office, presumably feeling it undignified that British citizens should be exported to do manual labour in a foreign country, at first raised objections but the Duke persisted; conditions in the Out Islands in particular were so desperate that there was little alternative except starvation. He recognized that the scheme 'would only be a temporary solution of our difficulties, and might well be the cause of a lot of discontent in the long run', but at least it would buy time in which his plans for the development of the Out Islands could be pursued.[1] By early 1945 five thousand Bahamians were working in Florida, with another five hundred on the way.[2] Since their wages were high by Bahamian standards, and their contracts stipulated that at least a quarter of their income had to be remitted home, the benefit to the islands' economy was considerable.

But for the war there would not have been room for the Bahamian labourers in Florida, otherwise there was only the presence of American forces in Nassau to indicate that the British Empire was involved in a desperate conflict. In March 1942, however, possibly because of some intercepted radio traffic, the Colonial Office suddenly took alarm at the thought of a German submarine landing a raiding party at Nassau and abducting the Duke.[3] To his surprise he was told that he was to be provided with a personal escort: 'It was my idea to send you a Company of Infantry to guard Government House,' the King wrote proudly, 'and I am glad that the 4th Camerons, my own special Battalion, should have been selected for the task.'[4] One of Hoover's agents reported that the Duke was 'very much worried for fear of being kidnapped by the Germans and being traded for the release of Rudolf Hess',[5] an interpretation of events which makes the Duke sound more alarmist than he was; he never asked for the guard and welcomed it mainly as providing some new faces about the place. He drew the line at having an electrified fence erected around Government House or at taking an escort with him whenever he travelled outside Nassau.[1] Churchill was inclined to accept the Duke's line on the second point but to insist on the fence: 'The right rule is, one may always take a chance but not offer a "sitter".'[2] The Duke persisted: local drunks would undoubtedly blunder into the fence and electrocute themselves and the black population would think it was aimed against them.[3] Churchill dropped the idea.

The Duke's own personal war with Bay Street was growing more violent, however little he might relish it. In response to his long profession of faith Stanley replied sympathetically but firmly. The constitution of the Bahamas was under severe scrutiny in London; it would only survive if it could be shown that under it there could be introduced 'the sort of reform which everybody today considers a minimum'.[4] In April the House of Commons debated colonial administration in the West Indies. The Duke personally got a good press, but Stanley wrote to tell him, 'there is a genuine feeling on the subject of politics in the Bahamas, which may well develop into very outspoken criticism unless appeased by substantial measures of reform'. Income tax and the secret ballot were the two most significant innovations urged by Stanley.[5] The Duke accepted that he must act; his only stipulation was that, since the introduction of income tax would be opposed by everyone affected, white or black, it would be better to isolate Bay Street by concentrating first on the secret ballot.[6] He spoke to everyone in the Assembly who was likely to be at all sympathetic to the cause, and explained to them that on the introduction of the secret ballot might depend the survival of the constitution. Then, on 30 November, he opened the Legislature with a speech in which the need for constitutional reform was starkly set out.

The response was more one of incredulity than of outrage; the proposal, it was generally supposed, could be no more than a bargaining counter which would be dropped in exchange for acceptance of some of the Governor's social legislation. Given half a chance, the Duke would have been happy to treat it as such. 'Quite frankly, I am not convinced that all the Out Islands are yet

478

ripe for the Secret Ballot in their present backward state,' he told Stanley. 'The whole question is most delicate and fraught with difficulties and is one which, if I take too firm a stand, is likely to produce a clash not only with the House of Assembly but with the unofficial members of my Executive Committee. This is a risk which I personally deem it imprudent to run at the present juncture.'[1] Two months later he had grown more robust. He had been converted, he told Stanley, by Professor Richardson, his economic adviser, who had arrived in the spring of 1943 and quickly established himself as a very considerable influence on the Duke in every field of activity. He now believed there was a chance that the Assembly might accept the secret ballot. But what if it was rejected? Should he dissolve the House? 'I have since childhood been taught to avoid politics like the plague,' he told Stanley, 'and as a brother of the King it would . . . be most undesirable were I to become involved in a highly contentious political conflict which is fundamentally a racial one.' Besides, he concluded rather touchingly, so far he had done well for the community in his charge: 'I wish my administration to be remembered as a constructive one when I leave and not clouded . . . by so unpopular an incident as dissolving the House of Assembly.'[2]

Stanley regretfully agreed, satisfied that even if the Duke did dissolve the House an election would be unlikely to change things very much, and the Governor would then either have to abandon the cause or suspend the constitution – not a course ever to be taken lightly, least of all in wartime. But he insisted that the Duke should first do his best to persuade the Assembly to accept the ballot – possibly the strength of opinion in London might induce some of the less recalcitrant to change their minds.[3] The Duke accepted the instruction, though he became ever more convinced, he told Richardson, that 'white Bahamian resistance to the Secret Ballot is the right one at the present time; for the alternative, namely the rule of Messrs Milo Butler, Bert Cambridge etc is too terrifyingly awful to contemplate'.[4]* As he expected, the House rejected any extension of the secret ballot, though it agreed that the device should become permanent in New Providence. As a quid pro quo it accepted the Duke's pet legislation, the Out Island

---

* Two leading black politicians: Cambridge was a jazz musician and Butler eventually became the first black Governor General.

Development Plan, by which £400,000 was allocated over a period of eight years for the improvement of these benighted areas. The Duke, at least, was satisfied that the bargain was a good one for the Bahamas. And when, in February 1945, he was able to tell Stanley that there had been a change of heart in the Assembly and it seemed likely that the secret ballot would after all be extended to all the Bahamians,[1] he had some right to reflect that he had done his job well and that Whitehall would in the end be able to have its cake and eat it too.

It was singularly unfortunate for the Duke that his very real achievements as Governor should have been overshadowed by a lurid scandal in which he played a less than impressive if peripheral role. His tenure of office in the Bahamas is associated in popular memory more than anything with the murder of Sir Harry Oakes. On 8 July 1943 the body of this rugged yet flamboyant magnate was found, charred and battered, in the bedroom of his house near Nassau. Oakes was 'a very fine and charming old man', the Duke told Marjoribanks; 'the Santa Claus of New Providence . . . very popular in the community'. He was a Santa Claus with enemies, however, and one of them had now murdered him, the Governor told Stanley, 'in circumstances as grim and gruesome as any crime concocted in the imagination of Edgar Wallace'.[2] When the news was brought to the Duke he at once made his first blunder and tried to clap an embargo on the news – a move that would have been pointless in any case and was made doubly so since word had already reached the American mainland, whence a flock of journalists was shortly to descend on the Bahamas.

Next he made a still worse mistake. He concluded that the local police force was 'entirely unequal and unequipped' to deal with such a crisis.[3] It is not surprising that he reached this decision. Even before he arrived in the Bahamas the Acting Governor had telegraphed him, in connection with the possible assassination attempt, that the local detectives were '*not* to be relied on to undertake skilled investigations'.[4] Heape confirmed that his view had not changed when he told the Colonial Office in November 1943 that a murder of such complexity was 'beyond the capacity of any small police establishment such as we have here'.[5] Hallinan, the Attorney General, also believed the Governor was probably correct in calling in reinforcements.[1] But it was in the choice of those reinforcements that the Duke erred sadly.

In peacetime it would have been automatic procedure to appeal to Scotland Yard. In wartime, however, with flights hazardous and spasmodic, it might have taken weeks before a detective had arrived in Nassau. A telephone call to Washington would have produced equally efficient assistance, but here too there would have been some delay. The Duke was consumed by a sense of urgency, believing that what evidence there might be would soon be destroyed in the heat of the Bahamian summer. It was essential that detectives come at once. It is a common weakness of those in the highest places to believe that people with whom they are personally acquainted possess some special quality denied to other mortals. While in Miami, the Duke had been impressed by the efficiency of Captain W. E. Melchen who had been assigned to guard him by the Miami police. He telephoned Melchen, a call which was intercepted and transcribed by the American authorities, told him Oakes was dead, and asked him to come out with one or two of his men to investigate. It was, he said, a 'very, very urgent matter'. There was no need to bring a passport and Pan American would hold the midday flight. It was imperative the investigation begin that day.[2]

The true horror of the Duke's blunder was not to become apparent for a little while, but he now compounded it by making up his mind who had done the murder before the investigation had even begun. Sir Harry Oakes was known to have quarrelled violently with his son-in-law, Alfred de Marigny. The Duke disliked de Marigny, who had been less than respectful towards the royal Governor.[3] He did not hide his views; the behaviour of the American detectives suggests strongly that they went to the scene of the crime determined to find de Marigny guilty. The Duke could hardly have expected, however, that Melchen's deputy, Barker, would manufacture evidence to help secure a conviction.

Who in fact killed Sir Harry Oakes is a mystery and probably always will be. A plethora of theories has been put forward, some convincing, some grotesque. What is certain is that when the murder came to trial, the case against de Marigny collapsed and Barker in particular was exposed as a dishonest bungler. The

Duke thought it wisest to leave Nassau while the trial was on, and talked to Halifax about the case. He told the Ambassador that he thought de Marigny was probably guilty but was unlikely to be convicted.[1] The evidence does not support the first part of his view. The jury had no hesitation in acquitting, though for reasons which were obscure then and remain so today they added a recommendation that de Marigny be deported forthwith from the Bahamas.

This recommendation the Duke pursued with vengeful eagerness. Since the United States would not receive de Marigny, he could not be deported by the Pan American flight; to wait for a suitable boat would involve a longer delay than the Duke could endure, Transport Command must send an aircraft to remove him.[2] The Colonial Office, who had been doubtful about the wisdom of importing American police from the start, approached Transport Command, but without much zeal. The Command predictably said that all their planes were needed for military purposes. He was convinced, the Duke then telegraphed, that a failure to deport de Marigny 'would constitute a deplorable evidence of the impotence of the local Government and have very serious effect on the Colony's reputation throughout the world'. Duly impressed by this prognostication, the Colonial Secretary approached the Secretary of State for Air. Sir Archibald Sinclair supported Transport Command. The Duke now threatened that unless a place was quickly provided he would appeal direct to Churchill. Stanley passed this on to the Air Minister. 'Your first reaction may, I fear, be to resent the tone of the telegram,' he wrote, 'but you will realize that in this particular case we all have to make allowances.' Sinclair showed no signs of yielding, and then the news came that de Marigny had already left the Bahamas under his own steam, leaving the Duke looking like a man who had been beating down a door with a sledge hammer only to find that it had never been locked.[3]

The Duke thickened the smoke of mystery that hung around the case by posting the Commissioner of Police, Colonel Erskine-Lindop, to another West Indian island before he was able to give evidence at the trial. The truth of the matter, the Duke told Stanley, was that the transfer had already been gazetted at the time of the murder. Lindop had been so upset by the criticism meted out to him in the Russell report into the riots that 'he lost heart and more or less sat down on the job awaiting transfer . . . The result was a general deterioration of the Police Force, both as regards discipline and efficiency, until it got to a very low ebb, and as the state of the Police Force is my direct responsibility, became a situation I could not tolerate.'[1] He would have done well to tolerate it for a few weeks more; the disappearance of Lindop inevitably led to rumours of a cover-up. In fact the Bahamian police had been so effectively divorced from the investigation that Lindop had little to contribute in the way of evidence and certainly nothing that could not have been said perfectly well by his deputy – but this did little to check the tide of gossip.

The Duke had made a fool of himself. There were those who suggested, and still suggest, that he had done far worse. Many accusations have been levelled at the Duke by those who thrive on sensation; most of them suggesting that he received some sort of financial reward for his performance and was operating, consciously or unconsciously, as the agent of international criminals, probably the Mafia. All that can be said of these is that no evidence has ever been produced which would stand up in court, and that such conduct would have been contrary to everything that is known about his character. Even if the distinctly shaky thesis that international crime was somehow involved in the Oakes murder be accepted, no one has ever produced any fact which even implies the possibility of the Duke's complicity, still less of any motive that could have been strong enough to impel him into taking so appalling a risk. He can fairly be accused of impetuosity and bad judgment, and of allowing his dislike of de Marigny to impair what should have been his complete impartiality. This is quite bad enough, without dredging up fantastic slanders from the sludge of unsubstantiated gossip.

26

What Comes Next?

S HORTLY AFTER THE NEW GOVERNOR ARRIVED IN
Nassau he found himself required to present a large photograph of the Queen to the Duchess, in her role as President
of the Red Cross centre. The portrait, he explained, had been
requested by his predecessor: 'I only regret that he is not here
to perform the unveiling ceremony,'[1] he stated, with no doubt
conscious ambiguity. He had forgiven his family nothing. Nor was
the atmosphere notably warmer in England. Lascelles was amused
when the Dean of Windsor, in a moment of aberration, invited his
congregation to pray for Edward, Prince of Wales – 'not at all a
success,' commented Lascelles.[2]

In August 1942 the Duke of Kent was killed in a flying accident.
In their common grief it seemed as if mother and son might be
brought closer together. 'My thoughts go out to you, who are so
far away from us all,' wrote Queen Mary, 'knowing how devoted
you were to him, and how kind you were to him in a difficult
moment in his all too short life, kindness I for one shall never
forget; he always remembered it, for he was very fond of you.' 'I
hope you will often write to me now, as you used to do,' she
continued, and then, most significant olive branch of all, 'Please
give a kind message to your wife, she will help you to bear your
sorrow.'[3]

The Duke's reply was quite as warm. 'Loving thanks for your
sweet letter,' he wrote, 'shining with your indomitable spirit of
course, which is of the greatest comfort to me.' The difficult times
he had gone through with his brother had brought them close
together: 'He was in some ways more like a son to me, and his
charm and gaiety brought great happiness to York House those
years he lived with me.' 'I have written to Marina,' he went on –
perhaps the letter was blown astray by some wind of war, for he
was often unfairly accused of having failed to send even a brief

message of condolence to his sister-in-law. The Duke of Kent's death had brought home to him forcibly 'the utter useless cruelty of this ghastly war . . . Remembering how much you and I hated the last war, I can well imagine how our feelings about this one must be the same – a deep-rooted conviction that it could have been avoided and then an intense craving for an end to all this misery, but which I am now afraid cannot come to pass until we have once and for all time frustrated the World domination plans of a single nation.' He promised to write regularly in future, and said how much he was longing to see her again, while 'always hoping that maybe one day things will change and that I shall have the intense pride and pleasure of bringing Wallis to see you'.[1]

Whatever her views on the final sentence, Queen Mary was delighted with the rest of her son's message. 'A perfectly charming, sympathetic letter,' she described it to the Countess of Athlone,[2] hoping that it would be the precursor of a warmer relationship in the future. If she saw the Duke's letter to King George VI, she must have realized that there was deep bitterness still to overcome. As he had done to his mother, he stressed how close he had felt to the Duke of Kent, but then continued: 'It is, therefore, a source of great pain to me now to think that on account of your "attitude" towards me, which has been adopted by the whole family, he and I did not see each other last year when he was so near me in America.'[3] The promised letters to his mother never came, or only in the shape of cursory notes. She had hoped for more, Queen Mary told Princess Alice, 'but oh! dear no, nothing of the kind, most disappointing. I believe he is angry because Bertie will not let her be called HRH, but why should she?'[4]

So long as this issue was unresolved – as the Duke saw it – or remained immutably settled as it had been in 1937 – as the King felt – there could be no true reconciliation between the Duke of Windsor and his relations. He never rested in his efforts to right what he felt to be a grievous offence against his wife and used every contact he enjoyed to bring pressure on the royal family. At the end of 1942 he persuaded Churchill to raise the issue again; foolishly, to Lascelles's mind – 'God knows, [it] is not going to make the world a better or worse place, whichever way it be answered.'[5] Even to consider the problem upset the King, Lascelles noticed. The King refused to reopen it. He was ready to leave the matter in abeyance, he told Churchill, 'but I must tell you quite honestly that I do not trust the Duchess's loyalty'.[1]

In the autumn of 1943 the issue re-emerged in a different guise. For some time the Duke had been playing with the idea that there might be oil in commercial quantities to be found on his Alberta ranch. Towards the end of 1942 a geologist conducted a survey and reported that prospects were good. The Duke involved some rich American friends in the affair and set up a company to drill for oil. But now problems arose. The lease granted him by the government of Alberta exceptionally included mineral rights, but it ran only so long as the ranch was farmed by the Duke or a member of the royal family. If the Duke died, the Duchess would inherit. What would happen then? The Duke wrote to King George VI to explain the problem, and to ask that, even though she was not to be granted the title of HRH, his wife should be officially designated as a member of the royal family.[2] His lawyer, Allen, raised the matter with Lascelles.

There was a real legal issue involved, but it was also an ingenious way of inserting the thin end of a wedge which ultimately seemed likely to win the Duchess her coveted distinction. Lascelles was immediately suspicious. The Duke's request implied that the principle by which the status of the Duchess had been decided might be changed on purely commercial grounds. Hostile American newspapers would be entitled to say that being a Royal Highness depended on whether or not there was money in it. 'To me, the Duke's suggestion seems indefensible from every aspect.'[3] It was, anyway, no concern of the King's, Lascelles argued; the question of the Duchess's legal status was one for the Canadian courts, or possibly for the law officers of the Crown.[4] The latter considered it and dodged the issue by saying that there was no legal definition of the royal family but that, anyway, the Duke's lease did not carry the implication which he had read into it – there was no reason why his heir should be a member of the royal family.[5] 'No action on my part can affect the issue,' the King told his brother.[6]

The problem now vanished away, with a softness and silence that suggested Lascelles might have been right in his surmise that for the Duke the question had been more one of his wife's position than of the legal title of his heir. By the beginning of 1944 negotiations with the government of Alberta had been completed, on terms, the Duke told Malcolm MacDonald, as satisfactory as could be expected from 'these exceptionally difficult and obstinate politicians'.[1] Drilling began, and a year later prospects looked bright. 'It would indeed be a pleasant surprise to wake up finding oneself an oil magnate instead of the impoverished owner of a mere cattle ranch!' the Duke told Queen Mary.[2] But there was to be no such happy ending. Oil was discovered but only in tiny quantities and the Duke found himself not only no oil magnate but $100,000 dollars the poorer. The Duchess's inheritance would hardly have been worth going to law for.

The Duchess herself had decided to intervene in her husband's long-drawn-out battle with his family. She profited by the fact that the Bishop of Nassau was departing for England and was an old acquaintance of Queen Mary, to send her mother-in-law a letter by his hand. The Bishop, she said, would be able to tell Queen Mary whether 'all the things David gave up are replaced to him in another way, and the little details of his daily life . . . The horrors of war and endless separations of family have in my mind stressed the importance of family ties. I hope that by the end of the summer we will be nearer that victory for which we are all working so hard and for which England has so bravely lighted the way.'[3] 'It is a nice letter,' admitted the King. His suspicions of his sister-in-law, however, were not to be so easily overcome. 'I wonder what is the real motive behind her having written,' he went on. '. . . I must say I do feel a bit suspicious of it!!' He added a postscript to say that he had just seen the Prime Minister, who had received a letter from the Duke asking for a change of post. 'A coincidence!!'[4]

King George VI did not relent with the passage of time. In September 1944 Churchill visited the United States. A meeting with the Duke was part of his schedule. 'The King sent a most cold reply to the PM's request for a fraternal greeting to the Duke of Windsor,' reported Colville.[5] At their meeting, and subsequently by letter,[6] the Duke urged Churchill to take up once more with the King the question of the Duchess being received at court and given the title of Her Royal Highness. The Prime Minister had little enthusiasm for an errand that he was certain would prove fruitless, but he did his best. The King, recorded Lascelles in his diary, 'apart from his engrained dislike for the woman, and also apart from his recollection that the D of W has, on more than one occasion, been extremely rude to (and about) the Q, Q Mary and other royal ladies, thinks that such a gesture is wrong in principal* and would imply that the abdication had been all a mistake'. Lascelles's suggestion was that the King should tell Churchill that, on personal and family grounds, he was averse to meeting the Duchess, but would of course do so if asked to by the government. That would mean the Prime Minister could only bring further pressure if the Cabinet endorsed his attitude, something which Lascelles was sure they would refuse to do (Churchill had already told the Duke as much two years before, when he regretted that 'it would be impossible to move the War Cabinet in that direction, and I should deprecate even bringing the matter before them'[1]). Churchill's sentimental loyalty to the Duke, Lascelles told the Home Secretary, John Anderson, was 'based on a tragic false premise – viz that he (Winston) really *knew* the D of W, which he never did'. Lascelles also warned both Churchill and Anderson that 'constant harping on this problem might have a really serious effect on the present King's health'.[2]

Probably Lascelles's advice made little difference; the Queen told him a few days later that she and Queen Mary had drawn up and signed a statement to the effect that 'they were *not* prepared to receive the Duchess, now, or at any time, for the same reasons that they would not do so in 1936'.[3] Churchill passed the news on to the Duke; personally he regretted the decision, he said, 'but my judgment may well be, as indeed it proved at the Abdication, quite different from that of the great mass of the British people'.[4] The Duke can hardly have been surprised but he was still bitterly distressed, particularly by Churchill's suggestion that it was not just his family who took this line but the British people as a whole. They would never return to Britain so long as that was the state of things, he told the Prime Minister.[5] He sent a copy of Churchill's letter to his mother. Was she really so inflexible? he asked. When they returned to Europe he would visit her alone. 'In view of your attitude it would be a very big concession on my part to go to see you; at the same time we could talk things over quietly and who knows but that an exchange of viewpoints . . . might not well be enlightening to both of us.'[6]

*

---

* [*Sic*] So unusual a slip from this most meticulous of writers suggests that Lascelles himself was rendered overwrought by any airing of this subject.

It was not only about his wife's status that the Duke constantly pressed Churchill. Almost before he had arrived in the Bahamas he was looking around for some other post where his talents could be put to better use. In October 1940 Philip Guedalla, now head of the Latin American section of the Ministry of Information, tried to put the Duke in charge of a high-powered mission that was to tour that area. 'The very fact that it would certainly be more interesting wartime employment for us, and possibly more useful, is just the reason why they would never send us to South America,' wrote the Duke sadly.[1] Whether or not he interpreted the reasons correctly, he was right in his conclusion: Lord Willingdon headed the mission. The Duke continued to play with the idea of some sort of roving ambassadorship in Latin America, however, and mentioned it to Monckton in September 1942.[2] The possibility had already been discussed and dismissed in London. Eden told Churchill he could see no advantage in the proposal; it would arouse American suspicions and, anyway, 'Any prominent visitor to Latin America must be able to speak with authority and first hand knowledge of what we are doing to win the war. Through no fault of his own, the Duke of Windsor could not do this.'[3]

Eden's memorandum presumably arose out of a letter the Duke had written to Churchill a little earlier in which he said that he could not contemplate remaining in the Bahamas for the duration of the war and asked for another job, preferably in the United States or Canada.[4] 'But what kind of work can he do and under whom can he work?' asked the King. 'Neither country will relish "her".'[5] Churchill suggested Southern Rhodesia as an alternative but Smuts quickly blocked the proposal. It would have a bad effect on public opinion; baffle the natives, who would not understand how a former monarch could be subordinate to a Secretary of State; and embarrass those whose object was the continued co-operation of South Africa in the Commonwealth. 'This is decisive,' minuted Churchill.[6] He could report no progress when he met the Duke in Washington in July 1942, but found him better disposed to the idea of staying in the Bahamas with occasional visits to the United States. Churchill told the King that he had noticed the Duke was uncertain of himself when not with his wife or under her influence. 'D was still very anti-me,' recorded the King, 'which Winston tried to put right.'[7] The respite did not last long, by

November the Duke was again clamouring for a change: 'The calibre and intellect of my associates . . . are not of a high order, and I miss the stimulation that is afforded by collaboration with men of affairs to which I have hitherto been accustomed.'[1]

The Duke deluded himself that Beaverbrook would be a useful ally in his quest. In fact Beaverbrook had no intention of interfering, but shrank from saying this openly. When in New York at the same time as the Duke in April 1943, he told his henchman David Farrer to say always that he was 'out for a walk' if the Duke called. Eventually he relented and agreed to have a meeting. Farrer rang the Duke's suite and asked for the equerry. 'The Duke speaking,' came the reply. Farrer lost his head, blurted out 'Oh God!' and put down the receiver. 'What the Hell do you think you're doing, speaking to the Duke like that?' asked Beaverbrook indignantly.[2] Whether or not as a result of the ensuing meeting, he did speak to Churchill; and whether or not through Beaverbrook's intervention, Churchill did bestir himself again to find another post. The result, in June 1943, was the offer of the Governorship of Bermuda: technically a promotion, but to an island which, though it had a better climate than the Bahamas, was even smaller and more remote. 'It seems to me that Your Royal Highness would have the opportunity of developing American contacts which would be of importance to us at the present time,' suggested Churchill.[3] The Duke was not impressed by this justification of a proposal which he felt to be on the verge of an insult. He refused politely enough[4] but the draft letter to Churchill which he prepared but never sent a year or so later, in which he referred to the offer as being 'further proof . . . of the limitations placed on my capabilities',[5] showed his real feelings.

He sent this draft to George Allen, in May 1944, with a covering letter in which he said that he was thinking of resigning and settling in the United States until such time as he could decide about his long-term future. 'If I got a job in America, there would be a good chance of the Duchess getting lost, taxwise, in the Diplomatic shuffle'; as for his own dollar securities, these had all been transferred to Beacon Agencies in 1942 – 'you will recall that my object . . . was to insure against the possibility of a more hostile British Socialist Government forcing me to surrender all my dollar holdings'.[6] It is unclear whether the job he had in mind was private or in the public service; presumably the former, since in the same letter he referred to the fact that 'family jealousy would oppose any suggestion of an appointment worthy of my experience' such as a 'roving commission' in the United States.

Allen was dismayed by the financial implications of this proposal. He warned the Duchess that if they settled in the United States they would face the possibility of 'almost complete confiscation of the whole of your current joint income as well as the danger . . . (since you are an American citizen) of a claim for payment of tax on your back income'.[1] As to the idea of finding some job in the United States in which the Duke would be sheltered from avaricious taxmen by an umbrella of diplomatic immunity, Allen wrote that he had consulted Beaverbrook, who felt that it would be unfair to the British Ambassador. What about governing Newfoundland? Beaverbrook had asked: 'It will be a real man's job,' or perhaps acting as Governor General of the proposed West Indian Federation?[2]

As the end of the war approached, the court became ever more preoccupied with the Duke's future. Lascelles was resolute in his determination that no public employment should be offered him. The two possibilities that would most appeal to the Duke were that he should be given some representational role abroad, or return to Britain to live as the younger brother of the King. Both were impracticable, Lascelles concluded: a man who had renounced the throne could not represent the monarch, and there was no room for two Kings in England. The only solution was for him to live abroad as a private individual and develop his own interests.[3] Churchill was unconvinced. One could not rule out the provision of some representative role being found for the Duke, he retorted, and as for residence in England: 'Nothing that I am aware of can stop him returning to this country.'[4] Nor was the King so rigid as his private secretary; at about this time he asked Halifax whether the Duke might not after all be made an ambassador in Latin America. 'I did not encourage the idea much,' recorded Halifax.[5]

The Duke and Churchill met again in September 1944, and the Duke wrote to him the following month. He could see it was too early, he said wistfully, to decide what kind of a job there might be for him after the war: 'I would not wish to be unemployed if there was any sphere in which it were considered my experience could still be appropriately utilized.' But he could agree with Lascelles on at least one point; there would be no question of his seeking to live in England again unless there was a drastic change of heart in the Palace. He could not resist a gibe at his brother on this score: 'Having been given to understand that they are by now so well and firmly established in the hearts of their people, I would not have thought that my presence in their midst could any longer be considered so formidable a nuisance to the solidarity of the monarchy.'[1] Churchill was still anxious to help, and realized that the time was approaching when it would not be possible to postpone the issue further. The Duke was now not only talking of resignation but actively discussing the kind of successor who was needed. He should be rich, he stressed, since Nassau was expensive and the need to entertain Americans was pressing; even more important, he should be drawn from outside the Colonial Service, since otherwise he would follow too slavishly the bidding of the Colonial Office. The Bahamas were different to other colonies, and the new Governor must act accordingly.[2] 'That special negro problem is a grim legacy which my successor must inherit,' he told Churchill, 'and in his post-war approach a career man might not possess the firmness, tact and vision that will be required to uphold the rightful power and prestige of a local white community . . . in the face of growing criticism in the House of Commons and the preaching of Harlem negro agitators.'[3]* When Stanley visited Nassau in January 1945 the Duke formally announced his resignation, and fixed it for the end of April, a few weeks before the five-year term of office traditional for a Governor would have run its course. A decision of some kind must rapidly be taken.

King George VI had made up his mind what was desirable. Lascelles told Stanley that 'the best solution was the one I have always advocated – that he make himself a home in the USA',[4] and the King came to share this view. When Churchill was due to meet the Duke in Washington, the King urged him to 'put forward my conviction . . . that his happiness will be best served by making his home in the USA'.[5] The Prime Minister was not disposed to take such instructions meekly: 'With humble duty,' he replied, 'Mr

---

* The government were not impressed by his arguments and appointed W. L. Murphy, a 'career man' without private means currently serving as Colonial Secretary in Bermuda.

Churchill feels that if he delivered himself of such a message, it might well have the effect of leading HRH to establish himself in England.' Besides, he added with a touch of menace: 'Mr Churchill has never abandoned the idea of the Duke discharging Ambassadorial or Governor functions if suitable openings can be found.'[1]

They were brave words, but when it came to the point 'suitable openings' proved as hard to find as ever they had been in the past. The Embassy in Washington had now been tacitly dropped from the list of possibilities, though Stanley thought the Duke still hankered after it.[2] Mackenzie King and other eminent Canadians had made it plain that the Duke would not be welcome as Governor General in Canada.[3] Churchill at one point suggested that he might become Governor of Ceylon – 'despite the fact that a perfectly good one has been newly appointed,' commented Lascelles.[4] Another variant was to make him Governor of Madras. Lascelles did as much as anyone to counter these proposals, arguing – with considerable force – that such an appointment would make the position of the Viceroy impossible and that 'as we are continually kicking Indian princes off the *gaddi* because they make unwise marriages, the Windsors' position would be, to say the least, equivocal'.[5] There were, indeed, excellent arguments to be advanced against any individual job that might be suggested; and yet Churchill had reason for stubbornly insisting that the Duke did deserve *something*, and that considerable talent would be going to waste if nothing were provided. Even Lascelles noted in his diary that Oliver Stanley had reported the Duke not merely looked remarkably well and young and was obviously still in love with his wife, but that he was 'a competent Governor and knew all there was to know about his islands'.[6]

If nothing official could be found for them to do, the problem of where the Windsors were to live became an urgent problem. They had houses in France which had now been liberated, but the political future of the country was obscure and the French themselves were not over-enthusiastic about the possibility that the Windsors might soon be in their midst. Oliver Harvey reported a conversation with Massigli, de Gaulle's Ambassador in London, in which it had been made clear that the Windsors should stay out of France until the situation cleared up: 'What M. Massigli had evidently in mind, although he did not say so, was that he feared the Duke and Duchess might seek to renew acquaintance with many who had turned out to be collaborators, and this would cause a most embarrassing situation.'[1] 'Any such objection could, I think, easily be overcome,' stated Lascelles blithely,[2] but it still put a disturbing question mark over the long-term projects of the Windsors.

Nothing had been decided when the Duke's resignation was publicly announced except that the Windsors would go first to the United States for a holiday. When asked his plans by the *Daily Tribune* the Duke answered vaguely that he expected to travel a lot: 'The Duchess likes travel and as for me I have never before spent five years in one place. And I hope that I shall never be in one place that long again.'[3] He was particularly anxious that nobody should imagine he had either been pushed into premature retirement or had abandoned his post for selfish reasons. The first text of the 'Note for the Guidance of the Press', which had been drafted in Nassau, contained the sentence: 'Others who, like the Duke, have freely given their whole time and energy during the war to special service under the Crown, have already found it necessary, with the approach of the end of hostilities in Europe, to resume charge of their personal affairs.' Someone in Buckingham Palace suggested substituting 'willingly' for 'freely', presumably in recognition of the salary that the Duke had drawn. Churchill said that the tone of the whole communiqué was far too defensive.[4] No amount of guidance could anyway stop the American press announcing that the Governor had been amazed when his resignation was accepted, that Churchill had promised him a more important post, and that he had already applied and been rejected for the posts of Governor General of Canada and Viceroy of India.[5]

The Windsors left Nassau on 3 May 1945. At the last meeting of ExCo which he attended, a resolution was passed mouthing all the appropriate clichés about the Duke's 'untiring effort', and 'wisdom, foresight and ability', and the 'affection and gratitude of all sections of the community'.[6] No doubt they were sincerely meant, and no doubt the Duke was duly touched. It is reasonable to assume, however, that he took greater satisfaction from the words of his old adversary Etienne Dupuch in the *Daily Tribune*. He had been critical of the Duke's original appointment, wrote Dupuch, and he had deliberately constituted himself a thorn in his side. But he had soon become convinced that the Governor was 'genuinely trying to do his best for the islands and the people – and especially for sections of the Colony that had long been neglected by selfish political interests centred in Nassau'.

There had been occasional clashes between the Duke and certain powerful interests. 'These clashes could have led to serious political consequences for the Colony. But, while the Duke has always been strong, definite and unswerving in his purposes, he has always been a gentleman under the most trying circumstances. The polished approach he has given to these situations has taken them far on the road to accomplishment without precipitating an open break with anyone.'

The Bahamas were now enjoying a period of great prosperity.

This situation is no accident. His Royal Highness has used his influence in the higher councils in the United States and in Great Britain to put the Colony where it is today. Obstacles that no ordinary Governor would have tackled in these difficult war times, His Royal Highness has taken in his stride and there has been no blowing of bugles at these accomplishments. They have just happened . . .

We know of many views held by His Royal Highness in which we are in strong disagreement but we have grown to respect him because he is no politician – he doesn't bluff and he is no hypocrite. Never matter how strongly we may disagree with a man, we can admire him if he lays his cards honestly on the table for all to see, and leaves no doubt in the public's mind as to the honesty and earnestness of his purpose.

We were sorry to see the Duke come to the Colony as its Governor. We are more sorry to see him leave.[1]

The sentiments could perhaps have been expressed with greater elegance, but it was not a bad epitaph to have earned after five difficult years.

27

'Some Sort of Official Status'

W HEN THE WINDSORS ARRIVED IN MIAMI ON 4
May 1945 life stretched in an alarming blank ahead of
them. Between the abdication and September 1939 the
Duke had been in waiting; quite what was going to turn up he did
not know, but that something would, he knew. The war did, and
for the next five years his life had been, if not wholly satisfactory,
then at least structured. He had always known what he was
supposed to be doing, unappealing though it might sometimes
be. Now he found himself with no commitment save that of
administering his own affairs. He was left with two overriding
ambitions: to find himself a job and to secure his wife's recognition
by the royal family. These were to dominate the next few years of
his life; in both he failed.

It was the autumn before they felt the time was ripe for a return
to Europe. In the meantime they spent an uneventful four months,
mainly in New York, with breaks in Newport and for fishing in
New Brunswick. The previous year the Duchess had been operated
on for cancer of the stomach; the operation seemed to have been
a total success, but worries about his wife's health added to the
Duke's concern about his own future. As if these preoccupations
were not enough, he was profoundly pessimistic about the future
of the post-war world. For five years he had predicted that the only
beneficiary from the conflict would be the communists. When he
stayed with Jock Balfour, the British Minister in Washington, he
made it clear that he still thought 'if Hitler had been differently
handled, war might have been avoided', and that the world in such
a case would have been a better and safer place.[1] He was convinced
that an already disastrous situation had been made immeasurably
worse by the surrender of the ailing Roosevelt to Stalin at Yalta,
and the subsequent irruption of Soviet power into the heartlands
of Europe.[2] He called on Roosevelt's successor, Truman, in August

and found him 'in a state of utter gloom'. Word had just come in that the Japanese had rejected the American ultimatum. 'I now have no alternative than to drop an atomic bomb on Tokyo,' said the President despairingly.[1] The Duke was impressed by his obvious determination and integrity, but alarmed by his naivety and ignorance of international affairs.

The greater part of his personal possessions was still in France, and it was there that most people expected him to settle, yet he viewed the future of that country with the utmost gloom. France had not been a first-class nation since the time of Napoleon, he told an American friend, Robert Young. She had lacked the stamina to resist the Germans in 1940, and that same lack of stamina was impeding her recovery in 1945. De Gaulle was 'not the leader he is portrayed and he would do a lot better if, instead of trying to lift France's prestige abroad by assuming high-hat attitudes, he concentrated upon exhorting the people to get on with the job of reconstruction'. But even if he did, the cards were stacked against him; he had 'the Communists on his neck and ... cannot take more than a superficial stand against them'.[2] A year later, in October 1946, he had almost lost hope; the 'Moscow-directed campaign to sabotage our free-enterprise system' was on the point of final success; de Gaulle was 'both too weak and too late to rally the French people sufficiently'.[3] The conclusion he drew for himself was that he should be extremely careful before he committed more of his resources to a doomed continent; before he even returned to Europe he was telling George Allen that he did not regard France 'as a healthy place of residence for anyone without an official job there ... I have in back of my mind a speedy return to America as soon as we have been able to make adequate dispositions regarding our possessions.'[4]

Though such jeremiads now seem extravagant, the situation in France was indeed precarious in the years immediately after the war, and the Duke was not alone in predicting a rapid descent into first chaos and then communism. He was more obviously wrong in his consistent misjudgment of the political situation in Britain, whose plight he felt to be little if at all less parlous than that of her continental neighbour. The general election of 1945, when Britain swept Churchill from power and installed a Labour government with an overwhelmingly large majority, seemed to him 'dis-

497

couraging and a great surprise'. Although he pronounced virtuously that 'tradition precluded any political comment on his part', he once again demonstrated that for him tradition was something to be ignored when he continued: 'I must admit to a sense of disappointment – not so much for Great Britain herself, who is well able to control the extent and tempo of new political and economical experiments with sanity and moderation, but as regards the effect of the British Socialist victory in this country [the United States] and on the continent of Europe, where the spread of Communism was the greatest danger confronting us and must now be a certainty.'[1] With Britain pink, France must inevitably take on the most lurid shade of red.

Soon he was not so confident about the 'sanity and moderation' of British government and people. The exponents of the free enterprise system, he told Queen Mary, would have to fight hard against 'the politically powerful advocates of nationalization or statism . . . I hope and believe the people of Britain will eventually rebel against the theoretical and ideological socialists they acclaimed and elected to power a year ago; only I hope it won't take too long to realize it backed the wrong horse, or before the present Government can enact too much unpractical and destructive legislation. And to add fuel to the general conflagration, the Socialist policy towards India is a disaster and will only create another vacuum which must eventually be sovietically absorbed.'[2] To Lord Portal, the Chairman of the Great Western Railway, he wrote sympathetically of 'the headaches this railroad nationalization scheme imposed by these crazy and dangerous Socialists must be giving you'.[3] 'Crazy and dangerous' were the epithets he used also in a letter about His Majesty's Government to His Majesty himself. How unfortunate for the King, he wrote, to have no option but to accept the Socialists' disastrous policies. Their 'concerted attack upon any form of wealth, their determination to nationalize many industries, and their continuation of rationing for rationing's sake, is as alarming as is the apathy of the people towards all the rules and regulations imposed on them'.[4] By the end of 1946 he was telling Queen Mary that Crossman and fifty other left-wing Labour members were communist in all but name, and that the political trends in Britain as well as France were 'very discouraging if not alarming'.[5]

The only minister in whom he had any confidence was Ernest Bevin, whose opposition to Soviet expansionism was robust enough to satisfy even the Duke. Adrian Holman, at the British Embassy in Paris, had a long talk with him in September 1945 shortly after his arrival in Europe and reported that 'his main preoccupation seems to be the growing menace of Soviet Russia'.[1] He welcomed enthusiastically Churchill's speech at Fulton, Missouri, in which the former Prime Minister proclaimed the existence of the cold war and warned the Western democracies to be on their guard. 'No one but you has the experience to tell the world the true implications of Soviet foreign policy,' he assured Churchill.[2] It was high time, he wrote to Queen Mary, that someone exposed 'Soviet Russia's manoeuvring and land and oil-grabbing aims'. Surely, even the 'ill-informed and misguided masses' of Great Britain would now see the danger before it was too late.[3]

The very fact that he wrote to his brother and his mother with such frankness shows that in the last two or three years there had been something of a thaw in the relationship between the former monarch and the court. Allen wrote to report that he had been summoned by the King, who wanted to know what plans his brother had, and that he had also seen Lascelles, 'who displayed the utmost goodwill'. The good will was limited. To Churchill, Lascelles wrote that, while he would not go so far as to state that the King was unwilling to meet the Duke, 'HM would not be sorry if his brother did not come to England for the next ten years'.[4] In saying this, he made the King sound more hostile to his brother than in fact he was. King George VI was always ready to see the Duke, if not looking forward to the meeting with any great enthusiasm. So were the Queen and Queen Mary. The King showed that the situation was in all essentials unchanged in a letter to his mother written shortly before the Duke arrived in London.

It seems to me that when he does come here . . . we must take the line that he cannot live here. We (the family) have told him we are not prepared to meet 'her' and they cannot live in this country without ever meeting us. I have always been told by Walter Monckton and Peacock that the taxation here will be a great deterrent to his settling over here, but the same thing applies in America if he settled there. I can well understand his not wishing to live in France or anywhere in Europe owing to the conditions prevailing there now, but none of us can relish the thought or contemplate the idea of those two persons living in this country even for a few months in the year without some misgivings. She does not like either us or this country, and the life she has been accustomed to live no longer exists here. He seems to think that when he gave up his work for which he was trained he could 'live' it down and return here as a private individual and all would be well. But he has to consider others beside himself, and I doubt whether even now he realizes the irrevocable step he took nine years ago and the ghastly shock he gave this country.[1]

The Duke deposited his wife in France, himself stayed two weeks in Paris, and then flew to London on 4 October. The auguries seemed propitious. He had written to his brother to announce the visit – the first letter beginning 'Dear Bertie' and ending, 'Yours, David' which had been received for several years[2] – and also to his mother to ask if he could stay with her at Marlborough House. The King had telegraphed to say that he would come down especially from Balmoral to meet him, while Queen Mary replied enthusiastically: 'I need scarcely assure you what a joy it will be to me to see you once again after all these years, for I have missed you very much indeed.'[3] The joy was genuine, but that it was not entirely unconfined was shown by the rather more cautious note of her letter to the Countess of Athlone: 'I hope he does not bother me too much about receiving her – as nothing has happened since to alter my views about that unfortunate marriage.'[4] The Queen, if no one else, realized what a turmoil of emotions the Duke's return must be arousing behind the immaculate facade Queen Mary presented to the world. 'I pray that his visit will give you pleasure,' she wrote, 'for whatever the sad events of the past, it is very hard for a mother to be parted from her son.'[5]

On the whole the Duke's stay in England did give pleasure, and a measure of reconciliation was achieved. King George VI told Peacock that he was greatly gratified by the way the visit had gone, 'and more than once he said it was a great comfort to him that matters had thus been restored to a more natural basis, and he looked forward with hope to this continuing'.[1] He said to Mackenzie King that he had been anxious about the visit before it took place, but now felt it had all been to the good and that the bitterness of the past was over.[2] Queen Mary was still more enthusiastic: 'It was the greatest pleasure for me to see you again after all these long years, looking so well and young, and so full of energy – and so nice to have had those nice talks on so many subjects in which both of us are interested. I have felt so much being cut off from you for such ages . . .'[3] They had probably never spent so long alone together in their lives before, mused the Duke, and he had enjoyed every minute of it. The only thing he had regretted about the years since the abdication had been his separation from his mother. But his last words set the limits to the reconciliation: as to the future, 'I can only ask you to remember that I am no longer a bachelor'.[4]

On the underlying problems that concerned the Duke, no progress was to be made. Ulick Alexander had recently married a divorced woman but retained his post at court, a development which the Duke believed, or professed to believe, must indicate some change of heart on the part of the royal family.[5] He was quickly disillusioned. King George VI was surprised to find that the Duke still could not see his wife as 'the villainess of the piece' or at least accept that that was how the British people saw her. 'I could tell that he is very happily married and that he wants to do his best for her in their future life together,' he told Queen Mary. 'But we cannot help him in this and I don't see how we ever can.'[6] Lascelles was equally struck by the Duke's 'intense devotion' to his wife, and saw in it some consolation for the King when he regretted the pain he was inflicting on his brother by thus keeping the Duchess at bay. 'As long as he and she are together, I don't think anybody need worry about his being happy or not,' Lascelles wrote to the King. 'All the more reason therefore that, having got what he wants, he should reconcile himself to accepting the drawbacks of his position as well as its advantages. One can't have everything in this life.'[7]

Lascelles had a long talk with the Duke and spoke to him with greater directness than King George VI or Queen Mary could ever have managed. They met at Marlborough House. 'The first thing that struck me about him was his voice,' Lascelles noted in his diary, 'wh. seems to have got shriller, and is now more pronouncedly American than that of many Americans ... He is noticeably, almost painfully thin, and his face is much lined though not unhappily ... I had had a hint from Allen that he looked on me as having been "obstructionist" towards his plans, but there was no suggestion of any hostility in his manner wh. was courteous and even friendly throughout, even when I spoke most frankly.' And he did speak very frankly. He said that he was convinced the King and Queen Mary would never receive the Duchess, and when asked what his own opinion on the matter was, replied categorically that he thought that for them to do so would have 'a very damaging if not dangerous effect on public opinion both here and all over the Empire'. When the Duke referred to Ulick Alexander's new wife and other cases of divorcees being received at court, Lascelles retorted that 'there is in this world one law for Kings and another for commoners'. The abdication had been necessary because of a conflict of principle, and that principle applied as much now as it did then. Could the Duke not accept this decision for once and for all and thus spare the King endless worry and embarrassment? He had already sacrificed his throne and had won himself happiness in so doing, could he not now make a further sacrifice 'on behalf of your brother, who, in order that you might lead your own life, took on, in your place, the most difficult job in the world, and saddled himself for life with cares and responsibilities, which he had never expected to assume, but for which you had always been prepared'?[1]

His conversations with King George VI and Lascelles did not finally cure the Duke of any wish to spend at least part of the year in England. In March 1946 he wrote to Alexander and referred to the possibility that Fort Belvedere might be sold by the Crown. If that were to happen, he asked, could he please be told, since he had ideas on the subject.[2] His idea seems to have been that he could spend the spring and autumn of each year in England, winter in Palm Beach, and visit France or the Mediterranean for the summer. Given the royal family's belief that the less time spent in Britain by the Windsors, the better it would be, it is not surprising that the Fort was never offered him. It languished without a tenant for several years, until finally in 1955 a ninety-nine-year lease was sold and the building passed from royal hands.

But if he could not live in Britain, perhaps he might at least return there after his death. In August 1946 he obtained the King's permission for the erection of a mausoleum in the grounds of the Fort where he and the Duchess could be buried.[1] Albert Richardson, the architect, was summoned to the Fort to discuss the project and was drawing up plans when he heard that, for fear of vandalism, the site had been changed to Frogmore. Then he was told that once again plans had changed, the Duke had decided to be buried in his wife's home town of Baltimore.[2] There the matter rested, until the final solution was arrived at some years later.

But the most pressing matter which the Duke had to decide on his visit to London was in what country, and on what terms, he would live, and what work he could find to occupy his time. When he saw Lascelles he told him that he did not feel confident enough of the future of Europe to make his home there, and that for the moment at least he and the Duchess proposed to return to the United States.[3] To Duff Cooper, who had now become Ambassador to France and who derived little satisfaction from the Windsors' sojourning in Paris, the idea seemed an excellent one. 'I dare say his presence will not render the task of future Ambassadors any easier, but I am sure it is the best solution of the problem,' he told Lascelles. 'He can do no good in this country. Neither of them have ever liked the French or will ever begin to understand them; and here he can only find a place in that little cosmopolitan world, the existence of which in Paris will probably always continue, and which can never do anything but harm. The best French people, as you know, avoid it.'[4] What seemed so sensible to Cooper in Paris, appeared very different to Halifax in Washington. He strongly deprecated any suggestion that the Duke should pay more than fleeting visits to the United States. Lascelles was alarmed at this intransigence. 'The King feels strongly – as I do myself – that USA is the only place in which he *can* live,' he told the reluctant Ambassador, 'and that he should be urged to make it his permanent home as soon as possible.'[5]

When Lascelles put this to the Duke he met with the plaintive query: 'I want to do something useful; if I do go and live in America, what am I going to do?' When asked what he wanted to do, he replied that he would like to help improve Anglo-American relations. Lascelles at once declared that this was precisely what he would be able to do, what nobody could do better. With his name, experience and contacts, he would be able to attract to his house all the most interesting people in America and mix them with British visitors, he would keep alive the old wartime friendships, he could foster whatever pet schemes for Anglo-American cooperation in the fields of education, agriculture, architecture, might appeal to him.[1] He could lead, suggested Lascelles, the life of a great nobleman of the eighteenth or nineteenth century, recreating somewhere in the southern states the elegance, distinction and, above all, usefulness of an English stately home. The Duke found some appeal in this vision of a Charleston Chatsworth or a Longleat reared above the waters of Lake Marian. Perhaps, he suggested, he might also provide the Ambassador with private reports on the individuals with whom he came in contact. An excellent idea, agreed Lascelles, then in an access of caution, 'always provided the reports *were* private'.[2]

The more that he thought about it, however, the more it appeared to the Duke that he could achieve nothing in the United States unless he was given some kind of formal appointment. He must have a 'proper background' for whatever work he was to undertake, he told the King. George VI would have to tell the State Department that his brother enjoyed his personal backing. 'The truth of the whole matter is that you and I happen to be two prominent personages placed in one of the most unique situations in history, the dignified handling of which is entirely your and my responsibility, and ours alone.'[3] But even the most forthright support from the throne would not be enough by itself. Life in America would be expensive in any case, any sort of representational work would be impossible 'without some form of tax relief which could be most easily and properly taken care of by the granting of diplomatic status'.[4] It was this financial angle which more than anything else convinced the Duke that, be it never so ill-defined, some sort of an official ambassadorial status must be assigned to him.

Peacock raised the matter with the King a week after the Duke had returned to Paris and reported that George VI had taken the point and wanted to help.[5] But as soon as he began to take advice on the subject, whether from his ministers or the intractable Lascelles, the King found that there were many formidable if not insuperable objections. Apologetically he wrote that he did not think it would be possible to create an official post specially for the Duke, but that he could still do important work in a private capacity: 'I honestly believe that you would get better results in this way than in a position which, however carefully camouflaged, would appear to have been invented for you alone.' Churchill was visiting Paris the following week, wrote the King, and would take advantage of the opportunity to discuss the matter with the Duke.[1] If the King had wanted to settle the matter for once and for all, he could hardly have found a more dangerous emissary. Churchill was never one to respect bureaucratic niceties, particularly when he was in opposition and would not have to suffer the consequences of his rashness. He told the Duke that, since as an ex-King of Great Britain his position was unique, there was no reason why a unique post should not be invented for him. What was needed, he insisted, was that the Duke should operate 'within the ambit of the British Embassy in Washington'. Joyfully, the Duke passed on this news to his brother, adding that 'it was essential that no hint or sugges- tion ever be made in America of the question of my taxation . . . for with the diplomatic status which functioning "within the ambit of the Embassy" . . . would automatically bestow, no taxation problem in America would ever arise'.[2] Churchill argued the same case when he got back to London, emphasizing the advantages of keeping the Duke 'under some general control' and with regular access to good advice. 'I would even go so far as to say that there might be serious disadvantages in utterly casting off the Duke of Windsor and his wife from all official contact with Great Britain, and leaving him in a disturbed and distressed state of mind to make his own life in the United States.'[3]

Like so many pleasant-sounding phrases, Lascelles complained a few months later, 'within the ambit of the British Embassy' was a will-o'-the-wisp which raised false hopes but had no real meaning.[4] At the time, however, the King took it seriously and instructed Lascelles to preach its merits to all and sundry. He got little reward for his pains. Halifax's opposition could have been taken for granted. The proposal would inevitably lead to trouble, he argued. It would cause embarrassment to the Ambassador and whatever Consul was responsible for the Duke's area of operation. It would mean that the Duke would have to see policy telegrams: 'I should myself feel little confidence in his discretion.' He might win a few friends for his country but the 'extent of press reports of society engagements in Newport, New York and Long Island would, as they have done before, tell heavily the other way'.[1]

It would have been surprising if the Foreign Secretary, Ernest Bevin, had taken a line substantially different from that of his Ambassador. Lascelles explained how anxious the King was that his brother should be given every possible encouragement and help to settle in the United States. Bevin was sympathetic but said that any official appointment would be unfair to the real Ambassador. In his diary Lascelles noted that Bevin 'laid bare the obvious nigger in the wood-pile – that if any sort of diplomatic status . . . were given to the Duke of Windsor, the Americans would immediately say that the chief reason for it was to get the Windsors immunity from taxation (and the Americans will not be far wrong)'.[2] To the King – and thus to the Duke – he stressed Bevin's concern about the status of the real Ambassador, and said that the Foreign Secretary had promised to review the matter after an unspecified period of time.[3] The Duke read this with chagrin; surely, he wrote to Monckton, his record over the last nine years 'and my retiring nature should be sufficient guarantee that I possess the goodwill, tact and experience of State affairs to prevent any infringement on the important and exalted post of British Ambassador in Washington'.[4]

Before any such riposte could be made, Attlee in his turn had rejected the idea, supported by the Permanent Under Secretary at the Foreign Office, Alec Cadogan.[5] Nor was the Prime Minister any more enthusiastic when Lascelles revived with him the suggestion that the Duke should become Ambassador to Argentina; a dream which had been rekindled in the Duke's mind when he dined with the outgoing Ambassador, Sir David Kelly, and spent a happy evening discussing domestic arrangements, allowances and such details.[6] Lascelles pointed out that the Duke had certain skeletons in his cupboard – 'Axel Gren, Bedaux and Ricardo Espírito Santo, all proven German agents' – which would be enough to bar any professional diplomat from employment under the Crown. Furthermore, when the Argentine government were asked for their *agrément* they could legitimately enquire whether the Duke's wife was received at the Court of St James. 'To this the only answer could be "No".' Not surprisingly, Attlee was impressed by this somewhat tendentious presentation of the case by the King's private secretary and agreed that the idea could not be contemplated.[1]

The Duke's hopes were temporarily revived when an old friend, Archibald Clark-Kerr, was appointed to replace Halifax in Washington. Bevin had hinted to the Duke that the attitude of the British Ambassador would always be a crucial factor; the Duke was sure Clark-Kerr would raise no objection.[2] Whether he was given a chance to do so is uncertain; Bevin and Attlee were adamant. 'I have used all my persuasive powers with both of them to make them see our point of view,' the King told his brother. 'I know this will be a blow to you and I am so sorry that I have not been able to arrange it for you.'[3] The Duke bore the rejection manfully. 'I am neither surprised nor disappointed,' he wrote, 'for I have sensed for some time that there was little chance of our plan maturing.' He must now look around for another job 'in whatever sphere and country I can find one suitable to my qualifications' – a statement that must have caused vague disquiet in the Palace.[4]

The King genuinely wanted his brother to be given some sort of official status in the United States and was disappointed that it could not be arranged. Lascelles had made up his mind from the start that there could be no place for the Duke of Windsor under the British Crown. The British Empire was like a clock which had to be kept ticking away, he at one time or another told the Duke, the King, Lord Halifax, and no doubt others too. Its mechanism was delicate. He and others had taken it to pieces a hundred times to try to fit in an extra wheel – the wheel of an ex-King. They had never found a way of doing so without damaging the works. In answer to this the Duke protested that the extra wheel had seemed to fit in perfectly well in the Bahamas, indeed had proved not to be an extra wheel at all. Ah yes, replied Lascelles, but that was in wartime; 'the experiment had worked once but could not safely be repeated'.[5] It is difficult not to agree with the Duke that the British constitution and the stability of the Empire would not have been in peril if some job had been created for him in the United States. Equally, Lascelles was right in thinking that such a post would have been of doubtful value and a considerable irritant to the incumbent Ambassador. In blocking it as effectively as he did he was fulfilling what he saw as being his role as an efficient private secretary; it was bad luck on the Duke, however, that he should have been the victim of Lascelles's unflinching rectitude.

The Duke did not follow up his threat – if threat it was – to look around for another job. Even after his rebuff by Attlee and Bevin he continued to believe that some day there would be a change of heart; at the worst, if he waited long enough, Churchill might return to power and his wrongs be redressed. This conviction curbed the enthusiasm with which he might have gone out in quest of something else, and the Duchess, who had no particular wish to see their seasonal programme interrupted by the demands of a husband's career, did not encourage him to fresh endeavours. Yet he was only a little over fifty; an age at which his more successful contemporaries were becoming ambassadors or admirals, ministers of the crown or captains of industry. Instead he seemed doomed to the life of a discontented Tennysonian lotus eater: why should he only rest, who was the first of things? In retrospect one can see that there would have been many jobs of a social or charitable nature which would have been suitable to his talents and to which he could have devoted as much or as little effort as he wished. At the time there seemed convincing arguments against any particular activity, and so he lingered on, filling the time agreeably enough and waiting for something to turn up.

Nothing saps the spirit so surely and so irrevocably as a failure to put one's abilities to work. Susan Mary Patten, wife of an American diplomat, sat next to him at dinner in Paris. He was pitiful, she found, 'looks young and undissipated, and the famous charm is still there, but I never saw a man so bored'. She talked of a club for enlisted men at which she worked and he said how much he would like to visit it. 'You know what my day was today?' he asked. 'I got up late, and then I went with the Duchess and watched her buy a hat, and then on the way home I had the car drop me in the Bois to watch some of your soldiers playing football, and then I had planned to take a walk, but it was so cold that I could hardly bear it . . . When I got home the Duchess was having her French lesson, so I had no one to talk to, so I got a lot of tin boxes down which my mother had sent me last week and looked through them. They were essays and so on that I had written when I was in France studying French before the Great War ... You know, I'm not much of a reading man.'[1]

They returned to Paris to find that the freehold of their house in the Boulevard Suchet had been sold and that they could not negotiate an extension of the lease beyond April 1946. Paris that first winter was a grim and uncomfortable city. 'It's not the same Paris, as you warned us,' the Duke wrote to an American friend, 'and the lack of food and fuel will be acutely felt.'[2] The electricity would be cut off, sometimes for five hours at a time; the exchange rate for the franc was ridiculously low; 'the most expensive discomfort she had ever known', the Duchess described it.[3] The restaurants were either closed or subsisting on the black market and charging outrageous prices for inferior food. Only the foreign embassies could afford to give dinner parties, otherwise cocktail parties were the usual form of entertaining, and to these the Windsors rarely went: 'However this lack of social life does not worry us any, and in fact the only time we are not depressed is when we are at home.'[4] Those who saw the Windsors together in Paris felt, as King George VI and Lascelles had done, that they were entirely content in each other's company. Noël Coward met them at dinner at the British Embassy. 'He loves her so much, and at long last I am beginning to believe that she loves him,' he wrote in his diary, and then a few months later: 'The Windsors were charming. I like her, and I think that now she is genuinely fond of him.'[5]

They were spared the worst of the privations by the fact that they drew British Army rations and had a resourceful and none-too-scrupulous chef to fill the gaps. There were seventeen for dinner on 2 January 1946, and fifty more came in after the meal: 'We had a buffet of hot dogs from the US, ham mousse from tinned ham, salade russe from tinned vegetables, sandwiches of cheese and cress and black market eggs stuffed – our only extravagance,' the Duchess told her aunt Bessie. They drank thirty bottles of champagne and three of whisky.[6] The *cuisine* could have been more *haute*, but nobody starved. Susan Mary Patten, who dined there a few weeks later, complained more about the level of the conversation. 'Awful evening,' she wrote. 'The Duchess determined to play word games, despite her complete lack of education and the competition of Lady Diana Cooper, who learned history with her mother's milk . . . The Duke couldn't remember Metternich and Castlereagh . . .'[1]

The presence of Duff and Diana Cooper at the British Embassy did much to ease what could have been a slightly awkward return by the Windsors to Parisian society. But though they were hospitable, and Lady Diana obstinately defied protocol by curtseying to the Duchess, the Coopers were sometimes critical of their royal succubi. 'The two poor little old things were most pathetic,' Diana wrote when she met them again in September 1945. 'Fear, I suppose, of losing their youthful figures, or homesickness, has made them Dachau-thin. She is much commoner and more confident, he much duller and sillier.' Second impressions were slightly less unfavourable: the Duchess was 'slim and svelte as a piece of vermicelli', while the Duke was 'common, of course, and boring, but not so puppetish as I thought' – but no sort of rapport was established.[2] Duff Cooper was forced to agree with Lascelles that the Duke could not properly fill a diplomatic post in the United States, but made it plain that he would not be unhappy to lose him from 'his own bishopric, Paris'.[3] 'I feel nothing but goodwill, and, indeed, affection and gratitude towards His Royal Highness,' wrote the Ambassador, 'but I must admit that his presence in Paris does not make things any easier . . . At the same time I am quite sure that he himself only wants to do the right thing and be helpful, and that they are both conducting themselves with the greatest propriety.'[4]

Soon after they arrived in Paris, Duff Cooper's deputy, Adrian Holman, gave the Duke a warning that the French press, in particular the left-wing papers, would be watching their activities closely and would be quick to report any evidence that they were making unsuitable friends among those suspected of collaboration with the Germans, or were obtaining supplies on the black market. The Duke promised to heed this advice, and though the Duchess might occasionally have regaled her guests with black-market eggs, any transgressions were on a scale that even the most censorious French journalists found venial. The worst that Duff Cooper could accuse the Duke of was a tendency to entertain official personages as if he himself had some role in public life. 'Important Canadians, American Senators, members of delegations . . . have all been received by him, one can only suppose that he feels it his duty to

510

receive them, because few of them possess any overwhelming social attraction.' Once he had got them to his house he tended to pontificate – lecturing the Prefect of Police, with all the authority of a former Governor, on police administration and the need for complete incorruptibility.[1] 'He was always given to holding forth,' wrote Lascelles in his diary, 'and indeed, as long ago as 1928, showed increasing signs of becoming a hearth-rug bore.'[2]

In April 1946, with the house in the Boulevard Suchet gone for ever, they had no recourse but to move south to their villa La Cröe in Antibes, another rented home but one which offered slightly greater hope of permanence. The move, in fact, suited the Duke well enough. His 'ultimate aim was to make his home in the south of France', Gray Phillips told Lascelles,[3] and La Cröe was more of a home to him than anywhere he had lived since Fort Belvedere. Though the Italians and Germans had billeted themselves in the garage, mined the sea front and cut down trees to provide a field of fire, the house itself had remained virtually unscathed until an American shell burst nearby, blowing in all the windows.[4] Other damage was negligible and the Duchess soon had the house in operation again. The scale was reduced but still impressive. By 24 April there were twenty-two people employed there: 'I imagine outside of embassies it is the only house run in this fashion in France and probably England today,' the Duchess told Aunt Bessie with mingled pride and ruefulness.[5] As a Major General, the Duke continued to draw rations from the British Army depot at Marseilles,[6] a dispensation which made it possible for them to entertain the stream of visitors who passed through the house.

The Metcalfes were not among the guests. For some long-forgotten reason the Duke at this time took violently against his old ally. When his millionaire American friend Robert Young arrived in Southampton the Duke warned him that he might be met by a 'certain Major E. D. Metcalfe', who was now employed by Arthur Rank and would undoubtedly swamp the new arrival with invitations. 'Well, Bob, you know my make up and that it is not vindictive, but if what I predict happens, I would appreciate your ignoring Metcalfe's invitations, until I have an opportunity of explaining my reasons for this request and telling you what a four-flusher Metcalfe is.'[7] He was justified in saying he was not vindictive, and this assault on someone he had known and cared about for so long was out of character. It did not endure. Within a year he was writing in the friendliest terms to suggest a meeting,[1] and when Metcalfe died in 1957 the Duke made a special visit to London for the funeral. 'He was, as you know, one of my oldest and closest friends,' he told Ali Mackintosh. 'We shall miss him a great deal.'[2]

It has been said that the Duke briefly played with the idea of living in Ireland. Nothing in his own papers suggests that this was so. The story probably arose from an exchange with Sir Shane Leslie at the end of 1945. In a letter to Leslie the Duke mentioned his admiration of the Church of Rome, which it seemed to him was one of the few sure bulwarks against communism in a distracted and divided world.[3] Leslie responded with a suggestion that the Duke should visit Ireland, so as 'to investigate the roots of Irish feelings, as expressed at home and abroad'.[4] Before he could have received any reply, he was excitedly telling Lascelles that the visit was as good as arranged. 'This is a good instance of the Duke of Windsor's irresponsibility and lack of political (and personal) judgment,' fulminated Lascelles, 'for it is a crazy idea which wd certainly do him harm.'[5] Crazy or not, there is no reason to believe that this particular idea was ever entertained seriously by the Duke, though Lascelles can hardly be blamed for believing Leslie. The urge to make himself conspicuously busy, and incidentally to irritate the British government, might easily have driven the Duke to Ireland, possibly with the same ill effects for his reputation as had been earned by his visit to Germany before the war.

Instead he began to pay more frequent visits to England, staying often with the Metcalfes. In the autumn of 1946 he brought the Duchess with him. The Duke made no attempt to secure an invitation to any royal residence, or even to establish contact with his family. They stayed, as they hoped inconspicuously, with the Dudleys at their house, Ednam Lodge, near Sunningdale. Their hopes were disappointed; ill fortune had it that their visit featured in the headlines of all British and most foreign papers. The Duchess had brought with her a large part of her jewellery, and one night a burglar climbed into the house and removed everything except what she was wearing and a few Fabergé boxes which were evidently felt to be too difficult to dispose of. Lady Dudley, her hostess, wrote that among the jewels stolen were 'a great many uncut emeralds which I believe belonged to Queen Alexandra';[1] she was as likely as anyone to have known the contents of the Duchess's jewel case, but even if the emeralds existed in the first place and had been made over to the Duchess, it seems surprising that they were still uncut at the end of 1946, or that, if they were, they would have formed part of her travelling collection. Emeralds or not, the theft was on a majestic scale and left the Duke and Duchess distraught. They had much enjoyed the 'charming hospitality' of the Dudleys, the Duke told his mother and their only regret was the 'bitter and costly discovery that Great Britain is no longer the secure and law-abiding country it used to be'.[2]

Rejected as he felt himself to be by his native land, it seems to have given the Duke some consolation to muse on the discredit that the robbery reflected on post-war Britain and on the tribulations that the British people were now experiencing. Britain at the end of 1946 was suffering austerity more grim than anything it had known during the war; the rich felt themselves oppressed and hard done by; the prospect of relief seemed infinitely remote. 'It has been quite a shock to notice how social and economic conditions have changed since 1936,' the Duke told Lord Portal. 'The old values have disappeared and been replaced by strange tendencies, and one senses an unfamiliar atmosphere throughout the country.'[3] He might have reflected that it was those very values which had created the conditions against which he had protested so valiantly in the 1930s, but he was in no mood to make allowances. He would not shake the dust of England altogether off his feet, but he was finally convinced that he must make his home elsewhere. It remained to decide how and where.

28

The Duke as Author

'T HE FUTURE OF THE WORLD IS INDEED OMINOUS,' THE
Duke wrote gloomily to Godfrey Thomas in March 1948.
Encouraged by their triumphs in Czechoslovakia and the
preoccupation of the Americans with their presidential elections,
it seemed certain that the Russians would 'have a bid for Italy and,
if successful, for France this coming spring'.[1] Since early 1947 the
troubles of France had led the Duke to question the wisdom of
putting even a small proportion of his eggs in so rickety a basket.
He persuaded the British Army to put three lorries at his disposal
so as to carry to London thirty-two packing cases of his most
cherished possessions from the vaults of the Bank of France. There
remained the furniture from the Boulevard Suchet and his property
in the south of France, but these, though their loss would be
painful, were of secondary importance. Viewed from the lofty
heights of the 1990s his fears may seem exaggerated, at the time
they were shared by many who were far from alarmist in their
general outlook. France 'is in the worst shape, politically and
economically, of all the countries outside the Iron Curtain', the
Duke told an American friend. The principal blame rested with
de Gaulle, who had done so much to sap the power of successive
middle-of-the-road French governments, with the result that 'there
is now no alternative to his return to power with the inevitable
clashes with the Communists, if not civil war, that his dictatorial
doctrines will precipitate'.[2] Two months later, with a coal strike
paralysing the country and armed troops storming communist-
occupied mines, he became still more convinced that a Soviet
takeover must be imminent; 'de Gaulle is certainly not the answer
to the revival of France's spirit or her economy'.[3]

But could he find anywhere more secure, which would offer the
same tax advantages as he enjoyed in France? He told the ex-
King Leopold of Belgium that he was thinking of Switzerland; a

proposition that caused sore alarm to another exiled monarch, Queen Ena of Spain, who had settled in Switzerland herself and did not relish the prospect of living cheek-by-jowl with the Duchess of Windsor.[1] He played with the idea of buying a plot of land and building in the south of Spain – 'Of course, I'm not a rich man like you,' a friend remembers him saying, when asking him to look out for a suitable site.[2] He looked about for a house on Long Island in which he could accommodate their furniture from La Cröe.[3] But always he hesitated before making any final commitment, and finally convinced himself that France would probably muddle through, without falling into the abyss of communism, or succumbing to a military dictatorship.

Even if the American taxmen had made it possible for him to establish a permanent home in Long Island, he would have had his doubts about the political future on that side of the Atlantic as well as in Europe. The years after 1945 show the Duke, haunted by the menace of communism and convinced that the democratic powers were effete and enfeebled, entrenching himself ever more deeply in a posture of rigid and irredeemable reaction. From New York he wrote to Beaverbrook that the United Nations were in 'fruitless session'; somewhat doubtfully he admitted that talking to the Russians might be better than shooting at them, but only 'at this stage, and until the Western Powers are more prepared'.[4] He blamed the state of the world on Franklin Roosevelt, deplored the fact that a statue in Grosvenor Square now honoured the memory of the man 'most responsible for the present impasse', and prayed for a Republican victory in 1948 that would remove 'the last dregs of the New Deal'.[5] When Truman disobliged him by defeating Dewey, he wrote that he was 'stunned', though not altogether surprised since he had sensed that leftist thinking was gaining ground throughout the world.[6] It was not just that a democratic administration would truckle to the communists abroad or pursue disastrous economic policies at home; worse still was that 'the departments in Washington and even the White House will escape the thorough house-cleaning of liberals and fellow-travellers, if not Communists, which is long overdue'.[7]

It was perhaps fortunate for his peace of mind that the one country where it was out of the question for him to live, seemed to him to become progressively more undesirable to live in. In May

1947 his brother-in-law, Lord Harewood, died and it seemed as if his vast wealth and estates would be almost entirely swallowed up by death duties. 'It is a crime how three decades of Liberal and Socialist legislation have completely destroyed a uniquely English way of life – the great country estates of Britain,' he lamented to his mother. 'But then so much of the traditional elegance we used to know has already vanished or is vanishing . . . until one hardly has the heart to revisit the haunts of one's youth.'[1] After a visit to England at the end of 1948 he told an American correspondent that all the people he knew were getting 'more sick and tired of the austerity and restrictions'. The most depressing part was that the British people obstinately refused to shed their illusions; a Labour victory at the next election seemed likely, which 'I am afraid, will hasten an eventual Communist dictatorship. I see no alternative.'[2] When Labour held Hammersmith at a by-election in the spring of 1949, he was more than ever convinced that Britain was lost for ever, and that the only thing that prevented an immediate communist takeover was that Russia was too busy consolidating her gains in Central Europe, the Balkans and the Far East.[3] It was not until the Conservatives narrowly won the general election of 1951 that the Duke conceded there might after all still be a tolerable future for his country: 'One can only hope that the misguided voting masses will realize that this new spell of austerity has had to be imposed as a result of six years of Socialist misrule based on class hatred.'[4]

And so the Windsors remained in France; with some reluctance abandoning La Cröe in the autumn of 1949, and renting a substantial if somewhat gloomy house in the rue de la Faisanderie in Paris, initially for two and later for four years. 'Wallis has as usual made it attractive and comfortable as she does to all houses,' the Duke told Queen Mary, but the house had many inconveniences and they were searching for another, so far without success. 'Everything is so discouragingly expensive nowadays.'[5] No economies were introduced when it came to entertaining. Though one of the drawbacks of the new house was that the dining room only seated twenty-four, they quickly resumed their former habits, giving luncheons or dinners to a procession of French or foreign dignitaries leavened with friends from England or the United States. Cy Sulzberger dined there in 1951 and found 'a weird collection of social derelicts'. This seems a little hard; the normal guest list read much as might have been expected in any important embassy when the ambassador had no particular artistic or literary leanings. The dinner attended by Sulzberger included René Pleven, then Prime Minister of France, and a visiting American senator, Warren Austin.

Certainly there was nothing second-rate about the fare. Post-war austerity had been put away. Cocktails were accompanied by canapés spread with caviar or covered with slices of lobster. There were ten courses washed down with sherry, white wine, red wine, pink champagne and 'huge slugs of brandy'. While the seventh course was being served, a string orchestra arrived. 'Happy Birthday to You' was sung in honour of the senator, and the orchestra played on merrily. 'From then on, the Duke couldn't eat because he was too busy waving his arms around in time to the music – his favorite habit. Whenever I have seen him anywhere near music, out comes his conductor's complex.'[1]

The Duke left La Cröe with less regrets than he had expected because it seemed to him that the south of France, or at least the Côte d'Azur, had deteriorated sadly. After a visit to the gala at Monte Carlo with Lord Rothermere and the journalist Alastair Forbes, he commented fretfully: 'The semi-nude people who congest all these joints are so tough and unattractive that going places and gambling really is not much fun any more. As a local hotelier is supposed to have remarked, "Yes, the crowd on the coast is getting worse and worse; in fact this year we have got next year's people." The French translation of the "GB" plate on British cars – mostly Rolls-Royces – is Ghetto Brittanique.'[2] In 1950 he returned to old loyalties and spent a month at Biarritz; they liked it so much that they resolved in future to patronize only the Côte Basque.[3]

Life in Paris was not made more agreeable by the disappearance of Duff and Diana Cooper from the British Embassy at the end of 1947. The Harveys, who took their place, made no bones about the fact that they disapproved of the Windsors and did not wish to receive them. It was only on direct instructions from London that they eventually and grudgingly invited them to dinner, and even then they only invited members of the Embassy staff to meet them.[4] After that the relationship between successive Ambassadors and the Windsors settled into a tranquil if hardly cordial pattern. The Duke and Duchess would dine at the Embassy perhaps twice a year, the Ambassador and his wife would return the compliment, the Windsors would attend the celebration of the royal birthday – honour was satisfied if little pleasure given to anyone.

They anyway spent less than half the year in Paris. Of the five years from 1947 to 1951 they spent almost two in the United States, for the most part at the Waldorf Towers in New York or at Palm Beach, sometimes renting a house, more often staying with friends. Until 1950 they spent two to three months a year at Antibes, and in 1951 went to Biarritz. Into the time that was left were fitted visits to Britain, holidays in Italy and Mexico, a tour of the British Army in Germany, and other lesser outings. It was a restless, itinerant life, but it suited the Duchess, and since the satisfaction of the Duchess was his chief concern, it suited the Duke as well.

The novelist Cecil Roberts dined with them both in Palm Beach and in New York and found that, with variations, they kept up the same state as in Paris. In Palm Beach they ate on a terrace by moonlight, amid flood-lit palm trees, while four musicians played ukuleles in the background. The Duke was dressed in Stuart plaid trousers with a magenta linen dinner jacket. After dinner he borrowed a ukulele and played it. 'He looked young and happy.' At their apartment in the Waldorf Towers it was another matter. There were full-length paintings of George III and George IV in their coronation robes, other royal portraits, two footmen in livery, napkins embroidered with the royal arms. 'This did not look like exile.' But once again there was music. 'The duke, in a plum-coloured velvet evening jacket, went to the grand piano and began to sing. He had a large repertoire, a good voice, and was excellent in some German, Lancashire, Scottish and Irish songs. His à la Harry Lauder "Oh, it's nice to get up in the morning . . ." was the *chef d'oeuvre*.'[1]

Harold Nicolson met him at lunch with Sybil Colefax in 1947. 'He is thin but more healthy looking than when I last saw him. He has lost that fried-egg look around the eyes. He is very affable and chatty. I notice that he has stopped calling his wife "Her Royal Highness" . . . I notice also that people do not bow as they used to and treat him as less of a royalty than they did when he had recently been King. He takes all this quite for granted. I have an impression that he is happier.' The Duchess also he found improved; softer and with the taut, predatory look almost disappeared. She talked wistfully of their wish to settle down – 'He likes gardening but it is no fun gardening in other people's gardens.' Above all, she said, he needed a job. 'You see,' she explained, 'he was born to be a salesman. He would be an admirable representative of Rolls Royce. But an ex-King cannot start selling motor-cars.'[1]

Two years later Nicolson met him again and thought him much older. 'His face was wizened, his teeth were yellow and crooked, and his golden hair was parched.' But he was in high spirits.[2] Beaton went to Paris to photograph them the same year. 'His face now begins to show the emptiness of life. It is too impertinent to be tragic . . . He looks like a mad terrier, haunted one moment, and then with a flick of the hand he is laughing fecklessly.'[3] Almost any account of him mentions his vitality and enduring charm. He descended on Windsor in April 1949. He 'was as captivating and effervescent as ever', reported Owen Morshead, the librarian and one of Queen Mary's closest confidants. He had a team of men unpacking and repacking his silver, 'and he keeps them happy with a lavish outpouring of chaff and treasury notes. He is extremely fond of the Castle, most kind in all his references to his father, instantly, recognizing old servants and asking after the wound in the right part of their anatomy: wherever he passes, people sigh.'[4] Sulzberger met him again at the end of 1951 and found him 'extremely informal and friendly', though he was disconcerted to find that the royal station wagon had 'The Duke of Windsor' displayed in metal letters on each door. 'After dinner there was a pianist. The Duke was transported with joy. He sang a few songs rather badly and joyfully initiated the playing of various instruments such as the cello and the violin, waving his arms around like a happy schoolboy. He knew a few Spanish and German songs partially.' At one point the Duchess leaned over to him and said: 'You promised you were going to listen tonight because there are a lot of brains around, but you are talking all the time.' 'I have to talk, or otherwise I would fall asleep,' he replied.[5]

Though Nicolson found the Duchess softer in manner, many accounts of the period testify to her formidable rancour against the British and above all the royal family. The Sulzbergers were treated to a lament about the shabby treatment that the Duke had received from his relations and her determination never to go back to England.[1] Jock Balfour sat next to her at dinner at Biarritz. He stooped to pick up her bag which had fallen to the floor. 'I like to see the British grovelling to me,' she remarked.[2] It was a joke, no doubt, but it left an unpleasant impression on her audience. The Duke's devotion to his wife was as obvious as ever. 'The Duke clearly adores her,' Sulzberger recorded. 'After dinner we were sitting together talking and every now and then he would look across at the Duchess and say: "It's so wonderful to see her. You know, I have not seen her for a week."'[3] Channon commented too that the Duke was still passionately in love. Three times, when Channon and the Duchess were talking, the Duke came up to bring her a drink, each time she accepted it smilingly but put it down untouched. 'There was certainly understanding and affection in her glance.'[4] In December 1951 the American Association of Marriage Brokers wrote to inform the Duke that the Windsors had been chosen as 'one of the happiest married couples in the land', and that it would be an honour to present them with a cupid loving cup at their forthcoming convention. The Duke replied politely, thanking them for the 'courteous and friendly gesture' but regretting that they could not be present.[5] The proposal was absurd, but to a man as romantic as the Duke it must also have seemed a touching and well-merited tribute.

It would be wrong to give too sugary a picture of an ideal marriage. The Duchess was a restless and discontented woman, sometimes the Duke's devotion must have cloyed, sometimes she hankered for madder music and for stronger wine. At the time the Marriage Brokers awarded the couple their loving cup, the Duchess was causing her husband some distress by her relationship with the American millionaire socialite and pederast, Jimmy Donahue. The Duke always maintained that his wife's relationship with Donahue caused him no concern. 'Don't you get jealous letting the Duchess go out every night with Jimmy?' Elsa Maxwell once asked him. He roared with laughter 'and, in his special semi-Cockney accent, said, "She's safe as houses with *him*!"'[6] In a sexual sense she no doubt was, but his wife meant much more to the Duke than merely sex, and he must have felt some jealousy over the pleasure she so obviously derived from the company of this flamboyant vulgarian. On the other hand, Donahue's riches and his insatiable appetite for night clubs and other species of nocturnal revelry – matched only by the Duchess's – made him a useful member of the ménage. It must have been a relief for the Duke when the association ended, if only because of the prurient interest taken in it by the American press, but he must also have regretted from time to time that this epicene gigolo was no longer to hand to share the burden of the Duchess's quest for pleasure.

At least he by then had something to do with any time left to him after he had finished dancing attendance on his wife. It was as early as May 1946 that he told Monckton it had been suggested 'from not uninteresting quarters' that he should write about his side of the abdication crisis. 'It seems that considerable doubt and conjecture still lives in the minds of many thinking people . . . concerning that episode.'[1] To resolve those doubts to his own advantage, to earn a lot of money, and to pay off a few scores along the road, would be an attractive way of filling the idle hours that lay ahead of him. Besides, the news that he was at work on his memoirs would send a shiver through the court, an idea also not without appeal. The offer, whatever it may have been, came shortly after his hopes of an official post in America had finally been dashed: a neater way of registering his anger at being left in idleness could hardly be conceived.

For some reason the idea was allowed to languish, then was revived early in 1947 in a modified form. The Duke contracted with Henry Luce, owner of Time-Life, to write four long articles dealing with his childhood and career up to 1914. At the same time he hinted that he might later extend his writings to cover the rest of his life, a possibility both more hazardous and even more inviting in commercial terms than the earlier exercise. When in October he told Thomas what was going on, he said that a full-scale autobiography might one day follow but that there was no commitment as yet. 'He said that as Mr Churchill was doing the same thing through this very group, he didn't see why he shouldn't, especially as he was constantly being asked by less reputable publishers in the States to write something for them.'[2] To his mother he adopted a slightly defensive note. He was hard at work on the three articles for *Life* magazine, he told her – three being the number originally envisaged – and was busily recalling details of his childhood and college days. 'I am fortunate as having to some extent inherited your prodigious memory. I am sure that an accurate story of our family life by one of its more prominent members can serve a useful purpose and make a good impression in America and wherever it is read. Otherwise I would not have accepted the offer.'[1]

To aid him in his task *Life* provided Charles Murphy, a journalist of considerable charm and experience, who at first worked fruit-fully and harmoniously with the titular author. The Duke did not need a 'ghost' in the sense that he found it hard to write; on the contrary, he had covered so many thousands of pages over the years with his clear, rather childish script that it sometimes seemed his problem was knowing when to stop. His style was undis-tinguished but clear and serviceable, with touches of wit and a pleasant self-deprecating irony from time to time leavening the slightly stolid text. He had a good eye for detail and enough common sense generally to avoid the perils of self-pity or an excessively partial presentation of his case. What he lacked was the experience or the inclination to undertake the necessary research, or to organize huge blocks of material into a lucid and readable narrative. In his early articles and autobiography it can be taken for granted that the views were his own, and probably the words as well, but that the accumulation of the material and the shaping of the work were the contribution of Charles Murphy. As so often with such partnerships, familiarity soured the relationship. The Duke began to take for granted Murphy's skills, Murphy to resent the Duke's sometimes cavalier treatment of his labours. The Duke accused Murphy of arrogance, tactlessness, incompetence, and an unsavoury sensationalism; Murphy found the Duke feckless, idle, irresponsible and wayward to an intolerable degree. Each, no doubt, tried the other high. Murphy had the last laugh, since in collaboration with another of the Duke's bookwrights, J. Bryan, he produced a biography of the Windsors which the Duke's friends found offensive and unfair but which contained so much convinc-ing detail not to be found elsewhere that other biographers will ignore it at their peril.[2] He was also well rewarded for his pains, receiving 21 per cent of the gross royalties from the autobiography, excluding sums paid by Time-Life.[1]

Predictably, the court were less sure than the Duke about the 'useful purpose' which the articles would serve. Lascelles was the most incensed. Poverty was no excuse, he told Bruce Lockhart. 'If you knew what that man had taken out of the country, you would know that he did not need money . . . He is in a royal trade union and the trade union rules are against this kind of thing. He is the meanest royalty that has ever been.'[2] The fact that the Duke had first resigned from the union and had then been ceremonially stripped of any remaining privileges of membership presumably counted for nothing. Bruce Lockhart may somewhat have embellished the conversation when recording it; when writing his views for the King Lascelles was more circumspect. But even in this memorandum his tone was damning. The articles, he said, could do nothing but harm — to the author and to the royal family generally. The only way to stop them would be by appealing to the Duke's better nature; 'but I am sorry to say that long experience has convinced me that he has no such feelings when the interests of the Monarchy or the Royal Family conflict with what he imagines to be the interests of himself and the Duchess'.[3]

By the end of 1947 the articles were finished. He had never had to work so hard or with such protracted concentration in his life, the Duke told Thomas, but — an ominous addition in the eyes of the court — he had enjoyed the task and gained valuable experience.[4] The articles appeared in *Life* in America and in the *Sunday Express* in Britain: good-tempered and colourful pieces that painted an attractive picture of the royal family and its daily life and certainly can have done nothing to damage the image of the monarchy in the public consciousness. To Queen Mary it seemed deplorable that any member of the royal family should reveal to the world intimate details — however innocuous — of the workings of the royal palaces and their inmates. 'I was surprised you thought it a pity I wrote of so many private facts,' replied the Duke. He claimed to have taken infinite pains to cut out any detail or anecdote which he felt intruded too far into the sanctity of their family life. 'I would submit that the personal memoir of Papa undertaken by John Gore at your and Bertie's request . . . contains far more intimate extracts from Papa's diaries and glimpses into his character and habits than I would have dared to use or thought suitable to include in the story of my early life.'[1] He paid more attention to the opinion of the editor of the *Sunday Express*, John Gordon, who wrote that the serialization had done the Duke 'immensely more good than anything in years'. The picture the articles had painted of his early life and the difficulties he had encountered had won him great sympathy. 'I should say that as a result of the success of the series he stands high in public affection today. And that there is a much wiser [*sic* wider?] understanding of the course of his life.'[2]

Emboldened by his success the Duke now hankered after greater things. In October 1948 he told Thomas that he was not thinking of writing any more for publication in the near future, but that at some point he would obviously want to carry his story a step further and that he was beginning to collect material. 'He again assured me that this, whenever it appeared, would be confined to his overseas tours and his official duties as Prince of Wales and would not go beyond 1935.'[3] If the Duke was quoted correctly he seems to have been disingenuous to say the least: three weeks before he saw Thomas he had told Monckton that his file for 1936 was 'growing ever bulkier'.[4] The contract with Time-Life was deliberately left vague so as to give the Duke the greatest possible freedom of action, but by the autumn of 1948, even though he may have envisaged a preliminary series of articles on his life as Prince of Wales, it was a full dress autobiography up to the time of the abdication that was in the course of preparation.

Any illusions the royal family may have harboured were soon dispelled. When Owen Morshead was approached by George Allen two months later and asked to give some help with the English sections of the story, he was left in no doubt that memoirs were being written. Murphy was brought to meet him and 'proved to be a gentlemanly and reasonable person: I liked him very much and formed the impression that he was trustworthy'. (Murphy had a way with courtiers. Thomas found him 'exceptionally nice, intelligent and cultured . . . he is far above the level of the ordinary American journalist'.[5]) Morshead felt certain that Murphy would do his best to keep the 'tone of the book pleasant and good natured, like the articles in *Life* . . . No doubt it were better that this book should not be written at all: but if it must be, then I think we are fortunate that it is in the hands of this decent-minded person.'[1]

Much of 1949 and 1950 – in the Duke's eyes almost exclusively, to Murphy's mind at irritatingly erratic intervals – were devoted to work on the memoirs. He refused an invitation from Lord Dudley, 'as I am carrying on with the research for my memoirs, and am at my desk at 9 o'clock every morning and work for four hours until lunch ... It is an interesting if exacting pastime.'[2] Murphy complained with increasing bitterness that it was proving difficult to fill out the essential features of his story. 'Please speak plainly to your former sovereign,' he urged Beaverbrook. 'He needs bucking up. And he needs to be told that writing must be done again and again. He also needs to be advised that much time and heartache will be saved if he reposes confidence in his collaborators. But I suppose this can never be.'[3] It is hard to be sure how far Murphy's strictures were justified, and how far he was merely frustrated by the Duke's reluctance to include delicate material which would have sold copies but also caused controversy. Murphy was to some extent working in competition with Monckton, who was constantly urging restraint on the uncertain author. 'If I go too far I shall lose what chance I have of exercising the pruning fork, which becomes more and more necessary at every stage,' Monckton told Lascelles.[4]

By the end of 1950 the work was almost done. The Duke stayed behind in Paris to finish the book while the Duchess went ahead to New York. The American newspapers had a field day with the news, and announced that the marriage had broken down and that Jimmy Donahue was enthroned in the Duke's place. Whether it was his distress at this malign publicity, frustration with Murphy, or just anguish at thus being parted from his wife, the Duke impetuously bundled up all his papers and pursued the Duchess. A conspicuously affectionate reunion on his arrival checked the worst of the gossip, and the work went ahead with hardly a break. 'We really did finish this damn book yesterday,' wrote his secretary, Anne Seagrim, with some relief on 11 March 1951. 'He had to write the whole of the author's note and acknowledgments in his own hand.'[5]

The articles in *Life* drawn from *A King's Story* had appeared the previous summer. The Duke sent copies to his mother; she thanked him cautiously; 'You know my ideas of that kind of subject, however I am reading the paper with interest.'[1] The articles, and the prospect of the book to follow, produced a flood of letters: most of those to the Duke congratulatory, most of those to the court deploring the publication. The Prime Minister's private secretary, Denis Rickett, passed on to Lascelles a letter from a Mr Pearson urging that publication be prevented. Lascelles said that this was but one of many. 'All of them express disgust at a former King of England selling for money his recollections of his family life, in a form that is indecent and for a motive that is squalid. But none of these has yet suggested any machinery whereby such a sale can be prevented. The only remedy that has ever occurred to me is that somebody should awake in the author the instincts of a gentleman; but, as I devoted the eight best years of my life to this end with signal ill-success, I fear I am not the man to make any constructive suggestion.'[2] What upset Lascelles most were the passages dealing with the Duke's love for Mrs Simpson – the omission of which would have made any history of the abdication read rather oddly. 'It is obscene to write gainfully about one's own love affairs,'[3] he told Monckton dogmatically; leaving open the questions of whether it was any less obscene to write about somebody else's love affairs, or to describe one's own free of charge.

As the centrepiece of the book's promotion the Duke had promised to address the annual dinner of the BPRA, the association of publishers' salesmen. Lord Cromer had previously written the Duke a letter which, coming as it did from a former Lord Chamberlain, reads oddly when compared with Lascelles's objurgations. He had praised 'the literary qualities and tactful choice of words that elevate this pathos-laden story to such a high and dignified plane', and protested that the book was presented with such 'verity, sincerity and graciousness of style that it cannot but command respect in the hearts of all the fair-minded'.[4] Now he urged the author to forgo the dinner, which savoured too much of the boosting of a commercial enterprise.[5] Besides, the King was seriously ill, so the timing would be singularly unfortunate. The Duke would probably have ignored Cromer, but Churchill too weighed in, urging him to avoid any public appearance until his brother was out of danger: 'It is so important that the first time you address the British public [you] shld have the most cordial welcome and be an unqualified success.'[6] Reluctantly the Duke gave way, grumbling that on the very day he was supposed to have spoken Princess Elizabeth and Princess Margaret had been seen at Ascot Races – 'Pretty blatant discrimination, wasn't it?'[1] It was perhaps as well that his oratorial ambitions had been curbed, since he had intended to launch an assault on those who criticized him for indulging in authorship and ask in what way he was different from his great-grandmother, Queen Victoria. His closing remark, however, deserved a hearing: 'My book is not a novel, but is a romance, and all I can say is that I hope it can end like most fairy tales – "and they lived happily ever after".'[2]

The book ended with the reign of Edward VIII, so the Duke was mercifully spared any temptation to enlarge on the various grievances that had poisoned the years since the abdication. On the whole it was a fair and well-balanced work, the only major figure who was conspicuously treated with less than justice being Baldwin. 'I think it was quite a good account,' the Earl of Athlone wrote temperately, 'but you were a bit too strong about Baldwin, who was really very fond of you.'[3] 'Without any overt expression of dislike,' the *Scotsman* judged in its review, the Duke succeeded, calmly and effectively, in 'roasting' his Prime Minister. To the contemporary reader the dislike seems all too overt, and the judgment ungenerous. But otherwise one can accept the *Economist*'s view that the book was 'most dignified, objective and historically valuable', or Roger Fulford's verdict in the *Manchester Guardian* that it was 'marked throughout by firmness and generosity'. 'The reader is conscious that it is the Duke's own book,' said the *Times Literary Supplement*, 'and that he has worked with care over every page; even if he has needed help to put his thoughts into words, his own personality, his likes and strong dislikes, spring to life as well as his keen sense of humour.' One of the more critical reviews came in the *Observer*, which found it 'frank and absorbing', but felt: 'The wisdom of publication is arguable . . . the hero emerges as rather a pathetic figure.'[4] Even Lascelles conceded that the Duke might have 'written a good book', though retaining his unshakeable conviction that 'it is wrong (and disloyal) for a former King of England to write such a book for profit, and to sell things that are not his to sell'.[5]

The profits were considerable – eighty thousand copies were sold in the United Kingdom in the first month – and the Duke was delighted by the outcome of his enterprise. One of the more gratifying features, he told Cecil Roberts, had been the conversion of 'a few of the old stuffed shirts of the hard upper crust who disapproved in principle of my writing my memoirs'.[1] But he could not have deluded himself that his success had in any way endeared him to the court. His complaints about the crimes the King's officials might be perpetrating against him grew no less paranoid with time: if he received bad coverage in the newspapers it was the Palace's fault; if he received none, they were just as much responsible. 'I shall be very interested to know if you are able to get the low down on the marked indifference of the Press in general to my presence in Great Britain,' he wrote to Dudley. 'It is difficult to believe that it was not acting on a direction from Buckingham Palace.'[2]

His chagrin was exacerbated by the fact that other royal families took their line from Buckingham Palace. Victoria's granddaughter, the ex-Queen Ena of Spain, would never see the Duke since, she believed, the Duchess would not let him come alone: 'Poor David, but perhaps it is better so, as like that he can never quote me, as having said this or the other to him about none of us receiving his wife, which he is very bitter about, it seems.'[3] Among the exiled monarchs, the only one whom the Windsors saw with some regularity was Leopold of the Belgians, who had married his former mistress, the Princess de Réthy. 'As far as the ladies are concerned, it seems to me a case of "birds of a feather flock together",' remarked Queen Ena.[4]

In London in May 1947 the Duke had asked if there was any truth in the rumours that Princess Elizabeth was to marry Prince Philip. Queen Mary replied that there was nothing definite to tell,[5] but early in July wrote to confirm that the engagement was now a fact. At once speculation began in the press as to whether the Windsors would be invited to their niece's wedding. To them it appeared obvious that they should be; to Queen Mary in particular it was equally obvious that if the Duchess was not fit to be received at Buckingham Palace it could hardly be supposed that she would be invited to take part in the celebration of a solemn sacrament in a church. George Allen, who had now replaced Monckton as the nearest approach to a mouthpiece the Duke had in London, was pestered by enquirers: he was instructed to reply that no invitation had been received. 'Believe me, Ulick,' the Duke wrote to Alexander, 'this form of publicity is as distasteful to the Duchess and myself as it is no doubt to the King. But so long as the Royal Family do not feel disposed to change the attitude they have adopted for more than ten years, these unpleasant exposés of a cheap and undignified family situation will inevitably flare up each time some relevant event occurs to ignite them, until all concerned are in their graves.'[1]

At about the same time the Duke made another appeal to his mother. 'I am always hoping that one day you will tell me to bring Wallis to see you, as it makes me very sad to think that you and she have never really met . . . it would indeed be tragic if you, my mother, had never known the girl I married and who has made me so blissfully happy.'[2] Queen Mary was unmoved. Nor did she prove more tractable two years later when the Duke renewed his battle over the Duchess's right to be styled Her Royal Highness. In 1937 the Duke had consulted the brilliant lawyer William Jowitt on the question and had received the reply that he had never ceased to be a Royal Highness himself, and that consequently there was no question of his wife not being entitled to the distinction. Jowitt maintained that the Letters Patent issued by King George VI, which had granted the title to the Duke but denied it to his wife, were nugatory and should never have been issued. Now, twelve years later, Jowitt was Lord Chancellor in the Labour government, and the Duke called on him to reaffirm his views and convince the King of the justice of the Duchess's case.

Jowitt shilly-shallied with all the expertise of one who was both a lawyer and a politician. The marks of respect which the subject pays to royal personages, he pronounced, were in no sense a legal obligation. They were rather a matter of good manners. To curtsey or not to curtsey to the Duchess was not a recognition of a legal position but arose from a desire to uphold the intentions of the King as the fountainhead of honour. Whatever the position might have been in 1937, it could now only be reversed by the issue of fresh Letters Patent. These could not be issued by the King alone but only on the advice of his ministers, who would probably feel it necessary to consult all the Commonwealth governments. 'What a difficult position for me,' Jowitt told Lascelles. 'I hope I did right.'[3] It was, Lascelles remarked to King George VI, 'the best example I have ever seen of a clever lawyer trying to eat his own words without giving himself indigestion'.[1] But Jowitt, he felt, had done right. That Jowitt himself felt he had done wrong is shown by the letter he wrote to Lascelles a week after his conversation with the Duke, in which he said that he still felt a legal mistake had been made. 'In reality he remained HRH notwithstanding the Abdication and the attribute to which he was entitled would automatically pass to his wife.'[2]

The Duke knew nothing of this later admission but refused to be deterred by the Lord Chancellor's discouraging reply. He now decided that the time had come to submit the question to the Prime Minister. King George VI pointed out to Attlee that the question had been exhaustively considered in 1937. If the Duke were to approach the Prime Minister, he went on, the King was sure 'you will not encourage him to think that any alteration can be made at this time'.[3] The Duke would get no support from Attlee, he told Queen Mary confidently: 'Anyhow, no one else can change the position except me, and I won't do anything.'[4] Lascelles took on the charge, and himself wrote to the Prime Minister arguing that this was not just a question for the Sovereign. To issue new Letters Patent would have wide constitutional consequences, would require consultation with all the Commonwealth governments, and 'might well evoke a considerable reaction among His Majesty's subjects in many parts of the world, for it would inevitably carry with it the implication that the Abdication itself was still a matter for discussion, or even modification'.[5] There was no need to make the Prime Minister's flesh creep with such far-fetched bogeymen. Attlee had no intention of risking the displeasure of the King for the sake of a woman of whom he disapproved quite as strongly as did any member of the royal family. He had given the matter careful consideration, he told the Duke a week after their meeting, and fully understood why it had been brought forward, 'but I feel bound to say that I don't think it advisable or opportune to take any action at the present time'.[6] 'Never apologize, never explain,' was an adage close to Attlee's heart.

As the Duke booked his appointment with the Prime Minister, Queen Mary sent the King a letter which showed vividly how little her attitude had changed over the last decade and how certain it was that she would never accept the Duchess of Windsor as a daughter-in-law.

> I cannot tell you how grieved I am at your brother being so tiresome about the HRH. Giving *her* this title would be fatal, and after all these years I fear lest people think that we condoned this dreadful marriage which has been such a blow to us all in every way. I hope you will be very firm and refuse to do anything about it, and that the Government will back you up. I was grieved that Leopold of the Belgians and his wife saw quite a lot of her in the South of France lately, but she is so pushing and she leaves no stone unturned to remain a thorn in our sides and advertise herself whenever she can. I feel furious that she is over here now, so unnecessary and tactless, and that you should be bothered in this way makes me furious, and I beg and beseech you to be very firm and refuse what he wants . . . With 2 husbands living still, I can't think how D can be so tactless.[1]

This was not a charitable letter, but charity had no place in Queen Mary's feelings towards her son's marriage. If the Duke had read it, even his determination might have wavered. As it was, he made one more approach to the King at the end of 1949. In what must have been a painful interview, the Duke seems to have accused his brother of making his life impossible and demonstrating in every way the hatred that he felt for the former King, and still more for the Duchess. Wearily the King recapitulated the shock that it had been for him and the nation when his brother abdicated. He had done throughout what he felt to be in the best interests of the country, the monarchy and the Duke of Windsor himself. His brother had never realized, never even considered, the 'ghastly VOID' his decision had left in his family's and everybody else's life. Then came the final rebuff:

> When you abdicated you accepted the view of the great majority of your subjects that your intended wife was not the right person to be Queen Consort. For that reason you renounced the throne for yourself and your descendants. What you now ask me to do would be to reverse that decision, which was your *own*. If your wife now became a member of

our family, there is no reason why she should not have become your Queen in 1937. It wouldn't make sense of the past, and it would be just as unacceptable to a great many people now as it was then . . .

You said that the present position was an insult to your wife. Please don't think this. When you married her she attained the highest rank in the English peerage. You won't believe anything I say to you . . . but you must remember that I made your wife a Duchess despite what happened in December 1936. You should be grateful to me for this. But you are not.[1]

Nothing could show more clearly the gulf of incomprehension that lay between the Duke of Windsor and his family. Starting from such different premises, how could they hope to reach the same conclusion? Even the words they used – love, duty, loyalty, sacrifice – meant different things to each of them. What to the Duke was callous persecution, was to Queen Mary and the King the course dictated by the inflexible demands of justice and morality. No one can ever be said to be entirely right or wrong in such a conflict of standards. Today, in a laxer generation, it may seem that Queen Mary was unnecessarily rigid, that no vital principle was at stake, that the 'dreadful marriage' had brought happiness to its members for a decade and seemed as strong as it had ever been. Yet according to the rules by which she had been bred and which she had followed faithfully all her life, there can be no doubting her total rectitude. Their minds could never meet.

The Duke replied briefly to his brother's letter, doing little more than protest at the King's statement that he had said his life was not worth living under these conditions: 'On the contrary I could not conceive greater happiness than Wallis has given me in these thirteen years of our married life.'[2] For the rest, he said that the subject had best be pursued face to face. There is no evidence that he did so. He never formally renounced his crusade to win acceptance for his wife, but from this time onwards he seems to have lost heart, and his efforts were perfunctory, as if made for the record.

Queen Mary tried conscientiously to keep her son in touch with the family. She sent him a long account of Princess Elizabeth's wedding and kept him posted on other items of domestic news: 'Lilibet's dear little girl Anne was christened yesterday, such a nice baby; as to the boy Charles, he is a very delightful child, full of high spirits and fun.'[1]

Early in 1951 the Duchess fell ill and cancer of the womb was diagnosed. She was operated on in New York for the removal of a fibroid tumour, and though the operation was a complete success it gave the Duke some agonizing moments. 'I feel so sorry for your great anxiety about your wife, and am thankful that so far you are able to send a fair account,' wrote Queen Mary;[2] not over-effusive, perhaps, but recognizing in her own way that, for the Windsors at least, the marriage had not been so 'dreadful' as she had recently styled it. The Duke acknowledged such overtures politely enough, the depth of his rancour would only be revealed when his mother was on her deathbed. For him there was only one way by which his relationship with his family could be properly restored – by their recognition of his wife. And that, he finally accepted, would never come.

29

The Final Years

B Y THE BEGINNING OF 1952 IT HAD BECOME FINALLY
evident that the Duke of Windsor would never be offered an
official post that would make any serious demand on his time
or energies. He would never be able to live permanently in Great
Britain. Of the countries in which he could contemplate living and
in which taxation made it feasible, France continued to seem the
most attractive. The parameters of his life were thus laid down; it
remained to live out the years that were left as agreeably and as
comfortably as possible.

To find a permanent home in France was the first priority. The
Duchess would have preferred to live in a house in central Paris,
perhaps with something rather less grand than La Cröe for stays in
the south of France, more probably renting houses or living in hotels
as the mood took them. The Duke preferred the country and would
have been happy to have his main residence somewhere reasonably
accessible but not too close to the capital. In the end they found a
solution which suited both of them remarkably well. First, early in
1952, they visited and were enchanted by the Moulin de la Tuilerie,
an old water mill in the valley of the Chevreuse, less than an hour's
drive from Paris yet in an as yet unspoilt pocket of country. The Mill
had been made habitable, but not much more, by the painter Etienne
Drian. The Windsors leased it, and then decided to buy. Without too
much difficulty the Chancellor of the Exchequer, then R. A. Butler,
was persuaded to make available the necessary £30,000 odd from
the Duke's capital in England, which was still blocked by currency
control.[1]

Then began the serious work of putting house and garden in order.
'Fixing houses is a headache anywhere,' the Duke complained a year
or so after they had taken possession, 'but it's an exhausting and
discouraging occupation in "Frogland" where there seems to be no
organization or supervision of work whatsoever. Plus the fact that

the *ouvriers* consume two to three bottles of red wine a day on the job; the sign saying "men working" should read "men drinking".'[1] Gradually the job got done, and the Mill was transformed into a comfortable and peaceful home. Its heart was the old barn, which was adapted as the main sitting room, called the Museum since it was there that the Duke kept his most precious relics: two large drums of the Grenadier and Welsh Guards, used as occasional tables; a frame containing specimens of every button used by the British Army during the First World War; an enormous wall map, equipped with flashing electric light bulbs which traced his travels as Prince of Wales; three golf balls mounted in silver to mark the three occasions he had done a hole in one.[2] It took three years' work and much expense before the house was completed to their satisfaction, but when it was done it ranked second only to Fort Belvedere in the pantheon of his affections.

The Duke told Harold Nicolson that he hoped the Duchess might be cured of her passion for New York and Paris if he provided her with a country seat.[3] In this he deluded himself, but while work on the Mill was still in progress, a solution was found to the problem of accommodation in Paris. In October 1952 the Duke was grumbling to his mother that houses or flats in Paris, not to mention their renovation and redecoration, were 'so incredibly expensive that one hesitates to take the plunge'.[4] Within a few months the City of Paris put at his disposal, at a very reasonable though far from nominal rent on a twenty-five-year lease, a solid white mansion set in two acres of grounds on the Neuilly side of the Bois de Boulogne. It offered privacy, quiet, splendid rooms for entertaining, limited but adequate accommodation for guests. He accepted the offer with alacrity.

The keynote of the Mill was informality, comfortable and expensive but in no way intended to impress the visitor. 4 Route du Champ D'Entraînement was a very different matter. If the Windsors could not live in a palace, then at least the Duchess was determined that the setting of their daily life should be palatial. Stéphene Boudin, who had first met the Duke and probably worked for him when he was Prince of Wales, and who specialized in producing aristocratic eighteenth-century French interiors for the affluent bourgeois of the twentieth century, was hired to manufacture a background fit for a man who had once been king.[5] The effect was artificial, theatrical even, but never vulgar; the portrait of Queen Mary by Llewellyn which dominated the principal salon seemed slightly out of place but not in the least disgraced by its surroundings. Some found the total effect over-ornate, others deplored its arid formality, but it avoided pomposity, the detail was of the highest quality, it provided a sumptuous setting for entertainment in the grand manner.

The fact that he was now settled firmly in France and had been treated with such generosity, both by the municipality of Paris and by the government, did not make the Duke any more disposed to like the French or to feel at home in their company. His command of French remained frail, and he was noticeably more eager to air his German or his Spanish. When the French in 1954 torpedoed the negotiations for a European Defence Community he exploded with indignation: 'And I guess that being in Germany right now, where there is no Communism and the work of reconstruction incredible, one despises the "Frogs" all the more. Taking into account that the Germans liquidated the French in 1940 as no nation ever has been before, the arrogance and stubbornness of their politicians passes all comprehension.'[1] It was partly the feeling that, though he was committed to living in France, he still wished to keep a toe-hold elsewhere that led him to reject an offer from Lord Brownlow in 1952 to buy his Alberta ranch. Possibly he still had some faint hope that the will-o'-the-wisp of an oil strike might one day after all prove a reality; but more seriously, he was reluctant to part with the only land which he owned apart from the Mill. He would not sell now, and he did not believe he ever would, he told Brownlow;[2] in fact he did, but not for another decade, and only after increasing ill health made it obvious that he could never get pleasure out of visiting the ranch again.

While the Windsors were thus digging themselves in in France, things changed dramatically in England. Early in February 1952 King George VI died suddenly at Sandringham. Even for those who had been closely in touch with him the news came as a surprise; for the Duke, who knew little more than any other newspaper reader about the King's health, it was a stunning shock. His rancour had been too great for too long, and the brothers had grown too far apart, for him to feel deep grief; but the death of a sibling who had once been so close to him was still profoundly disturbing. There were other considerations too. What effect would the death of the King have on the Windsors' standing in Great Britain? Not much, he reckoned – at any rate while Queen Mary lived – but might there not be some relenting on the part of the new generation? He hastened from New York, where he was staying when he received the news, to attend the funeral. His wife sped him on his way with sage advice and responded enthusiastically when he told her that he had been well received: 'Now that the door has been opened a crack try and get your foot in, in the hope of making it open even wider in the future because that is best for WE ... Do not mention or ask for anything regarding recognition of me.' She suspected that Queen Elizabeth* would be as much of an obstacle as Queen Mary to the Duke's ambitions, attributing her hostility to a particularly ferocious letter he had once written to his mother.† Queen Mary, she felt, should 'have kept it to herself', but instead she had shown it to King George VI, who had passed it on to his wife. She urged him to see Queen Elizabeth and try to explain what his feelings had been at the time: 'After all, there are two sides to every story.'[1]

To some extent, the Duchess's urging bore fruit. 'Of course, David rushed over at once, nice of him but a bit disturbing,' Queen Mary told the Athlones. 'However, he saw E and the girls, he had not seen them since *1936*, so that feud is over, a great relief to me.'[2] But the reconciliation did not go very deep. The Duke made brief notes of the principal conversations which he held during his stay in London. 'Mama as hard as nails but failing,' he noted. 'When Queens fail they make less sense than others in the same state. Cookie [the Windsors' nickname for Queen Elizabeth] listened without comment and closed on the note that it was nice to be able to talk about Bertie with somebody who had known him so well.'[3] He was not left with the feeling that the Duchess would be more welcome in London than she had been while King George VI was alive, or that his niece, the new Queen, would be likely to

---

* Only the consort of the King or the reigning monarch should be referred to as 'The Queen'; after the death of King George VI his widow was styled Queen Elizabeth or, by the public at least, the Queen Mother.
† Presumably the letter of mid-June 1937 (pages 360–1).

start her reign by defying what she knew to be the deeply felt convictions of her grandmother and mother. The most tangible consequence of his brother's death was that he lost the £10,000 a year which had been paid to him by King George VI as an allowance. The loss, at a time when he was expensively refurbishing the Mill and about to engage on the still more expensive decoration of the house in the Bois, was notably inopportune, even if it did not, as he told his mother was the case: 'necessitate a complete revision of the style of living we have maintained ever since our marriage, as befits the position of a son of a sovereign'.[1]

He was back in New York, a year or so after the King's death, when he received a letter from the royal doctor reporting that his mother was dangerously ill. After three harrowing weeks, in which Queen Mary, barely conscious and in considerable pain, fought death with the same tenacity as she had shown in every field of life, she finally died on 24 March 1953. The Duke arrived at her bedside a few minutes too late. At the sight of her, wholly out of touch at last and yet still without having said a word to accept her daughter-in-law into her family, a dreadful bitterness welled up inside her son. 'My sadness was mixed with incredulity,' the Duke told his wife, 'that any mother could have been so hard and cruel towards her eldest son for so many years and yet so demanding at the end without relenting a scrap. I'm afraid the fluids in her veins have always been as icy cold as they now are in death.'[2] It was a brutal comment; yet it must be read in conjunction with the grief that he expressed to his closest surviving friend, Lord Dudley, when he told him how he had dreaded the indefinite prolongation of Queen Mary's agony: 'Still, it was terrible when her end came, and her passing has left a great void for our generation, and a last great personal link with our past has gone.'[3]

Would he have bothered to be hypocritical to someone who knew him as well as did Lord Dudley? Did he, knowing what his wife must be feeling, exaggerate the animosity he felt as he stood beside his mother's body? Probably he scarcely knew himself. A part of him could never forgive Queen Mary's treatment of his wife, and that part spoke when he denounced her icy cruelty, but she had still been the first woman to have played an important role in his life, the first woman he had loved, the woman whose love and approval he had craved all his life. It was because he valued his mother's good opinion so highly that he was bitterly resentful when she withheld it from his marriage; if she had said even a word in recognition of the Duchess's membership of the family, he would have mourned her with all the passion of which he was still capable. But Queen Mary was not the woman to abandon a principle, even to win a last-moment reconciliation with her son.

His resentment festered within him so that, with his mother no longer there as principal target, he lashed out wildly at any that remained. For the funeral he stayed with the Gloucesters at York House. His sister, the Princess Royal, he told his wife, had 'been quite sweet and human on the whole and Harry and Alice have been friendly hosts here. But of course they don't talk our language and never will.' All his time in London he had been 'boiling mad' that the Duchess was not in her rightful place by his side. 'What a smug stinking lot my relations are and you've never seen such a seedy worn-out bunch of old hags most of them have become.'[1] He concealed his feelings well; the Duchess of Gloucester remarked how well he got on with his brother and sister: 'It was particularly moving listening to the Duke, because he was obviously so pleased to be talking with his own family again.'[2] Indeed, his pleasure was genuine. He did still yearn to be with his own family again. It would have taken only a few words to transform the 'smug stinking lot' into a cherished group of intimates. But those few words would not, could not ever be spoken, and so he reviled them in blind fury and slipped unforgivingly away.

To American friends he professed to feel total indifference towards the royal family, whether the new generation or the old, and to consider the whole concept of monarchy as a faintly comic anachronism. In October 1952 he told Robert Young that he had just been to London and had found the new regime well installed – 'not that I give a damn'.[3] But he did give a damn. He at first cherished the hope that he and the Duchess would be invited to the Coronation in June 1953, though with Queen Mary still alive and Lascelles installed as private secretary to the new monarch, it is hard to believe that he entertained it very seriously. Certainly he had abandoned it before the end of 1952. He prepared a statement for the press which he showed to Churchill, explaining that it would be contrary to precedent for any sovereign or former sovereign to attend the Coronation. Churchill confirmed that this was indeed the case and that the statement would provide a most dignified reply to anyone who asked whether or not the Windsors would be attending.[1] Possibly the Duke had hoped that his approach to Churchill would bring about a miraculous last-minute change of heart; his reply confirmed that he was 'disappointed and depressed that you foresee no change in my family's attitude towards the Duchess or to her rightful official status as my wife'.[2]

Instead he watched the ceremony on television from the house of American friends in Paris, regaling the company with a well-informed and only occasionally ribald commentary on what they saw. He told Princess Arthur of Connaught that he had found it very moving, 'and we thought Lilibet conducted herself superbly throughout the long and trying ceremony'.[3] To another friend he remarked that a Queen enjoyed a marked advantage over a King on such an occasion, when a combination of 'humility and resplendent jewellery play so important a role. A woman can go through the motions far more naturally and gracefully than can any man.'[4]

Though the Coronation was thus a source of fresh humiliation, it provided a temporary solution for what was now the principal problem of his life. Harold Nicolson identified this accurately when he met the Duke at lunch and observed: 'He pretends to be very busy and happy, but I feel this is false and that he is unoccupied and miserable.'[5] He would never be entirely miserable so long as he shared his life with the Duchess, but he was indeed bored and under-employed, knowing that his talents were going to waste, resentful of the fact, and yet unable to think what to do about it. He was therefore delighted when it was suggested that he should write a long article on the constitutional role of the monarchy, to appear at the time of the Coronation. He set about the task with relish, to such effect that he produced not only articles for the *Sunday Express* and the *Women's Home Companion*, but enough material to make up a slim book which, under the title of *The Crown and the People, 1902–1953*, was published in September 1953.

Much more than his autobiography, *The Crown and the People* was the Duke's unaided work. Once he had completed a first draft, he appealed to Harold Nicolson to cast a professional eye over his work. When Nicolson telephoned to make an appointment to come to see him he was cut off with some abruptness. Later that day the Duke wrote to apologize. The reason for his rudeness, he explained, was that 'my brother Harry was in the room. He knows nothing of the article, for in these matters I believe in the element of surprise!'[1] Nicolson mainly confined himself to modifying or urging the omission of some of the more astringent passages, including an unflattering reference to the British Labour Party.[2] 'He fusses so much about his article that it might be the President of the United States preparing an address to Congress,' commented Nicolson. 'But what he does not see is that it is wrong for him to write it at all.'[3] At least he accepted all Nicolson's proposed changes, as well as some still more drastic censorship imposed by George Allen. The final result was an uncontroversial series of recollections of the two Coronations in which the Duke had participated, with some reflections – perfectly sensible if neither profound nor original – about the nature and future of the monarchy. He wrote appreciatively of the contribution of his father and still more of his mother: 'She was not only the loving wife who bore him six children but also his gracious and enlightened Queen Consort.' King George VI, he wrote, had been a faithful reflection of his father; if his own reign had run its course 'it is possible that its mood and texture would have followed more that of Edward VII'. One remark must have seemed especially noteworthy to the royal family: after reflecting on the strain to which the late King had been subject during his reign the Duke added, 'and I am not insensible of the fact that through a decision of mine he was projected into sovereign responsibilities that may at first have weighed heavily upon him'.[4]

This slight offering was followed by another even slighter. In 1960 a series of articles was again cobbled into a book, this time entitled *A Family Album* and largely ghosted by Patrick Kinross. This curious little book contains a certain number of quite entertaining anecdotes but consists mainly of random recollections about clothes worn or not worn by the royal family. It abounds in incidents in which, as Prince of Wales, the author committed some sartorial solecism and was duly reprimanded by his father. That concluded the Duke's literary career. The year after *A Family Album* appeared a contract was drawn up for a biography of King George III which the Duke was to write with help from Charles Murphy.[5] A first draft of what had by then become 'My Hanoverian Ancestors' was completed in 1964 but does not seem to have found favour with its nominal author.[1] The project languished and died; it was hardly a promising enterprise from the outset. The Duke meanwhile had been taking a keen interest in progress on the Duchess's exceedingly profitable memoirs, which were published as *The Heart Has Its Reasons* in 1956.

The very considerable sums that the Windsors made by their writings were needed to support the lavish style of their life, but even if they had not been they would have given much satisfaction to the Duke. On the straitened canvas of his interests, the management of his investments bulked among the most conspicuous. He enjoyed the best advice. 'Many thanks for . . . the welcome check in the amount of $100,000,' he wrote to the railway mogul, Robert Young. 'With another of $75,000 to follow, it certainly is a quick and generous profit on an investment of £40,000 eight months ago.'[2] It certainly was, and though such spectacular conjuring tricks were never commonplace, they happened often enough to ensure that an already substantial fortune grew comfortably with the years. The Duke of Windsor was a rich man; he needed to be, and never felt that he was wholly secure, but by the standards of the generality of mankind, he had little to complain of. It was not all good luck and good advice. He was shrewd, well-informed, cautious without being timid: if the circumstances had made it possible he would have proved a formidable stockbroker.

Golf and gardening were the other diversions which made the greatest demands on his time and energies. Golf had always been a favoured pastime, gardening had languished since the days of Fort Belvedere but was resumed with enthusiasm after the acquisition of the Mill. A large and long-neglected walled garden was first purged of its few surviving vegetables and richer crop of weeds, then laid out with two typically English herbaceous borders filled with the traditional flowers he had favoured at the Fort – delphiniums, phlox, asters. On the other side of the stream that ran through the property he constructed a rock garden, set with alpine blooms, through which water piped from the river cascaded to the stream below.[3] When James Pope-Hennessy visited the Duke he found him supervising the erection of a sundial. He was led to the spot by 'a yelping noise (which I later identified as the Duke's theme when he is excited) and a stream of German oaths . . . I found the Duke, wearing a cerise felt baseball cap. He was jumping about rather wildly, and shouting "Jawohl! Jawohl!" and other military German expressions to a troop of French gardeners.'[1] The head gardener in fact came from Alsace, hence the choice of language; the only surprising feature of the scene was that the Duke was not himself helping to manhandle the sundial into position. In gardening he was very much of an interventionist proprietor, usually to be found digging or weeding as vigorously as any of his employees.

He kept up his Spanish, taking lessons twice a week; practised his German whenever an opportunity occurred; resolutely refused to improve his French. He wrote many letters, read newspapers and magazines, set his archives in order and then reordered them. The dogs demanded much attention: the cairns had been replaced by pugs – Disraeli, Trooper and Davey Crockett in 1958 – 'We did have a fourth, called Peter Townsend,' the Duchess explained to James Pope-Hennessy, with her least nice grin, 'but we gave the Group Captain away.'[2] It was not a crowded life, but no less eventful than that of most men of more than sixty; it is only when it is compared with what it might have been if the Duke had been more ambitious or dedicated that its triviality becomes so obvious.

Entertaining, or more accurately supporting his wife in her role as hostess, was a major preoccupation. The guest lists had not changed noticeably since the days of the Boulevard Suchet, a sprinkling of French or foreign guests of real distinction set amidst what Frank Giles with some hauteur described as 'a motley and not very attractive company: blue-rinsed widows of American millionaires, members of French cafe society, hangers-on of one sort or another'.[3] The food, drink and service were more to be relied on than the company; the Duchess's manner was very grand indeed, and she entered in a lavishly formal style that only rarely tipped over into ostentation. Kenneth Rose dined there in January 1972 and found it 'like stepping into a fairyland of fantastic luxury. Almost everything seemed to be made of gold or crystal. There are wonderful carpets, exquisite gilt furniture, little tables covered with thickets of jewelled bric à brac. The only light comes from candles, which cast their golden haze from chandeliers and sconces. Beautifully arranged flowers. Two pictures dominate the room – one of the Duke in Garter Robes and another of Queen Mary.'

The party moved on into dinner. 'The room is again lit entirely by candles. There are two tables of eight or ten each, covered with gilt and silver objects, painted porcelain candlesticks, delightful flowers and porcelain-handled cutlery that is rather heavy and difficult to manage. Endless butlers and footmen, all in white ties. Throughout the meal, the Duchess catches their eye from time to time so that they may receive swiftly whispered instructions, perhaps even rebukes.' The food was excellent: a rich fish stew with rice and olives accompanied by several different kinds of bread; saddle of lamb, 'which characteristically has sprouted ten kidneys instead of the usual two'; chocolate pudding, decorated with truffle chocolates; wafer thin pastry cups two inches high filled with hot cheese soufflé – 'They are unbelievably delicious.' They drank hock, claret, champagne, then claret again with the savoury. The women left once dinner was over, but within two or three minutes the Duchess was back, beckoning the men into the drawing room. Once there, a man sat down at the piano and began playing 'Smoke Gets in Your Eyes' and other tunes of that period.[1]

When they were not entertaining they were being entertained. Inevitably they were the guests of honour, and in most of the houses to which they went the Duchess was accorded something very close to royal status. Cecil Beaton remembered a dinner party early in 1960, when sequin crowns were distributed to the more favoured female guests. 'One of course was popped on to the Duchess of Windsor's head – a moment that would have been a flashlight photographer's scoop, but the Duchess looked quite a bit embarrassed as she smiled with her mouth turning down at the corners. Then, delighted at having a quotation to hand, she witlessly and clumsily and with wild little eyes shouted as she leaned across the table "Uneasy lies the head that wears a crown." '[2] On such occasions the Duke would drink as much as most, but rarely enough to be classified as drunk by any except the most censorious. When he did take too much, it showed itself in exuberance rather than bellicosity or alcoholic stupor. In St Moritz he danced the Charleston and a sailor's hornpipe with Noël Coward: Princess Sixte de Bourbon was decidedly shocked but 'there was no harm in it,' reflected Coward; 'it looked only faintly ridiculous to see us skipping about with a will.'[3] Anna Neagle, who was on the same liner for an Atlantic crossing, found him an exceptionally good dancer. They tried out a new and complicated rumba rhythm. She trod on his feet. They tried again. He trod on hers. 'We both laughed and he led me back to the table. "Difficult," he said, "but thanks for trying." No wonder they'd called him the Prince Charming.'[1]

Oswald and Diana Mosley were a couple whom they saw often, though more frequently in the country, where they were neighbours, than in Paris. Lady Mosley's sister, Nancy Mitford, considered the friendship was based wholly on a shared nostalgia for the days of the Third Reich: 'They want us all to be governed by the kind clever rich Germans and be happy ever after. I wish I knew why they all live in France and not *outre-Rhin.*'[2] No doubt Mosley and the Duke shared certain political assumptions but one does not need to look for any close affinity of views to explain why two exiled couples should seek each other's company; especially since, for the Duke, the Mosleys represented a society and a way of life from which he was now largely cut off but for which he still felt a wistful if almost reluctant longing. Diana Mosley noticed how eager he was to indulge in genealogical gossip whenever the occasion offered. 'He remembered people's sisters and cousins and aunts. He would say: "Now let me see. Lady so-and-so was Lord so-and-so's *great-aunt.* Recto?"'[3] The Duchess, perhaps in emulation of her husband, liked to gossip about the American upper crust, and at dinner regaled the British diplomat, Charles Johnston, with a laborious exegesis of inter-marriages between the Biddles and the Dukes.[4]

'I loved the Duke and have seldom met his like for charm,' wrote Lady Mosley. 'He was always ready to laugh and be amused and then his rather sad and anxious expression changed and his face lit up in a most engaging way. He had the almost miraculous memory that royal personages so cleverly cultivate and which everyone finds flattering.'[5] James Pope-Hennessy, who spent some time at the Mill when he was working on Queen Mary's official biography, was surprised to find that the Duke was 'exceedingly intelligent, original, liberal-minded and quite capable of either leading a conversation or taking a constructive part in one. He is also one of the most considerate men I have ever met of his generation.'[6] Nearly everyone agreed about his consideration, not all would have shared Pope-Hennessy's admiration of his intelligence or prowess as a conversationalist. J. K. Galbraith, for one, was not impressed. He met the Duke just before he left to take over as American Ambassador in New Delhi. The Duke claimed to be something of an authority on the Indians. 'You will find the people most agreeable in their own way,' he declared. 'They have been most uncommonly decent to my niece.'[1]

In this judgment, the Duke was being unusually polite about a race who suffered from the dual disability of being both coloured and left-wing. Though Pope-Hennessy found him 'liberal-minded', he often seemed reactionary to the point of caricature. Susan Mary Patten remembered a dinner at the British Embassy at which the Duke stung her diplomat husband to fury by announcing that General Marshall was unquestionably a communist. Patten demanded to know the Duke's evidence and a row ensued: 'At the end of it I happened to look at the Duchess. She was tight-lipped and cobra-eyed. I think we will not be invited to the Windsors again.'[2] They were not. When Eisenhower was nominated as the Republican candidate for President, the Duke was dubious and said that he would have felt safer with Taft. 'He is a sounder man, of independence and integrity . . . Besides, one doesn't know exactly to whom the General is committed, or whether he won't be the prisoner of some of the gang who control the present administration from behind the scenes in Washington.'[3] This opinion he soon revised. He wrote to Queen Mary after meeting Eisenhower in New York shortly before the inauguration and told her that he thought the new administration had already brought about a change of heart in America. 'President Eisenhower has lately revealed two encouraging and hitherto little known characteristics which may well have a profound influence on his foreign policy. One is the fact that he is a deeply religious man. The other is that, although he chose the army as a career, he is fundamentally a man of peace. Who knows but that these two estimable traits will make for a more effective approach to the solution of the "cold War", and a formidable spiritual counter-attack to ruthless Soviet aggression.'[4]

But his ideal among American politicians was that stalwart of the ultra-right, Senator Barry Goldwater. Early in 1962 he was telling a Republican friend that Goldwater inspired him more and more. 'He would make a wonderful President to our way of thinking. Still, I am afraid there are too many "liberals" in his party to stop his nomination.'[5] He never wavered in this belief, surprising Sulzberger two years later by his insistence that Gold-water was a great man. He added, 'I was against Dewey, but I am for Barry.'[1] The failure of the American people to share his point of view led to a gradual loss of faith in the future of the United States. By 1969 he was telling Loel Guinness that the country was on the road to revolution and that nothing was being done to check the process. 'Having disrupted the normal functioning of the universities and colleges and even the high schools, the white and black revolutionaries, aided by communist funds, are now going to focus [?on] their enterprise system and all other elements of the American Establishment and replace it by a communist state.'[2]

He judged the United Nations to be only a little less dangerous than the Soviet Union. He rejoiced at the death of Dag Ham-marskjold and predicted that, with 'Hammarskjold eliminated . . . that dying duck the U.N. is about to die too, to the relief of the American taxpayer'.[3] Adlai Stevenson seemed to him the paradigm of effete liberal, whose reckless determination to appease the Russians and support every kind of 'progressive' impulse was sapping America's power to stand upright in a dangerous world. Batista, the dictator of Cuba, was everything that Stevenson was not. 'I was intrigued to meet so forceful and yet so fair-minded a man who was a revolutionary only for his Country's sake,' the Duke told Arthur Gardner, United States Ambassador in Havana. 'I judge that the longer he remains in power the better for Cuba.'[4] They could have done with a Batista in Britain: the Conservatives, he was convinced, were not sufficiently aggressive to combat 'rabble-rousing demagogues like Bevan',[5] and when they did get back to power they seemed distressingly ready to acquiesce in all the misguided legislation that had been imposed on Britain under socialist rule. He saw nothing to deplore in the Anglo-French action against Egypt at the time of the Suez crisis, except in the British failure to take the United States along with it in support of the adventure. 'This serious difference in the official thinking of our two countries . . . couldn't come at a worse time.'[6]

His fears for Britain's future did not diminish his affection for its people, nor, it seemed, their affection for him. With the passing of time the bitterness of those who had felt themselves betrayed had faded and the Windsors began to benefit by the romantic light which suffuses all those who have renounced wealth or position for the sake of love. When they went to the theatre to see *Witness for the Prosecution*, the first play in London they had attended since the abdication, the audience stood and clapped when they entered their box and a large crowd assembled outside the theatre. 'Certainly to my mind,' wrote the play's producer, Peter Saunders, 'there was no doubt about the feeling of the people of England towards the couple.'[1] The relationship between them was perhaps not quite so idyllic as was believed by the more susceptible of their admirers, but on the whole it justified the faith of those who felt that the Duke's sacrifice had not been in vain. The Duke certainly felt himself bereft without her. At the end of 1955 she went alone to the United States in connection with the publication of her memoirs while the Duke stayed behind to supervise the replanting of the garden at the Mill. 'The lonely weeks have dragged since Wallis left, and I can hardly wait for her return,' he told one friend, and a fortnight later wrote to another: 'It is wonderful having the Duchess back with me after seven lonely weeks separation. It has been tough being left alone here ... a grim experience I am determined to avoid in the future.'[2] That her dependence on him was less great hardly needs restatement, but she too pined during his absence and the letters she wrote to him have the ring of sincerity. 'I hate, hate having you go away alone,' she wrote in 1952, 'but you are not really alone because I am so much a part of you ... Darling, I shall miss you each second and you know that I love you more than anything in the world for always.'[3]

On one of his visits to London the Duke was unpleasantly reminded of a passage in his past which he would rather not have resurrected. At the end of the war a vast collection of captured official archives had been removed from Germany for inspection by experts from Britain, France and the United States with a view to their eventual translation and publication. John Wheeler-Bennett, later to be the official biographer of King George VI, was in charge of the British end of the operation, and it soon became clear to him that some of the papers, if published, would be embarrassing to the Duke of Windsor. The despatches written by German ambassadors before the war might cause a few eyebrows to be raised but little more, the papers relating to the Duke's sojourn in Spain and Portugal in

1940 were more dangerous since these made it plain that the Germans believed the Duke could be induced to play a Quisling's role in an occupied Britain. They would inevitably give rise to unkind speculation as to how far that belief might have been justified. In August 1945 Attlee had sent Churchill a dossier containing the most mischievous of the papers, with a comment that 'little or no credence could be put on the statements made' but that publication 'might do the greatest harm'. Churchill replied the following day: 'I earnestly trust it may be possible to destroy all traces of these German intrigues.'[1]

It was, of course, impossible; the existence of the papers was already known to the Americans and even if they had not been, the official historians involved would have resigned rather than allow such important evidence to be suppressed. There was no question of publication until all the papers had been translated and properly edited, so the matter was allowed to rest. In the inner circle, however, there was much gossip about what was involved. Bruce Lockhart noted in his diary in November 1946 that Wheeler-Bennett had 'found some damaging material on the Duke of Windsor. There are various protocols of Nazi conversations with him, including one at Lisbon during the war. Jack is worried, because we are sharing documents with the Americans who will certainly publish this material. If we do not, we shall look very foolish.' Wheeler-Bennett, who had been given a completely free hand by the government to publish whatever he thought fit, was taking the line that he would tolerate no interference unless it stemmed directly from the King. Since it was obvious that George VI would not wish to intervene, it seemed the papers must eventually be published.[2]

In her important biography of King George VI Sarah Bradford has drawn attention to a request from Bevin to Marshall in March 1947 that a microfilm copy of a paper relating to the Duke of Windsor should be destroyed.[3] The archives at the Foreign Office and at Windsor contain no reference to such a request, and do not establish beyond doubt what the paper in question may have been. Sarah Bradford surmises that it may have related to some episode during the period in which the Duke was Governor of the Bahamas and was 'under American surveillance'. If this is correct it is hard to imagine why the Americans should have possessed only a microfilm of the document rather than the original, nor why the British should only have become concerned about its existence in 1947. It seems more probable that the same German dossier was in question. Two months before Bevin's approach to Marshall, the American Ambassador, John Winant, told Lascelles that he had finally been instructed to hand over the originals of the documents to the Foreign Office.[1] It is likely that Bevin, encouraged by this success, was now asking that the microfilm copy still in Washington should be destroyed. If so, he seems to have gained little satisfaction. In July of the same year the King finally ruled that the papers should be returned to the archives in Berlin for eventual publication if the editors of the German records felt it necessary.[2] Godfrey Thomas recorded that the King had warned the Duke, who made light of the whole affair, 'suggesting (as had already occurred to us as a possibility) that the German Ambassador was making up a good story on the lines that he thought would please his chief, Ribbentrop'.[3]

Legend has it that a cache of yet more sensitive documents was recaptured from various private German archives by a secret task force consisting of the art historian, Anthony Blunt, then working for Military Intelligence, and the Windsor librarian, Owen Morshead. The revelations contained in these documents, according to the most picturesque version of the story, were so hair-raising in their implications as to enable Blunt to blackmail the royal family and government into granting him immunity from prosecution even after his treasonable activities as a Russian agent had been detected. Reality is more prosaic. Blunt and Morshead did indeed visit Germany and later Holland on the instructions of the King; their mission, far from being secret, was widely reported in the press at the time. From Germany, with the approval of the Landgravine of Hesse, they brought back for temporary deposit in Windsor until conditions in Germany had settled down a trunk containing letters from Queen Victoria to her daughter, the Empress Frederick. These were returned in 1951. From Holland came various relics of the Kaiser of particular interest to the British royal family – his Garter star, Field Marshal's baton and so on – and, as an afterthought, photographic copies of a few nineteenth-century letters. No single paper brought to England by Blunt and Morshead related to the Duke of Windsor.

The Final Years

It was 1953 before the documents relating to 1940 were in a state where a final decision on publication was required. Churchill wrote to Eisenhower to urge that the Lisbon papers be suppressed: 'The historical importance of the episode is negligible, and the allegations rest only on the assertions of Germans and pro-German officials in making the most of anything they could pick up.'[1] Eisenhower was amazed to hear that the papers still existed. They had been called to his attention in 1945, he said, and his experts had then concluded that 'there was no possible value to them, that they were obviously concocted with some idea of promoting German propaganda and weakening Western resistance, and that they were totally unfair to the Duke'.[2] With both Churchill and Eisenhower intent on destroying the documents it might have seemed that their fate was certain, but when Monckton called on the French Foreign Minister, Georges Bidault, he was told that the French would agree to their publication being delayed, but not to their suppression.[3] With an obstinacy which, whatever the significance of the papers themselves, can only seem heart-warming, the British and American official historians defied their governments and threatened resignation if the papers were not published in full. King George VI, who shortly before he died had reconsidered the issue, insisted only that, if publication were inevitable, the Duke should be given warning and a chance to comment.[4] Churchill accepted the principle of publication, but ensured still further delay, and it was not until 1957 that Volume X of the *Documents on German Foreign Policy* containing the Lisbon papers finally appeared.

The Duke was distressed but not unduly disturbed. 'While it is a bore that Washington insists on publishing the "Lisbon documents",' he told Churchill, 'Walter Monckton and I examined them very thoroughly over the weekend and will have a *démenti* prepared . . . in advance of their publication.'[5] When they came out the Foreign Office issued a statement affirming that the Duke 'never wavered in his loyalty to the British cause . . . The German records are necessarily a much-tainted source. The only firm evidence is of what the Germans were trying to do in this matter and how completely they failed.'[6] The Duke for his part issued a statement, describing the communications which passed between Berlin and the German Ambassadors in Madrid and Lisbon as being 'in part complete fabrications and in part gross distortions of the truth'. The national press accepted this version, and the Germans involved in the affair were dismissed as self-deluded fantasists intent only on enhancing their own reputations.

Once a rumour has been launched it is not easily suppressed. Documents continued to trickle out, including the reports provided to Berlin by the absurd Duke of Saxe-Coburg,* which revived suspicions of the Duke of Windsor's political inclinations. 'Secret papers have disclosed his pro-Nazi perfidy which, of course, I was perfectly aware of at the time,' wrote Noël Coward with lofty omniscience. 'Poor dear, what a monumental ass he has always been!'[1] Ass perhaps, perfidious no: the papers show that the Duke felt the war could and should have been avoided, that he was defeatist about the prospects of victory in 1940 and 1941, that he preached the virtues of a negotiated peace. He had been indiscreet and extravagant enough in what he said to give the Germans some grounds for believing that he might be ready to play an active part in securing such a peace and returning to the throne after it had been negotiated. That is bad enough. What they do not show, and cannot show since no evidence exists, is that the Duke would ever have contemplated accepting such an invitation if it had been issued.

Lack of evidence rarely inhibits the more venturesome biographers. Many other fantasies have been voiced in the last thirty years. The laws of libel mercifully ensured that the most grotesque have been published only after his death and thus did not trouble him. Ever since his successful libel action against Geoffrey Dennis in 1937, he had, however, been obsessed by the need to protect his, and still more his wife's reputation. He was disturbed in 1953 by the publication in America of Iles Brody's *Gone with the Windsors*, and wrote indignantly: 'Whatever inspired him to write so vindictive and inaccurate a diatribe remains something of a mystery . . . Of course, the book never will be published in Great Britain; my lawyer assures me it contains sufficient libel to scare any publisher from doing so.'[2] His lawyers were right, but he fared less well with Geoffrey Bocca's *She might have been Queen*. In June 1953 he wrote to the proprietors of the American publishers,

* See page 267 above.

Henry Holt, to ask if his lawyers could see a typescript of Bocca's book so that he would have a chance to remove anything offensive – 'I have been trying to get the low-down on this guy Bocca's book since March.'[1] Next thing he knew was that it was to appear in Britain and, a cruel cut, to be published by Express Books: 'Old Max Beaverbrook certainly has reached an all time high in his unpredictability by publishing that lousy Bocca book about the Duchess.'[2]

But the book which caused him greatest concern, just because it was certain neither to be 'lousy' nor 'vindictive', was John Wheeler-Bennett's official biography of King George VI. The Duke had spent some time with Wheeler-Bennett while the book was being researched, and in 1956 asked that he should be allowed to see in typescript those passages that related to him; after all, he argued, 'in the references to me . . . you are actually writing part of the official history of a living former Sovereign'.[3] Wheeler-Bennett cautiously replied that he must put the matter to The Queen since it was she who had commissioned the book. The Queen equally cautiously ruled that she would read the biography herself before deciding whether any other member of the royal family needed to see it before publication.[4] The Duke's worst suspicions were aroused: obviously 'that evil snake Lascelles' had been working on Wheeler-Bennett to ensure that the author put King George VI on a pedestal and presented the Duke 'in as bad a light as possible'.[5] In the end he was sent a copy when the book was in proof and seems to have accepted that, though he would have liked certain things to have been expressed differently, there was nothing to which he could reasonably take exception. He asked for only two changes, one a minor error of fact, one no more than a typist's slip. Both the corrections were made.[6]

The Duke's complaints about the royal family's discourtesy in withholding Wheeler-Bennett's biography until it was in the final stages marked the only occasion on which he voiced any criticism of The Queen. On the whole he accepted that the vendetta which had marred his relationship with his mother's or his own generation of the royal family, did not carry through to the new regime. He never changed his view that the Duchess should be formally recognized but he no longer made the failure to do this an act of war. Indeed, he went out of his way to avoid anything which might seem unacceptable to the Palace. Dan Ingman wrote a play about the months before the abdication called *The Woman I Love* which was very sympathetic to the Windsors. Peter Saunders sent it to the Duke with a letter extolling its virtues. The Duke returned it unread, saying that he 'would not agree to any play being performed on the subject in question'. Saunders tried again, offering to arrange a private showing. His reward was a solicitor's letter, threatening legal action if the matter was pursued.[1]

There comes a point in nearly everybody's life when he must accept the fact that he is old; from that moment onwards all that is left is a melancholy process of decay, sometimes mitigated by remissions or apparent recoveries, sometimes proceeding headlong to total degeneration. With one victim the mind decays more quickly than the body, with another the physical collapse comes first, but always the path leads the same way, only the pace is different. For those less fortunate the fatal moment can come early, others may postpone it until they are seventy or much more. For the Duke of Windsor the point was reached in 1958, when he was nearly sixty-four and was harrowed by a long, painful and debilitating attack of shingles. 'Only those of us who have been thus afflicted know the physical and mental ravages of this wretched malady,' he wrote to a fellow sufferer.[2] He recovered, but suddenly he was conscious of his age, unable to take anything approaching violent exercise, lethargic where he had once been hyperactive, forgetting facts and faces with disconcerting rapidity. He was far from senile but he realized that, for once and for all, he was past his best. In 1964 he endured open heart surgery while in America, the following year he underwent a serious eye operation, each ordeal slowed him up and made him that much more aware of his mortality. While he was in the London Clinic for the second operation The Queen called on him and met the Duchess for the first time since the abdication.

The operation accelerated the gradual withdrawal from activity which is the lot of the elderly. An arthritic hip, which forced him to walk with a cane from 1968, deprived him of any role in gardening beyond the purely supervisory and drove him towards a still harsher sacrifice: 'We have almost sold the Mill,' he told

Aird. 'We are sorry to have let this attractive property go, but we must look for some place in the sun.'[1] He could still play nine holes of golf, he added proudly, but soon that pleasure also was denied him. The sale of the Mill dragged on interminably, and in the end fell through; sometimes they would go down to the increasingly shabby property and wander around, hating all they saw, yet unable to keep away. Not far from the house, blocks of flats were springing up and a petrol station, particularly offensive to the Duke. 'It had a row of flag poles in front of it which he called "those ghăstly măsts",' Lady Mosley remembered.[2]

He was concerned to protect his wife's position after he died. She would anyway have been a rich woman, but he was disturbed by the fact that, on his death, the £10,000 or so which he received each year, in lieu of rent for his life interest in Sandringham and Balmoral, would cease. In August 1968 he appealed to The Queen to continue this for the Duchess's life.[3] She agreed to go on paying £5000 a year and in the same letter told him of Prince Charles's coming investiture as Prince of Wales: 'I have hesitated to enquire whether you would like an invitation considering the circumstances,' she wrote, 'but if you would reply to this indirect form of invitation in whatever way you feel, I shall quite understand.'[4] 'As I do not believe that the presence of his aged great uncle would add much to the colorful proceedings centered upon Charles, I do not feel that I should accept,' replied the Duke. 'At the same time I do appreciate your nice thought.'[5]

If The Queen had specifically included the Duchess of Windsor in the invitation, he would perhaps have felt otherwise. When, a few weeks later, he was invited to the dedication of new Garter windows in St George's, he refused on the grounds that he would be on the way to the United States at the time. 'Although you did not include Wallis by name in the invitation,' he added, '. . . I presume that you would have expected her to accompany me. You see, after more than thirty years of happy married life, I do not like to attend such occasions alone.'[6] It was a mild rebuke, if a rebuke at all. Much of the bitterness had gone out of the issue since, in June 1967, The Queen had invited the Duchess to accompany her husband to the dedication of a plaque outside Marlborough House in memory of Queen Mary. It was a curious touch of irony that so intimate a family occasion, honouring the woman who had done most to ensure that the Duchess of Windsor should never be accepted as a member of the royal family, should be the occasion at which the Duchess first took her place in their midst. The newspapers were preoccupied above all by the question of whether the Duchess would curtsey to Queen Elizabeth (she did not); for the Duke the significance of the occasion was far more profound. He had not won his wife all that he had wanted for her, but at least the worst of the humiliation was behind them.

At an earlier meeting with The Queen, the Duke had asked if he and his wife might be buried in a private mausoleum in the gardens of Frogmore, the secluded Georgian house near Windsor Castle where he had spent much of his childhood. When, in 1968, he came over for the funeral of the Duchess of Kent, he was struck by the tranquil dignity of the royal burial ground at Frogmore, where since 1928 most deceased members of the royal family except the sovereigns clustered around Queen Victoria's sombre mausoleum. He asked The Queen if he could change his mind and be buried alongside his wife and amidst his relations. Permission was given in August 1970. The burial plot was not to lie vacant for long. Towards the end of the following year a tumour in his throat was found to be malignant. No operation was possible so cobalt therapy was prescribed – that dread treatment that is almost worse than the condition it is supposed to cure. His appearances in public became increasingly rare. On 24 November 1971, he failed to turn up at a dinner where he had been expected until the last moment. 'The poor fellow is dying of cancer of the throat,' wrote a fellow guest. 'He is such a frail little man that, at seventy-five, one would have hoped he could have died by having a stroke or a heart attack. Apparently the cancer is very near the jugular vein, so that he might go at any time or survive painfully for months.'[1]

He survived painfully for six months, knowing that he was dying, patiently accepting all the tedious and degrading rituals that afflict a fatal illness, awaiting his end with courage and determination. Some years earlier the Bishop of Fulham, in whose diocese Paris lay, had told him that changes in the Church of England's legislation meant that, if he wished, he could now be readmitted to communion. The Duke replied politely that he had discussed the matter fully with his wife: 'While we are both of us, at heart, deeply religious, we feel that in the light of all that has passed regarding our position with the Church, we would prefer to leave matters as they stand and not risk any more controversy.'[1] He experienced no deathbed change of heart. If religion was any solace to him as he lay dying, he gave no sign of it. As they had been for nearly forty years, his thoughts were all with the wife who had so filled his life and who would now have to face the future alone.

In May 1972 The Queen visited Paris and wished to pay a last call on her uncle. The Duke insisted on leaving his bed and dressing for the occasion.* He could not be deprived even for a few minutes of the drip that sustained his life, and so an elaborate arrangement was fitted up by which a long tube attached him to the fluid flasks concealed behind a nearby curtain. It was a precarious and ramshackle contrivance, and the doctor was aghast when the Duke insisted on getting up and bowing at his niece's entry. The connection remained in place and Queen and former King chatted cheerfully for a quarter of an hour. After she had left, the Duke asked his doctor, Jean Thin, whether he had been presented. 'When I replied that I had not, he seemed very annoyed. This was the only time I saw him display irritation throughout the whole of his long and difficult illness.' He survived another nine days, then one evening the doctor noticed that the pug, which had scarcely left its master's bed over the past few weeks, had moved away and was lying nearby on the floor. It was 27 May 1972. In the early hours of the following morning the Duke died.[2]

Three days later his body was flown by the RAF to Britain and on 1 June he lay in state in St George's Chapel. There he remained for two days, while sixty thousand mourners filed past the coffin. On the first day the queue waiting to enter the Chapel was said to be more than a mile long. The Duchess of Windsor arrived on the second day, visited the coffin of her husband, and stayed with The Queen at Buckingham Palace. She was shocked, frightened, ill, but at least she was where the Duke would have wished her to be.

At 11.15 a.m. on Monday, 5 June, the funeral service took place at St George's. The Archbishops of Canterbury and York, the

---

* Sydney Johnson, the Bahamian valet who had served the Duke devotedly for more than thirty years, remembered that he was unable to leave his bed on this occasion, but Johnson was not himself present during the interview and the weight of the evidence is against him.

Moderator of the Church of Scotland, and the Dean of Windsor headed the procession of church dignitaries; the royal family were there in force except for the Duke of Gloucester, who was too ill to attend; the King of Norway; Mountbatten; the Prime Minister; and a little band of the Windsors' personal friends. When the Duchess of Windsor appeared in the Choir with The Queen, Lady Avon told Cecil Beaton, 'she seemed very strange . . . did nervous things with her hands and kept talking. "Where do I sit?" "Is this my seat?" "Is this my prayer book?" "What do I do now?" . . . Clarissa said The Queen showed a motherly and nannie like tenderness and kept putting her hand on the Duchess's arm or glove.'[1] The service began with the hymn 'The King of Love my Shepherd is', followed by prayers and the ninetieth psalm, 'For a thousand years in thy sight are but as yesterday'. The most stirring moment came when Garter King of Arms proclaimed the style and titles of the late Duke: Knight of the Garter, of the Thistle, of St Patrick, Knight Grand Cross of a multiplicity of Orders, one-time King Edward VIII of Great Britain, Ireland and the British Dominions beyond the Seas, Emperor of India. To everyone in the congregation this roll-call of heraldic honours must have provided a vivid reminder of how much he had given up; the slim, wasted figure of the widow in black recalled with equal vividness why he had made the sacrifice. And so his coffin was removed to Frogmore where he was interred that afternoon in privacy, under a simple stone on a quiet lawn, awaiting the time, fourteen years later, when the Duchess would lie beside him.

*   *   *

> No! I am not Prince Hamlet, nor was meant to be,
> Am an attendant Lord, one that will do
> To swell a progress, start a scene or two,
> Advise the prince . . .

It was the peculiar tragedy of the Duke of Windsor that he *was* Prince Hamlet and was meant to be Prince Hamlet, but found himself temperamentally disqualified from playing the part. Prufrock's limitations were not his – 'politic, cautious, and meticulous'; his courtiers, indeed, might have said these were the very qualities required by a constitutional monarch in the twentieth century and would happily have traded them for the Duke's restlessness, recklessness and febrile rejection of any kind of discipline. But he could not, or would not meet the demands that the starring role imposed on him. He wrote his own script, made up his own rules, directed his own performance. At his best he could be dazzling in his style and his dexterity; at his worst he was disastrous.

> At times, indeed, almost ridiculous –
> Almost, at times, the Fool.

'Wonderful as the service was, I was not moved by the death of this man who for less than a year had been our King,' wrote Cecil Beaton when he wrote up the events of the day after the Duke of Windsor's funeral. He must have been almost the only person in the congregation to feel no emotion. For most of those present, and for many millions who were not, it was a moment of poignancy; poignancy because of the sense of opportunities lost, of talents wasted, of a heritage thrown away. There was much he could have done; he did so little. And yet he himself would never have seen it in such a light. To his own mind he had done the one all-important thing; he had rejected the stultifying trammels of a career which he detested to secure the greatest of human joys, the total commitment of himself to another being. 'This above all: to thine own self be true,' Polonius/Prufrock had advised; others might say that he had betrayed his people and his patrimony, he knew that he had been faithful to himself.

In those unregenerate days when narrative history was still in vogue, and children were taught of kings or battles rather than economic or demographic trends, it was permissible to attach to monarchs a convenient label which fixed them for ever in the minds of those who studied them. For those of a certain age Ethelred will always be Unready, Edward a Confessor, William a Conqueror, Richard a Lion Heart. How should one describe Edward VIII under such a system? Edward the Unworthy, the unkind might say, yet to do so would beg some fundamental questions, for while it might be argued that he was unworthy of the throne, it has also been maintained that no throne could have been worth the price he was required to pay for it. Edward the Obstinate would not be wholly unfair, for no man could cling more doggedly to a point of view or a line of action, and greet any attempt to move him as fresh reason for sticking to his guns. Edward the Amiable? Certainly, in the original sense of the word, for he was loved by many till the day he died, loved for his charm, his humility, his good will. Edward the Well-meaning? That perhaps most of all, for no monarch can have been more moved by the sufferings of his subjects, or more anxious to relieve them.

The limitations of such nomenclature are at their most obvious in this last example. Edward was indeed well-meaning; yet though no monarch can have been more anxious to relieve the sufferings of his subjects, few can have done less to achieve their aim. Whatever efforts he might make were quickly frustrated by his inability to resist distractions, a superficiality of thought and feeling that ensured he would rarely pursue any objective to the end, and none to the bitter end. His every virtue, and they were many, seems to have been complemented by a corresponding vice – or every vice by a corresponding virtue. He could be quixotically loyal – yet certain old friends he abandoned ruthlessly when the going, for one reason or another, became too difficult. He was notoriously mean – and yet at times he was capable of the most striking generosity. No man is consistent, yet more than most he seems to have been a kaleidoscope of conflicting elements; his character is evanescent, bewildering, rippling and swirling like a mountain stream which is whipped by the wind and broken by the boulders in its path.

Yet one objective he did pursue to the bitter end, one feeling was not superficial, to one ideal he was constant. Whether the Duchess of Windsor was worthy of the devotion which he lavished on her is a question to which no objective answer can be found. What sort of a king he would have made if he had remained a bachelor or had found a more suitable woman to sit beside him on the throne is a problem no more easy to resolve. But the greatness of the sacrifice he made for her, the fortitude with which he battled for her over the thirty-six years of their marriage, the steadfastness of his love until the day he died, are matters which should not be forgotten when any final judgment is essayed of the life and character, if not the reign, of King Edward VIII, later Duke of Windsor.

Nomenclature

The various metamorphoses experienced by members of royal families may cause confusion to those unversed in such questions (and sometimes to the versed as well). A brief note may be of use. The Duke of Windsor bore seven titles in the course of his life, though only four are of significance: Prince Edward, Prince of Wales, King Edward VIII and Duke of Windsor.

When he was born in 1894 his great-grandmother, Queen Victoria, still reigned. His grandfather and his grandmother were Prince and Princess of Wales. His father and mother were Duke and Duchess of York and he himself was styled Prince Edward of York.

On the death of Queen Victoria in 1901 his grandfather succeeded as King Edward VII and the Princess of Wales became Queen Alexandra (referred to as the Queen, a designation reserved for reigning monarchs or the wife of a reigning king). His father and mother briefly became Duke and Duchess of Cornwall as well as of York, during which period he was Prince Edward of Cornwall and York. Later in 1901 the Duke of Cornwall was invested Prince of Wales. Prince Edward then became Prince Edward of Wales; his brothers Princes Albert, Henry and George and his sister Princess Mary being princes and princess of the same house.

King Edward died in 1910. The Prince of Wales succeeded as King George V. His wife, Queen Mary, was from then until January 1936 known as the Queen; Queen Alexandra being always referred to by name. Prince Edward was Duke of Cornwall until 1911 when he was invested Prince of Wales. His brother Prince Albert was created Duke of York in 1920; Prince Henry became Duke of Gloucester in 1928; Prince George Duke of Kent in 1934; while Princess Mary married the 6th Earl of Harewood in 1922 and was created Princess Royal in 1932.

On the death of King George V in January 1936, the Prince of

Wales succeeded as King Edward VIII. His mother was henceforward known as Queen Mary. When he abdicated in December of the same year he was created Duke of Windsor. His brother, the Duke of York, succeeded as King George VI, the Duchess becoming Queen Elizabeth and known as the Queen.

George VI died in 1952 and was succeeded by his daughter, Princess Elizabeth. His widow was henceforward styled Queen Elizabeth or, more popularly, the Queen Mother.

Notes

2¹ James Pope-Hennessy. *Queen Mary*. London, 1959. p191.
3¹ Pope-Hennessy. *Queen Mary*. p222.
3² Kenneth Rose. *King George V*. London, 1983. p23.
3³ Harold Nicolson. *King George V. His Life and Reign*. London, 1952. p10.
4¹ The Duke of Windsor. *A King's Story*. London, 1951. p1.
5¹ 24 June 1894. RA GV AA 12/32.
5² Pope-Hennessy. *Queen Mary*. p299.
5³ RA Z 477/183.
5⁴ RA Z 477/184.
5⁵ *Journals and Letters of Reginald Viscount Esher*. Ed., Maurice V. Brett. Vol 1. London, 1934. p345.
5⁶ Marquis de Breteuil diary. Breteuil papers.
5⁷ RA GV AA 6/457.
6¹ *Hansard*. H of C. 4th Series. Vol 26. 28 June 1894.
6² 17 Feb 1896. RA GV AA 12/43.
6³ *Journals and Letters*. Vol 1, p301.
6⁴ Mabell Countess of Airlie. *Thatched with Gold*. London, 1962. p113.
7¹ 7 Aug 1894. RA GV CC 1/55.

7² 23 Sept and 17 Oct 1895. RA GV AA 6/469 and 470.

7³ RA GV CC 50/288.

7⁴ Duchess to Duke of York. 28 Oct 1896. RA GV CC 5/187.

7⁵ 18 Nov 1897 and 12 Feb 1905. RA DW 3 and 120.

7⁶ Arthur Marder. *Fear God and Dread Nought: the Correspondence of Admiral of the Fleet Lord Fisher of Kilverstone.* Vol I. London, 1952. p286.

8¹ Rose. *George V.* p57.

8² Rose. *George V.* p55.

8³ 1 Aug 1903. RA DW 91.

8⁴ James Lees-Milne. *Harold Nicolson.* Vol II. London, 1981. pp230 and 235.

8⁵ John Gore. *King George V. A Personal Memoir.* London, 1941. p211.

9¹ *Harold Nicolson. Diaries and Letters 1945–1962.* Ed., Nigel Nicolson. London, 1968. p167.

9² Conversation with Lady Laycock.

9³ J. Bryan III and Charles J. V. Murphy. *The Windsor Story.* London, 1979. pxvi.

9⁴ James Pope-Hennessy. *A Lonely Business.* London, 1981. p214.

9⁵ Pope-Hennessy. *Queen Mary.* p391.

9⁶ Windsor. *A King's Story.* p7.

10¹ Windsor. *A King's Story.* pp17–18.

10² *Memoirs of H.R.H. Prince Christopher of Greece.* London, 1938. p164.

10³ E to Queen Mary. 29 Oct 1897. RA GV EE 3.

11¹ Pope-Hennessy. *Queen Mary.* p394.

11² Genevieve Parkhurst. *A King in the Making.* London, 1925. p20.

11³ *Journals and Letters of Reginald Viscount Esher.* Ed., Maurice V. Brett. Vol 2. London, 1934. p53.

11⁴ Elizabeth Peters to Duchess of York. 28 April 1896. RA GV EE 3.

11⁵ Grand Duchess of Mecklenburg-Strelitz to Duchess of York. 10 Nov 1896. RA GV CC 27/70.

12¹ Nicolson. *King George V.* p51.

12² 22 April 1901. RA DW 27.

12³ RA Prince of Wales's diary. 22 Feb 1912.

13¹ W. and L. Townsend. *The Biography of H.R.H. The Prince of Wales.* London, 1929. p43.

13² E to Queen Mary. 18 Aug 1901. RA GV EE 3.

13³ E to Queen Mary. 2 April 1901. RA GV EE 3.

13⁴ Windsor. *A King's Story.* p12.

13⁵ Princess Charles of Denmark to Duchess of York. 3 Feb 1901. RA GV CC 45/229.

13⁶ The Duke of Windsor. *The Crown and the People.* London, 1953. p14.

Notes

14¹ Sir Shane Leslie to the *Sunday Times*. 23 Aug 1959. Copy in RA DW 10266.

14² Pope-Hennessy. *Queen Mary*. p393.

14³ Randolph Churchill. *Lord Derby, 'King of Lancashire'*. London, 1959. p157.

14⁴ Marquis de Breteuil diary. 24 Feb 1912. Breteuil papers.

15¹ 24 Oct 1951. RA DW 8046.

15² Harold Nicolson diary. 20 March 1953. Nicolson papers.

15³ E to Fleur Cowles. 3 Jan 1952. RA DW 8106.

15⁴ Pope-Hennessy. *Queen Mary*. p393.

16¹ 28 Oct 1906. RA GV AA 63/26.

16² 9 Dec 1907. RA GV AA 63/39.

16³ E to Princess of Wales. 27 April 1904. RA GV EE 3.

16⁴ Grand Duchess of Mecklenburg-Strelitz to Princess of Wales. 26 Feb 1906. RA GV CC 32/21.

16⁵ 22 March and 8 April 1906. RA DW 157 and 161.

17¹ Sir A. Lascelles's diary. 28 Oct 1942. Lascelles papers.

17² RA Queen Victoria's diary. 10 May 1898.

17³ *Journals and Letters*. Vol 1, p289.

17⁴ *The Memoirs of the Aga Khan*. London, 1954. p244.

17⁵ Parkhurst. *A King in the Making*. p27.

17⁶ Georgina Battiscombe. *Queen Alexandra*. London, 1969. p40.

17⁷ E to Prince of Wales. 2 April 1902. RA DW 66.

17⁸ Townsend. *Prince of Wales*. pp31–2.

18¹ RA GV CC 60/43.

18² 10 Dec 1936. RA KEVIII Ab. Box 1.

19¹ Nicolson. *King George V*. p14.

20¹ Hansell to Sir Vincent Baddeley. 5 Dec 1906. RA Vic Add F 155.

20² E. Hyde Parker to Hansell. 3 Feb 1907. RA Vic Add F 160.

20³ Duchess of Buccleuch to Princess of Wales. 19 Feb 1907. RA GV CC 47/129.

20⁴ 6 March 1907. RA GV CC 50/843.

20⁵ 16 Dec 1936. RA Vic Add F 201.

20⁶ 5 May 1907. RA DW 187.

21¹ 14 May 1907. RA DW 191.

21² 23 June 1907. RA GV CC 24/84.

21³ 5 Feb 1909. RA GV AA 63/51.

22¹ 27 Oct 1907. RA DW 247.

22² 26 June, 10 July, 26 July 1908. RA GV EE 3.

22³ 23 Feb 1908. RA DW 283.

22⁴ 24 July 1907. RA DW 220.

22⁵ 19 Jan 1908. RA DW 270.

22[6]   17 Jan 1909. RA DW 378.

23[1]   4 Feb 1911. RA GV EE 3.

23[2]   *Journals and Letters.* Vol 2, p305.

23[3]   Prince to Princess of Wales. 4 Aug 1907. RA GV CC 3/238.

23[4]   E to Princess of Wales. 9 May 1909. RA GV EE 3.

23[5]   15 May 1909. RA DW 410.

23[6]   23 May 1909. RA GV EE 3.

24[1]   Stephen King-Hall. *My Naval Life.* London, 1952. p47.

24[2]   E to Princess of Wales. 30 May 1909. RA GV EE 3.

24[3]   E to Princess of Wales. 10 March 1910. RA GV EE 3.

24[4]   Viscount Knutsford. *In Black and White.* London, 1926. p267.

24[5]   Windsor. *A King's Story.* p70.

24[6]   6 Oct 1910. RA DW 563.

25[1]   20 Nov 1910. RA GV EE 3.

25[2]   20 Nov 1910. RA DW 580.

25[3]   E to Queen Mary. 20 Nov 1910. RA GV EE 3.

25[4]   25 June 1910. RA GV CC 25/64.

25[5]   9 June 1910. Davidson papers. Vol XX, 202.

25[6]   Davidson to George V. 15 June 1910; George V to Davidson. 16 June 1910. Davidson papers. Vol XX, 204 and 205.

25[7]   26 June 1910. RA GV CC 47/211.

26[1]   RA Prince of Wales's diary. 7 April 1911.

26[2]   Queen Mary to Grand Duchess of Mecklenburg-Strelitz. 11 June 1911. RA GV CC 25/105.

26[3]   Windsor. *The Crown and the People.* p24.

26[4]   Townsend. *Prince of Wales.* pp56–7.

26[5]   John W. Wheeler-Bennett. *King George VI.* London, 1958. p51.

26[6]   Windsor. *The Crown and the People.* p26.

26[7]   Nicolson. *George V.* p147.

26[8]   John Grigg. *Lloyd George. The People's Champion.* London, 1978. pp303–4.

27[1]   Windsor. *A King's Story.* p79.

27[2]   RA Prince of Wales's diary. 2 July 1911.

27[3]   25 July 1911. RA DW 647.

27[4]   29 July 1911. RA DW 653.

27[5]   Queen Mary to Grand Duchess of Mecklenburg-Strelitz. RA GV CC 25/109.

27[6]   Sir Henry Luke. *Cities and Men.* London, 1953. p208.

27[7]   12 Jan 1914. RA DW 1195.

28[1]   Robert Rhodes James. *Memoirs of a Conservative. J. C. C. Davidson's Memoirs and Papers.* London, 1969. p19.

28[2]   RA Prince of Wales's diary. 29 March 1911.

Notes

28³ George V to E. 6 Oct 1910. RA DW 563.

28⁴ E to George V. 2 June 1913. RA DW 939.

28⁵ cit Hector Bolitho. *Edward VIII*. London, 1937. pp14–15.

29¹ RA Prince of Wales's diary. 4 Sept 1911.

29² RA Prince of Wales's diary. 26 Sept 1911.

29³ 2 Nov 1911. RA GV CC 47/276.

29⁴ 29 Sept 1911. RA DW 698.

30¹ James Lees-Milne. *The Enigmatic Edwardian. The Life of Reginald, 2nd Viscount Esher*. London, 1986. p214.

30² Windsor. *A King's Story*. p59.

30³ 21 June 1908, 13 Jan 1913, 25 Jan 1914. RA DW 319, 921 and 1204.

30⁴ 29 May 1910. RA DW 529.

30⁵ 22 June 1907. RA DW 206.

31¹ RA Prince of Wales's diary. 7 and 12 Sept 1913.

31² George V to E. 19 Jan 1912. RA DW 751.

31³ George V to E. 20 April 1913. RA DW 980.

31⁴ George V to E. 26 April 1913. RA DW 987.

31⁵ RA Prince of Wales's diary. 31 July 1913.

31⁶ E to George V. 13 May 1914. RA DW 1277.

31⁷ Edward Cadogan. *Before the Deluge*. London, 1961. p213.

32¹ Queen Mary to E. 12 May and 2 Nov 1912. RA DW 790 and 881.

32² RA Prince of Wales's diary. 16, 28 Sept 1913.

32³ RA Prince of Wales's diary. 6 Jan 1912.

32⁴ RA Prince of Wales's diary. 10 April 1914.

32⁵ RA Prince of Wales's diary. 25 Dec 1912.

32⁶ E to James Paterson. 25 Dec 1912. RA GV EE 8/24.

32⁷ Hansell to Queen Mary. 16 April 1912. RA GV EE 3.

33¹ Marquis de Breteuil diary. 24 Feb 1912. Breteuil papers.

33² RA Prince of Wales's diary. 4 July and 11 May 1912.

34¹ 21 June 1912. RA GV EE 3.

34² RA Prince of Wales's diary. 1 April 1912.

34³ George V to Marquis de Breteuil. 27 Feb 1912. Breteuil papers.

34⁴ E to George V. 8 April 1912. RA DW 768.

34⁵ E to George V. 7 May 1912. RA DW 788.

34⁶ RA Prince of Wales's diary. 19 May 1912.

34⁷ 22 April 1912. RA DW 779.

34⁸ *Memoirs of the Aga Khan*. p244.

34⁹ George V to Hansell. 10 April 1912. RA GV AA 63/89.

34¹⁰ *The Memoirs of Raymond Poincaré*. Tr., Sir George Arthur. Vol I. London, 1926. pp96–7.

35¹ Marquis de Breteuil diary. Breteuil papers.

35² Pope-Hennessy. *Queen Mary*. p445.

35³   15 Oct 1912. RA DW 867.

35⁴   RA Prince of Wales's diary. 10 Feb 1912.

35⁵   RA Prince of Wales's diary. 4 Sept 1912.

35⁶   RA Prince of Wales's diary. 15 Sept 1912.

35⁷   Churchill. *Derby*. pp156–7.

35⁸   George V to Hansell. 25 Nov 1911. RA GV AA 63/83.

35⁹   Compton Mackenzie. *The Windsor Tapestry*. London, 1938. pp102–7.

36¹   *Journals and Letters of Reginald Viscount Esher*. Ed., Maurice V. Brett.
       Vol 3. London, 1938. p108.

36²   RA Prince of Wales's diary. 5 Oct 1912.

36³   J. Brett Longstaff. *Oxford 1914*. New York, 1965. p186.

36⁴   Lang to Queen Mary. 27 July 1912. RA DW 844.

36⁵   Lord Grantley. *Silver Spoon*. London, 1954. p122.

37¹   RA Prince of Wales's diary. 12 Oct 1912.

37²   RA Prince of Wales's diary. 13 Oct 1912.

37³   Donald McLachlan. *In the Chair. Barrington-Ward of The Times*.
       London, 1971. pp35–6.

37⁴   E to James Paterson. 25 Dec 1912. RA GV EE 8/25.

37⁵   E to George V. 27 Oct 1912. RA DW 878.

37⁶   E to George V. 21 Feb 1913. RA DW 950.

38¹   RA Prince of Wales's diary. 24 Oct 1913.

38²   RA Prince of Wales's diary. 8 Nov 1913.

38³   C. L. Sulzberger. *An Age of Mediocrity*. New York, 1973. p147.

38⁴   RA Prince of Wales's diary. 10 Nov 1912.

38⁵   RA Prince of Wales's diary. 9 Nov 1912.

38⁶   RA Prince of Wales's diary. 23 Nov 1912.

38⁷   14 Jan and 25 Jan 1912. RA DW 749 and 753.

38⁸   RA Prince of Wales's diary. 4 Dec 1911.

39¹   RA Prince of Wales's diary. 6 Nov 1912.

39²   RA Prince of Wales's diary. 2 Feb 1914.

39³   E to Godfrey Thomas. 11 March 1914. Thomas papers.

39⁴   6 Feb 1914. RA DW 1214.

39⁵   RA Prince of Wales's diary. 28 May 1913.

39⁶   *The Crawford Papers*. Ed., John Vincent. Manchester, 1984. p319.

39⁷   RA Prince of Wales's diary. 16–21 June 1913.

40¹   RA Prince of Wales's diary. 15 Oct 1912.

40²   E to Queen Mary. 25 Jan 1913. RA GV EE 3.

40³   RA Prince of Wales's diary. 26 Jan 1914.

40⁴   RA Prince of Wales's diary. 18 Oct 1913.

40⁵   RA DW Box 4.

41¹   RA Prince of Wales's diary. 9 Jan 1914.

41²   RA DW Box 4.

41[3]   RA Prince of Wales's diary. 19 Nov 1912, 13 Feb 1914.

41[4]   Queen Mary to Grand Duchess of Mecklenburg-Strelitz. 15 Oct 1912. cit Pope-Hennessy. *Queen Mary.* p446.

41[5]   *The Times.* 18 Nov 1914.

41[6]   *Journals and Letters.* Vol 3, p105.

41[7]   RA Prince of Wales's diary. 19 Sept 1912.

41[8]   RA Prince of Wales's diary. 15 Dec 1913, 22 Jan, 29 April 1914.

42[1]   RA Prince of Wales's diary. 29 April 1914.

42[2]   The Duke of Windsor. *A Family Album.* London, 1960. p48.

42[3]   Windsor. *A Family Album.* p48.

42[4]   *The Diaries of Sir Robert Bruce Lockhart.* Ed., Kenneth Young. Vol 2. London, 1980. p43.

42[5]   RA Prince of Wales's diary. 27 March, 5, 6 April 1913.

42[6]   15 April 1913. RA GV CC 45/415.

42[7]   Pope-Hennessy. *Queen Mary.* p445.

42[8]   21 Feb 1913. RA GV CC 26/44.

43[1]   Prince Alexander of Teck to Queen Mary. 6 Sept 1913. RA GV CC 53/397.

43[2]   RA Prince of Wales's diary. 23 Aug 1913.

43[3]   Windsor. *A King's Story.* p100.

43[4]   RA Prince of Wales's diary. 31 Aug 1913.

43[5]   Bolitho. *Edward VIII.* p45.

43[6]   *Daisy Princess of Pless. By Herself.* London, 1929. p221.

43[7]   Katherine Villiers. *Memoirs of a Maid of Honour.* London, 1931. pp59–60.

43[8]   RA Prince of Wales's diary. 15 May 1911.

43[9]   Princess Viktoria Luise. *The Kaiser's Daughter.* London, 1977. p48.

44[1]   Princess Alice of Teck to Queen Mary. 18 Sept 1913. RA GV CC 53/399.

44[2]   RA Prince of Wales's diary. 7 June 1914.

44[3]   Godfrey Thomas diary. Thomas papers.

44[4]   E to James Paterson. 4 April 1913. RA GV EE 8/29.

44[5]   RA Prince of Wales's diary. 17 April 1913.

44[6]   RA Prince of Wales's diary. 22 March 1914.

45[1]   RA Prince of Wales's diary. 22 June 1912.

45[2]   RA Prince of Wales's diary. 13 March, 16 July, 9 May 1914.

45[3]   *The Memoirs of Raymond Poincaré.* Tr., Sir George Arthur. Vol II. London, 1928. p64.

45[4]   6 July 1913. RA DW 1036.

45[5]   E to Queen Mary. 17 June 1914. RA GV EE 3.

46[1]   RA GV CC 47/376.

46[2]   RA Prince of Wales's diary. 18 Sept 1913, 10 Dec 1911, 9 Sept 1913.

46³   1 Feb 1913. RA DW 933.

46⁴   22 June 1914. Thomas papers.

46⁵   RA Prince of Wales's diary. 13 April 1912.

46⁶   23 March and 1 April 1914. RA DW 1248 and 1256.

46⁷   26 March 1914. RA GV EE 3.

47¹   RA Prince of Wales's diary. 3 March 1913, 7 July 1914.

47²   John Evelyn Wrench. *Geoffrey Dawson and Our Times*. London, 1955. pp102–3.

47³   RA Prince of Wales's diary. 9 July 1914.

47⁴   Baroness Orczy. *Links in the Chain of Life*. London, 1947. p132.

47⁵   RA Prince of Wales's diary. 10 July 1914.

47⁶   RA Prince of Wales's diary. 2 July 1914.

47⁷   RA Prince of Wales's diary. 9 July 1914.

47⁸   E to Erskine. 30 June 1914. RA GV EE 8/91.

48¹   12 May 1938. RA DW 3623.

48²   E to Godfrey Thomas. 28 July 1914. Thomas papers.

48³   E to Erskine. 2 Aug 1914. RA GV EE 8/94.

49¹   RA Prince of Wales's diary. 3 Aug 1914.

49²   RA King George V's diary. 4 Aug 1914.

49³   5 Aug 1914. RA GV EE 13/2.

50¹   RA Prince of Wales's diary. 6 Aug 1914.

50²   RA Prince of Wales's diary. 8 Aug 1914.

50³   RA Prince of Wales's diary. 10 Aug 1914.

50⁴   23 Aug 1914. Thomas papers.

50⁵   RA Prince of Wales's diary. 8 Sept 1914.

51¹   16 Sept 1914. RA GV EE 8/56.

51²   9 Oct 1914. RA DW 1386.

51³   RA Prince of Wales's diary. 14 Sept 1914.

51⁴   *Journals and Letters*. Vol 3, p198.

51⁵   Undated. Glenusk papers.

52¹   RA Prince of Wales's diary. 5 Aug 1914.

52²   Peacock to E. 14 Aug 1914. RA DW 1347.

52³   Ponsonby to Benn. 28 Aug 1914. RA GV Q 690/2.

52⁴   17 Dec 1915. RA DW 1752.

52⁵   RA Prince of Wales's diary. 17 Jan 1916.

53¹   Godfrey Thomas diary. Thomas papers.

53²   RA Prince of Wales's diary. 21 Oct 1914.

53³   14 Nov 1914. RA GV Q 705/4.

53⁴   Godfrey Thomas diary. Thomas papers.

53⁵   20 Aug 1914. RA GV EE 8/10.

53⁶   E to Princess Alice of Teck. 11 Sept 1914. RA GV CC 50/1079.

53⁷   E to Godfrey Thomas. 23 Aug 1914. Thomas papers.

53⁸   E to George V. 10 Aug 1914. RA DW 1333.

53⁹   E to W. E. Houston-Boswell. 7 May 1915. RA GV EE 8/112.

54¹   Godfrey Thomas diary. Thomas papers.

54²   15 Nov 1914. RA GV Q 832/215.

54³   5 Feb 1915. Thomas papers.

54⁴   George V to E. 6 Feb 1915. RA DW 1473.

54⁵   RA Prince of Wales's diary. 27 Jan 1915.

54⁶   E to George V. 18 Dec 1914. RA GV EE 9.

55¹   E to George V. 5 March 1915. RA GV EE 9.

55²   25 March 1915. RA DW 1517.

55³   28 Dec 1914. RA DW 1444.

55⁴   RA Prince of Wales's diary. 21 Nov 1914.

55⁵   3 March 1915. RA DW 1501.

55⁶   Frances Donaldson. *Edward VIII.* London, 1974. p116.

55⁷   Sir Shane Leslie to E. 8 Oct 1959. RA DW 10271.

56¹   13–22 Jan 1915. RA GV Q 705/20.

56²   22 Jan 1915. RA GV EE 9.

56³   RA GV CC 47/448.

56⁴   *Editorial. The Memoirs of Colin R. Coote.* London, 1965. p60.

56⁵   RA Prince of Wales's diary. 16 Nov 1914.

56⁶   RA Prince of Wales's diary. 19 Nov 1914.

57¹   Osbert Sitwell. *Laughter in the Next Room.* London, 1949. p81.

57²   E to George V. 7 Jan 1915. RA GV EE 9.

57³   18 March 1915. Coke papers.

57⁴   15 March 1915. Thomas papers.

57⁵   23 June 1915. RA DW 1607.

57⁶   8 Feb 1915. RA DW 1476.

58¹   *A Good Innings. The Private Papers of Viscount Lee of Fareham.* Ed., Alan Clark. London, 1974. pp138–9.

58²   Valentine Williams. *The World of Action.* London, 1938. pp208–9.

58³   Donaldson. *Edward VIII.* p55.

58⁴   Parkhurst. *A King in the Making.* p142.

58⁵   RA Prince of Wales's diary. 22 Dec 1914.

58⁶   RA Prince of Wales's diary. 1 March 1915.

59¹   RA Prince of Wales's diary. 13 March 1915.

59²   RA Prince of Wales's diary. 14 March 1915.

59³   E to Queen Mary. 5 Feb 1915. RA GV EE 3.

59⁴   E to George V. 25 Feb 1915. RA GV EE 9.

59⁵   E to Queen Mary. 7 June 1915. RA GV EE 3.

59⁶   16 June 1915. Thomas papers.

59⁷   E to Queen Mary. 5 Feb 1915. RA GV EE 3.

59⁸   E to George V. 6 Feb 1915. RA GV EE 9.

59[9]   16 June 1915. Thomas papers.

59[10] RA Prince of Wales's diary. 1 June 1915.

59[11] E to Queen Mary. 8 June 1915. RA GV EE 3.

60[1]   16 June 1915. Thomas papers; 19 June 1915. Breteuil papers.

60[2]   *The Memoirs of Lord Chandos*. London, 1962. pp46–7.

60[3]   Kay Halle. *Randolph Churchill*. London, 1971. p137.

60[4]   24 June 1915. Coke papers.

60[5]   RA Prince of Wales's diary. 9 May 1915.

61[1]   18 July 1915. RA GV EE 9.

61[2]   21 July 1915. RA DW 1638.

61[3]   3 March 1915. RA DW 1501.

61[4]   20 March 1915. RA DW 1514.

61[5]   RA Prince of Wales's diary. 8 July 1915.

61[6]   E to George V. 13 July 1915. RA GV EE 9.

61[7]   E to Queen Mary. 7 July 1915. RA GV EE 3.

62[1]   3 Dec 1914. RA GV CC 4/129.

62[2]   18 Dec 1914. RA GV EE 9.

62[3]   25 July 1915. RA DW 1643.

62[4]   Godfrey Thomas diary. Thomas papers.

63[1]   RA Prince of Wales's diary. 18 Aug 1915.

63[2]   20 March 1915. RA DW 1513.

63[3]   RA Prince of Wales's diary. 16 July 1915.

63[4]   E to Lady Coke. 30 May 1915. Coke papers.

63[5]   E to Queen Mary. 23 Oct 1915. RA GV EE 3.

63[6]   E to Queen Mary. 22 Feb 1918. RA GV EE 3.

63[7]   E to Godfrey Thomas. 16 July 1915. Thomas papers.

63[8]   E to George V. 30 April 1916. RA GV EE 9.

64[1]   E to George V. 6 Feb 1915. RA GV EE 9.

64[2]   15 March 1915. Thomas papers.

64[3]   16 March 1916. RA DW Add 1/1.

64[4]   RA Prince of Wales's diary. 1 April 1915.

64[5]   4 Sept 1917. Coke papers.

64[6]   30 March 1916. RA DW 1833.

65[1]   21 and 27 June 1915. RA DW 1599 and 1612.

65[2]   E to Queen Mary. 6 July 1915. RA GV EE 3.

65[3]   E to George V. 10 June 1915. RA GV EE 9.

65[4]   George V to E. 16 July 1915. RA DW 1633.

65[5]   22 Sept 1915. RA GV EE 9.

65[6]   John Jolliffe. *Raymond Asquith. Life and Letters*. London, 1980. p219.

65[7]   RA Prince of Wales's diary. 1 Dec 1915.

66[1]   RA Prince of Wales's diary. 22 Sept 1915.

Notes

66² Cavan to George V. 29 Sept 1915. RA GV Q 832/59; RA Prince of Wales's diary. 29 Sept 1915.

66³ 1 Oct 1915. RA GV EE 9.

66⁴ George V to E. 3 Oct 1915. RA DW 1696.

66⁵ 20 Dec 1915. RA GV EE 9.

67¹ RA Prince of Wales's diary. 2 Oct and 20 Oct 1915.

67² 8 Dec 1915. RA DW 1744.

67³ E to Queen Mary. 10 Oct 1918. RA GV EE 3.

67⁴ E to George V. 11 Dec 1915. RA GV EE 9.

67⁵ Prince Alexander of Teck to Queen Mary. 31 Oct 1915. RA GV CC 53/428.

67⁶ RA Prince of Wales's diary. 28 Oct 1915.

67⁷ 22 Sept 1915. RA GV EE 9.

67⁸ 16 June 1916. Coke papers.

68¹ 12 April 1916. RA DW 1844.

68² 22 Jan 1916. RA DW 1789.

68³ E to Prince Adolphus of Teck. 29 Feb 1916. RA GV CC 50/1222.

68⁴ E to Queen Mary. 18 March 1916. RA GV EE 3.

69¹ 30 March 1916. Coke papers.

69² RA Prince of Wales's diary. 6 March 1916.

69³ Godfrey Thomas diary and Prince Albert to Thomas. 18 March 1916. Thomas papers.

70¹ RA Prince of Wales's diary. 18 March 1916.

70² E to George V. 18 March 1916. RA GV EE 9; E to Capt. W. E. Bailey. 25 March 1916. Glenusk papers.

70³ Geoffrey Serle. *John Monash*. Melbourne, 1982. p262.

70⁴ Field Marshal Lord Birdwood. *Khaki and Gown*. London, 1941. p300; Murray to Stamfordham. 20 March 1916. RA GV O 910/9.

70⁵ Mary Walrond to Queen Mary. 12 June 1916. RA GV CC 47/505.

71¹ 2 April 1916. Thomas papers.

71² RA Prince of Wales's diary. 3 April 1916.

71³ 4 April 1916. RA GV EE 9.

71⁴ 28 March 1916. RA GV O 910/17.

72¹ RA Prince of Wales's diary. 10 April 1916.

72² Ronald Storrs. *Orientations*. London, 1943. p194.

72³ 12 April 1916. RA GV EE 9.

72⁴ 9 May 1916. Salisbury papers.

73¹ 24 April 1916. RA DW 1857.

73² Prince of Wales's diary. 7 May 1916.

73³ Kitchener to George V. RA GV Q 705/19.

73⁴ Sir G. Arthur. *Further Letters from a Man of no Importance*. London, 1932. p43.

73⁵ Nigel Hamilton. *Monty. The Making of a General.* London, 1981. p114.

73⁶ Lord Newton. *Retrospection.* London, 1941. p223.

74¹ RA Prince of Wales's diary. 29 May 1916; E to Capt. W. R. Bailey. 25 May 1916. Glenusk papers.

74² 11 June 1915. RA DW 1578.

74³ 19 May 1918. Coke papers.

74⁴ *Sarah. The Letters and Diaries of a Courtier's Wife.* Ed., Alfred Shaughnessy. London, 1989. p82.

74⁵ Bruce Lockhart. *Diaries.* Vol 2, p689.

75¹ RA Prince of Wales's diary. 3, 7 and 9 June 1917.

75² 27 July 1917. RA GV EE 3.

75³ RA Prince of Wales's diary. 19 Aug 1916.

75⁴ RA Prince of Wales's diary. 19 July 1916.

75⁵ E to Lady Coke. 13 Sept 1916. Coke papers.

76¹ RA Prince of Wales's diary. 1 Sept 1916.

76² 7 Oct 1916. RA DW 1959.

76³ E to Queen Mary. 5 Aug and 15 Oct 1917. RA GV EE 3.

76⁴ E to Lady Coke. 23 June 1917. Coke papers.

76⁵ E to Lady Coke. 18 April 1917. Coke papers.

76⁶ RA Prince of Wales's diary. 13 Oct 1916.

76⁷ RA Prince of Wales's diary. 17 Oct 1916.

77¹ RA Prince of Wales's diary. 19 Nov 1916.

77² E to Capt. W. R. Bailey. 2 Nov 1916. Glenusk papers.

77³ 31 July 1916. RA GV GG 6 Box 3.

77⁴ 4 Sept and 17 July 1917. Coke papers.

77⁵ Stanley Jackson. *The Sassoons.* London, 1968. p194.

77⁶ 20 Sept 1918. RA GV EE 3.

78¹ 7 March 1917. RA GV EE 3.

78² E to George V. 28 June and 7 Dec 1916. RA GV EE 9.

78³ RA Prince of Wales's diary. 9 Dec 1916.

78⁴ E to Queen Mary. 21 July 1917. RA GV EE 3.

78⁵ 24 July 1917. RA GV EE 9.

78⁶ 1 April 1917. RA DW 2043.

79¹ 5 Nov 1918. RA GV EE 9.

79² RA Prince of Wales's diary. 13 March 1917.

79³ 15 Dec 1918. RA GV EE 3.

79⁴ Queen Mary to E. 6 Dec 1918. RA DW 2204.

79⁵ Queen Mary to E. 21 Feb 1915, 26 Jan 1919, 13 Oct 1917. RA DW 1490; RA DW Add 1/42; RA DW 2095.

80¹ Princess Mary to E. 19 Feb 1916. RA DW 1784.

80² E to Queen Mary. 12 Sept 1917. RA GV EE 3.

80³ E to Queen Mary. 27 Jan 1919. RA GV EE 3.

80[4]   Queen Mary to E. 6 Feb 1919. RA DW 2220.

80[5]   George V to E. 22 Jan 1919. RA DW Add 1/40.

80[6]   Stamfordham to George V. 21 Sept 1917. RA GV M 1224A/4.

81[1]   Cavan to George V. 28 Oct 1917. RA GV Q 832/61.

81[2]   10 Nov 1917. Coke papers.

81[3]   E to Queen Mary. 9 Nov 1917. RA GV EE 3.

81[4]   E to Godfrey Thomas. 10 Dec 1917. Thomas papers; and to Queen Mary. 12 Dec 1917. RA GV EE 3.

81[5]   E to George V. 22 Dec 1917. RA GV EE 9.

81[6]   20 June 1918. RA GV EE 9.

81[7]   10 Dec 1917. Coke papers.

82[1]   E to Lady Coke. 10 Nov 1917 and 16 Jan 1918. Coke papers; E to Queen Mary. 25 Jan 1918. RA GV EE 3.

82[2]   26 May 1918. RA GV CC 47/572.

82[3]   Sir James Rennell Rodd. *Social and Diplomatic Memories* (Third Series). London, 1925. pp360–1.

82[4]   4 June 1918. Coke papers.

82[5]   30 May 1918. RA GV EE 9.

82[6]   George V to E. 6 June 1918, and Queen Mary to E. 2 June 1918. RA DW 2146 and 2145.

82[7]   Stamfordham to Lloyd George. 28 May 1918. Beaverbrook papers. Series G 29/2/32.

82[8]   1 June 1918. RA GV EE 3.

83[1]   28 May 1918.

83[2]   Stamfordham to Lloyd George. 28 May 1918. Beaverbrook papers. Series G 29/2/32.

83[3]   25 Oct 1917. RA GV EE 9.

83[4]   E to George V. 28 July 1918. RA GV EE 9.

83[5]   E to Queen Mary. 27 Sept 1918. RA GV EE 3.

83[6]   Stamfordham to E. 2 Oct 1918. RA DW 2186.

84[1]   1 Nov 1918. Piers Legh papers.

84[2]   E to Queen Mary. 17 Oct 1918. RA GV EE 3.

84[3]   E to George V. 21 Oct 1918. RA GV EE 9.

84[4]   RA GV CC 47/611.

84[5]   11 Nov 1918. RA GV EE 3.

84[6]   E to Queen Mary. 17 Oct 1918. RA GV EE 3.

84[7]   E to George V. 18 Dec 1918. RA GV EE 9.

84[8]   30 Dec 1918. RA GV Q 2522/2/151.

85[1]   E to Queen Mary. 25 May 1915. RA GV EE 3.

85[2]   E to George V. 17 Feb 1919. RA GV EE 9.

85[3]   E to George V. 8 Jan 1919. RA GV EE 9.

85[4]   E to Queen Mary. 8 Jan 1919. RA GV EE 3.

86¹   13 Jan 1919. RA GV EE 9.

86²   18 Dec 1918. Piers Legh papers.

86³   8 Feb 1919. RA GV EE 9.

86⁴   14 Dec 1918. RA DW 2207.

87¹   10 Nov 1918. RA DW 2200.

87²   E to Lady Coke. 7 Jan 1918. Coke papers.

87³   *Speeches by H.R.H. The Prince of Wales 1912–1926*. London, 1927. p4.

88¹   27 June 1915. RA DW 1612.

89¹   E to Capt. W. R. Bailey. 25 May 1916. Glenusk papers.

89²   RA Prince of Wales's diary. 21 Feb 1916.

89³   Lees-Milne. *The Enigmatic Edwardian*. p301.

89⁴   RA Prince of Wales's diary. passim.

89⁵   E to Capt. W. R. Bailey. 2 Nov 1916. Glenusk papers.

89⁶   RA Prince of Wales's diary. 5 Jan 1917.

89⁷   RA Prince of Wales's diary. 5 July 1917.

90¹   1 Nov 1918. Piers Legh papers.

90²   RA Prince of Wales's diary. 9 March 1916. 10, 16 Jan 1917.

90³   E to Lady Coke. 26 July 1917. Coke papers.

91¹   E to Lady Coke. 27 May 1917. Coke papers.

91²   Notes on Lady Donaldson's copy of *Edward VIII*. Donaldson papers.

91³   Memorandum by Bruce Ogilvy. Donaldson papers.

91⁴   RA Prince of Wales's diary. 4 May and 20 March 1917.

92¹   RA Prince of Wales's diary. 21 April 1915.

92²   Prince Albert to Bryan Godfrey-Faussett. 23 and 25 Jan 1916. Godfrey-Faussett papers.

92³   16 March 1916. RA DW Add 1/1.

92⁴   RA Prince of Wales's diary. 5, 17, 31 Jan, 1 Feb 1916.

92⁵   RA Prince of Wales's diary. 22 Jan 1917.

93¹   Letter to the author from Lord Derby. 22 Oct 1987.

93²   RA Prince of Wales's diary. 27 May 1917.

93³   Godfrey Thomas diary. Thomas papers.

93⁴   George V to Queen Mary. 17 Aug 1922. RA GV CC 4/225.

93⁵   Lady Cynthia Asquith. *Diaries 1915–1918*. London, 1968. pp416–17.

93⁶   1 Oct 1917. Coke papers.

94¹   4 Sept 1917. RA GV EE 3.

94²   7 Sept 1917. RA DW Add 1/27.

94³   12 Sept 1917. RA GV EE 3.

94⁴   Lady Ednam to Duchess of Sutherland. Undated. Dudley papers.

95¹   Cynthia Asquith. *Diaries*. p421.

95²   Dudley Ward papers.

96¹   3 Feb 1921. Dudley Ward papers.

96² 16 May 1921. Dudley Ward papers.

97¹ Memorandum by Bruce Ogilvy. Donaldson papers.

97² 10 Sept 1923. Dudley Ward papers.

97³ Greville to Cromer. 18 Feb 1921. Cromer papers.

97⁴ Memorandum by Bruce Ogilvy. Donaldson papers.

97⁵ E to Freda Dudley Ward. 17 Oct 1921. Dudley Ward papers.

97⁶ E to Freda Dudley Ward. 7 Jan 1922. Dudley Ward papers.

98¹ E to Freda Dudley Ward. 5 Jan 1923. Dudley Ward papers.

98² Shaughnessy. *Sarah*. p116.

98³ E to Freda Dudley Ward. 27 April 1922. Dudley Ward papers.

98⁴ E to Freda Dudley Ward. 28 Nov 1920. Dudley Ward papers.

98⁵ 9 Oct 1944. RA DW 5619.

98⁶ Princess Mary to E. 27 Oct, 3 Nov 1918. RA DW Add 1/36 and 37.

98⁷ 16 Aug 1919. RA DW Add 1/43.

99¹ 16 May 1920. RA DW Add 1/53.

99² E to Freda Dudley Ward. Undated. Dudley Ward papers.

99³ 18 Oct 1921. Dudley Ward papers.

99⁴ 29 June 1922. RA GV CC 4/213.

99⁵ 13 Aug 1920. RA DW Add 1/59.

100¹ 5 April 1922. Dudley Ward papers.

100² 7 May 1922. Dudley Ward papers.

100³ 7 Aug 1922. Dudley Ward papers.

101¹ 18 July 1923. Dudley Ward papers.

101² 31 Aug 1923. Dudley Ward papers.

101³ 10 Sept 1923. Dudley Ward papers.

102¹ Winston to Clementine Churchill. 22 Oct 1927. Martin Gilbert. *Winston S. Churchill Companion Volume IV*. Part I, p1068; Brian Howard to William Acton. April 1928. *Brian Howard*. Ed., Marie-Jacqueline Lancaster. London, 1968; Aird diary. 5 June 1929. Aird papers.

102² 26 Feb 1922. Dudley Ward papers.

102³ Probably August 1929 or perhaps 1928. Dudley Ward papers.

102⁴ Dudley Ward papers.

102⁵ Ralph G. Martin. *The Woman He Loved*. London, 1974. p132.

103¹ e.g. E to Freda Dudley Ward. 17 Jan 1922. Dudley Ward papers.

103² Memorandum by Wigram of conversation with George V. 3 March 1932. RA GV GG 6 Box 3.

103³ RA King George V's diary. 7 July 1917.

106¹ Windsor. *A King's Story*. p132.

106² Windsor. *A King's Story*. p136.

107¹ Guy Paget. *Life of Frank Freeman, Huntsman*. Leicester, 1948. p24.

107² 6 March 1921. Lloyd George papers. Series F 60/4/14.

107³ Airlie. *Thatched with Gold*. p144.

107⁴ Airlie. *Thatched with Gold.* pp144–5.

107⁵ Walter Bagehot. *The English Constitution.* London, 1867. p79.

108¹ Max Beerbohm. *Works.* London, 1896. p74.

108² 3 Aug 1921. Dudley Ward papers.

108³ 5 Dec 1918. RA GV CC 8/229.

108⁴ 22 Dec 1918. RA DW 2209.

108⁵ Windsor. *A King's Story.* p134.

108⁶ 25 Dec 1919. Thomas papers.

109¹ E to George V. 5 Sept 1920. RA DW 2310.

109² Airlie. *Thatched with Gold.* pp144–5.

109³ E to Queen Mary. 6 Dec 1918. RA GV EE 3.

110¹ E to Queen Mary. 15 Dec 1918. RA GV EE 3.

110² Queen Mary to E. 29 Dec 1918. RA DW 2211.

110³ 19 Feb 1919. RA GV EE 3.

110⁴ E to Queen Mary. 19 Oct 1919. RA GV EE 3.

110⁵ E to Queen Mary. 31 Dec 1921. RA GV EE 3.

111¹ *The Times.* 25 June 1919.

111² E to Freda Dudley Ward. 8, 9, 10 March 1921. Dudley Ward papers.

111³ E to Freda Dudley Ward. 7 June 1921. Dudley Ward papers.

112¹ E to Freda Dudley Ward. 6 July 1921. Dudley Ward papers.

112² 19, 22 July 1919. RA DW 2227 and 2228.

112³ *Lloyd George. A Diary by Frances Stevenson.* Ed., A. J. P. Taylor. London, 1971. p205.

112⁴ *Lloyd George. A Diary.* p194.

113¹ Greville to E. 9 Nov 1919. RA DW 2266.

113² Windsor. *A King's Story.* p213.

113³ *The Times.* 2 May 1919.

113⁴ E to Capt. W. R. Bailey. 17 Jan 1919. Glenusk papers.

114¹ Windsor. *A King's Story.* p132.

114² 13 Jan 1919. RA DW 2216.

115¹ 10 Aug 1919. RA GV EE 3.

116¹ Grigg to Milner. 1 Aug 1919. Edward Grigg papers.

116² Mrs Alfred Shaughnessy diary. 11 Aug 1919. Piers Legh papers.

116³ Diary of Sub-Lt R. D. P. H. Hutchinson. 13 Aug 1919. Hutchinson papers.

116⁴ Windsor. *A King's Story.* p138.

116⁵ 16 Aug 1919. RA DW 2231.

116⁶ 20 Aug 1919. RA GV EE 3.

116⁷ 20 Aug 1919. RA GV EE 3.

116⁸ Robert Laird Bordern. *Memoirs.* Vol II. London, 1938. p988.

117¹ 31 Aug 1919. RA DW 2238.

117² *Speeches.* p15.

117³   16 Nov 1919. RA GV O 1548/264.

117⁴   6 Sept 1919. RA GV EE 3.

117⁵   E to George V. 31 Aug 1919. RA DW 2238.

117⁶   RA GV EE 3.

118¹   23 Sept 1919. RA DW 2243.

118²   Grigg to George V. 8 Sept 1919. RA GV O 1548/140.

118³   Halsey to Stamfordham. 18 Sept 1919. RA GV O 1548/154.

118⁴   Thomas to Queen Mary. 29 Sept 1919. RA GV EE 3.

118⁵   E to George V. 23 Sept 1919. RA DW 2243.

118⁶   Thomas to Queen Mary. 29 Sept 1919. RA GV EE 3.

119¹   E to George V. 23 Sept 1919. RA DW 2243.

119²   3 Sept 1919. RA GV O 1548/6.

119³   *Speeches*. p11.

119⁴   E to George V. 23 Sept 1919. RA DW 2243.

119⁵   20 Sept 1919. RA GV EE 3.

119⁶   George V to E. 27 Sept 1919. RA GV O 1548/165 and 28 Sept 1919. RA DW 2247.

119⁷   *Speeches*. pp18–19.

119⁸   19 Oct 1919. RA GV EE 3.

120¹   E to George V. 6 Oct 1919. RA DW 2250.

120²   E to Queen Mary. 3 Sept 1919. RA GV EE 3.

120³   R. E. Glazebrook to Grigg. 28 Aug 1919. RA GV O 1548/141.

120⁴   12 Oct 1919. RA DW 2253.

120⁵   *Speeches*. pp18–19.

120⁶   E to Queen Mary. 19 Oct 1919. RA GV EE 3.

120⁷   George V to E. 12 Oct 1919. RA DW 2253.

120⁸   E to Edward Grey. 14 Oct 1919. RA GV O 1548/208; cf Grigg to George V. 30 Oct 1919. RA GV O 1548/238.

120⁹   Cromer to Hardinge. 16 Oct 1919. Lloyd George papers. Series F 12/1/49.

121¹   Grigg to George V. 6 Oct 1919. RA GV O 1548/182.

121²   Thomas to Queen Mary. 29 Sept 1919. RA GV EE 3.

121³   Curzon to Stamfordham. 8 July 1919; memorandum by Curzon. 9 July 1919. RA GV O 1548/36 and 37.

121⁴   Lindsay to R. Graham. 20 June 1919. RA GV O 1548/23; Wiseman to Malcolm. 23 June 1919. Lloyd George papers. Series F 89/3/4.

121⁵   Stamfordham to Wiseman. 1 Aug 1919. RA GV O 1548/75.

121⁶   Sub-Lt R. D. P. H. Hutchinson diary. 18 Nov 1919. Hutchinson papers.

121⁷   *New York World*. 19 Nov 1919. cit Donaldson. *Edward VIII*. p73.

122¹   24 Nov 1919. Copy on RA GV O 1548/270.

122²   24 Nov 1919. cit Rose. *George V*. p304.

122³   Sub-Lt R. D. P. H. Hutchinson diary. 18 Nov 1919. Hutchinson papers.

122[4] 25 Dec 1919. Thomas papers.

123[1] Jan 1920. Copy in Thomas papers.

123[2] 3 Jan 1920. Thomas papers.

123[3] *The Leo Amery Diaries*. Ed., John Barnes and David Nicholson. Vol I. London, 1980. p266.

124[1] Lloyd George papers. Series F 39/2/3.

124[2] E to George V. 29 June 1920. RA DW 2291.

124[3] Lloyd George to Stamfordham. 22 Jan 1920. Lloyd George papers. Series F 29/4/2.

124[4] Conversation between Grigg and Kenneth Rose. 1 April 1954. Rose papers; cf *Lloyd George. A Diary*. pp198–9.

124[5] 28 March 1920. RA GV EE 3.

124[6] Donaldson. *Edward VIII*. p78.

124[7] H. H. Asquith. *Letters to a Friend*. Vol I. London, 1933. p122.

124[8] cit Kenneth Rose. *George V*. pp303–4.

125[1] 21 March 1920. Broadlands papers. M 61.

125[2] Edward Grigg diary. 24 March 1920. Grigg papers.

125[3] Everard Cotes. *Down Under With the Prince*. London, 1921. p99.

125[4] Edward Grigg diary. 26 March 1920. Grigg papers.

125[5] Edward Grigg diary. 30 March 1920. Grigg papers.

125[6] Sub-Lt R. D. P. H. Hutchinson diary. 31 March 1920. Hutchinson papers.

126[1] 10 April 1920. RA GV O 1548A/7.

126[2] Amery to Lloyd George. 1 Jan 1920. Lloyd George papers. Series F 39/2/1.

126[3] Grigg to Stamfordham. 25 May 1920. RA GV O 1548A/26.

126[4] Halsey to Stamfordham. 23 April 1920. RA GV O 1548A/15.

126[5] 27 April 1920. RA GV EE 3.

126[6] 9 May 1920. RA DW 2280.

127[1] Edward Grigg diary. 26 April 1920. Grigg papers.

127[2] *Speeches*. p41.

127[3] Edward Grigg diary. 4 May 1920. Grigg papers.

128[1] Munro-Ferguson to George V. 6 May 1920. RA GV P 284/155.

128[2] 3 June 1920. RA GV EE 3.

128[3] Windsor. *A King's Story*. p153.

128[4] Bede Clifford. *Proconsul*. London, 1964. p74.

128[5] 2 June 1920. RA GV O 1548A/28.

129[1] *The Diaries of Lord Louis Mountbatten, 1920–1922*. Ed., Philip Ziegler. London, 1987. pp129 and 130.

129[2] *The Diaries of Lord Louis Mountbatten, 1920–1922*. pp100–1.

129[3] 4 Aug 1920. RA GV EE 3.

129[4] E to Philip Sassoon. 3 Aug 1920. RA GV EE 8/67.

Notes

129⁵ Godfrey Thomas to Queen Mary. 12 Aug 1920. RA GV EE 3.

129⁶ Grigg to George V. 7 Aug 1920. RA GV O 1548A/60.

130¹ Thomas to Alan Lascelles. 9 Dec 1950. RA GVI 42/370.

130² 17 July 1920. RA DW 2296.

130³ Godfrey Thomas to Queen Mary. 24 July 1920. RA GV EE 3.

130⁴ 3 Aug 1920. RA GV EE 8/67.

130⁵ 11 June 1920. RA GV EE 8/65.

130⁶ 5 July 1920. RA GV EE 8/66.

131¹ Lloyd George papers. Series F 29/4/19.

131² *Lloyd George. A Diary*. pp205–6.

131³ E to Philip Sassoon. 9 April 1920. RA GV EE 8/64.

131⁴ 6 June 1920. RA DW Add 1/54.

131⁵ 25 May 1920. RA GV O 1548A/22.

131⁶ 21 July 1920. Lloyd George papers. Series F 39/2/16.

132¹ 23 July 1920. RA DW 2299.

132² 5 Sept 1920. RA DW 2310.

132³ 9 Sept 1920. RA GV EE 8/68.

132⁴ 4 May 1920. RA DW 2277.

132⁵ Mountbatten to Lady Milford Haven. 15 July 1920. Broadlands papers. Vol VIII.

132⁶ 24 June 1920. RA DW 2290.

133¹ Donaldson. *Edward VIII*. p81; cf *Diaries of Lord Louis Mountbatten*. p122; and letter to the author from M. D. de B. Collins Persse.

133² 6 Aug 1920. Cromer papers.

133³ Edward Grigg diary. 18 Aug 1920. Grigg papers.

133⁴ Undated. RA DW 2307.

134¹ *Speeches*. p65.

134² Queen Mary to Lady Mount-Stephen. 29 Sept 1920. cit Pope-Hennessy. *Queen Mary*. p516.

134³ Mountbatten to Lady Milford Haven. 30 Nov 1920. Broadlands papers. M 61.

134⁴ 7 Dec 1920. Lloyd George papers. Series F 29/5/8.

134⁵ E to Freda Dudley Ward. 3 Sept 1921. Dudley Ward papers.

135¹ E to Freda Dudley Ward. 18 Oct 1921. Dudley Ward papers.

135² *Lloyd George. A Diary*. p222.

135³ e.g. Willingdon to George V. 16 July 1921. RA GV P 1532/19.

135⁴ P. N. Furbank. *E. M. Forster. A Life*. London, 1978. pp100–1.

135⁵ S. D. Waley. *Edwin Montagu*. Bombay, 1964. p227.

135⁶ Montagu to Lloyd George. 26 Oct 1920. Lloyd George papers. Series F 40/3/27.

136¹ 8 Sept 1921. RA GV EE 3.

136² E to Freda Dudley Ward. 15 Sept 1921. Dudley Ward papers.

136³   1 Sept 1921. Thomas papers.
136⁴   24 Sept 1921. Cromer papers.
136⁵   Stamfordham to Cromer. 11 Aug 1921. Cromer papers.
136⁶   8 Nov 1921. Dudley Ward papers.
136⁷   E to Queen Mary. 24 Nov 1921. RA GV EE 3.
137¹   Windsor. *A King's Story*. p164.
137²   Stamfordham to Cromer. 11 Aug 1921. Cromer papers.
137³   Cromer to Wigram. 26 Nov 1921. RA GV GG 6.
137⁴   Donaldson. *Edward VIII*. p96.
137⁵   5 Feb 1922. RA DW 2383.
137⁶   *Diaries of Lord Louis Mountbatten*. p239.
137⁷   E to Freda Dudley Ward. 5 Jan 1922. Dudley Ward papers.
137⁸   *Diaries of Lord Louis Mountbatten*. pp189–90.
137⁹   E to Freda Dudley Ward. 11 Dec 1921. Dudley Ward papers.
138¹   E to Freda Dudley Ward. 25 Feb 1922. Dudley Ward papers.
138²   *Life of General Lord Rawlinson. From his Journals and Letters*. Ed.,
       Major-General Sir Frederick Maurice. London, 1928. p301.
138³   11 Dec 1921. Dudley Ward papers.
138⁴   Halsey to Lascelles. 1 March 1922. Lascelles papers. 3/5/6.
138⁵   E to George V. 16 Dec 1921. RA DW 2380.
138⁶   *Diaries of Lord Louis Mountbatten*. p263.
139¹   6 March 1922. Dudley Ward papers.
139²   Piers Legh to Lord Newton. 19 March 1922. Legh papers.
139³   E to Freda Dudley Ward. 11 March 1922. Dudley Ward papers; and to
       Queen Mary. 31 Dec 1921. RA GV EE 3.
139⁴   E to George V. 16 Dec 1921. RA DW 2380.
139⁵   Piers Legh to Lord Newton. 2 Feb 1922. Legh papers.
139⁶   E to Freda Dudley Ward. 16 Dec 1921. Dudley Ward papers.
140¹   E to Reading. 28 Dec 1921. Copy in Waley. *Montagu*. pp263–6; cf E to
       George V. 16 Dec 1921. RA DW 2380.
140²   22 Dec 1921. Dudley Ward papers.
140³   Reading to E. 9 Jan 1922. RA POW PS Tours India 1921–2.
140⁴   Reading to Montagu. 16 Feb 1922. IO EUR E 238/4/4.
140⁵   Surgeon-Commander Newport to Cromer. 26 Feb 1922. Cromer papers.
140⁶   Birdwood. *Khaki and Gown*. p368.
140⁷   E to Freda Dudley Ward. 23 March 1922. Dudley Ward papers.
141¹   E and Godfrey Thomas to Queen Mary. 13 Feb 1922. RA GV EE 3.
141²   Cromer to Wigram. 25 Dec 1921. Cromer papers.
141³   Legh to Lord Newton. 29 Dec 1921 and 18 Jan 1922. Legh papers.
141⁴   E to Freda Dudley Ward. 2 Dec 1921 and 6 Jan 1922. Dudley Ward
       papers.
141⁵   21 Dec 1921. RA DW 2383.

Notes

141[6] Stamfordham to Cromer. 13 Dec 1921. RA GV 31539.

141[7] Cromer to Stamfordham. 6 Jan 1922. RA GV 31539.

142[1] 14 Oct 1921. Cromer papers.

142[2] E to Freda Dudley Ward. 23 Jan 1922. Dudley Ward papers.

142[3] E to Freda Dudley Ward. 6 Feb 1922. Dudley Ward papers.

142[4] E to Freda Dudley Ward. 4 June 1922. Dudley Ward papers.

143[1] 5 March 1922. RA GV EE 3.

143[2] Halsey to Lascelles. 1 March 1922. Lascelles papers. 3/5/6.

143[3] Windsor. *Family Album*. p92.

143[4] 15 Sept 1922. Metcalfe papers.

143[5] 24 Nov 1921. IO EUR E 238/3/33.

143[6] 25 Nov 1921. Cromer papers.

143[7] 22 Nov 1921. Dudley Ward papers.

144[1] 16 Feb 1922. IO EUR E 316/2/8.

144[2] Reading to Montagu. 23 Feb 1922. IO EUR E 238/4/5.

144[3] E to Freda Dudley Ward. 16 Feb 1922. Dudley Ward papers.

144[4] Sir Almeric Fitzroy. *Memoirs*. Vol II. London, 1926. p780.

144[5] Viscount Peel to Reading. 6 April 1922. IO EUR E 238/5/2.

144[6] 2 April 1922. RA DW 2436.

145[1] Eliot to Curzon. 1 May 1922. IO MSS EUR F 112/224a.

145[2] Eliot to Curzon. 23 May 1922. IO MSS EUR F 112/224a.

145[3] 20 April 1922. Dudley Ward papers.

145[4] E to Queen Mary. 16 April 1922. RA GV EE 3.

145[5] 22 April 1922. RA DW 2444.

145[6] E to Queen Mary. 16 April 1922. RA GV EE 3.

145[7] Eliot to Curzon. 23 May 1922. IO MSS EUR F 112/224a.

146[1] 13 April 1922. Dudley Ward papers.

146[2] Thomas to Queen Mary. 22 April 1922. RA GV EE 3.

146[3] Eliot to Curzon. 23 May 1922. IO MSS EUR F 112/224a.

146[4] Eliot to George V. 27 April 1922. RA GV P 510/23.

146[5] Eliot to Curzon. 1 May 1922. IO MSS EUR F 112/224a.

146[6] Eliot to Curzon. 1 May 1922. IO MSS EUR F 112/224a.

147[1] Eliot to Curzon. 23 May 1922. IO MSS EUR F 112/224a.

147[2] Legh to Lord Newton. 20 April 1922. Legh papers.

147[3] 13 July 1922. Cromer papers.

148[1] *Speeches*. p169.

148[2] 6 Sept 1923. *Ernest Hemingway. Selected Letters*. Ed., Carlos Baker. New York, 1981. p92.

148[3] Bolitho. *Edward VIII*. p174.

149[1] 15 Sept 1923. Dudley Ward papers.

149[2] 25 Sept 1923. RA DW 2484.

149[3] Thomas to Ronald Waterhouse. 28 Sept 1923. Kenneth Rose papers.

149⁴ E to Queen Mary. 20 Sept 1923. RA GV EE 3.
149⁵ 5 Nov 1923. RA DW 2485.
149⁶ E to George V. 3 July 1924. RA DW 2499.
149⁷ 20 Aug 1924. RA GV CC 4/244.
149⁸ 3 Oct 1924. Thomas papers.
149⁹ Memorandum by Bruce Ogilvy. Donaldson papers.
150¹ 17 Oct 1924. RA GV O 1965/47.
150² Geddes to Curzon. 12 Feb 1922. IO MSS EUR F 112/224a.
150³ 28 Aug 1924. Thomas papers.
150⁴ George V to Queen Mary. 26 Aug 1924. RA GV CC 4/247.
151¹ Copy on RA GV O 1965/46.
151² 1 Dec 1924, sent to Thomas by Ronald Waterhouse. Kenneth Rose papers.
151³ Howard to Stamfordham. 28 Oct 1924. RA GV O 1965/54.
151⁴ Thomas to Waterhouse. 16 Dec 1924. Kenneth Rose papers.
152¹ 1 Sept 1924. Thomas papers.
152² Lascelles to Legh. 24 Sept 1924. Lascelles papers. 3/1/11.
152³ 3 Oct 1924. Thomas papers.
152⁴ Stamfordham to Howard. 15 Oct 1924. RA GV O 1965/44.
153¹ Solbert to Thomas. 8 Oct 1924. Thomas papers.
153² E to George V. 20 Sept 1924. RA DW 2503.
153³ Lascelles to Legh. 21 and 24 Sept 1924. Lascelles papers. 3/1/10 and 11.
153⁴ 18 Oct 1924. RA GV EE 3.
153⁵ Stamfordham to Howard. 15 Oct 1924. RA GV O 1965/44.
153⁶ 30 Sept 1924. RA DW 2504.
153⁷ Lascelles to Legh. 29 Sept 1924. Lascelles papers. 3/1/12.
154¹ 3 Oct 1924. Thomas papers.
154² Lascelles to Legh. 10 Oct 1924. Lascelles papers. 3/1/12.
154³ Jeffrey Williams. *Byng of Vimy*. London, 1983. pp296–7.
154⁴ 18 Oct 1924. Lascelles papers. 3/1/12.
154⁵ RA GV O 1965/59.
154⁶ Notes on Lady Donaldson's copy of *Edward VIII*. Donaldson papers.
155¹ Lascelles to Legh. 24 Sept 1924. Lascelles papers. 3/1/11.
155² Fisher to Stamfordham. 4 Dec 1924. RA GV O 1965/65.
155³ Howard to Stamfordham. 28 Oct 1924. RA GV O 1965/54.
155⁴ Wrench. *Dawson*. p233.
156¹ 30 Jan 1925. RA GV CC 53/501.
156² Ralph Deakin. *Southward Ho!* London, 1925. p6.
156³ Halsey to Wigram. 3 April 1925. RA GV 37430.
156⁴ G. Ward-Price. *With the Prince to West Africa*. London, 1925. p43.
157¹ G. Ward-Price. *With the Prince to West Africa*. p143; G. Ward-Price. *Extra-special Correspondent*. London, 1957. p175.

157[2] Halsey to Lascelles. 22 April 1925. Lascelles papers. 3/5/8.

157[3] G. Ward-Price. *Through South Africa with the Prince*. London, 1926. p60.

157[4] Clifford. *Proconsul*. p136.

157[5] Thomas to Queen Mary. 16 May 1925. RA GV EE 3.

157[6] 10 May 1925. RA GV EE 3.

158[1] 18 June 1925. Lascelles papers.

158[2] Ward-Price. *Through South Africa with the Prince*. pp131–2.

158[3] E to Queen Mary. 26 May 1925. RA GV EE 3.

158[4] Thomas to Ronald Waterhouse. 6 Aug 1925. Kenneth Rose papers.

158[5] E to Lascelles. 18 June 1925. Lascelles papers. 2/1.

158[6] E to Queen Mary. 6 and 11 April 1925. RA GV EE 3.

159[1] Clifford. *Proconsul*. p140.

159[2] Deakin. *Southward Ho!* p83.

159[3] 29 June 1925. RA GV EE 3.

159[4] North to Lascelles. 24 May 1925. Lascelles papers. 3/5/12.

159[5] 2 July 1925. Millicent Howard papers.

159[6] Thomas Boydell. *My Luck Was In*. Pretoria, 1948. p317.

159[7] Piers to Sarah Legh. 31 May 1925. Shaughnessy. *Sarah*. p136.

159[8] 4 June 1925. RA GV FF 3/1.

159[9] Boydell. *My Luck Was In*. p326.

159[10] Athlone to Queen Mary. 31 July 1925. RA GV CC 53/514.

160[1] 8 Aug 1925. RA GV GG 6 Box 2.

160[2] Athlone to Queen Mary. 31 July 1925. RA GV CC 53/514.

160[3] Thomas to Wigram. 8 Aug 1925. RA GV GG 6 Box 2.

160[4] 3 June 1925. Metcalfe papers.

160[5] Legh to Lascelles. 6 May 1925. Lascelles papers. 3/5/11.

160[6] 14 July 1925. RA DW 2526.

160[7] Halsey to Wigram. 17 Aug 1925. RA GV GG 6 Box 2.

161[1] 17 Aug 1925. RA GV EE 3.

161[2] Windsor. *A King's Story*. p209.

161[3] 1 Sept 1925. RA GV EE 3.

161[4] 30 Aug 1925. Thomas papers.

161[5] 1 Sept 1925. RA GV EE 3.

162[1] Halsey to Wigram. 1 Sept 1925. RA GV GG 6 Box 2.

162[2] Bryan and Murphy. *Windsor Story*. p49.

163[1] Lascelles diary. 29 Nov 1920. Lascelles papers.

163[2] 5 March 1943. Thomas papers.

163[3] Monica Baldwin's diary. 7 Oct 1937. Donaldson papers.

163[4] Helen Hardinge. *Loyal to Three Kings*. London, 1967. p32.

163[5] John Aird diary. 17 July 1929. Aird papers.

164[1] Bryan and Murphy. *Windsor Story*. p47.

164²   10 July 1922. Dudley Ward papers.

164³   Rosebery to Stamfordham. 9 Sept 1919. RA GV J 1366/8.

164⁴   E to Revelstoke. 28 June 1923. Baring papers. DEP 201/18.

164⁵   *Crawford Papers*. p437.

164⁶   John Aird diary. 26 June 1929. Aird papers.

164⁷   John Aird diary. 17 July 1929. Aird papers.

164⁸   *The Diaries of Sir Robert Bruce Lockhart*. Ed., Kenneth Young. Vol 1. London, 1973. p65.

164⁹   8 Aug 1922. Dudley Ward papers.

165¹   Kenneth Harris. *Kenneth Harris talking to . . .* London, 1971. p126.

165²   The Duke of Sutherland. *Looking Back*. London, 1957. p89.

165³   William Teeling. *Corridors of Frustration*. London, 1970. p18.

165⁴   John Aird diary. 7 May 1929. Aird papers.

165⁵   18 Aug 1926. RA DW 2547.

165⁶   5 Aug 1922. Dudley Ward papers.

165⁷   2 Aug 1922. RA DW 2467.

166¹   18 Nov 1920. cit Sarah Bradford. *George VI*. London, 1989. p126.

166²   John Aird diary. 8 April 1929. Aird papers.

166³   Queen Mary to George V. 8 May 1929. RA GV CC 8/335.

166⁴   19 Sept 1922. Lascelles papers. 2/1.

167¹   John Aird diary. 30 April 1929. Aird papers.

167²   John Aird diary. 15 April 1929. Aird papers.

167³   John Aird diary. 25 May 1929. Aird papers.

167⁴   Undated. Dudley Ward papers.

167⁵   Duff Cooper. *Old Men Forget*. London, 1953. p138.

167⁶   *The Diary of Beatrice Webb*. Ed., Norman and Jeanne Mackenzie. Vol IV. London, 1985. pp222–3.

167⁷   Captain Alastair Mackintosh. *No Alibi*. London, 1961. p62.

168¹   15 April 1927. Thomas papers.

168²   Rose. *George V*. p390.

168³   Patrick Howarth. *George VI*. London, 1987. pp36–7.

169¹   28 Sept 1920. Thomas papers.

169²   13 Aug 1920. RA DW Add 1/59.

169³   23 Dec 1922. Dudley Ward papers.

169⁴   27 Dec 1922. Dudley Ward papers.

169⁵   Stamfordham to Thomas. 28 Sept 1920. Thomas papers.

169⁶   E to Thomas. Undated, probably 1927. Thomas papers; Windsor. *Family Album*. pp42 and 93.

170¹   Rhodes James. *Memoirs of a Conservative*. p107.

170²   Stamfordham to Thomas. 28 Sept 1920. Thomas papers.

170³   E to Thomas. 28 Dec 1923. Thomas papers.

170⁴   28 Aug 1928. RA GV CC 4/289.

Notes

170⁵ E to Philip Sassoon. 9 Sept 1920. RA GV EE 8/68.

170⁶ Airlie. *Thatched with Gold.* pp144–5.

170⁷ Thomas Jones. *Whitehall Diary.* Ed., Keith Middlemas.Vol II. London, 1969. pp162–3.

170⁸ Queen Mary to Cromer. 6, 7 and 8 July 1924. Cromer papers.

171¹ 23 Nov 1921. Dudley Ward papers.

171² 28 Feb 1922. RA GV EE 3.

171³ 5 Jan 1922. RA DW 2392.

171⁴ 21 July 1920. RA DW Add 1/57.

171⁵ 26 April 1923. RA GV AA 61/156.

171⁶ 4 Oct 1922. RA GV CC 11/29.

171⁷ E to Freda Dudley Ward. 16 May 1921. Dudley Ward papers.

172¹ Rose. *George V.* p311.

172² 16 Jan 1923. RA GV EE 3.

172³ Philip Ziegler. *Diana Cooper.* London, 1981. pp174–5.

172⁴ E to George V. 21 Aug 1923. RA DW 2481.

172⁵ 13 Jan 1925. RA DW Add 1/76.

172⁶ 2 Oct 1925. RA DW Add 1/79.

172⁷ 28 April 1926. Legh papers.

173¹ Beaverbrook papers. Series G 25/13.

173² Eliot to Curzon. 1 May 1922. IO MSS EUR F 112/224a.

173³ Horace Rumbold to Stamfordham. 17 June 1927. RA GV P 591/67.

173⁴ Stanton B. Leeds. *Cards the Windsors Hold.* Philadelphia, 1957. pp92–3.

173⁵ Airlie, *Thatched with Gold.* p166.

173⁶ Athlone to Queen Mary. 22 Oct 1928. RA GV CC 53/574; cf Princess Alice, Countess of Athlone. *For my Grandchildren.* London, 1966. p187.

173⁷ 20 Feb 1924. Broadlands papers. S 395.

173⁸ 3 Oct 1924. Thomas papers.

173⁹ Athlone to Queen Mary. 31 July 1925. RA GV CC 53/514.

174¹ 12 Sept 1925. RA GV CC 53/517.

174² 28 Sept 1928. Dudley Ward papers.

174³ Beaverbrook papers. Series G 25/13.

174⁴ 15 Sept 1922. Metcalfe papers.

175¹ Wigram to Rawlinson. 3 April 1923. RA GV N 2555/12.

175² RA King George V's diary. 6 Nov 1924.

175³ 18 June 1925. Lascelles papers. 2/1.

175⁴ Wigram to Birdwood. 5 July 1922. RA GV N 2556/14.

175⁵ The Duke of Beaufort. *Memoirs.* London, 1981. p58.

175⁶ *Speeches.* p309.

176¹ Memorandum by Bruce Ogilvy. Donaldson papers.

176² 25 Aug 1926. Metcalfe papers.
176³ Paget to E. 1 Nov 1951. RA DW 8051.
176⁴ *Life of Frank Freeman.* pp24–5.
176⁵ Wigram to Birdwood. 3 Feb 1926. RA GV N 2556/41.
176⁶ 6 April 1923. Dudley Ward papers.
176⁷ 6 April 1924. Thomas papers.
177¹ 16 March 1924. RA GV AA 38/66.
177² 19 March 1924. RA DW 2494.
177³ *Speeches.* p119.
177⁴ John Aird diary. 14 June 1929. Aird papers.
177⁵ William Pearson-Rogers. 'The Flying Princes'. Unpublished typescript. p125.
177⁶ Lascelles papers. 2/1.
178¹ John Aird diary. 24 July 1931. Aird papers.
178² Bolitho. *Edward VIII.* p222.
178³ E to Freda Dudley Ward. Undated. Dudley Ward papers.
178⁴ Pearson-Rogers. 'Flying Princes'. p75.
178⁵ 28 Aug 1922. RA DW 2469.
178⁶ 20 April 1926. Legh papers.
178⁷ Bruce Lockhart. *Diaries.* Vol 2, p110.
178⁸ *Speeches.* p191.
179¹ *Crawford Papers.* p535.
179² *Crawford Papers.* p535.
179³ *A Good Innings.* pp300–1.
179⁴ *Crawford Papers.* p536.
179⁵ Kenneth Clark. *Another Part of the Wood.* London, 1974. pp225–6.
179⁶ Thomas to George Allen. March 1937. *Wallis and Edward. The Intimate Correspondence, 1931–1937, of the Duke and Duchess of Windsor.* Ed., Michael Bloch. London, 1987 (Penguin edition). p298.
181¹ *Speeches.* pp30–1.
181² 6 Jan 1921. RA GV EE 3.
181³ 14 Oct 1921. RA DW 2346.
182¹ *Further Letters.* p100.
182² Pope-Hennessy. *Queen Mary.* p536.
182³ 11 April 1924. Thomas papers.
183¹ 27 May 1923. RA GV EE 3.
183² Robert Rhodes James. *Victor Cazalet.* London, 1976. p110.
183³ Memorandum by Bruce Ogilvy. Donaldson papers.
183⁴ *Life With Lloyd George. The Diary of A. J. Sylvester.* Ed., Colin Cross. London, 1970. p55.
183⁵ Robert Low Orr. *Lord Guthrie. A Memoir.* London, 1923. p319.
183⁶ E to Queen Mary. Undated. RA GV EE 3.

Notes

183[7]   Gregory Blaxland. *J. H. Thomas. A Life for Unity*. London, 1964. p170.

183[8]   Ward-Price. *Extra-special Correspondent*. pp184–5.

184[1]   E to Queen Mary. 4 Aug 1925 and late 1925. RA GV EE 3; E to George V. 30 April 1926. RA DW 2545.

184[2]   Nourah Waterhouse. *Private and Official*. London, 1942. p274.

184[3]   Keith Middlemas and John Barnes. *Baldwin*. London, 1969. p977.

184[4]   Windsor. *A King's Story*. pp218–19.

184[5]   Stamfordham to E. 11 May 1926. RA DW 2544.

184[6]   28 Aug 1926. Metcalfe papers.

184[7]   E to Baldwin. 8 May 1926. Baldwin papers. 176/2.

184[8]   *Whitehall Diary*. p44.

185[1]   W. C. Bridgeman to E. 22 June 1926. RA DW 2546.

185[2]   Windsor. *A King's Story*. pp227–8.

185[3]   31 Jan 1929. Baldwin papers. 177/45.

185[4]   Curtis-Bennett to Eustace Percy. 3 Feb 1929. Baldwin papers. 177/52.

186[1]   Londonderry to Baldwin. 1 Feb 1929. Baldwin papers. 177/48.

186[2]   *Memoirs*. p165.

186[3]   Boydell. *My Luck Was In*. p324.

187[1]   8 Aug 1927. Dudley Ward papers.

187[2]   3 Aug 1927. RA DW 2560.

187[3]   9 Aug 1927. Thomas papers.

187[4]   Lascelles to Thomas. 25 Aug 1927. Thomas papers.

187[5]   Lascelles to Stamfordham. 2 Sept 1927. RA GV J 2123/17.

187[6]   Lascelles to Legh. 21 Aug 1927. Lascelles papers. 3/2/7.

187[7]   12 Aug 1927. Dudley Ward papers.

187[8]   John Aird diary. 12 Oct 1930. Aird papers.

188[1]   Lascelles to Legh. 9 Aug 1927. Lascelles papers. 3/2/4.

188[2]   11 Aug 1927. RA GV EE 3.

188[3]   9 Aug 1927. Thomas papers.

188[4]   Baldwin to George V. 24 Aug 1927. cit H. Montgomery Hyde. *Baldwin. The Unexpected Prime Minister*. London, 1973. pp283–4.

188[5]   28 Aug 1927. Lascelles papers. 3/2/9.

189[1]   16 June 1928. Grigg papers.

189[2]   *Leo Amery Diaries*. p538.

189[3]   16 June 1928. Grigg papers.

190[1]   Lady Grigg's diary. 28 Sept 1928. Grigg papers.

190[2]   19 Sept 1928. Dudley Ward papers.

190[3]   Isak Dinesen. *Letters from Africa*. London, 1981. pp362, 377, 387 and 395–6.

190[4]   5 Oct 1928. RA GV P 2053/7.

190[5]   Lady Grigg's diary. 10 Oct 1928. Grigg papers.

191[1]   *Letters from Africa*. p387.

191²   Lady Grigg's diary. 12 Oct and 30 Sept 1928, 26 Feb 1930. Grigg papers.

191³   28 Sept 1928. Dudley Ward papers.

191⁴   E to George V. 11 Oct 1928. RA DW 2587.

191⁵   Lascelles to Thomas. 10 Nov 1928. Thomas papers.

192¹   Patrick Chalmers. *Sport and Travel in East Africa*. London, 1934. pp64 and 74.

192²   Lascelles to Thomas. 19 Oct 1928. Lascelles papers. 3/3/13.

192³   19 Oct 1928. Dudley Ward papers.

192⁴   Lascelles to Thomas. 19 Oct 1928. Lascelles papers. 3/3/13.

192⁵   Baldwin papers. 177/36.

192⁶   17 Nov 1928. Lascelles papers. 7/1/2.

192⁷   RA KEVIII Ab. Box 2.

193¹   6 Dec 1928. RA DW Add 1/91.

193²   6 Dec 1928. RA DW 2602.

193³   Lascelles to Legh. 15 Oct 1928. Lascelles papers. 3/3/13.

193⁴   Lascelles to Legh. 30 Oct 1928. Lascelles papers. 3/3/16.

194¹   Lascelles papers. 3/9/4 p2.

194²   30 Dec 1928. Lascelles papers. 3/6/1.

194³   13 Jan 1929. Lascelles papers. 3/6/3.

194⁴   15 Jan 1929. Lascelles papers. 3/6/4.

194⁵   Feb 1929. Thomas papers.

195¹   Stamfordham to Thomas. 23 Feb 1929. Thomas papers.

196¹   Bryan and Murphy. *Windsor Story*. p545.

196²   Memorandum by Stamfordham. 12 Oct 1929. RA GV M 2229/38.

196³   *Diaries*. Vol 1, p110.

197¹   Gloria Vanderbilt and Thelma Lady Furness. *Double Exposure*. London, 1959. p262.

197²   Princess Alice, Duchess of Gloucester. *Memoirs*. London, 1983. p75.

197³   Lady Grigg's diary. 3 March 1930. Grigg papers.

197⁴   15 April 1930. Grigg papers.

197⁵   Lady Grigg's diary. 9 March 1930. Grigg papers.

197⁶   31 March 1930. Dudley Ward papers.

197⁷   8 Sept 1928. RA KEVIII Ab. Box 4.

197⁸   Lee. *A Good Innings*. p289.

197⁹   Monica Baldwin's diary. 7 Oct 1937. Donaldson papers.

198¹   Basil Dean. *Mind's Eye*. London, 1973. pp167–8.

198²   13 Jan 1933. RA DW 2677.

198³   Memoranda by Wigram and Halsey. 3 and 4 March 1932. RA KEVIII Ab. Box 4.

199¹   John Aird diary. 17 Jan 1934. Aird papers.

199²   Archibald Clark-Kerr to E. 5 Nov 1932. RA DW 2669.

Notes

199³   Middlemas and Barnes. *Baldwin.* p976.

199⁴   Leo Amery diary. 5 July 1937. Amery papers.

199⁵   Templewood papers. 210.

199⁶   Airlie. *Thatched with Gold.* p197.

199⁷   John Aird diary. 13 Oct 1935. Aird papers.

200¹   E to Queen Mary. 6 Sept 1935. RA GV EE 3.

200²   Undated, probably June/July 1929. Dudley Ward papers.

201¹   Undated, probably August 1929. Dudley Ward papers.

201²   16 Jan 1930. RA DW Add 1/93.

201³   4 Feb 1930. RA GV FF 3/1.

201⁴   E to Queen Mary. 6 March 1930. RA GV EE 3.

201⁵   John Aird diary. 24 Aug 1932. Aird papers.

201⁶   19 Aug 1933. RA GV EE 3.

201⁷   Memorandum by Bruce Ogilvy. Donaldson papers.

201⁸   10 Feb 1930. RA DW Add 1/100.

202¹   19 Sept 1934. Thomas papers.

202²   John Aird diary. 29 Nov 1934. Aird papers.

202³   Diana Cooper. *The Light of Common Day.* London, 1959. p161.

202⁴   Windsor. *A King's Story.* p235.

203¹   *Diaries.* Vol 1, p328.

203²   Vanderbilt and Furness. *Double Exposure.* p281.

203³   Charles Chaplin. *My Autobiography.* London, 1964. p392.

203⁴   E to J. M. Gow. 15 Feb 1960. RA DW 10328.

204¹   Conversation with Alfred Amos.

204²   Clark. *Another Part of the Wood.* p214.

204³   *Harold Nicolson. Diaries and Letters 1930–1939.* Ed., Nigel Nicolson. London, 1966. pp263–4.

204⁴   *Diaries.* Vol 1, p346.

204⁵   Arthur Rubinstein. *My Many Years.* London, 1980. pp219–22.

205¹   *Diaries.* Vol 1, p65.

205²   18 Jan 1923. RA DW Add 1/72.

205³   *Diaries and Letters 1930–1939.* p232.

205⁴   Duff Cooper diary. Jan 1936. Duff Cooper papers.

205⁵   George V to E. 21 Aug 1935. RA DW 2725.

206¹   Rose. *George V.* p391.

206²   Bruce Lockhart. *Diaries.* Vol 1, p263.

206³   Crown Prince Olav of Norway to E. 17 Dec 1935. RA DW 2732.

207¹   Walford Selby. *Diplomatic Twilight.* London, 1953. p42.

207²   G. E. R. Gedye. *Fallen Bastions.* London, 1939. pp172–4.

207³   Viktoria Luise. *The Kaiser's Daughter.* p188.

207⁴   *Documents on German Foreign Policy.* Series C. Vol IV. London, 1963. pp48–50.

208[1] 14 June 1935. RA KEVIII Ab. Box 4.

208[2] *Diaries*. Vol 1, p321.

208[3] Bingham to Roosevelt. 24 Dec 1935. *Franklin D. Roosevelt and Foreign Affairs*. Ed., Edgar B. Nixon. Vol III. Harvard, 1969. p142.

208[4] *Documents on German Foreign Policy*. Series C. Vol IV, pp1016–17.

209[1] John Aird diary. 31 May 1934. Aird papers.

209[2] *The Times*. 12 June 1935.

209[3] Wigram to George V. 12 June 1935. RA KEVIII Ab. Box 1.

209[4] Cabinet conclusions of 19 June 1935. Copy on RA GV M 2476/4.

209[5] *Documents on German Foreign Policy*. Series C. Vol IV, pp330–1.

209[6] Prince Henry XXIII of Reuss to E. 12 June 1935. RA DW 2714.

210[1] RA GV M 2476/10.

210[2] *News Chronicle*. 14 June 1935.

210[3] Beaverbrook papers. Series G 23/13.

210[4] Sir Alfred Munnings. *The Second Burst*. London, 1951. pp149–50.

211[1] Charles Higham. *Wallis*. London, 1988. pp108–9.

211[2] 14 Jan 1931. RA GV EE 3.

211[3] John Aird diary. 20 and 27 Jan 1931. Aird papers.

212[1] RA GV CC 48/1/44.

212[2] NA 033 4120 Prince of Wales 37 and 26.

212[3] NA 033 4120 Prince of Wales 42 and 33½.

212[4] NA 033 4120 Prince of Wales 50.

212[5] NA 033 4120 Prince of Wales 48.

213[1] NA 033 4120 Prince of Wales 47.

213[2] NA 033 4120 Prince of Wales 43.

213[3] John Aird diary. 21 and 14 March 1931. Aird papers.

213[4] E to George V. 25 March 1931. RA DW 2646.

213[5] Ronald Lindsay to John Simon. 13 Sept 1934. Copy in RA GV M 2434/32.

214[1] Michael Bloch. 'Philip Guedalla Defends the Duke'. *History Today*. Dec 1975. pp832–44.

214[2] E to George V. 12 Jan 1933. RA DW 2676.

214[3] 4 Sept 1931. RA DW Add 1/107.

214[4] Ramsay MacDonald to George V. 21 Sept 1931. RA GV K 2330(2)/107.

215[1] Robert Rhodes James. *Anthony Eden*. London, 1986. p133.

215[2] *The Times*. 19 March 1932. cf Martin Gilbert. *Winston S. Churchill. Companion Volume V*. Part III, p394.

215[3] Harold Nicolson diary. 13 Jan 1936. Nicolson papers.

215[4] Bingham to Roosevelt. 23 April 1934. *Franklin D. Roosevelt and Foreign Affairs*. Vol II, p79.

215[5] David Kirkwood. *My Life of Revolt*. London, 1935. pp257–60.

Notes

216¹ Margaret Brasnett. *Voluntary Social Action*. London, 1969. pp56 and 70.

216² 18 Jan 1933. RA GV EE 3.

216³ Windsor. *A King's Story*. p248.

216⁴ Donaldson. *Edward VIII*. p134.

217¹ 27 Jan 1935. RA DW 2669.

217² Wigram to Loraine. RA GV P 1659/42.

217³ Letter to the author from Lady Laycock.

217⁴ Thomas Jones. *A Diary with Letters*. Oxford, 1954. p65.

218¹ John Aird diary. 20 May 1932. Aird papers.

218² E to Queen Mary. 15 Nov 1932. RA GV EE 3.

218³ *Crawford Papers*. p553.

218⁴ John Aird diary. 22 May and 19 Dec 1935. Aird papers.

219¹ Bruce Lockhart. *Diaries*. Vol 2, p503.

219² *Lloyd George. A Diary*. p274.

219³ John Aird diary. 7 May 1935. Aird papers.

219⁴ Anthony Masters. *Inside Marbled Halls*. London, 1979. p97.

219⁵ John Aird diary. 21 March 1935. Aird papers.

220¹ Herbert Hensley Henson. *Retrospect of an Unimportant Life*. Vol II. Oxford, 1943. p358.

220² Undated draft. July 1935. Thomas papers.

221¹ Memo by Halsey. 10 Jan 1936. RA KEVIII Ab. Box 4.

221² Thomas to Wigram. 13 Feb 1935. RA KEVIII Ab. Box 4.

222¹ Lascelles to Thomas. 5 March 1945. Thomas papers.

222² 19 Jan 1931. Dudley Ward papers.

222³ *Diaries*. Vol 1, p185.

223¹ Vanderbilt and Furness. *Double Exposure*. p261.

223² *Double Exposure*. pp272–3.

223³ John Aird diary. 28 April 1931. Aird papers.

223⁴ Bruce Lockhart. *Diaries*. Vol 1, p190.

223⁵ *Chips. The Diaries of Sir Henry Channon*. Ed., Robert Rhodes James. London, 1967. p50.

224¹ *Wallis and Edward*. p3.

224² The Duchess of Windsor. *The Heart Has Its Reasons*. London, 1956 (references to Sphere edition of 1985). p6.

225¹ Hugo Vickers. *Cecil Beaton*. London, 1985. p195.

225² Cleveland Amory. *Who Killed Society?* New York, 1960. p237.

225³ Thomas Dugdale's Abdication diary. Written by Nancy Dugdale. Dugdale papers.

227¹ Memo by Mountbatten dated 1 Dec 1969. Broadlands papers. S 395.

227² *Wallis and Edward*. p35.

227³ Harold Nicolson diary. 2 Jan 1938. Nicolson papers.

227⁴   *Wallis and Edward.* p42.
227⁵   *Wallis and Edward.* p87.
227⁶   *Double Exposure.* p291.
228¹   *Double Exposure.* pp297–8.
228²   *The Heart Has Its Reasons.* pp85–6.
229¹   9 Oct 1944. RA DW 5619.
229²   John Aird diary. 9 April 1934. Aird papers.
229³   John Aird diary. 14 April 1934. Aird papers.
229⁴   Interview with Mr Alfred Amos.
229⁵   Memo by Mountbatten dated 1 Dec 1969. Broadlands papers. S 395.
229⁶   *Wallis and Edward.* p115.
230¹   John Aird diary. 1 and 5 Aug 1934. Aird papers.
230²   John Aird diary. 13 Aug 1934. Aird papers.
230³   John Aird diary. 2 Sept 1934. Aird papers.
231¹   cit Geoffrey Bocca. *She Might Have Been Queen.* London, 1955. p53.
231²   John Aird diary. 21 Sept 1934. Aird papers.
231³   19 Sept 1934. Thomas papers.
231⁴   Memorandum by Wigram. 12 April 1935. RA KEVIII Ab. Box 4;
        Cromer to Wigram. 26 April 1935. RA KEVIII Ab. Box 4.
231⁵   *Memoirs.* p162.
231⁶   John Aird diary. 27 Nov 1934. Aird papers.
231⁷   Rose. *King George V.* p392.
231⁸   Memo by Wigram. 12 April 1935. RA KEVIII Ab. Box 4.
231⁹   Halsey to Wigram. 12 Jan 1935. RA KEVIII Ab. Box 4.
232¹   Andrew Lyell. 'Skiing at Kitzbuhel'. *Angus Account.* June 1988.
232²   Memo by Bruce Ogilvy. Donaldson papers.
232³   Selby. *Diplomatic Twilight.* p42.
232⁴   Memo by Wigram. 12 April 1935. RA KEVIII Ab. Box 4.
232⁵   Halsey and Thomas to Wigram. 14 and 12 April 1935. RA KEVIII Ab.
        Box 4.
232⁶   John Aird diary. 5 April 1935. Aird papers.
232⁷   22 April 1935. Thomas papers.
233¹   Halsey to Thomas. 10 Jan 1935. Thomas papers.
233²   John Aird diary. 15 May 1935. Aird papers.
233³   Memo by Wigram. 11 May 1935. RA KEVIII Ab. Box 4.
233⁴   John Aird diary. 12 Sept 1934. Aird papers.
233⁵   Lascelles to Philip Moore. 27 Nov 1978. Lascelles papers. 3/9/12.
233⁶   John Aird diary. 14 May 1935. Aird papers.
234¹   John Aird dairy. 18 June 1935. Aird papers.
234²   *Corridors of Frustration.* p56.
234³   *The Reith Diaries.* Ed., Charles Stuart. London, 1975. p187.
234⁴   Amory. *Who Killed Society?* pp238–9.

Notes

234⁵ Memo of mid-1935. Thomas papers.

234⁶ Halsey to Wigram. 18 July 1935. RA KEVIII Ab. Box 4.

234⁷ RA George V's diary. 19 Aug 1935; George V to E. 21 Aug 1935. RA DW 2725.

234⁸ John Aird diary. 6 Aug 1935. Aird papers.

234⁹ John Aird diary. 18 Aug 1935. Aird papers.

234¹⁰ John Aird diary. 23 Aug 1935. Aird papers.

235¹ John Aird diary. 10 Dec 1935. Aird papers.

235² John Aird diary. 19 Dec 1935. Aird papers.

235³ Thomas to Wigram. 2 Jan 1936. RA KEVIII Ab. Box 4.

235⁴ John Aird diary. 31 Dec 1935. Aird papers.

235⁵ Harold Nicolson diary. 13 Jan 1936. Nicolson papers.

236¹ Cynthia Colville to Queen Mary. 28 March 1937. RA KEVIII Ab. Box 4.

236² Memo on above letter. 31 March 1937. RA KEVIII Ab. Box 4.

236³ Martin. *The Woman He Loved*. p149.

236⁴ Memo by Bruce Ogilvy. Donaldson papers.

237¹ Conversation with Alfred Amos.

237² Victor Cazalet diary. Early April 1936. Cazalet papers.

238¹ Conversation with Alan Fisher.

238² John Aird diary. 25 May 1935. Aird papers.

238³ *Wallis and Edward*. pp125 and 162.

238⁴ *Diaries and Letters of Marie Belloc Lowndes*. Ed., Susan Lowndes. London, 1971. pp145–6.

238⁵ Halsey to Wigram. 18 July 1935. RA KEVIII Ab. Box 4.

238⁶ John Aird diary. 25 May 1935. Aird papers.

238⁷ Memo by Bruce Ogilvy. Donaldson papers.

239¹ Duff Cooper diary. 29 Jan 1936. Cooper papers.

240¹ Duff Cooper diary. 16 Jan 1936. Cooper papers.

240² 15 Jan 1936. RA DW 2743.

240³ *Wallis and Edward*. p169.

240⁴ Neville Chamberlain diary. 20 Jan 1936. Chamberlain papers. NC 2/23.

240⁵ *A Diary with Letters*. p63.

241¹ J. G. Lockhart. *Cosmo Gordon Lang*. London, 1949. p391.

241² Memo by Wigram. 20 Jan 1936. RA KEVIII Ab. Box 4.

241³ *Loyal to Three Kings*. p61.

241⁴ Lockhart. *Lang*. p392.

241⁵ *Loyal to Three Kings*. p59.

241⁶ *The Letters of Virginia Woolf*. Ed., Nigel Nicolson. Vol VI. London, 1980. pp10–11.

242¹ John Aird diary. 21 Jan 1936. Aird papers.

242² *Hansard*. 5th Series. Vol 308, 14–15. 23 Jan 1936.

242³ Duke of Connaught to Princess Louise. 23 Jan 1936. RA Vic Add A 17/1590.

242⁴ C. R. Attlee. *As It Happened*. London, 1954. p85.

242⁵ Vickers. *Beaton*. p194.

242⁶ Paul Gore Booth. *With Great Truth and Respect*. London, 1974. p71.

242⁷ Dina Wells Hood. *Working for the Windsors*. London, 1957. p62.

243¹ 19 Feb 1936. RA GV P 1945/94.

243² Jones. *A Diary with Letters*. p163; cf Attlee. *As It Happened*. p85.

243³ *Chips*. p53.

243⁴ Diary of Alan C. Don. 20 Jan 1936. Lambeth Palace Library MS 2864.

243⁵ Lascelles papers. 3/9/4 p3.

243⁶ Alec Hardinge's narrative of the abdication. RA KEVIII Ab. Box 4.

244¹ Martin Gilbert. *Winston Churchill*. Vol V. London, 1976. p809.

244² Pope-Hennessy. *Queen Mary*. p559.

244³ *Chips*. p54.

244⁴ Duff Cooper diary. 29 Jan 1936. Cooper papers.

245¹ Leo Amery diary. 21 Jan 1936. Amery papers.

245² Neville Chamberlain diary. 25 Jan 1936. Chamberlain papers. NC 2123.

245³ Duff Cooper diary. 29 Jan 1936. Cooper papers.

245⁴ 4 Feb 1936. Thomas papers.

246¹ 4 Feb 1936. Thomas papers.

246² *Loyal to Three Kings*. p62.

246³ General Sir Michael Gow. 'King Edward VIII and the Household Troops'. Unpublished article.

246⁴ John Aird diary. 27 Jan 1936. Aird papers.

246⁵ Baroness Ravensdale. *In Many Rhythms*. London, 1953. p191.

246⁶ Harry Gratlidge. *Captain of the Queens*. London, 1956. pp262–3.

247¹ Wigram to Halsey. 16 Jan 1936. Maître Blum papers.

247² Memo by Wigram. 22 Jan 1936. RA KEVIII Ab. Box 4.

247³ Lascelles papers. 3/9/4 p3.

247⁴ Duff Cooper diary. Jan 1936. Cooper papers.

248¹ Duff Cooper diary. Jan 1936. Cooper papers.

248² *Crawford Papers*. p566.

248³ *A Diary with Letters*. p162.

248⁴ Lascelles papers. 3/9/4 p2.

249¹ Lord Birkenhead. *Walter Monckton*. London, 1969. p127.

250¹ Lockhart. *Lang*. p395; Windsor. *A King's Story*. p273.

250² Monica Baldwin's diary. Donaldson papers.

250³ Alan C. Don's diary. 4 March 1936. Lambeth Palace Library MS 2864.

250⁴ NA 841 001 Edward VIII 92.

251¹ Harold Nicolson diaries. 13 June 1936. Nicolson papers.

251² *A King's Story*. pp280–1.

Notes

251³   Pope-Hennessy. *Queen Mary*. p564.

251⁴   *Kenneth Harris talking to . . .* p141.

252¹   *Baltimore News Post.* 9 Dec 1936.

252²   2 Feb 1936. RA DW 2850.

252³   Leo Amery diary. 21 Jan 1936. Amery papers.

252⁴   *A King's Story.* p281.

252⁵   *A King's Story.* p282.

252⁶   Memo by Sir Austin Strutt. Kenneth Rose papers.

252⁷   Jones. *A Diary with Letters.* p189.

253¹   Hardinge. *Loyal to Three Kings.* pp93–4; cf *A King's Story.* p294.

253²   *A King's Story.* pp275–6.

253³   Alan C. Don's diary. 2 April 1936. Lambeth Palace Library MS 2864; Greig to Thomas. Undated. RA DW 2888.

253⁴   *Reith Diaries.* p187.

254¹   *Crawford Papers.* p568.

254²   Conversation with Lord Glendevon.

254³   Zetland to Willingdon. 2 March 1936. IO MSS EUR F 125/139/1.

254⁴   Linlithgow to Zetland. 4 May 1936. IO MSS EUR F 125/139/5.

254⁵   Zetland to Linlithgow. 27 July 1936. IO MSS EUR F 125/139/12 and 13.

254⁶   Zetland to Linlithgow. 27 Oct 1936. IO MSS EUR F 125/139/28.

255¹   Viscount Templewood. *Nine Troubled Years.* London, 1954. p215.

255²   Mountbatten to Wigram. 26 Dec 1936. RA GVI 020/2; cf Philip Ziegler. *Mountbatten.* London, 1985. p98.

255³   Cooper. *Old Men Forget.* p202.

255⁴   17 Jan 1937. RA GV EE 13/5.

256¹   Hardinge narrative. RA KEVIII Ab. Box 4.

256²   John Aird diary. 1 April 1936. Aird papers.

256³   Cicely Wyeth's diary. RA DW Add 3.

256⁴   Alexander to Morshead. 10 March 1942. RA KEVIII Ab. Box 4.

257¹   Notes by Sir Horace Wilson. PRO CAB 127/157.

258¹   John Aird diary. 15 May 1936. Aird papers; Notes by Sir Horace Wilson. PRO CAB 127/157.

258²   Alan Lascelles diary. 17 July 1943. Lascelles papers.

258³   21 July 1936. RA DW 2933.

258⁴   John Aird diary. 10 Sept 1936. Aird papers.

258⁵   *Crawford Papers.* p569.

259¹   Cromer to E. 9 July 1936 and E to Cromer. 14 July 1936. RA DW 2917 and 2921.

259²   Oliver Warner. *Admiral of the Fleet. The Life of Sir Charles Lambe.* London, 1969. p60.

259³   Bruce Ogilvy memorandum. Donaldson papers.

259⁴   11 June 1949. RA DW 7532.

259⁵   Lascelles to Thomas. 5 March 1943. Thomas papers.

260¹   Memo by Wigram. 20 Feb 1936. RA KEVIII Ab. Box 4.

260²   Memo by Hardinge. Jan 1937. RA KEVIII Ab. Box 4.

260³   Conversation with Alfred Amos.

260⁴   Harwood to Cromer. 25 April 1936. Cromer papers.

260⁵   Harwood to E. 20 June 1936. RA DW 2903.

261¹   John Aird diary. 18 Feb 1936. Aird papers.

261²   Memo by Hardinge. RA KEVIII Ab. Box 4.

261³   RA DW 2903.

261⁴   *A King's Story*. p292.

261⁵   York to E. 15 Oct 1936. RA DW 3012.

261⁶   Memorandum by Sir William Fellowes. Fellowes papers.

261⁷   18 Dec 1936. RA KEVIII Box 4.

262¹   Memorandum by Sir William Fellowes. Fellowes papers.

262²   York to Queen Mary. 13 Oct 1936. RA GV CC 12/35.

262³   York to Queen Mary. 4 Oct 1936. RA GV CC 12/33.

262⁴   Queen Maud to Queen Mary. 26 Oct 1936. RA GV CC 45/1060.

262⁵   Alexander to Lascelles. Lascelles papers. 3/9/4 p4.

263¹   Memo by Wigram. 28 March 1939. RA KEVIII Ab. Box 4.

263²   27 Jan 1936. RA Vic Add A 17/1592.

263³   Alan Don's diary. 9 April 1936. Lambeth Palace Library MS 2864.

264¹   John Aird diary. 16 July 1936. Aird papers.

264²   E to Major-General B. N. Sergison-Brooke. 16 July 1936. RA GV DD 2/49.

264³   Simon to E. 16 July 1936. cit Michael Bloch. *The Reign and Abdication of King Edward VIII*. London, 1990. p21.

264⁴   Memo by P. J. Philip. 25 May 1938. RA DW 3640.

264⁵   Philip Guedalla. *The Hundredth Year*. London, 1940. pp242–6.

265¹   *Diaries and Letters*. Vol I, p277.

265²   *Chips*. p74.

265³   *Crawford Papers*. p572.

265⁴   Alan Don's diary. 21 July 1936. Lambeth Palace Library MS 2864.

265⁵   Lockhart. *Lang*. p408.

265⁶   *Loyal to Three Kings*. p96.

265⁷   PRO 691 006/501.

266¹   *The Memoirs of Marshal Mannerheim*. London, 1953. p287.

266²   *A King's Story*. p277.

267¹   *Documents on German Foreign Policy*. Series C. Vol IV, p1023.

267²   *Documents on German Foreign Policy*. Series C. Vol IV, pp1062–4.

268¹   Duff Cooper diary. 19 Nov 1936. Cooper papers.

268²   Michael Bloch. *Operation Willi*. London, 1984. p35.

Notes

268³ PRO FO 371/20734.

268⁴ Sidney Clive to Cromer. 4 Dec 1936. Cromer papers.

268⁵ *Franklin D. Roosevelt and Foreign Affairs*. Vol III, p568.

269¹ Count P. F. Ahlefeldt Laurvig to Wigram. 16 Oct 1937. RA KEVIII Ab. Box 4.

269² Baron Palmstierna to Swedish MFA. 3 Dec 1936. Leifland papers.

269³ *Baffy. The Diaries of Blanche Dugdale*. Ed., N. A. Rose. London, 1973. p34.

269⁴ Osbert Sitwell. *Rat Week*. London, 1986. p36.

269⁵ Vansittart to Wigram. 23 Dec 1936. RA KEVIII Ab. Box 1.

270¹ Fritz Hesse. *Hitler and the English*. London, 1954. pp21–2.

270² *Documents on German Foreign Policy*. Series C. Vol V. London, 1966. pp193–4.

270³ *Documents on German Foreign Policy*. Series C. Vol V, p106.

271¹ *Documents on German Foreign Policy*. Series C. Vol V, pp119–20.

271² *The Ribbentrop Memoirs*. London, 1954. pp67–9.

271³ Rhodes James. *Eden*. p166n.

271⁴ *A King's Story*. p296.

272¹ E to Queen Mary. 4 June 1936. RA GV EE 3; Queen Mary to E. RA DW 2898.

272² *A King's Story*. p277.

272³ *Chips*. p76.

272⁴ *Franklin D. Roosevelt and Foreign Affairs*. Vol III, pp183–4.

272⁵ E to Queen Mary. 20 May 1946. RA GV EE 3.

272⁶ *Old Men Forget*. p202.

273¹ Hardinge. *Loyal to Three Kings*. p83.

273² *A King's Story*. p287.

273³ John Aird diary. 21 May 1936. Aird papers.

273⁴ Memo by Hardinge. Jan 1937. RA KEVIII Ab. Box 4.

273⁵ Martin Scanlon diary. 4 July 1936. Scanlon papers.

274¹ Memo by Wigram. 15 Feb 1936. RA KEVIII Ab. Box 4.

274² *Crawford Papers*. p573.

274³ Cromer to E. 25 June 1936. Cromer papers.

275¹ Bruce Lockhart. *Diaries*. Vol 1, p342.

275² Harold Nicolson diary. 23 Nov 1936. Nicolson papers.

275³ Memo by Hardinge. Jan 1937. RA KEVIII Ab. Box 4.

275⁴ Memo by Wigram. 15 Feb 1936. RA KEVIII Ab. Box 4.

276¹ *Wallis and Edward*. pp177–8.

276² 3 May 1936. Cromer papers.

276³ Bruce Lockhart. *Diaries*. Vol 1, p357.

276⁴ Victor Cazalet diary. 20 Nov 1936.

276⁵ *Reith Diaries*. p195.

276⁶ 9 Feb 1936. *Wallis and Edward*. p181.
277¹ Bryan and Murphy. *The Windsor Story*. p268.
277² Monckton papers. DEP MT 22/55.
277³ *Loyal to Three Kings*. p93.
277⁴ Memo by Wigram. 15 Feb 1936. RA KEVIII Ab. Box 4.
278¹ Memo by Wigram. 21 Feb 1936. RA KEVIII Ab. Box 4.
278² John Aird diary. 27 Feb 1936. Aird papers.
278³ Memo by Thomas. Undated. Thomas papers.
278⁴ Memo by Wigram. 4 Feb 1936. RA KEVIII Ab. Box 4.
278⁵ Birkenhead. *Monckton*. p128.
279¹ Memo by Wigram. 20 Feb 1936. RA KEVIII Ab. Box 4.
279² Memo by Wigram. 24 Feb 1936. RA KEVIII Ab. Box 4.
279³ John Aird diary. 18 Dec 1936. Aird papers.
279⁴ Memo by Wigram. 28 Feb 1936. RA KEVIII Ab. Box 4.
279⁵ Memo by Horace Wilson. PRO CAB 127/157.
280¹ Diana Cooper to Conrad Russell. 17 Feb 1936. Diana Cooper papers.
280² Memo by Wigram. 13 March 1936. RA KEVIII Ab. Box 4.
280³ *Wallis and Edward*. p319.
280⁴ Diana Cooper to Conrad Russell. 17 Feb 1936. Diana Cooper papers.
280⁵ *Rat Week*. p57.
281¹ Thomas Dugdale diary. 9 Dec 1936. Crathorne papers.
281² Duchess of Windsor. *The Heart Has Its Reasons*. p232.
281³ G. M. Young. *Stanley Baldwin*. London, 1952. p233.
281⁴ Nicolson. *Diaries and Letters*. Vol 1, p261.
281⁵ *Reith Diaries*. p188.
281⁶ E to Cromer. 2 July 1936. Cromer papers.
281⁷ Lees-Milne. *Harold Nicolson*. Vol II, pp77–8.
282¹ John Aird diary. 21 May 1936. Aird papers.
282² 3 Aug 1936. RA GV EE 3.
282³ John Aird diary. 28 July 1936. Aird papers.
282⁴ John Aird diary. 24 July 1936. Aird papers.
282⁵ John Aird diary. 30 July 1936. Aird papers.
282⁶ Hardinge. *Loyal to Three Kings*. p106.
282⁷ Lascelles to Thomas. 5 March 1943. Thomas papers.
283¹ 12 Nov 1936. NA 841 001 Edward VIII 89.
283² 2 Nov 1936. NA 841 001 Edward VIII 88.
283³ 22 Sept 1936. NA 841 001 Edward VIII 45.
283⁴ 8 Sept 1936. NA 841 001 Edward VIII 40.
283⁵ Piers Dixon. *Double Diploma*. London, 1968. p30.
284¹ Lord Kinross. *Atatürk. The Rebirth of a Nation*. London, 1964. pp481–2.

Notes

284²   Gordon Waterfield. *Professional Diplomat. Sir Percy Loraine*. London, 1973. pp212–15.

284³   John Aird diary. 8 Sept 1936. Aird papers.

284⁴   Vamik D. Volkan and Norman Itzkowitz. *The Immortal Atatürk*. Chicago, 1984. p327.

284⁵   John Balfour. 'Encounters with the Duke and Duchess of Windsor'. Donaldson papers.

284⁶   Victor Cazalet diary. Sept 1936.

284⁷   John Aird diary. 25 Aug 1936. Aird papers.

285¹   1 Sept 1936. RA KEVIII Ab. Box 1/19A.

286¹   Cooper. *The Light of Common Day*. pp174–90; Ziegler. *Diana Cooper*. p177.

286²   George Messersmith to Secretary of State. 11 and 18 Sept 1936. NA 863 OO/PR/129 and 130.

286³   John Aird diary. 13 Sept 1936. Aird papers.

286⁴   John Aird diary. 10 Sept 1936. Aird papers.

286⁵   Pope-Hennessy. *Queen Mary*. p568.

287¹   Bryan and Murphy. *Windsor Story*. p195.

287²   *A King's Story*. p313.

287³   John Aird diary. 7 Sept 1936. Aird papers.

287⁴   Bloch. *Wallis and Edward*. p219.

287⁵   Notes by second Earl Baldwin of conversation with Lascelles. RA KEVIII Ab. Box 2.

287⁶   Alan Don diary. 24 Sept 1936. Lambeth Palace Library MS 2864.

287⁷   Gilbert. *Churchill*. Vol V, p811.

288¹   Lascelles to Thomas. 5 March 1943. Thomas papers.

288²   26 Sept 1936. RA GV EE 3.

288³   2 Oct 1936. RA DW 2998.

288⁴   29 Sept 1936. RA Vic Add A 17/1615.

288⁵   Duchess of York to Queen Mary. 19 Sept 1936. RA GV CC 12/32.

288⁶   Godfrey Thomas diary. Thomas papers.

289¹   Anne Morrow Lindbergh. *The Flower and the Nettle*. New York, 1966. p50.

289²   John Boyd-Carpenter. *Way of Life*. London, 1980. p44.

289³   Lord Cilcennin to Lascelles. 25 April 1956. Lascelles papers. 3/9/26.

289⁴   PRO CAB 23/16(37).

289⁵   Duke of York to Queen Mary. 6 Nov 1936. RA GV CC 12/38.

290¹   11 Oct 1936. RA GV CC 12/34.

290²   Martin Scanlon diary. 31 May 1936. Scanlon papers.

290³   Thomas Dugdale diary. 7 Dec 1936. Dugdale papers.

290⁴   Monica Baldwin diary. Donaldson papers.

290⁵   4 April 1936. RA GV CC 45/1025.

291[1]   *Thatched with Gold*. p198.
291[2]   Lascelles papers. 3/9/4 p2.
291[3]   *Wallis and Edward*. p219.
291[4]   Gilbert. *Churchill*. Vol V, p811.
291[5]   Birkenhead. *Monckton*. p129.
292[1]   Memo by Goddard. RA KEVIII Ab. Box 4.
292[2]   Neville to Hilda Chamberlain. 17 Oct 1936. Chamberlain papers. NC 18/1/981.
292[3]   Neville Chamberlain diary. 25 Oct 1936. Chamberlain papers. NC 2/23.
292[4]   Memorandum by Sir William Fellowes. Fellowes papers.
293[1]   *Diaries and Letters*. Vol I, p282.
293[2]   Jones. *A Diary with Letters*. p284.
293[3]   Ramsay MacDonald diary. 21 Oct 1936. PRO 30/69 1753.
293[4]   Neville to Hilda Chamberlain. 14 Nov 1936. Chamberlain papers. NC 18/1/985.
293[5]   Memo by Lang. 1 Nov 1936. Lang papers. Vol 318.
293[6]   Memo by Warren Fisher quoted in Neville Chamberlain diary. 26 Oct 1936. Chamberlain papers. NC 2/23.
294[1]   Birkenhead. *Monckton*. p132.
294[2]   Neville to Hilda Chamberlain. 31 Oct 1936. Chamberlain papers. NC 18/1/983.
294[3]   Press summary in Beaverbrook papers. Series G 23/6.
294[4]   Lord Beaverbrook. *The Abdication of King Edward VIII*. Ed., A. J. P. Taylor. London, 1966. p30.
295[1]   A. J. P. Taylor. *Beaverbrook*. London, 1972. pp368–9.
295[2]   3 Nov 1936. RA GV CC 47/1544.
296[1]   Tweedsmuir to Hardinge. 27 Oct 1936. Hardinge papers.
296[2]   Wrench. *Geoffrey Dawson*. pp339–42.
296[3]   27 Oct 1936. Dawson papers.
296[4]   *Reith Diaries*. p189.
296[5]   *Chips*. p78.
297[1]   Templewood. *Nine Troubled Years*. pp218–19.
297[2]   13 Nov 1936. Complete text in *Loyal to Three Kings*. p133.
298[1]   Beaverbrook. *Abdication*. p49.
298[2]   *Loyal to Three Kings*. p136.
298[3]   15 Nov 1936. Baldwin papers. 176/10.
298[4]   Middlemas and Barnes. *Baldwin*. p990.
298[5]   Monckton to E. 18 Nov 1936. Birkenhead. *Monckton*. p136; Beaverbrook to Monckton. 4 Dec 1936. Beaverbrook papers. Series G 23/7.
299[1]   Simon to Baldwin. 8 Dec 1936. Beaverbrook papers. Series G 23/6.

Notes

299²   Neville Chamberlain diary. 13 Nov 1936. Chamberlain papers. NC 2/24.

299³   Ramsay MacDonald diary. 13 Nov 1936. PRO 30/69 1753.

299⁴   PRO CAB 23/86. Cabinet 68(36). 27 Nov 1936.

299⁵   *A King's Story*. pp331–2.

299⁶   *Loyal to Three Kings*. p139.

300¹   Templewood. *Nine Troubled Years*. p219.

300²   *A King's Story*. pp339–40.

300³   Neville Chamberlain diary. 17 Nov 1936. Chamberlain papers. NC 2/24.

300⁴   Templewood papers. IX 7.

300⁵   *A King's Story*. p340.

301¹   Duff Cooper diary. 17 Nov 1936. Cooper papers.

301²   Duff Cooper diary. 19 Nov 1936. Cooper papers.

301³   Memo by Wigram. 17 Nov 1936. RA KEVIII Ab. Box 4.

301⁴   20 Nov 1936. Baldwin papers. 176/12.

301⁵   21 Nov 1936. PRO 30/69 1753.

302¹   20 Nov 1936. RA KEVIII Ab. Box 4.

302²   Rhodes James. *Victor Cazalet*. p186.

302³   *Chips*. pp80–1.

302⁴   Ramsay MacDonald diary. 4 Dec 1936. PRO 30/69 1753.

302⁵   Middlemas and Barnes. *Baldwin*. p997.

302⁶   Lang's notes on abdication. Lang papers. Vol 318.

302⁷   *Diaries and Letters*. Vol I, pp276–7.

303¹   Neville Chamberlain diary. 26 Oct 1936. Chamberlain papers. NC 2/23.

303²   Leo Amery diary. Dec 1936. Amery papers.

303³   Beaverbrook papers. Series G 23/4; Alexander to Morshead. 10 March 1942. RA KEVIII Ab. Box 4.

303⁴   Jowitt to Lascelles. 14 April 1949. RA GVI 42/320.

303⁵   *The Heart Has Its Reasons*. p256.

303⁶   Rhodes James. *Memoirs of a Conservative*. p417.

303⁷   Jones. *A Diary with Letters*. p286.

303⁸   Monica Baldwin's diary. Oct 1937. Donaldson papers; PRO CAB 23/86. Cabinet 68(36).

303⁹   Jones. *A Diary with Letters*. p286.

304¹   Duff Cooper diary. 25 and 27 Nov 1936. Cooper papers.

304²   PRO CAB 23/86. Cabinet 68(36).

304³   Francis Williams. *Nothing so Strange*. London, 1970. p141; cf *Memoirs of a Conservative*. p416.

304⁴   Attlee. *As It Happened*. p86.

304⁵   Williams. *Nothing so Strange*. p141.

304⁶   Middlemas and Barnes. *Baldwin*. p989.

304[7] Neville Chamberlain diary. 25 Nov 1936. Chamberlain papers. NC 2/24.

305[1] Duff Cooper diary. 27 Nov 1936. Cooper papers.

305[2] Ramsay MacDonald diary. 27 Nov 1936. PRO 30/69 1753.

305[3] Middlemas and Barnes. *Baldwin.* p999.

305[4] Zetland to Linlithgow. 27 Nov 1936. Zetland papers. IO MSS EUR F 125/139.

305[5] Windsor. *A King's Story.* p347.

305[6] H. Montgomery Hyde. *Baldwin.* p477.

305[7] PRO CAB 127/155.

306[1] 5 Dec 1936. RA KEVIII Ab. Box 1/19.

306[2] 30 Nov 1936. PRO CAB 127/155.

306[3] 8 Dec 1936. NA 841 001 Edward VIII 95.

306[4] 8 Dec 1936. NA 841 001 Edward VIII 69.

306[5] 30 Nov 1936. PRO CAB 127/155.

306[6] 8 Dec 1936. NA 841 001 Edward VIII 67.

306[7] 8 Dec 1936. NA 841 001 Edward VIII 67.

306[8] 8 Dec 1936. PRO CAB 127/155.

307[1] 30 Nov 1936. PRO CAB 127/155.

307[2] 18 Dec 1936. NA 841 001 Edward VIII 97.

307[3] 2 Dec 1936. PRO CAB 127/155.

307[4] 2 Dec 1936. PRO CAB 127/155.

307[5] The Earl of Longford and Thomas P. O'Neill. *Eamon de Valera.* London, 1970. pp291–4; PRO DO 127/21 108504.

307[6] John Colville. *The Fringes of Power. Downing Street Diaries 1939–1955.* London, 1985. p716.

307[7] *Loyal to Three Kings.* p159.

308[1] *Baffy.* p32.

308[2] Jones. *Diary with Letters.* p289.

308[3] Neville Chamberlain diary. 2 Nov 1936. Chamberlain papers. 2 NC 2/23.

308[4] John S. Peart-Binns. *Blunt.* Queensbury, Yorkshire, 1969 (privately printed). pp153–4.

308[5] Alec Sergeant's notes. Lang papers. Vol 318.

308[6] *A King's Story.* p373.

308[7] *Diary with Letters.* p291.

308[8] cit Kingsley Martin. *The Crown and the Establishment.* London, 1962. p102.

309[1] *Baffy.* p35.

309[2] Martin. *The Crown and the Establishment.* pp108–9.

309[3] Bocca. *She Might Have Been Queen.* pp82–3.

309[4] Wrench. *Dawson.* p349.

Notes

309⁵ cit Duff Hart-Davis. *Peter Fleming*. London, 1974. p196.

310¹ Brownlow diary. 3 Dec 1936. Brownlow papers.

310² Conversation with Alfred Amos.

310³ Brownlow diary. 3 Dec 1936. Brownlow papers.

310⁴ *The Heart Has Its Reasons*. p263.

311¹ Birkenhead. *Monckton*. p142.

311² Edward Peacock's notes on the abdication. Baring Brothers' archives.

311³ Text in *A King's Story*. p397.

312¹ Memo by Horace Wilson. RA KEVIII Ab. Box 2.

312² Neville Chamberlain diary. 7 Dec 1936. Chamberlain papers. NC 2124.

312³ Thomas Dugdale diary. 7 Dec 1936. Crathorne papers.

312⁴ *A King's Story*. p398.

312⁵ Memo by Bertram Ogle. Donaldson papers.

313¹ *Chips*. p96.

313² *Crawford Papers*. p576.

313³ Bloch. *The Reign and Abdication of King Edward VIII*. p.187.

313⁴ Memo by Theodore Goddard. RA KEVIII Ab. Box 4.

313⁵ Thomas Dugdale diary. 9 Dec 1936. Crathorne papers.

313⁶ Copies in Monckton papers. DEP MT 20/29 and in Brownlow papers.

313⁷ Memo by Theodore Goddard. RA KEVIII Ab. Box 4.

313⁸ Horace Wilson to Monckton. 5 Feb 1949. RA KEVIII Ab. Box 1.

313⁹ Beaverbrook papers. Series G 23/3.

314¹ Hardinge to Lascelles. 3 Jan 1949. RA KEVIII Ab. Box 4.

314² 8 Dec 1936. PRO CAB 127/155.

314³ Edward Peacock's notes on the abdication.

314⁴ *Sunday Times*. 24 April 1966.

314⁵ Beaverbrook. *Abdication*. p42.

315¹ Taylor. *Beaverbrook*. pp370–1.

315² Beaverbrook. *Abdication*. p70.

315³ Leo Amery diary. 4 Dec 1936. Amery papers.

315⁴ Memo by Piers Legh. 3 Dec 1936. Legh papers.

315⁵ 10 Dec 1936. NA 841 001 Edward VIII 66.

315⁶ Lady Donaldson's notes on her copy of *Edward VIII*. Donaldson papers.

315⁷ Draft letter from Monckton to Roger Sencourt (removed from final version of 12 July 1957). Monckton papers. DEP MT 27/185.

315⁸ Lord Brownlow's diary. 3 Dec 1936. Brownlow papers.

315⁹ Memo by Piers Legh. 3 Dec 1936. Legh papers.

315¹⁰ Thomas Dugdale diary. 5 Dec 1936. Dugdale papers.

316¹ PRO CAB 70(36) of 4 Dec 1936.

316² Ramsay MacDonald diary. 4 Dec 1936. PRO 30/69 1753.

316³ PRO CAB 70(36) of 4 Dec 1936.

316⁴ Young. *Baldwin*. p242.

316⁵ Duff Cooper diary. 30 Nov 1936. Cooper papers.
316⁶ Belloc Lowndes. *Diaries and Letters.* pp154–5.
317¹ Gilbert. *Churchill.* Vol V, pp814–16.
317² Edward Peacock's notes on the abdication.
317³ Churchill to Boothby. 12 Dec 1936. Chartwell papers. CHAR 2/264 62.
317⁴ Duff Cooper diary. 4 Dec 1936. Cooper papers.
317⁵ 5 Dec 1936. Gilbert. *Churchill.* Vol V, p817.
317⁶ PRO CAB 23/86. Unnumbered meeting of 6 Dec 1936.
317⁷ 5 Dec 1936. RA DW 3045.
317⁸ Memo by Godfrey Thomas. Undated. Thomas papers.
318¹ On this point see Birkenhead. *Monckton.* p145 and Middlemas and Barnes. *Baldwin.* p1010.
318² Neville Chamberlain diary. 5 Dec 1936. Chamberlain papers. NC 2124.
318³ John Charmley. *Duff Cooper.* London, 1986. p96.
318⁴ Memo by Samuel Hoare. 6 Dec 1936. Templewood papers. IX 7.
318⁵ Cosmo Lang's notes on the abdication. Lang papers. Vol 318.
319¹ Birkenhead. *Monckton.* p145.
319² *Chips.* p94.
319³ Middlemas and Barnes. *Baldwin.* pp1007–8.
319⁴ *Chips.* p94.
319⁵ Cottenham to Thomas. 5 Dec 1936. Thomas papers.
319⁶ Cosmo Lang's notes on the abdication. Lang papers. Vol 318.
319⁷ RA KEVIII Ab. Box 5.
319⁸ Leo Amery diary. 10 Dec 1936. Amery papers.
319⁹ 7 Dec 1936. Thomas papers.
320¹ *Life With Lloyd George.* pp158 and 164.
320² Rhodes James. *Memoirs of a Conservative.* p417.
320³ 8 Dec 1936. RA DW 3052.
320⁴ 14 Dec 1936. RA DW 3092.
320⁵ Lord Halifax diary. 8 Sept 1942. Halifax papers. A 7/8.
320⁶ Baldwin to E. 1 June 1937. RA DW 3290.
320⁷ Young. *Baldwin.* p241.
321¹ Jones. *Diary with Letters.* p203.
321² 7 Dec 1936. Baldwin papers. 176/103.
321³ Williams. *Nothing so Strange.* p141.
321⁴ 7 Dec 1936. PRO 30/69 1753.
321⁵ Nicolson. *Diaries and Letters.* Vol 1, pp281–2.
321⁶ NA 841 001 Edward VIII 77.
321⁷ Leo Amery diary. 7 Dec 1936. Amery papers.
321⁸ 8 Dec 1936. Thomas papers.
322¹ Boothby to Godfrey Thomas. 7 Dec 1936. Thomas papers.
322² 7 Dec 1936. Gilbert. *Churchill.* Vol V, p823.

322³   Young. *Baldwin*. p242.
322⁴   Young. *Baldwin*. p242.
322⁵   Edward Peacock's notes on the abdication.
322⁶   George VI's notes on the abdication. RA KEVIII Box 2.
322⁷   Thomas Dugdale diary. 8 Dec 1936. Crathorne papers.
323¹   Memo by Samuel Hoare. 9 Dec 1936. Templewood papers. IX 7.
323²   *A King's Story*. p403.
323³   *A King's Story*. p336.
323⁴   *A King's Story*. p334.
324¹   17 Nov 1936. RA DW 3034.
324²   E to Queen Mary. 20 Nov 1936; Queen Mary to Wigram. 15 July 1938. RA KEVIII Ab. Box 4.
324³   *A King's Story*. p335.
324⁴   23 Nov 1936. RA DW 3035.
325¹   23 Nov 1936. RA DW Add 1/111.
325²   20 Nov 1936. RA KEVIII Ab. Box 4.
325³   25 Nov 1936. Thomas papers.
325⁴   Wheeler-Bennett. *George VI*. p285.
325⁵   Godfrey Thomas diary. 17 Nov 1936. Thomas papers.
326¹   Alexander to Morshead. 10 March 1942. RA KEVIII Ab. Box 4.
326²   Memo by Samuel Hoare. Templewood papers. IX 7.
326³   Michael Bloch. *The Secret File of the Duke of Windsor*. London, 1988. p47.
326⁴   Memo by Wigram. 10 Dec 1936. RA KEVIII Ab. Box 4.
326⁵   Wigram to Monckton. 10 Feb 1937. RA KEVIII Ab. Box 4.
327¹   Birkenhead. *Monckton*. p142; cf Edward Peacock's notes on the abdication.
327²   Draft of 10 March 1937. RA DW Privy Purse Box 3. It is uncertain whether this letter was ever sent.
327³   Alexander to Morshead. 10 March 1942. RA KEVIII Ab. Box 4.
327⁴   Birkenhead. *Monckton*. p143.
328¹   Meeting of 9 Dec 1936. Edward Peacock's notes on the abdication.
328²   Thomas Dugdale diary. 8 Dec 1936. Crathorne papers.
328³   Edward Peacock's notes on the abdication.
328⁴   Memo of 10 Dec 1936. RA KEVIII Ab. Box 4.
328⁵   George VI's notes on the abdication. RA KEVIII Ab. Box 2.
329¹   Edward Peacock's notes on the abdication.
329²   Thomas Dugdale diary. 17 Nov 1936. Crathorne papers.
329³   3 Dec 1936. RA DW 3041.
329⁴   Lancelot Percival quoted in Alan C. Don's diary. 19 Dec 1936. Lambeth Palace Library MS 2864.
329⁵   *A King's Story*. p365.

329⁶ Airlie. *Thatched with Gold*. p200.
329⁷ 11 Dec 1936. Baldwin papers. 176/17.
330¹ Memo by Wigram. 7 Dec 1936. RA KEVIII Ab. Box 4.
330² RA DW 3059.
330³ Edward Peacock's notes on the abdication.
330⁴ 11 Dec 1936. RA DW 3067.
331¹ 8 Dec 1936. PRO CAB 127/155.
331² George VI's notes on the abdication. RA KEVIII Ab. Box 2.
331³ *A King's Story*. p410.
331⁴ Reith to Monckton. 14 Dec 1936. Monckton papers. DEP MT 14/67.
332¹ Birkenhead. *Monckton*. p152.
332² Beaverbrook. *Abdication*. p92.
332³ Cosmo Lang's notes on the abdication. Lang papers. Vol 318.
332⁴ *Loyal to Three Kings*. p174.
332⁵ Ravensdale. *In Many Rhythms.* p201.
332⁶ Michael Thornton. *Royal Feud. The Queen Mother and the Duchess of Windsor*. London, 1985. p342.
332⁷ Leo Amery diary. 28 Dec 1936. Amery papers.
333¹ *Chips*. p100.
333² *Chips*. p103.
333³ 11 Dec 1936. RA DW 3067.
333⁴ George VI's notes on the abdication. RA KEVIII Ab. Box 2.
333⁵ Leo Amery diary. 28 Dec 1936. Amery papers.
333⁶ Conversation with Alfred Amos.
333⁷ Bruce Lockhart. *Diaries*. Vol 1, p362.
334¹ 10 Jan 1937. RA KEVIII Ab. Box 4.
334² Alfred Shaughnessy. *Both Ends of the Candle*. London, 1978. pp44–6.
334³ Lady Donaldson's notes on her copy of *Edward VIII*. Donaldson papers.
334⁴ Fisher to Hoare. 12 Dec 1936. Templewood papers. IX 7.
334⁵ Shaughnessy. *Both Ends of the Candle*. pp44–6.
334⁶ Beaverbrook. *Abdication*. p107.
334⁷ Memo of 9 Sept 1949. Beaverbrook papers. Series G 25.
335¹ RA GV CC 47/1563.
336¹ 18 Feb 1937. RA KEVIII Ab. Box 4.
336² Harold Nicolson diaries. 14 Dec 1936. Nicolson papers.
336³ *Chips*. p102.
337¹ Brownlow to Cromer. Undated. Cromer papers.
337² *Chips*. p101.
337³ Cecil Roberts. *Sunshine and Shadow*. London, 1972. p378.
338¹ 18 Dec 1936. *Wallis and Edward*. p256.
338² Selby to Godfrey Thomas. 15 Dec 1936. Thomas papers.
338³ Cosmo Lang's notes on the abdication. Lang papers. Vol 318.

Notes

338⁴ Lockhart. *Lang*. pp404–5.
338⁵ Alan Don's diary. 15 Dec 1936. Lambeth Palace Library MS 2864.
338⁶ 16 Dec 1936. RA DW 3098.
339¹ 15 Dec 1936. Thomas papers.
339² 23 Dec 1936. Monckton papers. DEP MT 14/100.
339³ George VI to Godfrey Thomas. 19 Dec 1936. Thomas papers.
339⁴ Lang to Wigram. 23 Dec 1936. RA KEVIII Ab. Box 1.
339⁵ Lascelles to Baldwin. 23 Dec 1936. Baldwin papers. 178/315.
340¹ Legh to Thomas. 15 Dec 1936. Thomas papers.
340² Memo of 6 Jan 1937. Baldwin papers. 276/57.
340³ Edward to Alexandra Metcalfe. 1 March 1937. Metcalfe papers.
340⁴ Edward to Alexandra Metcalfe. 7 Feb 1937. Metcalfe papers.
340⁵ Edward to Alexandra Metcalfe. 29 Jan and 7 Feb 1937. Metcalfe papers.
340⁶ 21 May 1937. RA GV CC 12/49.
340⁷ E to Laurence Foley. 6 Dec 1937. RA DW 3531.
341¹ Legh to Queen Mary. 15 Dec 1936. RA KEVIII Ab. Box 4.
341² George VI to Queen Mary. 18 Dec 1936. RA KEVIII Ab. Box 4.
341³ Jones. *Diary with Letters*. p299.
341⁴ Lloyd George papers. Series G 39/1/39.
341⁵ *Life With Lloyd George*. p174.
341⁶ 18 March 1937. Thomas papers.
341⁷ Bloch. 'Philip Guedalla Defends the Duke'. pp839–40.
341⁸ Mensdorff to Queen Mary. 21 Dec 1936. RA KEVIII Ab. Box 4.
342¹ Queen Marie to Queen Mary. 22 Jan 1937. RA GV CC 45/1086.
342² Leo Amery diary. 28 March 1937. Amery papers.
342³ John Aird diary. 18 Feb 1937. Aird papers.
342⁴ Douglas Reed. *Insanity Fair*. London, 1938. p337.
342⁵ Shaughnessy. *Both Ends of the Candle*. p64.
342⁶ Edward to Alexandra Metcalfe. 21 Jan 1937. Metcalfe papers.
342⁷ Edward to Alexandra Metcalfe. 24 Jan 1937. Metcalfe papers.
342⁸ Lambe to E. 28 Jan 1937. RA DW 3145.
342⁹ John Aird diary. 9 Feb 1937. Aird papers.
343¹ Iles Brody. *Gone with the Windsors*. Philadelphia, 1953. p8.
343² Edward to Alexandra Metcalfe. 3 Feb 1937. Metcalfe papers.
343³ John Aird diary. 10 Feb 1937. Aird papers.
343⁴ Roberts. *Sunshine and Shadow*. p379.
343⁵ 27 March 1937. RA DW 3180.
343⁶ 18 April 1937. Aird papers.
343⁷ John Aird diary. 9 Feb 1937. Aird papers.
344¹ 9 Feb 1937. RA KEVIII Ab. Box 2.
344² John Aird diary. 13 Feb 1937. Aird papers.

344³ George VI to Kent. 31 Dec 1936. RA GVI 342; George VI to E. 30 Dec 1936. RA DW 3127.

344⁴ 10 Jan 1937. RA KEVIII Ab. Box 4.

344⁵ Neville to Hilda Chamberlain. 13 Dec 1936. Chamberlain papers. NC 18/1/989.

345¹ PRO TS 22/1/A.

345² Journal of Anthony B. Cox. RA KEVIII Ab. Box 5.

345³ PRO TS 22/1/A.

345⁴ PRO TS 22/1/B and J.

346¹ 19 Feb 1937. RA DW Add 1/113.

346² Edward to Alexandra Metcalfe. 3 Feb 1937. Metcalfe papers.

346³ Letter to the author from General Sir Michael Gow. 30 Sept 1988.

346⁴ 14 March 1937. RA KEVIII Ab. Box 4.

346⁵ 3 April 1937. RA DW 3184.

347¹ 21 Jan 1937. PRO PC 12/163.

347² 6 Feb 1937. *Wallis and Edward.* p277.

347³ All in Thomas papers.

348¹ 17 Jan 1937. RA GV EE 13/5.

349¹ 22 Dec 1936. RA KEVIII Ab. Box 4.

349² Edward to Alexandra Metcalfe. 21 Jan 1937. Metcalfe papers.

349³ Birkenhead. *Monckton.* p164.

349⁴ New York *Sunday News.* 11 Dec 1966.

349⁵ Memo by E for conversation with George VI. Nov 1939. RA DW Add 1/154.

350¹ Chamberlain papers. NC 8/22/2; Memo by Edward Peacock. Undated. Peacock papers.

350² Dixon. *Double Diploma.* p35.

350³ Memo by Wigram. 10 Feb 1937. RA KEVIII Ab. Box 4.

351¹ 11 Feb 1937. RA DW Add 1/112.

351² 21 Feb 1937. RA GV EE 13/7.

351³ 9 March 1937. RA DW Add 1/114.

351⁴ Churchill to Chamberlain. 24 March 1937. Beaverbrook papers. Series G 26.

352¹ Churchill to Chamberlain. 8 April 1937. Chartwell papers. CHAR 2/300 19.

352² Memo by Wigram. 9 April 1937. RA KEVIII Ab. Box 4.

352³ Neville Chamberlain diary. 12 April 1937. Chamberlain papers. NC 2124.

352⁴ 30 April 1937. RA DW Add 1/118.

352⁵ *Wallis and Edward.* p260.

352⁶ Allen to Monckton. 22 Dec 1936. Monckton papers. DEP MT 14/77.

353¹ *Chips.* pp125 and 191.

Notes

353[2]   10 Jan 1937. RA KEVIII Ab. Box 4.

353[3]   25 Jan 1937. RA DW 3144.

353[4]   Duke of Connaught to Princess Louise. 29 March 1937. RA Vic Add A 17/1637.

354[1]   Mountbatten to E. 15 March and 5 May 1937. RA DW 3162 and 3206.

354[2]   Wigram to Lang. 5 April 1937. Lang papers. Vol 318; Monckton to Hardinge. 3 April 1937. RA KEVIII Ab. Box 4.

354[3]   Simon to George VI. 7 April 1937. RA KEVIII Ab. Box 2.

354[4]   Brownlow to E. 15 April 1937. Brownlow papers.

354[5]   10 April 1937. RA KEVIII Ab. Box 4.

355[1]   11 April 1937. RA DW Add 1/116.

355[2]   13 April 1937. RA DW Add 1/117.

355[3]   5 May 1937. RA DW 3206.

355[4]   28 May 1937. RA DW 3271.

356[1]   21 May 1937. RA DW 3238.

356[2]   John Aird diary. 19, 23 and 24 May. Aird papers.

356[3]   PRO FO 954 33/15 and 16.

356[4]   PRO FO 954 33/17 and 18.

356[5]   Memo by Lord Brownlow. Brownlow papers.

356[6]   22 May 1937. Brownlow papers.

356[7]   Conversation between Monckton and Thelma Cazalet. 26 Oct 1937. Cazalet papers.

356[8]   Telegrams of 22 May 1937. Brownlow papers.

357[1]   18 May 1937. RA DW 3222.

357[2]   21 Dec 1937. Birkenhead. *Monckton.* p155.

357[3]   Duke of Connaught to Princess Louise. 21 Feb 1937. RA Vic Add A 17/1632.

357[4]   13 April 1937. RA DW Add 1/117.

357[5]   14 Dec 1937. *Wallis and Edward.* p255.

358[1]   15 Jan 1937. RA KEVIII Ab. Box 1/19C.

358[2]   21 Jan 1937. RA KEVIII Ab. Box 1/19C.

358[3]   24 Jan 1937. RA KEVIII Ab. Box 1/19C.

358[4]   25 Jan 1937. RA KEVIII Ab. Box 1/19C.

358[5]   Wigram to Simon. 11 March 1937. RA KEVIII Ab. Box 1/19C.

358[6]   Simon to Wigram. 23 March 1937. RA KEVIII Ab. Box 1/19C.

358[7]   RA KEVIII Ab. Box 1/19C.

358[8]   22 May 1937. RA KEVIII Ab. Box 1/19C.

358[9]   Memo by Wigram. RA KEVIII Ab. Box 1/19C.

359[1]   4 May 1937. Baldwin papers. 176.

359[2]   Memo by Wigram. RA KEVIII Ab. Box 1/19C.

359[3]   Gwyer to Wigram. 26 May 1937. RA KEVIII Ab. Box 1/19C.

359[4]   Chartwell papers. CHAR 2/300 27.

359⁵   Memo by Hardinge. 26 May 1937. RA KEVIII Ab. Box 1/19C.

359⁶   RA GV EE 13/13.

359⁷   Neville Chamberlain diary. 30 May 1937. Chamberlain papers. NC 2124.

360¹   Birkenhead. *Monckton*. p166.

360²   2 June 1937. RA GV EE 13/14.

360³   26 May 1937. RA DW Add 1/119.

361¹   Undated, probably mid-June 1937. RA DW Add 1/120.

361²   3 July 1937. RA DW Add 1/121.

362¹   13 July 1937. RA DW Add 1/124.

362²   19 Dec 1937. RA DW Add 1/126.

362³   8 July 1937. RA DW Add 1/123.

362⁴   26 April 1937. Thomas papers.

362⁵   Janet Flanner. 'Charles Bedaux'. *The New Yorker*. Sept 1948.

363¹   Bedaux to Rogers. 18 Jan 1937. RA DW 3146a.

363²   Andrews to Monckton. 5 May 1937. RA DW 3203a.

363³   24 May 1937. RA DW 3240.

363⁴   Lang to Bishop of Pretoria. 29 July 1937. Lang papers. MS 2884/210.

364¹   Cecil Beaton diary. Beaton papers.

364²   Cecil Beaton diary. Beaton papers.

364³   Pope-Hennessy. *Queen Mary*. p142.

365¹   Birkenhead. *Monckton*. p162.

366¹   Winston to Clementine Churchill. 7 Jan 1937. Gilbert. *Churchill*. Vol V, p527.

366²   Winston to Clementine Churchill. 8 Jan 1939. Gilbert. *Churchill*. Vol V, p1340.

366³   Cicely Wyeth diary. 31 Oct 1937. RA DW Add 3.

366⁴   4 Nov 1937. *For the President. Correspondence between Franklin D. Roosevelt and William C. Bullitt*. Ed., Orville H. Bullitt. London, 1973. p230.

367¹   10 July 1937. Thomas papers.

367²   Monckton to Hoare. 27 Aug 1937. Templewood papers. X 2.

367³   Basil Liddell Hart. *Memoirs*. London, 1965. Vol II, p32.

368¹   E to J. Bernard Rickatson-Hatt. 18 May 1938. RA DW 3624.

368²   Hood. *Working for the Windsors*. pp42–3.

368³   Martin Scanlon's diary. 4 Jan 1939. RM 3.

368⁴   Winston to Clementine Churchill. 18 Jan 1939. Gilbert. *Churchill*. Vol V, p1347.

368⁵   Hood. *Working for the Windsors*. p36.

369¹   Vincent Sheean. *Between the Thunder and the Sun*. London, 1943. pp48–51.

369²   Nicolson. *Diaries and Letters*. Vol 1, p351.

369³ Lees-Milne. *Nicolson*. Vol II, pp106–7.

369⁴ Harold Nicolson diary. 4 Aug 1938. Nicolson papers.

369⁵ Hood. *Working for the Windsors*. pp45–6.

370¹ Lees-Milne. *Nicolson*. Vol II, p107.

370² Ted Morgan. *Somerset Maugham*. London, 1980. p420.

370³ Conversation with Sir Dudley Forwood.

370⁴ Lindbergh. *The Flower and the Nettle*. p568.

371¹ Baldwin to Monckton. 16 Dec 1937. Monckton papers. 326.

371² *The Diplomatic Diaries of Oliver Harvey*. Ed., John Harvey. London, 1970. p225.

371³ Lilli Palmer. *Dicke Lilli, Gutes Kind*. Zurich, 1974. p146.

371⁴ 16 Dec 1936. RA DW 3098.

371⁵ 23 Aug 1938. RA DW 3716.

371⁶ 11 Aug 1937. RA KEVIII Ab. Box 2.

372¹ H. Montgomery Hyde. *Baldwin*. p517.

372² George VI to Queen Mary. 14 Sept 1937. RA GV CC 12/57.

373¹ 22 Dec 1937. RA DW 3540.

373² 7 Jan 1938. RA DW 3550.

373³ 29 Aug 1938. RA DW 3722.

373⁴ Birkenhead. *Monckton*. p169.

373⁵ 18 Sept 1938. RA DW 3744.

373⁶ 11 Sept 1938. RA DW 3736.

373⁷ 24 Sept 1938. RA DW 3753.

374¹ 23 Oct 1938. RA DW 3777.

374² E to Monckton. 18 Nov 1938. RA DW 3815.

374³ Davidson to Monckton. 5 Sept 1938. Monckton papers. DEP MT 16/133.

374⁴ 20 Dec 1938. RA DW 3879.

374⁵ Hardinge to George VI. 19 Jan 1939. RA Hardinge papers.

374⁶ Report of 5 Jan 1939. RA KEVIII Ab. Box 3.

374⁷ 21 Dec 1938. RA DW 3895.

375¹ Chamberlain to George VI. 5 Dec 1938. RA KEVIII Ab. Box 2.

375² 14 Dec 1938. RA KEVIII Ab. Box 2.

375³ Monckton to E. 21 Dec 1938. RA DW 3880; Chamberlain to E. 23 Dec 1938. RA DW 3882.

375⁴ E to Chamberlain. 9 Jan and 24 Feb 1939. RA DW 3897 and 3961.

375⁵ George VI to Queen Mary. 3 Feb 1939. RA GV CC 12/87.

375⁶ 10 Feb 1939. RA KEVIII Ab. Box 2.

376¹ 30 April 1937. RA DW Add 1/118.

376² Monckton to Hoare. 27 Aug 1937. Templewood papers. X 2; and to George VI. 6 Sept 1937. RA KEVIII Ab. Box 2.

376³   Hardinge to Monckton. 6 Sept 1937. Monckton papers. DEP MT 15/257.

376⁴   Queen Elizabeth to Monckton. 21 Sept 1937. RA Monckton papers.

377¹   George VI to Farrer. 31 Oct 1937. RA DW Privy Purse Box 3.

377²   Memo by Farrer of April 1937. RA DW Privy Purse Box 3.

377³   22 Sept 1937. RA GV CC 12/58; George VI to Monckton. 22 Sept 1937. RA Monckton papers.

377⁴   Memo by Farrer of 2 July 1937. RA DW Privy Purse Box 3.

377⁵   A. G. Allen to Farrer. 14 Oct 1937. RA DW Privy Purse Box 3.

377⁶   A. G. Allen to Farrer. 10 Nov 1937. RA DW Privy Purse Box 3.

377⁷   Farrer to George VI. 19 Feb 1938. RA DW Privy Purse Box 3.

377⁸   Bloch. *The Secret File of the Duke of Windsor.* p65.

377⁹   Memo of 12 Nov 1937. RA DW Privy Purse Box 3.

378¹   Monckton to George VI. 11 Aug 1937. RA KEVIII Ab. Box 2.

378²   Farrer to George VI. 27 Oct 1937; Allen to Farrer. 10 Nov 1937. RA DW Privy Purse Box 3.

378³   Farrer to Allen. 22 Nov 1937. RA DW Privy Purse Box 3.

378⁴   Aide-mémoire of 10 Jan 1938. RA DW Privy Purse Box 3.

379¹   Monckton to George VI. 11 and 20 Aug 1937. RA KEVIII Ab. Box 2.

379²   Kent to E. 27 July 1937. RA DW 3390.

379³   E to Monckton. 17 Aug 1937. Monckton papers. DEP MT 15/241.

379⁴   Prince Paul of Greece quoted by Alastair Forbes. *Times Literary Supplement.* 4 Jan 1980.

379⁵   George VI to Kent. 16 Aug 1937. RA GVI 342.

379⁶   16 Aug 1937. RA GV CC 12/52.

379⁷   E to Monckton. 17 Aug 1937. Monckton papers. DEP MT 15/241.

380¹   George VI to Queen Mary. 18 Aug 1937. RA GV CC 12/53.

380²   George VI to Monckton. 21 Aug 1937. RA KEVIII Ab. Box 2.

380³   George VI to Queen Mary. 18 Aug 1937. RA GV CC 12/53.

380⁴   Kent to E. 8 Sept 1937. RA DW 3422.

380⁵   18 Oct 1937. RA DW Add 1/125.

380⁶   Hardinge to Monckton. 9 Sept 1937. Monckton papers. DEP MT 16/119.

380⁷   Princess Alice. *Memoirs.* p117.

380⁸   George VI to E. 28 Oct 1938. RA DW 3787.

380⁹   E to George VI. 30 Oct 1938. RA DW 3790.

381¹   31 Oct 1938. RA DW 3791.

381²   Davidson to Monckton. 13 Nov 1938. Monckton papers. DEP MT 16/202.

381³   Gloucester to E. 16 Nov 1938. RA DW 3812.

381⁴   Davidson to Monckton. 5 Sept 1938. Monckton papers. DEP MT 16/134.

381⁵ Lindbergh. *The Flower and the Nettle.* p503.

381⁶ Vansittart to Hardinge. 4 May 1937. RA GVI 42/2.

381⁷ Hardinge to Vansittart. 6 May 1937. RA GVI 42/1.

382¹ Hardinge to Vansittart. 23 Sept 1937. RA GVI 42/9.

382² 19 Jan 1938. RA GVI 42/33.

382³ Allen to Monckton. 15 Feb 1938. RA DW Add 1/132.

382⁴ Monckton to E. 2 Feb and 25 April 1938. RA DW Add 1/134 and 140.

382⁵ Minute of 16 Feb 1938. RA KEVIII Ab. Box 2.

382⁶ E to George VI. 30 April 1938. RA DW Add 1/141.

382⁷ Monckton to E. 6 and 11 May 1938. RA DW Add 1/142 and 143.

383¹ 18 May 1938. RA DW 3624.

383² Phipps to Hardinge. 28 May 1938. RA GVI 42/43.

383³ E to Rickatson-Hatt. 7 June 1938. RA DW 3658.

383⁴ 16 Aug 1938. Monckton papers. DEP MT 16/119.

383⁵ E to Queen Mary. 15 Jan 1938. RA GV EE 3.

383⁶ 6 March 1938. RA DW 3583.

383⁷ 14 Feb 1939. RA DW 3948.

383⁸ 2 April 1939. RA DW Add 1/151.

383⁹ E to Alexander. Undated. RA DW Add 1/152.

383¹⁰ E to Queen Mary. 15 March 1939. RA DW Add 1/148.

384¹ E to Queen Mary. 30 March 1939. RA DW Add 1/150.

384² E to Monckton. 12 May 1938. RA DW Add 1/144.

385¹ 5 July 1938. RA DW 3681.

385² 10 Feb 1939. RA KEVIII Ab. Box 2.

386¹ Brownlow to E. 15 April 1937. Brownlow papers.

388¹ Bloch. 'Philip Guedalla Defends the Duke'. p840.

388² Mallet to Vansittart. 14 Sept 1937. RA GVI 42/66.

388³ 25 Sept 1937. RA GVI 42/67.

388⁴ 22 Sept 1937. RA Monckton papers.

388⁵ Monckton to George VI. 4 Oct 1937. RA KEVIII Ab. Box 2.

389¹ 20 Sept 1937. RA DW 3423.

389² Vansittart to Hardinge. 1 Oct 1937. RA GVI 42/68.

389³ Henderson to E. 30 Sept 1937. RA DW 3435.

389⁴ Wigram to George VI. 4 Oct 1937. RA KEVIII Ab. Box 5.

389⁵ Monckton to George VI. 4 Oct 1937. RA KEVIII Ab. Box 2.

390¹ *Documents on German Foreign Policy.* Series C. Vol V, pp1032 and 1067–8.

390² 5 Oct 1937. RA Monckton papers.

390³ 4 Oct 1937. RA GV CC 12/60.

390⁴ 30 Sept 1937. PRO FO 954 33/55.

390⁵ 1 Oct 1937. PRO FO 954 33/62.

390⁶ 24 Sept 1940. RA DW 4668.
390⁷ Phipps to Eden. 12 Oct 1937. Phipps papers. PHPP 1/1/19.
390⁸ Phipps to F.O. 4 Oct 1937. RA GVI 42/53.
391¹ Ogilvie Forbes to Harvey. 13 Oct 1937. PRO FO 954 33/89.
391² Report by H.M. Consul, Dresden. 18 Nov 1937. RA GVI 42/63.
391³ 13 Oct 1937. RA GVI 42/77.
391⁴ *Daily Express*. 15 Aug 1938.
391⁵ David Irving. *Hess. The Missing Years*. London, 1987. pp36–7.
392¹ Emmy Göring. *My Life with Göring*. London, 1972. p88.
392² Paul Schmidt. *Hitler's Interpreter*. London, 1951. pp74–5.
392³ Duchess of Windsor. *The Heart Has Its Reasons*. pp315–16.
392⁴ Conversation with Sir Dudley Forwood.
392⁵ Schmidt. *Hitler's Interpreter*. p75.
392⁶ *The Heart Has Its Reasons*. p318.
392⁷ Alvin Owsley to Secretary of State. 10 Nov 1937. NA 862 002/313.
392⁸ 22 Nov 1937. *Diaries*. Vol 1, p403.
393¹ Nigel Law to Eden. PRO FO 954 33/131.
393² 28 Oct 1937. RA DW 3475.
393³ *Forward*. 13 Nov 1937.
393⁴ Lindsay to Vansittart. PRO FO 954 33/64.
393⁵ Memo by Harvey. PRO FO 954 33/102.
394¹ *Crawford Papers*. Appendix. pp616–21.
394² Vansittart to Mallet. PRO FO 954 33/113.
394³ Bullitt to Roosevelt. 4 Nov 1937. *For the President*. p230.
394⁴ *Crawford Papers*. pp616–21.
394⁵ William Shirer. *Berlin Diary*. London, 1942. pp76–7.
394⁶ Ian G. Walker to E. 22 Oct 1937. RA DW 3464.
395¹ Report of 22 Oct 1937. RA GVI 42/81.
395² Ogilvie Forbes to Harvey. 17 Oct 1937. PRO FO 954 33/94.
395³ Memo of 30 Sept 1937. RA GV EE 3.
395⁴ RA DW 3471.
395⁵ Lindsay to F.O. 5 Nov 1937. PRO FO 954 33/121.
395⁶ *New York Times*. 4 Nov 1937.
396¹ Lindsay to George VI. 8 Nov 1937. RA GVI 42/102.
396² Monckton to George VI. 7 Nov 1937. RA KEVIII Ab. Box 2.
396³ Bloch. *The Secret File of the Duke of Windsor*. p119.
396⁴ E to Bedaux. 6 Dec 1937. RA DW 3529.
396⁵ E to Oscar Solbert. Draft letter possibly never sent. RA DW 3566a.
396⁶ Monckton to George VI. 7 Nov 1937. RA KEVIII Ab. Box 2.
397¹ Hardinge to Lindsay. 22 Nov 1937. RA GVI 42/105.
397² Lindsay to Hardinge. 16 Nov 1937. RA GVI 42/103.
397³ 8 Nov 1937. RA DW 3505.

397⁴   9 Nov 1937. RA DW Add 2.

397⁵   Phipps to Eden. 28 Dec 1937. PRO FO 954 33/186.

398¹   *Baffy*. p127.

398²   21 Sept 1938. Monckton papers. DEP MT 16/150.

398³   18 Sept 1938. RA DW 3745.

398⁴   George VI to Chamberlain. 30 Sept 1938. RA GVI 047/13.

398⁵   19 Sept 1938. RA DW 3748.

398⁶   19 Oct 1938. RA DW 3773.

399¹   RA GVI 42/274. The complete text was published by Bloch as an Appendix to *The Secret File of the Duke of Windsor*. pp313–14.

399²   *Daily Express*. 8 May 1939.

399³   Kent to George VI. 16 May 1939. RA GVI 342.

400¹   Hardinge to George VI. 9 May 1939. RA Hardinge papers.

400²   Hood. *Working for the Windsors*. p143.

400³   E to Monckton. 24 Sept 1938. RA DW 3153.

400⁴   23 Aug 1939. RA DW 4195.

400⁵   26 Aug 1939. RA DW 4200.

400⁶   RA DW 4197.

400⁷   27 Aug 1939. RA DW Trunk 2.

401¹   28 Aug 1939. RA DW Trunk 2.

402¹   Duchess of Windsor. *The Heart Has Its Reasons*. pp329–30.

402²   Monckton to Wilson. 26 Aug 1939. Monckton papers. DEP MT 17/91.

402³   Memo by Monckton. 2 Sept 1939. RA KEVIII Ab. Box 3.

403¹   Edward to Alexandra Metcalfe. 3 Sept 1939. Metcalfe papers.

403²   28 Aug 1939. RA GV CC 12/108.

403³   RA George VI diary. 16 Sept 1939.

403⁴   Memo by Monckton. 5 Sept 1939. RA DW 4211.

404¹   31 Aug 1939. RA GV CC 12/110.

404²   7 Sept 1939. RA GVI 342.

404³   *The Heart Has Its Reasons*. p335.

404⁴   Kent to George VI. 22 Sept 1939. RA GVI 342.

404⁵   George VI to Kent. 26 Sept 1939. RA GVI 342.

404⁶   Birkenhead. *Monckton*. p172.

405¹   *The Heart Has Its Reasons*. p335.

405²   George VI to Kent. 26 Sept 1939. RA GVI 342.

405³   R. J. Minney. *The Private Papers of Hore-Belisha*. London, 1960. pp237–8.

405⁴   Martin Scanlon diary. 15 Sept 1939.

406¹   Article by the Duke of Windsor. *New York Daily News*. 13 Dec 1966.

406²   25 Sept 1939. Metcalfe papers.

406³   Harold Nicolson. *Diaries and Letters 1939–1945*. Ed., Nigel Nicolson. London, 1967. p38.

406⁴ Memo by Metcalfe. 23 Sept 1939. RA DW 4314.

406⁵ 24 Sept 1939. RA DW 4315.

407¹ 25 Sept 1939. RA DW 4319.

407² 26 Sept 1939. RA GVI 342.

407³ Lady A. Metcalfe's diary. 25 Sept 1939. Metcalfe papers.

407⁴ R. E. Vintras. *The Portuguese Connection*. London, 1974. p24.

407⁵ Gloucester to George VI. 22 Sept 1939. RA GVI 342.

407⁶ Howard-Vyse to Hardinge. 19 Sept 1939. RA KEVIII Ab. Box 3.

407⁷ Hardinge to Howard-Vyse. 20 Sept 1939. RA KEVIII Ab. Box 3.

408¹ Michael Bloch. *The Duke of Windsor's War*. London, 1982. pp28–9.

408² Memo by Metcalfe. 23 Sept 1939. RA DW 4314.

408³ Memo by Metcalfe. 23 Sept 1939. RA DW 4314.

408⁴ 2 Oct 1939. RA DW 4331.

408⁵ Bloch. *Duke of Windsor's War*. pp27–8.

408⁶ Edward to Alexandra Metcalfe. 4 Oct 1939. Metcalfe papers.

408⁷ Edward to Alexandra Metcalfe. 4 Oct 1939. Metcalfe papers.

409¹ Edward to Alexandra Metcalfe. 9 Oct 1939. Metcalfe papers.

409² PRO WO 106/1678.

410¹ 13 Oct 1939. RA DW 4348.

410² 14 Oct 1939. RA DW 4351.

410³ Philip Goodhart to E and E to Goodhart. 20 and 29 June 1952. RA DW 10753 and 10759.

410⁴ PRO WO 106/1678 3B.

410⁵ E to Ironside. 2 Nov 1939. RA DW 4376.

411¹ Memo by E. RA DW Add 1/154.

411² Gloucester to George VI. 19 Oct 1939. RA GVI 342.

411³ Pownall diary. 18 Oct 1939.

411⁴ Kent to George VI. 25 Oct 1939. RA GVI 342.

411⁵ Hardinge to Ironside. 24 Oct 1939. RA KEVIII Ab. Box 3.

411⁶ Memo by E. RA DW Add 1/154.

412¹ Churchill to E. 17 Nov 1939. RA DW 4396.

412² Gloucester to George VI. 12 Oct 1939. RA GVI 342.

412³ 8 Nov 1939. RA KEVIII Ab. Box 2.

412⁴ Memo by E. RA DW Add 1/154.

412⁵ *The Diplomatic Diaries of Oliver Harvey*. p325.

412⁶ Memo by E. RA DW Add 1/154.

412⁷ Monckton to E. 10 Nov 1939. RA DW 4380.

412⁸ E to Monckton. 12 Nov 1939. RA DW 4386.

413¹ E to Churchill. 14 Nov 1939. RA DW 4388.

413² Monckton papers. DEP MT 17/196.

413³ 14 Nov 1939. RA DW 4389.

413⁴ 17 Nov 1939. RA DW 4394.

413⁵   17 Nov 1939. RA DW 4396.

413⁶   E to Churchill. 18 Nov 1939. RA DW 4397.

413⁷   17 Nov 1939. RA DW 4395.

413⁸   21 Nov 1939. RA KEVIII Ab. Box 3.

414¹   E to Monckton. 19 Nov 1939. RA DW 4399.

414²   RA KEVIII Ab. Box 3.

414³   Howard-Vyse to E. 27 Nov 1939. RA DW 4406.

414⁴   E to Monckton. 9 Dec 1939. RA DW 4416.

414⁵   2 Jan 1940. Monckton papers. DEP MT 18/12.

414⁶   31 March 1940. RA DW 4475.

414⁷   Roger Bruge. *Faites Sauter La Ligne Maginot.* Paris, 1973. p97.

415¹   27 Jan 1940. *Documents on German Foreign Policy.* Series D. Vol VIII.
London, 1957. p713.

415²   19 Feb 1940. *Documents on German Foreign Policy.* Series D. Vol VIII,
p785.

415³   Bloch. *Operation Willi.* pp41–2.

415⁴   16 Oct 1939. RA DW 4355.

415⁵   Peake to Harvey. 26 Jan 1940. Harvey papers; Harold Nicolson diary.
1 Oct 1940. Nicolson papers.

415⁶   Edward to Alexandra Metcalfe. 27 Feb 1940. Metcalfe papers.

415⁷   Gloucester to George VI. 21 Feb 1940. RA GVI 342.

416¹   Bloch. 'Philip Guedalla Defends the Duke'. pp842–3.

416²   Howard-Vyse to Phillips. 20 May 1940. RA DW 4492.

416³   Virginia Cowles. *Looking for Trouble.* London, 1941. pp368–9.

416⁴   E to Phillips. 4 June 1940. RA DW 4497.

416⁵   24 May 1940. Metcalfe papers.

417¹   Harvey. *Diplomatic Diaries.* p365.

417²   Draft of telegram of 1 July 1940. RA KEVIII Ab. Box 3.

417³   29 May 1940. RA KEVIII Ab. Box 3.

417⁴   E to Howard-Vyse and Howard-Vyse to E. 7 and 11 June 1940. RA DW
4501 and 4502.

417⁵   27 May 1940. Metcalfe papers.

417⁶   3 June 1940. RA DW 4496.

418¹   6 June 1940. RA DW 4499.

418²   4 June 1940. RA DW 4497.

418³   Edward to Alexandra Metcalfe. 1 Feb 1947. Metcalfe papers.

419¹   Dodds to F.O. 23 Oct 1940. PRO FO 954 33/204.

420¹   *The Diaries of Sir Alexander Cadogan.* Ed., David Dilks. London, 1971.
p287.

421¹   19 June 1940. PRO CAB 65(7) 172(40)4.

421²   21 June 1940. PRO CAB 65(7) 174(40)11.

421³   21 June 1940. RA GV CC 12/128.

421[4] A. W. Weddell to Secretary of State. *Foreign Relations of the United States. 1940.* Vol III, 1939/4357 p41.

421[5] 30 June 1940. PRO FO 371/24407 74.

421[6] 1 July 1940. Chartwell papers. CHAR 20/9A 23.

421[7] 1 July 1940. Templewood papers. XIII 20.

422[1] Unpublished memoir. Templewood papers. Box XXIII. 'A Deep-laid Plot'. p12.

422[2] Bloch. *Duke of Windsor's War.* p82.

422[3] 24 June 1940. PRO FO 371/24491.

422[4] 24 June 1940. RA DW 4512.

422[5] 26 June 1940. RA DW 4514.

422[6] 28 June 1940. RA DW 4518.

423[1] 28 June 1940. RA DW 4519.

423[2] 26 June 1940. Chartwell papers. CHAR 20/9A 8.

423[3] 27 June 1940. Templewood papers. XIII 16/29.

424[1] 23 June 1940. *Documents on German Foreign Policy.* Series D. Vol X, p2.

424[2] 24 June 1940. *Documents on German Foreign Policy.* Series D. Vol X, p9.

424[3] 25 June 1940. *Documents on German Foreign Policy.* Series D. Vol X, p9n.

424[4] 2 July 1940. *Documents on German Foreign Policy.* Series D. Vol X, pp96–7.

424[5] Bloch. *Operation Willi.* p66.

425[1] Selby to E. 24 Sept 1957. RA DW 9529.

425[2] Pell to Cordell Hull. 20 July 1940. NA 844 E 001/52 Duke of Windsor.

425[3] PRO FO 954 33/212.

425[4] 11 July 1940. *Documents on German Foreign Policy.* Series D. Vol X, p187.

425[5] Bloch. *Operation Willi.* p96.

426[1] 25 June, 4 and 17 July 1940. *By Safe Hand. Letters of Sybil and David Eccles.* London, 1983. pp128, 132 and 139.

426[2] 27 June 1940. RA GV CC 12/129.

426[3] Colville. *Fringes of Power.* pp176–7.

426[4] 3 July 1940. RA DW 4520.

426[5] 26 June 1940. Chartwell papers. CHAR 20/9A 17.

426[6] George VI to Queen Mary. 7 July 1940. RA GV CC 12/130.

427[1] 4 July 1940. Bruce Lockhart. *Diaries.* Vol 2, p65.

427[2] Colville. *Fringes of Power.* p184.

427[3] 7 July 1940. RA GV CC 12/130.

427[4] Halifax to Hoare. 8 July 1940. Templewood papers. XIII 20.

427[5] Countess of Athlone to Queen Elizabeth. 11 July 1940. RA GVI 342.

Notes

427⁶ Duke of Kent to Prince Paul of Yugoslavia. 17 July 1940. cit Bradford. *George VI*. p436.

427⁷ Queen Mary to Countess of Athlone. 7 Sept 1940. RA GV CC 53/780.

427⁸ 31 Jan 1942. Metcalfe papers.

428¹ 19 July 1940. Colville. *Fringes of Power*. p197.

428² E to Phillips. 18 July 1940. RA DW 4570.

428³ 20 July 1940. RA DW 4582.

428⁴ J. H. Peck to Churchill. 20 July 1940. Chartwell papers. CHAR 20/9A 85.

428⁵ Chartwell papers. CHAR 20/9B 121.

429¹ Chartwell papers. CHAR 20/9B 122.

429² Lothian to F.O. 17 July 1940. PRO FO 371/24249.

429³ Memo of 20 July 1940. NA 844 E 001/52.

429⁴ Undated. RA DW 4567.

429⁵ 24 July 1940. RA DW 4593.

429⁶ 27 July 1940. RA DW 4605.

429⁷ 26 July 1940. RA DW 4600.

430¹ 11 July 1940. *Documents on German Foreign Policy*. Series D. Vol X, p152.

430² 30 June 1940. *Documents on German Foreign Policy*. Series D. Vol X, p66; cf Bloch. *Operation Willi*. pp58–9.

430³ E to Templewood. 15 Aug 1956. RA DW 10059.

431¹ 23 July 1940. *Documents on German Foreign Policy*. Series D. Vol X, p276; cf Bloch. *Operation Willi*. pp126–7.

431² Bloch. *Operation Willi*. p127.

431³ *Documents on German Foreign Policy*. Series D. Vol X, p290.

431⁴ Walter Schellenberg. *The Schellenberg Memoirs*. Ed. and trans., Louis Hagen. London, 1956. pp128–30.

431⁵ Schellenberg. *Memoirs*. pp138–9.

432¹ 26 July 1940. *Documents on German Foreign Policy*. Series D. Vol X, p317.

432² Bloch. *Operation Willi*. pp165–71.

432³ 26 July 1940. RA DW 4598.

432⁴ Birkenhead. *Monckton*. p180.

432⁵ 30 July 1940. *Documents on German Foreign Policy*. Series D. Vol X, p363.

433¹ Monckton to Churchill. 8 Aug 1940. Chartwell papers. CHAR 20/9B.

433² 9 Aug 1940. Templewood papers. X 4.

433³ 3 Aug 1940. *Documents on German Foreign Policy*. Series D. Vol X, p410.

433⁴ 15 Aug 1940. Bloch. *Operation Willi*. p227.

434¹ Bloch. *Operation Willi*. pp227–8.

434[2]   7 July 1940. RA KEVIII Ab. Box 3.

435[1]   Chartwell papers. CHAR 20/9A 34.

435[2]   PRO FO 371/24249.

437[1]   Michael Craton. *A History of the Bahamas*. Second edition. London, 1968. p11.

437[2]   Alfred de Marigny. *More Devil than Saint*. New York, 1946. p84.

439[1]   31 July 1940. RA DW 4613.

439[2]   Bloch. 'Philip Guedalla Defends the Duke'. p843.

439[3]   1 Dec 1943. Halifax papers. A4 410 4/18(1).

440[1]   George VI to Queen Mary. 22 Aug 1940. RA GV CC 12/133.

440[2]   27 July 1940. RA DW 4605.

440[3]   Frank Giles. *Sunday Times*. London, 1986. p24.

440[4]   Giles. *Sunday Times*. p26.

441[1]   26 July 1940. RA DW 4628.

441[2]   Undated draft. RA DW 4627.

441[3]   Giles. *Sunday Times*. p25.

441[4]   Giles. *Sunday Times*. p26.

441[5]   22 Aug 1940. Monckton papers. DEP MT 18/87.

441[6]   Giles. *Sunday Times*. p22.

441[7]   10 Aug 1940. RA DW 4625.

442[1]   Craton. *History of Bahamas*. p273.

442[2]   17 July 1940. BRO EXCO 20.

442[3]   15 Aug 1940. BRO EXCO 23.

442[4]   *Nassau Daily Tribune*. 17 Aug 1940.

442[5]   17 Aug 1940. NA 844 E 001/53.

442[6]   Rosita Forbes. *Appointment with Destiny*. London, 1946. p184.

443[1]   22 Aug 1940. Monckton papers. DEP MT 18/87.

443[2]   Bloch. *Duke of Windsor's War*. p128.

443[3]   31 July 1940. RA DW 4616.

443[4]   Frederick van Zeylen. 'My Boss the Duke of Windsor'. *Bahamas Handbook*. 1966–67. p54.

443[5]   E to Clifford. 30 Sept 1940. RA DW 4671.

443[6]   29 Aug 1940. Chartwell papers. CHAR 20/9B 181 and 184.

443[7]   Lloyd to E. Draft in Chartwell papers (possibly never sent). CHAR 20/9B 182.

443[8]   *Nassau Daily Tribune*. 14 Sept 1940.

444[1]   'My Boss the Duke of Windsor'. p54.

444[2]   Conversation with Irma Cosforth.

444[3]   René MacColl. *Deadline and Dateline*. London, 1956. pp123–5.

444[4]   Mackintosh. *No Alibi*. p185.

445[1]   Sir Etienne Dupuch. *Tribune Story*. London, 1967. pp89–90.

445[2]   Windsor. *A Family Album*. p69.

445³ Dundas to E. 31 July 1940. RA DW 4616.
445⁴ 18 Jan 1941.
446¹ 21 Aug 1940. BRO EXCO 24.
446² 28 Aug 1940. BRO EXCO 25.
446³ 10 July 1940.
446⁴ PRO CO 23/712. May 1940.
447¹ Bloch. *Duke of Windsor's War*. p145.
447² 9 July 1941. BRO EXCO 30.
447³ *Nassau Daily Tribune*. 28 Aug 1940.
448¹ Dupuch. *Tribune Story*. p83.
448² E to Sir Malcolm Robertson. 4 Sept 1941. RA DW 4915.
448³ Forbes. *Appointment with Destiny*. p193.
448⁴ Dupuch. *Tribune Story*. pp86 and 90.
449¹ E to Moyne. 26 July 1941. RA DW 4870.
449² Moyne to E. 14 Aug 1941. RA DW 4889.
449³ 10 Nov 1942. RA DW Add 1/165.
450¹ 28 Jan 1941. RA DW 4737.
450² Conversation with Oris Russell.
450³ Dupuch. *Tribune Story*. p84.
450⁴ *The Second World War Diary of Hugh Dalton*. Ed., Ben Pimlott. London, 1986. p739.
450⁵ John Balfour. 'Encounters with the Duke and Duchess of Windsor'. Donaldson papers.
450⁶ 1 Nov 1940. NA 844 E 001/60.
451¹ Bede Clifford to E. 28 April 1941. RA DW 4783.
451² 1 Nov 1940. NA 844 E 001/60.
451³ E to Clifford. 30 Sept 1940. RA DW 4671.
451⁴ 5 March 1941. Monckton papers. DEP MT 19/15.
452¹ E to L. W. Robert. 20 Jan 1942. RA DW 5022.
453¹ E to Moyne. 26 July 1941. RA DW 4870.
453² Bloch. *Duke of Windsor's War*. p201.
453³ 22 Sept 1941. RA DW 4937.
454¹ Stanley to Halifax. 6 Jan 1944. Halifax papers. A4 410 4/18(1).
454² 15 Jan 1941. RA DW 4726.
454³ *Nassau Daily Tribune*. 25 June 1942.
455¹ 10 Oct 1937. Wenner-Gren diary. Leifland papers.
455² RA GVI 141/35.
456¹ 24 July 1940. FBI report. Leifland papers.
456² Colville. *Fringes of Power*. p332.
456³ Commercial Counsellor, Stockholm to Ministry of Economic Warfare. 16 April 1942. PRO FO 837/875.
456⁴ NA 800 202 11 Wenner-Gren, Axel/210.

456⁵   18 April 1941. NA 800 202 11 Wenner-Gren, Axel/56.

456⁶   3 Feb 1942. Nassau. Government Gazette. Colonial Secretary's Office. No 34.

456⁷   Leifland papers.

457¹   Wenner-Gren diary. 18 and 25 Oct 1940, 3 Feb 1941. Leifland papers.

457²   *Daily Mirror.* 10 Dec 1940.

457³   Eastwood to Hardinge. 9 Jan 1941. RA GVI 141/34.

457⁴   Halifax to F.O. 14 March 1941. PRO FO 954 33/188.

457⁵   17 March 1941. RA DW 4756.

457⁶   30 Jan 1941. RA GV CC 12/150.

458¹   16 June 1941. RA DW 4833.

458²   23 June 1941. RA DW 4842.

458³   22 June 1941. NA 800 202 11 Wenner-Gren, Axel/48.

458⁴   5 Feb 1942. Copy in Leifland papers.

458⁵   20 Jan 1942. PRO FO 837/858.

458⁶   9 Sept 1942. PRO FO 837/875.

458⁷   H. Montgomery Hyde. *Secret Intelligence Agent.* London, 1982. pp116–17.

459¹   17 April 1941. Chartwell papers. CHAR 20/31A 70.

459²   Bloch. *Duke of Windsor's War.* p176.

459³   Bloch. *Duke of Windsor's War.* p199.

459⁴   Notes by Thomas and Hardinge. RA KEVIII Ab. Box 3.

460¹   23 Nov 1940. RA GVI 141/18.

460²   *Liberty Magazine.* 22 March 1941 and *Sunday Despatch.* 16 March 1941.

460³   *The Goebbels Diaries 1939–1941.* Trans. and ed., Fred Taylor. London, 1982. pp344–5.

460⁴   17 March 1941. RA DW 4756.

460⁵   18 March 1941. RA DW 4758.

461¹   27 March 1941. RA DW 4764.

461²   Halifax to Churchill. 4 Oct 1941. Chartwell papers. CHAR 20/31B 160.

462¹   Churchill to E. 27 July 1940. RA DW 4605.

462²   Monckton to Cadogan. 9 Oct 1940. PRO FO 371 24249/361.

463¹   Countess of Athlone to Queen Mary. 21 Aug 1940. RA GV CC 53/774.

463²   Monckton to E. 26 Aug 1940. RA DW 4647.

463³   11 Oct 1940. RA GV CC 53/789.

463⁴   Lloyd to Halifax. 20 Sept 1940. PRO FO 371 24249/353.

463⁵   F.O. to Lothian. 8 Nov 1940. PRO FO 371 24249/373.

463⁶   Bloch. 'Philip Guedalla Defends the Duke'. p843.

463⁷   Duchess of Windsor to Monckton. 2 Oct 1940. Monckton papers. DEP MT 18/112.

464[1] F.O. to Lothian. 29 Nov 1940. RA GVI 141/20.

464[2] Chartwell papers. CHAR 311 20/9B 199.

464[3] Colville. *Fringes of Power*. p332.

464[4] Bloch. *Duke of Windsor's War*. p168.

464[5] Wenner-Gren diary. 10 and 17 Dec 1940. Leifland papers.

465[1] 1 Dec 1940. NA 701 4111/1131.

465[2] 11 March 1941. PRO FO 371/26191.

465[3] 14 March 1941. PRO FO 954 33/188.

465[4] 17 March 1941. RA DW 4756.

465[5] 18 March 1941. RA DW 4758.

465[6] Eastwood to Colville. 22 April 1941. Chartwell papers. CHAR 20/31A 73.

466[1] 3 Aug 1941. RA DW 4879.

466[2] 10 Sept 1941. Monckton papers. DEP MT 19/202.

466[3] MacColl. *Deadline and Dateline*. pp124–5.

466[4] MacColl. *Deadline and Dateline*. p122.

467[1] *Washington Star*. 29 Oct 1941.

467[2] 17 Nov 1941. Metcalfe papers.

467[3] *Hansard*. 5th Series. Vol 376, 602. 25 Nov 1941.

467[4] E to Churchill. 27 Nov 1941. RA DW 4993.

467[5] Halifax diary. 2 Oct 1941. Halifax papers A7 8/9.

467[6] Halifax to Alexandra Metcalfe. 4 Oct 1941. Metcalfe papers.

468[1] 19 Oct 1941. RA GVI 053/USA/5.

468[2] Athlone to Queen Mary. 15 July 1941. RA GV CC 53/888.

468[3] 26 July 1941. RA GV CC 53/897.

468[4] 19 Oct 1941. Halifax papers. A4 410 4/11.

469[1] 19 Oct 1941. RA GVI 053/USA/5.

469[2] 1 March 1942. Halifax papers. A2 278 26/5.

469[3] Halifax diary. 9 Sept 1942. Halifax papers. A7 8/11.

469[4] Halifax diary. 15 Sept 1942. Halifax papers. A7 8/11.

469[5] Halifax to Stanley. 22 Nov 1943. Halifax papers. A4 410/4. 18(1).

469[6] Halifax diary. 19 July 1945. Halifax papers. A7 8/17.

469[7] 30 Aug and 1 Sept 1944. RA DW 5576 and 5580.

470[1] *The Private Diaries of Sydney Moseley*. London, 1960. p433.

470[2] 21 July 1942. NA 800 202 11 Wenner-Gren, Axel/59.

470[3] Halifax to F.O. 3 Dec 1941. PRO FO 954 33/207.

470[4] Monckton to E. 28 Sept 1940. Monckton papers. DEP MT 18/93.

470[5] Monckton to E. 26 July 1940. Monckton papers. DEP MT 18/48.

470[6] 8 Aug 1940. Chartwell papers. CHAR 20/9B.

471[1] Alexander to Morshead. 10 March 1942. RA KEVIII Ab. Box 4.

471[2] Wilson to Monckton. 15 Nov 1940. Monckton papers. DEP MT 18/144.

471³ E to Stanley. 30 Jan 1943. RA DW 5250.

472¹ Halifax to E. 2 June 1942. RA GVI 141/64.

472² Halifax to F.O. 2 June 1942. RA GVI 141/64.

472³ *Nassau Guardian*. 9 June 1942. *Nassau Daily Tribune*. 9 and 13 June 1942.

473¹ E to Cranborne. 6 June 1942. RA DW 5058.

473² Correspondence on PRO CO 23/731; cf E to Cranborne. 10 June 1942. RA DW 5061.

473³ Correspondence on PRO CO 23/736.

473⁴ E to Colonial Office. 24 March 1943. PRO CO 23/734.

473⁵ 7 Oct 1942. PRO CO 23/731.

474¹ Randol Fawkes. *The Faith that Moved the Mountain*. Nassau, 1979. p31.

474² Correspondence on PRO CO 23/731.

474³ 17 June 1942. BRO EXCO 23.

474⁴ Correspondence on PRO CO 23/731.

474⁵ Bloch. *Duke of Windsor's War*. p269.

474⁶ 28 June 1942. BRO EXCO 24.

475¹ E to Cranborne. 9 Dec 1942. RA DW 5220.

476¹ 1 Jan 1943. RA DW 5250.

477¹ E to Frank Norman. 4 Jan 1943. cit Frank Norman. *Whitehall to West Indies*. London, 1952. p221.

477² E to Halifax. 17 Jan 1945. RA DW 5381.

477³ Moyne to E. 4 March 1942. RA DW 5032.

477⁴ 30 Oct 1942. RA DW Add 1/163.

477⁵ Hoover to Berle. 23 April 1942. NA 740 0011 European War 1939/21295.

478¹ Cranborne to Churchill. 29 Aug 1942. Chartwell papers. CHAR 20/63 24.

478² Churchill to Cranborne. 31 Aug 1942. Chartwell papers. CHAR 20/63 25.

478³ Cranborne to Churchill. 2 Oct 1942. Chartwell papers. CHAR 20/63 29.

478⁴ Stanley to E. 1 March 1943. RA DW 5260.

478⁵ Stanley to E. 12 May 1943. RA DW 5286.

478⁶ E to Stanley. 10 Aug 1943. RA DW 5320.

479¹ E to Stanley. 24 Jan 1944. RA DW 5415.

479² E to Stanley. 8 March 1944. RA DW 5452.

479³ Stanley to E. 4 May 1944. RA DW 5477.

479⁴ 27 June 1944. RA DW 5534.

480¹ 6 Feb 1945. RA DW 5672.

480² 22 July 1943. RA DW 5309.

Notes

480³   E to Stanley. 10 Aug 1943. RA DW 5320.

480⁴   10 Aug 1940. RA DW 4626.

480⁵   Heape to Beckett. 14 Nov 1943. PRO CO 23/714.

481¹   Hallinan to Houts. 9 April 1971. Marshall Houts. *Who Killed Sir Harry Oakes?* London, 1976. p308.

481²   NA 844 E 001/120.

481³   10 Aug 1943. RA DW 5320.

482¹   Halifax diary. 11 Nov 1943. Halifax papers. A7 8/13.

482²   E to Colonial Office. 12 Nov 1943. PRO CO 23/714.

482³   Correspondence on PRO CO 23/714.

483¹   24 Jan 1944. RA DW 5415.

484¹   *Nassau Daily Tribune.* 26 Nov 1940.

484²   Lascelles diary. 9 Aug 1942. Lascelles papers.

484³   31 Aug 1942. RA DW Add 1/156.

485¹   12 Sept 1942. RA GV EE 3.

485²   14 Oct 1942. RA GV CC 53/1078.

485³   15 Sept 1942. RA DW Add 1/158.

485⁴   24 March 1943. RA GV CC 53/1129.

485⁵   Lascelles diary. 11 Dec 1942. Lascelles papers.

486¹   9 Dec 1942. RA KEVIII Ab. Box 2.

486²   27 Oct 1943. RA GVI 217/2.

486³   RA GVI 217/5.

486⁴   Lascelles to George VI. 29 Oct 1943. RA GVI 217/8.

486⁵   Simon to Lascelles. 5 Nov 1943. RA GVI 217/11.

486⁶   9 Nov 1943. RA GVI 217/15.

487¹   19 Jan 1944. RA DW 5412.

487²   13 Dec 1944. RA GV EE 3.

487³   Duchess of Windsor. *The Heart Has Its Reasons.* pp369–70.

487⁴   George VI to Queen Mary. 5 May 1942. RA GV CC 13/12.

487⁵   Colville. *The Fringes of Power.* p516.

487⁶   E to Churchill. 10 Nov 1942. RA DW Add 1/165.

488¹   22 Dec 1942. Chartwell papers. CHAR 20/63 92.

488²   Lascelles diary. 9 Nov 1944. Lascelles papers.

488³   Lascelles diary. 18 Nov 1944. Lascelles papers.

488⁴   31 Dec 1944. RA DW Add 1/170.

488⁵   12 Feb 1945. RA DW Add 1/172.

488⁶   Undated. RA DW Add 1/173.

489¹   Bloch. 'Philip Guedalla Defends the Duke'. p844.

489²   Halifax diary. 15 Sept 1942. Halifax papers. A7 8/11.

489³   14 May 1942. Chartwell papers. CHAR 20/63 57.

489⁴   E to Churchill. 18 April 1942. RA DW 5040.

489⁵   George VI to Queen Mary. 11 May 1942. RA GV CC 13/13.

489⁶   Smuts to Churchill. 29 May 1942. Chartwell papers. CHAR 20/63 69.

489⁷   George VI to Queen Mary. 4 July 1942. RA GV CC 13/19.

490¹   10 Nov 1942. RA DW Add 1/165.

490²   David Farrer. *G – For God Almighty*. London, 1969. pp118–19.

490³   10 June 1943. RA DW 5276.

490⁴   13 June 1943. RA DW 5289.

490⁵   Contained in letter from E to Allen. 3 May 1944. RA DW 5476a.

490⁶   E to Allen. 3 May 1944. RA DW 5476.

491¹   23 March 1944. RA DW 5463.

491²   Allen to E. 31 May 1944. RA DW 5501.

491³   Lascelles to Martin. 30 May 1944. Chartwell papers. CHAR 20/148 37.

491⁴   Churchill to Lascelles. Chartwell papers. CHAR 20/148 37.

491⁵   Halifax diary. 3 July 1944. Halifax papers. A7 8/15.

492¹   3 Oct 1944. RA DW 5615.

492²   E to Stanley. 18 Oct 1944. RA GVI 236/2.

492³   E to Churchill. 30 Oct 1944. RA DW 5615.

492⁴   Lascelles diary. 6 Feb 1945. Lascelles papers.

492⁵   16 Sept 1944. Chartwell papers. CHAR 20/148 55.

493¹   16 Sept 1944. Chartwell papers. CHAR 20/148 56.

493²   Lascelles diary. 6 Feb 1945. Lascelles papers.

493³   Lascelles diary. 12 Aug 1944. Lascelles papers.

493⁴   Lascelles diary. 18 Nov 1944. Lascelles papers.

493⁵   Lascelles diary. 9 Nov 1944. Lascelles papers.

493⁶   Lascelles diary. 6 Feb 1945. Lascelles papers.

494¹   Conversation of 8 Nov 1944. Chartwell papers. CHAR 20/148 64.

494²   Lascelles diary. 18 Nov 1944. Lascelles papers.

494³   *Nassau Daily Tribune*. 16 March 1945.

494⁴   RA GVI 236/11.

494⁵   American News Summary. 16 March 1945. RA GVI 236/9.

494⁶   25 April 1945. BRO EXCO 16.

495¹   *Nassau Daily Tribune*. 17 March 1945.

496¹   John Balfour. *Not too Correct an Aureole*. Salisbury, 1983. p108.

496²   Bloch. *Duke of Windsor's War*. p343.

497¹   Balfour. 'Encounters with the Duke and Duchess of Windsor'. Donaldson papers.

497²   22 Dec 1945. RA DW 6096.

497³   E to Young. 2 Oct 1946. RA DW 6454.

497⁴   E to George Allen. 30 July 1945. RA DW 5899.

498¹   E to Duncan Stewart. 24 July 1945. RA DW 5891.

498²   8 July 1946. RA GV EE 3.

498³   9 Nov 1946. RA DW 6550.

498⁴   10 Nov 1946. RA DW 6555.

Notes

498⁵ 15 Dec 1946. RA GV EE 3.

499¹ Holman to Harvey. 24 Sept 1945. RA KEVIII Ab. Box 3.

499² 5 May 1946. RA DW 6274.

499³ 25 March 1946. RA GV EE 3.

499⁴ Lascelles to Martin. 21 Dec 1944. Chartwell papers. CHAR 20/148 24.

500¹ 23 Sept 1945. RA GV CC 13/135.

500² Lascelles diary. 12 Aug 1945. Lascelles papers.

500³ 24 Aug 1945. RA DW 5919a.

500⁴ 27 Aug 1945. RA GV CC 53/1422.

500⁵ 18 Sept 1945. RA GV CC 13/133.

501¹ Peacock to E. 23 Oct 1945. RA DW 6018.

501² *The Mackenzie King Record.* Ed., J. W. Pickersgill and D. F. Forster. Toronto, 1970. p78.

501³ 17 Oct 1945. RA DW 6009.

501⁴ 13 Oct 1945. RA GV EE 3.

501⁵ E to Gray Phillips. 4 July 1943. RA DW 5872.

501⁶ 6 Oct 1945. RA GV CC 13/137.

501⁷ 9 Oct 1945. RA GV EE 13/35.

502¹ Lascelles diary. 9 Oct 1945. Lascelles papers.

502² 19 March 1946. RA DW 6224.

503¹ E to George VI. 25 Aug 1946. RA DW 6404.

503² Simon Houfe. *Sir Albert Richardson. The Professor.* London, 1980. pp137–9.

503³ Lascelles diary. 9 Oct 1945. Lascelles papers.

503⁴ Cooper to Lascelles. 26 Nov 1945. RA KEVIII Ab. Box 3.

503⁵ Lascelles to Halifax. 10 March 1946. Halifax papers. A4 410 4/10.

504¹ Lascelles diary. 9 Oct 1945. Lascelles papers.

504² Lascelles to Halifax. 10 March 1946. Halifax papers. A4 410 4/10.

504³ 18 Oct 1945. RA GV EE 13/32.

504⁴ E to Peacock. 20 Oct 1945. RA DW 6013.

504⁵ Peacock to E. 23 Oct 1945. RA DW 6018.

505¹ 10 Nov 1945. RA DW 6042.

505² 15 Nov 1945. RA DW 6051.

505³ Churchill to George VI. 18 Nov 1945. RA GV EE 13/41.

505⁴ Lascelles to Halifax. 10 March 1946. Halifax papers. A4 410 4/10.

506¹ Halifax to F.O. 4 March 1946. RA GV EE 13/48.

506² Lascelles diary. 30 Nov 1945. Lascelles papers.

506³ Lascelles to George VI. 30 Nov 1945. RA GV EE 13/42.

506⁴ 9 Dec 1945. RA DW 6083.

506⁵ Lascelles diary. 27 Nov 1945. Lascelles papers.

506⁶ Marie Noele Kelly to Kenneth Rose. 18 Jan 1970. Rose papers.

507¹ Lascelles diary. 5 Oct 1945. Lascelles papers.

507² E to Lascelles. 28 Jan 1946. RA DW 6151.

507³ George VI to E. 20 March 1946. RA DW 6227.

507⁴ E to George VI. 10 April 1946. RA DW 6254.

507⁵ Lascelles diary. 9 Oct 1945. Lascelles papers.

509¹ Susan Mary Alsop. *To Marietta from Paris*. London, 1976. p54.

509² E to General John Franklin. 2 Oct 1945. RA DW 5959.

509³ E to Peacock. 20 Oct 1945. RA DW 6013.

509⁴ E to Vernays. 24 Feb 1946. RA DW 6187.

509⁵ *The Noël Coward Diaries*. Ed., Graham Payn and Sheridan Morley. London, 1982. pp54 and 62.

509⁶ Bloch. *The Secret File*. p223.

510¹ Alsop. *To Marietta from Paris*. p67.

510² Ziegler. *Diana Cooper*. p242.

510³ Lascelles diary. 20 Dec 1945. Lascelles papers.

510⁴ Cooper to Lascelles. 5 Nov 1945. RA KEVIII Ab. Box 3.

511¹ Cooper to Lascelles. 5 Nov 1945. RA KEVIII Ab. Box 3.

511² Lascelles diary. 9 Nov 1945. Lascelles papers.

511³ Lascelles diary. 1 July 1945. Lascelles papers.

511⁴ E to Queen Mary. 20 May 1945. RA GV EE 3.

511⁵ Bloch. *The Secret File*. pp227–8.

511⁶ Major-General Sir Francis de Guingand. *From Brass Hat to Bowler Hat*. London, 1979. p240.

511⁷ 13 July 1946. RA DW 6358.

512¹ E to Metcalfe. 4 Oct 1948. RA DW 7336.

512² 22 Nov 1957. RA DW 9844.

512³ E to Leslie. 19 Nov 1945. RA DW 6057.

512⁴ Leslie to E. 25 Nov 1945. RA DW 6072.

512⁵ Lascelles diary. 30 Nov 1945. Lascelles papers.

513¹ Laura, Duchess of Marlborough. *Laughter from a Cloud*. London, 1980. pp104–5.

513² 5 Nov 1946. RA GV EE 3.

513³ 9 Nov 1946. RA DW 7336.

514¹ 9 March 1948. Thomas papers.

514² E to Charles Cushing. 27 Sept 1948. RA DW 7323.

514³ E to Beaverbrook. 4 Nov 1948. Beaverbrook papers. Series G 24/16.

515¹ Queen Ena to Queen Mary. 26 April 1948. RA GV CC 45/1585.

515² Conversation with Willoughby Norman.

515³ E to Queen Mary. 6 July 1948. RA GV EE 3.

515⁴ 4 Nov 1948. Beaverbrook papers. Series G 24/16.

515⁵ E to Vernays. 2 Sept 1948 and E to A. Perry Osborn. 8 Sept 1948. RA DW 7288 and 7292.

515⁶ E to Suydam Cutting. 3 Nov 1948. RA DW 7386.

Notes

515⁷   E to Beaverbrook. 4 Nov 1948. Beaverbrook papers. Series G 24/16.

516¹   15 Aug 1947. RA GV EE 3.

516²   E to Suydam Cutting. 3 Nov 1948. RA DW 7386.

516³   E to Queen Mary. 10 March 1949. RA GV EE 3.

516⁴   E to Queen Mary. 13 Nov 1951. RA GV EE 3.

516⁵   E to Queen Mary. 23 Nov 1949. RA GV EE 3.

517¹   C. L. Sulzberger. *A Long Row of Candles*. New York, 1969. p690.

517²   E to Lord Dudley. 11 Aug 1949. RA DW 7555.

517³   E to Thomas Emery. 12 March 1951. RA DW 7903.

517⁴   Ziegler. *Diana Cooper*. p262.

518¹   Cecil Roberts. *The Pleasant Years*. London, 1974. pp16 and 36.

519¹   Nicolson. *Diaries and Letters 1945–1962*. pp98–9.

519²   Lees-Milne. *Nicolson*. Vol II, p234.

519³   Vickers. *Beaton*. p340.

519⁴   Morshead to Queen Mary. 11 April 1949. RA GV CC 48/1559.

519⁵   Sulzberger. *A Long Row of Candles*. p673.

520¹   Sulzberger. *A Long Row of Candles*. p690.

520²   Balfour. *Not too Correct an Aureole*. p64.

520³   Sulzberger. *A Long Row of Candles*. p673.

520⁴   *Chips*. pp444–5.

520⁵   10 and 16 Dec 1951. RA DW 8073 and 8081.

520⁶   Noel Barber. *The Natives were Friendly*. London, 1977. p32.

521¹   31 May 1946. RA DW 6311.

521²   Memo by Godfrey Thomas. 8 Oct 1947. Thomas papers.

522¹   16 Oct 1947. RA GV EE 3.

522²   J. Bryan III and Charles J. V. Murphy. *The Windsor Story*. London, 1979.

523¹   Murphy to E. 25 July 1950. Copy in Cecil Beaton papers.

523²   Bruce Lockhart. *Diaries*. Vol 2, p641.

523³   19 Sept 1947. RA KEVIII Ab. Box 3.

523⁴   E to Thomas. 9 March 1948. Thomas papers.

524¹   8 March 1948. RA GV EE 3.

524²   Gordon to George Allen. 17 Feb 1948. Copy in Thomas papers.

524³   Thomas to Lascelles. 27 Oct 1948. Thomas papers.

524⁴   Bloch. *The Secret File*. p242.

524⁵   Thomas to Lascelles. 27 Oct 1948. Thomas papers.

525¹   Morshead to Lascelles. 28 Dec 1948. RA GVI 42/338.

525²   11 Aug 1949. RA DW 7555.

525³   19 Aug 1949. Beaverbrook papers. Series G 25.

525⁴   8 July 1949. RA GVI 42/344.

525⁵   Bloch. *The Secret File*. p251.

526¹   2 June 1950. RA DW 7785.

526² Lascelles to Rickett. 18 May 1950. RA GVI 42/348.

526³ 18 April 1950. Monckton papers. DEP MT 20/161.

526⁴ Cromer to E. 21 Aug 1951. RA DW 7988.

526⁵ Cromer to E. 19 Sept 1951. RA DW 8017.

526⁶ Churchill to E. 26 Sept 1951. RA DW 8023.

527¹ E to Ulick Alexander. 6 Oct 1951. RA DW Add 1/184.

527² Sulzberger. *A Long Row of Candles*. p691.

527³ Athlone to E. 5 Jan 1952. RA DW 8194.

527⁴ *Scotsman*. 27 Sept 1951; *Economist*. 29 Sept 1951; *Manchester Guardian*. 27 Sept 1951; *Times Literary Supplement*. 28 Sept 1951; *Observer*. 30 Sept 1951.

527⁵ Lascelles to Roger Fulford. 6 Oct 1951. RA GVI 42/368.

528¹ 25 April 1952. RA DW 8194.

528² 16 Oct 1947. RA DW 6958.

528³ Queen Ena to Queen Mary. 16 Aug 1949. RA GV CC 45/1644.

528⁴ Queen Ena to Queen Mary. 1 Feb 1949. RA GV CC 45/1621.

528⁵ E to Queen Mary. 11 July 1947. RA GV EE 3.

529¹ 7 Sept 1947. RA DW 6915.

529² 16 Oct 1947. RA GV EE 3.

529³ 14 April 1949. RA GVI 42/320.

530¹ Lascelles to George VI. 16 April 1949. RA GVI 42/318.

530² 21 April 1949. RA GVI 42/322.

530³ 20 April 1949. RA KEVIII Ab. Box 2.

530⁴ George VI to Queen Mary. 20 April 1949. RA GV CC 13/223.

530⁵ Lascelles to Attlee. 9 Dec 1949. RA GVI 42/329.

530⁶ 26 April 1949. RA DW 7497.

531¹ 18 April 1949. RA GVI EE 13/63.

532¹ Draft of 16 Dec 1949. RA GVI EE 13/69.

532² 6 June 1950. RA GVI EE 13/70.

533¹ 22 Oct 1950. RA DW 7845.

533² 27 Feb 1951. RA DW 7898.

534¹ E to Butler. 24 Nov 1952. RA DW 8396.

535¹ E to Cushing. 27 Nov 1953. RA DW 8611.

535² Windsor. *A Family Album*. p138.

535³ Harold Nicolson diary. 19 March 1953. Nicolson papers.

535⁴ 9 Oct 1952. RA GV EE 3.

535⁵ See John Cornforth's interesting 'The Duke and Duchess of Windsor's House in Paris'. *Country Life*. 25 June 1987. pp120–5.

536¹ E to Cushing. 2 Sept 1954. RA DW 8880.

536² E to Brownlow. 21 Oct 1952. RA DW 8361.

537¹ Bloch. *The Secret File*. pp261–3.

537² 23 Feb 1952. RA GV CC 53/1566.

Notes

537³ Bloch. *The Secret File*. p265.
538¹ 9 Oct 1952. RA DW 8348.
538² Bloch. *The Secret File*. p277.
538³ E to Dudley. 6 April 1953. RA DW 8497.
539¹ Bloch. *The Secret File*. p279.
539² Princess Alice. *Memoirs*. p174.
539³ 16 Oct 1952. RA DW 8357.
540¹ 19 Nov 1952. RA DW 8385.
540² 20 Nov 1952. RA DW 8387.
540³ Undated. RA DW 8549.
540⁴ E to Robert Young. 22 June 1953. RA DW 8562.
540⁵ Nicolson. *Diaries and Letters 1945–1962*. p290.
541¹ E to Nicolson. 7 April 1953. RA DW 8500.
541² Lees-Milne. *Harold Nicolson*. pp268–9.
541³ Harold Nicolson diary. 19 March 1953. Nicolson papers.
541⁴ Windsor. *The Crown and the People*. pp36, 41 and 42.
541⁵ Murphy to E. 5 July 1961. RA DW 10630.
542¹ Copy in Maître Blum papers.
542² 8 July 1955. RA DW 9169.
542³ Duchess of Windsor. *The Heart Has Its Reasons*. p376.
543¹ Pope-Hennessy. *A Lonely Business*. p212.
543² Pope-Hennessy. *A Lonely Business*. p213.
543³ Giles. *Sundry Times*. pp130–2.
544¹ Kenneth Rose diary. 29 Jan 1972. Rose papers.
544² Cecil Beaton diary. Jan 1960. Cecil Beaton papers.
544³ *Noël Coward Diaries*. p399.
545¹ Anna Neagle. *There's Always Tomorrow*. London, 1974. p160.
545² Selina Hastings. *Nancy Mitford*. London, 1985. p207.
545³ Diana Mosley. *A Life of Contrasts*. London, 1977. p264.
545⁴ Charles Johnston diary. 25 Oct 1953. Johnston papers.
545⁵ Mosley. *A Life of Contrasts*. p264.
545⁶ Pope-Hennessy. *A Lonely Business*. p210.
546¹ J. K. Galbraith. *A Life in our Times*. London, 1981. p265.
546² Alsop. *To Marietta from Paris*. pp220–1.
546³ E to Alfred Sloan. 14 July 1952. RA DW 8267.
546⁴ 29 Jan 1953. RA GV EE 3.
546⁵ E to Arthur Gardner. 17 Jan 1962. RA DW 10709.
547¹ Sulzberger. *An Age of Mediocrity*. p96.
547² 20 May 1969. RA DW 11752.
547³ E to William Pawley. 27 Sept 1961. RA DW 10672.
547⁴ 29 March 1955. RA DW 9085.
547⁵ E to Hore-Belisha. 14 May 1952. RA DW 8211.

547⁶ E to Harold Talbott. 3 Dec 1956. RA DW 9594.

548¹ Peter Saunders. *The Mousetrap Man*. London, 1972. p144.

548² E to General Franklin. 24 Nov 1955 and to Charles Cushing. 11 Dec 1955. RA DW 9263 and 9276.

548³ Bloch. *The Secret File*. p258.

549¹ 25 and 26 Aug 1945. Beaverbrook papers. Series G 25/21.

549² Bruce Lockhart. *Diaries*. Vol 2, p572.

549³ Sarah Bradford. *George VI*. London, 1989. p427.

550¹ 27 Jan 1947. RA DW Misc Box 2.

550² Bevin to Attlee. 31 July 1947. Copy in RA DW Misc Box 2.

550³ Memo of 10 July 1947. Thomas papers.

551¹ Churchill to Eisenhower. 27 June 1953. Beaverbrook papers. Series G 25/21.

551² Eisenhower to Churchill. 2 July 1953. Beaverbrook papers. Series G 25/21.

551³ Monckton to Churchill. 1 Sept 1953. Beaverbrook papers. Series G 25/21.

551⁴ Memo by Churchill. 12 Aug 1953. Beaverbrook papers. Series G 25/21.

551⁵ 17 Nov 1954. RA DW 8947.

551⁶ *The Times*. 1 Aug 1957.

552¹ *Noël Coward Diaries*. p520.

552² E to Colonel McCormick. 18 Nov 1953. RA DW 8608.

553¹ E to Clint Murchison. 19 June 1953. RA DW 8559.

553² E to Thomas. 30 June 1954. RA DW 8815.

553³ 20 July 1956. RA DW 9485.

553⁴ Wheeler-Bennett to E. 26 July 1956. RA DW 9488.

553⁵ Bloch. *The Secret File*. p296.

553⁶ Wheeler-Bennett to E. 8 May 1958. RA DW 9979.

554¹ Saunders. *Mousetrap Man*. pp144–5.

554² E to Mrs Peggy Talbott. 25 July 1958. RA DW 10027.

555¹ 13 Oct 1969. RA DW 11850.

555² Mosley. *A Life of Contrasts*. p266.

555³ E to The Queen. 17 Aug 1968. RA DW Add 1/204.

555⁴ The Queen to E. 26 Feb 1969. RA DW Add 1/204.

555⁵ E to The Queen. 3 March 1969. RA DW Add 1/204.

555⁶ E to The Queen. 11 March 1969. RA DW Add 1/210.

556¹ Sulzberger. *An Age of Mediocrity*. p791.

557¹ Bishop of Fulham to E. 27 Nov 1962 and E to Bishop. 1 March 1963. RA DW 10815 and 10851.

557² Memo by Dr Jean Thin. cit. Bloch. *The Secret File*. pp301–3.

558¹ Cecil Beaton diary. 5 June 1972. Beaton papers.

Bibliographical Notes

By far the most important collection of manuscripts relating to the life and reign of King Edward VIII is to be found in the Royal Archives at Windsor (RA). These include a substantial number of papers which the Duke of Windsor had with him in France at the time of his death and which the Duchess agreed should be deposited at Windsor because they concerned the affairs of the royal family (RA Duke of Windsor's papers and RA Duke of Windsor's papers Add Mss 1, 2 and 3). Certain papers of Lord Hardinge, Lord Monckton and Lord Wigram have also been deposited in the Royal Archives.

Many important papers on the subject are to be found in the Public Record Office, particularly in the PRO CAB, PREM, CO, FO and WO series, in PRO 954 33 (Lord Avon's papers) and 30/69 (Ramsay MacDonald's diary); in the India Office Library (IO MSS EUR E and F); and in the National Archives in Washington (in particular NA 841 001, 844 E and 033 4120).

There are many collections of letters, diaries and relevant papers deposited in public institutions, notably those of Earl Baldwin (Cambridge University Library), Lord Beaverbrook (House of Lords), Neville Chamberlain (University of Birmingham), Winston Churchill (Churchill College), Archbishop Randall Davidson (Lambeth Palace Library), Geoffrey Dawson (News International Record Office), Canon Alan Don (Lambeth Palace Library), Bryan Godfrey-Fausset (Churchill College), the Duc de Grantmesnil (Kenneth de Courcy) (Hoover Institution), the Earl of Halifax (Borthwick Institute), Lord Harvey of Tasburgh (British Library), Archbishop Cosmo Lang (Lambeth Palace Library), Alan Lascelles (Churchill College), Earl Lloyd-George (House of Lords), Lord Monckton (Bodleian Library), Harold Nicolson (Balliol College), Eric Phipps (Churchill College), Henry Pownall (Liddell Hart Centre), the Marquess and Marchioness of Reading (India Office Library), Martin Scanlon (Maxwell Air Force Base Archives), Lord Templewood (Cambridge University Library).

Among those collections of letters and diaries in private hands I have consulted those of John Aird, Leo Amery, Cecil Beaton, Maître Suzanne Blum, the Marquis de Breteuil, Lord Brownlow, Victor Cazalet, Lady Coke, Lady Diana Cooper, Duff Cooper (Lord Norwich), the Earl of Cromer, Lady Donaldson, Freda Dudley Ward, Thomas Dugdale (Lord Crathorne), William Fellowes, Lord Glenusk,

Edward and Joan Grigg (Lord and Lady Altrincham), Lord Hardinge, Millicent Howard, R. D. P. H. Hutchinson, Charles Johnston, William Lambton, Piers Legh, Edward and Lady Alexandra Metcalfe, Earl Mountbatten of Burma, Bruce Ogilvy, Edward Peacock, Patrick Reilly, Lord Revelstoke, Kenneth Rose, Mrs Alfred Shaughnessy, Godfrey Thomas, Axel Wenner-Gren.

The Duke of Windsor's memoirs covering his life up to the time of the abdication, *A King's Story* (London, 1951), and the Duchess's autobiography *The Heart Has Its Reasons* (London, 1956) are indispensable sources for any study of the life of Edward VIII. The Duke's other published works are *The Crown and the People* (London, 1953) and *A Family Album* (London, 1960).

The most important biography of King Edward VIII is that of Lady Donaldson, *Edward VIII* (London, 1974). Michael Bloch's contributions to the field are equally essential: *The Duke of Windsor's War* (London, 1982); *Operation Willi. The Plot to Kidnap the Duke of Windsor* (London, 1984); his editing of two volumes of the Windsors' correspondence, *Wallis and Edward. The Intimate Correspondence, 1931–1937, of the Duke and Duchess of Windsor* (London, 1986), *The Secret File of the Duke of Windsor* (London, 1988); and *The Reign and Abdication of Edward VIII* (London, 1990) which the author kindly let me read in typescript. J. Bryan III and Charles V. Murphy's *The Windsor Story* (London, 1979) contains much information not to be found elsewhere. Lord Beaverbrook's *The Abdication of King Edward VIII*, ed., A. J. P. Taylor (London, 1966) is unreliable but contains much of interest. Other books about the Duke and Duchess of Windsor are mentioned as necessary in the reference notes.

It would be superfluous to recapitulate all those other books which are cited in those notes, but it might be useful to mention a few of those which, for one reason or another, proved of particular value: Lord Birkenhead, *Walter Monckton* (London, 1969); Sarah Bradford, *King George VI* (London, 1989); *The Crawford Papers*, ed., John Vincent (Manchester, 1984); *Documents on German Foreign Policy*, Series C, Vols. IV and V and Series D Vols. VII, VIII and X; *Journals and Letters of Reginald Viscount Esher*, ed., Maurice V. Brett, Vols. 1, 2 and 3 (London, 1934–38); Martin Gilbert, *Winston Churchill*, Vols. 5, 6, 7 and 8 (London, 1976–88); John Gore, *King George V. A Personal Memoir* (London, 1958); Helen Hardinge, *Loyal to Three Kings* (London, 1967); *Lloyd George. A Diary by Frances Stevenson*, ed., A. J. P. Taylor (London, 1971); Keith Middlemas and John Barnes, *Baldwin* (London, 1969); Harold Nicolson, *George V. His Life and Reign* (London, 1952); James Pope-Hennessy, *Queen Mary* (London, 1959); Kenneth Rose, *King George V* (London, 1983); John W. Wheeler-Bennett, *King George VI* (London, 1958).

Index

With the exception of the British royal family, crowned heads are listed under the name of their country.

A comma rather than a semi-colon between page references denotes that both pages are covered by the preceding sub-heading.

King Edward VIII is referred to throughout as E.

Index

Index

Index

angry letters 359–62; travels to France 362; search for clergyman 363; marries 364–5. Lack of occupation 366; settles in France 367; rents La Croë 368–9; visitors in Paris 370–1; plans to return to UK 371–6, corresponds with Chamberlain 372–3, faces opposition 374, accepts postponement 375; sues for libel 376; continues financial negotiations 377–8; and abortive visit by Kents 379–80; Gloucesters visit 380–1; and royal visit to Paris 382–3; and memorial to George V 383–4; rebuffed by Queen Mary 384–5. Visits Germany 386–93, role of Bedaux 386–8, indignation of court 388–90, meets Nazi leaders 391–2, praised by Churchill 393; plans to visit USA 393–7, opposition of royal family 393–4, Americans hostile 394–6, accepts cancellation 396–7; and appeasement 397–9; broadcasts to USA 398–9; appeals to Hitler 400–1. Return to UK 402–3; calls at Palace 404; appointed to Military Mission 405–6; relationship with Howard-Vyse 406–8; visits French Army 408–11, Maginot Line 410; takes 'Royal Salute' 410–11; forbidden to visit British troops 412–14; defeatism 414–15; takes wife to Biarritz 416; leaves Paris 417–18; leaves for Spain 419; in Madrid 420–3, indiscretions 421, argues over return to UK 422–3, German plot to retain in Spain 424; in Lisbon 425–33, further indiscretions 425, and arguments over return 426; offered Bahamian governorship 427, haggles 428–9; German kidnap plot 430–1; visited by Monckton 432–3; sails 433; sends mysterious telegram 434; possible intentions 435–6. Views of Bahamian posting 437–9; in Bermuda 440–1; arrives Nassau 442; deplores state of Government House 443–4; style of life 444; gubernatorial role 445–6; views on race 447–9; social policies 449–52; reforms ExCo 452–3; encourages US bases 453–4; develops Out Islands 454; and Wenner-Gren 455–8; suspected of treason 459; gives controversial interview 460, annoys Churchill 460–1; wishes to visit USA 462–5; visits Miami 464; meets Roosevelt 464; in USA 466–9, accused of extravagance 467, 469–70; dispute over dollar holdings 470–1; and riots in Nassau 471–4; and secret ballot 475, 478–80; as cautious paternalist 475–7; possible kidnap victim 477–8; and income tax 478; and Oakes murder 480–3; and death of Kent 484–5; relationship with family 485–8, over HRH issue 486–7; seeks another post 589–94, offered Bermuda 490, hopes for job in USA 491–3; leaves Bahamas 494–5. Visits USA 496; doubts about future of France 497–8; deplores Labour victory 498–9; relationship with family 499–503; stays with Queen Mary 500–2; seeks job 503–8, supported by Churchill 505, frustrated 506–8; bored 508; life in Paris 509–10, and Antibes 511; contemplates visit to Ireland 512; visits UK 512–13. Political pessimism 514–16; settles in France 516–17; relationship with Embassy 517–18; visits to USA 518, and UK 519; state of marriage 520–1; commissioned to write articles 521–3; turns to memoirs 524–5; publishes *A King's Story* 526–8; not invited to royal marriage 528–9; reopens HRH issue 529–33; buys Moulin 534, and lent villa in Paris 535–6; attends George VI's funeral 536–8, and Queen Mary's 538–9; not invited to Coronation 539–40; writes *The Crown and the People* 540–1, and *A Family Album* 541; interest in money, golf and gardening 542–3; entertains 543–4; consorts with Mosleys 545; becomes reactionary 546–7; continued devotion to wife 548; and publication of German Documents 548–52; disturbed by hostile books 552, and biography of George VI 553; health declines 554; reconciliation with royal family 555–6; organizes burial site 556; final illness 556; dies 557; buried 557–8. Characteristics: Arrested development 163, 285; charm 56, 190–1, 197, 203, 212, 297, 406, 408, 545; courage/cowardice 58, 165, 230, 264; depression 75, 122–5, 130, 140, 163–4; drunkenness/abstemiousness 38, 160, 167, 212, 219, 276, 394, 444; energy 38–9, 47, 60, 69, 155, 167, 185, 342; humanity 17–18, 55, 77, 181, 186, 210; informality 18, 45, 62, 71, 83, 106–7, 134, 136, 146, 165–6, 189, 203; intellectual ability 15, 181, 510, 522, 545; linguistic skills – French 24, 33–4, 263, 543, German 20, 24, 263, 543, Spanish 211–12, 264, 543; memory 16, 242, 545; mortification of flesh 31, 47, 58, 60; oratorical powers 41, 45–6, 112, 116, 183; popular appeal 45–6, 55, 70–1, 117, 128; racism 158, 448–9, 476; radicalism 86–7, 110–13, 164–5,

Index

French, John (later 1st Earl of Ypres), 51; 53–6; 61; 63; 66–7
French, Sylvia, 321
Frogmore, 12; 14; 16; 503; 556
Fulford, Roger, 527
Furness, Marmaduke, 1st Viscount, 196; 222
Furness, Thelma, 196–8; 222–3; 226–9; 232; 235; on E's sexuality 236; 260; 368
Fury, HMS, 334

Galbraith, J. K., 545–6
Gambia, The, 156
Gamelin, General Maurice, 408
Gandhi, Mohandas, 135; 138–9; 143; 300
Gardner, Arthur, 547
Gaskell, Lady Constance, 234
Gathorne Hardy, General John, 76–7
Gaulle, Charles de, 410; 493; 497; 514
Geddes, Auckland (later 1st Baron), 107
Gedye, G. E. R., 207
General Strike, The, 184
George, Prince, see Kent
George III, King, 2; 275; 518; 541
George IV, King, 108; 255; 334; 518
George V, King (Prince George, Duke of York and Prince of Wales), Marries 3–4; character 4, 12–13; as a father 6–9, 30–2, 64–5, 79–80, 132; 10; becomes Prince of Wales 13–14; 15–16; and E's education 19–20, 29–30, 35–6, 38; 21–3; becomes King 24–6; 27–8; 33; 41; 45–7; 49; and E's military service 50–1, 53–8, 61–4, 66, 68, 77, 81, 83; 52; visits France 62, 67; 69; 72–3; 75–8; 82; 85–7; and E's marrying 88, 93, 98–9, 103–4, 173–4, 198–9; 107–9; and E's Commonwealth tours 114, 116–17, 119, 126, 128, 135–7, 144–5; criticisms of E 120, 131–2, 134–6, 141, 149–50, 152–4; congratulates E 160; 165; differences with E 169–72, over Metcalfe 174–5, and steeplechasing 175–7, and flying 177–8; 183; illness of 192–3, 196–7; differences with E 198–9; 203; 205; 207–10; 214–15; 219–21; and Mrs Simpson 224, 231–4, 238; dies 240–1; 243–4; buried 245–6; will of 246–7; 249; 251–2; 257–8; 260; 262–3; 266–7; 272; 277; 296; 329; memorial for 383–4; 523
George VI, King (Prince Albert and Duke of York), 6; 11; 15–16; at Osborne 22; closeness to E 32, 49, 64; 53; 69; 92; and Freda Dudley Ward 98–9; 131; 166; 168; on E's differences with George V 169; marries 171; 175; 193; 199;

distance from E 200; 203; and Mrs Simpson 234; 242; 244; 246–7; 253–5; at Sandringham 261, and Balmoral 262; and plans for Coronation 265; 288; alienation from E 289–90; and abdication crisis 322–33; defends E 339; 341; 343–4; estrangement from E 346–9; financial negotiations with E 349–52; and E's marriage 353–6, 362; and HRH controversy 357–60; abused by E 360–1; and E's return to England 371–5; financial negotiations with E 376–8; and Kents' visit to E 379–80; visits Paris 382–3; and George V's memorial 383–4; 385; E's visit to Germany 388–90, and to USA 393; 398–9; and E's return 402–3; E calls on 404–5; and E's job in France 407, 412–14; 421; on E's future 426–7, 429; 430; 434; 457; 462; 464; 467–9; 471; sends Camerons to guard E 477; 479; and HRH issue 485–8, 529–32; and new job for E 489, 492, 504–7; 498–500; on E's marriage 501; 502–3; 509; 523; dies 536–8; 541; and German documents 548–51; official biography of 553
Georges, General Alphonse-Joseph, 409
Germany, E visits 1913 42–4; 48; E's hostility to 49, 53, 85–6; E's sympathy for 205–10, 214, 266–72; 320; E visits 1937 388–93; 398–400; 415; 512; 518; E's admiration for 536, 545; publication of Official Documents of 548–52
Germany, Prince August Wilhelm of, 44
Germany, Empress Frederick of, 26
Germany, Princess Victoria Louise of, 43
Germany, Kaiser Wilhelm II of, 43–4; 53; 550
Giles, Frank, 441; 543
Gilgandra (New South Wales), 128–9
Gillot, Eugène-Louis, 34
Glasgow, 111; 182; 217; 296
Glenusk, Lady, 51
Gloucester, Alice, Duchess of, 200; 290; 323; visits Windsors 380–8; 539
Gloucester, Henry, Duke of, 6; 8; 38; 49; 62; 169; on safari 189–90; marries 200; 247; 271; 290; and abdication crisis 324, 330–1; and E's marriage 354–5; 374; visits Windsors 380–1; and E's job in France 407, 411–12, 414–15; 539; 541; 558
Goddard, Theodore, 291; 312–13
Goebbels, Joseph, 460
Gold Coast, The, 156
Goldwater, Senator Barry, 546–7
Gone with the Windsors, 552
Gordon, John, 524

645

Index

Index

Index

Munster, Count Paul, 367
Murphy, Charles, 9; 522; 524; 541
Murphy, W. L., 492n
Murray, Colonel Malcolm, 70–2
Mussolini, Benito 193; 210–11; 271; 417
Mysore, Maharaja of, 142

Nahlin, yacht, 282–7; 345; 369
Nairobi, 190–1; 197
Nassau, 429; 437–9; 441; E arrives in
 442; 443–4; 446–8; 450–1;
 Wenner-Gren in 455–6; 460; 463; riots
 in 471–3; fire in 474; 477–8; Oakes
 murdered in 480–3; 484; Stanley in
 492; E leaves 494–5
Nassau Daily Tribune, The, 442–6; 448;
 454; 464; 472; 494–5
Nassau Guardian, The, 472
National Council of Social Service, 182;
 215–16
National Gallery, 178–9
National Government, 214–15
National Relief Fund, 181–2
NBC (National Broadcasting Company of
 America), 398
Neagle, Anna, 544–5
Nepal, 141–2; 196
Neumann, Dr Heinrich, 286
Newfoundland, 491
New Providence Island, Bahamas, 437–8;
 475; 477; 479
News Chronicle, The, 294; 308
New Statesman, The, 309
Newton, Thomas Legh, 2nd Baron, 73–4
New York, 121; 127; 148; E visits 1924
 149–55; 227; 321; 395–6; 399; E
 wishes to visit 429; 459; Beaverbrook in
 490; E visits 1945 496; 506; 515; 518;
 525; 533; 535; 538
New York American, The, 295
New York Times, The, 153; 394
New York World, The, 121; 196
New Zealand, E visits 1920 126–7; 177;
 and abdication crisis 307
Nicolson, Harold, 8–9; 12; 15; 204–5;
 215; 235; 265; 275; 281; 292–3; and
 abdication crisis 302, 321; sees
 Windsors in France 368, and in London
 406, 518–19; 535; and E's authorship
 540–1
Nigeria, 156–7
Norfolk, Bernard Fitzalan-Howard, 16th
 Duke of, 265
North, Captain (later Admiral Sir Dudley),
 159
Norway, 44
Norway, Queen Maud of, 13; 262;
 290
Norway, King Olav of, 206; 558

Norwich, John Julius Cooper, 2nd
 Viscount, 267n

Oakes, Sir Harry, 438; 445; 455; 470;
 murder of 480–3
Observer, The, 527
Oesterreicher, Gusti, 225
Ogilvie Forbes, George, 390–1
Ogilvy, Bruce, 91; 97; 136; 149; 176; 183;
 201; and Mrs Simpson 231–2, 236,
 238; 259
Ogle, Bertram, 312
Operation Willi, 423
Orczy, Baroness, 47
Orlando, President, 82
Ormsby-Gore, William (later 4th Baron
 Harlech), 250
Osborne, Leonard, 280; 310
Osborne Naval College, 20–3; 30; 32
Ottawa, 154; 187; 306; 427; 463; 468
Oursler, Fulton, 460; 465–6
Out Islands, The (Bahamas), 438; poverty
 of 450–1, 454; development of 454–5,
 457, 477, 480; secret ballot for 475,
 478–80
Oxford University, 32; 35–42; 205; 214;
 253; 338

Paget, Guy, 176
Palm Beach, 205; 502; 518
Palmer, Lilli, 371
Panama, 125
Paris, 34; 89; 91; 174; 223; 237; 261;
 282; Mrs Simpson ill in 287; Windsors
 settle in 367; 370–1; Chamberlain in
 371, 374; Gloucesters in 380–1; royal
 visit to 382–3; 388; 390; 397; 405;
 409; 416–17; E returns to 499–500,
 503; Churchill visits 505; post-war life
 in 508–10, 516–19; 525; permanent
 home in 534–6; 545
Patriotic Fund, The, 52
Patten, Susan Mary, 508–9; 546
Patten, William, 546
Patton, General George, 410
Peacock, Edward, 311; 314; and
 abdication crisis 322, 326, 328–9; 350;
 meets E in Miami 465; 470; 499–500;
 504
Peacock, Walter, 27; 60
Pearson, Peter, 191–2
Pell, Herbert, 425
Pershing, General John, 84
Peru, 212
Peshawar, 138
Pétain, Marshal Henri, 419
Phelps, Rev Lancelot, 40
Phillips, Gray, 154; 416–19; 428; in
 Bahamas 441; 511

Index

Index